Puritan's Empire

By

Charles A. Coulombe

Bona Tempora Volvant

Arcadia
MMVIII

Printed in the United States of America

ISBN 978-1-944339-04-3

Puritan's Empire
© 2008 by Charles A. Coulombe

Third Edition

No part of this book may be reproduced in any manner whatsoever without written permission, except in the case of brief quotations embodied in critical reviews or articles.

Published by Tumblar House
All rights reserved.
Visit our website at www.tumblarhouse.com

ABOUT THE AUTHOR

Charles A. Coulombe was born in New York on 8 November 1960. At an early age, his parents took him to Hollywood, California, where they lived in an apartment building owned by famed television psychic, Criswell. Coulombe has lectured on a wide variety of historical, religious, and political topics on three continents, and did commentary for ABC News on the death of John Paul II and the election and installation of his successor. He is the author of numerous articles in many journals, and of 10 books on a variety of subjects including Puritan's Empire, a Catholic perspective on American history, and Vicars of Christ, a history of the popes.

Coulombe serves on the boards of the Queen of Angels Foundation and the Canadian Royal Heritage Trust, and is the Western United States representative of the International Monarchist League. He is or has been a member of the Knights of Columbus, the Knights of Peter Claver, the Newman Club of Los Angeles, the Mythopoeic Society, the Royal Stuart Society, and a number of others.

OTHER BOOKS BY CHARLES A. COULOMBE:

Vicars of Christ: A History of the Popes

Every Man Today Call Rome

Star-Spangled Crown

The Pope's Legion

The White Cockade

A Catholic Quest for the Holy Grail

Desire & Deception

TABLE OF CONTENTS

FOREWORD 1

INTRODUCTION 5
- *EUROPE* 8
- *THE AMERICAS* 14
- *AFRICA* 17
- *ASIA* 17
- *CONCLUSION* 18

THE FOUNDING OF CATHOLIC AMERICA 19
- *THE CONQUISTADORES* 30
- *THE MISSIONARIES* 35
- *THE SPANISH ACHIEVEMENT* 37
- *FRANCE COMES TO AMERICA* 41
- *NEW FRANCE MADE PERMANENT* 44
- *FRENCH AND SPANISH EFFORTS EVALUATED* 48

THE FOUNDING OF PROTESTANT AMERICA 51
- *THE ERA OF THE CIVIL WARS* 64
- *THE STRUGGLE AGAINST CATHOLIC AMERICA* 70
- *PRELUDE TO REVOLUTION* 82
- *THE RELIGIOUS PROBLEM* 85
- *SUMMARY* 85

THE FIRST CIVIL WAR 87
- *SUMMARY* 94
- *THE CONTENDING PARTIES* 94
- *WHAT CAME BEFORE* 102
- *THE WAR* 108
- *THE RESULTS* 126

THE YOUNG NATION 129

  THE START OF THE FEDERAL GOVERNMENT............................ 142
  THE FEDERALIST ERA 151
  THE REVOLUTION OF 1800.. 159

ADOLESCENT AMERICA 169
  UNITARIANISM, TRANSCENDENTALISM, AND THE AMERICAN NOVEL 178
  THE POLITICAL STRUGGLE.. 185
  CATHOLICISM EXPANDING.. 193
  THE MEXICAN WAR.. 204

DIVISION AND WAR 210
  GROWING DIVISION 227
  THE CIVIL WAR.. 236

RECONSTRUCTION AND IMMIGRATION 257
  THE CHURCH IN THE GILDED AGE.. 284

A NEW WORLD POWER 305
  NEW TECHNOLOGIES, NEW CHALLENGES............................ 315
  THE REIGN OF WOODROW WILSON 329

ISOLATION AND THE RISE OF FASCISM 345
  THE NEW DEAL... 397

WORLD WAR AND COLD WAR.................................... 423

ARSENAL OF DEMOCRACY 463
  CAMELOT, THE HIPPIE ERA, AND THE GREAT SOCIETY 487

AFTERWORD 503

APPENDICES... 516

BIBLIOGRAPHY 517

FOREWORD
by
Gary Potter

Those who do not remember the past, it is said, are doomed to repeat it. The saying, usually taken as an encouragement to learning about history, in fact suggests that the past was never as good a time as the present, that everything between then and now would be a record of unallayed progress except for the periodic failure to remember how bad the past was. This notion, far from turning anyone toward the study of history, tends to keep most persons fixed on the present, on now. In the present is not simply where they live and the time on which they will keep their minds focused, they end by believing that life could not have been better or happier than today—unless, perhaps, it might be in the future.

Writing early in the 20th century, the great G.K. Chesterton commented on how uncomfortable it actually is to try to live exclusively in the present because the present, the moment, is such a narrow amount of time. Trying to live in it, he said, is like sitting on a pin. Doubtless that is why some number wind up dreaming of life in the future. Of course the future is totally unlivable since the moment we arrive there it becomes the present. Still, there are those—especially persons of scientific or technological turn of mind—who persist in this dream. It is what space exploration is about. The scientists and technologists imagine that having wrecked this world, they finally will be able to build a perfect one in outer space.

Remaining Christians, as witness to G.K. Chesterton's comment, ought not to be fixed on the present, much less obsessed with the future. Living life as it is, enjoying it, real life, even life everlasting, is what they are supposed to be about. This is why, if they are serious in their Christianity, they will instinctively root themselves in the past. They will understand, if only instinctively, that there is where life exists most expansively, most abundantly. This is why tradition is so important to them, or should be. It is the past being lived. Of course we must adhere to tradition for it to be lived.

It is a parenthetical thought, but adhering to tradition, making the past live, if many more did it than do, would have wonderful political results. That is, the history of the past two centuries, ever since liberalism exploded politically at the end of the 18th century with the Revolution that began in France in 1789 and is still unfolding all over the world, ought to have taught us that the role of political power should not be to build paradise on Earth, to try to make the world perfect. Rather, those who wield power should be satisfied with preventing the creation of Hell on Earth. Adherence to tradition in religion and the cultural traditions that flow from that, would keep political leaders on that path. This, by itself, is a good reason to protect and cherish tradition.

In any event, if the past is as vital as it is for Christian living, persons who profess Christ as their Saviour ought to want to learn about it, and where may we do that? Where else but in that record of it known as history? Knowing this ought to make the study of history as exciting for the Christian as it is necessary. We study it when we read it thoughtfully, understanding that in the thought we are giving to it, what we are doing is bringing the past to life.

Doing that, it needs to be clear, is not the same thing as living in the past. It is not a matter of some poor guy entering middle age who keeps rerunning in his head the Friday night he scored the winning touchdown for his high school football team or of someone turning 40, not necessarily a woman, who cannot accept it that the face looking back from the mirror is not that of a 20-year-old. Nor are we speaking here of the notion—with some it verges on certainty—that almost any time or era of the past would in every way have been a better one in which to live.

The trouble with this fantasy, with believing that another time was so much better you wish you had lived during it, is that it ignores that human nature does not change from era to era.

Among remaining Christians are misguided ones who fantasize living during the time when Our Lord walked on Earth. One has heard them say, "How glorious it would have been to be alive at the same time as Our Lord, to see Him, to hear Him speak, perhaps to draw close enough to touch the hem of His garment." This sentiment ignores that most who did see and hear Him did not find it glorious. In fact, they—the majority—were perfectly ready to clamour for His crucifixion when given the choice between His and another's. It is why since then, as Bishop Bossuet once wrote, the Church has known that the rule of the majority can lead to any crime.

How can anyone be absolutely certain he would not have been among the majority—the anti-Christ majority—on the first Good Friday? He cannot be, not if he is honest enough to admit, if only to himself, how difficult it can be, how often he fails at being, merely good, let alone virtuous.

Yes, any one of us may like to think that standing there in Pilate's courtyard we alone would have cried "Give us Jesus" instead of "Give us Barabbas," forgetting that even Peter denied Him, forgetting that almost any day of our life we are liable to prefer something or someone (our own Barabbas) to Him.

In sum, living in the past may be something we fantasize, and circumstances then—education, social position, our state in life—could have made somewhat different persons of us, but as men and women, in our humanity, we would be as we are, fallen in our nature.

Charles Coulombe, the author of *Puritan's Empire*, understands all this. His understanding is reflected in the pages of his book. This is not to say his book is in any way one of philosophy or religion. It is history pure and simple, but written from a definite point of view—that of the believing Catholic who adheres to tradition. Moreover, the history he recounts is of the achievements of men (and women) inspired in their doings by what they believed as Catholics.

The achievements begin with the arrival in North America of the Catholic Spanish and French who were the first Europeans to reach the continent in appreciable numbers. They continue with the successful efforts of these Catholics, including the evangelization of native peoples, to settle and civilize the New World—efforts so successful that we may speak of them as producing a Catholic America. That is insofar as for more than a century there was no Christian presence in what we now know as the United States except the Catholic one.

We then see how that presence began to be diluted by the arrival on our shores of others, notably English-speaking Puritans. After that—and radically abbreviating here the far-ranging and detailed history Coulombe recounts—we see how, through a series of historical accidents, the newcomers' influence and power became dominant, eventually resulting in what we have today: a Puritan's empire. Along the way, by means of that far-ranging and detailed history, we are able to observe the constant interplay at home and in the nation's foreign affairs, in peace and at war, between the ideas, beliefs and standards of America's original Catholicism and all that has replaced them.

The reader may perceive here that we mispoke somewhat a few lines ago when we described this book as one of history pure and simple. That suggests nothing but a recitation of facts. In truth, what is detailed in *Puritan's Empire* is a real "clash of civilizations" or, more precisely, the clash of two very different views of men and how they ought to live in society. On the one hand is the view held by such as St. Thomas Aquinas of men (like life itself) as naturally good, though fallen, and on the other the view held by Calvin that we are hopelessly bad. To hold the first view and act on it can make right what ails America today, like a fifty-percent divorce rate, the alienation of young people who see no future role for themselves in society except as consumers, the drive to spread worldwide even by force of arms the ideology of democracy with its false promise of "freedom". To continue to hold the other will simply produce more of the same, and worse.

But let us be as succinct as possible in what we are saying: By enabling us to remember what was good in our past, beginning when America was Catholic, *Puritan's Empire* can help us repeat history; to do that by efforts to return the lands that form the United States to the original destiny from which they were tragically diverted; efforts, if undertaken, that no doubt would be abetted by the fact today's Puritan descendants are aborting and contracepting themselves out of existence anyway. In a word, the book can help us make America Catholic again. Thus would we do our part to fulfill the last commandment His followers heard direct from Our Lord's lips: to make disciples of all the nations.

Such a purpose is so high and noble, we risk its diminution by mentioning a secondary feature of the book. Yet that feature is not really so secondary, not nowadays when so many persons, especially young ones, lack the habit of reading serious books. It is that this volume, hefty as it is, is extremely easy, and often even exciting, to read. There is not an intelligent teenager in the country who cannot manage it.

One would hope for a multitude of Catholic parents who will see to it that their youngsters do read it. Furnishing these young persons with the knowledge and, more important, truths offered by *Puritan's Empire* will be a marvelous gift, and may go some way toward fulfilling the purpose we have named and which the book seeks to serve.

INTRODUCTION

We live in what has been, since 1945 at least, the most important and most powerful nation in the World. Trends, whether political or social, which start in the United States soon spread throughout the globe. But if this is a source of pride to Americans, it is also a great responsibility. For Catholic Americans, the responsibility becomes even greater. In the first case, there is the necessity of ensuring that this great power be a force for good; in the second, there is the added need to spread the Catholic faith in our native land—thus assisting it throughout the world.

History is the key to understanding men—whether as nations, families, or individuals. Without an employment record, we cannot evaluate a prospective worker; without genealogy, we cannot say much about a given family as it is today. Similarly, without a firm grasp of a nation's history, we cannot understand its present. In the case of America, so many of its present-day policies are based upon factors so deeply buried in our history, that without a good understanding of those factors the present is simply incomprehensible. Yet history (due in part to some of these factors) is probably our most poorly taught subject. Due to other of these factors, what little of it that is imparted to students is more in the way of a national mythology (with such episodes as Washington and the cherry tree and the Boston Tea Party given more attention than the underlying causes and forces) than serious history—useless for understanding, or for any other purpose than self-praise.

For Catholics, history has an even higher purpose beside. For them, history is the unfolding of God's Will in time, and the attempts of men either to conform themselves to or to resist that Will. As the great Dom Gueranger, author of the monumental *Liturgical Year* points out, "for the Christian there is no purely human History" since,

> ...man has been divinely called to the supernatural state. This state is his goal and the chronicles of human kind should therefore exhibit the traces of that supernatural life.
>
> Thus, the Catholic historian may rely upon the guidance provided by the Church which always goes before him as a column of light and divinely illuminates all his thoughts. The Christian knows that a close bond unites the Church and the Son of God made man; the Christian knows that the Church has the guarantee of Christ's promise against all errors in her teaching and in the general conduct of Christian society, and that the Holy Spirit animates and leads the Church. It is in

her, therefore, that he finds the rule for judging. The true Christian is not surprised by the weakness of churchmen or by their temporal abuses, because he knows that God has decided to tolerate the weeds in His field until the harvest... But he knows where the direction, the spirit, and the divine instinct of the Church are manifested. He receives them, he accepts them, he professes them bravely and applies them in his narration of history. Therefore, he never betrays them, he never sacrifices them, he considers good what the Church judges as good and bad what the Church judges as bad. He does not care about the sarcasm or clamor of short-sighted cowards. Other historians will stubbornly observe only the political side of events, and so will descend to the pagan point of view. But the Christian historian will remain firm, because he has the initial certainty that he is not mistaken. [He knows that] Christ is at home in history; [that is why] he must not fear condemning the thousands of calumnies which have made history a huge conspiracy against truth... It is necessary to be prepared to fight; if one is not brave enough to do that, then that person should refrain from writing history. (Gueranger, *The Christian Sense of History*, pp. 17-18, 53-54)

The good Benedictine gives us a second important premise.

> The supreme disgrace of the Christian historian would be to take the ideas of his time as criteria for evaluation and to apply them to judging the past. [In this way non-Christians] succeed in dragging Catholics into their systems, and are jubilant because of the progress they have made in imposing their language and their ideas (*ibid*, 36 and 59).

Adherence to these principles has produced such great historians as Hilaire Belloc, Bernard Faÿ, William Thomas Walsh, and Christopher Hollis, to say nothing of the great Dom Gueranger himself. But American Catholic historians have generally refrained from exploring their own national history with these principles, preferring instead to adopt the analysis of their non-Catholic colleagues, save when looking at purely Catholic topics (and sometimes not then). It is easy to see why.

Solange Hertz, perhaps the first Catholic writer to rigorously apply Catholic principles to American history, reached an uncomfortable conclusion:

> U.S. History shows how all Catholic government, whether English, French, or Spanish, was gradually crowded out... on a continent liberally watered by the blood of martyrs from all parts of Europe who first planted the Cross of Christ there and who sought no

other end than consolidating His peaceful possession (*The Star-Spangled Heresy*, p. 171).

This is not a pleasing summary. But it is this author's belief that a candid examination of the facts of U.S. history will bear Mrs. Hertz's contention out. For America is not as yet really a nation. It is in fact a religion—Americanism, described thusly by Dr. John Rao:

> "Americanism" is a religion in which both major elements of the American "soul"—secularized Puritanism and Anglo-Saxon conservatism—have helped to develop. "Americanism" is a religion that adores the United States as the incarnation of the secularized Puritan vision of paradise. It is a religion that simultaneously adores the bland, materialistic, catch-all unity that stems from the Anglo-Saxon drive for stability and integration. "Americanism" is an evangelical religion that wishes the rest of the world to be converted to its doctrines (Americanism, p. 3).

As a revealed religion Catholicism must claim a monopoly of truth; she cannot be tolerant of error, of false religions. Americanism, being a rival faith, must inevitably be an opponent of Catholicism. As Dr. Rao further opines, it "is, and always has been, a danger to the Church of Rome. Indeed, the threat that it poses to Catholicism may be the most pressing experienced in the past few centuries of revolution" (*loc. cit.*).

Having said all of this, it must be pointed out that opposition to the religion of Americanism is not the same thing as disloyalty to the country. If anything, pursuit of the Americanist religious ideals has involved this country in innumerable foreign and domestic disputes, any one of which could easily have destroyed us. Moreover, for a Catholic resident in a non-Catholic country, a desire to convert his nation from its error constitutes real patriotism, just as a convert's desire to see his parents accept the truth of the Faith is the cornerstone of his love for them.

It is vital then, for Catholics, especially young Catholics, to have a good and proper understanding of their country's history. To exercise their patriotism, they must work for the conversion of the U.S.; to do this effectively, they must understand the forces and events which brought forth not only the religion of Americanism and the country itself, but also the sort of Catholicism which, in 300 years, failed so dismally to bring this conversion about.

One of the most exciting and positive notes of our history, however, is that the American continents have provided a place wherein native and European, African, and Asian cultures have mingled, and from which a vital spirit emerged. In those areas evangelized properly, the results have been extraordinary. Two models have been offered for this mingling: the Catholic, wherein the constituent elements retain their integrity while enriching one another, and the Americanist, wherein the ultimate result is intended to create a conformity based upon the lowest common denominator: money.

In this book, it is hoped that a beginning will be made toward a Catholic view of American history. Obviously, such a vast topic cannot be adequately explored in the little space available to us. But what can be done (and what this author hopes to have accomplished) is to reinterpret the better-known episodes of our history in accordance with the Faith, and to point up lesser-known details which will give factual proof of the truth of this reinterpretation.

Unfortunately, so poor has so much of the standard historical education been in recent decades, that many names, places and dates which were common knowledge not long ago will have been forgotten. Hence, for best results, this book should be used alongside a standard encyclopedia. The names and places in italics can then be looked up for further knowledge.

The author does not pretend to have written the final word in this matter; it is no small task to reverse five centuries of misinterpretation and outright lies. But if this present work will inspire other, abler hands to lend their pens to this work, he will have succeeded.

At any rate, it will be helpful, before we begin our survey, to look at the continents of Europe, America, and Africa on the eve of the great discovery which would bring them all together.

EUROPE

The Europe of 1492 was a continent in the midst of change. In the West, Catholicism reigned supreme from Iceland to Russia. In many ways, the ideals of Medieval Christendom, although shaken by the Great Schism (with its scandal of three Popes at once) and the Renaissance (with its rediscovery of pagan literature and morality), remained. The Middle Ages were suffused with Catholicism in a way which the world has never seen—before or since. This does not mean that they were perfect, or that men were any less sinners than they are now. What it does mean is that they were clearer as to their goals than were either their ancestors or their descendants. As Kenelm Digby observes in *Mores Catholici*, "...the avowed object of all government in ages of faith was to secure glory to God, and peace on earth to men of good-will. The Catholic religion admitted of no other."

The Kings themselves, hereditary for the most part, were not merely the equivalents of our heads of state. For just as Papal and Imperial authority were considered to be divine in origin, so too was Royal. Yet the Kings often had little power: no power of income tax, nor of regulation, nor of the secret police, nor of so many of the myriad interferences we have come to accept as the rightful appurtenances of governmental power. Instead, as Kenelm Digby (*op. cit.* p. 99) says:

> ...the whole state was founded on the pacific type of the best kingdom. The pacific character of royal majesty was a religious idea, emanating from what was believed of the celestial dominations and powers; for it was a devotional exercise in reparation of the sins of anger, passion, and revenge, to offer to God the peace, mildness and tranquillity of the thrones. The Christian religion had put everything in its place, so that the hierarchy of men was as complete as that of angels in the order shown by Dionysius. As in the latter, thrones are after Seraphim and Cherubim, so in the state, physical force was regarded after love and science. In the ancient Christian sculpture, dominations, which command angels, and principalities, which rule over men, are represented with crowns and sceptres; but powers which command the Satanic race are shown with spear and shield, since the devil only yields to force. Therefore, the crown and sceptre were the symbols of royal power, and the maxim was "'Tis more kingly to obtain peace than to enforce conditions by constraint."

For this reason, the King had three roles: in a sense, he had a demi-priestly character, conferred by his coronation. He was firstly the defender of the Church within his realm. A sort of sub-diaconal character was his, and various kings were often traditionally canons of one or several of their cathedral cities. Kings also often had liturgical roles, such as foot-washing on Maundy Thursday, an honored place in Corpus Christi and other processions, and special Mass prayers said for them. In a few cases, he was believed to have miraculous powers. So the Kings of England and France cured scrofula (called "The King's Evil), the King of Denmark cured epilepsy, the King of Hungary jaundice, and the Holy Roman Emperor, successor of Charlemagne, was said to have some control over the weather (so in Germany fine warm weather is called *Kaiserswetter*). Isabella of Spain's ancestors, the Kings of Castile, were resorted to by the possessed for exorcism, as we see in Alvarez Pelayo's 1340 work, *Speculum regum*, written to King Alphonso XI:

> It is said that the kings of France and of England possess a [healing] power; likewise the most pious kings of Spain, from whom you are descended, possess a power which acts on the demoniacs and certain sick

persons suffering from divers ills. When a small child, I myself saw your grandfather king Sancho [Sancho II, 1284-1295], who brought me up, place his foot upon the throat of a demoniac who proceeded to heap insults upon him; and then, by reading words taken from a little book, drive out the demon from this woman, and leave her perfectly healed. (quoted in Marc Bloch, *The Royal Touch*, p. 88).

His Majesty's second role was as supreme judge. The Court of Queen's Bench is a relic of this in Commonwealth countries—indeed, our very word "Court" hearkens back to the King sitting in judgment over cases, with all his chief men around him. Yet he could not be arbitrary: each of his provinces must be ruled in accordance with their own laws—or Roman Law if that was accepted there. Law was considered to be something immutable which could be discovered, but never created. So true was this that the Assizes of Jerusalem, the legal code of the Latin Kingdom of that city, were declared to be a recovery of previous law, rather than a new creation for a new kingdom. Nor was the King above the Law: such things as Magna Carta and various Golden Bulls were not considered as new limitations of the King's power, but rather a return to previously existing balance. Since the King had little power at his command, he must either hear cases in his own residence, send out judges to the different provinces of his realm, or else invest various local notables with judicial power. Lack of a real standing army generally reduced his ability to discipline offending nobles to merely declaring such "outlaws" who might be preyed upon by any other noble strong enough to do so.

This last brings us to the King's third role: warlord. He was chief of whatever soldiery he happened to have on hand: if he wished to go to war with a neighboring nation or to go on Crusade, he must summon his chief nobles with their retainers, or else hire mercenaries. Both of these were often dangerous propositions. Thus it is that until the Hundred Years War, we see little in the way of major wars between Christian Kings, although there was plenty of local warfare between barons.

The King's role, then, was that of orchestra conductor. A good King, like St. Louis, was able to benefit his subjects greatly through force of personality; a bad one was unable generally, to do more than make the lives of his courtiers unpleasant. Would the same might be said of chief executives today! The Kings gathered around themselves courts. These consisted of the ruler's friends, servants, and the great men of his realm. One thinks immediately of King Arthur's Round Table, the Paladins of Charlemagne, and the warriors clustered around Hrothgar in *Beowulf*; but the much-attenuated descendants of such groups may be found today in institutions like the British Privy Council and the Danish Council of State. Within these amorphous bands, the King carried out his main functions: observing the rites of the Church, ruling on judicial cases brought to him, and occasionally deciding on military action.

As time progressed, these particular functions became more specialized, and eventually developed into quasi-departments or ministries of state. From this simple beginning have derived the great central administrations with which we are familiar; in time, these would do away with the Kings. Today, only the largely ceremonial British royal household, and the pragmatic Roman Curia survive in anything like their original form.

It is important to remember that just as Christendom was one body in religious matters, so it was in temporal matters also. This is admirably summed up by James, Viscount Bryce, in his *The Holy Roman Empire* (pp. 102-105):

> The realistic philosophy, and the needs of a time when the only notion of civil or religious order was submission to authority, required the World State to be a monarchy: tradition, as well as the continued existence of a part of the ancient institutions, gave the monarch the name of Roman Emperor. A king could not be universal sovereign, for there were many kings: the Emperor must be universal, for there had never been but one Emperor; he had in older and brighter days been the actual lord of the civilized world; the seat of his power was placed beside that of the spiritual autocrat of Christendom. His functions will be seen most clearly if we deduce them from the leading principle of medieval mythology [as the ignorant call it], the exact correspondence of earth and heaven. As God, in the midst of the celestial hierarchy, rules blessed spirits in Paradise, so the Pope, His vicar, raised above priests, bishops, metropolitans, reigns over the souls of mortal men below. But as God is Lord of earth as well as of heaven, so must he (the Imperator coelestis) be represented by a second earthly viceroy, the Emperor (Imperator terrenus), whose authority shall be of and for this present life. And as in this present world the soul cannot act save through the body, while yet the body is no more than an instrument and means for the soul's manifestation, so there must be a rule and care of men's bodies as well as of their souls, yet subordinated always to the well-being of that element which is the purer and more enduring. It is under the emblem of soul and body that the relation of the papal and imperial power is presented to us throughout the Middle Ages. The Pope, as God's vicar in matters spiritual, is to lead men to eternal life; the Emperor, as vicar in matters temporal, must so control them in their dealings with one another that they are able to pursue undisturbed the spiritual life, and thereby attain the same supreme and common end of

everlasting happiness. In view of this object his chief duty is to maintain peace in the world, while towards the Church his position is that of Advocate or Patron, a title borrowed from the practice adopted by churches and monasteries of choosing some powerful baron to protect their lands and lead their tenants in war. The functions of Advocacy are twofold: at home to make the Christian people obedient to the priesthood, and to execute priestly decrees upon heretics and sinners; abroad to propagate the faith among the heathen, not sparing to use carnal weapons. Thus does the Emperor answer in every point to his antitype the Pope, his power being yet of a lower rank, created on the analogy of the papal... Thus the Holy Roman Church and the Holy Roman Empire are one and the same thing, seen from different sides; and Catholicism, the principle of the universal Christian society, is also Romanism...

This has specific reference to our own continent. Gary Potter defines it admirably in modern terms (*In Reaction*, p. 55):

Words express ideas, and some of them now being quoted signify notions likely to be totally foreign to anyone unfamiliar with history prior to a few decades ago: "world emperor," "imperial office," ... This is not the place to lay out all the history needed to be known for thoroughly grasping the notions. However, the principal one was adumbrated by Our Lord Himself in the last command His followers received from Him: to make disciples of *all* the nations. In a word, the idea of a universal Christian commonwealth is what we are talking about.

To date it has never existed. Today there is not even a Christian government anywhere. However, from the conversion of Constantine until August, 1806—with an interruption (in the West) from Romulus Augustulus in 475 to Charlemagne in 800—there was *the* Empire. It was the heart of what was once known as Christendom. Under its aegis serious European settlement of the Western Hemisphere began, and the Americas' native inhabitants first baptized, which is why the feathered cloak of Montezuma is in a museum in Vienna.

The first time Christendom had set out to colonize a territory outside of Western Europe was during the course of the First Crusade in 1099. At that time, while the modern nationalities of Europe were in existence, they were seen by their members as being at least theoretically subordinate to their common obedience to the Holy Empire, the *Res Publica Christiana*. Although various of the armies of the First Crusade were led by Lorrainers, French, English Normans, and Italian Normans, and in later days German, French, and English rulers would lead swarms of multi-national crusaders to the Holy Land, there was never any questioning of annexing the new lands to one of the constituent kingdoms of the Empire. Instead, the lands freed from the Turk were organized into independent Crusader states: the Kingdom of Jerusalem, and its vassal counties of Edessa, Tripoli, and Antioch.

Being the common property of Christendom, the Kingdom of Jerusalem was organized as the prototypical feudal state. For all that the King was crowned in the Basilica of the Nativity in Bethlehem, his powers were limited. His three chief officers, the Seneschal, Marshal, and Constable, each wielded considerable power. The Lords of the constituent fiefs, gathered together in the High Court, were a strong check on the King's will, as was the Court of the Burgesses, to which belonged citizens of the different towns. The Patriarch of Jerusalem and the Grand Masters of the three Military Orders (Knights Templar, Knights Hospitaller, and Teutonic Knights) were similarly placed. All in all, the historian must agree with Donald Attwater's description of the Kingdom's administration as "a good example... wise, just, and moderate."

However, this first attempt at colonization would fail. Internal disunion could perhaps have been remedied. But the growing national disunity of the states of Christendom, whose joint effort was essential to the Kingdom's survival, doomed it. By 1291, the last cities held by the Crusaders had fallen. With the exception of the 1918-1948 British Mandate, the Holy Land has been out of Christian hands ever since.

This disunity continued; it led to the fratricidal Hundred Years' War between England and France, the War of the Roses in the former country, ongoing strife between Guelphs (Papal supporters) and Ghibellines (Imperial supporters) in Germany and Italy, and at last the Great Schism in the very Papacy itself. The same friction between emerging, centralizing nations led directly to the fall of Constantinople to the Turks in 1453, and permitted them to occupy all Europe south of the Danube River.

But by 1492, a great deal of this had been papered over; Alexander VI, the much-maligned Borgia Pope, was on the throne of Peter; Frederick III, last of the Emperors to be crowned at Rome, was reigning in Vienna. Charles VIII of France had married Anne of Brittany, uniting her land—the last major independent fief—to the French throne. In England, Henry VII, first of the Tudors, was imposing unity on the country after defeating and killing the rightful King, Richard III, in 1485. While all these men were attempting to consolidate their respective realms by centralizing power under the royal administrations we have just discussed, Ferdinand and Isabella of Spain, having united Aragon and Castile by their marriage, were ending the age-old struggle against the Moors. The year of 1492 saw the fall of the last Moorish stronghold, Granada, to the Spanish. The Canary, Azores, and Madeira Islands had already been discovered and partially colonized by this year. An Italian mariner, Christopher Columbus, wished to go further in that direction, and blaze new trade routes to the Far East; these would replace the ones occupied by the Turks, and allow the Faith to expand in heretofore unknown areas. Freed of the Moorish problem, Ferdinand and Isabella were disposed to back him.

The Portuguese, during the course of the 1400s, had been busy exploring themselves. Under the patronage of the King's brother, *Prince Henry the Navigator* (1394-1460), the Azores, Madeiras, and Cape Verdes were discovered as mentioned. Portuguese sailors continued to journey south along the African coast, until in 1486, *Bartholomew Diaz* discovered the Cape of Good Hope. The East lay waiting. But it should be noted that Prince Henry was not interested only in trade with the Far East. As Grand Master of the Order of Christ (the Portuguese branch of the Templars which survived when that order was suppressed), he committed his ships and sailors to finding out the strength of Islam in the regions they explored, to attempt to contact Christian allies (if any were present) and to spread the Faith among the heathen. So it was that his caravels bore the red Crusader's cross, as their voyages of discovery were considered continuations of that conflict.

THE AMERICAS

Due to the lack of written records, a veil is drawn across the face of pre-Columbian America. Although the commonly held belief among academics is that there was little or no contact between the Americas and the rest of the world, some scholars do maintain otherwise. The history of the Americas is quite as and even more interesting from this point of view. In the article "Mexico", in the *Catholic Encyclopedia*, (X, p. 252), there is a fascinating account of pre-Columbian Mexican religion. Some of their traditions closely parallel various stories from Genesis, and represent their particular remnants of the original revelation given the first men. But other elements have a later origin:

> In the history of the nations of ancient Mexico the coming of Quetzalcoatl marks a distinct era. He was said to have come from the province of Panuco, a white man, of great stature, broad brow, large eyes, long black hair, rounded beard, and dressed in a tunic covered with black and red crosses. Chaste, intelligent, a lover of peace, versed in the arts and sciences, he preached by his example and doctrine a new religion which inculcated fasting and penance, love and reverence for the Divinity, practice of virtue, and hatred of vice.

He went on to predict the coming of white men at a particular time and place (which "just happened" to be those where came Cortez) who would overthrow their old gods. He was driven out, and went to Yucatan with the same message; among the Mayans he was called Kukulcan. From his time in both areas dates the native veneration of the Cross, and in various places there were practiced rites he had introduced, suggestive of our baptism, confession, and communion. The Mayans who practiced the latter called the bread *Toyolliatlacual*: "food of our souls." The author of the article supposes that Quetzalcoatl was a 10th or 11th Century Norse priest, driven off course perhaps from the Northern voyages. Others suggest that he was some disciple of the Irish St. Brendan the Navigator, or even the Saint himself. Whatever the case, the implications of the song written by Cauch, High Priest of Tixcayon long before the Spanish came are clear:

> There shall come the sign of a god who dwells on high,
> And the cross which illumined the world shall be made manifest;
> The worship of false gods shall cease.
> Your father comes, O Itzalanos!
> Your brother comes, O Itzalanos!
> Receive your bearded guests from the East,
> Who come to bring the sign of God.
> God it is who comes to us, meek and holy.

It is interesting to note that Our Lady appeared at Guadalupe in the traditional garb of an Aztec princess. This 1531 apparition was the signal for mass conversion. Ancient Peru also had a Quetzalcoatl-like figure, Viracocha, who was said to have been an old bearded white man wearing a robe and carrying a staff.

The Vikings, while still pagan, had chased Irish monks from Iceland. Upon their settlement of Greenland, they found evidence that the same group had preceded them, and then fled westward. According to the *Vinland Saga*, the Indians the Norse later encountered on the coast of North America informed them of white bearded men in the interior, who while wearing robes, carried crosses in procession. The Vikings assumed that these were still more of the same. They themselves maintained a diocese in Greenland from the tenth Century until the 1400s, when the Greenland colony died out. We have, of course, no way of knowing what, if any, missionary activity they undertook, whether collectively or via lone individuals.

Then there is the famous tale of Madoc ap Owain Gwynedd, the legendary Welsh Prince who many claim led a party of colonists to North

America in 1170. The legends of "white Indians" bearing tattered Missals, crucifixes, rosaries, etc. appears to have some basis in fact: Roman coins (then in circulation in Wales) have been discovered in Kentucky, where such a group was rumored to exist around Louisville in the 18th Century. Lewis and Clark were very surprised by the Caucasian appearance of many of the Mandan Indians; artist George Catlin, who lived among them before their near destruction by smallpox and knew them better than any other white man, claimed their language contained a great many Welsh words. Whatever the case, the Daughters of the American Revolution felt the story had enough proof to erect a monument to Madoc at the supposed site of his landing in Mobile Bay.

There are further supposed traces of Japanese, Chinese, African, and even Phoenician visits to the American coasts before Columbus. But regardless of whether or not such voyagers arrived, it was Columbus who started the movement which would make America an integral part of the civilization of Europe.

There were, however, civilizations in the Americas already: the bloody theocracy of the Aztecs, and the ant-hill like despotism of the Incas. Whatever they may have owed to Old World contacts, they were certainly distinctive enough. Many other civilizations—the Olmecs, of Mexico, the Chimus of Peru, and of course, the Mayans of Yucatan, had risen and fallen. In North America, a similar culture, called either "Mound-builders" (so called from the enormous mounds they built) or "Mississippian" had reached practically the same technological level as the Incas or Aztecs about the year 850 A.D. But a few hundred years later it began to break up, under pressure from Plains and Woodland tribes. By the time the Europeans arrived, the Natchez Indians survived as a lone remnant, rather as the Byzantines were of Rome. Interestingly, as the Inca was called the "Son of the Sun," so the chief of the Natchez was titled "The Great Sun."

The North American Indians at the time of the discovery were much more primitive than either their Aztec and Inca contemporaries or their Mississippian predecessors. More settled tribes, such as those in the South and North East, grew pumpkins, beans, corn, and squash. Plains Indians, having no horses (none would arrive until the Spanish came), lived sedentary lives in earth lodges nestled along river banks. In the far West, the California Indians lived wretched lives, subsisting primarily off acorns and rabbits (the fires local tribesmen lit to frighten rabbits out of hiding in the L.A. area provided that future city's first smog). North Western Indians lived relatively comfortably. These latter were famous for *potlaches*, parties at which the host would give away most of his goods to his guests.

It was a continent teeming with game. Buffalo, deer, elk, rabbit, passenger pigeon, turkey, and many other animals and birds went into the tribesmen's larder, as well as various wild plants, and the four staple crops mentioned above. Further to the South, peanuts, chocolate, and potatoes all were raised. Their subsequent introduction to the rest of the world (from which they were absent) would cause as great a revolution in various old world countries' diet as importation of European foods and plants would in the Americas.

At any rate, it so happened that, at the time of the discovery, there were no Indian nations capable of real resistance to the Europeans, save the Aztecs and the Incas. The bloodthirstiness of the former and the rigid interior conformity of the latter seriously depleted their ability to defend themselves against any technologically superior culture with which they might come in contact.

AFRICA

The portion of Africa closest to America, West Africa, is naturally the part which would have, via the slave-trade, the closest connection to the New World. Divided among such incessantly warring peoples as the Ashanti, Fante, Dahomey, and Benin, the West African coast was nevertheless a rich source of gold. In 1471, the Portuguese arrived at what they soon called the Gold Coast (present day Ghana) and in 1482, they built Elmina Castle there, the first of four local forts designed to ensure that other Europeans did not trade in the region. From this depot they hoped to send the gold to Europe, rather than Muslim North Africa. On that particular occasion, an Italian seaman named Christopher Columbus was present.

The small local states had another interesting custom. Fighting continually as they did, they captured many prisoners. These they would sell as slaves, generally to the larger Muslim states to the North, particularly those in the Sudan. But of course, the change in direction of the gold flow away from these countries reduced their ability to buy slaves. Luckily for the petty coastal chieftains, the discovery of the New World would soon provide a whole new outlet for their wares.

ASIA

But what of Asia, of the glittering Far East which the Portuguese hoped to reach by sea going East, and Columbus by going West? In the 13th Century, *Marco Polo* had reached the court of *Khublai Khan*,

Mongol ruler of China. From then on, overland trade and communication between Europe and China grew for about a century, during which time Catholic dioceses were established. Foreigners themselves, the Mongol Emperors of China were friendly to Europeans.

But in 1368, they were driven out of the country, and the native Ming dynasty assumed the throne. Expansionistic, China under the Ming resolved to become a naval power. From 1407 to 1431, Admiral *Cheng Ho* cruised the waters of the Indian Ocean. He visited East African and Arabian ports, and reduced many countries in Southeast Asia to vassals of his Emperor. This was the beginning of the massive emigration of Chinese to those areas, of which their later migration to our West Coast was an eventual product.

But later Emperors did not consolidate the conquests of Cheng Ho. Moreover, the naval interests of China lay to her South and West, not East—where were the fierce Japanese pirates. Although, as earlier suggested, some Chinese may have reached the new world at one time or another, the China of 1492 was not interested in what lay beyond Japan.

Japan herself, in a state of civil war, produced as seamen pirates who were interested only in capturing Chinese ships—thus discouraging Chinese interest in their direction further, and causing them to look Westward. The rest of Eastern Asia was too divided to worry about what might lay beyond the Eastern horizon. If the Westerners were interested in Asia, and unable to dislodge the Turks from their control of the traditional overland routes, then they must find a way by sea themselves.

CONCLUSION

This, then, was the situation of the world on August 3, 1492, when Christopher Columbus and his tiny fleet of three ships set sail from Palos Harbor. They did not realize it, nor did any other human on the planet, but the world was set for a major revolution. Those three small ships, the *Niña,* the *Pinta*, and the *Santa Maria* carried as cargo the future of the world, the civilization of Christendom, and the Catholic Faith. Not only the Americas were to receive these benefits as a result of the voyage, but Asia and Africa too, as Portuguese efforts to keep up with Spain drove them to pursue their Eastern direction more avidly. Further, the cornerstone of our own country was set down that Summer day in Spain.

THE FOUNDING OF CATHOLIC AMERICA 1492-1763

GODMOTHER OF THE AMERICAS

The most obvious thing about Medieval Monarchy is that like the Society over which it presided, it was entirely suffused with Catholicism. The Faith was a living presence in every part of life, and the declared goal of State, as of Church, was the salvation of souls. In the words of historian Catherine Goddard Clarke:

> We have been slowly and deliberately taught that monarchies and kings are bad things, and papal supervision of any kind of government, even over its morals, is a *very* bad thing. The obvious truth, that a bad king can be a bad thing, but that a good king is always a blessedly *good* thing and that the Pope is the divinely constituted guardian of faith and morals for the whole world, is carefully kept from the realization of every school child and man and woman.
> Scarcely anyone is ever told any more that France, Spain and Portugal, Poland and Hungary, England and Sweden, all had kings and queens who were saints, and who ruled their lands gloriously and brought untold happiness and well-being to their subjects.
> (*Our Glorious Popes*, p. 59)

But this kind of government was doomed. The decline of feudalism, the emergence of a money economy, and the spirit of irreligion unleashed by the Renaissance all contributed to a this-worldly point of view. Many a King saw in the centralization of power under himself the only way in which his country (and himself) could be truly great. The Church, Guilds, Nobles, Estates—all must be brought under Royal control. From this emerged *James I* of England's idea of the "Divine Right of Kings." From it also arose the Scandinavian and English Kings' and North German Princes' determination to rule the Church in their countries as much as the State—which determination allowed the so-called Reformation to succeed in those nations. From this also emerged the Modern State apparatus with which we are familiar, whose masters at length either deposed the Kings who had called them into existence, or else reduced them to impotence.

This pagan view of the State, that it existed purely for itself and for the exaltation of its ruler, was much in the air in the 15th century. It is remarkable that *Isabella*, though forced at times to centralize, preserved the local liberties as much as was consonant with the good of the realm; she never succumbed to what was then the avant-garde philosophy. She attempted to rule as a good Catholic Queen—and that required proper handling of the office we have just described.

Spain Before Isabella

One other bit of stage setting required to explain her public career is the state of Spain at the time of her birth. Due to the 750-year-long presence of the Muslims in Spain, the country had long been a frontier of Christianity against Islam. In 711, the Muslims triumphed over the Visigothic King Roderick, and overwhelmed the whole country. Under the leadership of a nobleman, Pelagius (Don Pelayo I), a small group of Christians took refuge in the cave of Covadonga in Asturias. From that refuge they sallied forth to do battle with the Infidel. Thus began the eight-century long *Reconquista*, which was ended triumphantly by our heroine in 1492.

That small cave in Asturias was the beginning of the Kingdom of Castile (so called from the castles built against the Moors). Other centers of resistance similarly gave birth to Kingdoms as their rulers retook more territory from the Muslims. A French Count in the Pyrenees carved out what became the Kingdom of Navarre; another began what became the Kingdom of Aragon, which later absorbed the Frankish Province of Barcelona, once restored by Charlemagne to Christendom. Portugal started as a County freed by a Burgundian nobleman. The whole campaign was carried on in this fashion, with some fighting the enemy for one or the other of these Kings, and others doing it on their own, like the great hero *Rodrigo de Bivar—El Cid*. Proclaimed at last a Crusade like the ones raging in Palestine and Prussia, Orders of Knights were formed as they had been in those places—Santiago, Calatrava, Alcantara, Montesa, Christ, and Aviz. Like their prototypes, the Templars, Hospitallers, and Teutonic Knights, the orders were made by the lands they recaptured, and the castles they built powers to be reckoned with.

The result of this do-it-yourself reconquest was that each of these Kingdoms had wildly varying institutions and character exceptional even in an age our own carefully supervised society would consider anarchic. Each province guarded its rights of self-government (the *fueros*) jealously. The nobles were similarly turbulent; the oath of allegiance to the King of Castile by his lords was almost insulting: "To you, who are no better than we are, from us who are as good as you, true faith and allegiance as long as you obey our laws; and if not, no!"

Despite this, Castile still produced some remarkable Kings, such as Alfonso X ("the Wise," 1221-1281), and St. Ferdinand III (1201-1252) of whom the great Dom Gueranger writes in *The Liturgical Year:*

> Catholic Spain is personified in her Ferdinand. His mother Berengaria was sister to Blanche, the mother of St. Louis of France. In order to form "the Catholic Kingdom," there was needed one of our Lord's Apostles, St. James the Great; there was needed a formidable trial, the Saracen invasion, which deluged the peninsula; there was needed a chivalrous resistance, which lasted eight hundred years, and by which Spain regained her glory and her freedom. St. Ferdinand is the worthy representative of the brave heroes who drove out the Moors from their fatherland and made her what she is: but he had the virtues of a saint, as well as the courage of a soldier. (vol. VIII, "Paschal Time," Bk. II, p. 630).

St. Ferdinand had in Isabella a worthy descendant, who was always mindful of his example. His efforts restricted the Moors in 1238 to a last remnant of territory, the Kingdom of Granada in the far south of Spain. There they sat, occasionally sending out raiders, but for the most part stagnating in a melancholy fashion well captured by Washington Irving in his *Tales of the Alhambra.*

But this indolence was not to profit the Christians of Spain for another 254 years. Most of St. Ferdinand's successors were not nearly so great. Pedro the Cruel, for instance, while of unpleasant personal habits, was not the man to conquer Granada. But on April 22, 1451, John II, as ineffectual King as ever graced the throne of Castile, was presented by his new wife, Isabella of Portugal (niece of Prince Henry the Navigator) with a daughter. Named after her mother, she would regain for her country the glory of her ancestors, and spread it to lands they had never dreamed of.

Like his contemporary in England, Henry VI, John had been the pawn of rival factions of nobles throughout his reign. Just as the English counterpart of this conflict, the War of the Roses, inflicted untold suffering on Henry's subjects, so too did the Spanish version affect John's. "The Royal Baton," as King John was known, died when his daughter was two years old. He was succeeded by her elder brother, Henry IV, called the "Impotent" or the "Strange."

He was apparently homosexual, and gave his associates free reign—not unlike England's Edward II (1307-1327). Like that unhappy monarch, too, Henry's fecklessness and reliance on favorites led eventually to a revolt by another faction of his nobles, who took umbrage at his mismanagement. They proclaimed the King's heir and younger brother, Alphonso, as King. But when, in 1467, Alphonso died, leaving young Princess Isabella as sole heiress to the realm, the civil war ground to a halt.

How had Isabella fared? Her first eleven years were lived in seclusion with her mother, the dowager Queen; then she arrived at her brother's court, the most corrupt in Europe. When the civil war broke out between her brothers, although she maintained her love for Alphonso, she refused to join the rebellion, preferring to remain in a convent. After Alphonso's death, both sides relied on her as heiress.

Isabella as Queen

In an atmosphere filled with plots and counterplots, Isabella married in 1472 Ferdinand, Crown Prince of Aragon. Two years later, Henry died, leaving Isabella as Queen. Revolts broke out against her; the next few years is an exciting tale of escapes, sieges, and intrigue. But Isabella, Ferdinand at her side, triumphed over her enemies and secured her throne. In 1479, Ferdinand succeeded to the throne of Aragon, and the two largest countries of Spain were united. They would retain separate institutions for many centuries, and so late as the 19th Century, the common Spaniards referred to their country as "the Spains." But the emergence of the Spain of today had begun.

As has been noted, the turbulent Spanish nobility were an important force for anarchy. Triumphing over her opponents and safeguarding her throne were achievements for the Queen in itself. But something had to be done to maintain order and restrain those who, during the periods of civil war, had taken to robbery. This was, after all, in a day when Monarchs had no police force to watch the entire citizenry as we do today. Isabella's solution was typically Spanish, and typically Catholic.

In the Middle Ages, men and women gathered together in all sorts of Confraternities. These had as their aim generally both religious and temporal goals. On the religious side, all members were bound to pray for one another, attend Mass together at various feast days, and so on—sometimes one or another of these groups undertook miracle or mystery plays. Our Scapular Confraternities of today are survivals of this kind of thing. More temporally, they often provided for members' burial and support of survivors. Beyond this, though, there could be an almost dizzying number of ends. The Trade and Craft guilds regulated their professions; knightly confraternities did the same in a given district. Then, in areas torn by anarchy and domestic warfare between nobles, confraternities grew up with the goal of maintaining peace. It was an idea that had spread to Spain; various locals on the road to Compostela had formed themselves into confraternities devoted to protection of the pilgrims who wended their way there to venerate the bones of St. James the Great. Defense of such travelers became not merely a civic but a religious duty, with corresponding benefits after death if the job were performed well.

With the breakdown of order in Castile, these confraternities or "Holy Brotherhoods" had declined. But Isabella and her consort revived them in 1476. Companies of the *Santa Hermandad* were formed and subsidized throughout Spain. By 1504, the roads throughout the country were once again safe, and so commerce flourished. The Brotherhoods themselves lasted long enough to play a glorious part in the Peninsular War, acting as a local militia against the French invaders of Napoleon.

However, it was not enough merely to apprehend malefactors. They must also be tried—and in remote parts of Castile, where they might be working secretly with the local nobleman to whom judicial power had been delegated—this might be difficult. So Isabella traveled extensively in far away provinces like Extramadura and Andalusia, to sit in judgment over criminals. This was done at great personal risk; but the good of her subjects demanded it, and it was her responsibility as Queen. Here too, she was successful.

The Fall of Granada

The reign of justice restored after long years of labor, she and Ferdinand were now ready to turn their attention to the last remaining Moorish possession—Granada. Although no longer able to threaten most of Spain, the Moors were able to mount bloody raids on the borders. And while they themselves might be quiescent, their co-religionists, the Ottoman Turks, were not. Two years after Isabella was born, Constantinople, the great City of the East and center of the Byzantine Empire, fell to them. Greece, Serbia, and Bosnia all came under Turkish sway before Isabella took the throne; twenty-two years after her death they would be at the gates of Vienna. Their caravels were already prowling the Mediterranean, a problem which would not be relieved until Isabella's great-grandson, Don John of Austria, defeated them at Lepanto in 1571. As long as any part of Spain lay in Muslim hands—even in those of the enervated Moors—the peninsula could not be truly secure. The last struggle against the Moors began in 1488, and continued until January 1492. The entrance of Ferdinand and Isabella into the Alhambra marked the end of the age-long struggle begun when Don Pelayo emerged from the Covadonga eight centuries before. At last, all Spain was free.

One of the immediate results of this occurrence was the expulsion of the Jews from Spain. This happening has been frequently cited in recent years against the Queen, and it is an important question to address. In order to understand it in context, we must remember that the Spanish

Jews had, from the first invasion by the Moors back in 711, collaborated closely with the Muslim invaders, who were after all, also a Semitic people. This was considered an act of betrayal by the Spanish. During the long years of Moorish tyranny, Jews often served under them as governors of the Christian populace; Jewish culture in Spain flourished, Toledo and Cordova in particular becoming centers of Hebrew thought and learning. While such collaboration is easily understood, so too is the resentment toward it. When an occupying force is at last dislodged from a nation's territories, those who collaborated with the occupiers—as Pierre Laval and Vikdun Quisling found out after World War II—often do not fare very well.

But where Twentieth Century rulers faced with large ethnic minorities might launch genocide against them, as did the Turks with the Armenians and the Nazis with the Gypsies, Jews, and Poles (or else "ethnic cleansing" as the Serbian Communists call it), Isabella had no such desire. She feared possible future collaboration of the Jews with Muslims—and she had not defeated restive nobles, brigands, and the Granada Moors to see it all lost to Turks. But as a Catholic she would certainly not want them wantonly executed. What, then, to do?

At this point, in order to explain her motivations, a few points must be made about her and her contemporaries' understanding of Catholicism. They believed Our Lord's words "Unless a man be baptized of water and the Holy Ghost, he shall not enter the Kingdom of God," and "Unless a man eat my body and drink my blood, he shall not have life in him." They agreed with Pope Boniface VIII in his bull, *Unam Sanctam,* that "it is absolutely necessary to the salvation of every human creature to be subject to the Roman Pontiff." This is why the Protestant Henry of Navarre (later Henry IV of France) said in regard to his conversion to Catholicism, "the ministers say that I can save my soul as a Catholic, the priests that I cannot save it as a Protestant. Therefore I can surely be saved as a Catholic." Without this understanding, none of the Queen's actions with regard to the Jews or to the Guanches and Indians (of whom more presently) can be understood.

For like her Savior, she did not desire the death of sinners, but that they should live. She wished that all of her subjects might be members of the Catholic Church, outside of which she believed there was no salvation. If the Jews would convert (for Church law forbade her to force them to do so) they would be given all the privileges and rights of ordinary Spaniards. If not, they were a security risk, and must go. In the event, at most 160,000 left. Many of these, interestingly enough, were picked up by Ottoman vessels and brought to Thessalonica and Constantinople, in which city the anniversary of their arrival was celebrated in 1992. Others went to North Africa, and still others to the

Netherlands where, unhampered by the Church's laws against usury, they laid the foundations for that country's capitalist economy and eventual financial prowess. Those who converted, however, soon reached the heights of Spanish society. Many became bishops and nobles and high courtiers; St. Teresa of Avila, for example, was part Jewish.

The Discovery of America

But 1492 was not only concerned with the fall of Granada and the expulsion of the Jews: as every American school-child knows, it was the year that "Columbus sailed the ocean blue." In so doing, he opened up a new world, filled with new problems in administration.

Nevertheless, Isabella was not completely unfamiliar with colonies. In 1404, the Castilians had begun the conquest of the Canary Islands, which would not be completed until 1496. Their native inhabitants, a blonde, blue-eyed people called the Guanches, were and are something of a mystery. Fierce warriors, they are claimed by some anthropologists to have been pure Cro-Magnons, by some linguists to have spoken a language related to the equally mysterious North African Tuareg. However all that may be, they certainly were monotheists, extremely primitive, and dogged opponents.

In 1472, Pope Sixtus IV called the Christian powers involved in the Canaries (primarily Castile) to make every effort to convert them. Five years later, discovering that many of the Guanches were being sold into slavery (an institution only just being revived among Christians), Ferdinand and Isabella issued this decree:

> Know that we have heard that some persons have brought some natives of the Canary Islands, and, by the will of the lord of those islands and other persons, have sold them and divided them out among themselves as slaves, though some are Christians, and others on their way to converting to our Holy Catholic Faith. This is a great disservice to God and to us and is detrimental to our Holy Catholic Faith, and it would be a great burden on our consciences to consent to it, because it would lead to no one wishing to convert to the Holy Faith.
> (quoted in Warren Carroll, *Isabel of Spain*, p. 120)

Nor were they content to let their decree sit; they dispatched two trusted advisors to the Canaries to ensure compliance.

A 1490 uprising on the Canary island of Gomera was suppressed by Governor Pedro de Vera with great ferocity, most of the inhabitants being killed or sold as slaves, despite the fact that many of the survivors were Christian. When word of this outrage reached Isabella and Ferdinand, they moved into action. Although many of the men of

Gomera had been implicated in the revolt, those who had been were dead; the women and children were not involved, and being Christian had full civil rights. They could not be slaves. 5,000,000 maravedis were taken from the Governor as security for the transportation of the Gomerans back to their homes from wherever they had been sold. This order was scrupulously carried out. Never again would an attempt be made to enslave the Canary Islanders, and they settled down to become loyal Spanish.

The result has been that culturally, the Islands are almost identical to Spain. Still, the Canarios have a much higher incidence of blue-eyed blondes than does most of Spain, and on Gomera the strange Guanche "whistling-language" used to communicate from hill-top to hill-top is still used. Apart from exporting the canary bird, Canario settlers went to various spots in Latin America. Some of the oldest families in San Antonio, Texas are Canario descended, and the *Isleños* of St. Bernard Parish, Louisiana, settled there by the Spanish in the 1770s, still preserve old Canario folk songs and dialect. But the Canaries played one other great part in Spanish history; they were the base from which Francisco Franco launched his war against the Communist government in 1936. As they were the first part of Spain's overseas empire, so today they are the last.

What all of this meant was that when Columbus discovered America, Ferdinand and Isabella already had a plan for dealing with colonial peoples. When Columbus presented his project to them, it was not in terms of finding new routes to China, nor of proving the world round (which educated opinion believed in any case). It was to win souls for Christ. Let it not be forgotten that the militant Catholicism, encompassing within it the desire to conquer the world for Christ, built up over eight centuries of struggle, needed an outlet. The Portuguese had found one; starting with Isabella's uncle, Prince Henry the Navigator, they had voyaged down the West Coast of Africa. By the time a half-century had passed after Isabella's death, the Portuguese would have settlements all along the Indian Ocean, from Mozambique to Indonesia. While this effort gave rise to many abuses (as every human endeavor does) it allowed St. Francis Xavier alone the opening to baptize 3,000,000 in the countries he visited; and he would have many colleagues to follow his example. To this day, the Church in Japan, China and all the countries which touch the Indian Ocean owe their origin to these Portuguese efforts; the surnames of thousands of Catholic Sri Lankans, Indians, Malaysians, Pakistanis, Bangladeshis, and Indonesians are further proof.

It should not be surprising then that the same fervor could be found in Spanish hearts. After Columbus' discovery, in 1493, Pope Alexander VI divided the non-Christian world between the Spanish and the

Portuguese. To the latter was given responsibility for the evangelization and civilizing of the East Indies and Brazil; to the former, the same with regard to the Americas excepting Brazil. The words of the Pope's Bull, *Inter Caetera*, reflect well the spirit in which the great work was undertaken:

> Wherefore, as becomes Catholic kings and princes, after earnest consideration of all matters, especially the rise and spread of the Catholic faith, as was the fashion of your ancestors, kings of renowned memory, you have purposed with the favor of divine clemency to bring under your sway the said mainlands and islands with their residents and inhabitants and to bring them to the Catholic faith. Hence, heartily commending in the Lord this your holy and praiseworthy purpose, and desirous that it be duly accomplished, and that the name of our Savior be carried into those regions, we exhort you very earnestly in the Lord and by your reception of holy baptism, whereby you are bound to our apostolic commands, and by the bowels of the mercy of Our Lord Jesus Christ, enjoin strictly, that inasmuch as with eager zeal for the true faith you design to equip and dispatch this expedition, you purpose also, as is your duty, to lead the peoples dwelling in those islands and countries to embrace the Christian religion; nor at any time let dangers or hardships deter you therefrom, with the stout hope and trust in your hearts that Almighty God will further your undertakings.

Within the lifetime of Isabella, only the Island of Hispaniola was colonized. But there was laid the foundation of Spanish America which today extends culturally from Tierra Del Fuego to San Francisco Bay and Southern Colorado. The spirit of the legislation she and Ferdinand drafted for this first American possession has been well captured by historian C. H. Haring:

> The Papal Bull of 1493, which gave to the kings of Castile dominion over the Indies, imposed one supreme obligation: to spread the gospel and draw the pagans into the Church of Christ; and Isabella to the day of her death regarded the welfare of the American natives as a major responsibility. When, therefore, the new governor, Nicolás de Ovando, came out to America in 1502, he was instructed by Isabella to assure the native chiefs that they and their people were under the crown's special protection. They might go in entire freedom about the island, and no one was to rob them or harm them in any way, under severe penalties. They were to pay tribute only as the rest of the king's subjects. Only in the royal service in mines or on public works might they be compelled to labor. These orders were followed to the letter. But left to themselves, the Indians refused to work... They withdrew from all association with the colonists, with results that from the European point of view were disastrous. Within a few months

Governor Ovando wrote to Spain protesting that the only effect was the falling off of tribute, lack of labor, and inability to carry forward the work of conversion to Christianity.

The sovereigns replied with the famous orders of March and December 1503, which legalized the forced labor of free Indians but attempted at the same time to protect them from uncontrolled exploitation. The natives must be made to work, if necessary, on buildings and farms and in the mines, but in moderation and for reasonable wages. At the same time, to ensure their being civilized, they must be gathered into villages, under the administration of a patron or protector, and provided with a school and a missionary priest. Each adult Indian was to have a house and land which he might not alienate. Intermarriage of Spaniards and Indians was also to be encouraged. And in everything they were to be treated "as free persons, for such they are." Only cannibal Indians from neighboring islands if taken in war might be sold into slavery.

(*The Spanish Empire in America*, pp. 39-40).

The *encomienda*, as this system was called, was intended to spread the faith among the Indians; the first requirement for the *encomiendero* as the patron was called, was the instruction and baptism of the Indians entrusted to him. In practice, the system did not work well, and giving rise to many abuses was denounced by *Bartolome de Las Casas* to the Crown in 1517, after which it was abolished. After that, Indians in the Spanish territories were to be subject to the King himself, and live under their own chiefs or *caiciques*. Some of these, like Mexico's Princes of Tlaxcala or Peru's Marquesses of Oropesa, were to become great noblemen in their own right. The Tlaxcalans, for example, by order of Charles V, were given the title "Don," exempted from taxes, and were permitted to ride horses; they played an important part in the settlement of the Philippines, Northern Mexico, and New Mexico. It was not until Latin American independence dawned that the new centralizing governments destroyed Indian autonomy. But all of these developments were far off when Isabella died in 1504.

The Queen's Legacy

What is important in this context is the Queen's motivation in her legislation regarding the Indians. For Ferdinand and Isabella, the American territories were not Spanish colonies, actually, but separate realms. Eventually, after the conquests of Mexico and Peru, their concept of governance was carried out under their successors. So the King of Spain was in the end King really of the Spains: that is, Castile, Aragon, Navarre, the Canaries, New Spain (Mexico, Central America, the Spanish West Indies, the Philippines, Florida and the U.S. South West, as well as Guam and the Marianas), Peru (including Chile), New Granada (Colombia, Ecuador, Venezuela, and Panama), and Rio de la Platt (Argentina, Bolivia, Paraguay, and Uruguay). Each of these "Spains" were in theory equal, none subordinate to the other, but all subject to the same King. Subjects in each of these countries were full citizens if they were Catholic and spoke Spanish. Obviously, theory and practice, during the long centuries of Spanish rule, were rarely completely in accord. But the Spanish were much more humane in the overall to the Indians than were the English. This is due in no small part to the initial tenor of Isabella's legislation on their behalf.

Isabella was fully Catholic in both her public and private personae. As Queen she believed in the divinely bestowed responsibilities Spain's essentially sacral political order had endowed her with. As Queen it was part of her royal duties to found churches and monasteries, and to give gifts to already existing ones. The furtherance of the Faith was a major motif of her foreign and colonial policies. The Orders of Calatrava, Santiago, Montesa, and Alcantara were still possessed of enormous lands, despite the ending of the Moorish war. So powerful were they, and so fractious their membership, that they could have become a threat to the Crown. To forestall this from happening, but to also maintain their integrity as religious orders, she united their Grand Masterships with the Kingship. In this way royal patronage bolstered them and they supported the Crown.

But Isabella's religion was not merely public:

> Isabel has been called a mystic who managed to lead the life of a contemplative in the midst of an absorbing career, but there was nothing in her mysticism of that dreamy quietism from the east that denies the claims of reality and takes refuge in a subjective passivity. Like all the great western mystics—like Saint Teresa, like Saint Catherine of Siena, like Saint Ignatius Loyola—she was acutely conscious of the problems of this world and of her duties toward them, and like them she found in prayer the motive power for large and heroic actions. In every crisis she humbly laid her difficulties at the feet of God; but having appealed to Him with all confidence, she proceeded to do her part with an energy that would have commanded the admiration of those less articulate Yankee farmers whose motto was, "Trust God, and keep your powder dry." (Walsh, *op. cit.*, p. 246).

Despite the pressures which surrounded her continually, she kept both her personal devotion and her private and public morality intact, for which reason Washington Irving called her "one of the purest and most beautiful characters in the pages of history."

THE CONQUISTADORES

Coming as it did at the end of the long struggle with Islam, the Spanish colonization of the Americas was undertaken in the same manner as the *Reconquista,* and before that, the Crusades. As with those struggles, the story of the Conquest of the New World sees the highest motives mixed with some dreadful actions. But that has always been true of any human endeavor which has as its declared goal anything higher than basic survival. It is important to remember that the Conquistadore had much the same attitudes as did the Medieval knight; that is how we must understand them—as later flowers of chivalry. What Leon Gautier said of their Crusading forerunners is true of the Conquistadores also: "The faith of these rude warriors, that faith which was so precise, had nothing namby-pamby in it: nothing *dilettante* or effeminate. We have not to do with the little sugar-plums of certain contemporary devotion— but with a good and frank wild-honey. It is a grosser but loyal Catholicism" (*Chivalry,* p. 27). It is certainly true that in their number were unscrupulous and greedy men—like Francisco Pizarro. But over all, they were as idealistic and practical a group of men as any who have ever set out on a goal higher than themselves. We cannot look at all of them, but we will examine a few of the most important.

Christopher Columbus

We do not usually think of Columbus as a Conquistadore, but it was he who opened the way. An ancestor of his had been aboard the boat which received the dying Bl. Raymond Lully, when that mystic and missionary was stoned by a North African mob in Tunis in 1316. Lully's last words were to say that there lay another continent beyond the sea, and to admonish his hearers to send missionaries there to save souls. This account was preserved in the young Columbus' family and made a great impression on him.

Born in Genoa, Columbus went to sea at 14, sailing as far away as Iceland. He eventually made his way to Portugal to study at the school of Prince Henry the Navigator, doubtless receiving not only navigational skills but also the crusading and missionary zeal of the Knights of Christ who ran the school. With them, as we have seen, he sailed to the Gold Coast of Africa. He attempted to interest the Kings of Portugal, England, and France in his idea of sailing around the world to Asia; in this he failed. Luckily, Fr. Mendez, the Queen's confessor, took an interest in him and his work, and attained an audience with Ferdinand and Isabella. They were not very receptive at first. But the fall of Granada gave them leisure for other projects. Columbus received their backing, and the New World was duly discovered.

Columbus' landing on October 12, 1492 was significant in innumerable ways. Not least of these is the fact that it is the feast day of Our Lady of the Pillar. This commemorates the very first apparition of Our Lady, which occurred while she yet lived. St. James the Apostle, having had very little success with converting the Spaniards, was about to go back to Palestine. But in Saragossa (Caesarea Augusta, as it was in Roman times), the Blessed Virgin appeared to him, and assured him that, if he stayed, the Spanish would one day become a great Catholic people. He did, and they did, eventually revering St. James as their patron and treasuring his relics at Santiago de Compostela.

At any rate, much discouraged, and with his crew near mutiny, Columbus agreed to turn back to Spain if land was not sighted by sundown on the feast of Our Lady of the Pillar; doubtless he felt much like St. James. Like St. James, his perseverance was rewarded, and America discovered. He would make a total of four voyages to America, founding the first permanent settlement by Europeans in the Americas—Santo Domingo, on the island of Hispaniola. His career was difficult, and he faced much opposition, from enemies at court, from disobedient subordinates, and from the Indians the latter provoked. Many of the slanders his enemies made against him are used today as well by enemies of the Faith.

But the truth about Columbus is that his primary goal was to convert the Asians (as he thought the Indians to be) to Catholicism. He was very pious, being in fact a Third Order Franciscan and buried in the Franciscan habit. Although his enemies at last had him sent home to Spain in chains in 1504, he was not embittered. Indeed, he offered to set sail again, and to spend his last possession on what would have been his crowning voyage: an attempt to regain the Holy Sepulcher from the Infidels. But it was not to be, and death claimed him in 1506. He was even proposed for Sainthood; a storm of opposition from Protestant and other quarters stymied this attempt in 1892—not unlike that which beset his memory in 1992. It really does not matter, however. The day of his discovery is kept as a national holiday, Columbus Day, in the United States, The Bahamas, Belize, Chile, Colombia, Costa Rica, The Dominican Republic, Ecuador, El Salvador, Guatemala, Honduras, Mexico, Paraguay, Spain, Uruguay, and Venezuela. Thus the father of the Americas has, indirectly, been responsible for the erection of the Feast of Our Lady of the Pillar into a legal holiday in 16 countries. Given Columbus' character, it is an accomplishment which doubtless would have pleased him more than merely discovering a new continent.

Hernando Cortez

Ferdinand and Isabella's daughter, Juana, married in her turn the handsome Philip of Burgundy, himself the son of Maximilian I, the gallant and chivalrous Holy Roman Emperor. Unfortunately, Juana went mad after her husband's premature death; their son Charles I therefore succeeded his grandfather, Ferdinand, when the latter died in 1516. Having already been ruler of Burgundy and The Netherlands when his father died, he found himself ruler of a vast empire in the New World. The major islands of the West Indies were being colonized, and the shores of Mexico and Central America were being explored. In 1518, word was brought back to Havana of the Aztec Empire of Mexico. The next year, two great events happened: Charles I succeeded his grandfather Maximilian as Holy Roman Emperor (thus picking up the Habsburg territories in Central Europe and the responsibility of dealing with the Reformation—Martin Luther began his activities in 1517—and the Turks); and an expedition was fitted out in Havana to bring the Aztecs into Spain's dominion in accordance with the mandate of Alexander VI. The man chosen to lead it was Hernando Cortez.

Headstrong and impetuous, Cortez had the courage and daring necessary for such a quest. Landing at San Juan de Uloa near Vera Cruz on April 21, 1519, he had few troops. 600 infantry, 16 cavalry, 13 crossbowmen, and 14 cannon were the entirety of his force. As it turned out, however, he had arrived at precisely the time and place predicted by Quetzalcoatl; the Aztecs did not move immediately against him as a result. This delay allowed him to make contact with the Tlaxcalans and other Indian subjects of the Aztecs. Tired of long years of seeing their handsomest and most beautiful young men and women sacrificed in their thousands to the Aztec gods, they joined the Spanish. This turned the tide; by 1521, Mexico was in Cortez's hands.

This did not last long, however, for a man of Cortez's nature could not get along well with superiors. He was eventually removed from office, and returned to Spain in 1540, dying in Seville 7 years later. His was not as sterling a character as Columbus'. But he was a friend to the clergy; it is also notable that he named his first town, Vera Cruz, after the True Cross. If he was at times cruel and barbaric in his treatment of the Aztecs, it should be remembered that his Indian allies presented him with innumerable accounts of Aztec atrocities; his reaction was not unlike that of the American soldiers who liberated the German Concentration Camps in 1945.

Heaven, however, gave its sign of approval to the conquest. Ten years afterwards, Our Lady appeared dressed as an Aztec princess to the Indian Juan Diego, at the hill of Tepeyac outside Mexico City. She told him that she wanted a shrine built there in her honor, and that he was to tell the bishop of this request. The bishop demanded proof; this Our Lady provided, when she told Juan to gather roses on the hillside—a difficult feat in a Mexican Winter. But there they were; he gathered them in his *tilma* (a sort of poncho) and brought them to the cathedral. Releasing them from his cloak, all were struck by the image on it—that image known to us as Our Lady of Guadalupe. Reaction was immediate; by the time Cortez left Mexico, nine million Mexican Indians had converted. This came about at the very time that Kings and Princes in Europe were tearing their people out of Christendom, and taking total control of their realms. So, at least in terms of numbers, what was lost in the Old World was made up in the New.

Hernando de Soto and Francisco de Coronado

De Soto (1500-1542), discoverer of the Mississippi, was a Knight of the Order of Santiago and Governor of Cuba. Determined to advance the cause of Christ on "the Northern Rim of Christendom" (as the Spaniards were already beginning to call North America), he landed in Florida, and marched through that state, Georgia, Alabama, and Mississippi. Reaching the river which gives its name to the last state, he explored it up as far as the Ohio. Many skirmishes were fought with hostile Indians; fever claimed De Soto, and he was buried in the Great River he had discovered.

Michael V. Gannon in his *The Cross in the Sand* sums up De Soto's character very well:

> Although it is recorded that De Soto was not above the use of deception in his dealings with the Indians, nor averse to reducing them to slavery when it suited his purposes, to his credit it is also recorded that he sometimes assisted the priests in instructing Indian chiefs and tribesmen in Christianity. On one such occasion... De Soto fashioned and raised a towering pine-tree Cross at the town of Casqui on the western bank of the Mississippi, and proclaimed to the Indians of the place: 'This was He who had made the sky and the earth and man in His own image. Upon the tree of the Cross He suffered to save the human race, and rose from the tomb on His third day... and, having ascended into heaven, was there to receive with open arms all who would be converted to Him.'

Gannon goes on to evaluate De Soto as: "A brave soldier, a man of invincible spirit and high resolve, a rude but earnest missionary..." (pp. 8-9).

Francisco de Coronado (1500-1553), while De Soto was exploring the South-East, set off for the South West. Like De Soto, he was led on by Indian reports of wealthy cities which, mirage-like, seemed to recede ever further into the distance. Having left Mexico in 1540, he wintered among the Pueblo Indians, and then set off after reports of "Quivira." He moved ever northward through modern day Texas, Oklahoma, Kansas, and Nebraska. But at last, discouraged, he gave up and returned to Mexico City. But one item was left behind in Kansas, to be discovered in 1886: a Spanish sword from Coronado's expedition, inscribed with the name of its owner, Juan Gallegos, and on the blade these words: "Do not draw me without right. Do not sheathe me without honor." Here at once is summed up the essential chivalry of the Conquistadores.

Pedro de Menendez

Despite all of these and other explorers, Spain failed to establish a permanent settlement in the present United States. Meanwhile, Emperor Charles V, worn out with fighting the Protestants and the Turks, abdicated his thrones in 1555. To his brother, Ferdinand I, he gave the Empire and the Habsburg Austrian lands. To his son, Philip II, he gave Spain and its rapidly growing overseas empire.

To that empire and its shipping, English and French Protestant pirates constituted a grave threat. When a band of the latter established a nest at Ft. Caroline (present-day Jacksonville, FL), the better to menace Cuba with, Philip resolved on action. His military commander, Pedro de Menendez, was given a royal commission to clear out the pirates, and to found a Spanish town in the area which would serve to prevent the same thing happening again. On September 8, 1565, the town of St. Augustine was founded on its present site. The next month, the pirates of Ft. Caroline were wiped out. The first part of Menendez's job was completed.

The second, securing the safety and prosperity of St. Augustine, would take longer. Indeed, it would not be until 1606 that the town was on a firm foundation. But in the meantime, the most important thing was to secure a steady supply not only of colonists (hard to obtain—living in Spain at that time was very pleasant, and few wished to leave), but of missionaries. Menendez wrote a letter to the Spanish Jesuits, imploring them to send some of their number:

> They [the Indians] ask me to make them Christian as we are, and I have told them that I am waiting for your Honors, so you can make wordlists, and quickly learn their language, and then tell them how they are to be Christians, and enlighten them that if they are not they are

serving and having as their Lord the most evil creature of the world, which is the devil, who is deceiving them, and that if they are Christian, they will be enlightened and serve Our Lord, who is Chief of Heaven and earth; and then, being happy and content, they will be our true brothers, and we will give them whatever we may have.

Menendez did not live to see his vision become a reality. But it did. Eventually, although Spain's actual colonizing efforts produced only St. Augustine and Pensacola in Florida, her missionaries—Jesuit and Franciscan—Catholicized northern Florida, Western and coastal Georgia, and coastal South Carolina. Like the Princes of Tlaxcala and the Marquises of Oropesa whom we have already encountered, the caiciques of the twenty-seven converted tribes were direct vassals of the King, with whom some corresponded familiarly. Indeed, because the missionaries reduced the Indian languages to writing, they wrote one another, long before the pilgrims ever saw Plymouth Rock. In truth, much of Spanish power in the present U.S. rested on the shoulders of the mission padres, at whom we shall now take a closer look.

THE MISSIONARIES

There can be no doubt that the Spanish missionaries in the U.S. were much assisted in their efforts by many miracles, such as the one at Guadalupe. Most spectacular and best known of these is the experience of *Venerable Maria de Agreda* (1602-1665). At that time, the first Franciscan missionaries reached the tribes of West Texas and Eastern New Mexico. Much to their surprise, the padres found that a few of the tribes were already aware of Catholicism, knew its doctrines, and asked for Baptism. When asked how they knew, they replied that they had been taught by a lady in blue. Several of the Friars returned to Spain, and found Maria de Agreda, head of a convent of nuns who wore blue habits; she claimed to have bilocated to the New World to instruct Indians there. Questioned in detail about the appearances and customs of those she allegedly had taught, she described to them perfectly the tribes they had just left. The account is commemorated in a picture at the Cathedral of Fort Worth, Texas. But why did she go to those tribes, rather than others? Good Will, one must suppose. At any rate, one who was inspired by her example was the Apostle of California, *Bl. Junipero Serra.*

A professor of Bl. Raymond Lully's philosophy, he followed the example of his mentor, whom we met dying in view of one of Columbus' forebears, and went to California, eventually founding the string of Missions which were the start of its modern culture. Upon his arrival in 1771 at the future site of Mission San Antonio de Padua (near present day Jolon) in central California, he immediately unloaded a bell from a mule, hung it on a tree, and rang it. All the while he shouted "O ye gentiles! Come to the holy church!" His associates reminded him that there were neither Indians nor a church about, to which he replied that he just wanted to "give vent to my desires that this bell might be heard all over the World!" But shortly thereafter, an old Indian woman came into the camp, asking to be baptized. The padres were quite shocked, seeing that there had been no one there to explain the sacrament or its need to the Indians. But the woman explained that her father had told her about a man who appeared to him four times, explaining to him the doctrines of Catholicism. Satisfying their questions, she was forthwith baptized.

Missionaries as Colonizers

Just as the settling of Florida was primarily achieved by evangelizing the Indians rather than bringing over Spanish colonists, so too with the rest of Spanish North America. Thirty-three years after St. Augustine was founded, Juan de Oñate set off with a group of 400 colonists for New Mexico. He founded the city of Santa Fe, then as now, capital of the province. Then as now, Santa Fe was surrounded by Indian Pueblos. Rather than try to destroy them, as the English might later, the Spanish Franciscans set to work converting them. They taught them the Creation story by having them act it out; they had them perform their dances in honor of Our Lord and Lady, and the Saints. So Spanish and Indians lived side-by-side; each retaining their own ways, but sharing a common faith.

It was not until 1698 that Spain occupied Texas. With that first band came *Fr. Massenet*. While soldiers and Canary Islanders were founding the town of San Antonio, Massenet and those padres who followed him were founding missions, of which the Alamo is certainly the most famous. Two years later, *Eusebio Kino, S.J.*, entered Arizona, to found San Xavier del Bac near Tucson. So firmly did he and his successors plant the Catholic faith among the Pima Indians of the area, that when San Xavier del Bac lay abandoned for a century and a half, the Pimas kept it in perfect condition until the Jesuits returned.

In 1769, Bl. Junipero Serra began California. The founding of the twenty-one California missions did not cease until the last, San Francisco Solano in Sonoma, was opened in 1821. There were in addition, four *presidios* (forts), two towns (Los Angeles and San Jose) and many ranchos. Obviously, until they were secularized by the Mexican government in 1831, the missions and their Indian inhabitants were the bulk of Spanish California.

All of this achievement was not without its cost in blood. Eighty-three Spanish missionaries were martyred for the faith by hostile Indians or by the English in the course of their work, starting with *Fr. Juan de Padilla, O.F.M.* in the Fall of 1542, and ending with *Fr. Antonio Diaz de Leon,* killed by Texan-American frontiersmen for his religion in 1834.

Yet this was merely the tip of the missionary iceberg in Spanish America, and far from the most important region. We cannot do more than mention the Jesuit *Reducciones* of Paraguay, where from 1607 to 1768 the padres ruled over a veritable Mission state. Even an enemy of the Church, Voltaire, could say of them:

> ...they had arrived at what is perhaps the highest degree of civilization to which it is possible to lead a young people... Laws were there respected, morals were pure, a happy brotherhood bound men together, the useful arts and even some of the more pleasing sciences flourished; there was abundance everywhere.

The Dominican *Vasco de Quiroga* in the 1530s established a similar commonwealth in his chain of missions among the Tarascan Indians around Lake Patzcuaro in Mexico's Michoacan State. Many of the crafts he taught are still practiced by the Tarascans, who continue to venerate his name. There were many more examples throughout the Spanish Americas.

THE SPANISH ACHIEVEMENT

By 1763, the Spanish possessions in the New World constituted an incredible achievement. Stretching from the frontier in North America—"the Northern Rim of Christendom," Spanish rule continued down through Mexico and Central America, through the Andes mountains to the plains of the Pampas, ending at Patagonia, and hemming in Portuguese Brazil (where a similar achievement had been undertaken). Taking in every conceivable kind of environment, it was an area of peace for over 300 years, despite a very small military force. After the conquest, the main areas under Spanish control developed a life as advanced as Europe at the same time. Churches, monasteries, fine houses and public buildings, universities and the arts all flourished. To this day, although the University of Mexico City is ultramodern in style, it owes its foundation to Pontifical and Royal charters issued in the 1550s; the monumental cathedral of Guadalajara boasts a statue of Our Lady of the Roses given by Emperor Charles V, and eleven elegant side-altars donated by Ferdinand VII. Many more tangible examples of Royal favor dot Latin America. Indians who had acquired degrees in Spanish-

American universities went back to the mother country to teach. The wealth from gold and silver mines and from ranchos led to great beauty in the cities of the New World. But above all, the influence of the Church produced Saints—not just martyrs, but miracle-working contemplatives, just as she had in Europe. *Ss. Turibius, Rose, Juan Macias*, and *Martin de Porres* (himself of Spanish, Indian, and Black blood) all lived in 17th Century Lima, just as *St. Peter Claver* attended to the needs of Black slaves in Cartagena.

The Peoples of Spanish America

Most appointed officials in the Americas were *peninsulares*, natives of Spain. To prevent the growth of a native oligarchy which might one day take over control of the colonies (which in fact happened in the English colonies), political power was generally in the hands of *peninsulares*, who nevertheless constituted a small minority of the population.

The *criollos* (whence comes our word Creole) were the native-born Spaniards. Few rose to high position in the Spanish administration, but many were very wealthy. Quite a number bore Spanish titles of nobility.

Mestizos were people of mixed white and Indian blood. They tended to form a sort of middle-class, working as artisans, farmers, and foot soldiers. There were very many more of them then of the *criollos* or *peninsulares*.

Indians were governed by their own rulers, as we saw earlier.

The Blacks had been imported originally as slaves. In the beginning, Indians were used as cheap labor (as we use immigrants in factories). But mines and fields took a heavy toll. Their major advocate, *Fr. Bartolome de Las Casas*, had come to the New World in 1500. To relieve them of their burdens, he called on the Spanish to import Blacks instead. Since, as has been mentioned, the Slave marts of the Guinea Coast had few customers at the time, prices were low. Thus began the importation of African slaves to the New World. Obviously, Spanish, Portuguese, French, Dutch, and English all took part in the trade. But it should be emphasized that the influence of the Church in Catholic countries produced a much more humane version of the system than that which prevailed in Dutch or English possessions. Among the Spanish, there were protective regulations regarding housing, food, work, and punishment. Slaves could choose their own wives and change masters if they could find their own buyer. They were able to purchase themselves at the lowest possible rate; so it was that the end of the 18th Century, black freedmen outnumbered slaves in the Spanish colonies. Needless to say, the law required masters to bring their slaves into the Faith and assist them in observing it.

Government

As mentioned, the King of Spain was independently King of each of his Viceroyalties. To assist him in this, he maintained in Spain the Council of the Indies, which carried on the day-to-day running of affairs in the Americas, subject to the King's approval.

In New Spain, Peru, New Granada, and Rio de La Plata, the King was represented by the Viceroy, whose authority in his territory was theoretically as supreme as the King's. But every three years, a Visitor was sent by the Council of the Indies to audit his administration, and recommend improvements or personnel changes if necessary. In addition, each Viceroyalty possessed an *audencia*, which acted as the Viceroy's Council. The Viceroyalties were further divided into Captaincy-Generals and Provinces, presided over by Captains-General and Governors. Each major city had in addition a *cabildo*, a sort of city council, on which *criollos* could sit, and which was responsible for most of the every-day acts of administration.

The Spanish Achievement in Latin America

To put it bluntly, all of Latin America save Portuguese-speaking Brazil and French-speaking Haiti owe everything of value they possess to Spain. Religion, language, culture, learning, their very existence, all of this came from the mother country. Considering how few Spaniards actually came to the Americas, this is really amazing. Unfortunately, much of this legacy has been destroyed by many of the post-Independence governments in Latin America, often with the assistance or at the urging of, sadly, these United States. This is particularly tragic, since our debt to Spain is almost as great.

The Spanish Achievement in the United States

While, as we shall see in the next chapter, the unique civilization the Spanish developed in Florida was destroyed by the English, the foundations they planted in California, Texas, New Mexico, and Arizona, survived to be taken advantage of by the Americans in their Westward expansion. Numbers alone are intriguing:

SOUTH CAROLINA: 1 mission, 2 presidios;
NORTH CAROLINA: 2 missions, 3 presidios;

VIRGINIA: 1 mission;
ALABAMA: 1 mission, 4 presidios;
MISSISSIPPI: 2 presidios;
TENNESSEE: 2 presidios;
ARKANSAS: 2 presidios;
LOUISIANA: 6 presidios;
MISSOURI: 3 presidios;
GEORGIA: 31 missions, 6 presidios;
FLORIDA: 96 missions, 22 presidios;
TEXAS: 47 missions, 14 presidios;
NEW MEXICO: 58 missions, 5 presidios;
ARIZONA: 16 missions, 5 presidios;
CALIFORNIA: 21 missions, 5 presidios.

Intrepid explorers that they were, the Spanish linked many of the missions with trails, such as those extending from Sonoma, California to San Diego; from Santa Fe to El Paso, and thence to Chihuahua; and the one which linked Nagadoches to San Antonio and Laredo. Each of these was inevitably called *El Camino Real*: "The King's Highway," along which traveled both padres and soldiers of the King.

But there is more than this; notice the proportions of missions to presidios. Consider also how few Spanish settlers came here. Apart from St. Augustine and Pensacola in Florida, the major towns the Spanish settled were Los Angeles and San Jose, California; Tucson, Arizona; Taos and Santa Fe, New Mexico; and San Antonio, El Paso, Laredo, and Nagadoches, Texas. The Spanish were not interested in destroying the native peoples, but in making them Catholics and Spaniards, even while retaining the best parts of their indigenous cultures. How different indeed from English and subsequent American policy! The important thing to remember is that, apart from the initial conquest, Spain's rule of her American colonies was less dependent upon force than upon religion, culture, and the rule of law. That is certainly a description of good government. We shall see in subsequent chapters if anything better replaced her rule.

When the Spanish Habsburgs ended with the death of Charles II in 1700, the throne passed to Louis XIV of France's grandson, *Philip V* (1683-1746), thus starting the line of the Spanish Bourbons, who hold the throne of Spain today. A war was fought over this, the War of Spanish Succession. But the reign of the Spanish Bourbons introduced the "modernizing", centralizing methods of Louis XIV into the Spains. This tendency came to a head under *Charles III* of Spain (1716-1788), who moreover was friendly to the ideas of the Enlightenment, and expelled the Jesuits from his dominions. This in turn destroyed the Paraguay

Reducciones, crippled missionary activity in many parts of the empire, and helped weaken Spanish rule. But by the same token, Charles III in 1760 consecrated all his territories to Our Lady of the Immaculate Conception, and made all public officials swear an oath to uphold that doctrine. Such were the concerns of even the most worldly of Spanish monarchs in those days; well did they earn the hereditary title Alexander VI granted Ferdinand after the taking of Granada: "Most Catholic Majesty."

FRANCE COMES TO AMERICA

France also had a very turbulent history before she was able to send colonists to America. When America was discovered, France was a typical medieval kingdom. In the glorious days of the 13th Century, with St. Louis IX she had boasted of one of the greatest kings in Christendom. In France, there developed the *religion royale*, centering around the Holy Ampulla containing chrism delivered by the Holy Ghost to St. Remigius in 496 at King Clovis' baptism at Rheims, and used at the French coronations; the ability of the Kings of France to heal scrofula; devotion to the Sacred Heart and the Assumption; and the quasi-priestly characteristics of the French Crown, such as receiving communion in both kinds, being members of certain chapters of canons, and being allowed to touch the sacred vessels. France gloried in her title of "Oldest Daughter of the Church" (so called because the Franks under Clovis were the first of the post-Roman Western nations to convert) and in the fact that her kings were, like the Holy Roman emperors, successors to Charlemagne. Dom Gueranger tells us:

> In the baptistry of Saint Mary's at Rheims, the Frankish nation was born to God; as heretofore on the banks of Jordan, the dove was again seen over the waters, honoring this time, not the Baptism of Jesus, but that of the Church's eldest daughter; it brought a gift from heaven, the holy vial containing the chrism which was to anoint the French kings in future ages into "the most worthy of all the kings of the earth." (*op. cit.*, vol. XIV, pp. 308-309).

But the fair land of France had suffered much in the years after St. Louis. From 1339 to 1453, the Hundred Years War raged in France, as the English kings attempted to secure the French Crown (to which they did have some claim). Although at first defeated, the French rallied under St. Joan of Arc in 1429, and began the long process of freeing the lands the English occupied. By 1453, this goal was accomplished. But the country was much weakened. Nevertheless, in 1462, Pope Paul II awarded the monarchs of France the title, "Most Christian King."

Attempts at Settlement

From about 1504, French fishermen sought their livelihood off the Grand Banks of Newfoundland. Twenty years later, King *Francis I* (1494-1547) commissioned *Giovanni de Verrazzano* (1485-1528) to find a Northwest Passage through the Americas to Asia. He reached what is now North Carolina, and proceeded northward. Reaching New York Harbor, he was the first European to gaze on it (which is why the Verrazzano Narrows were given his name much later). He named it the Bay of Saint Margaret. After this he sailed into Narragansett Bay, and met the Wampanoag Indians who would befriend the Pilgrims a century later. His fleet sailed next along the Maine coast, encountered the Abnaki Indians; up to Newfoundland, and then back to France. But he had claimed none of this territory for France. Another ten years would pass before Francis saw fit to try again.

This time, he dispatched *Jacques Cartier* to the New World. Cartier's 1534 voyage led him to the west coast of Newfoundland, Prince Edward Island, and Anticosti Island. The next year he returned to discover both the Bay and River of St. Lawrence, the latter of which he sailed up as far as the Iroquois village of Hochelaga (present day Montreal). His next voyage was in 1540, whereon he built a fort. Two years later he was joined by the *Sieur de Roberval*. As the Spanish at the same time sought the gold-laden city of Quivira, so too did the French search the St. Lawrence for the wealth-laden Kingdom of Sanguenay, with whose riches Francis hoped to fight Charles V, lord of the Mexican and Peruvian wealth. But try as Roberval might, there was no sign of such a place. Preceded by Cartier, he returned to France in 1543.

Having European wars to worry about, Francis did not bother to send anyone else to the cold and forbidding river valley Cartier had claimed for France. Dying in 1547, he was succeeded by his son Henry II, who was not interested either. In any case, Henry II had problems closer to home. The Protestant Reformation, which had shorn off Northern Europe from the Faith, was threatening France from within. Many nobles and merchants joined the new religion, hoping to benefit from the theft of Church properties, as their counterparts had elsewhere. This resulted in secret plottings just below the surface of French public life. When Henry died in a tournament, his 16-year-old son, Francis II, came to the throne, and the plots quite literally thickened. He died the next year, and his young bride, the beautiful and tragic Mary Queen of Scots returned to her homeland to face the Protestants there—who would in the end engineer her judicial murder.

But in France, Francis' 10-year-old brother, Charles IX, became King with their mother, Catherine de Medici, as regent. Two years later, civil war broke out with the Huguenots (as French Protestants were called). Lasting until 1589, it was a bloody affair of shifting allegiances and atrocities breeding atrocities. The Huguenots took a particular joy in defiling Catholic shrines and sanctuaries, desecrating the Blessed Sacrament and relics of the saints whenever they could. When the war was over, France was again devastated, the last of Catherine's children, Henry III, (and the Valois dynasty) was dead, and the leader of the Protestant faction, Henry IV, converted to Catholicism. He was, after all, the closest heir to the throne.

Success at Last

Unlike his more immediate predecessors, Henry IV had the leisure to consider the lands Cartier had claimed for France more carefully. There was no gold there, but certainly there were furs and perhaps other useful things. More than this, there were souls to be saved, and brought into that Church which the King himself was a new member of. Near at hand was his remarkable Geographer-Royal, *Samuel de Champlain* (1567-1635). His father was a mariner, who took him on a number of voyages. When he was 20, he joined the Catholic Army against the Huguenots. The war ended, he returned to his father's trade, of which he said:

> Navigation has always seemed to me to occupy the first place. By this art we obtain a knowledge of different countries, regions, and realms. By it we attract and bring to our own land all kinds of riches; by it the idolatry of paganism is overthrown, and Christianity proclaimed throughout all the regions of the earth. This is the art... which led me to explore the coasts of a portion of America, especially those of New France, where I have always desired to see the lily [symbol of France] flourish, together with the only religion, Catholic, Apostolic, and Roman. (*Les Voyages du Sieur de Champlain*, Paris, 1613, Pt. V)

After serving in 1598 with the Spanish navy against English pirates off Puerto Rico, he was appointed Geographer Royal to Henry IV in 1601. Two years later, he visited Canada as second in command of an expedition which failed to establish a settlement. After more exploratory visits, he founded the city of Quebec on July 8, 1608. What Mexico City, capital of the Viceroy, was to New Spain, so Quebec would be to New France.

But where the Spanish authorities could build on the semi-civilized foundation left by the Aztecs, Incas, and Mayas, and use it as a base for improvement and expansion into less settled areas, the French could not do with the St. Lawrence Valley. Its native inhabitants, the Huron and Algonquin Indians, while friendly enough, were primitive hunters with the limited agriculture described in the Introduction. Whatever there would be of civilization in New France, the French would either have to import or make on the spot.

Champlain, however, became as intrepid an explorer of inland rivers as he was of the high seas, venturing down into the present United States. While camped near Ticonderoga, on the Lake which bears his name, he joined the Algonquins in a fight against their sworn enemies, the Iroquois. This skirmish in 1609 involved the French in a struggle that would bedevil them for the rest of their North American career.

The Five Nations of the Iroquois (Mohawk, Cayuga, Oneida, Onondaga, and Seneca) were a confederacy of five tribes centered in Upstate New York. They were better organized than the surrounding tribes, and were brave and ruthless warriors, delighting in torturing their captives (a habit also known by their neighbors, however). The allying of the French with their Huron and Algonquin enemies resulted in their eventually siding with first the Dutch and then the English against them. It was a great advantage, for the Five Nations were the most effective war-machine in North America. Nevertheless, the French missionaries would make converts among the Mohawk.

Although Henry IV had been assassinated in 1610, his son, Louis XIII did not come of age until 1617. The King faced opposition from some of the great nobles of the realm, from the Huguenots (who had certain fortified cities in their keeping, as given them by the Edict of Nantes, which ended the religious wars), and Germany was about to break out into the Thirty Years War, which pitted the Emperor and the Catholic Princes of Germany against the Protestant Princes. He could not give New France the attention it required.

The Church, however, was able to provide some help. Four Franciscan Recollects arrived in 1614. In 1625-26, eight Jesuits came to New France, and two years later, 400 settlers. After an English pirate seized the town in 1629, the colony was in their hands for three years, during which time Champlain was a prisoner. But he returned in triumph to the town he had founded, and served as governor until his death.

NEW FRANCE MADE PERMANENT

Once safely back in French hands, the colony was able to begin real growth. Louis XIII was able to take a real interest in New France's growth, as did his chief minister, *Cardinal Richelieu,* who invested heavily. The King, on the other hand, having taken the rebellious Huguenot city of La Rochelle, was as concerned with the spiritual health of his realm on either side of the Atlantic. In 1638, he consecrated his lands to Our Lady of the Assumption:

> We command the Archbishop of Paris to make a commemoration every year, on the Feast of the Assumption, of this decree at the High Mass in his cathedral; and after Vespers on the said day, let there be a procession in the said church, at which the royal associations and the corporation shall assist, with the same ceremonies as in the most solemn processions.
>
> We wish the same to be done also in all churches, whether parochial or monastic, in the said town and its suburbs, and in all the towns, hamlets, and villages of the said diocese of Paris. Moreover we exhort and command all the archbishops and bishops of our kingdom to have Mass celebrated in their cathedrals and in all churches in their dioceses; and we wish the Parliaments [Provincial high courts] and other royal associations and the principal municipal officers to be present at the ceremony. We exhort the said archbishops and bishops to admonish all our people to have a special devotion to the Holy Virgin, and on this day to implore her protection, so that our Kingdom may be guarded by so powerful a patroness from all attacks of its enemies, and may enjoy good and lasting peace; and that God may so well be served and honored therein, that both we and our subjects may be enabled happily to attain the end for which we were created; for such is our pleasure!

But the King wished to do more for the Faith in a practical way. Eight years earlier, he had given his patronage to a remarkable group called The Company of the Blessed Sacrament. Among its members were *St. Vincent de Paul, Ven. Alain de Solminihac, Bishop Bossuet,* and *Jean-Jacques Olier,* founder of the Sulpicians, as well as many of the greatest names in the realm. The association worked to correct abuses among the clergy, and to help prisoners and the poor. It was responsible for the founding of the General Hospital of Paris and the Seminary of Foreign Missions. Its members worked, moreover, to prevent the then rampant oppression of Catholics by Huguenots in the districts and towns allotted the latter by the Edict of Nantes. They wished also to promote the Faith in New France.

To this end they appointed the 30-year-old *Sieur de Maisonneuve* as governor of a new town, at which he and his settlers arrived in 1642: Montreal. Pious and courageous, he regarded the enterprise as a crusade. From Montreal, missionaries would go out to all the surrounding tribes, including even the Mohawk; that very year, they killed the Jesuit lay brother, *St. Rene Goupil.*

The next year, Louis XIII died, and was succeeded by his five-year-old son, *Louis XIV.* Over the next decade, the following North American

Martyrs were killed by the Mohawk: Ss. Isaac Jogues and John Lalande in New York State, 1646; St. *Antoine Daniel* in Canada, 1648; and *Ss. Jean de Brebeuf, Charles Garnier, Noel Chabanel,* and *Gabriel Lalemant,* all in the Huron Country in 1649. These latter, missionaries among the Huron, were all captured when the people they worked amongst were decimated by the Iroquois, who then subjected them to fiendish tortures. Yet their work did produce such fruit as *Bl. Kateri Tekakwitha,* the "Lily of the Mohawks"

Life in New France

But neither the French nor the Hurons were destroyed. They continued a long guerrilla warfare against the Iroquois, which made the French settlers outside the towns very hardy indeed, completing the process begun by the weather. In the towns, particularly in Quebec, an approximation of European culture was kept up, with the governor presiding over a splendid court, and after 1659, a bishop and cathedral.

From 1663 on, New France's administration was regularized. There was in Quebec a Governor-General, similar to the Spanish Viceroys. Under him in Acadia, Montreal, and Trois Rivieres were local Governors, again like the Spanish Captains-General. Assisting him in Quebec was an *Intendant,* responsible for finance, justice, and civil administration. The third important official at Quebec was the Bishop. These three were assisted by a Council, similar again to the Spanish Audencia.

Outside the towns, along the banks of St. Lawrence, the settlers or *habitants* farmed, generally under a *seigneur*, who, in return for 6 days of labor a year and nominal rent, directed their defense. During harvest and planting seasons, they worked unremittingly. But in the Winter and major feast days, they reveled in Masses, music, dancing, and tale-telling. Under the constant Iroquois threat, they refused to become a somber people, and soon became a match for their Indian enemies at irregular warfare. They would need to be.

Some of the settlers, however, cared little for the towns or farms of New France. Free spirited, they preferred to trap furs with the Indian allies, often taking wives from among them. These were the *Coureurs de bois*, and the *voyageurs*, who used the system of Great Lakes and of rivers, all of which flowed into the St. Lawrence, as their highways into the interior.

With them often traveled Jesuit and other missionaries, the former often encouraged to come to New France by reading of mission exploits in the famed Jesuit *Relations*. These established missions among the tribes contacted by their lay voyageur colleagues. Often the fort and the mission were close together; the first to trade furs, the second to evangelize.

Under the influence of such missionaries, many tribes adopted the Faith: the Hurons, the Abnaki, the Algonquins, the Illinois, the Ottawa, and countless others. As the Indians of Florida, New Mexico, and elsewhere provided the Spanish settlements in what is now the United States with support and protection, so too did those who encountered the French. Direct allies of the King, they were essential to the continuance of New France, combining the teachings of Catholicism with whatever of their lifestyle was reconcilable with it.

The Founding in Louisiana

In 1672, the most remarkable of New France's governors was appointed: *Frontenac*. Wishing to challenge English expansionism in North America, he began the construction of a chain of forts along the great lakes. When, in 1677, *Fr. Marquette* and the voyageur, *Joliet*, discovered the Mississippi, the governor was anxious to take advantage of it. The next year, *Robert, Chevalier de La Salle* began his explorations. Reaching the Mississippi himself in 1682, he descended to the river's mouth, crossing at some point over the grave of De Soto. He was the first European to reach the Delta.

From 1689 to 1697, France and Britain were at war. When hostilities ceased, the importance of settling the Mississippi valley became obvious. The brothers *Iberville* and *Bienville* set about doing so; by 1712, the towns of New Orleans, Nachitoches, Biloxi, Mobile, Kaskaskia, Cahokia, and Vincennes had been founded. More would follow.

But where New France was cold, Lower Louisiana was tropical, having more in common with the West Indies (where by this time Haiti, Martinique, and Guadeloupe were all French possessions) than Quebec. Instead of furs, sugar became the cash crop. Just as in the West Indies, however, plantation crops meant plantation labor—slavery. As in Spanish territory, slavery was ameliorated by the Church. The *Code Noir* which governed the institution among the French was similar to the Spanish legislation we examined earlier. The result was not only retention of family life among the Blacks, but the rise of a mixed class of Free Men of Color—*gens de coleur libre*. These often retained their French fathers' surnames, inherited property from them (including slaves) and enjoyed French educations.

New Orleans soon rivaled Quebec as a center of culture. It became world renowned in time, and despite the changes of flags it would suffer, as "the city that care forgot." This name survives today, and serves as a reminder of the gallant Frenchmen who attempted to reproduce the ways of Versailles in a swampy wilderness.

The Fall in New France

The War of the Grand Alliance, as the 1689-1697 conflict was called (King William's War, to the English colonists) was not the last of the conflicts between France and Spain. Fought as it was in Europe, America, Asia, and the High Seas, it has the dubious distinction of being the first actual worldwide war. It was followed by the War of Spanish Succession (Queen Anne's War) 1701-1713; the War of Austrian Succession (King George's War) 1740-1748; and the Seven Years' War (French and Indian War) 1756-1763. These too were all world wars, in the case of the Americas pitting French and Spanish colonies against English. On the side of the French, in particular, were all the affected Indian tribes save two: the Iroquois and the Cherokee. The French had the experience of being continually at war with the Iroquois, and of being conscious of their mission as bearers of the Faith in North America. But the English colonists, although their militias were no match for the French, had a much greater population (since, conditions in Great Britain being rather unpleasant at the time, many English, Scots, and Irish, as well as Germans, were all too eager to come to the New World) and much more military and monetary support from the Mother Country. The result was that by 1763, all the French possessions east of the Mississippi had fallen to the British (as we must call them after 1707); those west and lower Louisiana were given to King Louis XV's Spanish cousin, Charles III, to safeguard their inhabitants' religion.

FRENCH AND SPANISH EFFORTS EVALUATED

Although there were many differences between the two nations' policies, and although they sometimes came into conflict in the New World, on the whole the similarities are striking.

Under both powers, there was the same emphasis on correct and impartial administration; education, particularly higher, and the arts; and on public and private works of charity. Similarly, there was the same concern for the spiritual and temporal welfare of Indians and Blacks, to a degree simply unheard of in the English colonies.

Further, there was a certain similarity in the men who guarded and extended the frontiers against hostile Indians and Europeans alike. Among the Spanish, they were the *Soldados de Cuerro*, the "Leather-Jacket Soldiers," superb cavalrymen who with their lances and broad-brimmed hats kept Apaches and Commanches at bay through the trackless desert and mountain wastes of the "Northern Rim of Christendom." For the French, they were the *Coureurs de bois,* the "Runners of the Woods," who were fine boatmen, ever expanding Christendom along the great rivers of North America. The exploits of both groups reminds one of the Medieval crusaders, just as much as those of the first Conquistadores and navigators do. The reason is simple: the Faith always calls forth the same kind of soldiers for her defense.

Alike also was the official dedication of French and Spanish administration in the New World to the public observance and spread among the Indians of the Catholic Faith. Bishops were important figures, monks, friars, and nuns assisted in their work with public funds. The result in both New France and New Spain was a society eminently civilized and eminently humane. That there were lapses, even atrocities, is unquestionable. But these were not the norm, and were generally denounced by the people themselves. These words of Leo XIII in regard to Medieval Christendom are almost as applicable to its continuations in the New World:

> There was once a time when States were governed by the philosophy of the Gospel. Then it was that the power and divine virtue of Christian wisdom had diffused itself throughout the laws, institutions, and morals of the people, permeating all ranks and relations of civil society. Then too, the religion instituted by Jesus Christ, established firmly in befitting dignity, flourished everywhere, by the favor of princes and the legitimate protection of magistrates; and Church and State were happily united in concord and friendly interchange of good offices. The State, constituted in this wise, bore fruits important beyond all expectation, whose remembrance is still, and always will be, in renown, witnessed to as they are by countless proofs which can never be blotted out or ever obscured by any craft of any enemies. (*Immortale dei*, cap. 21).

Where the colonizers fell short of this vision, it was due to the already powerful spirit of secularism, unleashed ultimately by the Reformation. But by and large, the desire of Queen Isabella and subsequent rulers of Spain and France to erect another part of Christendom on the other side of the Atlantic was fulfilled. What great accomplishments would have resulted had this vision endured is anyone's guess.

In the next chapter, we shall see how that dream was frustrated, and what was built on its ruins.

THE FOUNDING OF PROTESTANT AMERICA 1607-1770

ENGLAND DURING THE PERIOD

The Catholic England of Henry VII, for which Cabot had claimed part of North America, was destroyed by the next king, *Henry VIII*. His declaring himself head of the Church of England began a long series of civil wars and rebellions in England, which would not finally end until 1746 (first of these was the 1536 *Pilgrimage of Grace*, when many North English Catholics, led by *Robert Aske,* demanded restoration of the monasteries; they were betrayed and slaughtered). By the time this occurred, England was both a Protestant nation and mistress of Scotland, Ireland, and an empire which spanned the globe.

Henry, although wanting both rule of the Church in his realm and money from seizure of abbeys and the like, was not in doctrine a Protestant. His Archbishop of Canterbury, Thomas Cranmer, was. After Henry's death in 1547, he was succeeded by his ten-year-old son, *Edward VI.* During this reign, Cranmer determined religious policy. In 1549, Cranmer introduced an English liturgy to replace the Mass, called *The Book of Common Prayer*. The Catholics of Cornwall and Devonshire rebelled in the *Rising in the West*. This too was defeated. But some Protestants were more radical than others; where Cranmer wanted to retain some prayers, ceremonies, vestments, and so on from Catholic worship, dissenting Protestants wanted to get rid of all of it, and even of bishops (which Cranmer, being one himself, obviously wanted to retain).

When Edward died in 1553, his successor was his older sister, *Mary I*, daughter of Henry's rightful wife, Catherine of Aragon. The next year Queen Mary married *Philip II* of Spain, whom we met in the last chapter. Together, they returned England to the Catholic fold. But their marriage was childless. Henry VIII had had one other daughter, however, by another of his "wives:" *Elizabeth I.* In return for her promise to uphold Catholicism in England, she was recognized as heiress by both Mary and the Pope. When Mary died in 1558, she thought that England's return to the Faith was secure.

In this, she was wrong. Elizabeth immediately disavowed her promises, and returned to her father's policies. But England was not the religiously united country Henry had ruled. There were determined Catholics, *Puritans* (who wished to "purify" the Church of all Catholic influence), and all sorts of shades between. So Elizabeth attempted to revive the Church of England in such a way as to make it a compromise between Catholicism and Protestantism, based upon the three pillars of the episcopate, the royal supremacy, and the Book of Common Prayer. These things being accepted, one was free to believe what one wished. Since loyal Catholics could not accept these last two, they were subject to intense persecution, and many were martyred both in England and in Ireland. Her hatred of the Faith was mirrored in her foreign policy: she supported rebels in the Netherlands against Spain, whose shipping she encouraged English pirates to attack; she did her best to subvert the government of her Catholic cousin and heiress, *Mary Queen of Scots*. When Mary was driven into exile in England, Elizabeth imprisoned her. A year later, the 1569 *Rising in the North* saw English Catholics rise in favor of the Scottish Queen, who, Elizabeth having broken her promises, was the rightful Queen of England as well. In 1587, Elizabeth had her executed. To punish his former sister-in-law for this unheard-of action, Philip II attempted an invasion of England with a fleet called the *Armada*. Battered by storms, the Armada was defeated by *Sir Francis Drake* in July 1588.

This last shattered Spanish naval supremacy, and made possible the establishment of English colonies in the New World. Just a year before, *Sir Walter Raleigh* dispatched 117 colonists to Roanoke Island in what is now North Carolina. There was born Virginia Dare, the first English-speaking native of the New World. Apparently, a number of these first settlers were refugee Catholics, and young Miss Dare may even have been born to and baptized by Catholic parents. Whatever the case, this was the famous "lost colony;" when a ship reached them the next year, all settlers had vanished without a trace. Only the word "Croatan," carved on a tree in the abandoned village, appeared to give some hint of their fate. Certainly, the Croatoan Indians of today claim to descend from the colony, and bear many of their family names—including Dare. The whole area north of the Spanish territories was named Virginia, after the "Virgin Queen," the unmarried Elizabeth.

The Stuarts

Nevertheless, it was only under *James I* (1603-1625), Protestant son of the murdered Mary of Scots, that English settlement in the New World began in earnest. James was a scholar, and commissioned the Protestant translation of the Scriptures called the *King James Bible*. But despite his commitment to Anglicanism, his wife, Anne of Denmark, was a Catholic (although he allowed her co-religionists to be persecuted from time to time). For this and other reasons, the Puritans began to agitate against the Church of England, demanding among other things the abolition of bishops. James opposed this for both political and religious reasons, holding that both crown and mitre came from God ("no bishop, no king"). At the same time, the Puritans as we shall see began their migration to the New World, even as they gathered strength in England.

It was left to James' son, *Charles I*, to oppose them. Since allied with the Puritans politically were many of the wealthiest merchants and landholders in the country who had control of Parliament, religious, political, and economic opposition to the remnants of the Catholic social order in England coalesced against the king. He too married a Catholic Queen, Henrietta Maria of France. Allied with him were Catholics, High-Church (that is, more Catholic minded, as opposed to Low-Church, more Protestant inclined) Anglicans, peasants, and much of the gentry and nobility of the more remote Northern and Western parts of England; similarly, he had the allegiance of the Highland Scots and Catholic Irish. These two factions, Parliamentarians and Royalists (called also *Roundheads* and *Cavaliers*) first intrigued against each other, and then fought an open conflict, the *English Civil War*. Lasting from 1642 to 1646, it resulted in the defeat of King Charles; in 1649 the triumphant Parliamentarians had him beheaded. England was ruled by a Puritan dictatorship much like that in Massachusetts, headed by *Oliver Cromwell*. Christmas was abolished in accordance with Puritan beliefs, and mince pies outlawed.

From 1649 to 1660 this state of affairs continued. But after Cromwell's death in 1658, his son Richard was unable to maintain order for more than a year. By popular acclamation, the son of the martyred king, *Charles II*, assumed the throne. Although the Puritans were no longer part of it, the remainder of the oligarchy which had deposed Charles I remained in place, even though on the surface it appeared that the old government had been restored. "The Merry Monarch" as Charles II was known, did not attempt to push the oligarchy, but preferred to operate in non-controversial areas, if possible. He too married a Catholic, the Portuguese princess, Catherine of Braganza. Although Catholics were persecuted at various times during his reign, Charles converted on his deathbed in 1685.

His brother, *James II*, had already done so, although his daughters, *Mary* and *Anne* were raised Protestant beforehand. Because Catholics were by this time a minority in England, James legalized toleration for all Christians, and attempted to strengthen the position of Catholicism in England by appointing many to high office (the same way in which Anglicanism had become so powerful at the hands of his ancestors). He also tried to rule as a traditional king. This was tolerated by the oligarchy as long as James' heiresses were Protestant princesses who would be amenable to control. But when in 1688 James' Catholic Queen, Mary of Modena, gave birth to a son, they knew that James must be deposed if they were to keep power. The result was the so-called *Glorious Revolution*. The King was deposed, and in his place were brought over from Holland his daughter Mary and her husband *William of Orange*. They became known as William III and Mary II. James' supporters were known as *Jacobites* (from the Latin for James—*Jacobus*). The Scottish Jacobites were defeated in 1689, and the Irish in 1690. William and Mary, and through them the *Whig* oligarchy, now ruled the three Kingdoms.

Under William and Mary (until she died in 1694, after which William ruled alone), Parliament (or rather, those who controlled it) really governed the country. They passed a law in 1689 settling the succession, and declaring that Catholics were ineligible for the English throne. Political power largely gone, William gave away the Crown's financial power to the Whig oligarchs who founded the *Bank of England* in 1694. James II died in exile in France in 1701, and his son, *James Edward*, was proclaimed James III by the Jacobites.

Upon William's death the next year, his sister-in-law Anne became Queen. In 1707, the Parliaments of England and Scotland were merged, and the countries renamed "Great Britain." Taking advantage of the dislike of the Scots for this last measure, James III attempted to land in Scotland in 1708, but his fleet was driven off by a storm. From 1701 to 1713, Britain was involved in a war against France, *the War of Spanish Succession*. The year after it ended, Queen Anne died, having left most of the business of government in the hands of her ministers, who in turn were responsible to Parliament, itself controlled by various factions among the oligarchy.

The Hanoverians

Had her half-brother, James III, been willing to renounce Catholicism, he would have ascended the throne at her death. As he was not, it went to the next closest Protestant relative, the Elector of Hanover, who became King as *George I*. Less than a year after his accession, the Scots Jacobites rose against him, and James III came over to lead them. But although there were pitched battles in Scotland and the North of England, the 1715 rising failed. James went back to France, and George settled down to routine. He spoke no English, and so left practically all matters in the hands of his ministers—preferring to spend time in Hanover, where at least he could speak the language. He died in 1727.

His son, *George II*, was at once better in English (although he did have a thick German accent), and rather more interested in his kingdoms generally. From 1740-1748, Britain was involved in the *War of Austrian Succession,* another worldwide conflict. During its course, Prince *Charles Edward*, "Bonnie Prince Charlie," son of James III, led the last Jacobite attempt at regaining the throne for the Catholic Stuarts. Although they invaded England (and George II was actually packing) Prince Charles' lieutenants forced him to retreat into Scotland where they were crushed at Culloden in 1746, a year after the adventure had begun. Although George II tended to clash with his ministers in small things, for the most part he followed his father's lead.

At his death in 1760, his grandson became *George III*. Although the reign started in the midst of the *Seven Years' War*, (begun in 1755), it ended triumphantly for Britain three years after the Third George ascended. From the beginning, this King showed a determination to be a true King, as had Charles I and James II. George exerted a certain amount of pressure upon his ministers; in 1765 they came up with the *Stamp Act* to help pay both for the huge debts incurred in defending the American colonies in the last war, and also for their continuing military protection. The next year, James III died, leaving Prince Charles to be hailed as Charles III by the dwindling number of Jacobites; much disappointed in his defeat of two decades earlier, Charles posed little threat to George. Through skillful politicking, George was eventually able to acquire a majority of friendly seats in the House of Commons. Thus, in 1770 he could appoint Lord North as Prime Minister—responsible to himself and not the Oligarchs. So began the era of the King's "personal rule."

The Foundation and Growth of the English Colonies

While all this happened in the mother country, colonies were founded, and grew steadily. The first successful settlement was commenced north of the failed Roanoke Colony, at Jamestown in 1607. It was begun at the instigation of the Virginia Company, a joint-stock business formed for the expressed purpose of settling and exploiting the supposed riches of the land. The first 100 colonists consisted primarily of gentlemen and criminals; workers were few, the more so since the colonists preferred hunting for gold to planting crops. The result was that the first few years were filled with poverty and starvation. Two years after Jamestown was settled, *Lord De La Warr* was appointed Governor of Virginia by King James. He encouraged the growth of the colony and the development of agriculture. By the time of his death in 1618, there were 600 colonists. But it was also during his reign that contact was made with the Powhatan Indians of Virginia, a confederacy of many tribes similar to the Iroquois.

John Smith, an English soldier assigned to help protect Jamestown, was taken prisoner by the Powhatans. His life was saved, however, by the chief's daughter, *Pocahontas*, who put herself between the braves who were going to kill Smith. The chief relented, and Smith was saved. Pocahontas herself later married another Englishman, and died in England. Although there was peace for many years after, increasing settler pressure on them provoked war in 1644. The Powhatans were defeated, and declined steadily; from 8,000 in 1607, to only 2,100 in 1669. Today there are about 3,000 descendants. Two of the tribes—Pamunkey and Mattapony—retain reservations from the Commonwealth of Virginia, rather than the Federal government.

The year after Lord De La Warr died, the new governor assembled with his council and representatives of the boroughs or districts which had formed. These representatives became the *House of Burgesses*, and acted as a parliament for the colony. Voting was restricted to property owners. Although Virginia received several other constitutions under the royal government, they were all roughly similar. In 1624 the Company was abolished, and the King appointed a Royal Governor. His council was to be made up of eleven members appointed by the King. The Burgesses would pay the Governor's salary, which made him dependent to a degree on them; he in turn could veto their legislation. Further, the Church of England was the established one in the colony. This meant that Anglican ministers were supported by the colonial government, and that all tax-payers—regardless of their own beliefs—contributed toward it. Just as the King governed the Church of England at home (through his ministers) so too did the Governor in Virginia. Also, all of the laws against Catholics applied in Virginia as well.

These *Penal Laws* restricted Catholics, and were intended to force them to leave the Church and become Protestants. They were very effective: £1 in the money of that time was roughly $US50 today. So the penalties were heavy: £100 fine and a month's imprisonment for hearing Mass; fine of £20 a month for not attending Anglican services; high treason to be or to make a convert—punishable by death in various unpleasant ways; high treason to be a Jesuit and felony to shelter one; those convicted of not attending Anglican worship were fined £20 the first month, £40 the next, and £60 the next after that; Catholics were banned from military commissions and public office, nor could they be executors of wills, guardians of children, lawyers, doctors, or pharmacists. Every convicted Catholic was incapable of either defending himself or prosecuting in civil courts, and was fined £100 if found within 10 miles of London—center of court, intellectual, and economic life in England.

Obviously, these laws were not enforced uniformly at all times. Certainly, the Catholics whom the Stuarts took to wife were not bound by them, nor were their friends. In many places, Anglican authorities turned a blind eye to Catholic activities. But the laws were on the books, just as anti-Catholic laws had been in the Pagan Roman Empire. Just as then, the laws could be used at any time by local or national officials, for whatever reason. It provoked in the Catholic community continual unease, since they could never know for sure when persecution would start. Many (particularly those with a great deal of money or property to lose) defected as a result.

The Founding of Maryland

Despite the laws against conversion to Catholicism, converts were made. One of these was a good friend of James I and his former secretary of state, *George Calvert, Lord Baltimore*. His son Cecil had already converted. Seeing his co-religionists persecuted so fiercely, he conceived the notion of establishing a New World refuge for them, where they would practice the Faith freely. As a former Protestant himself, however, he wished to give non-Catholics the same freedom in his planned colony. After trying unsuccessfully to establish such a place in Newfoundland's Avalon Peninsula, he turned his sights south. In 1632, on the eve of the granting of a charter to that part of Virginia north of the river Potomac (to be called *Maryland* after both Charles I's Queen, Henrietta Maria, and the Virgin Mary), he died. His son Cecil succeeded to both the title and the dream.

Despite heavy protest by the government of Virginia against the venture, 200 Catholic and Protestant colonists arrived at what is now St. Mary's City aboard the ships Ark and Dove. With them came two Jesuit priests as chaplains, who, after landing, erected a large wooden cross and sang High Mass. We do not know how the Protestant colonists reacted, but we do know that this action was in violation of Lord Baltimore's orders that: "all Acts of the Roman Catholic Religion... be done as privately as may be." However poorly those first Jesuits obeyed this decree, many American Catholics have made it the spirit of their religious practice ever since.

Still, the followers of Lord Baltimore set up a government in conformity with his wishes. Lord Baltimore had complete control, under the King. He had of course an agent in the colony, who had in turn a council and Assembly, in similar fashion to Virginia. Where Maryland differed, however, from her Southern neighbor was that neither the Church of England, nor the Catholic Church, nor any other, was established. Rather than subjecting Protestants to the same abuse they themselves had received, they made a great point of granting them equality. As we shall see, it was a tragic blunder.

Life in the Southern Colonies

Maryland and Virginia, and those southern colonies which would be founded later, had no gold nor other profitable minerals. What they did have were fertile soil, plentiful water, and a warm climate. But the very warmth of the climate, and certain other factors, made labor difficult, and small individual plots unprofitable—particularly because tobacco, which grew so well in Virginia and Maryland, and which sold so well in England, requires large scale farming. So developed the *Plantations*, huge farms which were self contained communities, headed by their owners. To work such plantations, however, labor was needed. In the beginning, this was provided by indentured servants, who, in return for having their passage to the New World paid, agreed to work on a plantation or at some other job (depending on their skills). Eventually, criminals and political prisoners (the latter particularly from among the Catholic Irish by Oliver Cromwell) were sent over as virtual slaves. Nevertheless, this was a limited source of essential labor. But in 1619, a Dutch ship landed at Jamestown and sold 20 black slaves from Africa. In time, these would come to dominate the fields of the South.

As we saw in the last chapter, this happened also in the French, Spanish, and Portuguese possessions. Whether we speak of the Plantations of the South and the West Indies, the *Ranchos* of the Southwest, the *Seigneuries* of Canada, the *Haciendas* of Mexico and Central America, the *Latifundias of* Hispanic South America, or the *Fazendas* of Brazil and the *Estancias* of Argentina, we are talking about similar phenomena. Large landholdings in the Americas tend to breed a similar sort of culture. The laborers are generally submissive to authority, hard-working, religious, and carriers of folklore. Often they are black or Indian by blood. The owners usually pride themselves on their family heritage, horsemanship, general culture, and connection to Europe. In much they resemble the feudal lords of Old Europe, of whom Paul Misner writes (*Social Catholicism in Europe,*p. 9):

> In an idealized view of this state of things, the squire or lord of the manor was paternally diligent in looking after the arrangements that would assure the prosperity of the little community (or large family). He and his immediate family would plan and supervise the common projects, allow the peasant families enough time and provisions to cultivate their own plots, and settle any problems and quarrels that arose.

The peasants in turn would see to it that the soil was properly worked, sown, and harvested with their labor.

Obviously, the ideal and the real are no more often the same in such places than they are anywhere else. But by and large, particularly in earlier times before the Enlightenment, such societies had a level of unity unthinkable to modern people, who think that the terms master and serf, or master and slave, must imply enmity.

Since in the South most non-Catholic Plantation owners were Anglican, they kept up many of the customs of old England, including the great holidays of Christmas and Easter. Money was considered a bad thing to worry about, and pleasure a good thing. As John Crowe Ransome put it:

> The South never conceded that the whole duty of man was to increase material production, or that the index to the degree of his culture was the volume of his material production. His business seemed to be rather to envelop both his work and his play with a leisure which permitted the activity of intelligence. On this assumption the South pioneered her way to a sufficiently comfortable and rural sort of establishment, considered that an establishment was something stable, and proceeded to enjoy the fruits thereof. The arts of the section, such as they were, were not immensely passionate, creative, and romantic; they were the... social arts of dress, conversation, manners, the table, the hunt, politics, oratory, the pulpit. These were arts of living and not arts of escape; they were also community arts, in which every class of society could participate after its kind. The South took life easy, which is itself a tolerably comprehensive art. (Twelve Southerners, *I'll Take My Stand*, "Reconstructed but Unregenerate," p. 13).

The Puritans, to whom we must now turn our attention, were quite different.

Puritan New England

In 1620, *the Pilgrims* landed at Plymouth Rock in Massachusetts, arriving on the good ship Mayflower. This was, in many ways, the real birth of the United States as we know them. The Pilgrim Fathers are stock-pieces of our national folklore. We celebrate in emulation of them Thanksgiving Day; our proudest families claim descent from them, and pride themselves on being Mayflower progeny. The names of William Bradford, John Alden, Miles Standish, and Priscilla Mullin are or were (before the decline of education in America) known to every schoolchild. But just who were they?

They were the same sort of Calvinists as the Puritans—which can be used as a synonym for their beliefs; but where the Puritans wished to change the Church of England, the Pilgrims held that she was so Catholic she could not be "Reformed." So, in 1609 1,000 of them settled in Leyden, Holland, where the Calvinist rebels against the Spanish would be only too happy to have them. But while they were with their co-religionists, they soon discovered that their children were becoming Dutch rather than English. After a decade, they made arrangements with the firm to whom King James had granted lands north of Virginia, the Plymouth Company. On August 5, 1620, they set off from Southampton. November 9 found them off Cape Cod, and two days later they signed the *Mayflower Compact,* an agreement which bound the signers together into a body for the purpose of forming a government when they should settle. It was in fact very similar to the "covenants" members of that religion would sign when forming a congregation. In late December, they at last reached Plymouth Rock. Of them, Perry Miller wrote:

> ...[Puritanism's] role in American thought has been almost the dominant one, for the descendants of the Puritans have carried at least some habits of the Puritan mind into a variety of pursuits, have spread across the country, and in many fields of activity have played a leading part.... Without some understanding of Puritanism, it may be safely said, there is no understanding of America. (Perry Miller and Thomas H. Johnson, eds., *The Puritans,* p. 1).

Because of their belief in predestination, and further that predestination to Heaven could be seen by material blessings given by God to His elect in this world, they set great store by wealth. Material success was a sure sign of moral superiority; so everything that contributed to this—thrift, industriousness, and so on, became not merely a means to an end but religious duty. Similarly, those who were poor or enjoyed pleasures other than those of labor were considered damned. Added to this was their hatred of much of the arts; initially because they considered them idolatrous (had they not resulted in Catholic statues and icons?), but finally because they did not in themselves conduce to wealth. To be fair, the Puritans did try to give their tools and implements a certain sparse beauty, but these were legitimate only because they were first and foremost tools, rather than mere ornaments. If a thing or action was pleasant or pleasurable on its own, it was suspect unless also profitable.

Further, identifying themselves with the children of Israel in the Old Testament, they considered all those whom they encountered—Indians, French, Spanish, and even non-Puritan English—to be the equivalent of the Canaanites, and so to be treated the same way, without mercy.

Lacking confession, personal sin was elevated from a question for the penitent and his confessor into a matter for the whole community. This in turn encouraged everyone in the settlement to have a much greater interest in the private affairs of their neighbors than would be tolerated in many places. What would have been considered a sin—malicious gossip—in Catholic Europe, became thereby a civic duty.

In much diluted form, these basic attitudes remain very much alive today in this country. In the early days, however, they produced quite an interesting type, as described by Nathaniel Hawthorne in his *The May-Pole of Merry Mount:*

> ...Puritans, most dismal wretches, who said their prayers before daylight, and then wrought in the forest or the cornfield, till evening made it prayer time again. Their weapons were always at hand, to shoot down the straggling savage. When they met in conclave, it was never to keep up the old English mirth, but to hear sermons three hours long, or to proclaim bounties on the heads of wolves or the scalps of Indians. Their festivals were fast-days, and their chief pastime the singing of psalms. Woe to the youth or maiden, who did but dream of a dance! The selectman nodded to the constable; and there sat the reprobate in the stocks; or if he danced, it was round the whipping-post, which might be termed the Puritan May-Pole.

It might also be pointed out, however, that due to the fact that their religion was centered on the Bible alone, the Puritans set great store on reading, and so each village had its school. Self-improvement became a large part of their creed also; with this dual idolatry of the written word and education we see another large part of their legacy.

Although they took eventually to annihilating the Indians, they were at first dependent on their good-will, particularly the first year. Two years later, settlements were made at Portsmouth and Dover, New Hampshire, by similarly minded "godly" folk. But in 1625, Captain *Wollaston* settled at Mount Wollaston or "Merry Mount" as it came to be known. Here was a small settlement and trading post much more like the English mainstream at the time. As with the French, Indians were welcome at Merry Mount; whatever was left of Catholic England's culture expressed itself there, and the place stood as both a social and religious alternative to Plymouth. Again, we defer to Hawthorne in the same story just quoted:

> Bright were the days at Merry Mount, when the May-Pole was the banner-staff of that gay colony! They who reared it, should their banner be triumphant, were to pour sunshine over New England's rugged hills, and scatter flower-seeds throughout the soil. Jollity and gloom were contending for an empire.

Alas, gloom triumphed! In 1628, a military column from Plymouth surprised the folk of Merry Mount, and sent most of them back to England. How different would have history been, had the Merry Mounters been as aggressive!

But they were not, and two years after the fall of Merry Mount, another group of Puritans (who retained a nominal connection with the Church of England) arrived and founded Boston. Salem had been founded the same year that Merry Mount fell. On October 19, 1630, the General Court of Massachusetts was convened for the first time, Boston and Salem both being represented. Throughout the following decade, settlers continued to arrive, and the colony of Connecticut was organized. Religious dissenters (including *Roger Williams*, first Baptist minister in the New World) founded Rhode Island as a haven for all Protestant sects and Jews—though not for Catholics. By 1642, Puritan New England, in its basic outline, was formed.

The Dutch in New York and the Swedes on the Delaware

The Dutch Protestant rebels against Spain carried their combat to the high seas. As with the English, Dutch piracy was a prelude to Dutch colonization. Throughout the 17th Century they snatched lands from Catholic powers, particularly the Portuguese. In this manner they seized the Spice Islands in the East Indies, Ceylon, Bombay, Malacca, the Gold Coast, and such West Indian Islands as Curacao. To keep open a means of communication with the East, they settled the Cape of Good Hope in South Africa; from these settlers descend the Afrikaaners of today, who retain membership in the Calvinist Dutch Reformed Church and still speak a dialect of Dutch. Early in the Century, though, the Dutch dispatched to North America an English sea captain, *Henry Hudson* (d. 1611), who sailed up the river in New York that bears his name in 1609. He failed to discover the Northwest Passage to China which he sought, but he discovered Manhattan Island. In 1613, a trading post was built there, followed the next year by a proper fort; in 1615 one was built at present day Albany, New York. At last, after *Peter Minuit* bought Manhattan in 1626 for 24 dollars (from the Manhattan Indians, who did not own the island anyway), he founded the settlement of New Amsterdam at the extreme south end of the island. This was the beginning of the great New York City.

To ensure the settlement of the colony, the *Dutch West India Company* which controlled the settlement, granted lands to those men (called *patroons*) who would undertake to settle colonists on them; these were to be quasi-feudal fiefs. The Dutch sold firearms to the Iroquois, and in return had little to fear from the Indians, the small tribes in their territories giving little resistance.

Just as the Netherlands became a refuge for Jews and Protestants from Catholic Europe, so too did the New Netherlands. Although the Dutch Reformed Church was established, Portuguese Jews, German and Dutch Lutherans, Protestant Walloons, and many other groups settled in the colony. But then as now, New Amsterdam had an identity of her own which superimposed itself upon its immigrants.

Although they were Calvinists, the Dutch of New Netherlands practiced their gloomy creed with much less gloom than did their Puritan neighbors to the East. Even the Reformation could not take every bit of jollity from the Dutch heart; although they hated the Church as much any good Protestant nation, they retained many of her customs. Not only did they retain Christmas, but as in Holland St. Nicholas continued to visit the children on his feast day, December 6. Indeed, it was through his importation by the Dutch to New York that St. Nicholas survives in this country in the bizarre apparel of Santa Claus. While this last gentleman may certainly be called a cheapened version of the Saint whose mangled name he bears, he is certainly a much more welcome custom than the Puritan non-observance of Christmas, which might have prevailed had the Dutch never come to these shores.

Further, the Dutch of New Amsterdam contributed an important word to American industry: *Baas,* which we call "Boss." The Dutch in New York moreover produced a body of native folklore, immortalized by Washington Irving in his "Rip Van Winkle." His *Dietrich Knickerbocker's History of New-York,* while perhaps more amusing than rigorously accurate, nevertheless portrays the Dutch as a pleasing contrast to Hawthorne's Puritans:

> The province of the New Netherlands, destitute of wealth, possessed a sweet tranquillity that wealth could never purchase. There were neither public commotions nor private quarrels; neither parties, nor sects, nor schisms; neither persecutions, nor trials, nor punishments; nor were there counselors, attorneys, catch-poles, or hang-men. Every man attended to what little business he was lucky enough to have, or neglected it if he pleased, without asking the opinion of his neighbor. In those days nobody meddled with concerns beyond his comprehension, nor thrust his nose into other people's affairs; nor neglected to correct his own conduct, and reform his own character, in his zeal to pull to pieces the character of others... (*op. cit.,* pp. 119-120).

Although obviously colored by romanticism, the passage does show what the Dutch in New Amsterdam prided themselves upon. Their stone houses were beautiful imitations of the ones they had left behind in the Netherlands, even down to the colorful tiles around the fireplace; these were often illustrated with scenes from the Bible which allowed the lady of the house to instruct her offspring.

Within four years from the founding of New Amsterdam, however, conflict arose with the colony's Puritan neighbors. The Dutch had established posts on the Connecticut River. But the colonizing efforts of the Puritans slipped past them in order to found the settlements which became the colony of Connecticut. Rather than fight over the land, the Dutch West India Company conceded it to the Puritans in 1638.

In the same year, pressure began to be felt in the South, at the mouth of the Delaware River—land already claimed by Lord Baltimore for his Maryland colony, although not as yet settled by his people. This important area was settled by Swedish colonists, who called their new territory New Sweden. Their first settlement, Ft. Christina (at present day Wilmington, Delaware) was named after Sweden's Queen, who later abdicated to become a Catholic, ending her days in Rome (her tomb is in St. Peter's). The Finns who accompanied the Swedes introduced the kind of house they lived in Swedish-ruled Finland: log cabins. So well adopted to the timber-rich American frontier were they that in time the log cabin became the preferred frontier residence for settlers of all nationalities.

In time, the little Swedish colony became a threat to New Netherlands; in 1655 the Dutch conquered it, and became masters of a realm stretching from Lord Baltimore's Maryland to the Connecticut Puritans. Such a colony would in normal times be a danger to the English colonial enterprise. But by 1655, the English were deep in other troubles.

THE ERA OF THE CIVIL WARS

As previously noted, 1642 saw the long simmering conflict between Charles I and his Parliament break out into open conflict. The New England colonies were always in more or less subtle tension with their King, and by their very existence gave moral strength to their co-religionists in England. They declared for Parliament immediately, and then federated as the United Colonies of New England, from which grouping Rhode Island was excluded because of its religious stance. In Maryland, William Claiborne, a Puritan, and Richard Ingle, a pirate, seized control of the government for a year, but were driven out by the populace. Nevertheless, Parliament took control of the colony in 1652, since the proprietor was a Catholic, and imposed the penal laws. The same year witnessed the overthrow of *Sir William Berkeley*, the Royal Governor of Virginia. With this last development, the colonies, like the mother country, were under the sway of Oliver Cromwell, who in turn exported many Irish as slaves to the New World.

The Restoration

Oliver Cromwell died in 1658; his son Richard attempted to continue the Commonwealth. But the next year Sir William Berkeley was restored to power in Virginia, and Charles II proclaimed King, foreshadowing his restoration in England itself in 1660. Maryland quickly returned to the rule of Lord Baltimore as well. However, in New England, careful negotiations were required, first to assure royal supremacy in the province, and then to convince the colonies there to accept new charters binding them more closely to the home government (thereby weakening the Puritan establishment). Eventually, agreements were come to; but the Puritans remained quick to seize whatever power they could from the crown.

Meanwhile, New Netherlands continued to grow and prosper, presenting at once a danger to the neighboring colonies and a tempting target. England and the Netherlands being at war, it was resolved that New Netherlands must be taken. They were granted by King Charles to his Catholic brother, James, Duke of York, who had reorganized the Royal Navy after the confusion of Cromwell. He was a good admiral and a skilled soldier.

His opponent was the Dutch governor, *Peter Stuyvesant:* a doughty old soldier, who had lost a leg fighting in South America, yet conquered New Sweden. When in August 1664 an English fleet of four ships appeared in the harbor and demanded surrender, Stuyvesant refused, replying in a letter:

> As touching the threats in your conclusion, we have nothing to answer, only that we fear nothing but what God (who is just as merciful) shall lay upon us, all things being in His gracious disposal; and we may as well be preserved by Him with small forces as by a great army; which makes us wish you all happiness and prosperity, and recommend *you* to his protection.
> My lords,
> Your thrice humble and affectionate servant and friend,
> P. Stuyvesant

Despite the valor of the governor, however, the walls of the little fort were tumbling down, and the Dutch troops were very few. So the populace and the governor's council demanded he surrender. He did so, but was dragged from the walls by the Dutch minister declaring that he would rather be dead.

Still, he stayed in the colony, and died many years later, loved and respected by both English and Dutch; his bones were laid in the church of St. Mark-in-the-Bouwerie, and his descendants too continued for several centuries as one of the first families of the city. Here again, though, as with Merry Mount, one wonders what might have happened had the influence of the jollier Dutch prevailed over that of the Puritans.

After the conquest, the Duke of York found himself in control of the Hudson Valley, present day New Jersey, eastern Pennsylvania, and Delaware. Both colony and its capital were renamed New York in his honor. Confirmations were given to the patroons of their status, and as Lords of the Manor, the same was given to later arrivals under the same rules. The Duke almost immediately granted New Jersey to two of his friends, however, who named it after the island of Jersey, over which one of them had been governor.

Indians, Spaniards, and Rebellion

In 1663, a group of eleven lords were granted the territory south of Virginia stretching to Florida, which they named "Carolina" for the King. After a few false starts, the first settlement, Charleston, was founded in 1670. The new town and its environs, being semi-tropical in environment, lent themselves to such plantation crops as rice and indigo. As a result, many of Charleston's first settlers were planters from Barbados and French Huguenots (after the latter were expelled from France in 1687) who gave the town an aristocratic tone it has never since lost.

But the ever-expanding Carolina settlers eventually came into contact with the Northern edge of Spanish Florida. Conflict was certain.

Meanwhile, the New England colonies also continued to expand, with ever more Puritan settlers occupying ever more Indian lands. Already in the 1630s the settlers in Connecticut had destroyed the Pequot tribe. In Massachusetts, the Wampanoags, the Indians with whom the Pilgrims had shared the first Thanksgiving, began to feel the increasing pressure of white expansion. Thus, the friendship of chief *Massasoit* turned eventually into enmity on the part of his son, *King Philip*. More and more the Indians were pressured to accept Puritan oversight of their tribes and regulation of hunting and so on. As a defensive measure, he leagued most of the Indians from Maine to Connecticut. But when three Wampanoags were executed for the murder of a spy by Massachusetts authorities, the young braves demanded revenge. War broke out in June 1675.

At first, with the element of surprise, the Indians had the upper hand. White settlements across the New England frontier burned, with men, women, and children dead. The militia retaliated with equally bloody assaults on Indian Villages. In December, The Great Swamp Flight in Rhode Island decimated the Narragansetts, Philip's closest allies. Nevertheless, the Indians managed to hold the upper hand until the Spring of 1676. The Summer was disastrous, and in August, Philip was captured and shot and his young son sold as a slave. Soon Indian resistance was broken—half the Wampanoags were sold into slavery in Bermuda, whence many a Bermudan has Indian features today. Whole villages had been massacred, and many of the remnants fled north to Canada and the French, or else sought refuge with the Mohawk, who had sympathized with the revolt. Those who remained were put on reservations, and most of their lands in southern New England opened for settlement. But more than 600 white men had been killed—over a sixth of the male population of New England. Still, it was a complete triumph for the Puritans.

Even so, there were reverberations elsewhere. Indians further south were agitated as a result—some of the Susquehanna, for instance, going on the warpath on the Maryland frontier. This led to defensive preparations in Virginia. There the governor, the long-serving Sir William Berkeley, attempted a sort of static defense by supporting presumed friendly Indians and monitoring possibly hostile tribes. One of the Burgesses, *Nathaniel Bacon,* urged an aggressive policy against all Indians in Virginia. On 23 June he appeared in front of the statehouse with 500 thugs, their weapons cocked and ready. They demanded that Bacon be given command of the provincial forces for a war against all the Indians in the colony. The assembly capitulated, Jamestown was in Bacon's hands, and Sir William fled across the Chesapeake to the Eastern Shore. Bacon meanwhile set off to attack the Pamunkeys, up to now steady allies of the English. Sir William recaptured Jamestown, which caused Bacon to cut short his plundering mission, and retake the capital, which he burned and evacuated. Dying of natural causes on October 26, he left his disorganized followers to be defeated by the septuagenarian Sir William. When troops arrived from England they found Virginia at peace. Later historians have often considered Bacon's rebellion to have been a rehearsal for the American Revolution.

At the same time, more settlers continued to arrive in Carolina. As they did so, English raids into the Florida province of Guale became more frequent. At last, in 1680, a band of English allied Creek Indians attacked the northernmost mission, Santiago de Ocone on Jekyll island. A few of the Indians of the mission were killed, but the remainder under a single Spanish officer held off the attack. Shortly thereafter, Santa Catalina on St. Catherine's Island was assaulted by 300 English-led Indians. One Captain Francisco Fuentes fended them off with five

Spanish and sixteen Indian musketeers. Despite these and other such acts of bravery, the Spanish governor at St. Augustine ordered the northernmost missions abandoned.

This was a mistake, because the Indians involved considered retreat cowardice. In 1684, these tribes defected to the English. They then in turn began raiding farther south into Spanish territory themselves. With only 290 Spanish soldiers, the governor in 1686 decided to withdraw troops and missions south of the St. Mary's River, then as now the northern frontier of Florida. But the English were not interested in evangelizing their new allies. Missions they could destroy; they would not replace them.

Penn's Woods

Sir William Penn was another friend of the Duke of York, and a convert to Quakerism. He wished to establish a colony where all men, even Catholics, could worship as they pleased. The Duke, being Catholic, was pleased by the idea of another place in the colonies where his co-religionists might be free, and granted Penn an area to be called "Penn's Woods"—Pennsylvania—in 1681. The next year the settlement of Philadelphia, the city of "Brotherly Love" was founded.

From the beginning, Pennsylvania was a melting pot. In addition to the Quakers, many Ulster Scots settled on the frontier, and closer to Philadelphia were Germans. These latter belonged to many different sects—Lutheran, Mennonite, Amish, German Reformed, and Moravian—as well as the Catholic Church. Calling themselves *Deutsch*, Germans, they were and are called "Pennsylvania Dutch." Their culture survives even today, and the Pennsylvania Dutch country is still a world apart.

Good King James

King Charles II had been much more successful than anyone had supposed he would be. J.M. Sosin observes:

> From almost the onset of the rule of Charles II, men in America, especially the more zealous Puritans in New England, had expected the restored monarchy to collapse. As one year succeeded the next, Charles remained on the throne, although the King and his ministers seemed unable to exert their will on the plantations across the Atlantic.... Charles II proved to be a much more adept politician and a more tough-minded ruler than his father. He survived the hysteria raised by the Popish Plot and broke the attempt by the Parliamentary opposition to control the throne by excluding his brother from the succession. During this extended crisis at home, king and ministers could devote little

attention to affairs across the Atlantic. By the close of 1682, however, the monarchy seemed in a stronger position as a result of the reaction to the extremist tactics employed by the political opposition in and out of Parliament.... Only then did Charles and his ministers attempt to impose some order. But time had almost run out; Charles had but a short time left to his life. (*English America and the Restoration Monarchy of Charles II*, p. 167).

Indeed, the Merry Monarch died, a repentant Catholic, in 1685. His brother, the Duke of York, succeeded him as James II. James was the first Catholic to ascend the throne since Queen Mary in 1553. But 132 years had changed much. Mary had ruled over a country still primarily Catholic, which rejoiced in a return to the old religion. James presided over a nation with a large Protestant majority. Further, Mary's opposition had been poorly organized; James' was not, and not only had the experience of running the nation already, but also possessed the precedent of having beheaded James' father.

For all this, while James wished to see Catholicism triumphant in England, he was well aware that this would take time, even as weaning Englishmen from the religion of their ancestors had taken time.

The religious question was not the only one which concerned the new king, however. Already he had appointed the Catholic *Thomas Dongan* as governor of his colony of New York before he was king. At that time he realized that the major weakness of the colonies was their disunity. He was resolved to remedy this.

At the time of James' accession, there were over 150,000 settlers scattered from Maine to Carolina. While England and France were at peace, their interests on the northern frontier often collided, and might precipitate conflict at any time. James was concerned that, as things stood neither the New England colonies nor New York could stand a determined assault on their own from Canada. They must be welded into one strong colony, therefore.

The King appointed *Sir Edmund Andros* as governor of New England. Sir Edmund arrived at Boston to take up the reins of Massachusetts government on December 20, 1686. A few days later, he assumed the rule over Rhode Island. On October 18, 1687, he received orders from London to annex Connecticut to the "Dominion of New England," as the new super-colony was to be called. Sir Edmund traveled to Hartford and took control of that colony on November 1. New Hampshire, New York, and New Jersey were also added to the Dominion. It appeared that James' plan would succeed.

But there were several problems brewing. One was that Sir Edmund's review of land titles went against the claims of various wealthy speculators in the Dominion. Another was his insistence that one of Boston's three Puritan churches allow Anglicans to worship there on Sunday morning.

The Un-"Glorious" Revolution

The overthrow of King James II in 1688 undid all the progress in colonial unity he had accomplished. Puritan New England had in any case hated both him and his brother, accepting them only grudgingly. When on 18 April the news of James' overthrow arrived in Boston, a mob including hundreds of militiamen arrived in Boston, disarmed Andros' guard of 15 men, and took them to prison. In each of the other New England colonies, those who had held office prior to the organization of the Dominion ejected Sir Edmund's officials and returned to power.

In New York, a group of rebels led by one *Jacob Leisler*, an apparently paranoiac rabble rouser, took control of the city. But Leisler's rule was confined to Manhattan. There however, anyone might be accused of being a "Papist" and removed from office or employment. Eventually, a governor was appointed from England, the city subdued, and Leisler tried for treason and executed.

In Pennsylvania, the local establishment took advantage of Penn's well-known friendship with James to take over effective rule of the colony, although Penn remained officially in charge. Carolina's and Virginia's governments simply proclaimed William and Mary as King and Queen.

Maryland was, of course, a different case. Like his father and grandfather, the third Lord Baltimore, Charles Calvert, allowed Protestants to freely settle in Maryland and enjoy full civil rights. By 1689, they were a majority of the population. When the news from London arrived, a group of the more wealthy and influential formed the Protestant Association. On July 27, the Association seized the capital at St. Mary's City. In 1690, King William officially took control of the colony, and voided the rights of the Catholic proprietor. The Assembly made it illegal for Catholics to hold office in Maryland.

THE STRUGGLE AGAINST CATHOLIC AMERICA

The major ally of James II, even in exile, was France's King Louis XIV. He was already engaged in war with the Grand Alliance of the Holy Roman Empire, Spain, Sweden, Bavaria, Saxony, and the Palatinate. When William usurped the throne, he immediately brought England into the conflict, known as "King William's War" in the colonies.

Toward the end of 1689, the Iroquois allies of the English staged the horrible Lachine massacre, against the little town near Montreal. The reaction of the French and their Indian allies was swift and deadly. On February 8, 1690, Schenectady, New York was similarly served by them. Raids hit other frontier villages, but in April of that year, *Sir William Phips* seized the French naval base of Port Royal in Acadia. The war then settled down into skirmishes.

Witchcraft at Salem

While more exposed areas were undergoing attacks by French and Indians, Massachusetts had little to fear from earthly enemies. But the Puritans, still imbued with the gloomiest Calvinism, attempted to continue building their "city on a hill." The encounter between the darkest European heresy and the dark and still pagan New England hills must have been a difficult one indeed. Fr. Montague Summers describes the problem well:

> There can be no doubt that the settlers in New England were not only firm believers in every kind of Witchcraft, but well primed in every malevolent superstition that could commend itself to their verjuiced and tortured minds. They looked for the devil round every corner, and saw Satan's hand in every mishap, in every accident. The Devil, in fact, played a larger part in their theology than God. They were obsessed with hell and damnation; their sky was cloudy and overset; their horizon girded with predestination and the awful consciousness of sin. It is almost impossible to conceive the effect of a new land, a strange mysterious bourne beyond the waves of the illimitable Atlantic, must have had upon the muddied morbid minds and tortured souls of these stern and stoic pioneers. (*The Geography of Witchcraft*, p. 256).

This provided a sort of mental pressure cooker which, from time to time, produced mass hysteria of various sorts. In the case of Salem, it began in the long Winter nights of 1691 and 1692, when friends and family of the Reverend Samuel Parris, minister at Salem, would gather to listen to the weird tales of voodoo and magic told by the Parris' female slave, Tituba. Soon, three of the young girls who had heard the tales declared themselves bewitched, and accused three women of Salem of doing it to them. More and wilder tales were told and fits performed. The number of bewitched grew slowly, that of the accused by leaps and bounds. After conviction, the witches were put to death by "pressing" with rocks or by hanging. Over 20 had been executed by October of 1692. Finally, the Royal Governor, Sir William Phips (the victor of Port

Royal) stepped in, and forbade the special courts to hear any more Witchcraft cases; further he decreed that the regular courts were no longer to accept spectral evidence. Finally, he ordered all prisoners discharged in May of 1693, and the 200 inmates returned to their homes.

The repercussions of the case have reverberated down to our own day. On the one hand, the great grandson of Judge Hawthorne, Nathaniel Hawthorne, was haunted by a sense of familial guilt which inspired much of his best work. Arthur Miller's play, *The Crucible* was set during the affair at Salem, and it is continually invoked in our popular culture. But as we shall see, it was not the last outbreak of mass hysteria in our country.

In this same year of 1692, however, as a sort of mournful counterpoint to the events at Salem, the Assembly of Maryland forbade Catholics there to act as attorneys.

The Martyrdom of Fr. Plunkett

After five more years of skirmishing, King William's War finally drew to a close. In that same year, however, there died in Virginia a martyr for the Catholic Faith, Fr. Christopher Plunkett, O.P., whose story should be better known. He was born to a noble Irish family in 1649. At 21 he became a Capuchin, and in 1680 he arrived in Virginia, and the estate of his cousin, John Plunkett. The *Annali Cappucini* tells his story (III, 540-542):

> Father Christopher undertook his voyage with a vigorous and cheerful spirit. He sailed happily, looking back to the shores of his beloved fatherland. Combining great prudence and zeal, he went to the enemies of the Catholic Faith and offered himself a courageous and indefatigable apostle.
>
> Penetrating deeply into the remote villages and inhospitable forests, he approached timid Catholics who had been frightened by the pressure of persecution. He encouraged them by his eloquent words and instilled in them resignation and faith in the power and goodness of God. And to many who had been ensnared by erroneous doctrine he brought light and explanation, so that he not only strengthened the holy faith of the many Catholics who had fallen into this deception, but even converted heretics and brought them into the bosom of the Catholic Church.
>
> And although he was very careful to avoid the snares of the Protestant princes who ruled the whole island, he fell into their hands and was harshly treated. Relentlessly they dragged him from one to another galley, with beatings and with sufferings of hunger and thirst.
>
> The intrepid Father Christopher bore all with an unconquerable spirit, rejoicing in his heart that he was able to suffer after the example

of our Lord Jesus Christ. They not only wanted to weaken his firmness of faith by coaxing and alluring him, but also to have him among the preachers of Calvinism; but in vain, for he was as solid as an immovable bulwark.

Seeing, therefore, that they were not able to defeat and subdue him, they condemned him to exile, confining him to a barbarous island on which there was no one but heretics and enemies of Catholics. In that place the invincible Fr. Christopher saw sorrow, until he ended the captivity of men by passing into the sweet and perpetual liberty of God.

He died alone and abandoned on that brutal island in the forty-eighth year of his age and the twenty-seventh in religion. His death is registered in this year of 1697.

Fr. Plunkett's sufferings were emblematic of what all English-speaking Catholics would have to go through, if in less unpleasant ways. Two years after the sainted Capuchin died, William III decreed even more restrictions for Catholics. 1) Any bishop or priest exercising his office or any Catholic keeping a school to be imprisoned for life; 2) £100 reward for the capture of any priest or the conviction of a Catholic sending his children overseas to be educated; and 3) no Catholic refusing the Oath of Supremacy and the Declaration Repudiating Transubstantiation could buy or inherit land.

The Ruin of Spanish Florida

The War of Spanish Succession having broken out, and Spain being allied with France, the English in Carolina resolved to finish the job begun twenty years earlier. On October 22, 1702, Governor James Moore arrived in front of St. Augustine with a thousand men—half English, half Indian allies. Unable to reduce the fort, the English made their revenge on outlying churches and missions, killing many of the Indians thereat, and taking 500 away as slaves.

Two years later, Moore returned, this time to what is now the Florida Panhandle, then the abode of the Apalachee Indians. He commenced his work there with an assault on a mission and its surrender. Then

> Word of the attack reached the nearby presidio of San Luis Patali, and Captain Alonso Dias Mexia, with thirty Spaniards, two friars, and four hundred Indians, rushed to give assistance. Twice they drove Moore back, but in the evening they... ran out of ammunition and had to surrender. Moore was immensely satisfied with himself... At Ayubale, and the next day at Patali, his men slew the three priests, and committed acts of gratuitous barbarity on the Christian Indians. Fray Juan de Parga Araujo was beheaded, and his body butchered. Fray Manuel de Mendoza's body was later found in a charred state, his

hands and a half-melted crucifix sunk into his flesh. Father Miranda's remains were never found. To a Spanish rescue party that reached the two towns several days later, the scene was one of indescribable horror: scalped and mutilated bodies of men, women, and children lay about the ground, or hung from stakes. The few survivors who came out of the blood-bath to tell the tale had consoling tales of heroism. The governor passed them on to the king: "During this cruel and barbarous martyrdom which the poor Apalache Indians experienced, there were some of them who encouraged the others, declaring that through martyrdom they would appear before God; and to the pagans they said, 'make more fire so that our hearts may be allowed to suffer for our souls. We go to enjoy God as Christians.'" (Michael V. Gannon, *The Cross in the Sand,* pp. 75-76).

The missions in Florida never recovered from these blows. By 1708 the remaining mission Indians had been gathered within the walls of St. Augustine. In the meantime, ten to twelve thousand Indians had been taken to Carolina as slaves. The beautiful hybrid civilization developed in Florida was completely destroyed.

One must wonder why no "Black Legend" ever grew up around James Moore.

The Rest of the War

1704 saw a political victory for the Protestants in Maryland as great as Moore's in Florida was for Carolina. In that year the Assembly passed the Act To Prevent The Growth Of Popery. This prohibited Catholic worship and forbade priests to make converts or to baptize any but children of Catholic parents. The wealthier Catholics of the colony petitioned for a temporary reprieve from the first clause in respect to private homes; in an extraordinary move, Queen Anne intervened to make the exception permanent. Because of this, Catholic Maryland survived. The peculiarly English Catholicism that yet remains in parts of Maryland like St. Mary's and Charles Counties, the Eastern Shore, and the area in the north of the State around Mt. St. Mary's and Emmitsburg, and which was later brought to the "Holy Land" of central Kentucky in such places as Loreto and Holy Cross, owes its survival thereby to Queen Anne.

On other fronts, the French and Spanish tried unsuccessfully to take Charleston in 1706; 1710 did see the successful capture of Port Royal by the English, who renamed it Annapolis Royal after their Queen. Two years later a revolt by the Tuscaroras of Carolina was put down with great bloodshed, and the survivors fled to the Iroquois, who made them a "Sixth Nation." At last, in 1713, peace was signed; in North America,

France ceded Hudson's Bay, Newfoundland, and Nova Scotia to Great Britain, although the French-Acadians who lived in the latter place were allowed to stay.

The Long "Peace"

Although peace had been declared, sporadic raiding by Indians allied with all sides continued. More immigrants continued to arrive from various parts of Europe to the English colonies, and agriculture and trade increased correspondingly. In New England, the Salem Witch trials had badly discredited much of the Calvinist establishment. As Fr. Montague Summers opines:

> The Genevan ministers had neither the spiritual nor the practical knowledge to deal with so dark and difficult a task. Naturally they blundered woefully and abundantly. As in England, their mistakes have provided the sceptic and the materialist with many a text for trite moralizing and meditation upon the ignorance of our forefathers (*op. cit.*, p. 348).

An element of doubt entered into the New English mind, which, when it encountered new, unbelieving currents of thought, would end by destroying faith in any sort of Christianity at all among many of the more educated former Puritans.

But internal demons aside, New England in the 1720s faced another foe: the Abnaki Indians of northern Maine and today's Maritime Provinces of Canada. The last had been converted to Catholicism by the French Jesuits and were steady allies of the nation who had brought them the true religion. Moreover, they had also supported King Philip, and gave refuge to many of the defeated in that war.

In 1694 there came among the Abnaki of the valley of the Kennebec a new Jesuit missionary, Fr. Sebastian Râle, S.J. He was a diligent pastor, beloved by his flock, for whom he composed in their own language a catechism, and in the same language translated the common Catholic prayers. Setting up his headquarters at the village of Norridgewock, he stayed with his people throughout King William's War, several times fleeing marauding English bands with them.

When 1713 brought peace, the English agreed to leave the Abnaki in peaceful possession of their lands. But before long the settlers began encroaching upon them again. War broke out in 1721 as a result, and the New Englanders resolved to capture Fr. Râle, whom they considered to be the heart of the resistance. In August of 1724, the English attacked Norridgewock while all the men were out hunting. To give his flock time to escape, he went out to meet the invaders. The old missionary was shot at the foot of the village cross, his body catching a hundred bullets. His body was then mutilated. Fr. Râle's scalp was taken back to Boston and paraded around the streets.

Elsewhere in the colonies, the same pattern of growth in settled areas and skirmishing on the frontiers continued. Northern Carolina had become home to many small farmers and merchants, whereas the southern part of the colony continued to develop along the lines of plantation economy. Strife between the two sections became so intense that at last the government in Britain separated the two areas into the colonies of North and South Carolina in 1729. Due to the highly stratified and aristocratic nature of society in Virginia and South Carolina, North Carolinians took to calling themselves "a valley of humility between two mountains of conceit."

Although Governor Moore and various other worthies of the same sort had devastated Spanish Florida's interior, St. Augustine remained inviolate due to its fortifications. Driven out of the south of Carolina by the English, the Yamasee Indians had sought refuge at St. Augustine with the Spanish. From there they had continued to harass the English, until a raid nearly wiped them out in 1727. But with the land between the Spanish frontier and Charleston being basically empty of all save warlike Indians and brigands, South Carolina was not secure.

An answer appeared in the person of James Oglethorpe, an English philanthropist. In Britain in those days, one could be imprisoned for debt. He would stay in Debtor's Prison until and unless his debts were paid. Naturally, it was rather difficult to earn money while imprisoned, and so for many debtors it was a life sentence, unless friends or relations could or would bail them out. Charles Dickens' father, in a later time, went there; this is why the young Dickens had to work as a child.

Oglethorpe conceived the idea of a refuge for such prisoners in America, where they could start over. The Crown, in the meantime, looked at the empty portions of South Carolina as a security risk, and longed for colonists to settle it. The two ideas were joined, and in 1733 Oglethorpe led the first band of settlers to the new town of Savannah, in the new colony of Georgia, named after King George II. All thirteen colonies were founded, and South Carolina had a buffer against the Spanish. Its effectiveness would shortly be tested.

King George's War

The hatred of Spain which had so long characterized the English was always easily inflamed. In the late 1730s, another wave of anti-Spanish hysteria gripped the British public. During a parliamentary debate on the topic in 1738, a certain Captain Jenkins appeared, exhibiting what he claimed was his ear, cut off by Spanish coast guards in 1731. Whatever the truth of the affair, it was enough to cause a declaration of war—a conflict called, appropriately enough, the War of Jenkins' Ear.

One year after the war began, James Oglethorpe tried his hand at generalship. With 1,200 men he set out to besiege St. Augustine. For 37 days he kept at it. Despite being outnumbered, however, the garrison and populace refused to given in. Whenever the British let loose a cannonade, the besieged Spanish, led by their bishop, Francisco de San Buenaventura y Tejada, would join in a chorus of *Ave Maria*! Discouraged at last, Oglethorpe and his men retreated to Georgia.

Semi-comic as this episode was, the war in general fanned the fanatical anti-Catholic hatred of the colonials. In 1741, New York City was rocked by an affair called the *Negro Plot*, which led to the death of one Fr. John Ury as yet another martyr to American Protestantism. It began due to rumors spread about a rash of unexplained fires. These, it was said, were being set by blacks at the instigation of priests as a prelude to burning the entire city. Panic began to set in. The Lieutenant-Governor, George Clarke, despite having proved that at least one of these fires was certainly an accident, a few weeks later claimed to have discovered a conspiracy to destroy the city. He offered a good deal of cash and a pardon to any white who would come forward with information about the plot. An indentured servant named Mary Burton claimed to have information and took the reward. Based on her evidence, three blacks were hung, although no real proof had been produced that there was any conspiracy at all. An atmosphere prevailed in New York not unlike that at Salem 49 years before.

Clarke then offered an amnesty to any black who would come forward and reveal what he or she knew. Hoping to free themselves from any possible accusation, many did so—telling wild self-contradictory tales which nevertheless were enough to cause arrests. At last, Mary Burton surfaced again with an accusation against one John Ury; both that he was in on the plot and that he was in fact a Catholic priest (for which offense alone he could be executed). Ury was arrested and tried. During his interrogation, although he denied involvement in any plot, he refused to answer whether or not he was a priest. He was accused of teaching children catechism in a secret school in New York, performing baptisms, and gathering folk in his room to celebrate Mass. There were no papers or any proof that he was a priest or even a Catholic, but his silence was enough to condemn him. There has been some question as to whether or not he was indeed a Catholic priest, but the fact that he maintained silence when a single word could have saved his life seems conclusive; he would not have admitted it however, in order to protect his secret flock. Some have suggested that perhaps he was an Anglican Jacobite who would not take the oath to King George—but he could have said so and saved himself from hanging. His last words were published in Philadelphia shortly after, and only the Catholic network of the time could have done this, some of their number having witnessed the hanging.

The deaths of the blacks were horrible. Eleven were burnt at the stake and twenty hanged. Most were raised in the English or Dutch colonies, without religion, and went to their deaths screaming in despair. But some had been freed by the Spanish and died as true Catholics, clutching their crucifixes. Typical of these is this account from the register of the day:

> Juan de Sylva, the Spanish Negro condemned for the conspiracy, was this day executed according to sentence: he was neatly dressed... behaved decently, prayed in Spanish, kissed a crucifix, insisting on his innocence to the last.

Thus died a group of Catholics, victims of the same murderous temper against the faith which from time to time breaks out in all heathen lands.

Back in the South, the Spanish attempted in 1742 to take Savannah with a force of 3,000. Just as they had repelled Oglethorpe two years earlier, so he returned the favor now. Exhausted, the two sides settled down to a war of attrition.

Two years later, the War of Austrian Succession broke out, pitting Austria and Great Britain against Prussia, France, Spain, Bavaria, and Saxony. Being yet another world war, it was called King George's War by the British colonists; it absorbed the sputtering War of Jenkin's Ear.

Although the French had ceded Acadia, the mainland of Nova Scotia, to Britain, she retained Cape Breton Island, called Isle Royale. On that island, to make up for the loss of the naval base of Port (called by the English Annapolis) Royal, was built the great town and fortress of Louisbourg, named after King Louis XV. As long as it remained in French hands, there would be possibility of a French fleet sweeping down on Boston. On April 30, 1745, a force of 4,000 British troops under *William Pepperell* landed and began to lay siege to Louisbourg. At last, on June 16 the city fell.

The rest of the conflict was marked by false starts and campaigns that never left the planning stage on both sides. Frontier warfare continued with all its horror and atrocity. At last, the belligerents in Europe made peace, and returned all conquests made. Louisbourg was again in French hands.

The End of New France

In the years after the peace accord, the French in Canada built a network of forts in the Ohio country (the present states of Ohio, Indiana, Illinois, Kentucky, West Virginia, and Western Pennsylvania) to secure their claims. In 1753, the Royal Governor of Virginia, which colony claimed those lands, dispatched the youthful colonel *George Washington* to protest the presence of the French in what they considered Virginian land. The French commander sent the protest to the Governor at Quebec. The next year, Washington returned with a body of troops, but was defeated and captured, although allowed to withdraw afterwards—ironically on July 4.

War clouds were stirring elsewhere in the world as well. On the frontier the first shots would be fired in the Seven Years' War. General William Braddock was sent from England to take command in North America. He chaired a convention of the royal governors which decided upon a three-pronged strategy requiring assaults on Ft. Duquesne (present day Pittsburg), Ft. Niagara, and Crown Point.

At that time, a detachment of 3,000 Massachusetts militia took the French forts Gaspereau and Beausejour on the Nova Scotia isthmus. That deed done, they turned their attention to the 7,000 French-Acadian settlers who had dwelt peacefully under British rule since 1713. These were given the choice of going into exile or renouncing their Catholicism and allegiance to the King of France. They chose exile. From Florida to Maine they were parceled out along the shore, with no regard to separation of families. Eventually, many made their way to the bayous and prairies of Louisiana where they were the ancestors of today's Cajuns. Others returned to France, settling on islands off France's West coast. Many others returned north. Finding their old country occupied by Puritan settlers from New England they settled parts of Cape Breton and the "French Shore" of Southern Nova Scotia. Still others went to Quebec's Magdalene Islands and southern Gaspe Peninsula, to Prince Edward Island, and to New Brunswick. Some of these last penetrated eventually deep into the interior, along the St. John's river valley, which today is the French speaking Madawaska region of Maine. The whole affair was immortalized by Henry Wadsworth Longfellow in his poem *Evangeline*.

At the same time, July 9 saw the massacre of the British troops attacking Ft. Duquesne in Braddock's Defeat. Marching European fashion through the forests, Braddock and his men were ambushed by the French and Indians. The colonial militia, led by Col. Washington, was able to make its escape.

The British had better luck the following August on Lake Champlain. Although Crown Point resisted them, they were able to defeat a French force in the Battle of Lake George on September 8. At the south end of that lake they built Ft. William Henry. In response, the French under the gallant *Marquis de Montcalm* built Ft. Ticonderoga between the two lakes. The expedition to Niagara was abandoned.

All of this activity had occurred during ostensible peacetime, war not being declared until 1756. As with the other colonial wars, the action was dependent upon events in Europe. Until this time, the rivalry between the two great Catholic houses of Bourbon and Habsburg had provided many of the reasons for these wars, with Britain supporting the Habsburgs. At last, however, this unnatural state of affairs which had ensured the triumph both of the Reformation and of the Ottoman Turks came to an end with a treaty between France and Austria in May of 1756. By its terms, the daughter of the Holy Roman Empress, Maria Theresa, was betrothed to the Dauphin of France (later Louis XVI). Europe was now divided into two camps: Great Britain, Prussia, Hanover, and Hesse, versus France, the Empire, Austria, Saxony, Bavaria, Russia, and Sweden. War was declared, and the events in the colonies became an integral part of the worldwide conflict.

August of 1756 saw Montcalm take the British Forts Oswego and George; this disaster led to a suspension of all British offensive plans. A year later, Ft. William Henry fell to the French and their Indian allies. Montcalm promised the garrison safe conduct from the fort, but he was unable to control his Indian allies—who after all were not directly subject to him; before his horrified eyes they massacred the garrison and their dependents, as depicted in James Fenimore Cooper's *The Last of the Mohicans*.

The next year was one of successive defeats for the French, as post after post fell to the continually reinforced British. Louisbourg fell after a two-month long siege on July 26; Ft. Frontenac was taken by the British August 27, followed by Ft. Duquesne on November 25.

If 1758 was bad, 1759 was worse. Ticonderoga fell a year to the day after Louisbourg. From that latter port, General *James Wolfe* sailed off to the St. Lawrence to try and take the French colonial capital, Quebec. He was at first repulsed at the Montmorency. But he conducted his troops stealthily by night up to the plateau behind the city, the Plains of Abraham, where battle was joined on September 13. The French were completely defeated, and both Wolfe and Montcalm were mortally wounded. There is today a monument on the site to both of them, surely the only place in the world where commanders of opposing armies are jointly and equally commemorated. But as the British were breaking through the walls into the old city which had held them off for a century and a half, an anonymous Frenchman carved into the fireplace of an inn called the *Chien d'Or*—the Golden Dog—the following lines:

> I am a dog that gnaws its bone;
> I sit and gnaw it all alone.
> A time will come, which is not yet,
> When I'll bite him by whom I'm bit.

Nevertheless, the city fell, and almost a year later Montreal and the rest of New France surrendered. In 1762, Louis XV gave Louisiana to Spain to save it from the British; everything France had owned east of the Mississippi save New Orleans was conceded to Britain in 1763, who in turn gave Spain Cuba (which they had captured) in return for Florida, which all the Spanish living there immediately left.

Pontiac's Rebellion

The defeat of the French left their Indian allies without guidance as to dealing with the changed political scene. While the new British King George III planned to be as much a father to the Indian nations as Louis XV had been (his proclamation in 1763 forbidding white settlement on Indian lands west of the Alleghenies was one sign of this), his intentions would take time to filter down to frontier. In the meantime, Indians were no longer welcome at the formerly French posts in the old Northwest where they had always been honored guests before. Settlers took the French defeat as an invitation to seize bordering territories. In the face of this arose an imposing figure: *Pontiac*. Like King Philip before him, he was that rather rare figure among Indians: a first-rate inter-tribal organizer. He was a chief by 1755, and commanded his tribe—the Ottawas—at Braddock's Defeat. Although in 1760 he had agreed to leave the English alone if they would respect him, he soon came to realize that what was at stake was not merely welcomes at forts but the ever-encroaching settlers. Encouraged by French traders and hunters who informed him that he would have help from France, he resolved to drive the British out of the Northwest. On April 27, 1763, he held a grand council of all the tribes from the Great Lakes to the Lower Mississippi. His plan was relatively simple. Each of the tribes would take the nearest fort, and then united they would turn on the settlements. He reserved for himself Ft. Detroit.

He attempted to take the fort by surprise on May 7, but failed. Two days later he began the siege. Elsewhere, his plan worked perfectly. In short order, the only forts left in British hands were Detroit, Niagara, and Pitt (the former Ft. Duquesne). In July the siege of Ft. Pitt was broken by the British. Pontiac himself broke off the siege of Detroit after receiving news from the French commander of Ft. Chartres on the Mississippi that no French aid would be forthcoming on October 30. After this the rebellion petered out, partially helped by distribution of small-pox infected blankets by the British officer Colonel Henry Boquet. By the end of 1763, however, 200 settlers and traders had been killed, and about £100,000 worth of property plundered or destroyed.

Pontiac himself made peace in 1766; three years later he was killed by a Peoria Indian brave who had been bribed to do so by an English trader. The result was a ferocious reprisal the next year against the Peoria by the Pottowattomis who had been loyal allies of Pontiac. But by that time the policies of George III had borne fruit, and the tribes had given him their allegiance, thanks in no small part to his remarkable superintendent of Indian affairs, *Sir William Johnson.*

PRELUDE TO REVOLUTION

At last, British America had no real enemies to fear from the outside. But the strains and stresses in the relationship between the ruling classes of the various colonies and the Crown, which had always been there, more or less obviously, began ever increasingly to show. Further, because George III wished to restore Britain's monarchical constitution which had been eroded from the English Civil War to the accession of George I, there would of course be conflict.

Struggles Over Taxation

The wars in America had cost the British government millions of pounds; moreover, the continued necessity of defending the colonies required even more money. Up until now, the British taxpayer had footed the entire bill. But the Crown cast about for some equitable way to have the colonies pay a part of it. The oligarchies in each of the colonies, while they had no objection—through their control of the Assemblies—to taxing all the unrepresented poorer settlers, objected to being treated in the same way by the home government.

Problems began in March 1764, when Parliament passed the Sugar Act, which placed a tax upon sugar sent to the 13 colonies. As the text of the law said, "It is just and necessary that revenue be raised in America." Immediately, *James Otis,* son of a wealthy lawyer in the province of Massachusetts, who had already made a name for himself agitating against enforcement of the Navigation Acts (which required the colonies to trade only with other British colonies—as all colonial empires did at the time), wrote a pamphlet which maintained that

Parliament could not tax the colonies because the colonies were not represented therein (he doubtless would have resented a similar case being made by a local against the Assembly Otis himself sat in). At any rate, the wealthier Boston merchants made a compact not to use British goods.

The Stamp Act

March of 1765 saw another attempt to prevail upon the colonial leadership to pay their fair share. This was the Stamp Act, which required that only paper for legal documents, newsprint, and pamphlets which bore the stamp signifying payment of a small tax could be sold.

Reaction on the part of the colonial leadership, most of whom were bound not only by self-interest but also membership in the various lodges of Freemasons, was swift. *Patrick Henry* gave a speech on May 30 in Virginia's Statehouse at Williamsburg denying Parliament's right to tax the colonies. October 7 saw the convening of the Stamp Act Congress in New York, whereat representatives of the wealthy opponents of the Act gathered from all the colonies save Virginia, North Carolina, and Georgia. The delegates drew up petitions to the King and Parliament, again asserting their immunity from taxation; they adopted a *Declaration of Rights and Liberties* plainly declaring this. In our own day of IRS supremacy, we can well see the importance of the right to tax.

The arrival of stamp officers to begin collecting the tax led to demagogue-incited riots in various cities. In Boston, the house of the tax officer, *Andrew Oliver,* was looted and burned, as was that of Lieutenant Governor *Thomas Hutchinson;* in the latter case Hutchinson's manuscript of his magisterial history of the colony, along with his vital source materials, was destroyed. He later rewrote it from memory. The ringleaders, many of whom were prominent and important men holding official positions, formed non-importation and non-consumption agreements which not only bound the signers not to use British goods, but to boycott or otherwise punish those who did. Thus, if a man refused to pay the tax, he broke the law; if he paid it, the thugs employed by the anti-Stamp Act folk would rough him up. Friends of the government in Boston were forced to lay low. In the end, the Stamp Tax brought in no money at all, and so was repealed in March of 1766. But it was done with a parliamentary reiteration of their right to tax the colonies.

The next year, Parliament levied a tax upon glass, paper, paint, and tea brought into the colonies. It is important to remember at this point that the increase in price to the consumer was minimal. The problem for many of the wealthier circles, particularly in New England, was that a good piece of their income came from smuggling much cheaper goods from French, Dutch, Danish, or Spanish possessions, and selling them at a tremendous profit over the going rate established for goods imported from other British colonies. If all goods sold were taxed, they would have to be imported legally. This was the major reason why the colonial assemblies, dominated by such men, were resistant to the idea of paying any tax to the Crown. Beyond this problem, however, some few of the ideologues among these folk had already decided upon independence. New England had in any case always had an uneasy relationship with her Kings due to the Puritan problem.

Thus, in protest the New York Assembly refused to make provision for the British troops sent to protect the harbor; Parliament suspended the Assembly's legislative power as a result.

Massachusetts was strife-torn in 1768. The Assembly there sent a circular letter to its equivalent bodies in the other colonies. The ministry in London demanded the letter, calling for joint resistance, be withdrawn. This demand refused (92 to 17), the Royal Governor, Sir Francis Bernard, dissolved it. The same sort of action occurred elsewhere.

In June, *John Hancock*, a known smuggler, had a sloop of his seized in Boston Harbor by the custom house officials. Hancock's allies provoked a riot, and the officials were forced to flee to Castle William on an island in the harbor. Sir Francis having left for England, Hutchinson, the Lieutenant Governor, was forced to deal with the crisis. The group centering around Hancock, Otis, *Samuel Adams, Paul Revere*, and other influential folk, had made the town and province ungovernable, putting everyone at the pleasure of a mob of their own devising. Hutchinson begged London for troops, which duly arrived in October. These restored order in Boston itself.

The same sort of men and their allies who sat in the colonial assemblies also sat on juries, both roles being in those days reserved for men of means. It was soon realized by the government that it was useless to bring before such men their friends on charge of treason. 1769 saw Parliament attempt to overcome this by resolving that acts of treason committed in the colonies could be tried in Great Britain. This was resented, of course. The Virginia House of Burgesses protested the action; Lord Dunmore, the Governor, dissolved it but similar resolutions were adopted in other colonies. Meanwhile, the Massachusetts Assembly refused to meet in Boston's Statehouse as long as there was a guard posted there; they adjourned to Cambridge.

For all this activity, however, worse had happened at other times in the history of the colonies. What changed the complexion of the struggle was the majority gained by the King's Friends in the House of Commons in 1770. George III was able at last to appoint a Prime Minister of his own choosing, and to assume personal rule. The whole struggle became involved, as we shall see, with much higher questions.

THE RELIGIOUS PROBLEM

Most political questions are, in essence, religious ones. The wars against the Spanish and French were religiously based, as was of course the persecution of English and other Catholics in the colonies. Beyond that however, it was the gradual erosion of belief in Christianity of any sort which characterized the history of the colonies. The excesses of the Puritans, the gentle tolerance of the Southern Anglicans, the Inner Light of the Quakers—all resulted in the Deism of men like John Adams, Thomas Jefferson, and Benjamin Franklin. As Bernard Faÿ says of the latter: "The God that Benjamin thus adored from the bottom of his heart was not in the least like the Christian God. Rather, he resembled a ... Deity that might have been dreamed of by a disciple of Plato." (*Franklin*, p. 115). Deism rejected completely the idea of revealed religion, toward existing examples of which it might be either amusedly contemptuous, as was Franklin, or actively hateful, like Tom Paine.

In the place of the God of the Christians was put instead the idea of the Watchmaker-god, who set creation going but does not intervene in it. In a sense, it was the inverse of Puritanism, whose Predestination effectively prevented God from acting in the present—only in the Past could He manifest actively, in the sense of saving one's soul. It is the Deist God, in fact, whom the Masonic order claimed and claims to revere as the Grand Architect of the Universe; this was an idea which also appealed much to the scientists of the day. All three tendencies—Deistic, Masonic, and Scientificist come beautifully together in the person of Franklin's English friend, *Joseph Priestley*. Priestley was at once an inventor and chemist, pastor of the first Unitarian church in Great Britain, a Freemason, and a noted supporter (when at last the time came round) of the French Revolution.

Since there were few Catholics in the British Colonies, the task of upholding in an effective way the dictates of revealed and dogmatic Christianity fell to the Anglican establishment. Since there were no bishops in the colonies, this meant to the Royal Governors, and ultimately the King their master. It will be obvious that they were in no way adequate to the task; but they were all there was.

SUMMARY

To conclude, the history of the English colonies is the story of the ultimate triumph of Puritanism—at first fanatical, and then latterly secularized or Deist. It is the record of a long line of defeats of glorious causes, the victory of any one of which might well have spelled a better present. Had the French and Spanish triumphed, we might today be a Catholic nation. Had the men of Merry Mount surprised Plymouth, New England and so all Anglo-America might be a happier place today. By the time we have reached in our story, only two things stood in the way of complete triumph for the sort of Deistic Puritanism we have described. One was the very different nature of the southern colonies, no matter how much political considerations might have led them to ally with New England for the moment; the other was allegiance to the King, with connection to a larger empire. We shall see the fate of the latter in the next chapter.

THE FIRST CIVIL WAR
1770-1783

CAUSES OF THE REVOLUTION

The Christian world in the late 18th Century was in the grips of a movement called *The Enlightenment*. Its most radical members believed that the state of affairs in European countries and their overseas colonies, influenced as they were (even in Protestant lands like Great Britain) by the Catholic Middle Ages, must go. God, if He existed, was not interested in men, having created them and then left them alone. As a result, the power of the state churches, and particularly of the Catholic Church, must be broken. Similarly, the authority of Europe's Kings must be overthrown, based as they were upon the sanction of the established churches. Such views were spread by writers like *Voltaire* and *Jean Jacques Rousseau*. The motto which summed up these beliefs was "a Church without a Pope and a State without a King."

Adherents of these ideas believed that nations should be ruled by those who had proved their ability to do so—the wealthy. Custom and tradition should be disposed of in favor of "rational" planning; local liberties and differences should be suppressed in favor of centralized rule. In public life, self-interest should replace personal loyalty. Man, after all, was supposed by these people to be merely a rational animal, important only for his money-making ability, rather than a creation of God with a soul.

But these were the Enlightenment ideas in their purest and most radical form—held by only a small minority (although often a rich and influential one). Many other people who would oppose this program if it were made completely clear to them, agreed with portions of it. The large number of pamphlets and books supporting these ideas in more or less diluted form won a large number of converts, and made others at least sympathetic. In time, the whole atmosphere of educated Europe (and America) became more or less influenced by these ideas. This is why the late 18th Century is often called *The Age of Reason*, although, as we shall see, application of Enlightenment principles often resulted in bloody and horribly unreasonable acts.

On Christmas Day, 1775, Pope Pius VI wrote a letter to all the Catholic bishops called in Latin *Inscrutabile*. In this letter, the Pope described the ideas we have been talking about. He detailed both their evil nature and evil results. He went on to say that:

> When they have spread this darkness abroad and torn religion out of men's hearts, these accursed philosophers proceed to destroy the bonds of union among men, both those which unite them to their rulers, and those which urge them to their duty. They keep proclaiming that man is born free and subject to no one, that society accordingly is a crowd of foolish men who stupidly yield to priests who deceive them and to Kings who oppress them, so that the harmony of priest and ruler is only a monstrous conspiracy against the innate liberty of man.
>
> Everyone must understand that such ravings and others like them, concealed in many deceitful guises, cause greater ruin to public calm the longer their impious originators are unrestrained. They cause a serious loss of souls redeemed by Christ's blood wherever their teaching spreads, like a cancer; it forces its way into public academies, into the houses of the great, into the palaces of Kings, and even enters the sanctuary, shocking as it is to say so. (cap. 7).

But the Pope's wise warning was ignored. Most of Europe's rulers—Holy Roman Emperor Joseph II, Russia's Catherine the Great, Prussia's Frederick the Great, and Spain's Charles III—believed in much of the Enlightenment (not the part about doing away with the Kings, but in everything that hampered the Church). With the French King Louis XV who died in 1774, most of the Catholic rulers had proven their "enlightened" beliefs by forcing Pius VI's predecessor, Clement XIV, to abolish the Jesuits. This loss to the Church of one of her strongest orders was a heavy blow to her and a correspondingly great victory for her enemies.

One especially dangerous means of transmitting these ideas at Royal courts and elsewhere was through various lodges of the Freemasons. Although at this time many good Catholics and others joined these lodges for social and other reasons they were unaware of the dedication of the Masonic leadership to spreading the Enlightenment. But in joining they gave the Masonic Order the benefit of their time, money, and prestige, and in turn became more inclined toward such ideas themselves. In this way, Masonry became very influential at the court of the French King, even after Louis XV, somewhat friendly to their ideas, died. His grandson and successor, Louis XVI, was both much more pious and moral than his predecessor. But he was forced to rely on the ministers and courtiers bequeathed him by Louis XV, with results that we shall see later.

Great Britain Under George III

In the British Isles and their colonies, things were more complicated. In any Protestant Country, the principles of the Enlightenment were especially welcome. This was truer still in Britain. The reason was that they provided justification for the Whig Oligarchy who actually ran the country, whom you will remember from the last chapter. They already had power; now the Enlightenment made this situation virtuous!

But England still retained the form of government she had always had. On paper, the King functioned much as the American President does. He appointed the cabinet to carry out his programs; just as skill is required for the President to get his bills passed by Congress, so the King's ministers had to be skillful enough to guide legislation through Parliament. In theory, Parliament acted as a check on the King's power, while the King himself provided unified leadership above party and faction. Since Parliament consisted of both Lords and Commons (the latter elected by the well-to-do), both people and nobility were part of the government. King, Lords, and Commons were to maintain a balance which would insure good government as much as anything human can.

However, due to earlier wars and insurrections, as well as the fact that the English throne had been occupied by foreigners since 1714, much had changed. Although the form remained the same, the substance was different. The King continued to go through the motions of appointing the Prime Minister and Cabinet, but in reality the Cabinet was put in place by whichever Whig faction could control a majority in Parliament. The modern equivalent would be the American Cabinet being appointed by the Party which holds the majority in Congress. Obviously, if this were the case, the President would have no power over the Federal government at all. Such was the case in Great Britain by 1760.

Since the House of Commons members were for the most part in the hire of wealthy oligarchs, and since the dominant faction among them was able to give out government positions to its supporters, the whole method of British government changed in reality, even while remaining the same on the surface. Policies and appointments were dictated purely on the basis of keeping a majority in the Commons; corruption grew incredibly, and the national interest was forgotten by politicians intent on wealth and power. George I and George II, being Germans much more interested in their Electorate of Hanover than in Britain, were content to let things go on in this way. But George III, who succeeded his grandfather George II in 1760, was different.

Unlike the last two Kings, George III "gloried in the name of Briton." Unlike them he was faithful to his wife, as pious as an Anglican can be, and more interested in Britain and its Empire than in Hanover. As a boy, his mother had often told him to "be a King." For him, that meant restoring his country's original constitution—in a word, functioning as the President does, rather than as a figurehead. That way, he could lift the government of Britain above petty factional greed and dispute; instead of self-interest, his realm would be governed for the benefit of his people and the glory of God (as far as he could see it). But this project would require a great deal of skill if it were to succeed. After all, arrayed against him were all the Whig factions who between them had complete control of Parliament, however much they might squabble and struggle among themselves when there was no effective King to fear; the owners of the Bank of England, whose control of the country's money supply (an essential part of governing) made them in effect more powerful than either King or Parliament; and those Freemasons and others who were disciples of the Enlightenment.

Against these seemingly all-powerful foes, however, the King had many important advantages. Above all, he was King. In those days, the majority of his subjects had retained from Catholic days the traditional reverence due a King. This was described a Century and a half later by John Healy, the Catholic Archbishop of Tuam, Ireland:

> The character of Kings is sacred; their persons are inviolable; they are the anointed of the Lord, if not with sacred oil, at least by virtue of their office. Their power is broad—based upon the Will of God, and not on the shifting sands of the people's will... They will be spoken of with becoming reverence, instead of being in public estimation fitting butts for all foul tongues. It becomes a sacrilege to violate their persons, and every indignity offered to them in word or act, becomes an indignity offered to God Himself. It is this view of Kingly rule that alone can keep alive in a scoffing and licentious age the spirit of ancient loyalty, that spirit begotten of faith, combining in itself obedience, reverence, and love for the majesty of kings which was at once a bond of social union, an incentive to noble daring, and a salt to purify the heart from its grosser tendencies, preserving it from all that is mean, selfish, and contemptible.
>
> (P.J. Joyce, *John Healy*, pp. 68-69).

The King's coronation at the beginning of his reign, his headship of the Church of England (in Catholic countries the King is instead the defender of and most important layman in the Church), and his continued liturgical role continued to impress upon his people the sacred character of his office, and instill in them a personal loyalty to him very unlike what we Americans feel toward our President. He was father of his country, and most Britons, either in the Mother Country or in her colonies loved him in a real though distant way. This was a great help in dealing with politicians who inspired in the people no loyalty, and whose only source of power was wealth and corruption.

Secondly, in Parliament there remained a small but compact group of the Whig's long-time adversaries, the Tories. Spiritual descendants of the Cavaliers, their policy was, according to *Dr. Samuel Johnson*, one of their most famous members, adherence "to the ancient constitution of the State and the apostolic hierarchy of the Church of England..." Since this required the closest possible loyalty to the sovereign, the reigns of the last two Kings, themselves creatures of the Whigs, had left them out in the political cold. Many had supported the exiled house of Stuart, at least until their final defeat at Culloden in 1746. But George III's accession breathed new life into them. Here was a reigning King whom they could follow!

However, the Tories alone had not enough members in Parliament to allow the King to form a government above faction. Fortunately, a large number of Whigs were public-minded enough to see the justice of the King's program. They joined with the Tories to form a loose group in Commons called "the King's Friends." For a decade after the accession of George III, this group grew in numbers of M.P.s. Amid factional strife, the King and his friends carefully worked. At last, in 1770, George III and his supporters in Parliament were strong enough to secure a Prime Minister, Frederick, Lord North, who would attempt to run the government along national and patriotic lines.

But the enemy was defeated, not destroyed. The Oligarchy remained powerful in Parliament, in the Army and Navy, in the control of the Bank of England, and lastly in the very intellectual climate of England. They would seek to return to complete power at any moment. If George III were to succeed, it would destroy them; if His Majesty failed, they would ensure that no monarch could ever again challenge them. As long as things went on in a relatively stable manner under Lord North's ministry, they would have no chance to move against the King. What was needed was a crisis. The ongoing attempts of the government to persuade the American colonies to pay a percentage of the money spent on them would provide that crisis.

The Colonial Oligarchies

None of the colonies were what we call democratic today. With few exceptions the colonial assemblies, upon whom the Royal Governors and other officials depended for pay, and who in general decided the courses of action for the colonies, were elected by those whose property or income qualified them. These constituted a governing class in each colony. Of course, they differed considerably from province to province. In New England they tended to be merchants, much concerned with shipping; in religion they held primarily to the Congregationalism their Puritan ancestors had brought over from England. New York's rulers were either wealthy merchants or else proprietors of the great manors.

Dutch or English by blood, they held either the Anglican or the Dutch Reformed religions of their progenitors. Pennsylvania, Delaware, and Maryland, being proprietary colonies granted in the first two cases to the Penn family and in the latter to the Lords Baltimore, their ruling classes were primarily those who had received grants of land from the Proprietors. In Maryland these were mostly English; in Pennsylvania they were a blinding kaleidoscope of nationalities and religions. Lastly, the southern colonies (Virginia, North and South Carolina, Georgia) were uniformly dominated by plantation owners centered in the Tidewater. All in all, they reflected the settlement patterns spoken of in the last chapter.

They were very much like their opposite numbers, the English Oligarchs, to whom they were related by interests, politics, and often, blood. Developments at home were eagerly followed by them, and they managed quite a civilized life for themselves in the colonies. As with their English equivalents, they were faction-ridden, depending on intensely local and personality issues to shape their shifting alliances. From their ranks came the judges, militia captains, and Assembly and Governor's Council members.

Again differing from colony to colony, this ruling class ran into more or less friction with the poorer folk whom it ruled. In the South, where the friction between the backwoods Piedmont region and the coastal Tidewater region reflected the poverty of the former and the wealth of the latter, conflict was especially violent, and broke out in open warfare at various times. The Royal Governors were often sympathetic to the plight of the disenfranchised in a way that many of the oligarchs found extremely uncomfortable.

The attempt of the King and his party in Parliament, and their subsequent efforts at reestablishing effective Royal government in the colonies was feared by many of the colonial ruling classes for four reasons: 1) they were political heirs to the Whig tradition of 1688, and believed that effective control of the state ought to be in the best, that is their, hands; 2) many (particularly such as *Benjamin Franklin, Samuel Adams* and *Thomas Jefferson*) were disciples to a greater or lesser degree of the Enlightenment. For such as these, all their activity aimed ultimately at doing away with the monarchy, not just in the colonies but in the Mother Country; 3) there was a great fear that renewed Royal authority in the colonies would not merely force them to pay something toward the upkeep of their defense but deprive them of their monopoly of local power; and 4) that such renewal would inevitably force them to share some power with their fellow colonists.

It should be pointed out at this juncture that the phrase "no taxation without representation" was coined purely as a slogan to beat the home government with. Most of those who paid local taxes at the behest of the colonial assemblies could not vote for them, and so were unrepresented.

Thus, for those of the colonial oligarchy who were ideologically motivated, the King's attempts were an attack upon progress; for those who were guided by more mundane concerns, they threatened their jealously guarded privilege and power. It was not difficult for them to make common cause with one another, both over colonial boundaries and with their English counterparts. The strong union of many of these Whigs was undergirded by their mutual membership in the Masonic Order, which swiftly became as prominent in America as it was at home.

Anti-Catholicism

Catholicism was hated in all the colonies, and legal in just three. Nevertheless, despite this, and the Penal laws against the Faith in the British Isles, it was continually feared that "Popery" could emerge at any moment to destroy the colonies. In part this was due to the age-long conflict between Britain on the one hand, and France and Spain on the other, which engendered the Black Legend spoken of in the last chapter.

But in New England, the actual spawning ground of the Revolution, it was not merely hatred of the French and Spanish that influenced anti-Catholicism. You will remember that the Puritans had wanted to purify the Church of England of anything remotely Catholic (except, indeed, the Bible). Failing in this, they came to New England. Since the arrival of Sir Edmund Andros in 1686, they had feared that the King merely awaited his chance to make Catholics of them. This was a fear waiting to be exploited.

Worse, when Quebec finally fell in 1760, and was handed over to the Crown by treaty in 1763, George III did not immediately disenfranchise the French-Canadians and hand them over to the New Englanders to run as they chose. Rather, he sat idly by while successive military governors permitted the hated Quebecois to practice their Catholic Faith and live in accordance with their own laws. Instead of putting into effect the Penal Laws immediately, the King was acting as though the newly conquered French were his subjects also! Good Puritans were much offended, as were the Enlightened. This too was a smoldering source of resentment. As Jonathan Boucher said in his appeal on behalf of the King to the Catholics of Maryland, as regarded the New England Puritans:

> ...hardly a book or an article of religion has been written, hardly a sermon or any controverted point has been preached, hardly any public debate or private conversations have been held on the subject of

religion or politics in which the parties have not contrived a thwack at Popery.

Hatred of the Indians

If it were bad enough that George III treated his new French subjects so well, his dealings with the Indians were worse. As you will remember, almost all the Indian tribes had allied with the French against the British, save the Iroquois and the Cherokee. But when the treaty with France was signed, George III undertook to occupy the same relationship with his former Indian enemies that the French Crown had had. This meant protecting the interests of his new Indian allies, even against the desires of his white subjects for more land. Hence the Proclamation of 1763, which declared all land West of the Alleghenies to belong to the various Indian tribes; therein no white man could settle without their consent.

Despite this Proclamation, as you will recall, Pontiac and the Northwest Indians rose in revolt. After their suppression two years later, the need to conciliate them even further became more apparent. But it roused a great deal of frontier opinion against the King.

SUMMARY

The accession to power of Lord North and the seeming triumph of the King's restoration policy alarmed Whigs on both sides of the Atlantic. The bickering over taxes with the colonial ruling classes which had marked the first decade of George III's reign provided a means to ruin his policy. If his measures in the colonies failed, they must fail in England; if he succeeded in restoring the colonies to non-oligarchical government, he would seal the oligarchy's fate in England. In a word, the stakes were not merely the right to tax colonies, but ultimately rulership of the whole British Empire.

Thus was the stage set for a struggle which began in the political sphere, became a civil war, and ended as a worldwide conflagration.

THE CONTENDING PARTIES

Civil Wars are always the bloodiest and cruelest. Brother fights brother, and often no quarter is given. When bound up with revolutionary activity, there is the added ingredient of conspiracy, of the imposition upon the majority of a minority's desire for power. So it proved in that war we call the American Revolution. Every such conflict has three major sides: those who defend the present regime, those who attack it, and those who are neutral. To understand the conflict we are discussing, which has played such an important part in the formation of the American national consciousness, it were well to examine all three sides.

The Loyalists

These were the defenders of what was at the time the duly established government. To understand them, imagine that a revolt broke out against the government in Washington; which side would you support—particularly if the revolt was led by those who already held most of the power in your state? This was the position the Loyalists were in.

Some favored the King just because he was King; others because they had taken oaths which they would not break. Still others feared being left completely in the hands of the oligarchy, with no King in London to appeal to. Many had disagreed with Royal policy on taxation, but did not see that as cause to commit treason. A few perhaps saw the good effects that would accrue should the King succeed in his attempt to restore the British Empire to its ancient constitution. And of course, there were opportunists, as there are on every side in every question.

The Loyalists were hampered by a great many drawbacks. Firstly, they were not organized on an Empire-wide basis, as the Whigs tended to be. Indeed, they were in the beginning completely unorganized. The movement of events took them by surprise, for seemingly over night the political landscape changed on them. Often, in the beginning, the better educated among them thought that it was only a matter of getting the facts of the situation (that the government wished to impose light taxes in order to offset the tremendous expense the colonies brought Great Britain) out to the public in an effective way. They did not realize that it was not a question of right or wrong, but of power. The majority came from groups and regions effectively left out of political affairs anyway. The one advantage that most supporters of established regimes have—the machinery of government—was of little use to them.

Firstly, there was little in the way of government in the colonies to begin with. Most of what there was—militia companies, courts, assemblies—were in the hands of the oligarchy. The Royal Governors had little in the way of organized support unless there was a garrison of regular British troops in the colony; these were usually too few to be of much use. Loyalists did not begin gathering into armed bands until after the war began; in the meantime, they and their property were at the mercy of the rebels.

It is an exploded myth that the Loyalists were men of wealth. There were some among them, it is true, but most were poor or middle class. They often came from economically disadvantaged areas, or from cultural minority groups. Anglicans in New England, for instance, where they were a minority, tended to be Loyal. But those in the South, where they were members of the Established Church, often were rebels. It will be very instructive to take a quick colony by colony survey of them:

New Hampshire

Here the Loyal cause was relatively weak. Most lived in Portsmouth, the capital, and were either office-holders or professional men. Typical was the native-born Royal Governor, *John Wentworth*.

Massachusetts

In New England, due to Puritanism, Loyalist strength was tenuous. But Massachusetts had a goodly number, including the also native-born Governor, *Thomas Hutchinson* and the pamphleteer, *Daniel Leonard*. Although Boston was their hub, as indeed it was of the colony, they could be found in numbers in Portland (Maine, then part of Massachusetts) and Worcester county. Commerce, the professions, and the royal service were their usual occupations, although some few patricians, like Hutchinson, also rallied. Many were driven from their homes to Boston even before hostilities broke out; the residents of what is now called Tory Row in Cambridge were forced to flee one night in 1774, purely for their adherence to the King. The first American Black female poet, Boston resident *Phillis Wheatley*, wrote a Loyalist poem:

TO THE KING'S MOST EXCELLENT MAJESTY

Your subjects hope, dread Sire—
The crown upon your brows may flourish long,
And that your arm may in your God be strong!
O, may your sceptre numr'ous nations sway,
And all with love and readiness obey!
But how shall we the *British King* reward?
Rule thou in peace, our father and our lord!
Midst the remembrance of thy favors past,
The meanest peasants most admire the last.
May *George*, beloved by all the nations round,
Live with heav'n's choicest constant blessings crown'd!
Great God, direct and guard him from on high,
And from his head let ev'ry evil fly!
And may each clime with equal gladness see
A monarch's smile can set his subjects free.

Rhode Island

Here the Loyalists were concentrated in Newport, and were the usual Anglican and merchant, New England Tory sorts. Here again, the Governor, *Joseph Wanton*, was native-born.

Connecticut

Stamford, New Haven, and Norwalk were the major Loyal strongholds. The Loyalists here were generally modest farmers or professional men. In this colony, even the Governor defected to the rebels—the only one of the thirteen to do so.

New York

Unhampered by Puritanism, New York was the bastion of the Loyal Cause in the North, particularly among the Scots Catholics and other settlers along the frontier, among the less assimilated Dutch speakers of the Hudson Valley, and people of all descriptions in the New York City and Long Island areas. A few of the great families—the De Lanceys, Philipses, and Crugers, rallied to the cause, as did pamphleteer and clergyman *Samuel Seabury*, the entire faculty of King's College (now Columbia University), and the families of *St. Elizabeth Anne Seton* and her husband.

New Jersey

Middle-class farmers were the bulk of the Loyalists here, although the Governor, *William Franklin* (son of Benjamin) had a well-known name.

Pennsylvania

This colony too had a great many Loyalists, particularly in Philadelphia and surrounding counties. Here as in New Jersey, they tended to be small farmers if in the country; if German, they tended to be less assimilated. *Joseph Galloway* was the best-known Loyalist in the colony. Here were raised two regiments of Catholic Tories, notably the Roman Catholic Volunteers, under Major Alfred Clinton.

Delaware

Here the Loyalists were scattered throughout the colony, but had a higher proportion of well-to-do in their number.

Maryland

This colony had a large number of Catholics, of whom most of the poorer sort were Loyal. Most of the population of the Eastern Shore was Tory. In the rest of the colony, Annapolis, Baltimore, and Frederick had the largest number of Loyalists. Prominent among them were *Jonathan Boucher* and *Daniel Dulany*.

Virginia

Except for the Eastern Shore, (here as in Maryland resolutely Loyal) the Loyalists were most influential in the Piedmont. Few among the Tidewater planters were Tory, although various Merchants and office-holders in Norfolk, Williamsburg, Gosport, Petersburg, and Portsmouth were. As elsewhere in the colonies, the King was popular among Blacks, both slave and free.

North Carolina

Here too, Loyalists among the dominant Tidewater planters were few. But merchants and office-holders in Wilmington and New Bern were often Loyal. The bulk of Tory strength, however, was in the Piedmont, among the small farmers called *Regulators* who had revolted against the colony's oligarchy in 1771. Also inland was a large colony of Scots Highlanders settled there after the Jacobite defeat at Culloden. Instrumental in rallying them for King George III was *Flora MacDonald*, who had helped Bonnie Prince Charlie escape Scotland after the defeat.

South Carolina

In this colony, the same pattern repeated itself, pitting Loyal Charleston merchants and Piedmont farmers (centered in the towns of Camden and Ninety-Six) against most of the oligarchy.

Georgia

Most Georgians remained Loyal, perhaps out of gratitude for the 30,000£ annual subsidy granted the colony by the Crown (since Georgia, you will recall, was the newest and weakest of the colonies). While Savannah was a Loyalist stronghold, it was also the base of rebel activities in Georgia.

Although significant numbers of the ruling class in the colonies rallied to the King only in Massachusetts, New York, and Georgia, the Tories numbered many talented writers, scientists, artists, academics, and professional men. But at no time did these ever try to cooperate on an America-wide basis, generally fighting and losing their political or military battles locally.

Catholics Among the Tories

There were only about 30,000 Catholics in the thirteen colonies in 1770. These included the Scots Highlanders in the Mohawk Valley of New York, German and English Catholics in Pennsylvania, and English Catholics in Maryland. Four regiments of Catholic Loyalist soldiers would be raised from their number. While the rank and file of the Catholic community tended toward Loyalism, the wealthier and more influential Catholics (such as Maryland's Carroll clan) sought their loyalties elsewhere. The French of Quebec were also Loyal. Among the better known Catholic Loyalists were Major Clinton, *Fr. John McKenna*, Irish pastor of the Mohawk Valley Scots and later first chaplain in the British Army since the Reformation, and Bishop *Olivier Briand* of Quebec.

The Rebels

The four wealthiest men in the colonies were *John Hancock,* George Washington, *Philip Schuyler*, and *Charles Carroll of Carrollton*. All four were rebels. As we have already noticed, there was a solid core of radicals among the oligarchy who wanted abolition of the monarchy, or failing that, independence from Britain. But in 1770, these were a small minority. Most of the oligarchs would be quite pleased to retain both their connection to the Mother Country and their allegiance to the Crown—so long as these were purely symbolic and did not require anything from them. In this, they were not unlike the Whigs in England. A larger number still did not think in these wide terms, but simply wished redress of what they considered to be grievances, particularly in regard to the Stamp and other taxes. These last were perhaps genuinely loyal to the Crown. Apart from the oligarchs there were various urban mobs, always ready to riot and loot.

The third named group was perhaps the largest, but they were not in control. The tide of events we are about to survey carried them much further than they wished to go, and they were caught between radical agitation and government reprisal. In the end, they threw in their lot with the radicals, who were, after all, well organized and knew precisely what they wanted. It is usually thus with revolutions and civil wars.

It should be remembered again that the Royal government in America in 1770 was considered no more foreign than the Federal government is in California today. Any who plotted to overthrow the American constitution, flag, and so on would be considered traitors. Those who would break their oaths to the Constitution would be considered perjurers. So it was in 1770. This is one other point to keep in mind; each of the rebels who had held public office, like Franklin, Jefferson, *George Washington,* and *Patrick Henry*, had to break their oaths to the King. Such Oaths of Allegiance meant as much or more then as they do to us today.

There was another factor in the decision of many Southern Planters to side with the rebels. Most were heavily in debt to British merchants for the sorts of manufactured goods their plantations needed but could not supply for themselves. Hence their support for independence, which would allow them to renege on such debts. This was summed up by Irish poet Thomas Moore:

> Who could their monarch in their purse forget
> And break allegiance but to cancel debt.

As a result of the Stamp Act agitation, the rebels in each colony had two organizations to spread rebellious propaganda and coordinate their activities. The *Sons of Liberty* were a loose organization, somewhat like the Ku-Klux-Klan or Chinese Red Guards of later years. Their mission was to terrorize Loyalists into submission or at least neutrality, using tarring-and-feathering, burning of property, and on some few occasions, murder, to accomplish this goal. Given that Royal officials could only depend on local militia (often infiltrated by the Sons of Liberty) or the ever too few British troops for security, they were usually unable to protect outspoken Tories, who tended to either keep silent or flee to safer havens. In either case, the Royal cause suffered.

The *Committees of Correspondence* were rather more respectable. These were a network of committees throughout the colonies, often based on the local Masonic Lodge, which served as a conduit of information for the rebels. If a Royal official attempted to perform his duties, word of the "outrage" would soon be spread, in highly exaggerated form, from New Hampshire to Georgia.

Add to these the rebel dominance of colonial government referred to, and it will become obvious that, in a sense, the peaceful continuance of the colonies in the Empire was doomed, if the oligarchs so decided. The assumption of government by Lord North and the momentary triumph of the King's Friends in England promised that the American Whigs would have to show their strength, if their English counterparts were to triumph over George III. War became inevitable, for the King would certainly not back down. But with an administration riddled with Whiggery, how reliable were the tools with which he would have to work?

Catholics Among the Rebels

While the rank and file of Catholics were Loyal, the most prominent Catholics in the colonies followed the lead of the wealthy with whom they were most closely associated. So Maryland's Charles Carroll of Carrollton, and Pennsylvania's *John Barry* (father of the U.S. Navy) and Generals *Stephen Moylan* and *Thomas Fitzsimmons*, all of whom were at least well-to-do before the War, joined the rebels. This would stand the rebel cause in good stead later with France and Spain.

The Neutrals

Although it is impossible to make any real estimate of numbers, committed Loyalists probably outnumbered committed rebels. But commitment is an unruly thing—doubtless the lukewarm outnumbered the committed on both sides; such as these awaited the outcome of things before deciding which side they would join.

Perhaps more numerous than any were those who were more or less neutral. Some of these were religious pacifists, like the Quakers. Others (and these are numerous in any civil conflict) did not really care who ruled, so long as they were left alone to pursue their own affairs. To use once again a modern example, most adults really do not like paying Income Taxes. How attached to the government would be those who think of it chiefly in terms of the Internal Revenue Service? How supportive would they be of would-be overthrowers of the government, if they thought that the revolutionaries would charge the same taxes or higher? Either way, they would be most concerned with staying out of such a conflict. Yet it is precisely such people, because of their numbers, who can spell the difference between victory and defeat.

In the case of the American Revolution, it is fair to say that the bulk of the people fell into this category.

WHAT CAME BEFORE

Due to the agitation against the Townshend taxes on glass, paper, printer's ink, and tea, the Whigs had succeeded in paralyzing the government of Massachusetts and in making the Governor, *Sir Francis Bernard,* return home in disgust. The Lieutenant Governor, Thomas Hutchinson, took his place. Despite Hutchinson's being the fifth generation in the province, he was no more able to restore tranquillity than Bernard had been. Already, the Assembly had arrogated to itself the power to disavow Parliament's tax laws. This would be the equivalent of the State Legislature doing the same thing as regards Congress. But that was only the beginning. As Hutchinson wrote:

> At first, indeed, the supreme authority (of Parliament) seemed to be admitted, the cases of taxes only excepted; but the exceptions gradually extended from one case to another, until it included all cases whatsoever. A profession of "subordination" [to Royal authority], however, still remained; it was a word without any precise meaning to it (Hutchinson, *History of the Prov. of Mass.*, p. 256).

Local assemblies in Massachusetts replaced the legal administration. In particular, those who persisted in buying the four taxed items (the "non-importation" agreement, you will recall, was a compact by the oligarchy in the colonies compelling merchants not to purchase the taxed items) were ordered boycotted by these assemblies, and subject to assaults by the Sons of Liberty.

The Boston Massacre

In January 1770, Lord North took office, and almost immediately, events began to heat up.

Inside Boston itself, the presence of *General Thomas Gage* and his two regiments had provided some peace. But on March 5, a mob made up of Sons of Liberty and some others began assaulting a sentry at the customs house. Seven soldiers from the garrison were sent to his aid. Goaded by the crowd (and mistaking some of its taunts for an order to fire), the soldiers fired on their assailants, killing three and wounding eight. This was the famed *Boston Massacre*, which has ever since grown in the telling. The Committees of Correspondence ensured that news of this "atrocity" was known the length and breadth of British America. So infuriated were the agitators in neighboring Massachusetts towns, that they declared they would lead the people in an assault on Boston to drive out the British troops. Since such an affair would have led to great loss of life, Hutchinson and Gage decided to withdraw the troops to Castle William (now Ft. Independence), a fort on an island in Boston Harbor. Shortly afterwards, a local jury absolved the soldiers who had caused the "Massacre" of murder, and found only two guilty of manslaughter.

Ever since the Stamp Act, the radicals had spread rumors that there was a plot on the part of the government to "enslave" America. These rumors were now spread with redoubled force, especially through the Committees of Correspondence and the many newspapers started up for the purpose at this time. Control of the media is key to the success of any revolution. Furthermore, the Massachusetts Assembly spoke of itself in terms up to now reserved to the Parliament in London.

In April 1770, news arrived from London that all of the Townshend taxes had been repealed, except the one on tea. Despite the attempts of the radicals to keep it up, nonimportation died a natural death by July 1771.

Two months earlier, a sort of civil war had broken out in North Carolina. There, resentment at the expensive fees charged for provincial services and extremely high local taxes charged by the Assembly, led the backwoodsmen to rebel against the Tidewater Planters. Demanding that the Assembly's taxation be regulated by the Crown, they came to be known as "Regulators." Although defeated in open battle by the provincial militia on May 16, they remained disaffected. The Regulators would be a primary force in North Carolina Loyalism in the conflict to come.

Apart from the continuing intimidation of Loyalists, and the continuing inability of Royal officials to help them, a period of relative quiet descended upon the colonies.

The Gaspee Incident

This was broken in 1772. Newport, Rhode Island was a large center of smuggling, engaged in often by some of the leading men of the colony. To rein in this illegal activity, a revenue ship, H.M.S. Gaspee, commanded by Lieutenant Dudingston, plied Rhode Island's waters. On the night of June 9, it ran aground near Providence. A group of men, containing some of the best-known faces in Rhode Island politics, attacked the vessel, wounded its commander, disarmed the crew and burned the ship.

This open assault on the government's authority could not be ignored. A Royal Commission was appointed to inquire into the matter and bring the guilty to justice. But due to the prominence of the affair's organizers, their influence in Rhode Island protected them from indictment.

Meanwhile, in reply to the formation of the Royal Commission, Thomas Jefferson, Patrick Henry, and some others persuaded their colleagues in Virginia's House of Burgesses to appoint a Committee of Correspondence which would be a governmental body. This in turn was to contact the speakers of the other colonial assemblies, and invite them to do the same. All save New Jersey's assembly responded, and formed their own committees. From being clandestine organizations of subversives, the committees had become government agencies.

Back in Boston, the struggle of wills between Hutchinson and the subverted assembly continued, as did harassment of Tories. In the Spring of 1773 the connivance of Whigs in England allowed certain confidential letters sent by Hutchinson to the London authorities in 1768 at the height of the nonimportation struggle to be sent back to the Massachusetts assembly. Misinterpreted, they became a great propaganda tool in the hands of the radicals, and were speedily shipped around via the Committees. Benjamin Franklin, then in London as a colonial representative, secured them.

The Boston Tea Party

May of 1773 saw the passage in Parliament of the Tea Act, which gave the East India Company the ability to sell tea cheaply in America, without any tax upon it. Worse, it would be cheaper than the smuggled tea upon which the income of many an oligarch depended. Thus, it was noised about in the usual channels that the real reason for the act was to force the American colonies into accepting yet another chain—this time, a tea monopoly. The Committees of Correspondence ordered the resurrection of nonimportation.

Seven ships filled with tea were sent to America by the East India Company. The two bound for New York and Philadelphia were sent back. The one in Charleston was permitted to unload its cargo, but the tea was simply kept in a warehouse. In Boston, real trouble developed.

Three ships arrived at Boston on or after November 27, and were prevented from unloading by Sam Adams' Sons of Liberty. Governor Hutchinson, despite the fact that not only the Assembly but his Governor's Council were arrayed against him, and although the troops at Castle William were of no use to him, refused to give in to the demand that the ships depart. The radicals, on the other hand, continued to prevent the tea's unloading. At last, as everyone knows, on December 16 a group of the Sons disguised as Indians boarded all three ships, broke open the tea-chests and dumped their contents into the harbor.

The assembly and Governor's Council openly endorsed this action. It was a direct defiance of the Crown. Moreover, it showed that the government had lost all power in Massachusetts, and was fast doing so in the rest of the colonies. For several years, Hutchinson had appealed to King and ministry, informing them of the machinations and plotting in the province, and begging them to take decisive action. Now, at last, they must.

The "Intolerable Acts"

On March 4, 1774, Lord North asked the King to convene Parliament for the express purpose of dealing with events in America. It must be understood that George and Lord North were confronted with the same dilemma faced by President Lincoln when the South seceded; should the national government act to prevent parts of the country from leaving? King and Prime Minister made the same decision that the President did 86 years later.

Debate over the issue raged strongly. The Whig spokesmen in Parliament, *Charles Fox* and *Edmund Burke*, were predictably against any measures of punishment at all. It was hoped that Lord North would not be able to command a majority in Commons and so be forced to resign. But the seriousness of the situation was obvious to most M.P.s. Between March 18 and May 2 a series of laws were passed, in hopes of dealing with the situation quickly.

The Boston Port Bill closed the port of Boston until compensation was paid to the East India Company for its tea by the people of Boston; the customs house was moved to Salem. Another bill was passed in response to the usurpation of the Massachusetts government by the Adams-Hancock-Otis clique. By its provisions, the Governor's Council was to be appointed, rather than elected. The Governor would now appoint sheriffs and inferior judges, and all other lesser legal officials; town meetings would be restricted, and juries chosen differently. Realizing that any officials who tried to enforce these bills might be arrested by the Assembly, tried and jailed, Lord North put through a third bill providing that any official accused of a capital crime in performance of his duty, might be tried in Britain or in another colony, according to the Governor's choice. The Gaspee incident, after all, had made Lord North suspicious of colonial justice. A fourth bill allowed the Governor to billet troops in buildings other than barracks, should such be more convenient to their tasks. Hutchinson was relieved as Governor, and allowed to emigrate to England; General Gage replaced him.

A last measure was passed, which is particularly interesting from the Catholic point of view. This was the Quebec Act. It expanded the boundaries of the Province of Quebec to include the French-speaking settlements of the old Northwest. Within Quebec, the French civil law was to be retained alongside English criminal law. Rather than an elected assembly, which the French had no experience of, an appointed legislative council was brought into being. Under British law, no one could sit on such a council without renouncing Catholicism—this was the Test Act. The Test Act was made inoperative in Quebec, so that Catholics could sit on the Council. More than that, not only was the Church legal, but it could continue to collect tithes and be given support by the State. In other words, the status quo worked out by the military governors was erected into law, and extended to include all of George III's new French subjects. In the colonies, the King was accused of being a Jesuit, and in a number of towns in America his statues were adorned with rosaries.

In response, delegates from all the Committees of Correspondence except Georgia's convened on September 5, 1774, in Philadelphia. This was the First Continental Congress. The avowed aim was to coordinate resistance to the "intolerable" acts, but the Congress also declared that all laws passed by Parliament with regard to the colonies since 1763 were unconstitutional. The Congress drew up three addresses. The first, written by *John Jay*, was addressed to the People of England, and declared the Congress' astonishment,

> ...that a British Parliament should ever consent to establish in that country [Canada] a religion that has deluged your island in blood, and disbursed impiety, bigotry, persecution, murder and rebellion through every part of the world.

Yet five days later a similar letter was addressed to the People of Quebec:

> What is offered to you by the late Parliament? ... Liberty of conscience in your religion? No. God gave it to you; ... We are all too well acquainted with the liberality of sentiment distinguishing your nation, to imagine, that difference of religion will prejudice you against a hearty amity with us.

The Congress went on to form an American Association, embracing all the colonies and ordering their inhabitants not to trade with the Mother Country. It declared that it was in support of the King, so long as he did not do anything Congress disagreed with; and it adjourned on October 26, after resolving to meet the next year, if "justice" had not been done.

Many objected to the Congress presuming to act in the name of all Americans. After all, it was in itself formed of members of Committees of Correspondence, themselves groups of doubtful legality, serving

Assemblies who were acting irregularly. In Quebec, Bishop Briand examined the two addresses of the Congress to the English and the Quebecois side by side, and reached the conclusion that continued loyalty to the King who had guaranteed his people their religion, language, and laws was preferable than alliance with a group of doubtful legitimacy and intentions.

The Bishop's fear appeared to be confirmed in various ways. The *Suffolk Resolves*, made by the convention of the county Boston is in, did not bode well for the Faith, particularly in Article 10:

> That the late act of Parliament for establishing the Roman Catholic Religion in that extensive country, now called Canada, is dangerous in an extreme degree to the Protestant religion and to the civil rights and liberties of all Americans; and, therefore, as men and Protestant Christians, we are indispensably obliged to take all proper measure for our security.

Worse still was the defense of the Congress, *Full Vindication of the Measures of Congress*, written by *Alexander Hamilton* (who appears today on the $10 bill):

> The affair of Canada is still worse. The Romish faith is made the established religion of the land and his Majesty is placed as the head of it. The free exercise of the Protestant faith depended upon the pleasure of the Governor and Council... They may as well establish Popery in New York and the other colonies as they did in Canada. They had no more right to do it there than here. Your lives, your property, your religion, are all at stake.

Prelude to War

While the Congress met, more British troops were being concentrated in Boston, and the town was fortified. Meanwhile, sympathetic groups in the other colonies sent donations and the like to the Bostonians. General Gage, as Governor, dissolved the Assembly on September 28. But the very day that Congress broke up, they met, voted themselves the Provincial Congress, and ordered the militia mobilized and armed.

There could be only one reason to arm the militia: to carry rebellion beyond mere boycott and terrorism into open warfare. General Gage resolved that the stores of ammunition and powder must be destroyed. On February 26, 1775, he sent a small detachment to Salem, where the Provincial Congress was convened; it returned empty-handed.

Finally, Gage received news in April that the munitions were being stored in the town of Concord, and with them were rebel leaders John Hancock and Samuel Adams. If leaders and war-material could be seized at once, it would break the back of the rebellion. Gage resolved that his troops should march on Concord on the 19th. Given this information, Hancock's and Adams' co-conspirator, *Paul Revere*, after determining that 800 British under Col. Francis Smith would proceed by boat to the mainland rather then by the longer land route, mounted his horse and rode off into the night. He would warn the militia that the British were coming.

THE WAR

The Shot Heard Round the World

Although Revere was detained by British troops early in the evening, others spread the word. Adams and Hancock fled to safer quarters, and the munitions were removed. By the time the British advance guard reached the town of Lexington, a group of militia-men or "minutemen" (so called from their having to be ready to fight "at a minute's notice") had drawn up on Lexington Green.

Major Pitcairn, the officer commanding the British advance guard ordered the minutemen to disperse; they began to do so. The British troops began cheering, and a few of their officers fired pistols in the air. This was mistakenly taken to be a signal to start firing at the rebels. The British shot at them, and they ran, leaving eight dead and nine wounded. This was the famous "shot heard round the World", which started the Revolutionary War.

It did not have to. If Colonel Smith and his men had marched back to Boston, the countryside would not have been roused against them. Of course, the ammunition would have remained at Concord and the situation which caused Smith's column to be sent out in the first place would have been unchanged. He decided to march on to Concord. Once there, he found both ammunition and Adams and Hancock gone. He waited several hours, and then began the return march. By that time the hundred British guarding Concord's North Bridge were under attack by 300 rebels. Smith came to the rescue, and by noon a pitched battle had developed, with more and more militia pouring in.

General Gage learned of the uprising very quickly. By eight o'clock in the morning, Lord Percy with 1,000 reinforcements had been sent out, reaching Lexington by 2 PM. Colonel Smith, having disengaged at the Bridge, was now marching back. All along the return route to Lexington, minutemen fired at his troops from behind walls and hedges.

Although perhaps no more than 250 militiamen fought any one time, they had accounted for 273 British. Finally, Smith and his men arrived at Lexington, where Lord Percy and his men awaited them.

In the meantime, the militia had gathered again, and it took artillery fire to clear the road back to Boston. Fearing (rightly, as it turned out) that a fresh militia company would be awaiting them in Cambridge, Lord Percy brought his men back by way of Charlestown. They were only free from sniper fire when they crossed over to Boston. Overnight, the Province's capital became a besieged city, and Royal authority vanished in the rest of Massachusetts.

The Collapse of Royal Authority

News took a long time to travel in those days, we would think now. There were neither telegraph, television, nor telephone. Couriers by land and ships by sea were the means used to convey letters, papers, and proclamations. It could take up to three months for information to cross the Atlantic. But the Committees of Correspondence were able to get news out through their network as quickly as humanly possible in those days. Thus, information about the events at Lexington and Concord (suitably slanted) was quickly made available, and resulted in the collapse of Royal authority in most of the colonies.

In New Hampshire, Royal governor *Sir John Wentworth* fled from a mob in Portsmouth to a fort in the harbor, and then to England. Rhode Island's *Joseph Wanton* resigned and retired to his home in Newport. In Connecticut, governor *Jonathan Trumbull* not only declared for the rebels (and kept his job) he became the model of "Uncle Sam." All three provinces sent troops to join the Massachusetts militia encamped at Cambridge.

In the rest of the colonies, either subverted assemblies or self-proclaimed Provincial Congresses took control. In some places the governors tried to coexist with the new rulers. In others they fled. Only Virginia's *Lord Dunmore* attempted some resistance against the rebels, particularly after Patrick Henry gave his *"Liberty or Death"* speech to the Virginia House of Burgesses after word of Lexington and Concord arrived. But he was forced to flee the Governor's Palace at Williamsburg for the Loyalist Port of Norfolk.

Meanwhile, on the night of May 10, *Ethan Allen* and his Vermont *Green Mountain Boys* took Ft. Ticonderoga on Lake Champlain, in the name of "the Continental Congress and the Great Jehovah." Shortly afterwards they took Crown Point. These seizures accomplished two important goals: they opened the road to Canada, and they provided the rebel forces with 183 cannon, 19 mortars, 3 howitzers, 51 swivels, and

52 tons of cannon balls. This was the only artillery available to the rebels, essential if they were to take Boston from the British.

North of that city was the Charlestown peninsula, which contained the city of that name and two hills, Bunker and Breed's. On June 17, General Gage was informed that during the previous night the rebels had fortified the two hills. The Charlestown peninsula was essential to the security of Boston. He ordered the position on Breed's Hill to be taken. Twice the British marched up the hill, and twice they were forced to withdraw because of heavy casualties. At last, with the rebels having both sustained heavy losses and run out of gunpowder, they withdrew in the face of the third assault. Exhausted, the British allowed the rebels to escape. But the Battle of Bunker Hill, as it is always miscalled, was the first major pitched battle between the revolutionaries and the Royal forces. Among the British dead was Major Pitcairn of Lexington; among their opponents, *Dr. Joseph Warren*, Master of the Masonic Grand Lodge of Massachusetts, who had done so much to bring Massachusetts into rebellion.

A few days before this (although news had not yet reached New England) the Continental Congress had accepted the forces gathered at Cambridge as its army. It appointed George Washington of Virginia, the most distinguished American officer in the war against the French, as commander in chief, as well as five Major-Generals, and eight Brigadier Generals. These arrived at Cambridge on July 2. There to greet them was a new flag. Under the British, the most commonly used flag was the Red Ensign (also called Queen Anne's flag), which bore the Union Jack in the upper corner with a red field. Since at this stage the rebels claimed still to be loyal to George III, and only at war with his ministers (they called the British troops "ministerial" soldiers), they differentiated their flag with six horizontal white stripes. This formed seven red ones in between, which taken together were to represent the 13 associated colonies. The Union Jack was kept in the corner to show continued loyalty to the Crown, and the whole called the "Grand Union" flag. Under it, Washington began the organization from the various militias gathered at Cambridge, of what we must now call the Continental Army.

The Invasion of Canada

After Bunker Hill, events settled for a while into a sort of stalemate. Apart from drawing up lists of Loyalists to be guarded against in every community, the new authorities were content to spend their time trying to continue with the tasks of administration. The British army besieged in Boston, and still in charge of small posts on the frontier and detachments in ports like New York, was content for the moment to await developments. The Royal Navy's control of the Sea gave the British and Loyalist Americans every confidence that they could win by waiting for the rebels to "come to their senses."

Congress had other plans. To break the deadlock, an invasion of Canada was resolved upon. Word had reached Cambridge that Governor Carleton had only 1,000 men to hold the whole province. Given that the French were sure to join them, the Continental leadership thought it would be an easy invasion.

It was decided that two columns would set out. A left wing, under *General Richard Montgomery*, would set out from Crown Point and advance north to take Montreal; from there they would proceed to Quebec City. The right column, under *Benedict Arnold*, would proceed north along the Kennebec River in Maine, proceeding more or less directly to Quebec City. Meeting Montgomery's army there, the two forces would jointly take the walled city.

What appeared so easy in theory was not in reality. Setting out on September 20, 1775 from Ft. Pownal, Maine, Arnold's column marched alongside the Kennebec and Chaudiere rivers. In those days, that area was deepest wilderness. Cold and hunger were so demanding that one detachment of 350 men, led by a Col. Enos, simply returned home. Of the remainder, 75 more died before the column reached the shores of the St. Lawrence on November 8—only 675 men made it out of the original 1,100.

But Quebec was reinforced by 200 troops a day before Arnold reached it. Secure within its walls, well-provisioned, the city could not be taken by Arnold's tired, hungry soldiers alone—even though they wasted a good deal of powder and shot trying to. At last, having heard that Montreal had fallen to Montgomery, they sat down to wait for his troops.

These had made their way down Lake Champlain by boat. When they landed they were ambushed by a force of French Canadians and Indians, who after some heavy firing pulled away into the woods. The Continentals then marched north to Ft. St. John, where the British and French Canadians were dug in. Montgomery's men dug in themselves in early October, and the two armies fired artillery at each other with little result. However, the deadlock was broken when a small party of Continentals captured Ft. Chambly further down the river, thus cutting Ft. St. John off from Montreal. A British relief column was repulsed; Ft. St. John surrendered on November 3rd. Nothing now lay between the invaders and Montreal.

On November 12, Montgomery and his men entered Montreal, Carleton having withdrawn the night before. The British commander then went downriver to Quebec. Between regular British soldiers, French militia, Scots militia, Marines, and sailors, Carleton had about 1,168 men to defend a city better suited to 3,000.

But Arnold and Montgomery together had less than 1,000 men themselves. The French Canadians refused to help them, and battle was finally underway by December 31. However, Montgomery was killed, and Quebec City's defenders fought hard. The Continentals lost 48 killed, 34 wounded, and 372 were made prisoners; this was more than half of Arnold's command. He had to think of a way to extract his men from Canada.

The Fall of Boston

Although Quebec had been saved, and Boston remained in British hands, the King and his ministers realized that if the colonies were to be kept they would have to be fought for. For this, troops were needed. Where to find them? Ireland was a traditional recruiting ground for the army; and the leadership of the Irish Catholics rallied to the King's cause. They presented an Address to the King:

> ...justly abhorring the unnatural rebellion which had lately broken out among some of his American subjects against his most sacred person and government. We hardly presume to lay at his feet two million loyal, faithful, and affectionate hearts and hands.

The leaders of the Catholic Committee (which, much encouraged by the Quebec Act was working for an end to the Penal Laws), offered to raise funds for recruiting volunteers in Ireland. The Catholic Lord Kenmare offered to raise 1,100 men himself. But not only did the Northern Irish Protestants prevail upon the Cabinet to reject these offers, they would not join the army themselves. Many of their kindred were settled in America, and generally supported the rebels (these were the "Scotch-Irish").

This left the Highlands of Scotland as a source of troops. But there were only so many available. Where to turn?

At first, the government hesitated to arm and supply the Indian allies. But with such a lack of men, it was decided to do so. While this did provide more fighting men immediately, it helped weaken the Royal cause among the frontiersmen, who soon learned to identify the Crown with an Indian terror the British were powerless to control, the Tribes being allies rather than subjects.

One traditional means of raising troops the British government had used in other conflicts (including the Jacobite wars) was the hiring of mercenaries. 30,000 troops from small German states (called Hessians from Hesse-Kassel, where the largest number came from) were hired and brought over to the colonies. This too was probably a mistake; while they were effective soldiers, the rebel propaganda machine made much of this use of foreigners to fight British Americans. It made Americans more accepting of alliance with foreign nations against the King.

The best source of troops the British did not consider until it was already very late to organize them: the Loyalists. In every colony these had organized "Associations" of "friends of government." These in turn applied to the Cabinet to be organized as regiments and armed groups to prevent rebel takeover of colonial governments. But Lord North's cabinet was too overwhelmed by the course of events to act on these proposals. It was not until late 1775 that plans of this sort were even considered in London, and it was early 1776 before anything was done. In the meantime, as we have seen, the Royal administrations collapsed.

But Boston remained. If the rebels were to triumph it had to be taken; this was shown by the raid on Portland, Maine on October 17, 1775. The burning of the town served to turn more Americans against the Crown, and gave rise to the false rumor that the British intended to burn all the coastal ports.

Meanwhile, General Gage was replaced by *Sir William Howe*. His hopes were raised by events in Canada, where the Continental governor at Montreal, General Wooster, had outlawed Catholicism. This led to resistance on the part of the French, and the collapse of the American army. What remained of it was led back up to Crown Point by Arnold. Further, without opposing artillery, Boston could not be taken by assault.

Unfortunately for Howe, the artillery taken at Ticonderoga was on its way over the mountains by sled to Cambridge. Once there on February 26, 1776, it was used to shell British outlying positions. Under cover of this barrage, artillery was set up March 2 on Dorchester Heights, from which all of Boston could be shelled. Howe considered trying to take the Heights, but in the end decided he would not be able to do so with the troops he had. On February 7, he informed his officers that he had decided to save his army by evacuating the city. Over the next month, preparations were made for the evacuation by military and by Loyalists, many of whom preferred exile to remaining under the rebels. On March 17, the heavily-burdened fleet left Boston for Halifax. The next day, the city was occupied by the rebels.

The Rebels Consolidate

Although the Canadian debacle was just becoming well known, the Congress had reasons to celebrate. In December 1775, Lord Dunmore had been forced to evacuate Norfolk, although he continued aboard ship to haunt Chesapeake Bay.

Early in 1776, Philip Schuyler and his troops had descended upon the estate of Sir John Johnson near Albany. A leading Tory and the King's agent for Indian Affairs, he not only possessed Iroquois allies but a number of Scots Catholic tenants. These were disarmed, and all of them forced to make their way in the dead of winter to Montreal, a journey which killed many of their women and children. Their priest, Fr. John Mckenna, reported to Bishop Briand all that had happened, while the men constituted themselves a regiment, the Royal Yorkers. Based at Ft. Niagara and led by Sir John, they vowed revenge on their former neighbors.

At last the need to employ the Loyalists had sunk in on the cabinet in London. Since the bulk of Loyal strength in the Southern colonies lay inland, an elaborate plan was hatched by the British military as early as October 1775. A fleet from Cork, Ireland, would arrive off the coast of North Carolina. The Regulators and Scots Highlanders of the interior would rise, and make contact with the fleet. From there they would take South Carolina; Georgia would follow of its own accord. Then Lord Dunmore's friends in Virginia (and the Black slaves he freed on condition that they fight for the Crown) would be supported in retaking that colony. The South would then serve as a base for the reclamation of the rest of the colonies.

But the fleet was delayed time and again. In February, the Highlanders and Regulators rose anyway. But on February 18 the little army was defeated at Moore's Creek Bridge. It was not until late Spring that the British fleet finally arrived. Finding their original landing place at Cape Fear unsuitable, they sailed south to Charleston. Here the guns at the mouth of the harbor drove them off. For the moment, the revolution was secure.

The Declaration of Independence

From the beginning the rebels had protested their loyalty to their King, declaring that their quarrel was solely with his ministers. This was a situation which could not last. Early in 1776, *Thomas Paine*, a transplanted Englishman who had won Benjamin Franklin's favor prior to coming to America, wrote a pamphlet called *Common Sense*, in which he expressly charged the King with full responsibility for the war. More than this, he insulted George in language never before used of a King ("the Royal Brute"). Beyond this, he attacked the institution of Monarchy itself as "the Popery of government." From then on, radical propaganda advocating independence came out into the open.

The Continental Congress was made up of many different types of men, however. Many, such as George Washington, opposed independence: "I am as well satisfied as I can be of my existence that no such thing is desired by any thinking man in North America." But the military action which followed drove the most conservative delegates into the arms of the radicals.

In June 1776, various of the Provincial Congresses began declaring their independence from Britain. On June 24, the Continental Congress declared that all colonists who adhered to or fought for Great Britain were guilty of treason and should be punished. Thomas Jefferson, perhaps the most talented writer among the Delegates, was set to writing a declaration of independence. This set down in forceful language that authority comes from the people, who have the right to alter or abolish their government, in accordance with the ideas of the Enlightenment. It then went on to describe the supposed crimes of King George III; how he had imposed taxes, incited the Indians, abolished English Law in a neighboring Province (Quebec), and so on. It is from this *Declaration of Independence* that most Americans today derive their views of George III.

When the Declaration was published in England, Thomas Hutchinson wrote a reply to it, based upon his experience as Royal governor of Massachusetts. In this pamphlet, he maintained that the cause of the struggle was not the "abuses and usurpations" of which the declaration accused King George, but the agitations of "men in each of the principal colonies who had independence in view before any of those taxes were laid or proposed which have since been the ostensible cause for resisting the execution of acts of Parliament." He maintained in the future that,

> The tumults, riots, contempt and defiance of law in England were urged to encourage and justify the like disorders in the colonies and to annihilate the powers of government there. Many thousands of people who were before good and loyal subjects have been deluded and by degrees induced to rebel against the best of princes and the mildest of governments.

The Declaration, Hutchinson claimed, was intended "to reconcile the people of America to that Independence which always before they had been made to believe was not intended. This design has too well succeeded."

Whether Jefferson or Hutchinson was right, Congress passed the Declaration on July 4, 1776. Ever since, this has been our national holiday, Independence Day. The flag was altered, 13 white stars on a blue field replacing the Union Jack in the corner. Church bells pealed throughout the colonies, and bonfires lit the night. There were cheers, parades, public speeches. The wooden image of the King in Baltimore was carted away and burned, while the statue of the King on horseback at New York's Bowling Green was pulled off its pedestal and taken to be melted. At Boston's Province House (now the Old State House) and public buildings throughout America, the Royal Arms were hacked off or defaced. In the New England colonies, "King Street" in every town and village was renamed "State Street." With an Army, the Continental Congress, and now the Declaration, America seemed a real country at last.

The Fall of New York

Immediately after the Declaration, things seemed to go well for the new nation. Tories and Indians in both South Carolina and Georgia were defeated.

But the British were not defeated. The first thing they required was a proper land base in the colonies. The obvious choice was the finest harbor in America, New York City. On August 22, they landed in Brooklyn from their base on Staten Island. Among these were Hessians, the first to be employed in the war. Guided by local Loyalists, the British and Hessians defeated the Americans on August 26, and after another battle at Brooklyn Heights, found themselves masters of Long Island. The Americans had withdrawn to New York City on the night of the 29th.

Interestingly enough, General Howe, commander of the British forces, was an outspoken member of the King's Whig opposition at home. He did nothing after the Americans withdrew for two weeks. Finally, on September 15, the British landed on Manhattan Island. The Americans withdrew from New York (at the time only covering the southern tip of Manhattan) and pulled back to Harlem Heights, where the next day they fought the British again. Howe once more made no further move, this time for a month.

At the other end of the colony, the remains of the American force sent to Canada had fallen back to Crown Point at the southern end of Lake Champlain. Over half of them were sick, when *General Horatio Gates* took command.

Back in Manhattan, Howe finally stirred on October 12. Outflanking the American positions, a strong force sailed up the Hudson river, landing at New Rochelle. Moving swiftly, the British and Hessians outmaneuvered and outfought the Americans, forcing Washington to abandon all of Southern Westchester County and the parts of New Jersey facing New York.

Then Washington and his men retreated across New Jersey, hotly pursued by the British. The Americans arrived in Newark on November 23 and left on the 28th; their pursuers arrived the same day. The day after that, Washington and his men passed through Brunswick, staying until December 1. Two days later, the British arrived. December 2 saw the Continentals go through Princeton, where the British arrived five days later. The Americans having paused in Trenton on the 2nd, they rested until the 8th. Faced with capture by their opponents, they crossed over the Delaware River to Pennsylvania, abandoning most of New Jersey to the British. Then the news arrived that a British force of 6,000 had occupied Newport, Rhode Island.

With New York firmly in British hands, and the Continental Army an exhausted, chilled, hungry band, it appeared to the British that the war was almost over, and that Christmas, 1776, would be a happy one for them. So too thought the Hessians guarding Trenton.

Washington Crosses the Delaware

The American army was in a very bad position; the pursuit across New Jersey had not merely exhausted the troops and starved them, it had strained their morale so much that many deserted. An army which has suffered as much and has as little in the way of equipment as the Continentals did is generally on the way to defeat. But it was here that Washington's greatness as a leader became apparent.

It was one thing to command the army in Cambridge, when all that was needed was the conduct of a siege. Commanding a beaten force (particularly one as poorly organized as the Continentals were) and keeping it intact was quite different. But Washington rose to the occasion. He inspired his men in the midst of that dreary winter, despite the fact that many did not even have boots, but wrapped their feet in rags.

On Christmas Day, he led his men in a surprise move across the Delaware. The Hessians, still recovering from their Christmas Eve feasting, were completely unprepared. In 40 minutes without losing a single man, the Americans killed 22 and wounded 84 Hessians, taking the remaining 868 prisoner. It was one of the most complete victories ever gained by American soldiers.

General Howe allowed the Hessians to plunder New Jersey homes— whether rebel or Loyalist, indiscriminately. The result was to lose civilian support for the Royal cause. American counterattacks persuaded the British to withdraw from most of New Jersey by January 10, 1777. Washington's order to his men forbidding them to rob even Loyalists' houses did much to convert New Jersey to the Revolution.

In the meantime, Howe was once again delaying. Where would he strike? Would it be another attack from New York? An assault in the South?

In fact, the British had a much more complex plan. New England was the center of the revolt. Separate it from the other colonies, and they would sooner or later, given the large number of Loyalists in them and the Royal Navy's command of the sea, return to obedience. New England could then be reduced at leisure. To bring this about, General Howe would march north along the Hudson, Col. St. Leger would sweep along the Mohawk Valley, and *General John Burgoyne* would march south from Montreal. The three armies would meet at Albany, New York, and the plan would be accomplished.

Obviously, to be successful, all three commanders had to do their part. Unfortunately for the Royal cause, Howe once again decided to do something unexpected. In the short run, it appeared an easier and better target he aimed for; in the long run, it was disastrous. Leaving 9,000 troops in New York, he embarked 17,000 aboard ships bound for Chesapeake Bay. He had decided to attack Philadelphia, seat of the Congress.

Failure of the Three-Pronged Plan

On August 22, the British fleet appeared in the Chesapeake. They landed at Head of Elk, Maryland on the 25th. After defeating the Americans at the Battle of Brandywine Creek, Howe's troops made a slow and leisurely advance, entering Philadelphia on September 27. As usual, Howe's slow methods allowed many American troops to escape. The Congress, having fled their capital, reconvened at York, Pennsylvania.

Up North, the actions of the British were not as yet hampered by Howe's change of plans. The Americans evacuated Ft. Ticonderoga without a shot on July 6. Burgoyne's column continued to advance, and the American defense of Lake Champlain collapsed, as position after position was given up without much struggle. By July 17, General Schuyler had withdrawn his men all the way to Saratoga, while Burgoyne marched steadily South. But on August 4, Schuyler was replaced with *General Horatio Gates.*

During the same period, St. Leger advanced with his Canadians, Indians, and Loyalists. Among the latter were Sir John Johnson and his Royal Yorkers, accompanied by their chaplain, Fr. John McKenna. By August 3, they had laid siege to Ft. Stanwix, last major post on the road to Albany.

The Americans sent a column to relieve Ft. Stanwix that same day. This was ambushed by Johnson's Royal Yorkers, Col. John Butler's Queen's Rangers, and Chief Joseph Brant's Mohawks. While the Loyalists and Indians were beaten off, over half the rebels were killed, the remainder having to seek refuge in the fort. Still, Oriskany is considered an American victory. The siege continued sixteen more days, but the Loyalists' guns were too light to break down the fort's walls. Tiring of this kind of warfare, most of the Mohawks left, forcing the Loyalists to end the siege and withdraw to their bases in Canada. Thus, neither the western nor the southern prong of the invasion would be available to support Burgoyne.

The same day, a mostly Hessian detachment from Burgoyne's army was defeated at Bennington, Vermont. Neither Bennington, Oriskany, nor the failure to take Ft. Stanwix boded well for Burgoyne. Worse, the further south he advanced, the farther his supplies had to travel from Lake Champlain.

On September 19th, the British and Americans began the first battle at Saratoga. for almost a month the battle raged, but at last the Americans won. Overextended and undersupplied, Burgoyne surrendered with his 5,791 remaining troops. This defeat, as we shall see, was the turning point of the war.

It did not seem so immediately, however. On October 4, Washington's attempt to drive Howe from Philadelphia failed at the battle of Germantown. Further attempts to dislodge the British failed, and in November the Americans withdrew to their Winter Quarters at Valley Forge. It was a hard Winter, indeed. But in November, the Congress adopted a constitution for the new country, called *The Articles of Confederation*. Further, the rag tag army which camped out at Valley Forge received a drill master, *Baron von Steuben*. The traditions of the modern American army were started amid the snow of Valley Forge.

The Beginning of the End

Philadelphia under the British was a town filled with celebrations. While the Continentals froze in Valley Forge, the Philadelphians enjoyed Balls and all sorts of entertainments. This was the period when Major Clinton raised his Roman Catholic Volunteers from the among the city's Catholics, to fight for the Crown.

But the home government refused to send Howe reinforcements. He sent in his resignation, and left in May 1778 for England. Once home, he took his seat in Parliament among the Whigs, and spent the rest of the War trying to bring down Lord North's Cabinet and defeat the King on the homefront.

He had certainly done his part in America. The Philadelphian adventure almost certainly ensured the defeat at Saratoga, which bore fruit on February 8, 1778. King Louis XVI of France signed a treaty of trade and friendship with the United States, becoming the new nation's first ally. The effect in America was tremendous. Already, there were many French volunteers, such as the *Marquis de Lafayette*, serving with the Americans. In addition, there was a single regiment of French Canadians, Congress' Own Canadian Regiment, which had served at Saratoga. But this action of Louis XVI's served to legitimize the Congress for many. With French Recognition, the United States no longer appeared to be merely a string of rebellious colonies. On March 13, the French government informed the British of their recognition of the United States, and a month later a fleet was sent out to America under the *Comte d'Estaing*.

Louis XVI committed his country to war with England for several reasons. France had fought and lost a long series of wars with England, which had cost the French much in men and money. Under King Louis, various reforms had been undertaken in the military which made victory seem possible. And Benjamin Franklin, American Ambassador at King Louis' court, had many friends in the French Government who added their pleas to Franklin's.

News of the coming French fleet impelled the British to withdraw from Philadelphia on June 10. Otherwise, they could have been bottled up in Chesapeake Bay. The French intervention changed the nature of the war completely. Britain and France were rivals not just in the West Indies, but in India and Africa as well. The Congress' attempts to win the French Canadians by conquest had failed, so too did their diplomatic mission in 1776. Before going to France, Franklin had gone to Quebec with Charles Carroll of Carrollton and his cousin, Fr. John Carroll. However charming the French Court thought Franklin, their cousins in Canada did not. Bishop Briand (remembering the previous American actions) forbade any of his clergy to receive Fr. Carroll, and suspended one priest who did. But might not the French alliance change his and his people's mind?

At any rate, the British withdrew from Philadelphia across New Jersey, back toward New York. While on their way back, they were attacked with great losses at Monmouth Courthouse. At last, the British army, and the fleet which they had been afraid would be bottled up, arrived safely in New York on July 6. By the 11th, when the French Fleet appeared off the New Jersey coast, there was nothing left for them to catch.

It was soon agreed between French and Americans that the British-held town of Newport, Rhode Island must be taken. D'Estaing set off for it, arriving offshore on July 29. The New England militia had been called to help in the siege. But on August 9 the British fleet arrived from New York. D'Estaing broke off the siege, and fought the British on the high sea. The French fleet was severely damaged, and sailed to Boston for repairs on August 24. Four days later, the commander of the American forces who had been besieging Newport from the land received news that the British fleet had returned to New York to bring reinforcements to Newport. The Americans withdrew.

The French ships had arrived in Boston in the meantime. Needing a place to say Mass, the French were assigned the Anglican church, King's Chapel. Having been the church of the Royal Governor before the war, it had lost most of its congregation after the evacuation. But the French dared not leave the Blessed Sacrament overnight in the church; the Bostonians, being fanatical anti-Catholics, would have desecrated it. So every day there was a procession from the French ships with the Host carried in a monstrance with incense, canopy, bell—all the signs of Popery the good Puritans of the town hated. The mob would line the street screaming abuse. Finally, on September 15, they attacked the procession, hoping to get at the Blessed Sacrament. But the *Chevalier de St. Sauveur*, a French officer, successfully defended it, being killed in the process. He was buried outside King's Chapel, where his monument may be seen today.

After this, relations between the French and Americans steadily improved in Boston, where a shocked reaction set in after the Chevalier's murder. On November 3, the French set sail for the West Indies, where they captured the islands of St. Vincent (June 16, 1779) and Grenada (July 4).

Events in the West

The French Alliance and the Congress' recommendation to the states to seize all Loyalist property (to say nothing of increasing abuse of Loyalists in general) embittered those Tories who were under arms even more. On the frontier, those who had seen their children and wives perish in the Winter of 1776 returned to burn and pillage with their Indian allies in the summer and autumn. Among these actions were the Cherry Valley and Wyoming Valley Massacres, where the Tories and Indians showed little mercy toward their rebel former neighbors. Westchester County, between the British lines north of New York City, and the American positions further north, became known as the "Neutral Ground." Irregular bands of Loyalists (called "Cowboys") and rebels vied with each other in cruelty and atrocities. Civil War is like that; for some reason, men are never as cruel to foreign foes as they are to their own people.

The Old Northwest (the present states of Ohio, Indiana, Illinois, Wisconsin, Michigan, and part of Minnesota) was mostly unsettled Indian Country. Because the few posts (Kaskaskia, Cahokia, Massac, Detroit, Green Bay, Michlimakinac, Ft. Chartres, Ft. Miami, Ft. St. Joseph, and Prairie du Chien) were inhabited by French settlers, the area had been made part of Quebec by the Quebec Act. All of these scattered settlements were served by a single, much-traveling priest, Fr. Pierre Gibault.

As a war measure, the British commander at Detroit, *Col. Henry Hamilton,* offered his Indian allies money for the scalps of rebel frontiersmen (hence his nickname, the "hairbuyer"). Apart from this annoyance, the whole area was claimed, on the basis of their Royal Charter, by the State of Virginia. The state authorities commissioned *George Rogers Clark* to conquer the Old Northwest for them. On July 4, 1778, he took Kaskaskia without firing a shot. There he met Fr. Gibault, whom he persuaded to join the American side. Cahokia fell bloodlessly also, and then, through Fr. Gibault, Vincennes. The Americans marched on, but Hamilton swept down from Detroit, and retook the town. However, a surprise attack by the Americans on February 23, 1779, forced Hamilton to surrender. Most of the Northwest was now in American hands. As for Fr. Gibault, he reconsidered his actions after the war ended, and Protestant settlers began to pour in. "I always regretted and do regret every day the loss of the mildness of British rule" he said, considering what the exchange of the Quebec Act for the Articles of Confederation really meant.

The Summer of 1779 was spent by American forces devastating the land of the Iroquois in New York. By September, the land of the Six Nations was burned out, the Iroquois themselves were dependent on British handouts, and the frontier was freed of Indian terror.

The War Drags On

New York remained under British occupation a bustling port. It was a center of Loyalism, as Tories from Continental-held areas sought refuge there. A number of Loyalist regiments were quartered there, one of which was the Catholic Volunteers of Ireland, led by Lord Rawdon. On March 17, 1779, they held the first St. Patrick's Day Parade, at which was sung this song:

> Success to the shamrock, and all those who wear it;
> Be honor their portion wherever they go.

May riches attend them and stores of good claret,
For how to employ them sure none better know.
Every foe surveys them with terror,
But every silk petticoat wishes them nearer.
So Yankee keep off or you'll soon learn your error,
For Paddy shall prostrate lay every foe.
This day, but the year I can't rightly determine,
Saint Patrick the vipers did chase from the land.
Let's see if like him we can't sweep off the vermin,
Who dare 'gainst the sons of the shamrock to stand.
Hand in hand! Let's carol the chorus,
As long as the blessings of Ireland hang o'er us,
The crest of rebellion shall tremble before us,
Like brothers while thus we march hand in hand.

In December of 1778, the British had taken Savannah, which was immediately reinforced by a column from the British garrison at St. Augustine, Florida. Within a few months, most of Georgia was in the hands of Loyalists. Such American forces as remained in the State were too weak to retake it.

The next step was the invasion of South Carolina. Moving rapidly, British troops reached Charleston on May 8, and three days later demanded the city's surrender. In return, the State government replied that if the British would withdraw from South Carolina, they would become neutral, and go with the winning side after the war. The British commander refused, and the siege began. But a determined defense, partly commanded by the Polish officer *Casimir Pulaski,* led the British to call off the attack. They withdrew to Georgia in June.

That same month, Louis XVI's cousin, Charles III of Spain, also declared war on England and immediately began besieging the British naval base of Gibraltar. On August 16, a combined French and Spanish fleet arrived off Plymouth, England; all the while, *Admiral John Paul Jones* was sinking British ships wherever he found them in British waters. Although the Allied fleet was called off from Plymouth, it showed the erosion of British naval power—the country's main strength —in this war.

This had repercussions in America. Not only did the British evacuate Newport, D'Estaing had returned to American waters after his victories in the West Indies. The plan was to attack the British at Savannah from both land and sea. On September 8, the French fleet arrived off Savannah. By the 16th, the city was surrounded by land. It was not until October 3, however, that the cannon were emplaced. News came that a British fleet was on its way to relieve the city; the Americans and French stormed Savannah on October 9. It was a complete failure—and Pulaski was killed.

It mattered little to the Americans that the Spanish Governor of Louisiana, Bernardo de Galvez, had spent the Summer conquering Baton Rouge and Natchez from the British, with a mixed force of Spanish, Irish, Cajuns, and Mexicans.

Victory from Defeat

Never had American fortunes seemed at such a low ebb. In the immediate, things were to get worse. Because the new nation had no coinage, and its paper money was soon worthless, keeping the army supplied was difficult, despite French and Spanish aid, and the latter's conquest of Mobile on January 10, 1780. In the North Washington was kept pinned around New York; the defeat at Savannah and the departure of the French Navy left the South at the mercy of the British and Loyalists, who had become the bulk of the Crown's forces there.

Howe's successor, *Sir Henry Clinton* decided to take Charleston at last. Borne by ship from New York, the British landed near Charleston on March 29, and began their siege in early April. The British fleet cut off the city from any hope of rescue, since D'Estaing was nowhere near. Finally, on May 9 Charleston, with the only regular American army in the South, surrendered.

The long war had produced many strains in England itself. 1779 had been a very bad year for the Crown, considering all the defeats and difficulties. The King's enemies in Parliament were clamoring for both an end to the war and to the King's personal rule through Lord North. Meetings were held throughout the land, and Britain was near bankruptcy. Things reached the boiling point in June 1780 when Lord George Gordon, an apostate Catholic, led the London mob in rioting in an attempt to bring down the King and his cabinet. After burning Catholic chapels, setting fire to Newgate Prison and attacking the Bank of England, the rioters attempted to storm the House of Commons.

George III reacted quickly. Troops were dispatched to London, and 450 rioters killed or wounded. Shortly after calm was restored, news of the victory at Charleston arrived. For the moment, the war would continue. Yet it could not last forever. A large French army, under *General Jean Baptiste de Rochambeau* arrived at Newport on July 12, 1780.

In the South, the struggle between Tories and rebels became ever bloodier. Atrocities were committed on both sides as they became increasingly embittered toward one another. It was guerrilla warfare, of a type that the world has come to know all too well since.

Apart from these struggles, 1780 passed into 1781 without any more major campaigns in North America. In the West Indies, Senegal and the Guinea Coast, and particularly in India, France and Spain fought Great Britain on a similar scale to the fighting in North America. In early 1781, the Netherlands joined France and Spain, and promptly began losing West Indian, African, and Indian possessions to the British.

The British commander in the South, *Lord Cornwallis*, was determined to finally conquer the area, once and for all. The remaining American forces, under *General Daniel Morgan* received their supplies from Virginia. Cornwallis resolved to cut Morgan's supply lines, deciding to invade North Carolina. But on January 17, at a decisive battle called the Cowpens, his light cavalry were destroyed. This was disastrous, because the Americans decided to lure the British after them in typical guerrilla fashion; if they could avoid being defeated, they could wear the British down. Without light cavalry, it was doubtful if Cornwallis' troops would be able to catch up with the Americans.

A second problem was that the invasion of North Carolina was done without alerting the resident Loyalists in time. This blunder meant that much in the way of intelligence and the recruiting of more light troops was not done. At any rate, Cornwallis pursued the Americans toward Virginia for months, inflicting a defeat on them at Guilford Courthouse, where his own losses were nevertheless very heavy. Afterwards, Cornwallis retreated south along the Cape Fear River to Wilmington to recover at a seaport where the Royal Navy could supply his exhausted forces. The Americans he had been pursuing returned to South Carolina to begin seizing the British posts outside of Charleston.

Cornwallis left Wilmington, reaching Virginia in early May. Plantation rich, the State seemed to offer unlimited spoils, and the British lost no time in taking them. There were few troops capable of resisting Cornwallis' army; more and more the campaign became an affair of pure plunder. Washington decided to move his own and Rochambeau's armies south; similarly, the French Admiral De Grasse moved his ships toward Chesapeake Bay.

To avoid a pitched encounter with these armies, Cornwallis moved his army to Yorktown in early September. Strategically placed on a peninsula, it offered a secure haven to await a British fleet and be evacuated. Of course, the plan depended on British control of the sea. But on September 5, De Grasse defeated and drove off the British fleet. The trap was sprung, and Cornwallis' troops were under siege, surrendering on October 17. The surrender ceremony was serenaded by the Scots bagpipers playing a funeral dirge, *The World Turned Upside Down*. Afterwards, those officers of the British, French, and American armies who happened to be Freemasons held a banquet together. For all practical purposes, the loss of Cornwallis' large army doomed the British land effort in North America. A few weeks afterwards, the French recaptured from the British the Dutch island of St. Eustatius in the West Indies, with the sum of 2,000,000£.

The Summer had seen the increasingly outnumbered Loyalists and British swept out of the interior of South Carolina. On September 8, 1781, at the battle of Eutaw Springs, the last pitched battle of the war was fought. The British won, but withdrew to Charleston; they were not in a position to follow up their victory. Shortly afterward, they evacuated Wilmington.

In London, news of Yorktown and St. Eustatius was a heavy blow to Lord North's cabinet. In February 1782, the Whigs had gathered enough strength in Parliament to "authorize" (in reality, to order) the King to seek a truce with the Americans. Soon after this, the Island of Minorca in the Mediterranean fell to the French and Spanish, and word arrived of the fall of the British West Indian islands of St. Kitt's, Nevis, and Montserrat. Lord North's government could not survive these disasters. He resigned on March 20, and a Whig cabinet, filled with the King's enemies, came to power. The new Prime Minister, Rockingham, informed George III that peace with the colonies must be made, even if it meant independence. The war was over, although the treaty was not signed until 1783. A new nation had been born.

THE RESULTS

Why did the British lose? First, because they did not understand the nature of the threat posed by the pro-independence leaders; the warnings of men like Hutchinson were ignored. Second, because they did not attempt to organize Loyalists in the way the Committees of Correspondence and Sons of Liberty were organized. Third, because of the poor generalship of Sir William Howe. Fourth, because of the intervention of France and Spain.

The first result of the Revolution was, with the evacuation by the British of Savannah, Charleston, and finally New York, the exile of those Loyalists—about 100,000 or so—who could not reconcile themselves to the new regime. Many went to Ontario, New Brunswick, Nova Scotia, and the "Eastern Townships" of Quebec; these were the founders of English-speaking Canada. Many others went to the Bahamas, Bermuda, Barbados, Jamaica, and other West Indian islands. In the first named, they were as influential as they were in Canada. Still others went to England. But the original 13 States lost much by this emigration. Other Loyalists (like St. Elizabeth Anne Seton's family and in-laws) stayed, making the best they could of things.

George III's attempt to restore his country's constitution was ruined, the Whigs returned to cabinet, and the oligarchy regained control of power in Great Britain, which they have held ever since. Further, due to the war with France and Spain, and the activities of the Carrolls and other Catholic leaders in the colonies, the King became opposed to Catholic Emancipation. This would serve in time to alienate most of the Catholic Irish from the throne forever.

France had won—but was bankrupt. The French received little from their share of the war, except an enormous debt and a great many noblemen who served in the army in America infected with dangerous ideas. Yet the war had proved Louis XVI's abilities as a wartime leader. To him, more than any other one man, might be given the credit for the independence of the United States. In return, he would find his own crown threatened a mere six years after the peace treaty.

The Spanish received Florida, and a claim to a good part more of the American West—Mississippi, Alabama, and Tennessee. They would soon find themselves in friction with the country they had helped create.

America now had a legal existence as a country. But only the slightest framework of nationhood was present as yet, although an American nationality had begun to emerge during the war years. The States were considered the important units of the country. National borders were still in dispute, and the Indians in the unorganized territories of the Old Southwest and Northwest still were allied to Spain and Britain. National life still remained to be defined. We will see that definition in the next chapter.

THE YOUNG NATION
1783-1815

AT THE BEGINNING

The end of the year 1783 saw a new nation universally recognized among the countries of the world: the United States of America. Where the seat of sovereignty in the British Empire had been, on the surface, the King, in the United States matters were not so clear. For on declaring themselves independent states, the state governments considered themselves to have taken the place of George III. This meant that the Continental Congress was no more than a gathering place for emissaries from such regimes, rather than a sovereign body in its own right.

Every revolution is fought for two reasons: the declared reason, usually having to do with freedom in the abstract; and the real reason, involving merely the transference of power from one group to another. More of the revolutionaries are interested in the first than the second reason, but it generally is the leadership which is concerned with the latter. So it was with our revolution. Many of the idealistic had joined it thinking that "freedom" from the Crown would mean the freedom of each state to do as it pleased—the states after all being more answerable to their people than a large federal government would be. For such folk, authority came, not from God, as all Christian countries at that time claimed, but from the people themselves. But where a King is an individual, and may be held accountable for his wielding of God's authority, the people are too numerous to be responsible for anything. Further, since their desires rather than God's are to be the standard against which all must be judged, anything the majority appears to wish must be good. Naturally, since it is physically impossible for all the people to man the positions of governance, their powers must be used on their behalf. Those who actually do so are perforce the real rulers of the land.

So it was and so it is in this country. But with the states as the real powers under *The Articles of Confederation* (as the first constitution was called), this was a much more difficult affair. While it is true that the local oligarchy in each state had taken complete power during the revolution, they tended to be extremely limited in their worldview; less interested in spreading the doctrines of the American Revolution around the world than in making a profit at home. But for the more ideologically motivated among them this was not enough. Massachusetts was too small for John Adams, Pennsylvania for Franklin, Virginia for Jefferson, and so on. For such as these, it was not enough to have a string of little countries hugging the Atlantic coast: they wished to lay the foundations of a great commonwealth which, dedicated to the principles of the Enlightenment and Freemasonry, would serve as model for and steppingstone to a world state based upon the same ideals. For such as these, the American was to be a new kind of man. Like their Puritan predecessors, who had wished to sever themselves completely from Catholicism, they wished to cut off all connection to old Europe and to the revealed religion which had formed her. We shall look more closely at this presently.

But in 1783, the material at hand did not look very promising. The Articles safeguarded the powers of the states carefully. Although each of them could have from two to seven representatives at Congress, the states had no more than one vote apiece, in the unicameral body. There was no chief executive to administer and execute laws passed: the President of the Congress was no more than an official charged with enforcing parliamentary procedure, like today's Speaker of the House. Neither was there any national court system, each state's judiciary being completely independent. Nine out of the thirteen states had to agree for a bill to become law, and Congress could neither levy taxes nor tariffs. It could not regulate commerce, and so each state could (and did) tax goods coming in from the next state (this was particularly hard on the New Jersey farmers; those in the north traded in New York City, and those in the south in Philadelphia. They described their state as "a barrel tapped at both ends"). All the states had to consent to amending the Articles, which were in any case merely a "firm league of friendship" among the states, rather than basic law.

Had all thirteen states been identical in economic interests, social structure, and ethnic make-up, such a legal arrangement alone would have been a fertile source of difficulty and dissension. But they were far from identical.

STATE OF THE UNION

New England had been the starting point of the revolution. Men like turncoat Royal Governor Jonathan Trumbull, John Hancock, Sam Adams, Paul Revere, and of course, John Adams continued to play an important part in local affairs, serving as assemblymen, governors, and the like. Massachusetts, Connecticut, and New Hampshire were dominated by the same groups of urban merchants and bureaucrats who had been the mainstay of power under the Crown (although many individuals of these classes—including a large number of Harvard and Yale alumni—had fled to Canada as Loyalists). Correspondingly, many of the rural inhabitants of these states, no longer having a Royal Governor to appeal to, found themselves over-taxed and foreclosed upon by the same men they had helped to bring to complete power in the recent conflict. The Vermont farmers, whose lands were still disputed by New Hampshire and New York, simply carried on as an independent country, not recognizing and unrecognized by the Congress.

Although the New Englanders were ethnically homogenous—British Isles with a little French Huguenot, like the Reveres—they had religious tensions. In Massachusetts, the Congregational remained the State Church. Article III of the Commonwealth's 1780 constitution declared that:

> ...the happiness of a people, and the good order and preservation of civil government, essentially depend upon piety, religion, and morality; and... these cannot be generally diffused through a community but by the institution of the public worship of God, and of public instructions in piety, religion, and morality.

To this end, the same article gave the legislature the right to make the towns of the Commonwealth levy taxes to support "public protestant teachers of piety, religion, and morality," these latter being the Congregational ministers.

But while this establishment (which endured until 1833) was essentially the same which had prevailed before the revolution, it had a very different end in mind from that of the Puritan fathers. They had made theirs the state church to safeguard what they thought was Christianity; their descendants retained the arrangement to protect the civil order. This was a reflection of the decline of belief in the doctrines of the Congregational religion, and the corresponding growth of what would later be called Unitarianism. Even so, the established church was opposed by the Baptists, who were the largest religious minority in the Commonwealth. Yet both united in maintaining the Test Acts which excluded Catholics from public office (although, in view of the contributions of France and Spain, they were graciously allowed to exist). Yet some were annoyed by this last liberality; the Town Meeting of Dunstable, for example, called upon the legislature to deny "Protection to the Idolatrous worshippers of the Church of Rome."

Connecticut and New Hampshire also retained establishments like Massachusetts, as well as the Test Acts. The Republic of Vermont, while not having a State Church, nevertheless required its office-holders to believe in God, the Old and New Testaments, and the Protestant religion. Rhode Island's status quo merely continued.

The Middle States were quite different. New York, with its cosmopolitan population, and Pennsylvania and Delaware with their large German minorities, were dominated by an urban merchant class in New York City and Philadelphia, and by great landed estate holders. In New York, for example, while Loyalist patroons like the De Lanceys had been forced out, the rebel Van Rensselaers, the Livingstons, the Gardiners and others continued to rule their manors as they had for generations. New Jersey was still the domain of her British, Dutch, and German small farmers. In Delaware, New Jersey, and Pennsylvania, as no religion had been established prior to the revolution, neither was any afterwards. But the latter's 1776 constitution did require office-holders to believe in God and the Old and New Testaments—thus excluding Jews. Franklin among others led a drive on their behalf, and in 1790 this was amended to belief in God and "a future state of rewards and punishments."

New York was significantly different from these other states in two ways. First, that in the southern four counties the Anglican Church had been established, which state of affairs was ended in the state's 1777 constitution. Second, that specific opposition to Catholicism, led by such American heroes as William Livingston and John Jay, was particularly vicious. Jay's party advocated exiling all Catholics. Having failed in this, they were able to obtain in 1788 a Test Oath requiring all officeholders renounce all foreign powers "ecclesiastical as well as civil." This prevented Catholics from holding office there.

Where New England depended heavily on shipping and the slave trade, and the Mid-Atlantic looked to both trade and agriculture, the South was overwhelmingly rural; except for North Carolina, these states were dominated by the Plantations. The mountaineers and small farmers continued to resent the great landholders as they had before the revolution. Germans were found in the Piedmont of Virginia and Maryland, in the interior of South Carolina, and in ports like Charleston, Baltimore, and Savannah; Scots Highlanders (many speaking Gaelic) could be met in the New Scotland area of North Carolina, and Georgia's Darien settlement; and Ulster Scots prevailed in the Hill Country. But with these exceptions, as well as Charleston's Huguenots, most Southern whites were of English descent.

Thus, the Church of England was established in all these states at the beginning of the revolution. In 1784, the Virginia assembly transformed this into a requirement that all Virginians be taxed, not for the support of the Episcopal Church, but for the Christian denomination of their choice—as is done in Germany today. Unrelenting propaganda by the Deists in the Assembly however, brought about the passage two years later of Jefferson's Act For Establishing Religious Freedom, which severed all connection between the government of the Commonwealth of Virginia and any religious body.

South Carolina's 1778 constitution established "Protestantism" as the state religion, and barred all non-protestants from public office. Thus, in addition to the Anglican-Episcopal church, Baptists, Presbyterians, Independent Calvinists (Congregationalists), and Methodists were all registered as established churches. In 1790, the state's new constitution abolished all mention of church establishment, and ordered the "free exercise and enjoyment of religious profession and worship, without discrimination or preference." North Carolina's 1776 constitution ended the establishment of the Episcopal church as well, frankly forbidding establishment of any church; but offices were restricted to Protestants and remained so well into the 19th Century. Georgia's 1777 constitution was similar. Maryland, however, while opening offices to all Christians in 1776, retained the Episcopal church as the established one, with all provisions giving the state control of it to remain in force—except for funding. It was not until 1810 that the last vestige of establishment was abolished. Only Christians could hold office until the early 19th Century, and office-holders were still required to believe in God until the 1950s.

The states had abdicated their claims to the western lands in favor of Congress. But in 1783, Congress had no troops of its own to patrol the frontier, a job left to the militias. The result was that both Great Britain and Spain felt no need to recognize American sovereignty in large parts of the Old Northwest and Old Southwest. The British continued to occupy posts at Michilimakinac, Detroit, Niagara, Oswego, and elsewhere. These posts kept order, functioned as trading posts, and acted as liaison points with the Indian tribes of the area, who retained their attachment to George III despite being within American jurisdiction, even as their fathers had two decades before attempted to maintain their loyalty to Louis XV after the British victory.

Spain, meanwhile, had a legitimate complaint against the United States. Under British rule, the northern border of West Florida had been extended considerably. In a secret agreement, the Americans agreed to the British retaining the new boundary, should they regain the province at the peace table (Spain having conquered it during the Revolution). The Spanish, however, both kept West Florida, and later learned of the agreement. They then claimed the wider borders for their own. Large tribes of the area, such as the Creek, Choctaw, and Chickasaw allied with the Spanish.

Nevertheless, American penetration continued. In Ohio, Kentucky, and Tennessee in particular, large numbers settled. The French settlers of the old posts of Vincennes, Kaskaskia, and Cahokia found themselves joined by many of the newcomers, who would eventually outnumber them. As might be supposed, neither they nor their Indian neighbors were pleased by this prospect.

This, then, was the state of the new nation at the commencement of its career.

The Faith of the Founding Fathers

Despite the apparently ramshackle nature of the country, those who had been its ideological mentors in the revolution—some of whom (Adams, Jefferson, and Madison) would later preside over it—had great plans for it. It would be, as we have said, a country based not upon any sort of Christianity, but upon the ideals of the Enlightenment. This is a statement which will shock some, and so it were well to quote Franklin, Jefferson, and Adams on religion, so as to make the position of the most important of the founders clear.

A few weeks before he died, Benjamin Franklin wrote a letter to Yale's president, Ezra Stiles:

> Here is my creed. I believe in one God, Creator of the Universe. That he governs it by His providence. That He ought to be worshipped. That the most acceptable service we render Him is doing good to his other children. That the soul of man is immortal, and will be treated with justice in another life respecting its conduct in this. As to Jesus of Nazareth, my opinion of whom you particularly desire, I think the system of morals and his religion, as he left them to us, the best the world ever saw or is likely to see; but I apprehend it has received various corrupt changes, and I have, with most of the dissenters in England, some doubts as to his divinity; though it is a question I do not dogmatize upon, having never studied it, and think it needless to busy myself with it now, when I expect soon an opportunity of knowing the truth with less trouble. I see no harm, however, in its being believed, if that belief has the good consequence, as it probably has, of making his doctrines more respected and better observed...

This is a classic statement of Deism. The God of whom Franklin writes is not the Christian God, Whose Second Person incarnates of a Virgin and remains in Church and Sacraments. Rather, he is the Muslim Allah or the Masonic Grand Architect, essentially aloof from his creation. Revealed Christianity is spurious, but serves a useful social function. This last, essentially dishonest notion, led many of Franklin's co-theorists to support the Congregational establishment in New England. It is astonishing that Franklin never studied the question of Christ's divinity, especially when he had spent so much time with his friend, Fr. John Carroll—particularly when they went together to Canada to attempt to seduce the French there from their allegiance to the King. One assumes they had other things to speak of during their long acquaintance.

Where Franklin, however, saw in Christianity merely a harmless, perhaps even useful lie, Jefferson saw a definite evil. As he wrote to Mrs. Harrison Smith on August 6, 1816:

> My opinion is that there would never have been an infidel if there had never been a priest. The artificial structures they have built on the purest of all moral systems, for the purpose of deriving from it pence and power, revolts those who think for themselves, and who read in the system only what is really there.

But he saw signs of hope in the country which he both helped to create and which he ruled over for a time. To it, in a letter of June 26, 1822 for Benjamin Waterhouse, he imputed a messianic mission:

> I rejoice that in this blessed country of free inquiry and belief, which has surrendered its creed and conscience to neither Kings nor priests, the genuine doctrine of one only God is reviving, and I trust that there is not a *young man* now living in the United States who will not die a Unitarian.

Thus spake the author of the Declaration of Independence, who even wrote his own "de-mythologized" version of the Bible to prove his point. While he and John Adams had been intense political opponents in office, their shared religious opinions served as a means of reconciliation in retirement. Their correspondence has been preserved; the intriguing thing about it all is that where Jefferson was the more radical politically, in religious matters it is Adams who appears in the correspondence as the more bitter opponent of Christianity, and of Catholicism in particular.

On December 3, 1813, Adams informed Jefferson that:

> Indeed, Mr. Jefferson, what could be invented to debase the ancient Christianism, which Greeks, Romans, Hebrews, and Christian factions, above all the Catholics, have not fraudulently imposed upon the public? Miracles after miracles have rolled down in torrents, wave succeeding wave in the Catholic Church, from the Council of Nice, and long before, to this day.

In the same letter, he goes on to describe a book of Chateaubriand's (which he nevertheless admitted to reading "with delight") as "enthusiastic, bigoted, superstitious, Roman Catholic throughout." He saw an innate conflict between his and Jefferson's religion, and Catholicism, as he wrote to Jefferson on July 16, 1814:

> If the Christian religion, as I understand it, or as you understand it, should maintain its ground, as I believe it will, yet Platonic, Pythagoric, Hindoo, and cabalistical Christianity, which is Catholic Christianity, and which has prevailed for fifteen hundred years, has received a mortal wound, of which the monster must finally die.

And again on June 20, 1815:

> The question before the human race is, whether the God of Nature shall govern the world by his own laws, or whether the priests and kings shall rule it by fictitious miracles? Or, in other words, whether authority is originally in the people? Or whether it has descended for 1800 years in a succession of popes and bishops, or brought down from heaven by the Holy Ghost in the form of a dove, in a phial of holy oil? [This latter refers to a miracle which occurred at the coronation of Clovis, King of the Franks.]

February 2, 1816 finds him referring to "that stupendous monument of human hypocrisy and fanaticism, the church of St. Peter at Rome..." (Presumably he had no such opinion about the public buildings in Washington, such as the Capitol and White House, first used in his administration).

The principal author of the constitution, James Madison, wrote to a Reverend Adams in 1832 that: "In the Papal System, Government and Religion are in a manner consolidated, and that is found to be the worst of Government."

These sentiments required for their practical execution the creation of a distinct American character, made-to-order rather than organically developed over long centuries influenced by the Faith, as happened in Europe. There must be, in as many ways as possible, a radical divorce from both the mother country and the rest of Old Europe. Foremost in the pursuance of this goal was *Noah Webster*, famous as the creator of *Webster's Dictionary of the American Language*. The very name of the book tells us something about his intentions in altering the spelling of such words as honour, centre, and recognise to honor, center, and recognize. This change he called a "reform." In a 1789 essay he justified it on several grounds, but the one which most concerned him was simply that it "would make a difference between the English orthography and the American... I am confident that such an event is an object of vast political consequence." What was his goal?

> ...a *national language* is a band of *national union*. Every engine should be employed to render the people of this country truly *national;* to call their attachments home to their own country; and to inspire them with the pride of national character. However they may boast of

independence, and the freedom of their government, yet their *opinions* are not sufficiently independent; an astonishing respect for the arts and literature of their parent country and a blind imitation of its manners are still prevalent among the Americans.

Webster's efforts in this area soon received official commendation, and eventually prevailed. Here he realized a fact grasped by later revolutionaries: if all traces of the old regime are to be blotted out, the language and its manner of writing must themselves be changed. So Kemal Ataturk ordered Turkish to be written in Latin rather than Arabic letters; the Soviets "reformed" the Russian alphabet; and Mao had the Chinese characters "simplified." The result was to make their nations' literatures difficult or impossible for the younger generations to read, in hopes of cutting them off from affection for the former state of their lands. It was an extension of this principle which led George Orwell to his horrific vision of "Newspeak" in *1984*.

But Webster and his kind were not merely concerned with how things were spelled. They were also concerned with rejecting the inheritance of Christendom in education. In another essay, written in 1790, Webster argued for the banishing of classical and British literature from classrooms, and for their replacement with something else:

> Another defect in our schools, which, since the Revolution, is become inexcusable, is the want of proper books. The collections which are now used consist of essays that respect foreign and ancient nations. The minds of youth are perpetually led to the history of Greece and Rome or to Great Britain; boys are constantly repeating the acclamations of Demosthenes and Cicero or debates upon some political question in the British Parliament...
>
> But every child in America should be acquainted with his own country... As soon as he opens his lips, he should rehearse the history of his own country; he should lisp the praise of liberty and of those illustrious heroes and statesmen who have wrought a revolution in her favor.

In a word, education ought not to be the expansion of the mind so as to assist both in life and salvation, but at base, ideological indoctrination. Rather than teach the student, via the great minds of Western Civilization, how to think (and so evaluate things himself) he was to be initiated into the sort of nation-worship which was then being formulated, but which has been the mainstay of education in this country ever since.

It has been said that the public schools have been one of the major instruments of assimilation in this country. Indeed, they have been, for their job has been precisely that outlined by Webster. They have ensured that the basic ideas of the Enlightenment (as held by Franklin, Jefferson, and company) so opposed to Christianity in general and Catholicism in particular, became and remain the basic intellectual currency of this country. We will now see the response of the Catholic Church to this.

The Founding of Americanist Catholicism

The Catholic minority, centered as it was in Maryland, Pennsylvania, and Delaware, could not help but be affected by their country's independence. Prior to the war, American Catholics had been under the remote jurisdiction of the Vicar Apostolic of London, and served in large part by ex-Jesuits. The Vicar Apostolic himself (as with the Irish bishops and the Scots and other English Vicars Apostolic) was chosen by the Pope usually on the advice of the Cardinal-Duke of York, Henry Stuart. Brother of Bonnie Prince Charlie (Charles III, according to the Jacobites; his brother would inherit his claims in 1788, and would be called Henry IX afterwards), he was the highest-ranking English-speaking prelate. Would he not be consulted on the appointment of an American bishop, now that the States were a separate country?

No. Although Fr. Carroll had not apparently discussed the divinity of Christ with Franklin on their Quebec trip, he had made himself useful in other ways. Already aged, Franklin wrote on the trip that "I find I grow daily more feeble, and I think I could hardly have got so far but for Mr. Carroll's friendly assistance and care for me." Here we see a pattern which has dominated the Church in America from that day to this—practice of the corporal works of mercy to the exclusion of the spiritual.

At any rate, although Carroll had kept himself aloof from his brother priests after his return from Europe (where he was educated and ordained) in 1774, his brother Daniel's and cousin Charles of Carrollton's prominent positions as revolutionaries won him the appointment to the Canadian mission. With theirs and Franklin's continued support, he became afterwards de facto head of the body of priests functioning in America. This was made official in 1784. Franklin's journal for July 1 of that year has these words:

> The Pope's Nuncio called and acquainted me that the Pope had, *on my recommendation*, appointed Mr. John Carroll superior of the Catholic clergy in America, with many powers of bishop; and that, probably he would be made bishop *in partibus* before the end of the year.

Franklin's view of his part in the affair is confirmed by the letter of appointment sent to Carroll himself, wherein Cardinal Antonelli writes:

> ...it is known that your appointment will please and gratify many members of that republic, and especially Mr. Franklin, the eminent individual who represents that republic at the court of the Most Christian King.

So rather than depending on a holy Cardinal who had forfeited a temporal kingdom for the sake of his vocation, the choice of first bishop of this nation was made by a man who did not believe in the divinity of Christ.

But what sort of beliefs did Carroll have regarding the Faith? He considered two great problems in the Church of his time to be "the boundaries of the spiritual jurisdiction of the Holy See," and "the use of the Latin tongue in the publick Liturgy." On these he wrote to Fr. Joseph Berington in 1787:

> I consider these two points as the greatest obstacles to Christians of other denominations to a thorough union with us, or at least to a much more general diffusion of our religion, particularly in N. America... With respect to the latter point, I cannot help thinking that the alteration of the Church discipline ought not only to be solicited, but insisted upon as essential to the service of God and benefit of mankind. Can there be anything more preposterous than an unknown tongue; and in this country either for want of books or inability to read, the great part of our congregations must be utterly ignorant of the meaning and sense of the publick office of the Church.

As to the former point, Carroll had made himself very clear prior to his appointment as head of the clergy, in an April 10, 1784 letter to Fr. Plowden:

> ...that no authority derived from the Propaganda will ever be admitted here; that the Catholick Clergy and Laity here know that the only connexion they ought to have with Rome is to acknowledge the Pope as Spiritual head of the Church; that no Congregations existing in his States shall be allowed to exercise any share of his Spiritual authority here; that no Bishop Vicar Apostolical shall be admitted, and if we are to have a Bishop, he shall not be in partibus (a refined Roman political contrivance), but an ordinary national Bishop, in whose appointment Rome shall have no share; so that we are very easy about their machinations.

From such sentiments, it may even be inferred that had Rome not given him the appointment later that year, he might even have formed his own schismatic church. In any case, it is obvious that he wished not only a vernacular liturgy but the Pope reduced to the position of the

Anglican Archbishop of Canterbury—in a word, that the Catholic Church in America should be an imitation of the Episcopal Church. Today, he seems to have obtained his wish.

But what was this worthy prelate's stance on conversions, which, in a non-Catholic country like this one, is presumably the clergy's first interest? An answer may be found in his famed prayer for the Civil Authorities. After praying for the deliberations and conduct of the President, Congress, and so forth, the following paragraph is recited:

> We recommend likewise, to Thy unbounded mercy, all our brethren and fellow-citizens throughout the United States, that they may be blessed and sanctified in the observance of Thy most holy law; that they may be preserved in union, and in that peace which the world cannot give; and after the blessings of this life, be admitted to those which are eternal.

There is here no mention of conversion, or indeed of anything spiritual, save observance of the Divine Law. This is redolent of the sort of moralistic Deism which we saw promulgated by the Founding Fathers. Franklin himself could have recited it in good conscience. In place of the salvation offered by the Church's sacraments we seem to see here a temporal one envisaged. What is this union in which Americans must be preserved? It is not one of faith, obviously.

Yet herein was established the attitude towards conversion of America which has prevailed in the U.S. Church until the present: that the country does not need to be converted at all, because in some mysterious way it is already joined to the Church.

Problems of Confederation

The Congress being ineffective, jurisdictional bickering broke out between the states continually, such as that between New York and New Jersey over operation of a light house at Sandy Hook. Spanish, Indian, and British activity against American settlement could not be countered for lack of a standing army. No national coinage meant that the country had to rely on worthless paper notes and a dizzying array of French, Spanish, British, and other foreign coins.

This last was symbolic of the country's economy as a whole. Unable to levy taxes, the only way Congress could operate (let alone repay the debts incurred during the revolution) was to either borrow yet more money or ask the states to contribute—voluntarily, of course. Foreign nations would not negotiate over trade with Congress because each state had its own tariff policy. Despite the high hopes held for the new nation by the ideologues, the future did not look bright.

Within three years after the treaty, signs of impending ruin began to make themselves felt. Desperate for money, the Congress leased control of both shores of the Mississippi to Spain for a period of 25 years in 1786. While the needed gold and silver did help shore up the country's rocky finances, it was a terrible blow to national pride.

New England began to show signs of severe instability. In 1786 a band of New Hampshire farmers marched on their state capital to demand lowering of their taxes and issuance of more paper money. Massachusetts was rocked by Shays Rebellion. Bunker Hill veteran *Daniel Shays* led a band of farmers in the western part of the Commonwealth, who protested the lack of real money, high interest rates, widespread foreclosures, and a taxation rate which unfairly placed the greater part of the burden on farmers to the benefit of the merchants of the towns who controlled the legislature. He roused the whole of the west, and the governor declared a state of rebellion. On January 25, 1787, an attack was mounted on the Federal arsenal at Springfield. Shays' 1,200 men were repulsed, and scattered. But despite their defeat, they were pardoned under popular pressure.

On the frontier, meanwhile, feeling abandoned by the Congress in New York (where it had moved from Philadelphia), the settlers, surrounded as they were by trackless wilderness and potentially hostile Indians, looked elsewhere for protection. The settlers in what is now eastern Tennessee had already established a provisional government as the "State of Franklin," with revolutionary war hero *John Sevier* as provisional governor. Others in the newly opened areas of present day West Virginia, North Carolina, Georgia, and Alabama attached their small settlements to the new "state." Enraged by Congressional neglect and realizing the need to open trade on the Mississippi if the new state was to survive, Sevier appealed for help to the Spanish ambassador, the Captain-General of Cuba, and the Governor of Louisiana. Writing to the first-named, he declared:

> The people of this region are aware which is the nation from whom their happiness and safety will depend in the future, and foresee that their interest and prosperity are thoroughly linked to the protection and liberality of your government.

Similarly, yet another revolutionary veteran settled in Kentucky, General James Wilkinson, also made moves toward Spain. The general fomented an independence movement in his area, based again upon abandonment by the national authorities and lack of protection against Indians. He wrote twice to King Charles III of Spain, swearing allegiance to him, asking for help and trading rights on the Mississippi. But as with

Sevier's case, the King, although sympathetic to the plight of the western settlers (and not adverse to maintaining what he considered his rights in West Florida), was not interested in destroying the United States. He had in fact subsidized the building of St. Peter's church in New York City (where St. Elizabeth Anne Seton later converted) two years earlier, and took a sympathetic view to the new nation—provided of course that it did not attempt to seize his own dominions. We shall see how he was repaid later.

While it would be easy today to see Shays, Sevier, and Wilkinson as traitors, it was not so apparent then. Had not the government which they opposed itself been created in a revolution—a revolution which all three had themselves fought in? Did not Shays' farmers and Sevier's and Wilkinson's pioneers have the right to judge whether it had become necessary for them "to dissolve the political bands which have connected them with another...," even as the Declaration of Independence proclaimed?

Prior to the revolution, loyalty to the Crown was considered, as we have seen, to be both the bond of union between the diverse peoples of the Empire and a religious duty; this view was retained by the Loyalists. Their opponents, however, maintained (at least for public consumption) that self-interest on the part of the people was the sole criterion in government. But however effective this belief was in breaking down an established order, it was not a stable foundation for a new one. It was in fact the same dilemma faced by the Protestant leadership after their revolt against the Church. Private judgment was the rallying cry which enabled people to leave the Church—but how could one have any kind of religious structure based on it? The answer in both cases would be the same: continuing to pay lip-service to the ideal which was used to justify the revolt, while rejecting it in practice.

THE START OF THE FEDERAL GOVERNMENT

It was apparent by 1787 that the United States could not long continue as they were. Sooner or later the states and the pioneers would go each their separate ways, after which Great Britain or Spain would absorb all or part of them. The leaders in each of the states decided that the Articles of Confederation must be revised. So, in 1787, the states sent delegates to Philadelphia in order to do so. George Washington was made chairman of the Constitutional Convention, and such notables as Franklin, Madison, and Alexander Hamilton were present. To avoid any criticism on the part of the public, the meetings were held in secret.

As they deliberated, the delegates' purpose changed. Rather than revising the Articles, they determined that what was needed was the creation of a Federal government with effective powers—in a word, of a government that would take the place of the Crown. Naturally, many of the states, particularly the smaller ones, feared that such a government would be dominated by the greater states and run for their profit. The larger ones pointed out that they would be expected to bear the brunt of the new government's expense. The compromise worked out was that of a two chamber Congress. The Senate would consist of two senators from each state, appointed by the state government; this body would serve as both the protector of the smaller states' interests, and of the states as a whole against the Federal government. The lower chamber, the House of Representatives, would consist of congressmen chosen on the basis of population; there the larger states would prevail. To become law, a bill would have to be passed by both houses. Thus, a major block was broken.

But there were a few others. One was that, as the states were to be assessed their taxes and receive their number of representatives on the basis of population, some agreement had to be reached on the status of slaves. If they were not to be counted because of their unfree status, the slave states (which at this time included such northern states as New York and Pennsylvania, as well as the South) would pay much lower taxes. But if they were counted as part of the population, the slave states' representation in Congress would be much larger (even though the slaves would not vote). The compromise was typically American: five slaves would be counted as the equivalent of three free men. Further, the Slave Trade would become illegal in 1808 (a measure opposed as much by the New England shippers who brought the human cargo in as by those who bought it).

Another bone of contention was the commerce question. While it was obvious to the delegates that if the Congress were to function at all it must be able to regulate trade, the Southerners feared that the North, with its greater population, would for its own benefit strangle the trade necessary for Southern survival. The compromise attained here was that Congress was forbidden to tax exports, to favor one port over another, or to interfere with the Slave Trade until its 1808 abolition. Apart from these reservations, Congress would have the power "To regulate commerce with foreign nations, and among the several States, and with the Indian tribes." Interestingly enough, this last provision conferred a sort of status upon the Indian tribes analogous to that of foreign nations or the states. But the precise nature of that status has never been determined, and has been a source of difficulty ever since.

To prevent, as was said, tyranny, the government was divided into three sections: legislative, judicial, and executive. This last was to be the President. One conflict over this position was whether it should be directly elected or else appointed by Congress. It was pointed out that if

Congress appointed him, the President would be dependent upon that body, and the independence of the post would be lost. On the other hand, Shays' Rebellion was fresh in the minds of the delegates. Moreover, many had been involved with whipping up popular anger against the King, and knew from personal experience how popular opinion could be manipulated. How to prevent others from doing what they themselves had done? The solution was found in the creation of an Electoral College, made of prominent local people who would themselves be popularly elected, and would in turn elect the President and Vice President (who would be the candidate with the second highest number of Electoral votes). These would be, it was supposed, the same sort of substantial men who had brought about the revolution, continued to dominate many of the state governments, and had in fact been selected as delegates to the Convention itself.

The Supreme Court and inferior courts were envisaged as the third branch of government, which would have judicial power. To them would go disputes between states, and appellate power to decide on such cases brought them from lower courts as they were willing to hear. But note that the power of judicial review, through which abortion, for instance, has become the law of the land (through the Supreme Court determining that laws against it are somehow "unconstitutional") is nowhere to found in the constitution. It developed. It is precisely in this field of law, however, that an important factor in American history was implanted.

In Great Britain, where party strife between Whig and Tory, and between factions in those parties, was so acrimonious, the Monarchy served (and serves) as a stabilizing factor. Being in theory above mere party politics, it provides a focus of loyalty to authority available to those whose party is out of power—thus reducing the chance that they will take to violence to seize power. Indeed, the revolution against George III's personal government which was accomplished through bloodshed in this country was done through peaceful means in the mother country. An important part of this system is the law courts of the Crown, who are supposed to administer justice impartially and above all apolitically. Before them, a man stands not as a Whig or a Tory, but as a subject with rights thereby. This idea of an apolitical judiciary, so important for a stable society, was adopted along with the English Common Law by the states and then by the Federal government. From that time until our own day (when the courts have been increasingly politicized) it has provided much of the stability that a government otherwise dominated by party strife would normally lack; it has been an important factor in establishing the United States as a great power as a result.

There is another stabilizing factor which Monarchy brings, and which the United States must somehow supply if they were to prosper.

That is the sacredness of civil authority, seen as coming from God (which we described in the last chapter). The criticism of C.S. Lewis regarding opponents of Monarchy is very apt:

> Monarchy can easily be debunked, but watch the faces, mark well the debunkers. These are the men whose taproot in Eden has been cut: whom no rumour of the polyphony, the dance, can reach—men to whom pebbles laid in a row are more beautiful than an arch. Yet even if they desire mere equality they cannot reach it. Where men are forbidden to honour a king they honour millionaires, athletes or film stars instead: even famous prostitutes or gangsters. For spiritual nature, like bodily nature, will be served; deny it food and it will gobble poison.

While the truth of Lewis' charges in America's cultural sphere is obvious, it is not quite so politically. Indeed, the political application of the principle in most countries has generally resulted in the elevation to power of men like Napoleon, Hitler, and Peron. This has not happened here. Why?

The answer may be found in the creation of a sort of secular religiosity, whose object of worship is the abstract will of the people, and which takes the place of much of the liturgy offered to God which surrounds Christian Monarchy. In place of the Crown Jewels, we have the flag and icons like the Liberty Bell, and originals of the Declaration of Independence, the Constitution, and the Bill of Rights (of which more presently). These are all considered more or less sacred (all nations have flags, but few if any indulge in the sort of flag-worship we do—hedged about as it is with an elaborate ritual; obviously this fulfills a basic human need). The Inauguration of the President has come to have all the pomp of a Coronation. The Pilgrim and Founding Fathers are now saints whose opinions are tantamount to holy writ, and the 4th of July and Thanksgiving which honor them are the equivalents of Christmas and Easter for many. Obviously, this was not consciously planned; but it has had the result of supplying to these states the other great bulwark against anarchy and dictatorship. For the Catholic it does have one major drawback: it is a religion which is not Christian, and smacks of false worship. But it has been absolutely essential to the growth of a country whose unity has no real spiritual foundation, and has ensured that foreign strongmen have had here merely pale shadows like Andrew Jackson and Franklin Roosevelt. Its decline since the 1960s has been very dangerous to the well-being of the nation as it is presently constituted; from that point of view, President Reagan's call in his 1988 farewell address for a revival of civic ritual makes perfect sense.

Be that as it may, the development of this civic ritual was at once an eventual product of and an essential ingredient for the success of the Constitution composed in 1787. Without it, several flaws in the document would have ensured a great deal more civil strife than we have actually undergone. For while the Constitution did set up the framework of a government, it made no attempt to define the values under which that government would be administered. There was no mention of God, for example. So what system of morality would determine the conduct of public life? Religiously, the Founding Fathers were a varied bunch, the more important being Deists, and the remainder having varying degrees of attachment to the tenets of wildly diverging faiths. All alike had a certain adherence, however, to an aristocratic code of conduct, that code of honor which a Deist like Franklin and a Catholic like John Carroll could both agree on. But this code, based not upon an actual religion but upon a particular expression of European, specifically English, culture, could not long endure by itself. The American national religion arose to replace it, and for long provided the spiritual underpinnings without which the Constitution cannot operate successfully.

The Emergence of Parties

Although the Constitution was adopted by the Convention delegates, it had to be ratified by at least nine of the states. Since the state legislatures would be extremely reluctant to give up their power to the proposed central government, the delegates recommended that the document be submitted to special popularly-elected state conventions. The Constitution itself provided that if it was adopted by nine states, it would take effect in those states; practically, however, it had to be ratified by the four large states of Massachusetts, New York, Virginia, and Pennsylvania.

The opponents of the document were called *Anti-Federalists*. These were a loose coalition of debtors, farmers, and paper money supporters, who feared that the creation of a powerful Federal government would lead to ruin of state and local governmental independence, dominance by the wealthy, and eventual extinction of personal freedom. They were what would come to be known as populists. Patrick Henry, one of their foremost spokesmen, put their case with his usual eloquence:

> Here is a revolution as radical as that which separated us from Great Britain. It is as radical if in this transition our rights and privileges are endangered, and the sovereignty of the States will be relinquished...

> This Constitution is said to have beautiful features; but when I come to examine these features, sir, they appear to me to be horribly frightful. Among other deformities, it has an awful squinting. It squints toward monarchy; and does not this raise indignation in the breast of every true American?

The *Federalists* were the Constitution's supporters. They tended to comprise coastal populations, particularly merchants who were concerned with having a government capable of protecting their trade; those who lived more closely to the frontier or the borders and in regions fought over during the revolution, for military reasons. Particularly, those who believed most firmly in the United States as an instrument of world progress and redemption favored it. In any case, arguments such as Alexander Hamilton's summed up their position:

> There is an idea, which is not without its advocates, that a vigorous executive is inconsistent with the genius of republican government... Energy in the executive is a leading character in the definition of a good government. It is essential to the protection of the community against foreign attacks; it is not less essential to the steady administration of the laws; to the protection of property against those irregular and high-handed combinations which sometimes interrupt the ordinary course of justice; to the security of liberty against the enterprises and assaults of ambition, of faction, and of anarchy... A feeble executive implies a feeble execution of the government. A feeble execution is but another phrase for a bad execution; and a government ill executed, whatever it may be in theory, must be, in practice, a bad government.

It was a compelling argument, well articulated in the series co-written by Hamilton and Madison, *The Federalist Papers*. Through the course of 1788, all the states except Rhode Island and North Carolina adopted it; reluctant states like New York being assured that, should the Constitution indeed bring about despotic government, the states would be able to secede. Without this understanding, several would not have ratified it. For the next 77 years, secession remained the ultimate threat whenever tension between various of the states and the Federal government grew extremely hot.

Within two years Rhode Island and North Carolina both acceded to the Union. But the opposition of the Anti-Federalists was not without effect, because it brought about the adoption of the first ten amendments to the Constitution, the Bill of Rights. These were intended to safeguard the personal freedoms of the people against possible despotism. Let us look at each in turn.

The first amendment declares that Congress "shall make no law respecting an establishment of religion, or of prohibiting the free exercise thereof..." While this is taken today to mean that there was to be a "wall of separation between Church and state," (leading to the conclusion that religious symbols may not be erected on public property, prayers and Christmas pageants may not be permitted in public schools, and so on), this is not so. Rather, since several of the states had their own established churches and others had none, Congress was not to have the right to establish one of their own; this was a question reserved to the states. Similarly, Congress could not proscribe any religion. The amendment went on to declare that Congress could not restrict freedom of speech or of the press, nor the right of the people to assemble or petition.

Next came the second amendment, which protected, in the interests of providing a well-armed militia, the right of private citizens to bear arms. Today, this amendment is at the center of the arms-control debate. Proponents of gun-control maintain that the existence of the National Guard as the State Militia satisfies this amendment; opponents declare that the right of individuals to own guns is essential to American freedom.

The third and fourth amendments required respectively that a) no troops could be quartered in private homes in peace time; and b) that such homes could not be entered by authorities without search warrants issued by a judge upon proof of just cause.

Trial by jury was required and double-jeopardy cases forbidden, by the Fifth Amendment. The sixth ordered speedy trials, forbade trial of the accused outside the district where the alleged infraction occurred, and required that he be able to confront his accusers. He was also guaranteed, among other things, the right to defense counsel. Amendment VII guaranteed that trial by jury was preserved in major lawsuits, and the common law was given force here. The eighth forbade excessive bail or fines, as well as "cruel and unusual punishment." At the time of adoption, this latter was held to consist of torture, boiling in oil, drawing and quartering, and that sort of thing. Today it is often declared to be the death penalty itself.

The ninth amendment said that the rights given the people in the Constitution were not intended to deny others. The tenth is today the most forgotten: it restricts the powers of the federal government to those expressly given it in the Constitution.

The Federalists remained a party, considered more aristocratic and oriented toward Britain. They favored a loose construction of the Constitution. Hamilton and John Adams became some of their more prominent leaders. The Anti-Federalists became known eventually as members of what were called the Democratic-Republicans; apart from Patrick Henry, such supporters of the Constitution as its author Madison and Thomas Jefferson became its leaders. The D-Rs would favor a strict construction of the Constitution and friendly relations with France—the more so after the French Revolution. But while they were considered the equivalents of conservative and liberal at the time, and as we shall see their struggles would become extremely bitter, at base, they shared an ideology. There was a hollowness, an artificiality about their opposition to one another which has always characterized American politics.

Whence comes this strange unity, despite the often strident disagreements between parties? Apart from shared adherence to the secular American religion, it stems from three sources. First, the struggle is always over means rather than ends. No major political faction has ever seriously questioned the basic beliefs of the founding fathers, that the country exists solely to promote "life, liberty, and the pursuit of happiness," or in other words, economic growth. Profit for some, and at least subsistence for the majority; than this there is nothing higher, so that all questions of public morality are purely relative. There are never political principles but rather opinions, which the two major parties (whose names have changed over the course of history) exchange on a regular basis. When the two have a consensus on a given issue (such as that developing between Democrats and Republicans today on the merits of abortion) those who disagree simply do not exist politically.

Secondly, the extremely nebulous and ever-changing nature of the country's ruling class makes it adaptable to virtually any situation. While the folk who engineered the revolution were either landholding aristocrats or merchant patricians, their descendants did not necessarily remain part of the nation's ruling class. Stephen Birmingham in his *America's Secret Aristocracy* (pp. 9-10) treats of their withdrawal from public life:

> In the early days of the Republic, the American aristocracy simply assumed that its members would run the new country—as presidents, governors, senators, cabinet members, ambassadors—just as the British Aristocracy ran England. It was not until America's seventh president, the log-cabin-born Andrew Jackson, that a man entered the White House who was neither a member of the old Virginia landed gentry nor an Adams from Boston...
>
> In the years since Jackson, Americans continued to elect occasional members of the aristocracy to the presidency—up to and including Franklin D. Roosevelt—but the aristocracy itself had already become sorely disillusioned about the notion of American rulership and running for high political office... Gradually, it became merely prudent for the American aristocracy to turn to other less visible—and less vulnerable—forms of public service. Today, the American upper class shuns politics, and whether that is the country's gain or loss can only be a subject for speculation.

While, as we shall see, this retirement was not always as graceful as Mr. Birmingham suggests, it certainly did occur. In America, the upper class and the ruling class may contain a few of the same individuals, but they are emphatically not the same thing.

For entrance into the ruling class is solely dependent upon two things: money and adherence to the basic ideology of the existing membership. It is certainly not hereditary, nor is it based upon where the money comes from. At one time its leading professions were agriculture and trade, then banking and industry, and today they appear to be high finance and media. But the source of the funds is secondary to the thing itself. Obviously, however, such a diverse crowd is difficult to identify; moreover, there are an infinite number of degrees of "ins" and "outs", not unlike an onion. Where one belongs in the onion often changes back and forth during one's career.

The third factor in this underlying unity is the Masonic Order, which carries on today many of the functions of a state church. Most of our presidents have belonged to it, the White House, Capitol Building, and Washington Monument were all dedicated with its rites, and Washington himself swore the oath of office upon a Masonic bible (the same one, incidentally, used by George Bush). Apart from this overarching presence (and the pride which the Order takes in its part during the Revolution), it is also an important force outside the centers of power. Across the country, wherever the small towns are not primarily Catholic (and in some which are) lack of membership in the local lodge is the equivalent of social and economic ostracism. Nor must it be overlooked that with the division of American Freemasonry into the York and Scottish rites, many different degrees and innumerable affiliated organizations, it is a difficult thing to characterize. Suffice it to say that it exists to safeguard the principals of Freemasonry, which have become the generally accepted principles of the United States. Except at its highest levels, American (and British, Canadian, and Australasian) Freemasonry has no need to adopt the nastily anti-Catholic attitudes and tactics employed by their brethren in Europe and Latin America. Here they are the establishment, and can afford to be apparently nice. Further, it must also be recognized that most of their membership here are not concerned or even aware of the Order's ultimate goals; just as it ought also be remembered that they frequently bicker with one another.

All of which having been said, both Anti-Federalists and Federalists united to throw all the electoral votes behind George Washington, who became President in 1789, the same year as the beginning of the Revolution in Europe, which would topple our ally Louis XVI, and many another sovereign.

THE FEDERALIST ERA

The first Congress elected under the new Constitution likewise met in 1789. Despite Washington's offer to serve without pay, they voted him a salary of $25,000 per year. Further, it was voted to form the Federal court system, and to set aside a ten-square mile district to serve as the site of a capital to be built. Consisting of land donated on either side of the river Potomac by Maryland (which lost thereby Georgetown) and Virginia (similarly bereft of Alexandria), it was to be called the District of Columbia.

Soon after his inauguration at New York (shortly after which the capital returned to Philadelphia), Washington appointed a cabinet. In this, he departed from the British practice. With them, the cabinet was responsible not to the King but to whichever party was in control of Parliament. The Prime Minister was and is leader of that party, and responsible for selecting the other ministers and determining governmental policy. While the King or Queen continues to "appoint" the own Prime Minister, it is done solely on the basis of parliamentary majorities, the Monarch's preferences being immaterial.

But Washington set the precedent whereby the cabinet was chosen by himself (although Congress confirmed it), and acted as his own Prime Minister. Every President has done so, down to this day. But wanting to ensure that various opinions were represented, he appointed Jefferson as his Secretary of State, and Hamilton as his Secretary of the Treasury. The moderate federalist General Henry Knox became Secretary of War.

Where Washington differed from more recent Presidents was in his reluctance to express views on legislation before it went before Congress, or to try to influence national opinion. In his view, the chief executive was not empowered to interfere in the business of Congress.

Hamilton's economic policy, which Washington supported, centered on the creation of a national bank which would hold public funds, and issue bank-notes to ensure a solid currency for the country. The power to create such a bank was nowhere to be found in the Constitution; but on this point Washington favored the Federalists and "loose" construction. It was not expressly forbidden, after all. So, despite Jefferson's bitter opposition, the Bank of the United States was chartered in 1791. The same year saw the admission of Vermont as the 14th state.

Another of Hamilton's economic measures approved by Congress were taxes on whisky, carriages, slaves, lands, and houses. There was no income tax, this being forbidden as confiscatory taxation in the Constitution. Additionally, tariffs were put on imports; not merely to raise money but to protect American made products against cheaper foreign products.

A sign of growth on the frontier was the admission of the Commonwealth of Kentucky as the 15th state in 1792. Another sign of things to come in that momentous year was the invention of the cotton gin, which, by revolutionizing the growing of cotton, provided a stimulus for plantations devoted to the crop. The result was to make slavery, for long an unprofitable enterprise in slow decline, once again economically attractive. This in time would blow new life into "the peculiar institution."

The French Revolution

Events in France, in the meantime, had risen to a fever pitch. In 1789, the Old Regime in France was ended, for the most part due to action by wealthy bourgeoisie and nobility—folk very similar to and with many of the same ideas as those who had brought about the American revolution. Such figures as La Fayette were prominent in both actions. Louis XVI was expected to continue to rule as a constitutional monarch, similar to George III since the fall of Lord North's government. But it was not to be. The revolution in France became ever more radical, and the King was deposed in 1792. He would be executed early the next year. Soon after, a slave revolt decimated the French colony of Saint Domingue (ending eventually, after much bloodshed and several invasions, with the establishment of the black republic of Haiti). The French Revolution had several direct results in the United States and adjoining areas.

In the West Indies, French refugees settled in the Spanish possessions of Santiago de Cuba and Trinidad, Gallicizing them. Large numbers of both Saint Dominguan planters and their slaves and Royalists from France arrived and set up plantations in New Orleans and St. Martinville, Louisiana. The second named became so sophisticated as a result that it was long called "Petit Paris," and many of its present-day inhabitants pride themselves on their noble descent. Within the boundaries of the United States, the emigres arrived in all the major ports: Boston, New York (where the saintly black barber Toussaint arrived with a French family), Philadelphia, Wilmington (where settled the famed du Pont de Nemours clan), Baltimore, Charleston, and Savannah all received French emigres who at once refined manners in their places of refuge and either reinforced or introduced Catholicism there. Such towns as Gallipolis, Ohio were founded specifically as refuges for the French.

With these layfolk came also a flock of clerics, among whom were such names renowned in Catholic history as Bruté, Flaget, and Cheverus. To them do we owe the rapid extension of the Church into frontier territories—not merely to the French-speaking settlements in the old

Northwest, but also to the extensive ones in Kentucky settled by Marylanders. Under their aegis, the anti-Roman spirit of Carroll was for a time diluted.

However unfortunate their uprooting was to themselves, the presence of these exiles in America was an unmixed blessing. But still the United States had to adopt some attitude toward the French Republic, which, having declared war against both altar and throne, was soon embroiled with Great Britain, Spain, Prussia, Austria, Russia, and various other lands, in a series of conflicts which would not end until 1815, at Waterloo.

The United States were allied to France by the 1778 treaty. Yet strong trade links with Britain had been reestablished, and many of the Federalists deplored the atheistic, anti-aristocratic, and anti-property aspects of the new regime. The dilemma was solved in 1793, when Washington, on his own authority, issued a proclamation of neutrality. This aroused great annoyance on the part of the Democratic-Republicans, who favored the ideals of the Jacobins, and who saw the European conflict as an excuse to seize Spanish territory. From this time, the two parties were in open opposition to one another, particularly as Jefferson resigned from the cabinet in protest at Washington's French policy. So the origin of our party system may in reality be set at the feet of the French Revolutionaries.

Rebellion and Diplomacy

While the new federal taxes were accepted in most places with little complaint, they were bitterly resented in western Pennsylvania, where the manufacture of whisky in home stills was an important source of income to the Scotch-Irish farmers of the area, who often had no other profitable means of disposing of their grain. After a few years of building resentment, a group of these farmers armed themselves, threatened the revenue agents, and refused to pay the tax. Washington ordered federal troops dispatched to the area, and the rebellion was crushed. The new government had shown it could resist internal insurrection. Yet it was ironic that the government's troops were led by officers who a mere two decades before had themselves been rebels.

Nevertheless, relations with Great Britain were steadily improving. On November 19, 1794 John Jay signed in London a "Treaty of Amity, Commerce, and Navigation" with the British. This provided for a settlement of certain financial claims the British had remaining against the United States, in return for which they at last evacuated the posts on American soil which they had occupied for so long.

The next year saw another treaty signed, this time with Spain. Under its provisions, Spain recognized the American claims in northern West Florida, and agreed to evacuate all posts in the formerly disputed territory (although Natchez, Mississippi, for example, remained in Spanish hands until 1798). Even more importantly, however, the right of free navigation on the Mississippi and deposit at the port of New Orleans was conceded to the Americans.

Washington's second term was crowned with admission in 1796 of Tennessee as the 16th state. But the "Father of His Country" was disgusted by and fearful of the increasingly nasty tone of debate between Federalists and Democratic-Republicans. In addition, he was getting older and his health was failing. He resolved to retire to Mount Vernon, and on September 18, 1797 delivered his farewell address. In this speech, he warned against both foreign entanglements and political factionalism —advice generally ignored by his successors. In the ensuing election, John Adams garnered the larger number of electoral votes and the presidency, with Jefferson coming up second, and so becoming vice president.

The Adams Administration

John Adams had a very large set of shoes to fill, and a set of problems which daunted even his great predecessor. The Terror in France had made its mark on public, especially Federalist, opinion. Democratic Republicans were very vocal in their support of the French Revolutionaries in their attempts to conquer all Europe, spearheaded by a newly famous General, Napoleon Bonaparte. Further, while many of the new immigrants came to this country to escape the revolutions in Europe, others came to foment strife here. How to deal with a threat which had sunk so many older and stronger countries in blood?

Adams had the Alien and Sedition Laws passed through a Federalist dominated Congress as frightened of upheaval as he was. The Alien Act permitted the president to expel from the United States any foreigner he thought dangerous to the United States; the Sedition Act forbade any criticism of the President or Congress, and under its provisions a few newspaper editors were jailed. Although they provoked a hysterical reaction in many quarters and cost the Federalists a number of supporters, they were in fact the mildest national security measures ever adopted in the United States during a national emergency. It was a more innocent time.

Nevertheless, since the folk of those times could not foresee the future, many were enraged. The result were the Virginia and Kentucky Resolutions, co-authored by Jefferson and Madison. These declared that the Alien and Sedition Acts were void in the named states, being a violation of their sovereignty under the Constitution; these resolutions were in fact classic expositions of States' Rights theory.

Meanwhile, an undeclared naval war broke out with the French Revolutionaries on the high seas, adding to the general atmosphere of gloom, a gloom heightened by the death of Washington on December 14, 1799. There is a fairly well-known story that Washington converted to the Faith on his deathbed, being received by Fr. Leonard Neale, S.J. Let us hope it is true.

The election of 1800 saw the defeat of Adams by Jefferson, and the filling of the Vice-Presidency by Aaron Burr, the runner-up. The election of Jefferson was felt by the most extreme Federalists to presage the fall of this country into the horrors of the French Revolution. But although these fears went unfulfilled, enough changes would result from it that the name "Revolution of 1800" is justified.

On November 22, 1800, Congress met for the first time at Washington, in a capitol as yet uncompleted. As one of his last acts, John Adams appointed *John Marshall* as Chief Justice of the Supreme Court. A Federalist loose constructionist, Marshall would continue to hand down decisions based upon his and Adams' shared philosophy of law for the next thirty-four years while the Federalist party withered, died, and at last vanished from memory. But as we shall see, he made the Supreme Court what it was until the middle of this century, and served longer than any other Chief Justice.

The Failure of the Federalists

Although no one knew it at the time, the inauguration of Jefferson on March 4, 1801 spelled the end of the Federalists. They would continue on as an ever-diminishing minority for the next fifteen years, but they would not be an effective force again (although their ghost would continue on the Supreme Court). It will be instructive to look at the reasons for their failure.

On the surface, part of their problem was simply in being the party of strong government. It was one thing to boast that they were the men of experience, an aristocracy, in the sense of a ruling class by virtue of being better at ruling. But what if the Democratic-Republicans in office should in the end prove as or more successful than they were themselves?

From a Catholic point of view, it is rather a complex thing to try to determine which of the two was the party most in accord with the Church's teaching; both had good elements and ideas; both had bad ones; both were dedicated to a system basically in conflict with the social doctrines of the Church.

Subsidiarity is one of the most basic of these last. It is the belief that in governance, acts are best carried out by the smallest unit capable of doing so. In Catholic Europe, this meant that, in ascending order, the parishes (in a civil sense), the bailiwicks, and the provinces of the different kingdoms, with their parallel religious hierarchies of abbots, bishops and archbishops, and noble ones of barons, counts, dukes, and so forth, all administered affairs to the height of their capacity. To the King was reserved the ultimate appeal in justice, war and foreign affairs, roads and posts, and certain forests and waters. Centralizing tendencies on the part of various Kings played a large part in the Reformation, and the French Revolutionaries perfected it in the "One and Indivisible Republic." So it was that the opposition to them, as in Tyrol and the Vendee, demanded their local liberties back, along with their Church and King. The same was true in the 19th and early 20th centuries of the Legitimists in France, the Carlists in Spain, the Miguelists in Portugal, and of course the opponents of Bismarck and Cavour in the German and Italian states.

In American terms, the closest that we may come to subsidiarity under the religious, economic, social, and political conditions which have prevailed from 1783 to the present is States' Rights. So in this aspect, the Democratic-Republicans, when they remained true to their stated platform (which as we will see did not always happen—for good as for ill—when they were in power) were correct, and the Federalists were wrong.

But as regards their views on the French Revolution, we must change sides. For the Federalists believed it to be evil, and Democratic-Republicans supported it. So great was the horror of the Federalists at the atrocities in France, that it even caused some of them to reexamine their attitudes toward the Catholic Faith. In a sermon of July 4, 1798, the rigid Calvinist minister and president of Yale, Timothy Dwight, among many charges against the Jacobins listed: "2. The overthrow of the religious orders in Catholic countries, a step essentially necessary to the destruction of the religion professed in those countries." While the truth of the statement had always been maintained by his co-religionists, its denunciation as a crime if put into practice would have been unthinkable a decade or two before, when all New England would have considered it "a consummation devoutly to be wished."

But the realities of revolution led by others (as opposed to that led by themselves) forced many to think more sensibly on political topics than they had while engaged in rebellion against King George. *Fisher Ames*, for example, one of the most brilliant Federalists, wrote in 1805:

The people, as a body, cannot deliberate. Nevertheless, they will feel an irresistible impulse to act, and their resolutions will be dictated to them by their demagogues. The consciousness, or the opinion, that they possess the supreme power will inspire inordinate passions; and the violent men, who are the most forward to gratify those passions, will be their favorites. What is called the government of the people is in fact too often the arbitrary power of such men.

This is in fact an analysis which, while perhaps strange to Catholics of today, is perfectly in keeping with the Church's traditional teaching on the point. Compare these words of Pius VI in his allocution of July 17, 1793, *Pourquoi Nôtre Voix*:

The most Christian King, Louis XVI, was condemned to death by an impious conspiracy and this judgment was carried out. We shall recall to you in a few words the ordering and motives of this sentence. The National Convention had no right or authority to pronounce it. In fact, after having abolished the monarchy, *the best of all governments*, it had transferred all the public power to the people—the people which, guided neither by reason nor by counsels, forms just ideas on no point whatsoever, assesses few things in accordance with the truth and evaluates a great many according to mere opinion, which is ever fickle, and ever easy to deceive and to lead into every excess, ungrateful, arrogant, and cruel...(cap. 2).

Very similar, indeed. The Pope's words, and others like them, brought forth reactions from Catholics of all classes throughout France and the rest of Europe. When his peasant tenants came to his chateau in 1793, d'Elbée, soon to be renowned as a key leader of the Vendee revolt, told them:

My children, you know I have never deceived you; and I shall not deceive you now in this most important matter. The revolution is a fact: it will not, it cannot be undone. It will devour all that is good in France; and our efforts can be but feeble against a power which strengthens every day. I am ready to die for God and my King; but I will not command men who are not worthy of being martyrs. Go back for this night to your cottages; reflect that an act of yours may set them on fire, and ruin your families; and weigh well what I have said to you. Tomorrow morning come back again, if God inspires you with courage to die; and then I will go with you.

Thus spoke a Catholic aristocrat; an eminent realist, who nevertheless shared the sentiments of Pius VI, and presumably, Fisher Ames. But what did the eminent Mr. Ames think was the proper course of action, given the principles he held? Replying to the attack by his logically-minded Democratic-Republican opponents that ideological Federalists must be Monarchists, he wrote in the essay earlier quoted:

> It will weigh nothing in the argument with some persons, but with men of sense it will be conclusive, that the mass of the Federalists are the owners of the commercial and moneyed wealth of the nation. Is it conceivable that such men will plot a revolution in favor of monarchy, a revolution that would make them beggars as well as traitors if it should miscarry; and if it should succeed ever so well, would require a century to take root and acquire stability enough to ensure justice and protect property?

Here then, was the difference between Catholic counter-revolutionary and Protestant conservative; the one saw the battle with the Revolution as a fight of good against evil, truth against falsehood, and so a struggle worth any price; the latter saw in it merely a conflict between prudence and good sense on the one hand, and anarchy and demagoguery on the other. For this last-named, surely submission was wiser than resistance to the last? This has been the recipe for English speaking conservatives in the British Isles since the Jacobite cause went down to defeat at Culloden, and on these shores either since the last Tory went to Canada or Lee surrendered at Appomattox. One may die for a principle, but never for an opinion. The Federalists, alas, had only opinions.

There is a reason for this, however. It is a maxim that all political questions are in essence religious. Although the Federalists often invoked the language of Christianity to bolster their arguments against the supposedly "Godless" Democratic-Republicans, their leadership often had precisely the same opinions as their opponents. This we have seen with John Adams and Jefferson. But this was true of many lesser ranking Federalist potentates as well. A typical case was Theodore Sedgwick, the biggest man in Berkshire County, Massachusetts. As recounted by David Hackett Fischer:

> The means by which Sedgwick controlled his county ought not to be confused with the methods of a modern party machine. The principal prop beneath his power was the habit of deference in the people. It was slipping, as Shays' Rebellion showed, but not yet down. Every act of Sedgwick's was designed to buttress it. Firstly, he sought to strengthen "the influence of numerous connexions formed into a phalanx by family compact," as Jefferson described it. Sedgwicks, Dwights, Van Schaights, Worthingtons, Masons, and Sergeants were intertwined in one extended cousinage, one "union of political influence" which allowed of no alternative to "rule by the wise and the good."

Secondly, Sedgwick endeavored to promote "good order" in Berkshire County by means of an alliance with the established Congregational Church. Though he personally found Unitarianism attractive, his heresy remained a closely guarded secret until he made a deathbed confession to William Ellery Channing.
(*The Revolution of American Conservatism*, pp. 13-14)

There is the problem in a nutshell. Of what did Sedgwick's Conservatism consist? Loyalty to his sect? No, this was a mere hypocritical ploy to maintain "good order," whatever that might be. Loyalty to his King? Although he was, in Mr. Fischer's words, "a most reluctant rebel," "Doubts and mental reservations notwithstanding, Sedgwick committed himself unequivocally to the Whig cause." Yet how can an aristocrat who is loyal neither to his God nor his King call himself wise or good? It is a conundrum, but one may be sure that Sedgwick himself felt very idealistic indeed, while pursuing naked self interest—in which he shows he was a typical human being.

But the point here is that to succeed, a political party or faction requires a spirit of self-sacrifice. That is something which the Federalists, in common with many American "conservatives" since, lacked entirely. The more idealistic of them continued to enjoy their positions in local society, all the while denouncing their opponents futilely; the more pragmatic became Democratic-Republicans in order to "change the party from within." Whatever the case, the result was the same. The Federalists lost out to the Democratic-Republicans for one major reason. No matter how hotly they denounced them, or how much hatred they felt for them, they were in all that mattered identical to them—simply not as good at it as the Democratic-Republicans were. In the final analysis, that has been the story of the two parties ever since.

THE REVOLUTION OF 1800

When Thomas Jefferson took the oath of office on March 4, 1801, radicals rejoiced and conservatives darkly prophesied. Both were doomed to disappointment. For Jefferson although an opponent of the powers the Federalists had acquired for the government when they were in control, was only too glad to retain and even extend them when he was President himself. He supported the use of Federal money for the building of roads and canals to bind the regions of the country more tightly together, a policy which, continued by his successors, led to the rapid settlement of the West.

An example of this may be found in Ohio. The present state of Ohio had become a sort of refuge for many tribes (like the Delaware) driven from the East. Together with Indians already resident, such as the Shawnee, they were a powerful impediment in the way of western settlement. War broke out between them and the ever-encroaching settlers in 1790, and in the following two years they inflicted two crushing defeats on the American army. But in 1794, they were in turn defeated by the energetic veteran, "Mad" Anthony Wayne, at the battle of Fallen Timbers. The next year, the associated tribes signed an agreement with the United States, ceding most of southern and central Ohio to the government. Settlers from New England and the Pennsylvania Dutch country poured in via the opening trails, and by 1802, Ohio had a large enough population to be admitted as the 17th state. Western expansion was a large part of Mr. Jefferson's program.

Of course, he did make certain cosmetic bows to his principles. The court etiquette of the Federalist regime in the President's Palace was done away with. The Alien and Sedition Acts were repealed, as was the Internal Revenue measure that so annoyed the whisky producers. Jefferson never let an opportunity go by without praising the "common man."

Above all, his antagonism to the Federalists was most obvious in his dealing with the judiciary. Just prior to leaving office, Adams had appointed many "midnight judges." Jefferson instructed Madison, his Secretary of State, not to grant the commissions of several of these. One of them, William Marbury, asked the Supreme Court for a court order which would force the government to render the commission. Finding for Marbury in 1803, Chief Justice Marshall established the doctrine of judicial review, under which the Supreme Court has decided whether or not laws brought before it are valid or "Constitutional." Marshall declared that:

> The constitution is either a superior paramount law, unchangeable by ordinary means, or it is on a level with ordinary acts, and, like other acts, is alterable when the legislature shall please to alter it.
>
> If the former part of the alternative be true, then a legislative act contrary to the constitution is not law...
>
> It is emphatically the province and duty of the judicial department to say what the law is. Those who apply the rule to particular cases must of necessity expound and interpret that rule. If two laws conflict with each other, the courts must decide on the interpretation of each.

From that day to this, the Supreme Court has made judicial review its greatest privilege; indeed, it is now what most Americans think of as its primary function. But it is important to remember that while today (as in the case of abortion) Supreme Court decisions are held not merely to determine constitutionality but also intrinsic morality, it was not always so. There is nothing in the Constitution to warrant it.

The Louisiana Purchase

However unconstitutional Jefferson may have thought Marshall's decision, he was able to equal it in his action in buying the French colony of Louisiana that same year.

Spain had been defeated by France under Bonaparte. As part of the Treaty of San Idelfonso in 1800, Spain agreed to give Louisiana back to France. As Bonaparte was engaged in trying to reconquer Saint Domingue at the time, he planned to use Louisiana as a source of food for the highly profitable sugar colony Saint Domingue would become once again, after he subdued its rebellious blacks. But two years of fighting had failed to do so, and when he went to war with Britain once again in 1802, the military and naval supplies and troops (to say nothing of free use of the sea lanes to transport them) essential to eventual reconquest of the island had to be employed elsewhere. He would never be able to use Louisiana. Worse, the British might feel compelled to seize it themselves, and Napoleon had no real means of defending it.

Meanwhile, Jefferson was very intent on gaining control of the city of New Orleans and the Floridas (which remained Spanish; Louisiana also had not been officially transferred to France). He opened negotiations with Napoleon on the topic of acquiring New Orleans and whatever claims France might have in West Florida. Needless to say, this was not provided for in the Constitution. Nevertheless, Jefferson felt it imperative for the country's long-range development. Moreover, American frontiersmen were moving into Louisiana; swearing allegiance to the Spanish Crown, of course, but taking their oaths as lightly as did their fathers their oaths to the British Crown at the time of the revolution. Jefferson was astounded when, instead of just New Orleans, Napoleon offered the whole of Louisiana for $15,000,000. The President bought, and on December 20, 1803, the Stars and Stripes were hoisted in New Orleans' *place d'armes.* Creoles wept, and the French commissioner, Laussat, burst into tears, saying "What a magnificent New France we have lost."

Indeed they had. But just what had Jefferson bought? The boundaries of Louisiana were very unsure; except for the island of Orleans upon which the city itself sits, the boundary of the territory to the east was the Mississippi. On the north and west, it was supposed to include all the lands drained by the great river and its tributaries. But as much of this was unexplored, no one really knew quite where Louisiana's frontiers really were. More than this, Jefferson claimed that the purchase entitled the U.S. not only to this large territory, but to West Florida, Texas, and the Oregon country, thus bringing the country into land disputes not merely with Spain but with Great Britain and Russia also. But wherever the truth might lie, the area that was indisputably American doubled the size of the country at one stroke. Within this vast area were forests and prairies, rivers and the Rockies.

Settlement in this realm was quite varied. New Orleans itself was the equal of any European city in terms of sophistication; the city's Creole and emigre inhabitants had perfected the art of living to a degree unequaled anywhere on the continent outside the walls of Quebec. The public worship of the Church, balls, fine wines and food, music, literature, indeed, all that makes life pleasant were found there in a degree unknown to the United States, save perhaps those ports where the French emigres had already begun their work. It is also true that the city suffered from recurrent bouts of yellow fever, filthy streets and various other ills; but the city's flaws were as much common property to cities of that day as its virtues were its own. Then as now, the graceful Spanish architecture of what was then the whole of the city and is now the Vieux Carré was unequaled.

Apart from the town of St. Martinville, the bayous and prairies nearest New Orleans were the domain of Acadian refugees. Much simpler than their Creole neighbors, they were strongly attached to their religion and way of life. Subsisting in isolation, their gentle demeanor and friendly acceptance of outsiders led them, until the pressures of assimilation after World War I began to take their toll, to absorb the outsiders who came their way. So today such un-French names as Schnexnayder and Abshire are considered as "Cajun" as Broussard and Hebert.

Up the river, in places like Arkansas Post and the Missouri towns of Ste. Genevieve, St. Louis, and St. Charles, attempts were made by the Creoles there to live with some of the *joie de vivre* their cousins maintained in New Orleans. There too, and everywhere the rivers extended in Louisiana, Creoles were joined by French Canadian trappers and traders, who carried both the French language and the Catholic faith ever further into the interior. By this means, several tribes received a preparation for the Gospel which later missionaries like Fr. De Smet would benefit from.

What would have happened if the Louisiana territory had remained in French or Spanish hands? We cannot know. But surely the easy manner of living and intense piety which even today can be found in the southern parishes of Louisiana would extend throughout the center of nation; instead of being repeatedly moved and massacred, the Indians of those region might well have become, as Fr. De Smet wished, the inhabitants of something like the mission state of Paraguay.

In any case, Jefferson and his cronies had little but contempt for the Creoles (as the President's hatred for their religion would make obvious). Although the Treaty of Cession obliged the Americans to give the inhabitants of Louisiana the same rights as their new fellow-citizens, Jefferson opined that they were "as yet as incapable of self-government as children." As a result, in March of 1804, when the purchase was divided in two (along the present Louisiana-Arkansas boundary), the southern Territory of Orleans, although specifically indicated as a possible future state, was denied any sort of self-government. The northern District of Louisiana, being primarily Indian territory, was not to become a state. So a people of immense culture were deprived of any political voice, while the hordes of illiterate frontiersmen who soon poured in had the rights of citizens. Apparently Jefferson had forgotten the words he had written so long before in the Declaration, about the "just consent of the governed."

Immediately, Jefferson began fomenting trouble for the Spanish in West Florida, inciting various of their Anglo-American subjects to rebel, so as to be able to send in American troops to "restore order." Luckily, the Spanish had been able to suppress these without too much difficulty. But Spain also retained the post of Los Adaes east of the Sabine river in present day Louisiana, where lived a number of Spanish settlers and their Apache and Choctaw Indian allies. In 1806, Jefferson resolved to expel them. His Governor, William Claiborne, was all too aware that if war broke out between the Spanish and the Americans the disenfranchised Creoles would side with the Spanish. But he was able to outbluff the Spanish commander, and their troops withdrew into Texas.

Diplomacy Elsewhere

Meanwhile, events overseas also took a great deal of Jefferson's attention. For several centuries the Barbary pirates of North Africa had taken slaves during raids on remote parts of Ireland and Iceland, and had bedeviled the shipping of European nations. Usually they were bought off from time to time with tribute. But the Americans refused to pay, and so found themselves involved in difficulties with the Pasha of Tripoli in 1804. In reprisal, Jefferson dispatched a force of 7 marines under a Captain O'Bannon to assist a pretender to the throne in unseating the Pasha. The result of the war was a treaty with Tripoli in 1805, and the presentation of a scimitar to O'Bannon. Since then, U.S. Marine officers have carried similar weapons, called today "Mameluke swords."

At the same time, Britain and France from time to time in the course of their fighting one another would molest American ships and occasionally impress American sailors into their service. Things rose to a head after Jefferson's reelection in 1805. In 1806, the British forbade any ships to enter ports held by Napoleon; he in turn forbade any trading with Great Britain. American merchants thus fell between two stools. An attack by the British on an American ship in 1807 led to a total embargo on all trade with foreign nations; this act was passed by Congress on December 22, 1807.

The Embargo continued in full force until March 15, 1809, when it was repealed except with regard to France and Britain themselves. In that time, the American economy foundered. From Portland to New Orleans, ships and cargoes rotted at the docks. It soon became apparent that, despite the United States being the last best hope of mankind, the rest of mankind were somehow able to struggle on without them. But the Embargo did have the result of reviving for a time the Federalists, who at last had an issue. But the promise of James Madison to loosen the Embargo were he elected took even that from them. Thus, on March 4, 1809, James Madison was duly sworn in, and the Embargo duly ended 11 days later.

President Madison—Empire Builder

There were two major concerns facing Madison: foreign trade and national expansion. The first primarily revolved around the activities of the French and British warships. In 1810, the French swore off poaching American ships, and the Embargo was lifted as regarded them. But it was reaffirmed for Great Britain on February 2, 1811.

While all of this was underway, events in Spain were going from bad to worse. Napoleon on March 17, 1808 compelled both Charles IV and his son Ferdinand VII to abdicate the throne of Spain, whereupon he placed his brother Joseph on the throne. A revolt broke out almost immediately, and a parliament gathered in Seville which declared itself loyal to Ferdinand VII. In Spain's Empire, local officials were forced to choose between the two sides, shipments of arms and money from the motherland were cut off, and rebellions for or against Ferdinand broke out. In 1810, for example, the priest Hidalgo in Mexico led a bloody rising against the Spanish. While eventually suppressed, it had the effect (due to the blockade the rebels imposed on the Mexican port of San Blas) of isolating California from the rest of the Spanish world for eleven years. The Spanish officials and garrisons carried on, supported by the missionaries and rancheros there.

In the Floridas, so close to a United States which coveted them, and filled as they were becoming with American settlers, the situation was very dangerous. At last, on August 13, 1810, a convention of American settlers in Baton Rouge declared itself in charge of the district. They were in touch with Madison through the governor of the Mississippi Territory. On September 24, the conspirators seized the fort in Baton Rouge, captured the Governor, and three days later sent to Washington a "declaration of independence" detaching themselves from Spain and asking to be annexed to the United States. On October 27, Madison directed Claiborne to take control of Baton Rouge. From that time on, the area has been known as the "Florida Parishes" of Louisiana. This method having worked so well, Madison, leaving the Spanish in Mobile and Pensacola unmolested for the moment, turned his attention to East Florida and its capital of St. Augustine.

After Spain took control of East Florida from the British, the area between its northern boundary—the St. Mary's River—and St. Augustine began to fill up with settlers of various nationalities, all of whom took the oath to His Most Catholic Majesty (as indeed did the West Florida settlers). The northernmost port of Florida, Fernadina, had become very wealthy in assisting Americans to evade the Embargo. There Madison's stroke fell.

In March of 1811, a group of American irregulars took Fernadina, overpowering its nine-man garrison. Declaring the Republic of East Florida, they set off to conquer St. Augustine. The Americans first took Moosa, the site of a settlement of Catholic free blacks which had been destroyed by Oglethorpe in 1740. Proceeding to the walls of St. Augustine, they demanded that the Spanish surrender. The latter refused, and so the besiegers settled down. For over a year this situation continued. But as relations with Britain grew rockier (and Canada appeared more tempting), Madison decided to disavow the East Florida situation—particularly after Spanish reinforcements broke the siege in June of 1812.

After the War of 1812 broke out, the Spanish armed the Creek and Seminole Indians, and the many blacks who had fled slavery to go to Florida. Although the Americans duly occupied Mobile and Biloxi in 1812, reducing Florida to its present boundaries, and though the East Florida conflict eventually merged into the War of 1812, the rebels were eventually cleared out. Florida would remain Spanish for a few more years.

War with Britain

While Madison was busy with grabbing what Spanish territory he could, yet another Indian organizer in the tradition of King Philip and

Pontiac had arisen. He was the Shawnee chief, Tecumseh. Organizing a confederation of Western tribes that stretched from the Canadian to the Spanish borders, he had also the support of the British. While in 1811 the governor of Indiana Territory, William Henry Harrison, defeated him at the battle of Tippecanoe, he merely withdrew into Canada and bided his time.

At the same time, the clamor in Congress for war with Britain among the *Warhawks,* a group of young congressmen led by *Henry Clay* and *John C. Calhoun* grew ever more strident. They were not concerned with the continuing impressment problem, but thought it would serve as a good pretext to seize Canada.

At that time, Canada was made up largely of two very different groups: the French Canadians and the Loyalists who had been expelled from the United States. As these two groups were quite different from one another, and generally did not get along well, the two provinces of Ontario (shorn off Quebec) and New Brunswick (taken from Nova Scotia) were created to accommodate the English speakers. The supposed disunity of the two groups would, so the warhawks thought, make the invasion of Canada easy.

They were wrong. After war was declared on April 4, 1812, an invasion of Canada was mounted. It ended sooner than it began. The British with Tecumseh seized Detroit, and the American troops refused to leave Ft. Niagara. The next year the U.S. won control of Lake Erie, but lost the Niagara forts. Nevertheless, control of the lake allowed the Americans to burn the Canadian capital of York (now Toronto). An attempt to take Montreal was foiled at Chateauguay by the gallant Colonel de Salaberry and a handful of French-Canadian militia. The British blockaded the Atlantic ports. On the other hand, Tecumseh was killed at the Battle of the Thames. This noble character, who had early distinguished himself by risking his life to prevent the slaughter of captives, by Indian custom, was an enormous loss both to the British and to the Indians. But his allies the Creeks carried war to the Americans in the South, only to come up against one of the most remarkable figures America has produced: General *Andrew Jackson*. After defeating the hostile Creeks, he stripped both them and those who had fought for the United States of an enormous amount of acreage in Alabama. In this, of course, he was following the example of his commander in chief; after all—had not Spain been our ally too?

But 1814 also saw a great disaster befall American arms. A British fleet sailed up the Chesapeake. One column sailed off to attack Baltimore, the other Washington. Baltimore was preserved through the refusal of Ft. McHenry to surrender (an event witnessed, as everyone knows, by Francis Scott Key. So inspired by the event was he that he wrote the *Star Spangled Banner* to commemorate it. The tune he used was that jolly old drinking song *To Anacreon in Heaven*. Where the national anthem has, "O say does that star-spangled banner yet wave, o'er the land of the free and the home of the brave," the original says, "And so I will teach you like me to entwine, the myrtle of Venus with Bacchus' vine"). Washington did not fare so well. Four thousand American troops met the British at Bladensburg; all ran save 400 Marines, who were overwhelmed. When the British burned Washington in reprisal for the burning of York the previous year (one good capital deserves another, so to speak), they left untouched the house of the Commandant of the Marine Corps as a tribute to Marine valor at Bladensburg. In any case, Dolly Madison fled the President's Palace with a portrait of Washington (when she returned to the burnt-out shell, she had the building white-washed, hence the present name of White House).

All this time, New England had been left to shift for itself. Between the Embargo and the War, the region's economy had been ruined. To save themselves, the New England states sent representatives to Hartford, Connecticut to discuss secession from the Union. As Madison was driven by these calamities to seek peace, so too were the British, exhausted by years of struggle against Napoleon. A peace treaty was signed at Ghent on December 24, 1814, leaving all issues of contention basically undecided.

Unhappily, the news did not reach the New World in time to prevent the Battle of New Orleans, which raged around New Year's of 1815. General Jackson was able to repel an attempted British invasion—which, had it succeeded would have meant nothing as the treaty obligated Britain to withdraw from all U.S. territory. But nevertheless, the victory of Jackson, with his scratch force of militia, regulars, Creoles (who, having become outnumbered were entrusted with statehood in 1812), and Laffitte's pirates, was nothing short of miraculous. The people of the Crescent City have always regarded the victory as being due to the intercession of Our Lady of Prompt Succor. It was well for Jackson that he had so many pious Creoles praying for his victory—otherwise, what interest would Heaven take in a conflict between infidel armies?

By 1815, the United States were indeed a nation with an identity of their own. Much of the credit for this must go to Jefferson and Madison. But in the end, how must we evaluate them? Joseph Burkholder Smith gives a fair estimate in his account of the Florida plotting:

> Thomas Jefferson and his two disciples, James Madison and James Monroe, were promoted to the pantheon of the Founding Fathers, the American nationalist religion's temple, while all of them still lived. To

bolster this status, sculptors of the time portrayed them in the costumes of ancient Rome...

As for telling the truth to the American people, all three were Olympian when writing political philosophy. When running the government, their regard for the niceties of frank communication was Nixonian.

So it was, so it has been.

ADOLESCENT AMERICA
1816-1848

THE NATION IN 1816

The end of the War of 1812 found these United States greatly divided. New England merchants had received two great financial blows. The first was the abolition of the Slave Trade in 1808. As the human cargo was generally transported to America in New England ships, the loss of such profitable commerce was considerable, although some continued it secretly. On the other hand, the way was paved for New Englanders to eventually feel moral superiority to the South.

The second was the British blockade during the War of 1812. Cut off from British and other textiles, many New England merchants were forced to open cloth factories of their own, which continued after the war. Within ten years after the peace, the region was well on its way to becoming a great industrial center. This was to have several important effects.

The mass migration of Yankee farmers to the Ohio country commencing after the Revolution depopulated New England's countryside; just at the time when a large cheap labor force was needed, it vanished. The result was that factory owners had to look overseas and to French Canada for workers. Their migration would, within a century, completely transform the area from a Puritan stronghold to a numerically Catholic one (although the Puritan imprint on local culture would never be uprooted; the immigrants would conform to it instead).

A particularly fateful effect was that this change from trade to manufacturing would put New England into direct conflict with the South. Before, Yankee politicians had opposed any tariffs which would restrict the free flow of profits to and from Boston, Salem, and the area's other ports. Despite the development of Whaling and the China Trade, when the economy shifted, regional politicians came to support high tariffs as a way to protect their products from foreign competition. Such profits for Boston, however, could only mean losses for the South, forced to rely on more expensive New England manufactured goods essential to the Southern plantation economy (which could not make such things for itself). Beyond this, the beginnings of New England's industrialization marks a development which would lead not only to Northern dominance over the South but in time would propel the United States to the position of most powerful nation in the world.

The South, in the meantime, continued to develop its unique culture. Unlike New England, the Southern states were geographically able to expand their way of life directly into the western frontier. As a result, Southern politicians tended to favor territorial expansion toward the Pacific. For the continuance of their economy, they required a flow of cheap manufactured goods; low tariffs would ensure this. The Southerners were therefore more than a little suspicious of Federal power.

The Middle States, sitting between the first two areas and blessed with the harbors of New York City and Philadelphia, had the potential for real wealth. This area serving also as natural outlets for the West's trade, their politicians were anxious for national roads and canals which would make such travel easier. Already, their merchants had acquired a great deal of local power. But in 1816, New York and Pennsylvania were still slave states, and very much dominated by the agricultural oligarchies which had run them since settlement.

The West was being settled fast. Mississippi was admitted in 1817, Illinois the next year, and Alabama the year after that. Pioneers both from Europe and the East filled up land as quickly as the Indians could be moved off of it. As might be expected, the latter were none too pleased at the prospect.

The election of 1816 brought in James Monroe and sealed the end of the Federalist Party; for the next eight years all the major figures in American politics would belong to the Democratic Republicans. This period would go down in history as *The Era of Good Feelings*.

Where Spain had been a real opponent prior to the French Revolution, her American possessions had been severely shaken by local revolts and occupation of the homeland by the French. Florida had been repeatedly invaded and portions shorn off by American forces. Some American settlers were already arriving in Texas, and dreams were even now being dreamed of its annexation by the United States. Under the Americanist Archbishop of Baltimore, John Carroll, America's few Catholics were not too concerned about their Spanish co-religionists.

The States and Europe

The defeat of Napoleon at Waterloo in 1815 meant the restoration of the various dynasties in Europe to their thrones. Centering on the friendship of the Emperors of Austria and Russia, and the King of Prussia, *the Holy Alliance* eventually was joined by all the rulers on the continent save three: the Pope, because he could not ally with non-Catholics; the Prince-Regent of Great Britain (who nevertheless declared his agreement with the Alliance's principles); and the Sultan of Turkey, who would not join with Christians. Despite being initially suggested by the Tsar of Russia, the Alliance ultimately owed its origin to the writings of Catholic German lay theologian *Franz von Baader*.

The treaty which established it may be found in Appendix D[1]. From the Catholic point of view, there were a number of problems with the treaty. There was no mention of the Church of Christ; presumably Catholicism, heresy, and schism were all to have equal standing. The leading diplomats of the day, *Metternich, Castlereagh*, and others, all proclaimed it to be "sublime mysticism and nonsense."

Still, when all that can be said against the Alliance be said, there remains much in its favor. Whatever they may have thought privately, all Europe's sovereigns felt it necessary to sign. Such religious language had not been seen in a treaty since before the Reformation split Christendom—and the treaty's second article anticipated by over a century Pius XI's words in regard to the social Kingship of Christ in his 1925 encyclical, *Quas primas*.

Moreover, the Alliance signaled a desire for a return to the *Res Publica Christiana*, a Europe which was really one Christendom—united temporally as well as spiritually. It was supported not only by von Baader, but by all the best Catholic political writers of the era—*Joseph de Maistre, Chateaubriand, Louis de Bonald, Adam Müller, Karl von Haller*, and many more. Most significant of all were those who opposed the Alliance in Europe; it was universally hated by all who hated the Church. Secret societies took oaths against it, liberal politicians derided its principles.

Where stood these United States? In common with their ideological allies in Europe, most politicians and newspapermen in America condemned the Alliance as both Catholic and monarchical—a tool of tyranny. Moreover, the adherence of Spain to the Alliance appeared to mean that Spanish America would henceforth be not quite so easy to annex. Indeed, might not a revived Spain, assisted by the rest of Europe, attempt to regain her lost territories in Louisiana and West Florida? John Quincy Adams commented in 1817 on the revolts against the Spanish:

> The republican spirit of our country not only sympathizes with people struggling in a cause so nearly if not precisely the same which was once our own, but it is working into indignation against the relapse of Europe into the opposite principle of monkery and despotism (*Writings of John Quincy Adams*, vol. VI, p. 274).

Speaker of the House Henry Clay urged in May 1821:

---

[1] All of the Appendices may be accessed at:
http://www.tumblarhouse.com/puritans-empire-appendix.php

...that a sort of counterpoise to the Holy Alliance should be formed in the two Americas... to operate by the force of example and by moral influence, that here a rallying point and an asylum should exist for freemen and for freedom (*Papers of Henry Clay*, vol. III, p. 80).

It ought to be noted that both Clay and Adams were considered Conservatives in American terms.

Florida, Mexico, and the End of Spanish America

Whatever fears the Holy Alliance might raise in American hearts, the reality was that the Spanish edifice in the New World was tottering. In every way that they could, the United States encouraged the Latin American rebels. San Martin and Bolivar, leaders of the revolt in Argentina and Colombia respectively, considered themselves heirs of Washington and Jefferson. Like them, they were members of the area's Creole elites, who tended to support independence for the same reasons as did the colonial oligarchies in the 13 colonies. In many places (most notably Venezuela, Mexico, and Chile) the forces of the Spanish Crown were recruited extensively from the Blacks and Indians.

This was demonstrated by the first colony to declare independence: Venezuela. When the supreme Junta of Caracas threw off their allegiance to Spain on June 25, 1811, the Royalists at Valencia abolished slavery, and soon incorporated innumerable Blacks into their forces. Within a year the revolt had ended. But peace was short-lived.

The same year Paraguay revolted under the psychotic Jose Francia; in 1816 Argentina's elite led by San Martin pushed out the Spanish. Except for the frontier regions of Valdivia and Chiloe (loyal to Spain just as the backwoods Regulators had been to Britain in our revolution) in the south, Chile had fallen to the rebels in 1818. Bolivar succeeded in quashing Royalist resistance in Colombia, Ecuador, and Venezuela by 1819. Mexico and Peru (including Bolivia) remained loyal to Spain, even as they were the first colonized. Attached to the former was Florida:

> The Spanish position in Florida was totally untenable after the War of 1812. Deserted by the British and incapable of defending—much less administering—the Florida province, the Spanish played a waiting game. They had long since identified the man intent on their expulsion. Andrew Jackson was only the latest in a long series of conspirators who lusted after Spanish possessions. And they were quite convinced—correctly so—that he was prepared to sweep across the Gulf from Florida to Texas and then to Mexico. Other Americans had had such

dreams of empire, but Jackson, with his demonstrated military skills, was the man who could realize them.

So the Spanish waited, watched, and wrote hundreds of reports that were copied and recopied but generated nothing in the way of action to protect a crumbling empire. The first move belonged to the Americans. What pretext would trigger that move and incite Jackson and his troops into crashing into Florida the Spanish pondered and wrung their hands over. (Robert W. Remini, *Andrew Jackson and the Course of American Empire*, p. 344).

The Spanish had given refuge both to runaway slaves and broken remnants of Indian tribes (the latter eventually coalescing into the Seminoles) from the United States. These would in turn revisit their former enemies to the north, raiding and pillaging, which actions the Spanish were powerless to restrain. This came to a head with the First Seminole War. On January 22, 1818, Jackson invaded Florida.

In the course of pursuing the Seminoles, Jackson seized the Spanish fort at St. Mark's on April 6. Using it as a base, he defeated the Seminoles, and then executed two British traders he accused of supplying the Indians. On May 24, he pushed on and took Pensacola, seat of government in West Florida. He then established an American military government for the region. The War in South America going poorly, the Spanish bowed to what appeared inevitable, and sold Florida on February 22, 1819. The treaty also established the border between Louisiana and New Spain. The Stars and Stripes rose over St. Augustine.

Meanwhile, as earlier noted, Bolivar succeeded in conquering Colombia, Ecuador, and Venezuela. While Mexico, Peru and Bolivia remained firm, both Bolivar and San Martin showed every intent of conquering them. King Ferdinand VII ordered a large army to be sent to the New World in 1820 to defeat the rebels (up to this time, the King had had to rely primarily on local Royalists). But during the Napoleonic Wars, Masonic lodges had been especially formed to propagate liberal ideas among army officers. When the army was assembled to send to America, its officers mutinied, and declared in favor of a liberal constitution, which among other things was anti-clerical. Ferdinand was forced to accept it.

The generality of Mexicans refused the constitution, and the commander of the Spanish army in Mexico, General *Agustin de Iturbide* united with General Vicente Guerrero, commander of the insurgents (what remained of revolutionary forces launched by Fr. Hidalgo in 1810), in declaring the independence of Mexico. Thus, unlike the rest of Latin America, where independence came as the result of direct assaults on altar and throne by men like Bolivar, it was brought about in Mexico to defend them.

Iturbide and Guerrero produced on February 24, 1821 the Plan of Iguala (from the town where it was proclaimed). This plan had three guarantees: 1) Mexico was to be an independent monarchy—under a Spanish or some other European prince; 2) Native and foreign-born Spanish were to be equal; and 3) Catholicism was to be the religion of the state and no others were to be tolerated. The following August 24, the Viceroy, Don Juan O'Donoju surrendered, and Mexico became an independent empire. No European prince would accept the throne, however, and so Iturbide became Emperor Agustin I on May 19, 1822.

But influences from the north opposed the idea of a Catholic Mexican Empire; these inspired certain elements to back *Antonio Lopez de Santa Ana* against Agustin, who was deposed on March 19, 1823, and went into exile. He returned a year later, attempted unsuccessfully to regain the throne, and was executed. The next year saw the appointment of Joel Poinsett as first American Consul in Mexico.

In this country, Poinsett is remembered as the importer of Poinsettia, which is so much a part of our Christmas celebrations. But in Mexico he is recalled as the originator of "Poinsettismo," as the interference of the United States in the internal affairs of Mexico is often called there. He introduced the Masonic lodges into Mexico, and helped organize and strengthen the anti-clerical Liberal Party. From that day to this, the Mexican Liberals have always looked to the United States for assistance in battling the pro-Catholic Conservatives.

Peru and Bolivia remained in Spanish hands. Their peoples retained their ancient loyalty to the Spanish Crown.

> And loyal they were. [Latin] Americans were the majority of Spain's Peruvian army throughout all phases of the wars. At least half of the troops sent to reconquer Chile under General Manuel Osorio in 1818 were Peruvian-born. Peruvians, including free blacks in the military, had subdued revolts in the early years of the war. Peru had to be conquered militarily before it would become independent. Small towns and rural areas in northern Peru revolted against San Martin's liberating conquest. This broadly based royalist resistance included all social classes. More than one-quarter of the members of the Peruvian Congress of 1823 had to be drawn from Colombia, Argentina, and Chile. Of the fourteen Peruvian congressmen who remained during the brief Spanish reoccupation of Lima in 1823, eight switched to become royalists. The Peruvian Congress had elected Jose de la Riva Aguero president in February 1823. Nine months later Riva Aguero proposed to the Viceroy that Peru become a monarchy under a Spanish Prince selected by the Spanish King; in the meantime, the Viceroy would govern Peru. Bolivar arrested Peru's first traitor President. Jose Bernardo Tagle, Marquis of Torre Tagle, who had been a deputy to the Cortes from Lima and later Intendant of Trujillo, replaced Riva Aguero

as President of Peru. Early in 1824 Peru's second head of government committed treason by defecting to the Spanish side during the second Spanish reconquest of Lima.

The masses also remained loyal to Spain. Even as Peruvian independence approached, most of the fighting for Peru's independence was done by non-Peruvians (*Insurrection or Loyalty*, p. 262).

With the majority in favor of it in Peru and Bolivia, retention by Royalists of strategic centers (Chiloe Island and Valdivia in Chile, Puerto Cabello in Venezuela, the fortress of San Juan de Ulloa off Vera Cruz, Mexico) and the possible adherence of Mexican Conservatives and large groups elsewhere in Latin America, in 1822 restoration of Spanish rule was not impossible. Two things were required, however; the Liberal government in Madrid must be overturned, and Spain's partners in the Holy Alliance must give support. Then and only then could the majority of Peruvians and Mexicans (to say nothing of the other countries) exercise self-determination and remain under a Catholic monarchy.

On October 22, 1822, the representatives of Great Britain, France, Austria, Prussia, and Russia gathered at the Congress of Verona to consider, among other things, the revolutions in Spain and her colonies. A counter-revolutionary movement had already emerged in northern Spain, but it would certainly require foreign assistance to succeed. The same was true of the Spanish colonies, whose Royalists also needed aid. While the four continental powers were agreed on intervention, the British government did not. The Spanish Liberals, advocating limits on the Church and Crown, had looked to Britain for inspiration. Further, the revolutions in the colonies had opened their ports to British shipping; hundreds of British mercenaries served with the rebel armies. From this time on, Great Britain ceased to be a member of the Holy Alliance.

The remaining powers authorized the French to invade Spain and restore Ferdinand VII to full power. In 1823 Louis XVIII sent the "hundred thousand sons of St. Louis" under his nephew the Duke of Angouleme, and Marshal Bourmont. The weak grasp of the Liberals became apparent when their armies melted away at the approach of the French and Spanish Royalists. Madrid entered and Ferdinand once again in full control, the stage was set for the relief of the beleaguered colonial Royalists and reconquest of those American colonies where the revolt had succeeded.

The Monroe Doctrine

For the reasons outlined, Britain was opposed to the Holy Alliance restoring Spain's position in the New World. Knowing that the United

States were of the same opinion as themselves, the British proposed a joint declaration against the planned intervention. President Monroe wrote to Jefferson asking his advice; the reply contains the following revealing lines:

> With Great Britain withdrawn from their [the Holy Alliance's] scale and shifted into that of our two continents, all Europe combined would not undertake such a war, for how would they propose to get at either enemy without superior fleets? Nor is the occasion to be slighted which this proposition offers of declaring our protest against the atrocious violations of the rights of nations by the interference of anyone in the internal affairs of another, so flagitiously begun by Bonaparte, and now continued by the equally lawless Alliance calling itself Holy.
>
> But we have, first, to ask ourselves a question. Do we wish to acquire to our confederacy any one or more of the Spanish provinces? I candidly confess that I have ever looked on Cuba as the most interesting addition which could ever be made to our system of states. The control which, with Florida point, this island would give us over the Gulf of Mexico and the countries and isthmus bordering on it, as well as all those whose waters flow into it, would fill up the measure of our political well-being (H.A. Washington, ed., *The Writings of Thomas Jefferson*, vol. VII p. 317).

Thus, we see married in foreign policy two themes which have been with us ever since: high sounding idealism masking naked greed.

Rather than ally directly with Britain in the matter, however, President Monroe instead made a unilateral declaration: while currently existing European colonies would not be molested by the U.S., under no circumstances would new ones be permitted; nor would reconquest of the new Latin nations. While at the time only possible because the British were resolved on the same course, this "Monroe Doctrine" basically declared to the world that the Americas were henceforth open only to United States exploitation. This would have a tremendous influence on the subsequent internal history of Latin America. As in Mexico so in the rest of the region—the Liberals looked to the U.S. for support, while the Conservatives gazed towards a Europe rendered powerless to help them (unless the Europeans didn't mind a war with the ever-stronger United States).

The result in the immediate was that in 1824 Peru was finally forced into independence. The following year Bolivia was subjected to "liberation" with great loss of life. At last, in 1826, Chiloe, Puerto Cabello, San Juan de Ulloa, and Callao, Peru all surrendered. Spain's empire in the New World was reduced to the Philippines, the Marianas, Puerto Rico, and *Cuba siempre leal*— "ever loyal Cuba."

Under cover of the Monroe doctrine, American interests worked ever for the triumph of anti-clericals over the Catholic interest. As a result, many Latin American Conservatives would share the following sentiments of leading Catholic Argentine philosopher Antonio Caponnetto:

> Regarding Pan-Americanism and the *Monroe Doctrine* which sustains it, much has been said and written. It is, in fact, a hypocritically manipulated topic of the Left, since they *neither mention the historical support of the United States for Communism, nor do they ever mention International Monetary Imperialism* of which the United States is a seat as well as a branch but not its totality. Nonetheless, the Pan-Americanist doctrine has produced and produces fruits of perdition. In *the military order*, its big stick policy has meant the loss of territory for American nations, when there was no invasion, occupation, or support for other similar deeds. Still fresh in our memory—and difficult to erase—is the Yankee military display favoring England in the war for the Falkland Islands in 1982. In *the economic order*, systematic exploitation and the strategy of forced indebtedness has provoked, artificially in some cases, situations of dependence that imply a real obstacle to sovereignty... And, in *the legal order*, we have the creation of the OAS and other related organizations and entities that in practice only respond to the combined interests of the super-powers...
>
> For these and other reasons, Pan-Americanism does not constitute any serious guarantee of American unity. Above all else, there is a deeper question and it is *the explicit Protestant and Saxon philosophy that plans the extinction of the Catholic and Hispanic world vision*. This is a task for which over a long time they have been mobilizing a force worse than the military, than usury or any legal fallacies: *the penetration by sects which confuse, corrode and consume the remaining vestiges of Christian civilization.* (*The Black Legends and Hispanic Catholic Culture*, pp. 124-125).

Although this passage may seem harsh, it were well to compare the first portion with the quotation from Jefferson to Monroe, and the last with this one by President John Quincy Adams in 1826:

> There is another subject upon which, without entering into any treaty, the moral influence of the United States may perhaps be exerted with beneficial consequences at such a meeting [a proposed conference of American nations in Panama]: the advancement of religious liberty. Some of the southern nations are even yet so far under the dominion of prejudice that they have incorporated with their political constitutions an exclusive church, without toleration of any other than the dominant sect. The abandonment of this last badge of religious bigotry and oppression may be pressed more effectually by the united exertions of those who concur in the principles of freedom of conscience upon those

who are yet to be convinced of their justice and wisdom, than by the solitary efforts of a minister to any one of the separate governments (James D. Richardson, *A Compilation of the Messages and Papers of the Presidents*, vol. II, p. 319).

As Mary Hargreaves observes:

> Patriotism and religion marched in tandem during the mid 1820s, correlating the cause of developing freedom in Latin America with the opening of Catholic lands to Protestantism and translating republican leadership as a mighty force to hasten worldwide spiritual regeneration in accordance with God's will (*The Presidency of John Quincy Adams*, p. 114).

From that day to this, it has been the same story; politically, socially, culturally, American influence in Latin America has been at the disposal of whoever has wished to destroy the heritage of Spain and Portugal (whose daughter Brazil became an independent Empire under a Portuguese Prince in 1822). It has been a long hard struggle, with American-backed forces generally triumphing in the end. But the endurance of the Catholic Iberian tradition may be seen by the fact that the battle is not over yet.

One thing has changed: the nature of the non-political forces the U.S. backs. In the beginning, our government subsidized Protestant Bible Societies in Latin America, in hopes that Catholics would change their religion; today, although private funding from this country still assists the growth of Protestant sects in Latin America, government aid has shifted. Now USAID funds contraception and abortion. Rather than trying to get Latin Catholics to give up their Faith outright, our government will settle for their simply ceasing to practice it—doubtless in hopes that any children they may have will lose it entirely.

The change in the nature of American meddling reflects the decline of even the remnants of Christianity among U.S. Protestants in general and the descendants of the Puritans in particular. We will see how this came about in the next section.

UNITARIANISM, TRANSCENDENTALISM, AND THE AMERICAN NOVEL

Deism or Unitarianism was the belief of Jefferson, Adams, Franklin, and others of the Founding Fathers. In 1785, King's Chapel in Boston was the scene of an intriguing election: the existence of the Holy Trinity was voted upon by the congregation. The former having lost, this one-time church of the Royal Governors became the first Unitarian church in the country. To this day, it describes itself as "Anglican in liturgy, Unitarian in theology, and Congregational in polity."

Armed with the prestige lent it by the worthy Founding Fathers, Unitarianism spread throughout New England's Congregational churches. By 1815, it had become a strong enough movement within the denomination to warrant an attack by prominent minister Jebidiah Morse. It was at the time defended by *William Ellery Channing*, minister at Boston's Federal Street Congregational Church. Four years later he assumed the leadership of the movement by his statement of principles at the ordination of one Jared Sparks in Baltimore.

As a result, elections like King's Chapel's were held in all New England's Congregational churches. Where (the majority of cases) the Trinity lost, the trinitarians would give up the old church to their opponents and move across the town common to build a new site. Where the Trinity won, the opposite occurred. This is the reason that all over the region today one will see the First Parish or Church (marked either Congregational or Unitarian) frowning at the other on the common's opposite side. It is an almost inevitable pattern. By 1825 there were enough Unitarian churches to warrant the formation of the American Unitarian Association as a separate denomination. The appointment of a Unitarian theologian as professor of divinity at Harvard College in 1805 had already sealed that institution's connection with the new movement. Unitarianism itself became a sort of orthodoxy in New England, and was represented throughout the country—even Charleston, South Carolina boasted a Unitarian church.

Having rejected the Trinity, Original Sin, the inerrancy of Scripture and the Divinity of Christ (as well as the redemptive nature of His death on the Cross—an idea carrying with it "strong marks of absurdity" in the words of Channing) Unitarians nevertheless maintained that they were Christians. Their Christianity consisted of attempting to follow what they considered to be the moral teachings of Christ; thus, they tended to continue to follow more or less the Puritan code without any real doctrinal foundation for doing so. Moreover, they continued the familiar pattern of Protestant worship inherited from the Congregationalists (or Anglicans in the case of King's Chapel) suitably altered. With those forms they continued to celebrate Baptism and the Lord's Supper as symbols of entrance into and the unity of their religious community. Unitarianism produced a belief that was rationalistic, materialistic and moralistic, but lacked fervor; in a word, it was very dry.

The Transcendental Revolt

It is in the nature of revolutions that they must continue in stages, growing ever more radical, until at last they either burn themselves out or are put an end to. So it was with the French Revolution; so it was with the American (which continues to this day); and so it was with the religious revolution of New England. As Anglicanism gave way to Puritanism, which fell prey to Deism and then Unitarianism, so the latter must be succeeded.

The latest revolt was signaled in 1832 by a young Unitarian minister named *Ralph Waldo Emerson*. Arguing that the continued use of the Lord's Supper smacked of worshipping Christ as God, he confessed himself unable to celebrate it any longer. He declared that it was an outmoded form which, however valuable it might have been in the past, was no longer valid—at least not for Emerson himself. Since he could no longer perform the rite in conscience, he would only continue as a minister if his church would allow him to do so without it. As they refused, he gave up the trade.

Emerson was much influenced by a vast shadowy trend in literature, art and music, called *Romanticism*. Originating in Germany in the last portion of the 18th Century, Romanticism opposed the ideals of the Enlightenment by declaring the primacy of the individual's emotions over the dictates of reason and the state. The areligious moralizing of Deism came under special assault by the Romantics, who quickly spread throughout intellectual circles in Europe and the Americas. As part of their creed, the Romantics idolized nature, the (particularly Medieval) past, folklore, and the far away and exotic. After the mental straight jacket of the Age of Reason and the horrors and blood of the Revolution and Napoleonic Wars, the Romantics came to have a real dislike of the here and now.

Leading Romantic philosopher A.W. Schlegel wrote:

> ...the romantic delights in indissoluble mixtures. All contrarieties: nature and art, poetry and prose, seriouness and mirth, recollection and anticipation, spirituality and sensuality, terrestrial and celestial, life and death, are by it blended together in the most intimate combination... Romantic poetry... is the expression of the secret attraction to a chaos which lies concealed in the very bosom of the ordered universe, and is perpetually striving after new and marvellous births; the life-giving spirit of primal love broods here anew on the face of the waters (*Dramatic Art and Literature*, Lecture XXII).

Such sentiments fell upon the ordered mental world of late 18th Century Europe like a thunderclap. Scotland saw Sir Walter Scott evoke her storied past, while Ireland's Thomas Moore resurrected many of his country's old songs and wrote others of his own. In Germany, the Brothers Grimm gathered the stories of nursery and fireside, while E.T.A. Hoffman wove his tales of terror. France witnessed Chateaubriand compose his *Genius of Christianity*. So it went in every nation of Europe.

But out of the vast pot of Romanticism, two contradictory tendencies soon appeared. On the one hand, the nostalgia for the Middle Ages it engendered among such as Chateaubriand, Sir Walter Scott, and Novalis led to many conversions to Catholicism or at least to dogmatic Christianity; in such cases political Conservatism (as summed up in the phrase "altar and throne") soon followed. The Holy Alliance was a concrete expression of such Romanticism; the English Oxford Movement which led many of its members to Catholicism and others to try to "Catholicize" Anglicanism, was another.

This was not, however, the only current stemming from Romanticism. For some Romantics, the emphasis on the individual's total autonomy and the superiority of feeling to thought led to complete disbelief in authority, whether civil or political. Such Romantics as Victor Hugo and Lord Byron came to look upon political revolution as a form of individual self-liberation and expression. Religiously, men like Schliermacher decided that faith was simply a way to evoke and express Man's deepest feelings. What mattered was not intellectual belief but making contact—via the feelings and contemplation of nature—with the "spark of the Divine", whatever that might be, within all of us. This last fell heavily upon a New England made suspicious of objective dogma by its Puritan past, and of religious emotion and mysticism by its Unitarian present.

By the 1830s, "the life of the mind" pursued for its own sake was very popular among a certain set in Boston (centering around Harvard) and Concord, Massachusetts. In addition to Emerson, they included in their number George Ripley (1802-1880), Orestes Brownson (1803-1876), Bronson Alcott (1799-1888; his daughter, Louisa May, wrote a number of famous children's books, including *Little Women*), and Henry David Thoreau (1817-1862). Together they are generally referred to as *Transcendentalists*. Although Transcendentalism has been described by Perry Miller as a "sort of mid-summer madness that overtook a few intellectuals in or around Boston about the year 1840", it has had a lasting impact on our culture.

Although each held different views, they held in common belief in an "order of truths that transcends the sphere of the external senses". They rejected all external authority because "the truth of religion does not depend on tradition, nor historical facts, but has an unerring witness in the soul..." Belief in man's perfectability led them to form in 1842 a sort of commune called Brook Farm, where they hoped to demonstrate their principles concretely. They failed.

Despite the failure of Transcendentalism to function practically, its ideas nevertheless came to form with Puritan conformism and attitudes, part of the basic American character. Emerson's 1841 essay *Self-Reliance*, for instance, is filled with platitudes which have come to be part of American popular wisdom: "Society everywhere is in conspiracy against the manhood of every one of its members...", for instance, or "Whoso would be a man must be a nonconformist." From these sentiments come our national lip-service to Rugged Individualism. Similarly, generations of High School children have thrilled to Thoreau's lines in *Walden*: "I went to the woods because I wished to live deliberately, to confront only the essential facts of life, and see if I could not learn what it had to teach, and not, when I came to die, discover that I had not lived." Here we see a continuation and popularization of the notion that Man is somehow set free by the wilderness. Of course, we are a very conformist folk who for the most part live in urban areas, so the attraction of such ideas is obvious. But Emerson the nonconformist was a prominent Brahmin, as the Boston WASP elite were called; and Thoreau's cabin at Walden was a snug little retreat paid for by his aunt. Things are not always what they appear to be.

One other attitude the Transcendentalists were able to pass on to Americans was that of imbuing political issues with religious fervor. Abolitionism was the great conflict of the day; the Transcendentalists considered opposition to slavery to be a quasi-religious duty. Indeed, it led Thoreau to refuse to pay his poll-tax. He languished in jail overnight until his aunt bailed him out, but the occurrence was immortalized forever in the play, *The Night Thoreau Spent In Jail*. One thing is certain; the necessity for both sides in any American political dispute to clothe the issue in terms of a great moral crusade comes from these folk.

The Transcendentalists turned out reams of poetry and tons of essays. But one thing they generally did not do well: prose fiction.

The Birth of American Prose

As earlier noted, Romanticism brought forth two currents; the first, the nostalgic sort, was not completely lacking in America either. By 1800, there were any number of literary elements to work with in America, in addition to the common European background. Stories of the Indians and the Revolution, English, German and Dutch folklore transformed by the New World environment, and over a century and a half of university and intellectual life all laid the necessary background for the emergence of a native American Conservative Romanticism in literature.

Washington Irving (1783-1859), has won unending fame as the author of *Rip Van Winkle,* and *The Legend of Sleepy Hollow*. He rocketed to contemporary notoriety in 1809 with his *Dietrich Knickerbocker's History of New York,* in which he assumed the persona of an old New York antiquary of Dutch descent in order to parody the stuffy histories so prevalent at the time. A hilarious book, it was a real start for American letters, and was a first intimation that the country was truly capable of producing literary genius. In his many subsequent works like *The Sketch Book* and *Tales of the Alhambra* Irving explored the American West, Spain under the Moors, British customs, legends of his native state and many other curious things. In his work, wonder, horror, and humor were juxtaposed and mixed in true Romantic fashion according to the dictate set down by Schlegel.

Irving showed himself a true American equivalent of the Conservative wing of European Romanticism. As Van Wyck Brooks points out: "...he had antiquarian tastes and a liking for old customs and was therefore, in a sense, a natural Tory" (*The World of Washington Irving*, p. 164). His artistic voice was in no small part built upon the traditions he imbibed growing up in the New York of his era:

> ...the Hudson river valley and all the country about New York teemed with legends of the Dutch. At Hell Gate, a black man, known as the Pirate's Spook, whom Stuyvesant had shot with a silver bullet, was often seen in stormy weather in a three-cornered hat, in the stern of a jolly-boat, or so it was said; and from Tappan Zee to Albany, especially in the Highlands, every crag and cove had its story. The zee was supposed to be haunted by the storm-ship of the Palisades, whose misty form blew from shore to shore whenever a gale was coming up, as well as the ghost of Rambout van Dam, the roistering Dutchman of Spuyten Duyvel, who had desecrated the Sabbath on a drunken frolic. Rambout had never appeared again, but the muffled sound of his oars was heard on evenings when, among the shadows, there was no boat to be seen, although some people thought it was one of the whale-boats, sunk by the British in the war, that was haunting its old cruising-grounds. Point-no-Point was the resort of another storm-ship, often seen towards midnight in the light of the moon, when the chanting of the crew was heard as if they were heaving the lead; and the Donderberg and Sugar Loaf, Storm King and Anthony's Nose bristled with legends as with trees and rocks. The captains of the river-craft, when they approached the Donderberg, lowered their peaks in deference to the keeper of the mountain, the bulbous Dutch goblin, the Heer, with the sugar-loaf hat, who was supposed to carry a speaking-trumpet. With this, when a storm was rising, he gave orders in Low

Dutch for the piping up of a gust of wind or the rattling of a thunderclap. Once he was seen astride of the bowsprit of a sloop, which he rode full butt against Anthony's Nose; and once the dominie of Esopus exorcised him, singing the hymn of St. Nicholas, whereupon the goblin threw himself up like a ball in the air and disappeared as suddenly in a whirlwind. He carried with him the nightcap of the dominie's wife, and this was found on the following Sunday morning hanging on the steeple of a church that was forty miles off. Sometimes this foul-weather urchin was surrounded by a crew of imps who, in broad breeches and short doublets, tumbled about in the rack and the mist. They buzzed like a swarm of flies about Anthony's Nose when the storm was at the height of its hurry-scurry; and once, when a sloop was overtaken by a thunder-gust, the crew saw a little white sugar-loaf hat on the masthead. This, everyone knew at once, was the hat of the Heer (Brooks, *op. cit.*, pp. 48-49).

Like his European counterparts, Irving drank deeply from the legendry of his native land, transmuting it into brilliant fiction.

So too did *Nathaniel Hawthorne* (1804-1864). While Hawthorne knew the Transcendentalists (indeed, he even lived for a time at Brook Farm) he did not share their outlook. Where Irving was influenced by the often whimsical legends of Dutch New York, the shadow of Puritan New England lay heavily on Hawthorne. Descendant of a judge in the Salem witch-trials, Hawthorne produced from his native place's darker lore such classics as *The House of the Seven Gables* and *The Scarlet Letter*. It is further noteworthy that, when assuming the persona of a revolutionary war loyalist in "The Old Tory," he wrote that it was necessary to "transform ourself, perchance, from a modern Tory into such a sturdy King-man, as once wore that pliable nick-name." He too considered himself "Conservative."

Darker still at times (although he also wrote very amusing humorous stories—not well read today) is the fiction and poetry of *Edgar Allan Poe* (1809-1849). Unlike the other two authors, he was more cosmopolitan than regional. Born in Boston, he spent five years at school in England, and lived by turns in Charleston, Richmond, New York, Philadelphia, and Baltimore. Yet, despite this, he considered himself a Southerner, and sympathized with that region in its political struggles. Whatever the setting of his stories, they owed more to his internal landscape than to their supposed location. Poe was the first American writer to be widely acknowledged in non-English-speaking countries. By the time of Poe's death, in company with such as Cooper and Paulding, these three had inaugurated a distinctive American prose literature.

All three showed (like their Conservative Romantic confreres in Europe) a certain sympathy with the Faith. Hawthorne, in *The Marble*

Faun, set in Rome, praises various aspects of Catholicism, especially Confession, at great length. Irving, particularly in writing about the Spanish, whom he maintained to be, "...on many points the most high-minded and proud-spirited people in Europe," was similarly inclined. Poe, indeed, wrote a beautiful poem to Our Lady:

> HYMN OF THE ANGELUS
>
> At morn, at noon, at twilight dim,
> Maria, thou hast heard my hymn!
> In joy and woe, in good and ill,
> Mother of God, be with me still!
> When the hours flew brightly by,
> And not a cloud obscured the sky,
> My soul, lest it should truant be,
> Thy grace did guide to thine and thee;
> Now, when the storms of fate o'ercast
> Darkly my present and my past,
> Let my future radiant shine
> With sweet hopes of thee and thine.

Despite all of this, however, and similar effusions by such contemporary poets as Longfellow and Lowell, none of this sort of Romantic in America converted, as so many did in Europe. The reason was simply that the very idea of conversion to Catholicism, a religion so hated by the traditions from whence these folk sprang, was unthinkable to them. The only notable converts to the Faith from American Romanticism were Transcendentalists and former Brook Farmers Orestes Brownson and Isaac Hecker (the latter of whom has the sad distinction of being a father of the Americanist heresy, as well as founder of the Paulist Order).

So the quest for self-fulfillment led, for Brownson and Hecker, eventually to the Faith; but Conservative nostalgia did not do so for Irving, Hawthorne (whose daughter, however, did convert, later founding an order of sisters), and Poe. Something further is revealed herein about American Conservatism.

THE POLITICAL STRUGGLE

As literature in this period was dominated by three men, so too were politics. The first of these was *Daniel Webster* (1782-1852), a New Hampshire native whose skill at debate was immortalized in Stephen Vincent Benet's short story, "The Devil and Daniel Webster" (in which the old orator defeats Satan himself in a law-case). He began his political career in 1813 as a Federalist in the House of Representatives. In his subsequent roles as congressman (1823-1827) and senator (1827-1841) from Massachusetts, Secretary of State (1841-1843), and once more senator from the Bay State (1845-1852), his great object was the forging of the United States into a single nation greater than its constituent parts. To this end, he opposed States' Rights and the extension of slavery into new territories, and favored the right of the U.S. government to impose high tariffs.

Henry Clay (1777-1852) we have already met as an enemy of the Faith and the Holy Alliance. Like Webster, he was a zealous promoter of the Union against the States. Congressman from Kentucky at various times between 1811-1825 (occupying the Speakership of the House), Secretary of State from 1825 to 1829, and Senator 1831 to 1842, and again from 1849 until he died, he was called, because of his knack for obtaining compromise, "the Great Pacificator." He favored a "National System" of roads, canals, and improvements to unite the resources of the West with the ports of the East, and generally high tariffs. On the question of slavery, he favored its gradual abolition; but so adroit was he at compromise that the abolitionists accused him of supporting slavery, and the slaveholders believed him to be a radical abolitionist.

The last of the triumvirate was *John C. Calhoun* (1782-1850). A native of South Carolina, Calhoun was Congressman from that state, 1811-1817; Secretary of State under Monroe 1817-1825; Vice-President for both John Quincy Adams and Andrew Jackson from 1825 to 1832; senator from South Carolina 1833-1843; Secretary of State again 1844-45; and senator once again until his death. Unlike the other two, he retained a belief in the sovereignty of the individual states. He pioneered the doctrine of "nullification," which taught in effect that if a state government found a Federal act to be unconstitutional, it could void it by an act of the legislature. He opposed high tariffs, and sought to defend the South's economic mainstay, slavery. He was himself a kind master, and was considered to be a man of spotless integrity. Calhoun reminds one much of a Roman republican figure, austere and highly moral with no real religion.

These three in themselves summed up the regional struggles which in time would tear the Union apart. Many different political issues superimposed themselves one upon another, creating innumerable factions—a group might stand one way on the tariff issue, but differently on the slavery issue. The questions of aristocracy versus democracy, States' Rights versus Federal power, and slavery versus abolitionism, to name a few, agitated each of the States and the government in Washington. In the end, most of these questions would be solved not by agreement nor by compromise, but by bloodshed.

Compromise and the Adams Presidency

From the end of the Slave Trade in 1808, New England, as we have mentioned, became ever more anti-slavery. While New York and Pennsylvania were lukewarm in their opposition (indeed, the "peculiar institution" lasted into the 1840s in New York and until 1850 in Pennsylvania), Yankee-settled states like Ohio, Indiana, and Illinois were dead set against it. By 1819 the balance was 11 slave states to 11 free states (among whom were counted New York and Pennsylvania, who were pledged to eventual abolition) thus dividing the Senate equally. As long as this was the case, neither side need fear being dominated by its opponents in the Federal government.

But this was a precarious balance. Not only were the Western territories being settled by both northerners and southerners each desirous of forming their new homes into images of their old ones (thus getting in the way of one another) but the formation of new states would decide control of the Senate. This would in turn lead either to a Federal government which would be the servant of the States—or their master.

Missouri was slated to be admitted as a slave state. This would throw the Senate into the hands of the Southerners by one vote. Since the folk of the South had shown more of the pioneering spirit than their Yankee counterparts, it was feared that they would soon fill up the West with ever more slave states. Rather than see this happen, the North was willing to keep Missouri a territory indefinitely—which, given that both sides were evenly matched in the Senate, they would be able to do. At last a compromise was worked out, to no little degree because of Henry Clay. Missouri would be admitted as a state, but so too would be the District of Maine, at the time a part of Massachusetts and virulently anti-slavery; the balance would be maintained. In addition, except for Missouri, slavery would not be permitted north of the parallel forming the line between Arkansas Territory and Missouri.

When President James Monroe stepped down in 1825, he was the last Revolutionary War veteran to hold the office (hence his nickname of "The Last Cocked Hat"). His successor, John Quincy Adams, whom we have already met, although the son of John Adams and having been a long-time Federalist stalwart, was now a Democrat—as were virtually all the other politicians. He favored a strong union, rule by the "best suited" (and so maintained a certain aristocratic tone to his administration), and opposed slavery. Favoring the same sort of National System as his Secretary of State, Henry Clay, he saw gladly the building of the famed Erie Canal which united the trade of the Hudson River with that of the Great Lakes. In this way the path of settlement in such places as Michigan and Wisconsin was made possible. He was also responsible for the adoption of an extremely high tariff—the "tariff of abominations" in 1828. This cost him the election of that year. His opponent, General Andrew Jackson, whom we last saw annoying the Spanish, succeeded him, despite a strong anti-Masonic movement which opposed Jackson. The fact that Jackson's main opponent Henry Clay was also a Freemason paralyzed them.

The Revolution of 1829 and the Reign of Jackson

Not since Jefferson's "Revolution of 1800" had the capital seen such a change. The March 4th inauguration exemplified what many people considered Jackson's popular style as opposed to Adams'. Hordes of lower class and poor folk from all over the country descended upon the White House for a post-inauguration party. They danced on tables, smashed furniture and crockery, and in general did their best to give an impression of social revolution.

When the smoke cleared, the class system was still intact. But Jackson did intend a real change. Within his first year in the presidency, 690 office-holders were dismissed and replaced by Jackson's cronies; this is contrasted with only 74 removals by all six of his predecessors together. "To the victor belong the spoils" was his motto.

Jackson came into office with a number of interests: he wished to move all the Indians (particularly the "Five Civilized Tribes"— Cherokee, Choctaw, Chickasaw, and his old friends the Creek and Seminole) west of the Mississippi; to end the Bank of the United States, which he considered unconstitutional (as in the beginning he was a States' Righter and friend of Calhoun, whose support had been crucial in defeating Adams); and the annexation of Texas.

The first of these goals was rather complicated. The Constitution had conferred upon the Indian tribes a sort of sovereignty comparable to that of the States or foreign nations, the nature of which, however, was not precisely defined. The Five Civilized Tribes had formed themselves into little republics; many of their citizens lived like white men, some even owning black slaves. Jackson wanted to banish them to the West by purely congressional action; they had however the knowledge to bring their case to court.

Jackson proposed Indian removal in his first message to Congress. The National Republicans (as the opponents of Jackson's Democrats now called themselves) immediately organized opposition. But the Democrats had a majority in both houses, and on May 28, 1830, the Indian Removal Act became law. It authorized Jackson to have the Five Tribes removed by the army from their ancestral lands in Georgia, Florida, Alabama, and Mississippi, and send them to what are now

Kansas and Oklahoma. Four of the tribes capitulated, but the Cherokee took the government of the State of Georgia to the Supreme Court. On March 3, 1832, that Court under Chief Justice Marshall, ruled the law unconstitutional. Jackson's reply was; "Well: John Marshall has made his decision: *now let him enforce it!*" The Indians were forced to take the "Trail of Tears" to the West; many died of hardship along the way. But they did manage in the end to rebuild their tribal governments in their places of exile.

The Bank of the United States was his next target. This body, similar in many ways to our Federal Reserve Bank of today, held a monopoly of power over foreign and domestic exchange. Jackson felt it to be both unconstitutional and a threat to liberty. It came up for a renewal of its charter in 1832, which renewal passed the Senate on June 11 and the House on July 3. On July 10, the President vetoed it, thus ending the BUS when its charter ran out. In the message accompanying the veto, Jackson restated his belief in a limited state. But he was shortly to show that he believed rather in an unlimited one.

It was whether or not his veto should be overturned that the election of 1832 was fought against Henry Clay. Jackson won.

But no sooner was he settled down into another term, than there arose a dispute in which he showed the limits of his belief in States' Rights. Another Tariff act raised the burden upon the South imposed by the Tariff of Abominations which had cost Adams the Southern vote and the Presidency. Calhoun had enunciated his doctrine of nullification in response that year. The latest tariff was the last straw. November of 1832 saw South Carolina's legislature pass an ordinance declaring the tariffs of 1828 and 1832 unconstitutional, "and are null and void, and no law, nor binding upon this state."

Jackson was outraged. On December 10, he issued the nullification proclamation, in which he abandoned States' Rights and adhered to the theory of Federal Supremacy. He further declared his readiness to enforce the tariffs militarily. Tempers flared, but neither State nor President really wanted a showdown; on February 13, 1833, a compromise tariff was worked out by Henry Clay which allowed both sides to claim the victory.

Apart from an 1835 revolt by those Seminole Indians in Florida who had refused to go into exile (and which lasted actively until 1842—some Florida Seminole not signing a peace with the government until 1962) the remainder of Jackson's reign was relatively uneventful (except for congressional squabbles in the aftermath of the fall of the BUS) within this country's boundaries. Arkansas was admitted in 1836 as a slave state and Michigan in 1837 as a free state—thus maintaining the balance in the Senate.

But Jackson did encourage the activities of Americans over the Mexican border in Texas. The mercurial Santa Ana had come in and out of power in Mexico. Permitting unrestricted settlement of Texas by Anglo-Americans who fraudulently accepted baptism (at the knowing hands of one Fr. Whelan; recipients of his ministrations were called "Whelan-Catholics") he thus paved the way for the revolution there. (Incidentally, the Texas declaration of independence delicately describes the priesthood as one of "the eternal enemies of civil liberty, the ever-ready minions of power, and the usual instruments of tyrants").

The Mexican government, becoming fearful at the influx, took steps to keep Texas an integral part of the country. The Anglo-Americans revolted, declaring their independence in the anti-Catholic document just cited. It should be mentioned for the record that they were after all foreign settlers who had been required both to convert to Catholicism and to swear allegiance to their new country before being allowed to settle in Texas. Most did so fraudulently. If a group of Mexicans were to settle one of our states today, falsely convert to Baptistry or Methodism and swear a perjured oath to our constitution, and then repay our hospitality by taking the state over, we would feel betrayed. So too did the Mexicans in 1835 and 1836. Death is generally the penalty for treason, and this was the reason for the so-called massacres at Goliad and the Alamo. When Sam Houston captured Santa Ana at the Battle of San Jacinto, he intended to put the Mexican ruler to death in reprisal. Santa Ana was to escape execution by flashing the Masonic distress signal at brother-in-the-craft Houston.

The result, however, was to bring about Mexican recognition of the independence of Texas. But Mexico considered Texas' boundaries to be the Nueces River on the South and a closely restricted line on the West; the Texans claimed everything up to the Rio Grande, including half of New Mexico. The huge disputed tract in between would be the cause of much difficulty later.

Van Buren, Harrison, and Tyler

Jackson was replaced as standard bearer of his party in 1837 by his second Vice-President, Martin Van Buren. After the sound and fury of Jackson's reign, Van Buren's seemed a bit anti-climactic. The end of the BUS produced a yearlong depression in 1837. But while his tenure was relatively quiet, the Whig Party, (organized from the remnants of the National Republicans) prepared to make a grab for the White House.

They nominated for the election of 1840 William Henry Harrison, called "Old Tippecanoe" from the site of his 1811 victory over Tecumseh and the Shawnee. He was lauded as a simple man, supposedly born in a log cabin, as against Van Buren's aristocratic Hudson Valley Dutch ways. As a result of having John Tyler as his running mate, the Whig election phrase was "Tippecanoe and Tyler, too!"

Van Buren was defeated, and on March 4, 1841 Harrison was inaugurated. But he gave a long speech in the rain, caught pneumonia, and after a little over a month in office, died. This was the first presidential death of a series: for Harrison, elected in 1840, died in office—as did Lincoln, elected in 1860; Garfield, in 1880; Mckinley, in 1900; Harding in 1920; Roosevelt in 1940; and Kennedy in 1960. All sorts of theories were advanced to explain this strange phenomenon, from Indian curses to astrological anomalies. Whatever the case, Ronald Reagan, elected in 1980, broke the series; it is just possible, one supposes, that it was all coincidence.

The death of Harrison brought Tyler to the Presidency. A number of interesting things occurred during his time which he had little to do with, but which would nevertheless play key roles in the country's future history.

Rhode Island had maintained its 1663 charter despite the revolution. What this meant was that all of the towns had equal representation in the legislature, and among them only property owners could vote. By 1840, the result was to completely discount the fact that Providence had grown enormously, and to keep the large population of artisans in town disenfranchised. Power remained in the hands of the Protestant farmers, while the largely Catholic urban workforce counted for nothing.

In 1840, a young Providence lawyer named *Thomas Dorr* (1805-1854) began agitating for constitutional change. Without being summoned by the legislature, a group elected by universal manhood gathered as a constitutional convention in Providence and passed what was called the People's Constitution on November 18, 1841. The legislature in turn called a similar convention at Newport in February 1842 and adopted what was called the Freeman's constitution. The People's was submitted to the popular vote and accepted, while the Freeman's was rejected. On April 18, 1842, Dorr was elected Governor, but neither the state supreme court nor President Tyler recognized him. With some supporters, he went into rebellion, trying unsuccessfully to seize the state armory in Providence. This attempt was defeated, after which he went into exile in Connecticut, came back and was tried for High Treason and imprisoned in 1844, being released the next year. But by that time the imposed Freeman's Constitution had been altered in many respects, and for the most part the rule of the agricultural oligarchy in Rhode Island was at an end.

An even more dramatic episode happened in New York. The descendants of those great patroons who had rallied to the revolution still retained their power in the state. Their extensive manors on the Hudson were kept with all the rights given by the King. A proprietor's tenants were bound with perpetual leases, leases for 99 years, or leases for from one to three lives. Apart from rent, the tenants had to render certain feudal services to the proprietor, and if he sold interest in a farm to another tenant he had to pay a tenth to a third of the cost to the proprietor.

Now Stephen van Rensselaer, proprietor of Rensselaerwyck, largest and grandest of the manors, had been so wealthy he did not care if the rents were paid or not. But when he died in 1839 his poorer heirs attempted to collect the monies owed them. Their agents were violently repulsed. Governor Seward called out the militia, but directed the legislature to look into the tenants' grievances. Arbitration was unsuccessful, the violence spread to other manors, and the deputy sheriff of Delaware County was murdered in 1845. In that year, an anti-rent governor was elected, who called a constitutional convention. The document thus produced was promulgated in 1846; it abolished feudal tenures. The legislature passed a battery of bills designed to break up the leaseholds, and the great proprietors quickly sold most of their land.

The results of these last two events were both local and national. In both cases, the power of an aristocratic landed interest with primary power on a state level was destroyed. Whether or not that was a good thing depends upon how much one feels the mystic rites of the ballot box really contribute to the running of anything anyway; a case might be made that an oligarchy one can see and touch could be better than an invisible one which hides behind a faceless mass called "the people."

But the second national result was disastrous. The New York manorlords had played an important mediating role between the interests of the Southern planters whom they recognized and were recognized by as social equals, and the governing circles of the North with whom they were also intimately connected. In good part the congressmen and senators whom they controlled had played a major role in the compromises which kept sectional strife down a bit. Now they were gone, and there were few who could speak to both Southern planters and Northern bankers and industrialists. The polarization of the regions went on all the quicker.

In 1845 the balance of states was disturbed by the admission of Florida as a slave state. This was further exacerbated just before Tyler was due to step down in favor of his Democrat successor, James K. Polk, when Texas was annexed. Not only was Texas a slave-holding region, but the republic's becoming a United State meant that the nation as a whole must inherit the territorial problem with Mexico. It was a dispute the new President wished to end in the U.S.'s favor. The stage was set for this nation's third war.

CATHOLICISM EXPANDING

Meanwhile, Catholicism had expanded greatly since Carroll's death in 1815. Where the 1st Baltimore Provincial Council of 1829 was attended by the Archbishop of Baltimore and the bishops of Bardstown, Boston, New York, and Philadelphia, the sixth in 1846 saw His Grace of Baltimore joined by 16 suffragans. This tremendous growth was not brought about by mass conversions (although some extraordinary converts were made in that time) but by immigration, chiefly from Ireland, French Canada, and Germany. While such newcomers flocked to the great seaports and Northern industrial towns, various others began to establish colonies further inland, becoming an integral part of the pioneer history of our land. Often these would be led by one or another Catholic leader whose memory ought to be revered by us today. Let us survey the Catholic activities on the frontier in the period 1816-1845.

The Louisiana Purchase

It were well to start with what had been the Louisiana purchase. To be sure, the state of Louisiana itself hardly merited being called a "frontier" area. New Orleans was as civilized as any city in Europe at the time, and centered on its Cathedral of St. Louis fronting on the Place d'Armes—later renamed Jackson Square. Creoles, Cajuns, Isleños, Baratarians, Free People of Color, and more recent European Catholic immigrants had together evolved a unique matrix of cultures unlike anything else in the other States. Christmas, New Year's, Epiphany, Mardi-Gras, Lent, Holy Week, Easter, Corpus Christi, and All Saints' were kept publicly with a fervor reminiscent of Catholic Europe and Latin America. Although the Northern part of the state was filling up with Anglo-Saxon Protestant settlers, the Creoles of New Orleans fought hard to maintain their cultural and political supremacy. But in the southern part of the state too there were new settlements. The town of Abbeville was founded by Fr. Antoine Desire Megret in 1845. He built the church of Ste. Marie Madeleine, and laid out streets and farm plots around a central square, just like the towns of France. St. Martinville boasted the Church of St. Martin de Tours, built in 1765 and equipped with a baptismal font given by King Louis XVI. In Grand Coteau were both St. Charles College for Boys and the Convent and Academy of the Sacred Heart for Girls; its closest rival was the similar institution run by the Ursulines in New Orleans. The Cajuns were still in the process of spreading along the bayous and prairies of the southern part of the state, while Creoles and others continued to build plantations.

Arkansas had been sparsely settled under the French and Spanish, with only a few settlers at Arkansas Post and Pine Bluff; by the 1840s, that was where most of the state's Catholics were still—and usually of French descent. But as early as 1830, Mass had been said for the handful of Irish in Little Rock.

Missouri too had a Catholic past. The old French settlement of St. Louis became a diocese in 1826, and an archdiocese in 1847. Like the Creoles of Vincennes, Indiana and those across the Mississippi in Cahokia, Kaskaskia, and Prairie du Rocher, Illinois, those of Missouri were and are a fun-loving bunch:

> Local raconteurs at Old Mines [Washington County] are especially fond of medieval French animal stories and tales of magic... At both Florissant and Ste. Genevieve, the Host is borne through the streets in a solemn and colorful ceremony at the observance of Corpus Christi in June. Christmas is celebrated with firecrackers in the southwestern parts of Missouri, and at Old Mines and Ste. Genevieve the celebration of *La Guignolée* marks New Year's Eve, as masked revelers make the rounds of homes and business places, singing a song centuries old (WPA, *Missouri,* p. 132).
>
> Thomas Ashe, visiting the Creole settlement at Ste. Genevieve on a summer's evening in 1806, found the inhabitants gathered about their dooryards, "the women at work, the children at play, and the men performing music, singing songs, or telling stories..." Between numerous special occasions for group festivities, such as balls and holy or feast days, the music loving Creoles gathered night after night for the pure joy of singing together. They sang of the tragedy of a mother who unknowingly murdered her son in "La Retour Funeste"; of the trials of love in "L'Amant Malheureux" and "Belle Rose"; and of a more reflective theme in "Le Juif Errant." (WPA, *op. cit.*, p. 158).

St. Charles, Missouri, first capital of the State, was the American headquarters of *St. Rose Phillipine Duchesne* (1769-1855). Born in Grenoble, she entered the Order of the Visitation in 1797. Due to the unpleasantness of the French Revolution, her religious life was disrupted; in 1805 she entered the newly founded Madames of the Sacred Heart. On March 20, 1818, she left with four other sisters to begin missionary work among the Indians, who called her "the Woman Who Prays Always."

The Creoles at Ste. Genevieve (who for a time had Audubon for their Governor) were typical of their race; we cannot forebear to delve a little more deeply into their integrally Catholic way of life:

> ...the best index of [Ste. Genevieve's] life and manners is its festivals. On New Year's Eve, masked revelers dressed as Indians or

blacked as Negroes shuffle from house to house, accompanied by a fiddler and singing "La Guignolée," an ancient French song with unwritten music and traditional words. At one time it was sung to solicit food and drink for the King's Ball, held on Twelfth Night; today, however, the masked singers demand only wine.

At the *Gloria* of the Mass of Holy Thursday, before Easter, when the bells are silenced, the altar boys call the congregation to service by marching around the church square three times, rattling their rick-racks (wooden rattles) and calling out, *premier coup* (first bell), *deuxiéme coup* (second bell), and *dernier coup* (last bell). Later, in May or June, depending on the date of Easter, the Feast of Corpus Christi is celebrated. On this day, small shrines are erected in front of the houses, and the town is decorated with flowers. At midmorning, accompanied by his assistants, the priest, bearing the Eucharist, and dressed in the most resplendent robes of his office, leads a procession through the streets. Singing children precede the parade, scattering flowers. The procession ends with a special Mass and blessing in front of the church on the public square (WPA, *op. cit.*, p. 269-270)

By 1845, the City of St. Louis had already acquired a large German population. Its Greek-Revival cathedral of the same name built in 1831-34, had been enriched by Pope Gregory XVI with a special privilege: the same indulgence obtained by visiting the seven Roman basilicas could be obtained by praying at each of St. Louis Cathedral's three altars. King Louis XVIII of France, unable to confer spiritual favors gave artistic gifts instead—three pictures, including a very beautiful one of his ancestor, St. Louis IX.

Florissant, northwest of St. Louis, would be particularly important in the history of the Church on the frontier. From 1814 on, the French inhabitants held a Corpus Christi procession similar to that of Ste. Genevieve's; their Church of St. Ferdinand was originally built by the Spanish in 1788, although a new stone building was erected in 1821. Nearby was another convent built by St. Rose Phillipine Duchesne; also thereat was the Jesuit Seminary of St. Stanislaus, where was ordained *Fr. Pierre de Smet* (1801-1873) in 1827. We shall see more of him in subsequent chapters. For now, let it be said that he was certainly the greatest Indian missionary to have worked in this country since Independence.

In addition to these long-established Creole settlements, however, there were newer German ones which formed a pattern for later German Catholic colonies. One of the first of these was Taos (Cole County), whose founding the WPA Guide describes well:

> When Father Helias D'Huddeghem, born in Ghent in 1796, came here from Belgium as a Jesuit missionary in 1838, he found a colony of 200 Hanoverian and Bavarian immigrants in the region west of the

Osage River. After four years of service among them, he gave up his missionary duties and settled in Taos, where in 1840 he had built a stone church, financed partly by his mother, the Countess of Lens, and by the Canon de la Croix of Ghent and the Leopoldine Association of Vienna. In 1874 Father Helias died and was buried in the local cemetery; his grave is marked by a tall marble shaft, simply inscribed in Latin....

In 1847, largely through the efforts of Fr. Helias, 50 Belgians under the leadership of Pierre Dirckx, settled at Taos. They were trained craftsmen and contributed much to the prosperity of the community. Their descendants, who form the majority of the present inhabitants, preserve many religious customs not generally practiced in other parts of Missouri. On the afternoon of November 1, which is both All Saints Day and the eve of All Souls Day, a procession, headed by a cross-bearer and acolytes, follows the winding road from the church to the cemeteries, where the graves are blessed by the priest. On December 6, the Feast of St. Nicholas, a member of the congregation dresses as St. Nicholas, with a bishop's mitre, cope, and staff, and, accompanied by a costumed retinue, goes from house to house, asking parents how their children have behaved during the year, and distributing candy, fruits, and nuts. On Christmas Day, after early Mass, pistols, guns, and firecrackers are shot off in the churchyard (pp. 396-397).

Prior to settling in Taos, Fr. Helias evangelized German settlers in Osage and Maries Counties. Such towns as Westphalia and Rich Fountain owe their origin to him; but in this he was typical of many pioneering priests. In any case, Scott County's New Hamburg possesses a similar story:

[It is] a German community dominated by the bulk of the St. Lawrence Roman Catholic Church. The close-packed, square, one- and two-story white frame houses are owned by descendants of German immigrants who settled here in 1846. Because of their isolation, they remained a racial, religious and economic unit until a comparatively recent date. On New Year's Eve, masked villagers in fancy dress go from house to house, singing old German songs and being treated to wine and cakes. Belief in witchcraft is common. Spells are laid, the future told, and charms are often worn. Most serious is the hex or curse placed on individuals by their enemies. If one wishes to dream of a future mate, he need only sleep with nine different kinds of leaves beneath the pillow. Signs and omens are carefully observed before planting or reaping crops, or undertaking any other important venture (pp. 455-456).

The center of Catholicism in Iowa in this period was Dubuque. In 1835 Fr. Samuel Mazzuchelli reached the town and built St. Raphael's for the local Irish and German settlers, on land donated by a miner named Thomas Kelly. Fr. Mazzuchelli also served their countrymen in other towns on the river, like Davenport and Muscatine. The year before he came to Dubuque, a group of Irish farmers founded the nearby village of Key West. Nineteen miles southwest, more of the same group settled Cascade, where Gaelic was still spoken into the 1930s. North of Dubuque, Germans settled New Vienna and St. Petersburg in 1844, and with Irish settlers founded nearby Holy Cross; south of the city along the Mississippi Luxembourgers built St. Donatus. In all of these hamlets, the feast days and customs of their people's homelands were transplanted.

What is now Minnesota was, until 1847, served by three churches only: at St. Paul, St. Anthony (Minneapolis), and Mendota for the French settlers in those places.

The Old Northwest

Of course, there was a great deal of open space within the 1783 boundaries which was being settled during these years. Let us now turn our attention to the Old Northwest. Ohio was the State of the region least affected by French settlement. Fr. Edward Fenwick was sent as first resident priest to Cincinnati in 1817. At the time the city ordinances forbade building a Catholic church within city limits. He was made Bishop of the place in 1821, after which Germans began to pour in and to transform Cincinnati from a Yankee settlement into a German stronghold. The year after Fenwick came to the state, a band of Dominicans set up St. Joseph's Priory near Somerset in Perry County. With them came a royal gift; a chalice donated by Ferdinand VII of Spain. Five years prior, German Catholics settled Fayetteville in the north of Brown County.

Indiana also obtained a large number of Catholics from abroad. For many years, of course, the old French town of Vincennes was the center of the Faith in that state. Of its people the WPA guide to Indiana says:

> The Creoles were a musical, fun-loving people, caring little for either formal government or tilling the soil. All they wanted was a living, which was easy to get in those days—hence they became known as a race of pleasure-loving idlers. Life in a frontier outpost could not have been one of complete ease, but these people always seemed to take the line of least resistance and in spite of inevitable hardships they remained gay and easygoing. Certainly they were driven by no compelling urge to accumulate lands or goods (p. 273).

To a puritanical people, the charge of being pleasure-loving idlers levied against the Vincennes Creoles would have been most insulting; as it was, the same charge and innumerable others of the same sort (licentiousness, drunkenness and the like) were launched against not merely the French of Indiana but also against their Irish and German co-religionists throughout these United States, of which more shortly. But what is notable is that the Vincennes Creoles, for all that they were pleasure-loving idlers, managed for their bishops Bruté (1834-1839) and de la Hailandiére (1839-1847) to complete the magnificent Romanesque cathedral of St. François-Xavier in 1841, to build the first library in Indiana in 1842, and to contribute mightily to the foundation of Notre Dame University in 1843.

Nor were Vincennes and South Bend the only towns in Indiana to receive Catholic foundations; in Allen County (the seat of which is Ft. Wayne), the 1840s saw the foundation of Besancon with its church of St. Louis by French immigrants. At the other end of the state, Jasper, seat of Dubois County was settled in 1838 by a band of Germans led by a Fr. Joseph Kundeck. In the churchyard of St. Joseph's, another huge romanesque structure named after Fr. Kundeck, is the Cross of Deliverance erected by sculptor Joseph Baumann in fulfillment of a vow made during a stormy crossing of the Atlantic in 1847. Tucked away in the southeast corner of the state is Dearborn County, whose towns of Dover and New Alsace were settled in 1837 by Irish, French, and Germans; the latter built in that year New Alsace's St. Paul's Catholic Church. In the same year still more German Catholics settled Oldenburg in neighboring Franklin County; ever since a center of the Faith in Indiana, it boasts a shrine of the Sorrowful Mother.

Noel La Vasseur (1799-1879) is an example of a great Catholic pioneer. A fur trader, he established in 1832 a trading post at Bourbonnais, Illinois, south of Chicago. He arranged for large scale French-Canadian immigration to the area in the following decade, of which an early local historian wrote: "From Bourbonnais went people who established every other French town in Kankakee and Iroquois counties. Kankakee in a large measure, St. Anne, L'Erable, St. Mary, Papineau all acknowledge Bourbonnais as the mother." In later years these folk would be responsible for the building of a miraculous shrine of Ste. Anne in the town of that name, and two Catholic colleges in Bourbonnais itself. But the French-Canadians were not the only folk to start Catholic colonies in Illinois. Fayette County saw a group of English-descended Catholics from Kentucky settle St. Elmo in 1830; nine years later German Catholics founded Teutopolis in neighboring Effingham County. In 1828, the discovery of coal at Belleville attracted hosts of primarily Catholic Germans to the town, laying the foundations for it eventually to be come a diocese of its own.

Wisconsin's first towns were the usual French settlements; in her case, Green Bay and Prairie du Chien. Father Mazzuchelli whom we met in Iowa was to be the most prominent priest in Wisconsin from 1830 to 1860. Catholic immigrants came in; beginning in 1836, Germans and Irish flocked to Milwaukee. From thence the former people spread out. In 1843, the diocese of Milwaukee was separated from that of Detroit. All of this was facilitated by the opening of the Erie Canal.

The French were also responsible for the first church in Michigan, Ste. Anne's, Detroit. *Fr. Gabriel Richard* (1767-1832) served as pastor there for the last thirty years of his life. He was responsible for the founding of the University of Michigan, the first State University in the nation, and went to Congress as a delegate from the Michigan Territory. He also worked to expand the Church outside of Detroit, as when in 1824 he bought the site for a Catholic church in what is now Marine City. Sault Ste. Marie, St. Ignace, and Monroe (Frenchtown) were old French settlements which served as gateways of migration. In 1836 a German priest and five companions explored the wilderness in what is now Clinton County. They chose a site for German settlers, named it Westphalia, and with their help built St. Mary's Church, the State's first German Catholic parish. At the same time, missions were being established among the State's Indians—Ottawa, Ojibway, and Pottawattomi, most notably by the Bohemian born *Father (later Bishop) Frederick Baraga*.

The Old Southwest

New Catholic settlement was not nearly so prominent in the Old Southwest—but it did occur. The "Holy Land" of Kentucky continued to grow internally, centered on Jefferson, Campbell, Nelson, and Kenton Counties. Rural folk of Maryland-English descent, its inhabitants continued to practice the plain piety of their ancestors. Among them were already such institutions as Nazareth College at Cox's Creek, founded in 1814 and the Convent at Loretto, center of the first native American order of nuns. Louisville, by contrast, had attracted a number of French emigres during their Revolution. They were followed by many Germans in the 1840s, a large number of whom were Catholic. The center of the Faith was the See city of Bardstown, whose St. Joseph's Cathedral, begun in 1814 and dedicated by Bishop Flaget in 1816, was unequaled on the frontier. Complementing its impressive Classical architecture were interior gifts from King Louis-Phillipe of France, the King of Naples, and various other royal donors.

The first Catholic priests to visit Tennessee arrived in 1810. Eleven years passed before a bishop would visit the area. The first parish was founded in Nashville in 1830—and the town became a diocese seven years later. St. Mary's in that town was built in Greek Revival style in 1844-47.

In Alabama, Mobile had been since French colonial days a center of the Faith; so ingrained was it that Mardi Gras was as popular there as in New Orleans—and the Faith was similarly associated with aristocratic Creole society. Bishop Michel Portier, first bishop of the new diocese of Mobile, lay the cornerstone for the imposing Immaculate Conception Cathedral in 1836. He had founded Spring Hill College in 1830. In the coastal settlements south of the city, places like Bon Secour, Mon Louis Island, and Bayou La Batre, poor fishermen descended from the French and Spanish kept up their practice of Catholicism. In the rest of the state, the Faith was confined to large urban centers like Montgomery, where a few Catholics of good family might be found.

Like Alabama, Mississippi's coastal region was the focus of her Catholic life. Biloxi was a center of French and Spanish descendants. Other coastal towns like Pass Christian, Delisle, and Bay St. Louis all had their parishes. Natchez was made the site of a diocese by Pope Gregory XVI in 1837; the red brick Gothic Revival St. Mary's Cathedral was commenced in 1841, and would take a decade to complete.

The Seminoles kept the Church, along with other institutions associated with the Whites, from expanding too greatly into the interior of Florida, which after all had only come under nominal American control in 1819. The old Spanish towns of St. Augustine and Pensacola remained centers of Catholicism, as was the wrecker's settlement of Key West. Despite being a slave state, the Spanish and Black mixed-bloods of Pensacola (called by that elastic phrase, "Creole") were very important socially, and bulwarks of the Faith. St. Augustine's Minorcans also retained their loyalty to the Church, and produced a number of clergy who worked throughout the Gulf states.

The Thirteen Oldest States

Maine still counted in its Northern section as frontier territory. The oldest standing Catholic Church in New England was built by Irish in Damariscotta in 1808. The Penobscot and Passamaquoddy Indians, who lived on state reservations, had been Catholic since colonial times. Maine's northern border with Canada was not delimited until the Webster-Ashburton Treaty of 1842. With that, the British Crown conceded to the United States a number of Acadian French settlements who kept both their language and a very public expression of the Faith (Corpus Christi processions and the like) —scandalous to the good Unitarians of southern Maine.

There were also in 1816 wild unsettled areas remaining in Pennsylvania, New York, and Virginia, which Catholics would help to civilize in the ensuing years. In the last named Commonwealth, much of the area which is now West Virginia was yet a wilderness when the War of 1812 ended. The first Catholic church was built at Wheeling in 1821, but by 1845 there were only four others: at Parkersburg, Harper's Ferry, Weston, and near Kingwood. There are a few incidents from Catholic history there worth recalling. The most bizarre occurred at Middleway in Jefferson County, and is recounted by the WPA Guide to the state in the following terms:

> According to local stories, strange happenings took place in Middleway in 1790. Adam Livingston, a settler, gave shelter to a traveler, who fell desperately ill during the night and begged Livingston to call a priest. He refused, saying that there was no priest in the neighborhood, and if there were, he would not have one in his house. The traveler died; no wake was held, for candles brought into the room were mysteriously blown out; and the nameless stranger was hastily buried. Shortly afterward horses were heard galloping around the house at night; flaming logs jumped from the fireplace and danced around the kitchen; the heads of Livingston's horses, cows, pigs, and chickens mysteriously fell off; his barn burned to the ground; his money disappeared. Clothes, linens, and rugs, locked in chests and closets, were found cut to shreds or with tiny holes snipped in them. The snipping sound of shears could be heard night and day. Curious neighbors who called at the Livingston house went away with their clothes full of holes. Livingston appealed to his minister, but the clergyman was as mystified as the others. Finally, in a dream, Livingston saw a man in flowing robes who offered to help him. Convinced that he was a priest, Livingston went to Shepherdstown to consult Father Dennis Cahill, who returned with him to Middleway, and said Mass in the house. The manifestations stopped immediately. In gratitude Livingston deeded to the Roman Catholic Church 34 acres of ground, and specified that a chapel was to be was to be erected thereon. Trustees were appointed; years passed but no chapel was built. Livingston later sold all his property, except the broad field on the banks of the Opequon Creek, known as Priest's Field, and moved to Pennsylvania. After his death the field was claimed by his heirs; to hold the property, the Catholic Church erected about 1925 a small gable-roofed gray frame building, known as Priest's Field Chapel (pp. 311-312).

Although the Hudson River Valley had been settled from the 17th Century, the rest of the State of New York was wide open in 1816. Starting in the 1820s, the rash of canal building (especially the Erie Canal) brought droves of Irish laborers into western New York. By 1840 they had dug 13 canals totaling 900 miles. With them came missionary priests. Beyond their announced work, these Irish "were working on the foundations of three episcopal sees, were choosing sites for five hundred churches, were opening the interior of the state to the empire of religion, as well as of commerce."

The Commonwealth of Pennsylvania was blessed with Fr. Demetrius Gallitzin, the princely Russian convert priest who established the German Catholic settlement of Loretto, and Bohemian-born St. John Neumann who would later be Bishop of Philadelphia. But perhaps the most notable Catholic effort of the period we are actually discussing was the foundation of St. Mary's in Elk County. For this town was laid out in 1842 on land owned by the German Catholic Brotherhood. It was specially prepared as a refuge for German Catholics who had fled Philadelphia and Baltimore as a result of the Know-Nothing riots; we shall look at these more closely in a moment.

Frontier Lessons

The story of Catholicism on the frontier is very inspiring, if little known; we have barely scratched the surface. We should learn more about our fathers who came across the ocean and tried to reproduce the Faith of the lands they left in a strange and often hostile environment. They were precisely the reason for the enormous growth spoken of earlier.

But there is another, darker side to that growth. It came about almost entirely as a result of this tide of immigration—not because of conversion of the native Anglo-Americans. This was unfortunate, because starting in the 1790s and continuing for at least sixty more years, the frontier from North to South was agitated by what was called the Second Great Awakening or the Great Revival. Just as much of mainstream Protestantism today takes its lead from the Unitarians and Transcendentalists of this era, so too do many of the Fundamentalists look to Revivalism.

The relatively rapid settlement of the frontier had left many of the Eastern Protestant churches behind. Having outstripped their clergy, the settlers found themselves alone and spiritually bereft in a savage land. Starting in Kentucky about 1799, Revivalism was and is characterized by "Camp Meetings." These were large gatherings at a given time and place; families would come from as far as 30 or 40 miles away. They would pitch their tents around a clearing where a preacher would give his version of religion. Lasting for three or four days, these meetings would include prayer meetings, preaching, hymn singing, baptisms and weddings. Very often folk were expected to feel converted and to come up and "testify" about it. Sometimes as many as 10,000 to 20,000 would turn out for these affairs, which sometimes degenerated into mass hysteria. The Shakers, Methodists, and Baptists profited by them to spread throughout the West; the Disciples of Christ owe their origin to them. However strange they might appear to us, they certainly showed a hunger for religion—a hunger Catholics did not attempt to supply them on any large scale.

While not attempting the difficult task of mass conversions, effort was made to interest some few. In 1844, the noted Brook Farmer Orestes Brownson came into the Church. In the next decade and indeed until his death he would be a stalwart—if not always consistent—fighter for the Faith. Theodore Hecker, who would one day found the Paulists and become identified with the Americanist heresy was a friend of Brownson and had been at Brook Farm, converted also in 1844. The next year, James McMaster (1820-1886) became a Catholic. He too pursued Catholic journalism. Unlike Brownson (with whom he differed in philosophy and politics) he was a States' Rights Democrat and anti-abolitionist.

The same year that Brownson and Hecker converted, Philadelphia was wracked by the Know-Nothing riots, which would give the first inhabitants of St. Mary's, PA, a reason to go there. The increasing flood of largely Catholic immigrants had led in 1835 to the formation of the Native American Movement in New York. Over the next nine years the Nativists continued an ever-increasing propaganda campaign against Catholics.

Things came to a head in May of 1844, in Philadelphia. A Nativist mob burned two Catholic churches in the city. In the days that followed, Catholic homes were torched, and Catholics shot on their doorsteps and hung from lampposts. They could have saved themselves and their property by hanging out American flags, or signs saying "Native Americans;" but the Nativists had made the Stars and Stripes a sign of apostasy. Bishop Kenrick, fearful that more violence might occur, ordered all the city's Catholic churches closed on May 12. He had relied on the civic officials for protection.

In New York, things were a bit different. When news arrived at Bishop John Hughes' office about the events in Philadelphia, he warned the Nativist mayor: "If a single Catholic Church is burned in New York, the city will become a second Moscow."

"The mayor snidely replied, "Are you afraid that some of your churches will be burned?

"No sir," answered the redoubtable prelate. "But I am afraid that some of yours will be burned. I have come to warn you for your own good!"

The warning served its purpose, and nothing happened in New York.

But the United States was still an anti-Catholic country, whose army was not permitted to have priests as chaplains. This was a problem, for in little while America's Catholics would once again be asked to shed their blood—this time against fellow-Catholics.

THE MEXICAN WAR

As mentioned earlier, the annexation of Texas had made the United States heir to its new territory's land dispute with Mexico. Further, newly elected President James K. Polk had also to deal with the British in the Oregon country. In 1818, the two nations had agreed to joint occupation of the Oregon country, which included the present states of Oregon, Washington, Idaho, and parts of Montana, as well as the southern portion of the Province of British Columbia. Both American fur traders and agents of the Hudsons' Bay Company set up trading posts to fetch pelts from the Indians of the area.

The Company, which effectively administered all of what is now Western Canada as well as the Oregon Country, sent out as its "factor" or chief official one *Dr. John McLoughlin* (1784-1857) in 1824. McLoughlin was one of the noblest characters in the history of the Old West; his interest was not only to make profits for the Company, but also the development of the land given to his care, and additionally the spiritual welfare of the French half-breeds who worked for the H.B.C., and the Indians. He converted to Catholicism himself, and helped Fr. De Smet and other Catholic missionaries.

He immediately began the building of Ft. Vancouver (now Vancouver, Washington) as his headquarters. In 1829 he began the settling of Oregon City, welcoming all newcomers to the Oregon Country, regardless of nationality; he aided them all indiscriminately. As with the Mexicans in Texas, the price of such aid would be high.

McLoughlin had helped Protestant missionaries as well; in 1838 one of these returned with 50 more from the Eastern U.S., partially financed by the American government secret service fund. By 1841 there were enough American settlers to form a provisional government. British and Canadians were not pleased, but in 1843, 900 more Americans arrived from Independence, Missouri. The next year there were 1,400 new arrivals from thence, and in 1845 3,000. These began to show great hostility to McLoughlin and the H.B.C. The Western States began to agitate for annexation, and at the Democratic National Convention of 1844 it was declared that the U.S. had "clear and unquestionable" title to "the whole of the territory of Oregon." The Party, referring to the parallel which formed the northernmost boundary of the Oregon Country, made

"Fifty-four forty or fight!" a campaign motto. Polk was elected on the promise of obtaining it.

Negotiations were carried on, and at last it was decided to extend the frontier along the same line already dividing the two nations further east. But the whole of Vancouver Island was conceded to the British; at its southern tip H.B.C. transferred its headquarters in the new settlement of Victoria. McLoughlin ended his days in a mansion in Oregon City. Polk was free to turn his attention south.

In Mexico

The continual tug of war between the Liberals or Federalists and the Conservatives or Centralists had continued, with the ever-opportunistic Santa Ana serving as President for the Liberals. In November 1844, Conservative General Mariano Paredes went into open rebellion. Santa Ana left Mexico City to fight him; while the President was in the field, Mexico City went into revolt and the Congress deposed him. He surrendered in January of 1845, and after a few months in prison, was allowed into exile in June.

After a short period, Paredes became President of Mexico. He favored the continued relationship between Church and State in Mexico, and the implementation of the Three Guarantees. One of these, of course, was the securing of a foreign prince as Emperor. Moreover, he was in favor of maintaining Mexico's territorial integrity. Thus, President Polk's ominous remarks concerning the United States' destiny to expand to the Pacific were not received too well by him—any more than a declaration on his part that Mexico wished to expand to the Atlantic via Florida would have been by Polk. One thing we often forget in studying our history is that the expansion of our country has been at others' expense. Those others were quite as resentful as we might be under the circumstances.

American settlers had filtered into California from Oregon; there they would play the same part their confreres had played in that region and in Texas. After the annexation of the latter state, Polk ordered Zachary Taylor and his 3,900 troops from the Sabine River of Louisiana to Corpus Christi Bay in Texas. On February 3, 1846, Polk ordered them to move to the Rio Grande, thus ensuring the outbreak of war. On March 28, they arrived unopposed at their goal. Across the river lay the town of Matamoros and a Mexican garrison.

At first, the two armies sat. Nearly half of Taylor's forces were foreign born: 24% were Irish; 10% German; 6% English; 3% Scots; and 4% Others. Memories of the outrages in Philadelphia were fresh, and the Catholics in the army were all too aware that Chaplains of their Faith were not permitted in the American army. Over 200 deserted to the Mexicans. That their feelings about the war were not restricted to immigrants may be seen by this diary entry of Lieutenant Ethan Allen Hitchcock, one of Taylor's officers, and grandson of Ethan Allen:

> ...I have said from the first that the United States are the aggressors. We have outraged the Mexican government and people by an arrogance and presumption that deserve to be punished.... We have not one particle of right to be here. Our force is altogether too small for the accomplishment of its errand. It looks as if the government sent a small force on purpose to bring on a war, so as to have a pretext for taking California and as much of this country as it chooses; for, whatever becomes of this army, there is no doubt of a war between the United States and Mexico.... My heart is not in this business... but, as a military man, I am bound to execute orders.

The Course of the War

On May 8, the Mexicans crossed the Rio Grande, and were defeated at the Battle of Palo Alto; the next day they were drubbed again at Resaca de Palma. When news reached Washington, the war would begin in earnest. A week later, Taylor occupied Matamoros.

Meanwhile, events developed in California. General Mariano Vallejo, head of Mexican forces in Northern California at Sonoma Presidio (whither he had removed the troops from San Francisco), was a wealthy man. Such wealth had come to him through using for his own purposes Mission properties of which he was trustee for the Indians following secularization in 1833. He had already befriended the local Yankee settlers, insuring a place for himself under the new regime should there be a Texas-style change of governments. In the early morning hours of July 14, 1846, a group of these settlers went to Vallejo's house and affected to arrest him. He broke out drinks for all, and the California Republic was proclaimed; the flag they had already prepared for the occasion was run up the flag-pole of the Presidio. Meanwhile, the American officer John C. Fremont, who had been undercover, so to speak, with a party of U.S. soldiers, took command of the revolt. A small force of Mexicans coming from Monterey to suppress them was repulsed, and by the end of the month Fremont was master of all California north of San Francisco Bay (in those days, this meant former missions San Francisco Solano in Sonoma and San Rafael, the former Russian Ft. Ross, Sonoma Presido, Sutter's Fort in what is now Sacramento, and many, many trees).

A few days later, the U.S. Pacific fleet under Commodore Sloat demanded and received the surrender of the Californian capital at

Monterey. Two days later, the U.S.S. Portsmouth which had arrived in San Francisco Bay took possession of Mission San Francisco de Asis and the deserted Presidio. The stars and stripes were raised over the plaza of the little village between the two, Yerba Buena. Today that plaza is called Portsmouth Square, and is the center of San Francisco's Chinatown.

Southern California remained defiant, however. Fremont and his California Battalion were dispatched by sea to take San Diego, while a force of sailors was sent to San Pedro. Hard-riding Fremont rode quickly up the coast, joined forces with the naval party, and on August 12 received the surrender of the pueblo of Los Angeles. It appeared that California was completely in American hands.

When the city fell, Mexico already had a new president. After the defeats in the north, Paredes went to assume personal command. On July 31 the Vera Cruz garrison revolted and appealed to Santa Ana to return; four days later pro-Santa Ana troops entered the capital. On August 6, Paredes resigned. Thanks to American intervention, a genuine patriot's vision for Mexico was scotched, and a consummate if charming opportunist returned to power.

Two days after the fall of Los Angeles, an American column under General Stephen Kearny appeared outside Las Vegas, New Mexico, having marched all the way from Kansas. The next day the army entered Las Vegas and the small village of Tecolote; the oath of allegiance to the U.S. was administered to the inhabitants. On the 16th, San Miguel's citizens received the oath, and the march toward Santa Fe continued. Two days later, the capital was occupied without resistance. New Mexico had fallen without a shot being fired.

Meanwhile, Taylor's men continued the southward march into Mexico. Their objective was the city of Monterrey. They arrived at its gates on September 19. The changes in government had been mirrored in the city by changes in command, which reduced the abilities of the defenders considerably. For four days they fought the Americans, but on the 24th, Monterrey, Capital of the state of Nuevo Leon, fell to the invaders.

The fall of Monterrey resulted in one interesting development. More Irish deserted to the Mexicans. At length, these formed an Irish unit called the San Patricio Battalion, whose standard bore on one side the Mexican coat of arms with the motto "Long Live the Republic of Mexico;" on the other side was the figure of St. Patrick. No less than 1,011 deserted by March of 1847.

In late September, the Californios revolted against the American occupiers, and retook Los Angeles. The war in California was far from over. Fremont gathered about 430 men from the Monterey vicinity, and prepared to reconquer L.A. But by the time he reached Ventura on January 11, it was revealed to him that Kearny, having marched overland from El Paso (which they had taken peacefully on December 27 after fighting a skirmish with Mexican troops) had retaken Los Angeles themselves; this after being defeated by Californios armed with lances at San Pasqual. Their honor served, they accepted American occupation.

In the meantime, Taylor's army had desultorily occupied the areas around Monterrey and Saltillo. Santa Ana had gathered a large army at San Luis Potosi, and intended to attack the Yankees at a town called Buena Vista. February 22-24, the battle raged. It was one which the Mexicans should have won. But Santa Ana was outgeneraled, and the Battle of Buena Vista proved as crushing a defeat to the Mexicans, as Saratoga had been to the British during the revolution. Meanwhile, more American troops in El Paso marched south and took Chihuahua on March 2.

This was the same day that General Winfield Scott landed with another army near Vera Cruz. After a siege, the city fell on the 29th. Then the Americans turned inland on the road to Mexico City. On April 18, Scott's troops won the battle of Cerro Gordo; two days later they triumphed again at Churubusco. With the latter, the Americans were at the gates of the city, and expected surrender. Denied this, they began an assault on the castle of Chapultepec, key to Mexico City, on September 13. By the 14th, it was in American hands.

There they annihilated among other formations the Cadets at the Military School of Chapultepec and the San Patricio Battalion. Those of the latter who were not killed in battle were hanged after capture by the victorious Americans. The battles around Mexico City are immortalized in the U.S. Marine Corps hymn with the words "From the Halls of Montezuma..."

On the 15th, Winfield Scott's army entered Mexico City, and Santa Ana fled. For all practical purposes, the war was over. What was left of the Mexican government convened at Queretaro to await the orders of the victor. Santa Ana left the scene—to return a few years later.

On February 2, 1848, the Treaty of Guadalupe Hidalgo was signed, giving California, Texas, and New Mexico to the United States. The boundary was much like the one today, save that what are now Arizona south of the Gila River, and a strip including present day Las Cruces, New Mexico, remained in Mexican hands. For this, the U.S. would give Mexico 15 million dollars. The validity of the treaty, however, required three conditions: respect for the property of the local inhabitants; maintenance of their Spanish language, culture, and customs; and freedom for Catholicism. These would be disregarded.

It would be impossible to overemphasize the impact this conquest made on the conquerors. As Bishop David Arias points out:

> The taking of this vast region by the United States is not like coming into an uncivilized land, but into a territory that is explored and unified. It is a territory with a language and culture deeply rooted in its people and cities. Also, this is a territory with mining, agriculture, cattle raising, and economy in progress. It is a territory with its Indian population, to a large extent, settled, civilized, and Christianized from a slow but steady labor of Spain for over three hundred years. It is also a great legacy of Spain, which is now an integral part of its geographical, anthropological, and cultural identity. To realize that, one only has to formulate this question: "Would the United States be the same without Texas, New Mexico, Arizona, Colorado, and California?" (*Spanish Roots of America*, pp. 256-257).

Certainly, before 1848, the mother country of the United States was Great Britain, with France providing a secondary role in Louisiana and the Old Northwest. But Spain would join the ranks of America's mother countries as a result of this war. We would be joined to Latin America from then on.

But if the war was unjust, the Mexicans had partial revenge; the newly acquired territories would worsen the sectional conflict between North and South to the point of bloodshed. James K. Polk, who had single-handedly brought the war about did not profit at all. His conduct of it created many enemies and brought about his defeat in the next election by Zachary Taylor, the man whose career he in a sense created, by giving him the opportunity to become "the Hero of Buena Vista."

For the Church, the problem of integrating these Catholic newcomers in the new lands was daunting. We shall see how Church and State dealt with their new acquisitions, and the ever-increasing sectional strife in the next chapter.

DIVISION AND WAR
1849-1865

THE NEW TERRITORIES

At last Thomas Jefferson's dream of "Manifest Destiny" had been achieved; the United States lay from sea to sea. In the north, the British had been banished to Canada once and for all. Even Dr. John McLoughlin, former Factor of the Hudson's Bay Company, was content to live out his life in Oregon City, as a subject in the land he had once ruled so benevolently and so well. "Green gold", timber, from the Northwest would permit expansion of the American economy in innumerable ways, and the fertile soil of the region would stimulate immigration from all over the world.

Acquisition of the Southwest was a different matter. Whereas the Oregon Country had an Indian population that could fairly easily be subdued, and a small white population made up of British and French ex-H.B.C. employees and Anglo-American settlers, Texas and the lands most recently acquired from Mexico already had an established culture. While it had been much diluted by Anglo-American immigration in Texas, this Spanish and Catholic ethos was still predominant in California, New Mexico, and Arizona. Moreover, until the American conquest, Catholicism was the only legal religion there. Although later events would guarantee that the Southwest would become an integral part of the country as a whole, it would alter the nature of that country to a degree even as possession of Louisiana had.

Texas

The new "Lone Star State," admitted the same year it was annexed, had been an independent republic for nine years. The spirit of independence and self-sufficiency that this built among Texans has never disappeared.

The effect of Independence on the Church was catastrophic, however—as might be expected from a revolution which denounced the priesthood as an instrument of tyranny. In 1838 there were only two priests resident in the state; while this situation would improve, Methodist, Baptist, and Presbyterian ministers rushed in in large numbers. Although there were few defections from among the Mexicans, there were many among the Irish colonies in San Patricio, Refugio, Aransas, Bee, and Goliad counties. As a result, there are many anti-

Catholic folk settled there with beautiful Gaelic names, whose religious views would shock their distant cousins in the Old Sod.

But despite the lack of clergy, the *Tejanos* retained their Spanish language, culture, and heritage. Around the old capital of San Antonio (whose Spanish governor's palace, although converted into a store, retained and retains the Habsburg double-eagle over the door), Laredo, Nacodoches, El Paso, and the lower Rio Grande valley, the rancheros attempted to continue their gracious and refined manner of life. They continued to hold *fandangos*—public dances—on the plazas. Then as now, the feasts and customs of the Church retained their hold on public life, as the Texas WPA guide quoted in Appendix E tells us. All of which shows how much of Medieval Spain had been brought over to Mexico and thence to Texas. The *ricos*, great landholders, presided over their tenants as did the grandees in Spain. But rich and poor alike, the *Tejanos* were and to a large degree still are regarded as inferior and uncivilized by the Anglo-Texans, for all that they represent an unbroken tradition of centuries.

Some of these latter, however, had more in common in some ways with their Spanish-speaking compatriots than either would like to admit. Early on, settlers from the Cumberland and Ozark mountains arrived in the Austin hills and the piney woods of East Texas. They were great believers in the use of conjure balls to dry up wells, and kerosene oil to cure most illnesses. They told strange and frightening tales of ghosts and monsters in an almost Elizabethan English; from the old country too came ballads like "Barbara Allan." Like the peons moreover, they also looked up to a class of great landowners.

For even as the hill and wood dwellers had come from the Southern hills and woods, way of life intact, so too did great plantation owners. Building cotton plantations along the Brazos, Trinity, Neches, Sabine, and Colorado River bottoms, they sought to reproduce the way of life their peers had brought to Alabama and Mississippi from Georgia and the Carolinas. Moreover, due to their superior fortunes, these soon came to dominate the political life of the new state. Their slaves were much like those in the rest of the south, with an imaginative folk-life all their own—filled with "conjure," and charms, and extra-biblical stories of Moses. This planter aristocracy ensured that Texas would line up, in any conflict, with the other slave states. But there were other groups whose loyalty was not so certain.

The European uprisings of 1848 sent fleeing to America large numbers of Germans, Czechs, and Poles. Many of these came to Texas; the Catholics among them established settlements where the religion and traditions of their homelands could be maintained. The Czechs came to

Praha, Fayetteville, Dubina, and many other places. Of them our indispensable guide says:

> Neighbors gather to prepare goose feathers for bedding to be given newly-married couples; when the feathers have been stripped from their stems, the hostess serves a feast. On Christmas Eve, one youth will dress as St. Nicholas, another as an angel, a third as the devil, and as they question the children, St. Nicholas rewards the obedient ones, while Satan administers a few light blows to the less worthy. In rural sections of this region young boys dip all the girls in water on the Saturday night before Easter. Czech national dances, including the Beseda, are performed, especially on festival days. (p. 432).

So too did other groups retain their ways. Even before 1848, large groups of German colonists, many Catholic, were already coming to Texas. Three years previously, the settlement of New Braunfels was founded, near San Antonio; in Appendix F this event is described in detail.

We have dealt with this affair at length because it is emblematic of Catholic colonization efforts, not just in Texas, but across the frontier. How little, when we think of the pioneers, do we remember the Catholics among them! Note further that these Catholics attempted to preserve in what was then trackless wilderness an age-old way of life, even as their Spanish predecessors had. Lastly, such men as Prince zu Solm-Braunfels, Baron von Meusebach, and their noble colleagues ought to be remembered as fathers of Texas at least as much as Sam Houston and Stephen Austin are.

But in addition to such hardy Catholic settlers, many Liberal Germans came to Texas after the revolts failed. These were highly educated folk (called "Latin farmers" for their habit of reading the Classics in between plowing) who, as the Catholics came to carve out a new Catholic world, wanted to establish a Liberal and Protestant one. Their loyalties lay not with Old Europe, or even the neighboring Southern states, but with the Federal government of the new land in which they dwelled, dedicated as it was supposed to be to the same principles of revolution for which they had fought in Germany. In the years to come, this would be an ominous point for their English-speaking neighbors.

Settled as they were in colonies separated by unpleasant wilderness, the Catholic colonies in Texas looked little to playing a larger role in the state. Despite their religion and way of life, they did not look to convert the state in which they lived; neither did they seek to form a united stand between themselves in their German, Czech, Polish, Alsatian, and so on multiplicity, and the *Tejano* populace.

Apart from El Paso and the Rio Grande Valley, West Texas was still the haunt of tribes like the Commanche. During the 1850s a chain of forts was built across the state to ward off raids and serve as base for further expansion. This meant the presence of Federal troops on Texan soil, which also would have an effect in the future.

New Mexico

While the Spanish had only begun the settlement of Texas in the 18th Century, they had been in New Mexico a much longer time. Further, there was very little outside immigration to the remote province under Mexican rule. The Apache and Commanche had waged endless warfare against the colony and its allied Pueblo Indians since the beginning.

The Pueblos, while converted to Catholicism, retained many of their ancient customs, adapted to their lives as Christians. The traditional annual dances, for example, would be performed on the eve or feast of the given Pueblo's patron saint. It would be followed by a Mass and athletic events. Each of the Pueblos was and is presided over by a Governor, all of whom were initially confirmed in their powers by the King of Spain; this confirmation would be renewed by President Lincoln.

The *Hispanos*, as the white Spanish inhabitants are called, were similar to the *Tejanos* in the realm of religion and folklore. But there were a few major differences. The Third Order of St. Francis had become separated from the supervision of the padres when regular administration of the order broke down under the Mexican government. Nevertheless, they had continued and even augmented the public penances once so common in Medieval Europe and at the time still popular in the Hispanic world. The folk were called *Penitentes;* their little chapels, called *Moradas*, were generally off limits to outsiders. During Holy Week they would stage reenactments of the Way of the Cross, with the man playing Christ actually being scourged and crucified—non-lethally. If these practices seem harsh to us, it should be recalled that many of these were recommended by Saints.

North of Santa Fe lay the Sanctuary of Chimayo. Its twin shrines still exist, and many miraculous cures are yet wrought in them. In their way they are emblematic of the whole Catholic Spanish and Indian folk-culture of northern New Mexico. For here, despite the constant menace of Commanches and Apaches and isolation from Spain and Mexico, a high level of civilization was maintained. Although resources were few—limited mining and quarrying, cattle, sheep, and goat raising, and vegetable and grain farming—churches and public buildings were built unequaled in, say, colonial New England. The Palace of the Governors in Santa Fe, the great churches of villages like Santa Cruz, Laguna, and

Las Trampas, the carved furniture and statues of the Saints, all reflect not only religious devotion but an artistic taste and ability far in advance of the Puritans who gave the English-speaking areas their tone.

Chimayo's patron, the Santo Niño of Esquipulas, is significant. The Black Christ of that town was carved by order of the Conquistadors in 1594, and placed in a local church the next year. This was replaced in 1737 by a magnificent colonial edifice erected by order of the Archbishop of Guatemala; since then the shrine has remained the foremost pilgrimage center in Central America. The presence of the two shrines, virtually at opposite ends of the old Viceroyalty of New Spain, underscores the unity of devotion and culture brought by the Spanish to the New World. Initially cut off by Independence from Spain, this unity withered further with the increasing secularization of Mexico. The process would be well nigh completed by the annexation of New Mexico to the United States. In the end, New Mexico's uniquely Catholic and Spanish heritage would become much like the French and Catholic one of Louisiana: a jealously guarded treasure for those fortunate enough to be born into it or to immigrate to it, but emphatically not a springboard for the conversion of the North American continent to Catholicism, as its founders had hoped. The reward for passivity would be bare tolerance and progressive, if slow, assimilation. Even today, however, Spanish New Mexico is far from dead.

Arizona

Although the ongoing separation of what had been the Spanish frontier— "The Northern Rim of Christendom" —from its erstwhile hinterland to the south had stagnating effects in New Mexico, it was almost catastrophic for what remained of the Hispanic presence in southern Arizona. Unable to prevent the raids of the Apaches, the Mexican government after 1821 watched as Hispanic settlers were forced out of isolated ranchos into the secure refuges of Tucson and Tubac. Although the Papago and Pima Indians preserved the beautiful missions of San Xavier del Bac and Tumacacori, continuing to practice their Faith even without missionaries, it appeared by the end of the Mexican War that Tucson and Tubac would soon fall; the work of the saintly Padre Kino and his successors would be made in vain. The Gila River had been designated as Mexico's northern border by the treaty, but the defeated nation was in little position to garrison it.

But in 1853, what are now southern Arizona and a strip of New Mexico (the latter centering on the sleepy town of Mesilla and the Indian village of Tortugas) were sold to the United States by Santa Ana in the Gadsden Purchase. The arrival of American troops in Tucson, already abandoned by Mexican forces, signaled the end of the long siege and gave the old pueblo's inhabitants hope that their town would survive. It would, but in what form remained to be seen.

California

The California conquered by the Americans was much more cosmopolitan than either the remote New Mexican hills and valleys or the deserts of Arizona. An extensive sea coast with many harbors had brought traders from all over the world—albeit illegally—to Alta California. There were in 1848 only three incorporated towns: San Jose, the largest; Los Angeles; and Branciforte, destined to be absorbed by Santa Cruz. In addition to these, the presidios at San Diego, Santa Barbara, Monterey (site of the province's capital), San Francisco, and Sonoma had attracted Hispanic settlers who had built communities around them. The 21 secularized missions had also served as nuclei for new towns (even while large numbers of their pictures, statues, vestments, and the like were saved from the general plunder by zealous Indian or Spanish families; many of these would be returned later, when the missions were again in Church hands). Outside these widely separated islands of activity were the great ranchos; like their counterparts in New Mexico and Texas, the rancheros ran their holdings as great feudal estates—even as did their counterparts on the haciendas and latifundias elsewhere in Latin America. But in addition, a trickle of immigrants from every corner of the U.S. and many places overseas had begun to flow in even while California was Mexican. The conquest turned up that trickle to a steady stream.

One of the trickle was the Swiss-born *John Sutter*, who carved out an economic empire based upon his fort at what is now Sacramento. Although Sutter had managed to steer his realm peacefully through the American takeover (and to buy Ft. Ross from the Russians in Alaska), his doom was spelled by an employee's discovery in 1848 of gold on his land. The news spread around the world: the result was the famed California Gold Rush of 1849.

From a stream immigration became a torrent; one which submerged Sutter's holdings and changed the face of California forever. Men of every nationality flocked to the gold fields of northcentral California. Mining towns sprang up overnight, and failed as quickly when the gold gave out. Fortunes were made and lost in days; but millions upon millions of dollars in the precious metal could not help but enrich the national economy, no matter whose private hands it was in.

The little village of Yerba Buena, halfway between the mission and the presidio of San Francisco, benefited by her strategic location as the major port of entry to the gold fields to become an enormous city. She grew up around the two institutions which had given her birth, and took their mutual name. As the glorious city of San Francisco, she became in a short time a cultural center which could claim equality with places like New York and New Orleans. As the notorious "Barbary Coast," the city acquired a rough reputation for immorality and violence. But alongside the crime flourished opera and ballet; within a decade of the discovery of gold, San Francisco had become a recognized stop for performers engaged in national and world tours.

One product of the Gold Rush was the unofficial division of California into north and south. In those days, the Californios of the north being swiftly outnumbered and superseded politically, that area became the dominant section, particularly after the mass immigration brought statehood in 1850. The south remained pastoral and more Spanish much longer. But her time of mass immigration would come too, leaving her the dominant half. Nevertheless, the differences between the two halves of the Golden State, no matter how reinforced by later power struggles, find their essential roots in the Gold Rush era. It was also the Gold Rush which first brought non-Hispanic Catholics to the State. These mainly Irish folk would soon come to dominate the Church in California; they would build beautiful edifices like St. Mary's and St. Patrick's, both in San Francisco.

Colorado and Utah

The Spanish settlers of New Mexico had continued to settle northwards into what is now Colorado, particularly the San Luis Valley. The WPA Guide to Colorado well describes the genesis of the village of San Luis itself:

> The first successful attempt to found a town on the grant was made in 1851 when six Spanish families settled north of the present town. Their adobe houses were built around a square, both for protection against Indians and promotion of social life. The outer walls were without openings, and all doors and windows faced the square, in which wells were dug. The surrounding land was divided into ranches. A tract of 860 acres, reserved as a town common in accord with the system then in vogue in Mexico, has been retained. The Ute made numerous raids on the colony, stealing livestock and supplies, until the establishment of Fort Massachusetts...
>
> San Luis has changed little since its early days. The inhabitants have preserved their culture, social life, foods, and dress, drawing inspiration from Spain and New Mexico.

This was what there was of Colorado until gold was discovered at Pike's Peak, unleashing the Gold Rush of 1859. Like its California prototype, it would rapidly transform the area, establishing Denver in similar wise as San Francisco.

There was, however, in the newly conquered territory one other European descended group. Unlike the Hispanics, these were very recent arrivals, and were mostly English-speaking. Possessed of a new religion, the Mormons (a name given them by non-Mormon neighbors; they call themselves the Latter-Day Saints) were followers of one *Joseph Smith*. Smith had maintained that he had received a visit from an angel who had lent him a pair of spectacles. Armed with these he claimed to have read and translated what has become known as the Book of Mormon. Teaching among other things polygamy, Smith's followers were soon persecuted; he himself was murdered in Nauvoo, Illinois by an angry mob. But his followers, led by *Brigham Young*, migrated westward. In 1847, they settled in the valley of the Great Salt Lake.

It was hoped by Young that this would be the foundation of the "State of Deseret", which would encompass all the Great Basin. In the decades to come, Mormon pioneers would settle not only Utah, but large portions of southern Idaho, eastern Nevada, and northern Arizona. They would range as far afield as San Bernardino, California. Their skill in agriculture would make the desert bloom, and attract converts to Utah from all over northern Europe. In time, they would become a serious rival to Catholicism in many parts of the Americas. But that time lay far off in the future.

SUMMARY

What America received from Mexico was nothing less than an empire. At one stroke, the entire future of the nation was changed. For in these new territories lay unimaginable mineral and agricultural wealth. Properly exploited, it would transform the heretofore financially challenged United States with the funds necessary to propel them into the topmost rank of nations.

The legacy bequeathed the United States was not only material, however, but cultural. From the resident Hispanics, Americans would learn the trade of the cowboy. For many, coming to the newly acquired regions would be not only an economic improvement but a personal revelation. In time, the heritage of Spain would give to Catholicism a cachet for Protestant Americans she had not had when identified purely with hordes of immigrants from foreign lands.

But this cachet was acquired at a dreadful price: the removal of Southwestern Catholicism as a potential agent of conversion in the

United States. Through fraud, and in direct violation of the terms of the Treaty of Guadalupe Hidalgo, many Californios, Tejanos, and New Mexican Hispanos found themselves deprived of the land grants their ancestors had received in many cases from the King of Spain. The grants were then duly apportioned to Anglo-Americans.

In a society where land-ownership still meant political power, this meant the effective removal of the Hispanic "Dons" from public life. This was a two-fold loss. First, it was a loss to the Faith and to the poorer Hispanics. Despite individual cases of disloyalty to religion and tenants (such as Mariano Vallejo) the majority of the Dons were at once pious and protective of their dependents. Their loss of influence opened up the peons to exploitation and the Church to discrimination—in a region where she had been the only legal faith.

Secondly, the loss of political power by a class so imbued not only with Catholic tradition and deep ties to the soil, but also with a high regard for fine art and music, for food and wine, in a word, for all that makes life pleasant, was a grievous loss for the country as a whole. It is not merely that their persistence might have done much to alleviate racial tension in the Southwest, and to ease our relations with Latin America. Had they remained a significant part of this country's elite, they might have done much both to increase the influence of the Church and to make the U.S. more humane. A culture must inevitably reflect its elites; if they are given up entirely to banking, industry, and the making of money, it is just as inevitable that the society in question will not be that pleasant a place. And so it has proved.

IMMIGRATION AND THE PIONEERS

Much of the rest of the country was as empty as the new conquests. Official policy was to "extinguish" Indian title to a tract of land (usually by treaty following a short war, which would result in the given tribe's exile further West), open it for settlement, and allow whoever would come to take possession. There was a veritable avalanche of land speculation, which would not end until the closing of the frontier. Towns sprang up in the wilderness; some prospered and remain today. Others withered as quickly as they had come. Often, the new colonists would come from Europe in groups—particularly after (as we saw in Texas) the failure of the 1848 revolutions in continental Europe, and the Potato Famine in Ireland.

Catholics of other nationalities beside Irish and Germans began to arrive in numbers, alongside the first two stocks. We are often told of the non-Catholics who settled the frontier; but theirs is a tale so often told and so well elsewhere, we will leave it (save in brief) for a more detailed consideration of the Catholic settlements. The men, women, and children who settled them, those who led them (often priests and/or noblemen, as we have seen already) ought to be known by every Catholic American. They are our heritage, and often our direct ancestors. While the privations of other groups were often just as severe, they were undergone for the sake of economic gain or a false religion. To the Catholic settlers from Ireland, Germany, Poland, Bohemia, and elsewhere goes the imperishable honor of attempting to plant the light of the True Faith in a hostile environment—and to do so, not with the loving aid of a French or Spanish King with the wealth of an Empire behind their effort, but with only their own small pooled resources, in the face of an at best benignly neglectful regime in Washington.

The Old Northwest

Here settlement continued as it had before, with various colonies occupying tracts of land long cleared of Indians. Ohio in particular had (as we saw earlier) played host to a number of Catholic settlements. German Catholics flocked to the Indiana border from Darke County up to Putnam County—and are heavily Catholic to this day. One example of this effort is the village of Delphos, straddling the borders of Allen and Van Wert Counties.

In 1836, Fr. John Bredeick dispatched his brother Frederick to find a tract suitable for settlement. Frederick purchased 92 acres for the proposed settlement. In 1842 the first wave of 42 colonists arrived, joined the following year by a larger party. Fr. Bredeick himself arrived with another group in 1844. Despite the fact that non-Catholics also entered the village early on, to this day the Catholic High School is larger than the Public one. A similar undertaking in Mercer County to the south of the state was spearheaded by Fr. John Brunner. Germans—Catholic and Protestant alike—were not confined to rural colonies, however. Cincinnati and Cleveland became large centers for them in the 1840s and 50s; after the Famine, an ever-increasing number of Irish joined them. The former city in particular presented quite an intriguing picture as a river emporium. Filled with Germans and their singing and cultural societies, it looked to Europe; but intimately connected with the South both by the river and its position opposite Kentucky, it had nevertheless been founded by New Englanders. Cincinnati, like Ohio herself, was and remains a microcosm of the United States. While this resulted in an enjoyable cultural diversity, it could also give rise to sharp internal conflict. Just how sharp would soon become apparent. At any rate, the Catholics of the city were building fine churches like the Greek Classic St. Peter-in-Chains, graced as it was with a Murillo painting looted from the Cathedral of Seville by the armies of Napoleon; it also contained the marble tomb of Fr. Sebastian Badin, first priest ever to be ordained in the United States.

To some extent, the immigrants were already having an impact upon their native-born neighbors. As we saw earlier, Christmas was a holiday looked at with much suspicion by the Puritans. Although no longer illegal after the Revolution, it was not celebrated after the Revolution by native New Englanders, whether in their place of origin or the Ohio frontier. But in 1847, Wooster, Ohio, saw in a Bavarian immigrant home what is claimed to have been America's first Christmas tree. The home's owner, young immigrant August Imgard, was saddened by the lack of celebration on Our Lord's birthday. Accordingly, Imgard cut down a small spruce from the nearby woods, placed on its top a star he had a blacksmith make, and covered the tree with paper decorations and candles, just the like the ones he had trimmed at home. Soon the custom spread throughout Ohio and then the rest of the States.

It is interesting at this point to reflect that American Christmas celebrations truly reflect our polyglot origins; the tree is German, Santa Claus is New York Dutch. Poinsettias are Mexican, while holly, mistletoe, and most of our carols are English via the South, or else directly imported through Charles Dickens—the use of ham, turkey, and pumpkin and mince pies to grace the Yuletide table is pure Southern. And of course, late-night Christmas Eve services now offered by virtually all main-line Protestant sects (although not resorted to by all their membership) are completely alien to post-Reformation practice. They are entirely the result of observing Catholic Midnight Masses. Surely there is no greater irony than the elevation in the popular mind of a New England Congregational church, mantled in snow, to the position of supreme icon of the holiday season on Christmas cards. One wonders how John Calvin, Cotton Mather, or William Ellery Channing would have reacted to the sight, so common in Massachusetts since World War II, of a Nativity scene on a Unitarian church porch.

Indiana had much the same story to tell as Ohio. Like her, she had large numbers of Southerners crossing the river from Kentucky and points east; like her too she had plenty of Yankees and Pennsylvania Dutch Amish. But she differed in having already a small but well-established French Catholic populace, who welcomed immigrants of the same religion, if different blood. Vincennes, which in the first few decades of the 19th Century was a remote outpost of French culture, became much more cosmopolitan during the 40s and 50s. At first, Bishop Hailandiere accommodated the Germans with a special Mass and a priest of their own nationality at the Cathedral. But in 1852, they completed their own church, St. John the Baptist (named, one surmises, out of deference to the patron of their French co-religionists). As the WPA Guide to Indiana tells us, the future was then fast approaching:

> By 1853, when the first free public schools were inaugurated in Vincennes, the town was divided, so to speak, into three parts. "Frenchtown," which covered all the town below Main Street and from the Wabash to 8th Street, was still populated almost entirely by descendants of the town's Creole founders, who with their farmer cousins in the Cathelinette Prairies were still carrying on the customs of their forefathers to a noticeable extent. In the "Dutch Flats" stood the homes of the Germans, mostly members of the parish of St. John the Baptist. The remainder of the town, north of Main Street, was typically American and predominantly Protestant (p. 272).

In the end, of course, it was the customs and mores of the north part of town (save for the Faith herself) which would come to dominate all Vincennes, and many a similar town and city throughout the United States. The reason for this was the first-named phenomenon: the free public school.

It were well, while we are looking at the peopling of America, to consider the role of the Public School in melding the most diverse human elements into one—at least as far as national ideology is concerned. We have seen in an earlier chapter the desire of Noah Webster to give an ideological base to American education. If this was necessary to the purposes of the nation's rulers in 1790, when the population was relatively small and to some small degree homogeneous, how much more so would it be when the flow of immigrants became a flood tide? From the heartland of New England Unitarianism, however, an answer arose.

Six years after Webster outlined an American ideology, *Horace Mann* was born in Franklin, Massachusetts. Raised in poverty, he was nevertheless highly intelligent and industrious, and was admitted to Brown University, graduating thence in 1819. This was, as you may recall, the High Noon of Unitarianism and Transcendentalism. Mann imbibed these currents deeply, and left Brown determined to save the world. After a short career as a lawyer he turned to politics, serving in the Massachusetts Senate until 1837 (the prior year he was President thereof). He retired from that body to take up a post as head of the new State Board of Education. Self-made and self-educated himself, he wished to extend the benefits of education as he had received them to all.

For the next nine years (until resigning to take up John Quincy Adams' seat in Congress), Mann preached a six point program both in print and in lecture. He maintained that: 1) universal education was essential if this republic was to remain free; 2) the public must maintain and supervise this education; 3) that such education should bring together children of all sorts of backgrounds, so as to assimilate them; 4) it should be "moral" (in the odd generalized Unitarian meaning of that term) but non-specifically religious; 5) it should be animated by the spirit of a "free" society—no harsh punishment; and 6) it must be provided by well-trained teachers.

Although Mann's ideas were criticized by clerics of all denominations, by teachers, and by those who feared that school boards would undermine local and parental authority, they became in short order the dominant educational doctrine in the United States. Through them, the fundamental tenets of the American ideology discussed earlier became as unquestioned a part of the student's—and later the adult's—worldview as the Times Table and the Alphabet. Especially, religion was seen to be a private affair, with little bearing beyond family custom. Like the German, French or whatever of the home, Catholicism was an "Old Country" custom which was all right in its way, but not really necessary. For about a century and a half, attendance at Public Schools was a leading source of apostasy for young Catholics. For the populace as a whole, it led to a certain rigidity of mind about America; it reinforced the tendency to deify the country, rather than examine it critically as well as lovingly.

Partly to offset this development in his diocese, the Bishop of Vincennes begged the Abbot of the great Swiss Benedictine Abbey of Einsiedeln to send monks to the diocese. Their presence would bring many spiritual benefits, and anchor the Catholic identity of the region. On St. Benedict's Day, March 21, 1854, the monks founded St. Meinrad's Abbey, around which grew up the village of the same name. For over a century after, the German Catholics of that village and nearby Ferdinand looked to the Abbey as their center and spiritual stronghold. In the days of its greatness, St. Meinrad produced many a great monk, and well-kept the spirit and rule of St. Benedict alive in the new land. Moreover, in the early 1850s, the Holy Cross Fathers at South Bend founded what would become the University of Notre Dame. In Indiana, at any rate, it appeared that the disciples of Horace Mann would not go completely unchallenged.

The settling of the Old Northwest, which we now must call the Midwest, although facilitated greatly by National Roads and the canals, was spurred even further by the coming of the railroads in the 1850s. If more immigrants were pouring over the sea to Eastern ports, there were now quicker ways of getting them to their appointed wildernesses. Illinois profited greatly from this; Germans and Irish arrived throughout the 50s in ever larger numbers. The predominance of the Irish at that time in Chicago was signaled by the erection in 1856 of St. Patrick's.

Wisconsin had for long been a refuge for Indian tribes expelled from the East, who held the State in common with the Sauk, Fox, and Menominee tribes. But after the 1832 Black Hawk War (in which Abraham Lincoln had his only taste of military life) the first two tribes departed, and by 1856 the remaining tribes were on small reservations. Catholic immigration to the new state (achieved in 1848) became a torrent, as elsewhere. Not only Irish and Germans, but Dutch and Belgians flocked to various areas. Prior to this time, Catholic priests served the Indians and the old French parishes at Prairie Du Chien and Green Bay. But in 1848 Fr. Theodore Van Den Broek, a missionary among Indians at Green Bay induced a group of Dutch Catholics to settle at Little Chute; prospering, they numbered 1,400 five decades later. Marquette University was founded at Milwaukee (well on its way to acquiring the German Catholic flavor it is still renowned for today) in 1855. The original French populace of Green Bay found themselves heavily reinforced during the 50s by Germans, Dutch, and Belgians. After the failure of the 1848 rebellion against the Habsburgs in Bohemia, so many Czechs came to Racine that it was called the "Czech Bethlehem." The Door Peninsula jutting out from Green Bay into Lake Michigan began to be settled by Belgians in 1854-55. There they founded their town of Brussels. Faithful to their traditions, they retained their religion and such things as Maypoles and Kirmesses (harvest festivals). But about twenty miles away, not too long after they came to Door County, Heaven saw fit to reward them, as the WPA's description of the Robinsonville Chapel informs us:

> ...a popular Belgian shrine established in the 1860s by Sister Adele Brice who is buried in an adjoining cemetery. Sister Adele had a childhood unremarkable save for her reputed modesty and religiousness. The Virgin appeared to her twice without speaking, but on October 9, 1858, while she was returning from Mass, the Virgin appeared a third time and spoke to her in French, requesting her to devote her life to the service of the Virgin and the Catholic Faith and to build a chapel on the spot. Miss Brice followed her instructions. "From farm to farm, from one log cabin to another she went through rain, snow, and heat. She gathered the children in one place and gave them instructions; then she went forth for another meeting. God blessed her work, and soon, through the help of some generous souls, she found the means of building a little school and chapel." Sometime in the 1860s the first chapel was built and later it was surrounded by a church, schoolhouse, and convent. The present chapel was built in 1880 and the present convent in 1885.
> Sister Adele died on July 5, 1896. Her companions continued the work until October 1902, when the two remaining sisters joined the

Sisters of St. Francis of Bay Settlement, who took over the school (pp. 304-5).

But this is not the only spot in Wisconsin where the miraculous results arose from the immigration of the 50s. Near Menominee Fall is the height called Holy Hill. Crowned today by a church and monastery of Carmelite Friars, the shrine was founded in 1855 by Fr. Franz Paulhuber for the German Catholics settled round; he built a log chapel on the hill's brow. Later came a brick one to replace, the establishments on the top of Holy Hill, and an outdoor Stations of the Cross. There are many inspiring stories connected with this shrine. One of the best known is that of Quebecois monk François Soubris. Traveling to Holy Hill, he became totally paralyzed. He nevertheless climbed the slope on his hands and knees, and recovered completely after a night of prayer.

Still other German Catholics in the State attempted to carve out a place for Catholicism in the wilderness. One of the most extraordinary settlements was St. Nazianz, near Manitowoc. Here too, our WPA friends have left an engaging account:

> In 1854 Father Ambrose Ochswald, saintly idealist who hoped to free his co-religionists from governmental interference and to build a society patterned after the communistic life of the early Christians, led 113 people, members of his parish and others, from Baden, Germany, and purchased 3,840 acres of land in the forests here. On August 27 the company raised a tall wooden cross on the hillside; by New Year's the settlement had a church, four log houses, a large shed, blacksmith shop, smokehouse, barn, and 20 head of cattle.
>
> From the first life was organized on a communal basis. All worked, ate, and prayed together; money and land were jointly owned. Religion, the motive for the colony's founding, so governed life that in 1857, influenced by Father Ochswald, the unmarried Brothers and Sisters formally organized under the Third Order of St. Francis. A convent and the Loretto House were erected, and by 1866 there were 80 members of the male branch and 150 members of the female branch at St. Nazianz.
>
> The Christian community prospered until the death of Fr. Ochswald in 1873 destroyed the bond that held the group together. The property of the community had been held in Fr. Ochswald's name, but on his death a joint stock company was created under the name of the Roman Catholic Religious Society of St. Nazianz. Immediately dissension arose; many members sued the Society for their original investment and some demanded back wages for labor. Policies were changed. No married people were admitted after 1874, no new members after 1896. Eventually a part of the property was taken over by the Salvatorian Fathers who still possess it.

Community life has not greatly changed, however. Although the Utopian hope for Christian communism is gone, St. Nazianz is still dominated by its church, seminary, and convents. On special fest days solemn processions of the devout wind their way through the village, college grounds and fields to the Shrine of Our Lady of Loretto; the mellow tones of church bells still regulate the simple and active life of the inhabitants (pp. 366-7).

Although, as we have seen, economic progress at St. Nazianz was swift, Fr. Ochswald lay down this oft-repeated maxim to his flock: "We did not come to America to get rich, but to save our souls." This effort was, moreover, part of a trend all over the frontier: Utopianism. From the Shaker colonies and Brook Farm, to the Icarians and the Mormons, the notion of founding a "perfect" society in the wilderness was a dream shared by many Americans. Of St. Nazianz it may be said that it did better than most such attempts. Certainly, in terms of concrete achievement, it was a much greater success than Brook Farm, which is nevertheless held up as the acme of idealism (and whose notions, as we have seen, are important today).

Michigan also was filling up in the 50s. So many Irish settled the district south of Jackson that to this day it bears the name of "Irish Hills." Catholics were a large minority—large enough to gain considerable political influence, although Protestant unity would emerge just long enough to prevent complete control.

The tide of German and Irish Catholic immigration poured over the Mississippi into Minnesota as well. The arrival of Benedictine monks from St. Vincent's Abbey at Latrobe, PA (itself founded with considerable financial aid from King Louis I of Bavaria) in 1856, marks the origin of the city of St. Cloud. Determined to carve out from the wilderness an educational center, Fr. Demetrius De Maragona and his brothers started what would become both a network of institutions in St. Cloud, and the Abbey of St. John's, Collegeville. Their sponsor, Bishop Cretin (first ordinary of St. Paul) was responsible for the settling of Czechs at New Prague and Bavarians at New Munich (renowned ever after for their Corpus Christi processions). More Germans settled New Ulm under his benign regard. In this, he set a pattern of directly encouraging Catholic colonization in Minnesota which his successors would follow.

As the Czechs came to Texas and Minnesota in this era, so too did they to Iowa, settling after 1852 in Cedar Rapids and Linn County in general, as well as to remote settlements like St. Ansgar and Calmar. Like Bishop Cretin, Bishop Mathias Loras of Dubuque wanted monastic life in his diocese to help safeguard the spiritual life of his subjects in a materialistic environment. He offered the Abbot of Mount Melleray (a

Trappist house in Ireland) a tract of land; the offer was accepted, and Trappists from Ireland founded New Melleray in 1849. Part and parcel of the Catholic pioneering effort on the frontier was the establishment of religious houses—as it had been in Old Europe after Rome's fall.

Although Minnesota and Iowa became states fairly soon, by virtue of the enormous number of immigrants pouring in, immigration continued beyond them into the areas of the Louisiana Purchase remaining outside of Indian Territory and the chain of states extending north from Louisiana to Minnesota. Immigrants settled this region's eastern fringes, so that Congress felt compelled to organize it as the Kansas-Nebraska Territory. Already, in the 1850s, Irish, German, and Czech immigrants had begun to settle along the Missouri River. Even while their compatriots were still filling up the cities and forests of the East, these folk looked to the wind swept prairie ahead of them, and dreamed of when they might be open for settlement.

But of course, before these folk arrived at towns like Lawrence, Kansas City, Omaha, and Nebraska City, there were Catholics who had preceded them: French voyageurs, who took Indian wives and established ephemeral empires in the wilderness. While this was a type well known in the deep forests and river valleys of North America, it was far from uncommon on the prairie. An example of the breed is described by the WPA Guide for Nebraska, in their description of the man for whom the village of Barada in that state was named:

> [Antoine] Barada, son of Count Michel Barada, a Frenchman, and Laughing Water, a pretty Omaha Indian girl, once pinched a man with his toes until he begged for mercy. He was so strong he could snap a canoe paddle in two with his hands.
>
> Barada spent his childhood in eastern Nebraska. He ran away from Indians when kidnapped, from Army officers when taken to military school. He moved to St. Louis, grew to manhood there, and worked in a flour mill. He then returned to his tribe and his parents in central Thurston County, married a French woman in 1837, and joined the California gold rush in 1849. Six years later he returned to Nebraska and in 1887 [at age 80] died at Barada. His wife is buried by his side. His descendants still live in the vicinity (p. 276).

Nearby is the small town of Rulo, named after a similar character, Charles Rouleau:

> Rouleau was born in Detroit of French parents. He joined the Fremont expedition, came West, and married an Indian girl. Later he to his wife to Rulo and took up land... He was hotheaded, kind, and generous, and is said to have given an entire block in the heart of a city

to a stranger who sang a song that captured his fancy. When he died he had squandered a fortune (p. 277).

Such stories could be multiplied a hundred-fold. The important thing to bear in mind, however, is that while we are told of frontiersmen like Daniel Boone and Davy Crockett, and Western "heroes" like Wyatt Earp, it is essential to remember that we have our own, little known though they may be. Like Rouleau and Barada, or for that matter Prince zu Solm-Braunfels, they are often more exciting (and perhaps inspiring) than the figures we are usually exposed to.

The frontier is another enduring theme in our history. The experience of settling it reinforced many national attitudes: suspicion of tradition, individualism, self-reliance, violence. The myths and legends of the West are an important part of our national cultural patrimony. But we need to remember the important part played by Catholics in this drama. Not merely because the Catholic settlements and personages point to what might have been an alternative, possibly better path for the nation's development, but also because in large part modern Catholic America is the product of these settlers. All of the towns we have been describing still exist, and still retain something of their original character. Due to the ever-changing nature of urban and suburban areas (home to most Catholics, as non-Catholics, today) it is in them that something of a genuinely and traditional Catholic life is likeliest to be found in this nation.

One aspect we have left out is the work of Catholic missionaries among the Indians, and their attempts to form the first Americans under their care into communities—not unlike those of their Immigrant co-religionists, or the Spanish missions of the Southwest. This we will cover more comfortably in the next chapter.

GROWING DIVISION

One thing which will be apparent from what has just been covered is the extremely diverse nature of U.S. society in the 1850s. Not only did the several states regard themselves as sovereign nations, but the accidents of distance and cultural differences (exacerbated in areas of foreign settlement) tended to give each locality a very different ethos and a fiercely independent spirit. Overlaying these were the regional differences: New England, the Mid-Atlantic, the South, and the emerging Midwest were all quite different from one another. In those days, we still thought grammatically, and said, "the United States *are*..." instead of "the United States *is*..." as we do today.

There were, of course, forces for unity; a shared ideology, inculcated through the ever-increasing public schools, and expressed through such symbols as the Declaration of Independence was important. So too were economic ties.

But there was one irreducible problem. The ruling elites in the Northeast were based upon banking, industry, and the use of cheap foreign labor in factories. The Southern elite was based upon free trade overseas, agriculture, and the use of cheap slave labor on plantations. For the former, the continued power of the latter was an impassable roadblock on the road to national conformity and domination; to the latter, independence was vital. It was a dilemma which, in the long-run, was insoluble politically and peacefully.

The acquisition of the Southwest, in addition to bringing the Union all the other things we saw earlier, also brought the threat of imbalance between North and South. The Missouri Compromise had set up such a balance. In 1846, Iowa was admitted to the Union, and in 1848 Wisconsin. This brought the ratio of Free to Slave states up to an even 15 to 15. But what would the new territories become when they were admitted? Obviously, whichever system was exported to the larger part of the new lands would in time dominate Congress. Should the Abolitionists prevail, they could end slavery all at once, they could bankrupt the Southern economy. If the conquests became slave states, the system would last as long as it remained profitable. Folk were not long in grasping the significance of all of this.

In addition to the Northern abolitionists, the Southerners faced also opposition from the West. As we have just seen, the settlement thereof was made by possible by massive immigration fueled by Federally-funded roads and free land—both opposed by Southern politicos as extending overly Federal power. The Westerners sought ways thus to impede Southern projects. One immediate result in 1846 was the bringing before Congress of the Wilmot Proviso, which declared that slavery would not be permitted in whatever territory should be acquired from Mexico. This violated the Missouri Compromise; the Proviso passed in the House, and was only narrowly defeated in the Senate. The result was that Southern leaders like John Calhoun were enraged, and that abolitionists redoubled their efforts at organizing. This was followed by the foundation in 1848 of the Free Soil Party, ancestor of the present-day Republicans.

The election of 1848 saw the discredited Polk replaced with the Whig Zachary Taylor, the hero of Buena Vista. The new president was almost immediately faced with a crisis. As we saw, California's population mushroomed with the Gold Rush. Plans were underway to admit the new territory to statehood. The problem was that southern

California lay south of the Missouri Compromise line. Free staters swore that California should enter as a single Free state, no matter what it violated; Southerners, who saw in this their doom, demanded that slavery be legal in southern California.

Calhoun's major disciple, young Jefferson Davis of Mississippi thundered at the time:

> It is a struggle for political power [where] concession has been ever the precursor of further aggression, and the spirit of compromise has diminished as your relative power has increased. The sacrifices which the South has at other times made to the fraternity and tranquillity of the Union are now cited as precedents against her rights.
>
> If the folly and fanaticism and pride and hate and corruption of the day are to destroy the peace and prosperity of the Union, let the sections part like the patriarchs of old and let peace and good will subsist among their descendants.

Here we see a whisper of secession.

But the time was not yet. In the midst of the struggle, which featured angry meetings throughout the nation and acrid debates in Congress, President Taylor died on July 9, 1850. He was replaced by his Vice President, Millard Fillmore. Already, however, work on a Compromise was underway, spearheaded by none other than Henry Clay.

The aged Kentuckian's proposals permitted California to join as a Free state, but allowed slavery in the New Mexico and Utah territories, until such time as their inhabitants would decide their status as states. Although the slave trade would cease in the District of Columbia, slavery itself would remain legal there, as would the trade in all Slave states. Lastly, slaves who escaped to Free states were to be returned to their owners; this was the famed Fugitive Slave Law.

The dying Calhoun opposed it, but Clay and Webster backed the Compromise of 1850. In due course it became law, and California was admitted to the Union. Despite the misgivings of Calhoun's followers, who saw that conflict had merely been put off (before dying, Calhoun predicted that the Union would split within 12 years) the majority of Southerners were reassured. But the Compromise drove abolitionists to a fierce intensity, knowing as they did that, demographically, time was on the side of the North.

The Fugitive Slave Law was indeed the only concrete benefit the South derived from the Compromise. The Georgia legislature went so far as to say that only its faithful execution could preserve the Union. But from the beginning many Northern locales and individuals declared that they would not enforce it. One must say, parenthetically, that, harsh as it all seems to us, non-enforcement of this Law would mean that a certain number of discontented slaves must escape, with ruinous results to the Southern economy. No doubt the desire of the planters to hold on to their human property strikes us moderns as immoral; but it should then be pointed out that later, when the question of slavery was decided, the Northern Industrialists showed themselves quite as quick to employ force brutally to break strikes against the inhuman conditions in their sweatshops. It is not too much to say that the Southern planters regarded Northern encouragement of runaway slaves in much the same light as the Industrialists would have regarded Canadian encouragement of striking workers—or, for that matter, as our government regarded Canadian sanctuary for draft evaders during the Vietnam War.

Moreover, with the publication of *Uncle Tom's Cabin* in 1851, a steady stream of anti-Southern propaganda poured out of Northern presses. Emerson, Longfellow, Lowell, Whittier, and many others of New England's literati poured forth abuse on the South. Temperatures rose steadily on both sides. The Methodists, Baptists, and Presbyterians all split into Northern and Southern factions over slavery. In the election of 1852, the Whigs went down to defeat, and the Democrat Franklin Pierce was elected.

The year 1852 was one of real transition: both Clay and Webster died, and the old politics over which they and Calhoun presided died with them. All pretense of civility between differing positions would soon vanish. Nevertheless, Pierce was an ideal compromise candidate, regionally speaking. A non-abolitionist (and Know-Nothing opponent) New Englander, he was moreover a gentleman farmer from New Hampshire, who understood Southern aspirations quite well. Once ensconced in the White House, he appointed Jefferson Davis as Secretary of War.

Pierce's administration scored several notable successes in foreign policy. As we have seen, the Gadsden Purchase brought the U.S. Tucson and the area round; in 1854, Commodore Perry opened up Japan to American shipping. The same year also, a treaty was concluded with Great Britain regarding trade.

But personal good-will and diplomatic success could not prevent the continued unraveling of the Union. In 1854 also, Congress passed the Kansas-Nebraska Act. As we have seen, both areas were attracting settlers. The same vexing question arose—would the territories be Slave or Free?

Yet another compromise was reached. *Stephen A. Douglas*, Democrat Senator from Illinois, originated the notion of "popular sovereignty." This doctrine he incorporated into the Kansas-Nebraska Act. What this meant was that while the now-to-be-separated territories of Kansas and Nebraska would remain open to slavery, when the time came for admission, they would be Slave or Free depending entirely on whether their inhabitants voted it—regardless of their location on the Missouri Compromise Line. For abolitionists, this represented a possible extension of slavery; for Southerners, it held out a hope that the tide of immigration to the North and Midwest could be countered, and complete Northern control of the Federal government forestalled. President Pierce happily signed it into law after its due passage through Congress.

Initially, the Act precipitated a rush of Northern and Southern immigrants to the two territories, particularly Kansas. Both sides wanted to dominate at the polls. Inevitably, the two factions came to blows. An election for a territorial government in Kansas was held in 1855, at which the Southern faction prevailed, duly forming a pro-slavery administration. Abolitionist forces then organized one of their own.

Both governments relied on the services of the sort of frontier ruffians who would go on to make places like Dodge City and Tombstone famous. When the town of Lawrence, Kansas adhered to the abolitionist side, the pro-slavery forces burned it, albeit without loss of life. In return, a group of fanatical anti-slavery men led by one John Brown, encouraged by New England abolitionists, resolved to drive all Southerners out, killing them as necessary.

The first fruits of this was the Pottawatomie Creek Massacre, in which John Brown, his sons and allies attacked two pro-slavery families, murdering five men and boys and mutilating their bodies. In return, friends of the dead raided Brown's headquarters. In the shooting which followed, one of Brown's sons was killed, and the place burned. Declaring the attack unprovoked, Brown swore undying vengeance against all Southerners, and toured the North, lecturing to appreciative Abolitionist audiences.

In the meantime, with the election of 1856 coming up, a band of Free Soilers, Know Nothings, Whigs, anti-Southern Democrats, and abolitionists formed themselves into the Republican Party. Their nominee was Fremont, the conqueror of California. Ironically, given that the Know Nothings were a founding segment of the Party, a major opposition charge against Fremont was that he was a Catholic. Even more ironic was the fact that at the time he was actually an Episcopalian.

Pierce, whose attempts at reconciliation were not appreciated, was not renominated; instead, his successor as both nominee and then President was James Buchanan, the first (and so far only) bachelor to occupy the White House. Pierce's last speech to Congress outlined what he considered the major threat to the Union:

> Pierce placed full responsibility for the troubles in Kansas, first, on northern "propagandist colonization" designed to promote its "peculiar views of policy" and, second, on the attempt of free-state

settlers "to erect a revolutionary government" with the sedulous aid of "outside agents of disorder." In an... attack on the Missouri Compromise, he came close to claiming the right of slave-holders to carry their slaves into *all* the territories. Lashing out at the Republicans, he accused them of seeking not only to prevent the expansion of slavery but to achieve its abolition in the southern states as well. They sought to prepare the country for civil war "by appeals to passion and sectional prejudice, by indoctrinating its people with reciprocal hatred, and by educating to them to stand face to face as enemies rather than shoulder to shoulder as friends" (Kenneth M. Stampp, *America in 1857*, p. 6).

Pierce expressed the fears of many Americans, North and South; he pointed out that Buchanan's election win over Fremont showed that most Americans agreed with him. Even so, Buchanan was inheriting a difficult post, indeed.

The Union Unravels

The nation was in a mood for compromise; the Republicans had been defeated in the North, and the Fire-eaters, those Southerners who were convinced that the survival of their way of life required secession, were likewise defeated at the polls. Furthermore, President Buchanan himself wanted internal peace more than anything else.

This was not to be. Before the Supreme Court was a case involving a slave named Dred Scott. Scott, as a slave, had been taken by his army doctor owner to live in a Free state. When the doctor died, Scott changed hands among several heirs. Eventually, his legal ownership came to rest with the brother of the doctor's widow. Scott, in the meantime, had failed to make a living on his own, and was being supported by the doctor's sons in St. Louis.

Nevertheless, in a pattern very familiar to those of us living in later years, he was selected as a "test case" by a group of abolitionists. They sued Scott's legal owner, J.F.A. Sanford of New York, for the slave's freedom. Sanford's defense was that Scott was not a citizen, and so could not sue in Federal Court. When a U.S. Circuit Court ruled in Sanford's favor, Scott's sponsors appealed to the Supreme Court, declaring that four years residence in a Free state made Dred Scott free. The majority on the Court, including octogenarian Catholic Chief Justice Roger Brooke Taney, declared strictly on the particular case: since Scott had lived and returned to a Slave state, he was subject to its laws.

But as in our own day, when those who bring up ideological test cases are not interested so much in the actual case at hand as in obtaining a constitutional precedent, so too the Northern Justices Benjamin R.

Curtis and John McLean dissented, and demanded that the Court deliver an opinion on the Territorial question.

Chief Justice Taney ruled in response that not only slaves but their descendants could not be citizens. Therefore they could be transported anywhere, and not lose their slave status. This appeared to rule the Missouri Compromise unconstitutional from the beginning.

Abolitionists had a field day. Although the aged Taney had freed his own slaves when he inherited them (save two old ones whom he supported financially), he was painted as a Black-hater. Since he was a Catholic Marylander, he could be denounced on religious grounds as well. Both abolitionists and Fire-eaters were able to get fuel out of the decision.

Meanwhile, Kansas sputtered on. Buchanan wished to admit the territory with its pro-slavery administration. Senator Douglas, however, although the author of popular sovereignty, knew that he would lose votes in the upcoming 1858 Illinois Senatorial race if he did not assist in bringing about the new elections the Kansas abolitionists were clamoring for. Accordingly, he split with the President on the issue, and assisted the calling of the August 1858 election which voted down the pro-slavery constitution. Kansas was settled, but Douglas was considered a traitor by both the Administration and Southern Democrats.

His opponent in the 1858 election was another well-known Illinois politician and veteran of the Blackhawk War, Abraham Lincoln. Lincoln was no abolitionist; he did not believe slavery could be abolished where it already existed. Still less was he a believer in equal rights for Blacks:

> I am not, nor ever have been, in favor of bringing about in any way the social and political equality of the white and black races which I believe will forever forbid the two races living together on terms of social and political equality.

He believed that the ultimate answer to the racial problem was the deportation of blacks to Liberia—a solution which would have deprived this nation of the ancestors of some of its greatest artists, musicians, scientists, and writers. Easy answers are not always the best.

Moreover, Lincoln was an extremely astute politician. In his most famous speech against Douglas, Lincoln declared, "I believe this government cannot endure permanently half slave and half free..." In so declaring, Lincoln gathered to himself both the hatred of the South and the love of the abolitionists. But it was in neither case deserved. The word "permanently" was the operative one. Lincoln believed that slavery would die out on its own gradually; in the meantime he opposed its expansion into the territories. Had he moderated his language more in accord with his beliefs, he would have been neither demonized by the Fire-eaters nor lionized by the abolitionists.

But his interest was in defeating Douglas; to do this he must attack the latter's "Popular Sovereignty" notion, and discredit both it and its originator in the eyes of the Illinois electorate. If Douglas defended Popular Sovereignty, he would lose his seat; if he did not, he would alienate the Southern Democrats for good. In the end, he maintained that while anyone could legally transport his slave throughout the nation, this was "a barren and worthless right unless sustained, proclaimed, and enforced by appropriate police regulations and local legislations." He thereby admitted that his stand was an empty charade, designed for purely political reasons.

The result was that, while Douglas satisfied the Illinoisans and defeated Lincoln, he doomed his chances for the Presidency. The Southern Democrats, considering him a traitor, would not accept him as the nominee for the election in 1860 even if it meant splitting the Democratic Party.

Meanwhile, Minnesota and Oregon were admitted as Free states, putting the ratio at 17 Free to 15 Slave. With the growing strength of the Republican Party in the North, and the increase for Free States in the Senate, the specter of an abolitionist-controlled White House, Senate, and House began to loom large in the minds of Southerners as a clear and present danger; the wildest cries of the Fire-eaters as to Yankee determination to destroy the South began to seem more reasonable. What had been a worrisome possibility, however, seemed to become a probability in 1859.

On October 17, the Federal Arsenal at Harper's Ferry in northern Virginia (now West Virginia) was seized by John Brown (whom we last saw lecturing to adoring abolitionists) and 21 followers. With the weapons of the Arsenal, they intended to lead the slaves in Virginia in revolt; their masters were to be slaughtered. Whites were taken hostage, some with a freed Black were killed. But the slaves Brown and his men "freed" refused to leave their masters. No White nor Black man joined him. Militiamen and an Army Company sent out from Washington and commanded by Col. Robert E. Lee surrounded and finally stormed the Arsenal. In 36 hours the revolt had been suppressed.

In any other political climate, perhaps, the affair would have been a minor one. But for this one, it was like setting a match to dry tinder. Brown himself wished to unleash a bloody race-war on the South; his abolitionist backers in the North knew this, knew the sort of man he had proved himself to be in Kansas, and approved of it all—although most denied any knowledge later. Brown was tried for treason against the Commonwealth of Virginia, and sentenced to be hanged.

Although most Northern opinion was horrified by Brown's plot, the most vocal among them, the Transcendentalists, were not. After he was sentenced to be hanged, Louisa May Alcott called him St. John the Just; Emerson declared that Brown would "make the gallows glorious like the Cross." Such writers appeared to make all the Fire-eaters had claimed true; in a short time, these latter captured control of most of the Democratic Party in the South. When Brown was hanged, the abolitionists claimed him as a martyr ("John Brown's Body Lies A-Moldering in the Grave" was a catchy tune, itself immortalized in the "Battle Hymn of the Republic," and learned early in life by this writer).

The election of 1860 loomed large. For Southerners, the Republicans were supporters of John Brown. Should they be elected, without a doubt, the South was doomed. The only peaceful solution to the problem was therefore another Democratic President. But Buchanan would not take again the job which had seemed so glorious when he won it four years before.

When the Democrats gathered in Convention in Charleston, the Southerners were determined to force into the platform a plank proposing the very kind of legislation Douglas had declared would be needed if popular sovereignty were to be more than a slogan. Moreover, they were bound and determined to keep Douglas, who as a national candidate had the best chance of defeating Lincoln, from being nominated. The convention split on geographical lines. The Southerners nominated Vice President John Breckinridge; the Northerners tapped Douglas. In Virginia and Tennessee the Border Democrats put forth John Bell, and reorganized as the Constitutional Union Party. All to no avail; the split vote ensured the victory of Abraham Lincoln.

On all sides in the deep South, the cry rose for Secession; surely the Apocalypse had come. At the last minute several moderates of all parties came together under the leadership of Kentucky Senator John J. Crittenden to propose a Compromise which would basically restore the Missouri Compromise line, enforce the fugitive slave laws, and maintain the status quo as part of a series of Constitutional amendments. Republican legislators asked Lincoln what to do about it; he quietly recommended against it. Thus the Crittenden Amendment died, and with it the last hope that the Union would hold.

On December 20, 1860, South Carolina seceded from the Union. In short order she was followed by Alabama, Mississippi, Georgia, Florida, Louisiana, and Texas. The Union was dissolved.

THE CIVIL WAR

The conflict which resulted was, with the Revolution and the New Deal, one of the major factors creating the nation we know today. It was the bloodiest and bitterest war this country has ever been engaged in; yet (surely a measure of our character as a people) it has left surprisingly little mark on the attitudes of contemporary folk. Such a conflict fought elsewhere in the world would scarcely be unfought today, but would hover just under the surface of national debate, ever-ready to burst again into flame. Nevertheless, the American Civil War, the War Between the States, is a defining point. It was the last of the great Civil Wars which, beginning with the Pilgrimage of Grace in 1536, and proceeding through the 1549 and 1569 Risings in the West and the North; the 1641-45 English Civil War; the 1688-91, 1715, 1719, and 1745-46 Jacobite Wars; and the 1775-83 American Revolution, transformed the English-speaking world. At their commencement, England was a small European, decentralized, Catholic Monarchy. At their close, the Anglo-American powers were two mighty Oligarchies arching over the Earth, and dedicated to the spread of the principles of the Enlightenment and materialism throughout the globe. Moreover, the conclusion of the Civil War put the Union on a new basis, which, however at variance with the original notion of a Union of independent States, would eventually guarantee the eclipse of the Mother Country—still wedded to ancient if desiccated forms—in favor of the Daughter, completely formed as she was in the principles which animated the rulers of both lands.

Let us look a bit more closely at the contenders.

The Catholics

During the series of crises we have been discussing, Catholics were rather more closely united than members of other denominations. The hierarchy tended to oppose abolitionism, on the one hand, as being supported by the same folk who supported nativism. Northern bishops might be more critical of slavery, but then as in Apostolic times the Church saw slavery as a possible source of many evils, but not as necessarily sinful in itself. On the other hand, the bishops were committed to maintenance of the Union. When the South seceded, however, the Southern bishops loyally supported their new government.

Among layfolk, things were a bit more complex. Both Orestes Brownson and James McMaster opposed the extension of the Federal government's power at the expense of State sovereignty. Brownson considered slavery itself in somewhat the same light as did his Transcendentalist ex-colleagues, although he had no use for John Brown.

He did advocate the use of force to maintain the Union. McMaster, on the other hand, believed slavery to be on the wane in any case, and considered that the whole affair was purely an attempt to exalt the regime in Washington. Military force to compel the South to remain he declared to be both unconstitutional and immoral.

In the South, although relatively few in number, lay Catholics tended to be part of the upper classes, and to have an influence out of all proportion to their numbers. Thus they were much in favor of secession. Northern Catholics, while much more numerous, had little political power, being for the most part poor recent immigrants. Moreover, they saw the Blacks as rivals for the sort of low-paying jobs they themselves were able to secure only with difficulty in the face of Protestant contempt. Should abolition come, they feared that hordes of poor Blacks would come North willing to work for even less than the pittance currently being paid Northern industrial workers. The notion of fighting for such a development was obviously repugnant.

The North

Secession left the government in Washington in much the same situation as George III and his cabinet had been. Should the South be permitted to leave peacefully? Did the U.S. government have the authority to compel States to remain in a Union which they had entered freely? President-elect Lincoln asked a comedian who was a friend of his in Washington what his opinion was on the events. His reply was, "well, sir, if secession be a valid principle, then my sympathies are with the South; if not, then I say, 'God bless His Majesty!'" Surely, this was not a reply Lincoln could have appreciated. But it nevertheless pointed up a powerful consideration which, in the event, was ignored. Yet for many, the Union was a sacred thing which it was treason to break—even as the British Empire had appeared to the Loyalists.

Abolitionists hailed secession as a chance to mount a holy crusade against slavery. For the folk who considered John Brown a hero, nothing would do but to drag the South back into the Union a smoking, bloodied ruin. As the war progressed, the rhetoric they had manufactured came to be more and more the standard government line.

For the industrialists and bankers who were already the dominant force in the North, the War was a great opportunity. Victory would mean the destruction of the only real competition for national dominance they had; control of the Federal government would be a sweet additional prize.

Yet it must not be supposed that all Northerners supported the War. Given the rather nasty name of *Copperheads*, these latter comprised a wide variety of people. Many were Catholics, who for the reasons outlined above opposed the War; these were often led into conflict with their bishops who became staunch supporters of the government. But there were other reasons for opposition.

Some believed that the Constitution simply did not permit the Federal government to intervene militarily—after all, the Tenth Amendment to the Constitution forbade the Federal government to do anything not expressly permitted it in the rest of the Constitution. Nowhere did they see a proviso permitting armed force against secession They feared that such action would not merely bring back the South unwillingly, but enslave the Northern states as well. Unprecedented actions of the President during the course of the War appeared to justify them—never had it been thought that an American President would be able to arrogate to himself the right to arrest citizens and hold them without trial. Of these, the most prominent was *Clement L. Vallandigham*, of Ohio.

The North had the preponderance of the country's industry, and ready cash and bullion. A closely knit railroad net made transport of men and materiel very easy. Possession of the Federal government's Posts, Army, and Navy were certainly a distinct advantage. Should either Presidents Buchanan or Lincoln elect to move against the South, they would surely have the upper hand.

The South

For Southerners, it appeared that the moment had come to depart, indeed. The Federal government was in the hands of men who, as they believed, were determined to destroy the South; not merely by the abolition of slavery (preferably through a bloody race war), but economically, by using the Federal power to raise tariffs so high as to make foreign imported goods (upon which the cotton economy was dependent) simply impossible to buy. Behind this, of course, there was the perceived destruction of the Constitution. It was indeed maintained by Southerners that slavery was not the cause for the break, but merely the occasion. In the words of Jefferson Davis:

> [In regard to the Dred Scott decision.] Instead of accepting the decision of this then august tribunal—the ultimate authority in the interpretation of constitutional questions—as conclusive of a controversy that had so long disturbed the peace and was threatening the perpetuity of the Union, it was flouted, denounced, and utterly disregarded by the Northern agitators, and served only to stimulate the intensity of their sectional hostility.
>
> What resource for justice—what assurance of tranquillity—what guarantee of safety—now remained for the South? Still forbearing, still

hoping, still striving for peace and union, we waited until a sectional President, nominated by a sectional convention, elected by a sectional vote—and that the vote of a minority of the people—was about to be inducted into office, under the warning of his own distinct announcement that Union could not permanently endure "half-slave and half-free;" meaning thereby that it could not continue to exist in the condition in which it was formed and its Constitution adopted. The leader of his party, who was to be the chief of his Cabinet [William Seward], was the man who first proclaimed an "irrepressible conflict" between the North and the South, and who had declared that abolitionism, having triumphed in the Territories, would proceed to the invasion of the States. Even then the Southern people did not finally despair until the temper of the triumphant party had been tested in Congress and found adverse to any terms of reconciliation consistent with the honor and safety of all parties [the Crittenden Compromise].

No alternative remained except to seek the security out of the Union which they had vainly tried to obtain within it. The hope of our people may be stated in a sentence. It was to escape from injury and strife within the Union, to find prosperity and peace out of it (*The Rise And Fall Of The Confederate Government*, vol. I, pp 84-85).

It may be pointed out that they perhaps would have not been in such a state if the Southern Democrats had not split the party; or if the Republicans had not vocally supported the abolitionists, and the latter John Brown. Nevertheless, the fact remains that the majority of Southern voters believed themselves to be in the same relationship with the Federal government that their fathers' leadership had declared themselves to be with the Crown. The result was Revolution.

As will be obvious, it was to the Declaration of Independence that the South looked to first for justification. Moreover, had not the Founding Fathers expressly said in various places and ways that, were the Constitution to be voided and the welfare of the people to demand it, that sovereignty returned to the States? Several States had required assurances of this before adhering to the Constitution in the first place, to say nothing of the New Englanders at the Hartford Convention in 1814. So far as the Southern leadership was concerned, there could be no question of both the justification and legal right of secession.

But if the Federal government decided to fight them? The first seven Southern states had virtually no industry, few railroads, and indeed, little in the way of resources save cotton and sugar. But they were fighting on their own ground, and they reasoned, all they would have to do is defend their own soil until the European nations, particularly Great Britain and France, needing their cotton, would intervene on their behalf. In any case did not right make might?

Yet even as there were Copperheads in the North, there were Unionists in the South. These were in the main residents of the mountainous and/or poorer regions: West Virginia actually seceded from Virginia, and Eastern Tennessee very nearly followed suit. The poverty struck Winn Parish of Northern Louisiana (whence came Huey Long) was similarly inclined; there were other spots scattered about. Many of the inhabitants of these places had always felt alienated from the slave-holding aristocracy which dominated their States; this was what had led their fathers to back the Crown against the slave-owning rebels in Williamsburg, New Bern, Charleston, and Savannah.

As we shall see, Catholics figured prominently in the Southern War effort; particularly on the literary front. Fr. Abram Ryan, "poet-priest of the Confederacy" wrote a number of stirring tributes to the Cause. All three of the best known Southern songs (*Dixie* by Daniel Emmet, *The Bonnie Blue Flag* by Harry McCarthy, and *Maryland, My Maryland* by James Ryder Randall) were written by Catholics.

Foreigners, Communists, and Freemasons

The conflict in North America could not help but have consequences in the rest of the World. For one thing, the large numbers of foreigners—particularly Irish and Germans, but French and others as well already resident in this country, were naturally drawn into the conflict. Refugees from the 1848 Revolutions in Europe were inevitably in favor of the Union, and the Federal government made it a practice after some time to recruit Irishmen from the Old Sod to leave their poverty and join the Union Army. This latter course resulted in a very large Catholic and Irish representation indeed. This was particularly the case among the State militias, often organized along ethnic lines. Massachusetts boasted two Irish regiments; New York, ten; Pennsylvania and Illinois two each; and Connecticut, Indiana, New Hampshire, Michigan, Minnesota, Wisconsin, and Missouri one apiece.

> Most of the leaders of these regiments became famous for their gallantry, notably Colonel (afterwards General) Patrick R. Guiney of the Ninth Massachusetts Regiment, father of the poetess, the late Louise Imogen Guiney; Colonel (afterwards General) St. Clair Mulholland of the One hundred and sixteenth Pennsylvania; Colonel Patrick O'Rorke of the One hundred and fortieth New York, killed at Little Round Top in heroic defense of that critical point; Colonel O'Kane of the Sixtieth Pennsylvania, who likewise perished at Gettysburg; Colonel (afterwards General) Michael Corcoran, of the Sixty-ninth New York, and the "Corcoran Legion,"...; General Thomas F. Meagher, of the New York Irish Brigade,...; Colonel James A.

Mulligan of the Chicago Irish Brigade,... (Henry Grattan Doyle, "Catholicism in the Civil War and Reconstruction,"*Catholic Builders of the Nation*, vol. I, p. 169).

These and many other Catholic Union soldiers carved out a glorious name for themselves. But many other foreigners flocked to the colors. Such was the Garibaldi Guard, the 38th New York, made up of veterans of the European revolts. Anti-Catholic to a man, many would go back to fight again in such wars as the conquest of Rome in 1870, which deprived the Pope of his temporal power. Three grandsons of the Liberal Orleanist French King, Louis Phillipe, served for precisely that reason; one, the Comte de Paris, wrote a particularly biased history afterwards.

As might be expected, reactions toward the War in Great Britain were mixed. On the one hand, since Britain had abolished slavery in her Empire back in 1838, and used her navy to attack slave-ships and free their cargoes for three decades before that, most Britons condemned slavery and felt morally superior to the States as a result. But this did not necessarily mean a dislike of the South as a result; the American ships they had to seize were all from New England, and so the Yankees were considered just as addicted to the peculiar institution. Moreover, the Southern Aristocrats, with their code of honor, their British ancestry, and their nostalgia for Sir Walter Scott, were considered to be of the same sort as themselves by many of the British nobility and gentry. Large numbers of British Liberals saw the Southern struggle for independence in the same rosy light as they saw the Polish, Italian, and German struggles for it.

Trade relations between Britain and the South were close; the mills of Lancashire were run on Southern cotton. To safeguard this, the Confederate leadership was sure that Britain must recognize them in the end, and perhaps come into the War on their side. But with a worldwide Empire at her command, Britain began to grow cotton elsewhere. Sure that the South would win without her intervention, the British government was never ready to recognize or intervene until victory was out of the Southern grasp.

The France of Napoleon III was another proposition, however. Having just defeated Austria in 1859, Napoleon III was looking for new worlds to conquer. He was looking seriously at Mexico, where the Conservatives were being trounced by the Liberals under Juarez, heavily armed as they were by the United States. The notion of French intervention in Mexico began to take shape—an intervention which would succeed more easily if the South broke free. All Napoleon III wanted to commit himself to the Southern cause would be a major Southern victory, like Antietam, Gettysburg, or Monocacy Junction; that is, a victory in the North which would put Washington in Southern hands and signal an approaching end to the War. But those three battles were lost, and the great event never came.

Russia, humiliated by France and Great Britain in the Crimean War of 1853-1856 (in the course of which the Light Brigade made their famed Charge), was only too happy to support diplomatically the United States. Alexander II had a deep regard for President Lincoln, and would follow his lead some years later in ending serfdom in Russia.

Only one foreign power actually recognized Southern independence: the Holy See. In 1863, Pius IX had written Archbishops Hughes of New York and Odin of New Orleans, in the course of which (for reasons which shall become apparent shortly) His Holiness referred to Lincoln as a tyrant and usurper, and expressed a desire for peace. Confederate President Davis sent back a letter thanking him for his statements, conveyed by Ambassador Dudley Mann. Pius's reply was addressed to "The Illustrious and Honorable Jefferson Davis, President of the Confederate States of America, Richmond." This was the only open communication ever received from a foreign government which actually addressed Davis as Head of State of an independent country.

Another Confederate diplomat, J.T. Soutter, informed Pius IX that his government was aware that no other government had been as sympathetic. The Pontiff replied that, "he had done all he could, and regretted that he could not do more." When the War was ended, and Jefferson Davis was a prisoner in Fortress Monroe, Pius IX sent him a picture of himself with the words in Latin from Scripture: "Come to me all you who are heavy-burdened and labor..." With it was a replica of the Crown of Thorns Pius had made himself, and a scapular and medal. This writer has seen these objects in the Confederate Museum in New Orleans, even as he has seen Davis' rosary at his home, Beauvoir, near Biloxi, Mississippi.

One rabid supporter of the North overseas, however, was Karl Marx. Although he despised the Blacks, he saw the Civil War as being a classic example of his theory of Class Struggle. Just as the Revolution, he believed, had inaugurated the rule of the Bourgeoisie in the U.S., the Civil War would destroy it. In this, as in much else, he was mistaken. Nevertheless, Socialists and Communists throughout Europe hoped for Union victory.

So too, for the most part, did Freemasonry. Yet an important point must be made here; Freemasons were prominent on both sides, just as they are in every political dispute in English-speaking lands. The notorious *Albert Pike*, who would later formulate American Masonic beliefs after the War, was a Southern General. In this regard, it would be useful to include two very different quotes about Pike. The first is from the WPA Guide to Arkansas, describing the Albert Pike Recreational Area, near Norman in that State:

> After Albert Pike (1809-1891), explorer, newspaperman, poet, general, and Indian Commissioner for the Confederacy, had led troops from the Five Nations in the Battle of Pea Ridge, he quarrelled with his superiors, lashing the Arkansas military leaders in a letter to the Confederate Congress, and resigned his command. His movements thereafter until the close of the war are obscure, but considerable evidence indicates that toward the end of 1862 he retired to this wild and beautiful spot on the Little Missouri. One account describes him as arriving in magnificent style in a buggy drawn by white horses, followed by a wagon loaded with furniture and gold and a procession of two score slaves. Here he built a house, according to old settlers, and commenced the major work of his life, the writing of the philosophy of Freemasonry. His labors were interrupted after several months by a band of guerrillas that drove him from his home, destroyed his belongings, and threw his excellent library into the river. At the conclusion of the war he reappeared in Little Rock for a time, moved to Memphis, and eventually completed his Masonic writings in Washington, D.C. (p. 338).

This is a most baffling passage. Who were these guerrillas who treated the good general so unkindly? Certainly not Union sympathizers, for the War had not yet penetrated that part of Arkansas. This was a description which bothered this writer a great deal. But it often happens in historical research that a chance reading will shed unexpected light on an obscure topic. So it proved this case. While reading a book on American folklore, this illuminating passage appeared:

> The tenacious and secretive witch-lore pervading the Ozarks involves spells and poppets, the initiation of witches through orgiastic rites, and the preparation of counter-spells by witch-masters. In his "Unprintable Collections," Randolph reveals lascivious traditions about the nineteenth-century Arkansas poet, editor, and public figure, Albert Pike, covenanting with the Devil. The virile Pike sat on a throne in the woods, while naked women danced about in wild orgies. The naked women were all witches, a Confederate veteran told Randolph, and some of them were the wives of Pike's best friends (Richard M. Dorson, *American Folklore*, p. 100).

It is obvious enough, then, that the "guerrillas" who burned out Pike had more in common with the peasant mobs storming the Castle in the movie "Frankenstein" than they did with typical bushwhackers of the time. Of course, the Supernatural content of the tale ought not to disturb us unduly—President Lincoln would attempt to seek advice from beyond in the course of seances held in the White House.

The point here is that both sides had idealists, both sides had criminals and opportunists, both had madmen and fanatics. Still, when all is said and done, it is hard for the believing Catholic who has examined the background of the struggle to disagree with Solange Hertz's summation:

> ...a situation exist[ed] here from earliest times, when the on-going English revolution between Roundheads and Cavaliers was transported wholesale to America. The Roundheads, with their short haircuts and clean-shaven faces, established themselves in the North, which became the seat of a tight-lipped, Calvinist theocracy where Capitalism founded on rampant usury could flourish unhindered in a basically manichaean culture. Sex and alcohol were regarded as intrinsically evil, and virtue was rewarded by God with material prosperity. It was the logical terrain on which to begin Marxist agitation. In the South, alongside the Catholic cultures established by the French and Spanish in Louisiana and Texas, English Cavaliers and Jacobites, curled, bearded and unashamedly fun-loving (according to song and story) settled by instinct. Although most were Church of England, as in Virginia, they were far from considering themselves Protestants, whom they detested.
>
> We must beware of separating North and South unilaterally into "bad guys" and "good guys," for Masonry was prevalent in both camps... But facts are facts. One aspect of the Civil War which has been studiously ignored by establishment historians is its character as a *war of religion*. Protestants found themselves pitted against Catholics and Anglo-Catholics in a death struggle over two incompatible ways of life. The South retained far more vestiges of the old hieratic Christendom than did the North (*The Star-Spangled Heresy*, p. 110).

The Course of the War

President Buchanan tried in vain to hold things together until Lincoln should relieve him of the burden. In the meantime, delegates from the seven seceded States gathered in Montgomery, Alabama to form a government and a new nation. Together they drafted a document much like the one they had abandoned. Its differences for the most part were concerned with rectifying problems experienced in dealing with Washington. The new government of the Confederate States of America was prohibited from levying protective tariffs to safeguard certain industries; further, they were not to subsidize public works. Importation of slaves from foreign nations was strictly forbidden. The Confederate President was limited to a single six-year term of office. By far, the greatest difference was in the Preamble. Here it is, with differing language from that of the U.S. Preamble in italics:

> We, the people of the *Confederate* States, *each State acting in its sovereign and independent character, in order to form a permanent Federal Government*, establish justice, insure domestic tranquillity, and secure the blessing of liberty to ourselves and our posterity—*invoking the favor and the guidance of Almighty God*—do ordain and establish this Constitution for the *Confederate* States of America.

Apart from the affirmation of State sovereignty, the most glaring difference is the invocation of Almighty God. Surely this was a seed which might have borne good fruit, had the new nation been allowed to live.

In any case, once the Constitution was written the choice for President fell on the reluctant Jefferson Davis, who had then the responsibility for negotiating independence and creating a government out of nothing—a daunting task, to say the least. But Davis had great organizational ability, and would do the job, if anyone could. His cabinet secretaries were by and large able men; Stephen Mallory, a Catholic from Key West, was given the post of Secretary of the Navy. Knowing full well that he could not hope to outnumber the Union Navy, Mallory specialized in seeking technological advances that would nullify the North's superior number of ships.

Afterwards, Confederate officials began the peaceful seizure of forts, arsenals, post offices, naval yards, mints, and so on. But one installation which could not be taken peacefully was the fort at the entrance to Charleston Harbor, Ft. Sumter. Buchanan sent a ship to reinforce Sumter; the ship being fired upon, it withdrew. Rather than provoke war on the spot, Buchanan did not react. The fort's garrison continued to buy provisions in town.

On March 4, 1861, Abraham Lincoln was inaugurated as President. He immediately turned his mind to Ft. Sumter. General Pierre Beauregard, a Catholic Creole from Louisiana, had taken command of the Confederate troops in Charleston. He ensured that Major Anderson and the Sumter garrison were treated courteously. Anderson hoped that Lincoln would evacuate himself and his men.

The President himself refused to see the emissaries sent him from President Davis. He was in fact determined to bring the South back into the Union by force—whatever the legality of the move. On April 6, a message was sent to the Governor of South Carolina informing him that the U.S. would resupply Sumter. The implication was that the garrison would remain there. He well knew that however much he himself might deny the independence of the new nation, the Confederates themselves believed in it, and could not tolerate the retention of Ft. Sumter, key to the Confederacy's best Atlantic port, by a foreign nation. In a real sense, for the Confederates Ft. Sumter must bear the same relation that the British posts did for the rebels after the Declaration of Independence in 1776.

Informed that the resupply ships were coming, Beauregard issued on April 11 an ultimatum to Anderson; he must evacuate the Fort. Anderson's reply was that he would do so unless reinforced within two days time. With the ships just outside the harbor, Beauregard was aware that the time had come. On April 12, he began the shelling of Ft. Sumter; in thirty-six hours Anderson surrendered, and a Confederate ship took the garrison to one of the U.S. ships outside the harbor.

The firing on Ft. Sumter galvanized the North—anti-Southern emotion ran red hot. The President wrote the commander of the relief expedition:

> You and I anticipated that the course of the country would be advanced by making the attempt to provision Fort Sumter, even if it should fail; and it is no small consolation now to feel that our anticipation is justified by the result.

In such a climate, Lincoln was able to ignore the Constitution entirely. His first act was to issue a call for 75,000 90-day volunteers to invade the South. In response to this call, which was considered unconstitutional by many, Virginia, North Carolina, Tennessee, and Arkansas seceded. Most of the inhabitants of Missouri, Kentucky, and Maryland wished to do the same. With the four border states, the new nation received industry, a territorial buffer, additional manpower, and many fine officers, including *Robert E. Lee, Stonewall Jackson*, and *Jeb Stuart*.

In Missouri and Kentucky, legislatures split; both sides soon had governors of their own, and both soon raised troops for Confederacy and Union alike. In Maryland, the Governor, aware that if convened the legislature would vote for secession, refused to call it. Instead, he waited until the State was so filled with Federal troops that secession was out of the question. Even so, the South raised a number of Maryland volunteer units. Out of deference to Virginia, the Confederate capital was removed to Richmond; militia units from all over the South converged on Harper's Ferry.

Meanwhile, Lincoln called on Congress to convene on July 4. In the meantime, he rushed through a number of measures on his own authority—again, in defiance of the Constitution. He ordered a blockade of Southern ports (hence one of Mallory's major activities during the

War was to outfit fast blockade runner ships to bring urgently needed imports; the blockade runners made both the Bahamas and Bermuda very wealthy for the time being). He authorized an increase in the Regular Army, expenditure of Federal funds without Congressional approval or appropriation, and unilaterally suspended habeus corpus. The last measure allowed him to order the arrest without trial of noted secessionist leaders in Maryland, Kentucky, and Missouri. Whatever the outcome of the War, the Constitution became a permanent casualty—from that time on, Americans expected, permitted, and approved of their Presidents becoming dictators in war-time. Later, in 1862, such opponents of the War as James McMaster would be thrown into jail for their opinions. In such a climate, Copperheadism flourished.

Old General Winfield Scott, commander of the Union forces, recommended that the South be reconquered by first applying economic pressure via a thoroughgoing blockade. Troops could be landed at New Orleans. These would advance up the Mississippi; at the same time another force would proceed South along the same river. Between them they would cut the South in two, and squeeze the life out of the Confederacy. This plan was ridiculed as the "Anaconda Plan" by experts who "knew" better. These declared that all that was needed was the seizure of Richmond.

An attempt to do so was halted by the Confederates at the Battle of Big Bethel on June 10. A more determined attempt under Irvin McDowell was routed by Beauregard. This is the battle known as First Manassas in the South or First Bull Run in the North. The Union troops fled back to Washington; Scott was unfairly blamed, and retired on November 1. The first major tactical mistake of the Confederate army was made here; they did not follow the panic-stricken troops into the Capital. The Confederate leadership were under the delusion that all that was required for them to win their independence was to hold their own territory. But they faced an opponent who would not be satisfied with anything less than reabsorbtion of the Confederacy into the United States.

The result was inaction on all fronts. The "Free Staters" in the West of Virginia delivered their area over to Union forces in the Winter of 1861 to 1862, and eventually seceded from the Commonwealth of Virginia to become the State of West Virginia (admitted in 1863; this was accomplished by grabbing a few pro-slavery counties—such feuds as the famous Hatfield-McCoy fight were the result). The U.S. Navy began seizing coastal positions, most notably Roanoke Island (site of the lost colony of Sir Walter Raleigh and key to controlling both Virginia and North Carolina waters) on February 2.

The focus of War shifted West. In Missouri, Union forces had early struck at the militia gathering for the South under the Governor. A number of those captured were murdered in the streets of St. Louis by Germans who were themselves Liberal Refugees from 1848. The remaining Confederate militiamen (one of whom was the young Samuel Clemens, better known as Mark Twain, who immortalized his adventures in "A Memoir of a Campaign That Failed") turned to the Southwest of the State, from whence under General *Sterling Price*, they waged guerilla warfare.

Kentucky pursued a policy of neutrality; interestingly, it was the birthplace of both Presidents Davis and Lincoln. But its pro-Unionist government wished to abandon this neutrality. The question was merely which side would invade first. In the event, it was the Confederates. In a short time the Union forces under General *U.S. Grant* had pushed the Southern troops out of the State. He struck south into central Tennessee, seizing Ft. Henry on February 6; ten days later he obtained the "unconditional surrender" of Ft. Donelson, thus introducing a new phrase into the language.

More disasters followed for the South in quick succession. The Battle of Pea Ridge in Northwestern Arkansas destroyed Confederate Missouri as an organized force, although Missouri troops carried on until the end of the War; moreover, the defeat led to General Albert Pike's taking up the activities earlier referred to.

Union forces continued to press south through Kentucky and Tennessee. Particularly fierce was the push down the Mississippi. By Spring the Northern troops were in sight of Memphis, and had rolled down the Tennessee River as far as Pittsburg Landing. From there they were in a position to take Corinth, Mississippi. This city was an important railroad junction on a line stretching from Memphis to Charleston; severing it would be a great coup for the Union, and Grant was determined to have it. Sending a force to occupy Nashville (first Confederate State Capital to fall) he set off, and was met by a Confederate force near Shiloh Church on April 6 and 7. The Confederates delivered a stinging defeat to Grant initially, but the Union troops held, and the Confederates were forced to withdraw to Corinth.

Meanwhile, significant things were happening elsewhere. In the Chesapeake Bay, a Confederate Ironclad ship, fruit of Mallory's scientific program, the *C.S.S. Virginia* sunk a number of wooden ships. The Union, in the meantime, had accepted a Swedish inventor's design for an ironclad, the *Monitor*. The two met in combat on March 9. Although the battle was a draw (the two nullified each other), the end of the era of "iron men and wooden ships" was at hand.

More conventionally, the U.S. Navy took the North Carolina town of New Bern, thus beginning to make of the blockade a coastal occupation as well. On April 24, Admiral *David Farragut* ran his fleet past the forts at the mouth of the Mississippi and took New Orleans. This was an unmitigated disaster for the South. In short order Baton Rouge and Natchez fell, leaving the town of Vicksburg, Mississippi as the connecting point between the Confederacy's two halves. After Union troops seized Corinth, they waited quietly, believing that the planned offensive in Virginia would make further action in the West unnecessary.

In March, General *George McClellan* initiated what would be called the "Peninsular Campaign. He dispatched most of the Army of the Potomac (100,000) to Fortress Monroe at the very tip of the peninsula formed by the James and York rivers in Virginia. Since the Confederate ironclad protected Norfolk, there was only one direction McClellan could advance in—toward Richmond, governmental and industrial center of the South. At the same time McDowell began advancing from Alexandria to Fredericksburg.

The Confederates hurriedly threw up defenses around Richmond, with a garrison of 55,000 facing almost double that number. A single brigade was sent up to Fredericksburg to guard against McDowell's 50,000.

Stonewall Jackson's successful trouncing of the Union troops in the Shenandoah Valley, however, led President Lincoln to retain McDowell's men to defend Washington. The result was that the pincer movement did not occur, and Richmond's defense was secured. Yet McClellan's troops remained. On May 30, 1862, Robert E. Lee was given command of the Confederate army. His first task: save Richmond.

For a month, and culminating in the Seven Days Battles (ending with Malvern Hill on July 1), Lee outgeneraled McClellan. The Union troops withdrew 18 miles down to the James River. The besiegers were now the besieged. So many supplies were left behind by the retreating forces that the Confederate Army was benefited as much by the goods taken as by the ground won. At last McClellan withdrew his troops from the Peninsula; Lee looked North.

In Northern Virginia, the Union troops were led by *John Pope*. He had carried on a campaign of terror against the residents. In August 5, Lee hit him at the Battle of Cedar Mountain. On August 30, the Battle of Second Manassas or Bull Run was fought, Pope was defeated and retreated to Washington. Once again, Virginia was practically free of Union troops. The supplies captured from the Union warehouses at Manassas Junction were a badly needed shot in the arm. Unlike Beauregard in the aftermath of the First Manassas, however, Lee had every intention of taking Washington. By now it was well realized that such a victory would result in the entrance of France and probably Britain into the War, and doubtless victory and freedom. But Pope's army had been defeated, not destroyed; Washington had been heavily fortified since the First Manassas. The city would have to be outflanked.

In the West, there was similar good news. After the fall of Corinth, *Braxton Bragg* reorganized the Confederate forces and drove the Union out of most of Tennessee and deep into Kentucky. The siege of Vicksburg was broken, and the Confederates retook Baton Rouge. On September 5 and 6, Lee and his army crossed the Potomac into Maryland, singing *Maryland, My Maryland*. But he was defeated at South Mountain, and suffered horrible losses at Antietam on September 17. Union losses were heavy too, but Lee withdrew back into Virginia.

That same month, President Lincoln issued the Emancipation Proclamation, freeing the slaves—to a point. On April 16, it had been abolished in the District of Columbia. But the effects of the Proclamation were expressly limited to those areas under control of the Federal government. It was not abolished in Maryland, Delaware, Kentucky, or Missouri, nor in those areas of the Confederacy occupied by Union troops. It was to apply only to those areas controlled by the Confederates, who would obviously ignore it. Indeed, the major reason why it was done was because Copperhead sentiment grew with the casualty lists, and the sacred crusade to hold the Union together was fast losing popular appeal. As Lincoln wrote to Horace Greeley, "If I could preserve the Union without freeing the Negro, I would do so."

To the Union effort, then, was given a high moral tone. Certainly, it was a move which made foreign intervention less likely: while the British and French might intervene to save a nascent country throwing off oppression, fighting to preserve slavery was a different matter.

But reaction in the North was not favorable in all quarters. Antiblack rioting occurred in places where laborers feared competition.

All the while that the Mississippi Valley and Virginia had been battlefields in 1862, the Confederates had not been idle elsewhere. Beginning in February, they had occupied most of New Mexico, raising the Stars and Bars (as their flag was called) over both the Palace of the Governors in Santa Fe, and the Plaza in Tucson. It was hoped that they would reach California, where secessionist sentiment had grown (either to join the Confederacy or to unite with Oregon and the Washington Territory in a separate Republic of the Pacific). But defeat came at Glorieta Pass on March 26 and 28. The Union troops rushed in from California and Colorado, and by June even El Paso was in Union hands. As with all else in this War, Confederate Victory in New Mexico could only come about through swift action. Lack of men and materiel ensured that any successful Union halting of Confederate advance would result in Southern defeat.

Near the end of 1862, the Union made preparations to reopen hostilities in Tennessee and Virginia. Yet another attempt to take Richmond was mounted under *Ambrose Burnside*. Burnside led an army of 125,000 against the fortifications of Fredericksburg, a city he could have outflanked. He was driven off with great losses.

In Tennessee, the Union Army drove south toward Murfreesboro; they met the Confederates at Stones River on New Year's Eve. The Southerners fought the Unionists to a standstill. But in February of 1863, Grant was ready to move. The key to taking Vicksburg and cutting the South in two was landing troops south of the city. He managed to cut a canal from one bend of the Mississippi to another, so allowing the soldiers' passage. This done, he took Port Hudson and Jackson, Mississippi, and on May 18 settled down to besiege Vicksburg, having surrounded it on all sides.

Already, on May 3 Lee had crushed another attempt to take Richmond at Chancellorsville. But while he won the day, his great subordinate Stonewall Jackson was killed, an incalculable loss to the South. There appeared to be a stalemate. Lee resolved once again to invade the North.

On June 3, the Confederates set out from Fredericksburg. Through Maryland they marched, short of arms and material as usual. One column, once they crossed the Pennsylvania line, was sent off to the State capital, Harrisburg; the purpose was to capture a shoe factory, which commodity was in short supply. But as the main part of the army encountered the Unionists at a town called Gettysburg, the shoe-seekers were recalled. From July 1 to 3, the Battle of Gettysburg raged. It is considered to have been the Confederate "high-tide." The decisive stroke in the battle was the charge by Confederate General *George Pickett*. Pickett's Charge broke down the Union ranks; but there were no reinforcements sent after them, and the Blue-coats overwhelmed them. The battle was lost, and the long and horrible retreat to Virginia begun. The next day, July 4, Vicksburg fell. The South was cut in two.

In September, the Union forces returned to the attack in Tennessee. On September 9, they took Chattanooga, the gateway to Georgia. The Confederates hit back at Chickamauga; the battle raged two days, September 19-20. The Union was defeated, at great cost; but the victory was wasted, and not followed up—and the Union troops won the ensuing battles of Lookout Mountain and Missionary Ridge (November 24 and 25). Chattanooga was securely in Union hands. Moreover, there was a new Union commander there: *William Tecumseh Sherman*.

On March 12, 1864, Grant was made Commander-in-Chief of the U.S. armies, which henceforth would function according to one plan. He would attempt yet another Richmond campaign. Surely the ever-increasing Union supplies and manpower would break the Confederate defense? Not this time. The Battles of the Wilderness (May 5-12), Spottsylvania (May 12-21), North Anna (May 21-31), and Cold Harbor (June 1-3), dissipated Grant's assurance, and caused appalling casualties on both sides. At length, Grant settled down to besiege the suburb of Petersburg. June 15 to 18, Grant attempted to batter down the back door to Richmond, but here too, he failed. To draw off his army, *Jubal Early* was sent off with 14,000 men to invade the North again.

Early crossed the Potomac, and took the town of Frederick. The road to Washington lay virtually open; here was another opportunity to end the War. But Early delayed too long in extracting money and supplies from the folk of Frederick. Union troops hastily gathered together under the severely underrated General *George "Pap" Thomas*, and his nominal superior *Lew Wallace* (later famous as the author of *Ben Hur*) attacked Early at Monocacy Junction on July 9. Although the Union was tactically defeated, the delay permitted Grant to reinforce Washington. The last opportunity to bring foreign powers into the War was lost. On September 19, Early was defeated at Opequan by *Phil Sheridan*, who drubbed him again at Fisher's Hill, two days later, and again at Cedar Creek on October 19. Sheridan then ravaged the Shenandoah Valley, breadbasket of Virginia and source of badly needed economic supplies and cavalry horses for the Confederacy. He rejoined Grant near Petersburg. The picture looked bleak for the South.

It was worse elsewhere. On August 4, Admiral Farragut repeated his exploit in New Orleans, and ran his fleet past the harbor defenses of Mobile to take the city. This left the Confederacy only two major ports: Charleston and Wilmington. From Chattanooga, Sherman pressed steadily Southward, taking Atlanta on September 2. He burned the city (a scene made famous in the movie *Gone With the Wind*), then began his celebrated "March to the Sea." The Union had already made themselves obnoxious to the residents of occupied areas by looting and destruction. But the March to the Sea was unequaled by anything in the annals of Christian Armies. It was in fact the first example of unconditional warfare against civilians, which has become since a standby in modern battle. We Americans may be honored (or otherwise) by the fact that it was invented by the U.S. Army against fellow-Americans. A swath of destruction thirty miles wide was literally burned through. Plantations were torched, railroads broken up and their rails heated red hot and wrapped around trees ("Sherman Neck-ties"). Everything of value was destroyed or seized. On December 12, Sherman reached the sea, and on

December 22, he took Savannah. The South was now cut in three. In the meantime, Lincoln was re-elected in the North on November 8.

Sherman struck North. He took Charleston on February 17, and burned the State Capital of Columbia the same day. By March 23, he was in North Carolina. The first day of April saw Grant defeat Lee at the Battle of Five Forks. The next day, Petersburg fell, and Richmond, evacuated by its government on April 3, surrendered. Davis and the Cabinet adjourned to Danville on the North Carolina border. Lee attempted to join him with the remnants of the army, but was hotly pursued by General Grant. On April 9, at Appomattox Court House, Lee surrendered. On April 26, the last large Confederate army surrendered to Sherman at Raleigh, North Carolina.

But Davis and his cabinet continued their flight through the western Carolinas; after most of the cabinet had returned to their respective homes to be arrested, Davis, his family, and a few companions were apprehended by Federal cavalry in the Pine Barrens of Georgia. He was taken to Fortress Monroe and chained to the wall, where the picture and crown of thorns were sent him by Pius IX. He was released eventually, and ended his days held in great affection. When he died, his body traveled by train all over the South, and his funeral in New Orleans was the largest ever held in that funeral-loving city.

All over what was left of the Confederacy, bands of troops and independent commands surrendered. Some rode into Mexico to serve under Maximilian; others fled to Canada or Brazil, in which latter country their descendants remain a distinct group.

With the South vanquished, there was a difference of opinion between President Lincoln, who wished the Southern states to return to the Union intact, and the radical Republicans who wished to ensure their financial ruin (no doubt so that the financial oligarchy of the North would never again have to worry about competition).

On April 15, Lincoln was assassinated as a result of a very strange and obscure conspiracy. He had dreamed of his death several times during previous weeks; a great believer in portents, he was troubled. To this day, many questions regarding his death have never been answered; it is whispered that Secretary of War Stanton was involved. Whatever the case, the truth of the matter is, it is certain that with the death of Lincoln, the South had ironically lost its last defender; Vice-President Johnson, although committed to Lincoln's policies, did not have the same influence his murdered chief did. The South was delivered over to its enemies.

SUMMARY

The War of Southern Independence had ended disastrously for the South. Just as the victory of the rebels in the American Revolution would have been impossible without foreign intervention, so too was victory in this one. The price paid for defeat was a terrible one.

But it was a price paid by all the States, North and South. From now on, they were not to be considered as sovereign States, but as administrative divisions. Of a certainty, the Government in Washington succeeded to all the prerogatives of the Crown. Moreover, that Government was to be completely the tool of the financial and banking oligarchy of the Northeast. The only other significant power grouping remaining were the farmers of the Midwest; they were hardly the threat to the Oligarchy the Southern planters had been.

We are never allowed to know "what might have been." But it is tempting always to speculate. Had Britain and France come to Southern aid, the new nation would, without a doubt, have been culturally a much more European nation, a more Catholically-oriented nation, than the one which we have. When the Yankees invaded Louisiana, they shot at priests (Fr. Jan of St. Martinville was shot at while saying Mass and beaten by Union troops; in one town Union troops put on the priest's vestments and danced on the altar—elsewhere Irish troops mutinied rather than burn a Catholic church) and did various other unsavory things.

But in an independent Confederacy, Catholics would have counted for much more. The Indians of Oklahoma had fought in the War as Confederate allies, and it is quite likely that Confederate Indian policy would have been more humane. Since Emancipation was scheduled five years after the end of hostilities, the likelihood is that slavery would have ended gradually, with compensation for the owners and preparation for the slaves—as in the West Indies. Surely the result would have been a less vicious racial problem. Maximilian would perhaps have retained the throne of Mexico, since there would have been no Union government to rush arms to Juarez. The prospect of a Catholic and prosperous Mexico is a welcome one. Above all, it cannot be supposed that the two halves of the former Union could have remained separate also, given their economic ties. What a nation might have come from that reunion! Free of an oligarchy dedicated only to its own power and extension of its ideology over the Earth, both Americans and overseas nations could well have benefited immensely. Imagine: an America more concerned with self-development than foreign adventure!

As everyone knows, none of these things have happened. But there were a few good developments, as must happen with every occurrence.

Here is one chronicled by the WPA Guide to Mississippi, in regard to the town of Paulding:

> When the men of Paulding went off to fight in the War between the States, their wives visited with the women of Rose Hill, an Irish settlement, several miles N. It is said that when the men returned they found their wives converted to Catholicism, and since that time the population has been largely Catholic (p. 426).

At any rate, the War was over. The masters of the newly reunited nation decreed that the South must be reconstructed and the West's Indians subdued. More than this, the way was cleared for this nation, consecrated as it was to the ideals of Masonry, to "a Church without a Pope and a State without a King," to spread its influence throughout the world. However, favorable conditions would attract ever more Catholic immigrants from a wide variety of nations. All of these topics and several more we shall explore in the next chapter.

Before we take our leave of the defeated Southerners, however, it were well to give the last word to Fr. Abram Ryan. His poem, *The Conquered Banner* reflects perfectly the state of the South at the end of the bloody and devastating conflict:

> Furl that Banner, for 'tis weary;
> Round its staff 'tis drooping dreary;
>   Furl it, fold it, it is best;
> For there's not a man to wave it,
> And there's not a sword to save it;
> And there's not one left to lave it
> In the blood which heroes gave it;
> And its foes now scorn and brave it;
>   Furl it, hide it—let it rest!
> ...
>
> Furl that Banner! furl it sadly!
> Once ten thousands hailed it gladly,
> And ten thousands wildly, madly,
>   Swore it should forever wave;
> Swore that foeman's sword should never
> Hearts like theirs entwined dissever,
> Till that flag should float forever
>   O'er their freedom or their grave!
> ...
>
> Furl that Banner, softly, slowly!
> Treat it gently—it is holy—
>   For it droops above the dead.

Touch it not—unfold it never,
Let it droop there, furled forever,
  For its people's hopes are dead!

RECONSTRUCTION AND IMMIGRATION 1866-1899

AFTER THE WAR

With the surrender of the South, it had been President Lincoln's intention to reintegrate the Southern States into national life as quickly as possible, with a minimum of damage to what remained of their existing social and economic system. The Radical Republicans in Congress had other ideas, however, as did their ideologues in the general populace:

> In the great [Episcopalian] church of the Trinity in New York City the Reverend Doctor Vincent assured his congregation that the martyred President had been "unfitted, by the natural gentleness and humanity of his disposition to execute the stern justice of Christ's vicegerent." For Christ's vicegerent, the President of the United States, was "to hew the rebels in pieces before the Lord," and cast them out of the Kingdom of God. "So let us say, God's will be done" (Paul H. Buck, *The Road to Reunion*, p. 12).

The result of the assassination was to rally many of the country's best-known writers—Emerson, Melville, Whitman, for example, to a policy of vengeance—in complete opposition to the wishes of the man they so stirringly eulogized in poetry and prose.

Once again, it is important to bear in mind that while there were Oligarchs behind the scenes who used their financial and political power to manipulate events as well as they could, the actions of all sides were clothed in ideological robes. The Radical Republicans themselves purveyed (and many sincerely—for what that is worth—believed) a noble sounding doctrine called "The New Nationalism." A magazine called *The Nation* was launched to promulgate its ideals. As far as the New Nationalists were concerned, the United States are (or rather *is*, since this particular violation of the rules of grammar was adopted at this time to show the victory of ideology over fact) a single nation, whose government is supreme over any and all other—or lesser, as we must now say—sources of authority. In a word, the *Federalist Papers'* use of States' Rights as a means of selling the Constitution to suspicious States became a fraud. Henceforth, the States' creation was to be their master.

To this apparently bald and crude line of reasoning, however, was given a messianic tone; having destroyed slavery in the South, the government of the purified and regenerated United States would proceed to end racial prejudice, industrial abuse, ignorance, and all the other ills besetting Man. In a word, the United States and its government were God's instruments for the social redemption of the World. One Jesse T. Peck in his 1868 *The History of the Great Republic, Considered from a Christian [sic!] Stand-Point* wrote what may be considered the clearest religious exposition of this idea. For Peck, God had created the Republic "to advance the human race beyond all its precedents in intelligence, goodness, and power;" beyond this, "religion is the only life-force and organizing power." Americans had learned through their sufferings in the war that slavery was an "enormous individual and national crime." Nevertheless, the Almighty "determined to extend to the nation the regeneration which had long been recognized as the privilege of the individual only." Like Israel of old, the U.S. developed in stages: Preparation, Independence, Development, Emancipation; at last it had reached its final point—Mission. With universal education breeding a universal electorate, with a national Protestantism purified of slavery, the United States would be "the grandest missionary of progress ever known among men."

It was an intoxicating vision. For those attached to the ideology of New England, the New Nationalism was seen as the ennobling descendant of the ideals of 1776, itself a providential event. Of these idealists, perhaps the best known was Henry Adams. Allied with them in origin, but quite separate from them prior to the war, was ex-Brook Farmer Orestes Brownson. He had in ante-bellum days, although against slavery, supported States' Rights as the American expression of the idea of subsidiarity—so central to later Papal social teachings. But the events of the War (including the deaths of two sons fighting for the Union) altered his views, as expressed in the 1866 *American Republic*. Therein he not only supported in high-flown and would-be prophetic language the supremacy of the Federal Government over the States, he asserted for a Catholic audience the messianic nature of the United States. Where before the conflict Brownson had stridently written of the supremacy of Church over State (as exemplified in Papal writings up to that time), afterwards he embraced the notion that Separation of Church and State, far from being a mere expedient due to the non-Catholic nature of American Society, was a positive good. The special mission of America under God was to extend political democracy throughout the world—thus the nation's political goals were erected into quasi-religious ones; all of these notions would be repeated over and over in the following years, receiving their final enunciation in the period before Vatican II by

Fr. John Courtney Murray, S.J. In a word, Brownson was one of the first prophets of Americanism, which heresy we will deal with later.

Behind the sweet-sounding phrases of the New Nationalism lurked the powerful folk who used it to further their ends. Thus the period immediately following the War—the horrors of Reconstruction, the corruption and graft involved in giving government contracts to millionaires, and sundry other malfeasances being so prominent—filled the idealists with horror. Aristocratic folk like Henry Adams recoiled with loathing from the new society which was forming under the aegis of centralization and industrialization unleashed after the War. His classic *The Education of Henry Adams* is filled with the despair of a man who really believed in the high-sounding phrases, and who tried all his life to follow them and serve his country—with pathetic results.

Brownson too recanted. After registering his whole-hearted agreement with the *Syllabus of Errors* of Pius IX, and his dislike of "Liberal Catholicism," he wrote:

> Time was when I paraded my Americanism, in order to repel the charge that an American cannot become a convert to the Church without ceasing to feel and act as an American patriot. I have lived long enough to snap my fingers at all charges of that sort. I love my country, and, in her hour of trial, I and my sons, Catholics like myself, did our best to preserve her integrity, and save her Constitution; and there is no sacrifice in my power that I would not make to bring "my kinsmen after the flesh" to Christ; but, after all, the Church is my true country, and the faithful are my real countrymen. Let the American people become truly Catholic and submissive children of the Holy Father, and their Republic is safe; let them refuse and seek safety for the secular order in sectarianism or secularism, and nothing can save it from destruction (*Brownson's Quarterly Review*, January 1873, pp. 2-3).

Charity would require us to think of Brownson as the man of 1873, not of 1866.

Still, disillusion was in the future for such as Adams and Brownson. The millennium had dawned, and the New Nationalism appeared supreme. Yet it had its opponents.

These were called (both by themselves and their opponents) "Conservatives." A lawyer from New York, Vine W. Kingsley, laid down their views in his 1865 book, *Reconstruction in America*. Therein was, opposed to Radical Republicanism, the South's restoration rather than reconstruction; a vision of a culturally and politically diversified nation, rather than a homogeneous bloc; and prevention of the use of Blacks as political catspaws for the country's rulers. Who were these folk?:

Few important intellectuals, publicists, or clerics promoted these views in the postwar years. But they had wide popular—and hence political—appeal. Conservatism spoke for those who had the smallest stake in the war, or were least in sympathy with its outcome: white southerners, hardscrabble northern farmers, Irish Catholic laborers, merchants whose interests lay with the prewar economy; Baptists, Lutherans, and Old School Presbyterians skeptical of human perfectibility. They made up, in Carl Schurz's words, "essentially a party of the past" (Morton Keller, *Affairs of State*, p. 49).

In this country, of course, the insult hurled by Schurz that the Conservatives were the "party of the past" has a unique sting; for Americans the unconscious supposition is that the past is bad, and the future good. But that aside, it was an untrue charge, unless merely being the party kept out of power by military force automatically relegates a group to the past. For the Conservatives had an alternative vision of America which might very well have produced a more humane nation than the one in which we live in at present.

But they had an Achilles' heel. Their monthly *The Old Guard* carried on its masthead the phrase, "Devoted to the principles of 1776 and 1789." They had to justify and express themselves in terms of a philosophy of which their opponents were much more truly the heirs. This is a problem which has dogged the American Right since the days of Fisher Ames—and which, as we will continue to see, has kept up with us even to this day. In any case, it is now time to see Radical Republicanism and the New Nationalism not as mere high-sounding words, but in action.

Reconstruction and the Creation of the Race Problem

President Johnson was a Southerner and a States Righter, although he had been Unionist governor of Tennessee before becoming Lincoln's Vice President. He was a Conservative, but unable to affect the course of the Radically-controlled Congress. Over his veto on April 9, 1866, Congress passed a Civil Rights Bill which guaranteed Blacks legal and civil rights, but not suffrage. The following June 16, the 14th Amendment to the Constitution was proposed by Congress. A month later, once again over Johnson's veto, Congress made the Freedmen's Bureau, an institution devised in wartime to look after both the newly emancipated Blacks and Unionist Whites in the South, a permanent fixture.

This Bureau was an interesting creature, indeed. Emancipation had thrown millions of Blacks throughout the South out of the support system which had existed under slavery. Whereas old slaves had been kept and cared for on the plantations, the dawn of freedom meant poverty and even starvation for many of them. The Bureau was formed initially to meet this need. Direct medical assistance was given to over a million people, and over 21,000,000 rations distributed.

Beyond this, the Bureau founded over 1,000 schools for Blacks, and spent in excess of $400,000 on the training of teachers to staff them. After the Bureau's abolition in 1872, this educational network was sustained by the Black community itself—an achievement rarely commented upon today.

But there was a less pleasant side to the Bureau also. For its courts, established to hear complaints by the new freedmen against former Confederates, made little pretense to fairness, and yet took precedence of all other courts in the conquered South. A bleak but rather accurate picture of this period is given in the classic novel, *Gone With Wind.*

Although the reconquered states had put together civilian governments almost immediately after the cessation of hostilities, these were voided by the March 2, 1867 Reconstruction Act (passed, predictably, over Johnson's veto). This latter divided the former Confederacy into five military districts which would be each commanded by an army officer having jurisdiction over life and property. Civilian government would be restored in a state after a Constitutional Convention was held, made up of delegates "elected by the male citizens, ...of whatever race, color, or previous condition," except those disenfranchised by participation in rebellion. Then, according to the new document's terms, a state government would be constituted.

Since, however, the majority of the White male population in these states had been Confederate, they were automatically deprived of political rights. In each Southern State, the Black men became the bulk of the electorate. Unused to governing or voting, they were easy targets for manipulation by unscrupulous Northern profiteers, called *Carpetbaggers* from the Carpetbags they brought South with them. Southern White collaborators of these folk were called *Scalawags*.

The Carpetbaggers used Blacks as figurehead governors and legislators (although some of these were actually men of real ability, such as *Samuel J. Lee* of South Carolina and *Henry M. Turner* of Georgia). Unfortunately, these were often no match for their less able counterparts who were in Carpetbagger pay. It is not too much to say that in some places a veritable reign of terror developed, with state and local governments being run for the profit of the Carpetbaggers and their allies. They sold railroad contracts in return for kickbacks, and effectively squelched any opposition. To indoctrinate the newly Freedmen politically (and sometimes religiously; in Louisiana and elsewhere Catholic Blacks were encouraged to switch to Protestant sects) the Union Leagues were inaugurated. Secret Societies with rituals and so on of their own, they formed a powerful tool for keeping the Black electorate voting as a single mass, rather than as intelligent individuals.

With no legal or political way of defending themselves, many White Southerners turned to illegal tactics. In imitation of and rivalry with the Union Leagues, the Ku-Klux-Klan was founded at Pulaski, Tennessee in 1866 by a group of Confederate veterans chaired by General Nathan Bedford Forrest. Calling themselves "The Invisible Empire of the South," the Klansmen were headed by a grand wizard and a hierarchy of grand dragons, grand titans, and grand cyclopes. Dressed in their trademark sheets and hoods, which at once frightened the superstitious and prevented identification by authorities, the KKK drove out Blacks, Carpetbaggers, and Scalawags from their towns and homes. Crops were burned, as were crosses; murders too resulted in some places. Horrified at this latter occurrence, Grand Wizard Forrest ordered the organization disbanded in 1869. Nevertheless, it continued to act in some locales (it was always a decentralized sort of thing). So effective did it become that Congress passed the Force Act (1870) and the Ku Klux Klan Act (1871) which allowed the President (now U.S. Grant, Johnson having served out—despite an attempt to impeach him—Lincoln's term until 1869) to suspend habeas corpus, suppress disturbances by force, and severely punish Klansmen. These measures were ineffective, however, and only the gradual restoration of Southern White Civil Rights ended the KKK in its original manifestation (the one we know today was founded in 1915).

It ought not to be too surprising that such an organization soon graduated from redressing grievances to wholesale murder and crime. As with the Fenian Brotherhood and the Orange Lodges of Ireland, or the Broederbond of South Africa, such groups—generally of Masonic inspiration—respond to a leadership beyond the membership's control, and are particularly manipulable. It might be pointed out that the single real political effect gained by the Klan was to give an excuse for yet another voiding of Constitutional rights by legislative decree. It also served to focus the hatred of the disenfranchised small White farmers on the Blacks, rather than on their White users in the South and Washington.

This hatred was not shared by the Aristocratic politicians who were reorganizing the "Democratic-Conservative" Party throughout the South. In many cases the same men (or their sons) who, through land-ownership and education had dominated the political and social scene before the War, they generally were free of the sort of racial hatred which was to be found among their less well-to-do fellow citizens. Acceptance of the Reconstruction Amendments and Black Suffrage were, they believed, essential both to their recovering control of their states from the imposed Republican regimes and the continued growth of the Party.

So they would accept them in good faith. This was called "The New Departure." The result was twofold; the former Confederates were for the most part re-enfranchised, and the Democratic Party as a whole could become once again a credible opposition to the Republicans.

By 1876, the Democratic-Conservatives had regained control of all the Southern States from the Carpetbaggers, who left their Black allies to their fate. The new governments indulged in an orgy of constitutional revisions, which featured most prominently prohibition of state funds to assist railroads and industry. On the one hand, this had the effect of closing up a significant source of corruption. On the other, it assured that the South would remain agrarian for the foreseeable future.

The election of Rutherford B. Hayes to the Presidency in 1877 was secured with Southern support. In return for this, and the guarantee of the Southern aristocratic leadership that the Blacks would be unmolested, Hayes agreed that the South would return to legal equality with the rest of the country. The "Bourbons" as the planters' faction was called, settled down to power:

> The most successful of several experiments in substituting Southern patricians for Carpetbaggers as leaders of the Negro masses... was that conducted by Wade Hampton in South Carolina. The policy was called "breaking down the political color line." Promising the Negroes justice, better schools, protection from the white race fanatics, and minor offices, Hampton made a strong and, for a time, remarkably successful appeal for their support. The Carpetbagger ex-Governor Robert K. Scott admitted in August that Hampton "was honestly carrying out the promises he made," and had "already appointed more colored men to office than were appointed during the first two years that I was governor." And a Radical Negro leader, once an associate justice of the State Supreme Court predicted that Hampton would "get nine-tenths of the colored vote" in the next election. In his political and race policy Hampton received the hearty support of President Hayes and the bitter opposition of the upcountry whites and race extremists who eventually overthrew him under the leadership of Ben Tillman (C. Vann Woodward, *Reunion and Reaction*, p. 227).

This alliance of the old aristocracy and the Blacks was perhaps the most hopeful possibility for the South. But it was doomed. To their hatred and envy of the planters, the small farmers now added their hatred of the Blacks. When the generation grew to voting age that only remembered the horrors of Reconstruction, the political doom of the Black in the South was sealed. Not only their voting rights would be taken from them, but most interactions with whites. Reconstruction was the legitimate father of Jim Crow; the bitterness over the ending of the Jim Crow laws in the 1950s and 60s has lasted to the present day. Yet even while the Racial question was being spawned in the South, developments were taking place up North that would change the face of the nation as a whole forever.

The Robber Barons and the New Economy

If the Radical Republicans were unmerciful to the South, they were nevertheless kind to one segment of the population: Big Business. Beginning during the War, Federal, State, and Local subsidies to railroads resulted not only in ever faster communications between the various regions, but in the formation of huge railroad corporations. This tendency toward concentration of business in the hands of corporations was the single most noted economic development after the Civil War. It would have the effect of disrupting many of the facets of American life upon which the accepted national values were built—particularly individualism. In an economy dedicated to the notion of freely competing individuals, the major corporation could easily squeeze out smaller competition. As governmental power was becoming increasingly concentrated, so too was economic.

There were a number of important results from this. The small artisan or merchant has to be at once receptive to his customers and concerned with his employees. A large corporation need not be. As the election of President Grant in 1872 showed, through Grant's reliance on major industrial—particularly railroad—money in his campaign, the line between governmental and economic power was porous indeed. The corruption scandals which scarred his administration underlined this.

Such men as railroad tycoons Jay Gould and Cornelius Vanderbilt, steel magnate Andrew Carnegie, and Standard Oil founder John D. Rockefeller carved out huge corporate empires for themselves. Often they would make agreements with other such men in the same business to squeeze out competition. The result was the creation of a "Trust," a sort of unofficial monopoly which could determine prices and quality without reference to anything save profit. Successive discoveries of gold, silver, and other precious metals, the ever-growing network of rails made possible as the frontier advanced, and the development of new technologies employing such things as fuel oil and electricity opened up a boundless area for the well-placed to make fortunes in. The political clout conferred by millions of dollars in turn allowed them to make more, legally or otherwise, and in many places turned local and sometimes even state and federal governmental bodies into their tools. As *Charles Francis Adams, Jr.,* Henry's brother, wrote:

> The system of corporate life and corporate power, as applied to industrial development, is yet in its infancy.... It is a new power, for which our language contains no name (with Henry Adams, *Chapters of Erie*, p.96).

The Adams brothers had first encountered this powerful combination in action in 1869, when Jay Gould attempted to corner the market on gold; something he could only do with Federal collusion. It then came out that several highly placed figures around Grant (though not the President himself, an apparent babe in the woods) were the gentlemen to whom Gould looked for protection while he did the cornering. Idealists that they were, the brothers and their friends went out to expose the crime. The result may be found in *The Education of Henry Adams:*

> Grant's administration had outraged every rule of ordinary decency, but scores of promising men, whom the country could not well spare, were ruined in saying so. The world cared little for decency. What it wanted, it did not know; probably a system that would work, and men who could work it; but it found neither. Adams had tried his own little hands on it, and had failed. His friends had been driven out of Washington or had taken to fisticuffs. He himself sat down and stared hopelessly into the future (p. 280).

It is ironic that these two lineal descendants of the oligarchy which had triumphed over George III and Governor Hutchinson should find themselves likewise among the dispossessed. But we should remember that it did not appear to them in that way. The nature of America's ruling class is that it is ever-changing. It is not an aristocracy of blood; superseded Adamses and ruined Southern planters alike are the closest we come to such. Neither is it an aristocracy of learning. Rather, it is sort of like a fraternity, whose members are revolving, whose means are revolving, but whose goals remain the same.

The old American Aristocrats regarded the new tycoons of this money-making era ("The Gilded Age," as Mark Twain called both it and a novel he wrote about it) as "Nouveau Riche," a term which enters the language about this time. Accustomed as we are today to thinking of Rockefellers, Vanderbilts, and so on as the height of gentility, they were much looked down upon at the time by descendants of earlier oligarchs.

They went about trying to better themselves. Often of humble, they gave much money to transform prep schools like Andover and Exeter into copies of the British Public Schools, and the Ivy League Colleges into versions of Oxford and Cambridge. The reason was simple: that their sons might behave like English gentlemen, and at least be exposed to what passes for high ideals (fair-play, and so on) in that country. These centers of education, which prior to the Civil War had been relatively small and undistinguished, took on the veneer of age-old ivy covered gothic stone and mullioned windows, and the air of tradition, which marks them today. It should be realized, however, that for all their appearance of venerability they are rather recent.

Similarly, the Robber Barons aspired to live like real aristocrats. They built for themselves such palaces as the Vanderbilt mansions: the Breakers in Newport, Rhode Island, and Biltmore in Asheville, North Carolina. All sorts of artworks were brought over from Europe to adorn them, and full staffs of servants hired to look after them. To them such resorts as Newport and Palm Beach owe their origin as centers of elegance.

Nor were their building projects confined to their own comforts. Whether for sincere personal reasons or to curry favor with the public (who after all did use their wares) such men engaged in acts of philanthropy. The Carnegie Libraries, for instance, a chain throughout the country, were started by Andrew Carnegie in order to provide poor towns with libraries (and thus educational opportunities for their young) which they could never afford themselves. Many mock Gothic Episcopal, Unitarian, Presbyterian, and Methodist churches around the country owe their beautiful buildings to the munificence of such men.

Their activities during the Gilded Age had great impact abroad, particularly on the traditional landed elites they so wished to emulate:

> During the first three-quarters of the nineteenth century, the British landed establishment had been the wealthy elite of the richest nation in the world. But during the seventy years that followed, it was noticeably disturbed and diminished by new and international developments that it could not control, and in some cases could not survive. As the world became smaller, more competitive, and more unified; as distances were shortened by the steamship, the wireless, the telegraph, and the aeroplane; and as the economic autonomy and self-sufficiency of nations was eroded and undermined, the landowners of Britain were exposed to the full and icy blast of the global economy. Their economic circumstances were much less determined by the state of the harvest in Barset or by the health of their bank account in London, than by the price of wheat in Chicago and by financial dealings on the New York stock exchange. As Charles George Milnes Gaskell put it in an acute, prophetic, and pessimistic article, "the vast increase in the carrying power of ships, the facilities of intercourse with foreign countries, [and] the further cheapening of cereals and meat," meant that, economically as politically, the patricians were no longer lords of the earth.
>
> One ominous sign of this was the explosive growth of a new international plutocracy, especially in the United States. As W.H.

Lecky explained, "there has probably never been a period in the history of the world when the conditions of industry, assisted by great gold discoveries in several parts of the world, were so favourable to the formation of fortunes as at present, and when the race of millionaires was so large." From the late 1870s to the First World War, there was a sudden expansion of quite unprecedented American fortunes—billionaires like Henry Ford, Rockefeller, and centimillionaires such as the Vanderbilts, the Astors, and Andrew Carnegie. And where these giants led, the lesser wealthy—like J.P. Morgan, who died in 1914 worth a mere eighty million dollars, Henry Clay Frick, and Samuel P. Huntington—soon followed. Not only on the east coast, but in the Midwest and California, these "Transatlantic Midases" amassed their millions: in railways, mining, iron and steel, urban real estate, chemicals and automobiles--but not, significantly, in agricultural land (David Cannadine, *The Decline and Fall of the British Aristocracy*, p. 90).

Spurred by trade with the U.S., a similar caste grew up in Britain, which was soon displacing the landed nobility. In the rest of Europe, at faster or slower rates, the same thing was happening. Yet in the case of England, it is interesting also to see that many of the great noblemen who gradually suffered loss of position and power were the descendants of the Whig grandees who fought to bring down George III's personal government.

At the same time, however, the period after the Civil War saw the expansion of the British Empire in Africa, Asia, and around the world. Even as Britain's traditional leadership began its long decline, the nation's fortunes rose—and with Imperial expansion came a rush of plutocratic fortunes to Britain also, based upon wealth from and investment in the colonies. This in turn gave rise to the "New Imperialism," a messianic ideology much like our own New Nationalism. Probably its most notable exponent was *Cecil Rhodes* (1853-1902). He had made a fortune in the South African Diamond Mines (in fact, he founded the De Beers Consolidated Mine Company, which holds a near monopoly to this day on the world diamond supply), and went into politics, striving to annex as much of Africa to the Empire as he could. His importance to our story is that he endowed the Rhodes Scholarships to allow British, German, American, and Colonial students to study together at Oxford. This was symptomatic of the way plutocrats in both countries had come to think of the "Anglo-Saxon" joint world mission.

At the same time, various of the British nobility were marrying American heiresses in attempts to shore up the failing family fortunes earlier described. So the Duke of Marlborough married Consuelo Vanderbilt; his brother, Lord Randolph Churchill wed Jenny Jerome—their son Winston treasured his American descent.

This confluence between the two groups is often cited by those interested in such things as being a sort of British seduction of America's rulership. Subsequent events (like the two World Wars) are seen as the wily British Aristocracy's tricking of the poor Americans. The truth is much more subtle. The fact of the matter is that while in 1897 the British Empire was at possibly its psychological and economic highpoint (the Diamond Jubilee of Queen Victoria), already the flow of power and influence, financial and otherwise, was turning from the City of London to Wall Street. No matter how dismayed Charles Francis and Henry Adams were at the alteration in their country, one cannot help but feel that Great-Grandpa John would approve.

We should also bear in mind, while speaking of groups and conspiracies, the part that individual whim often plays in these kinds of developments. While Vanderbilt, Rockefeller and the rest were busy trying to cover their rapacity (which won such folk the title "Robber Barons") with a veneer of English culture, one at least wanted to go all the way. William Waldorf Astor emigrated to England in the end, and was made Viscount Astor in 1916. His daughter-in-law was the famed Lady Astor who was Churchill's recurrent antagonist.

Without a doubt, theirs was a glittering manner of life which has determined for most Americans their idea of what wealth is. The phrase "the 400," used to mean society today, refers to the 400 people who could fit into Mrs. John Jacob Astor's ballroom. On the one hand, because of their doings, we have come to think of wealth as something generally acquired by dishonest means; on the other, that it comes with no responsibility, save that of being flashy tabloid-bait. The idea of a well-to-do or even rich elite, tied to the neighborhood by heritage and duty, and doing its best to elevate the area round is completely unknown. In a word, wealth in America became as powerful as any feudal regime, but without any ties to society of blood or tradition. The English veneer, unfortunately, did not bring over in any effective way *noblesse oblige*. Moreover, their political power was enough to allow them the ability to bring about war.

The sad truth is that beneath the glittering mansions and balls, the fortunes of these men were built upon inhuman conditions meted out to cheap labor. To answer the call of the factories, French-Canadians, Italians, Poles, Czechs, Russians, and many more flocked to the cities and industrial towns. As we have seen, the Germans and Irish already were ensconced in them. But ever more labor was needed to man the factories, mines, and railroads. The cities grew, and the economy and society in general ever more and more functioned around them to the detriment of the farm. Urban squalor joined agrarian discontent to feed radicalism of various kinds.

Radicalism and Reform

Even as before the War the Southern Planters felt themselves in competition with a Banking-Industrial complex with which they could not compete, so too did the generality of small farmers after the War. They believed that the railroad men who transported their goods, the manufacturers who provided the implements necessary to raise crops, and the middle-men who sold them, were all exploiters—often allied with government. Although prices for their crops often fell, expenses did not. The result was an enormous amount of rural debt:

> The importance of debts in determining the fate of the farmer can be demonstrated by looking at the history of certain agricultural clubs and organizations. In 1867 Oliver H. Kelley, a postal employee, founded the Patrons of Husbandry, primarily in an effort to broaden the intellectual horizons and brighten the social life of rural citizens. After a slow start, the organization grew rapidly in the early seventies: between 1872 and 1874 no less than 14,000 local "granges" were established. The Grangers, as members were popularly called, inevitably became involved in attacking the problems of farmers. They established co-operatives to market their own crops and to buy farm machinery and other manufactured goods, and agitated in behalf of agricultural research, better schools, and more equitable tax laws. They became a powerful political force over-night, obtaining the passage of state laws regulating railroads and grain elevators and otherwise restricting practices of businessmen engaged in marketing and transporting farm products (John A. Garraty, *The New Commonwealth 1877-1890*, p. 52).

During the repeated cycles of boom and bust in the years following the War, rural discontent, particularly in the Midwest and South, grew ever hotter. Settlement of the West had been primarily by farmers from the East and Europe (particularly Scandinavia and Germany) on free public land. The results were impressive: in 1867, Nebraska became a state; in 1875, Colorado. The year 1889 witnessed both Dakotas, Montana, and Washington make the same step, as did Wyoming and Idaho the next year. The farmer had to endure not only the purely economic woes we have indicated but plagues of locusts and Indian attacks. Despite occasional victories such as those won by the Grange, he remained convinced that the Eastern Capitalist wished to destroy him. Such fears were not allayed by the pronouncements of men like Eastern Republican leader William Walter Phelps, who declared in an 1890 speech in New York:

> The export of agricultural products must find a limited and failing market; the export of manufactured articles must find an increasing and permanent market. The lowest grade labor can raise corn and wheat and pork. It does not require the intelligence and skill and invention in which American labor surpasses the world. Ultimately, then, we must lose these markets for our wheat, but not for our wares (*The Nation*, Oct. 9, 1890, p. 275).

What this meant was that a leading Republican Congressman and plutocrat as much as declared himself in favor of the American farmer's extinction. This symbolized the frustration of the farmers with both parties. In 1890 a convention gathered at Topeka, Kansas to launch a new political party, the Populist Party. It was a quite a gathering indeed; something of "a religious revival, a Pentecost of politics in which a tongue of flame sat upon every man, and each spake as the spirit gave him utterance." One of those who so spake was not a man, but Kansas lawyer and housewife Mrs. Mary Ellen Lease, who summed up the feelings of the attendees eloquently:

> Wall Street owns the country. It is no longer a government of the people, by the people, and for the people, but a government of Wall Street, by Wall Street and for Wall Street. The great common people of this country are slaves, and monopoly is the master. The West and South are prostrate before the manufacturing East. Money rules, and our Vice-President is a London banker. Our laws are the output of a system which clothes rascals in robes and honesty in rags. The parties lie to us and the political speakers mislead us... the politicians said we suffered from overproduction. Overproduction when 10,000 little children, so statistics tell us, starve to death every year in the United States, and over 100,000 shop-girls in New York are forced to sell their virtue for the bread their niggardly wages deny them!
> There are thirty men in the United States whose aggregate wealth is over one and one-half billion dollars. There are half a million looking for work... We want money, land and transportation. We want the abolition of the National Banks, and we want the power to make loans direct from the government. We want the accursed foreclosure system wiped out.... We will stand by our homes and stay by our firesides by force if necessary, and we will not pay our debts to the loan-shark companies until the government pays its debts to us. The people are at bay, let the bloodhounds of money who have dogged us thus far beware (J. D. Hicks, *Populist Revolt*, p. 160).

Populism had its roots in the Protestant Evangelical reformer tradition. Thus it is not surprising to find that it was closely connected in many places in the North and Midwest with Prohibitionism and anti-Catholicism. In the South, it was to a great degree tied up with racialism;

thus Wade Hampton was swept out of office in South Carolina by Ben Tillman, a Populist who stood for small farmers and White Supremacy. Thus, ironically, the political ruin of the Southern planters wrought by the Civil War at the behest of the Northern Oligarchy was completed by that Oligarchy's latest would-be opponents, the Populists. Further, the anti-Catholic strain in Populism ensured that Catholic farmers (especially in Kansas and Nebraska) would for the most part remain loyal to either of the two parties—thus tying them ever closer to political business as usual. This lessened ever more the likelihood of their trying to break the mold in the direction of the Church's social teachings.

In any case, the discontent among farmers was mirrored among Industrial Workers in the Gilded Age. The appalling conditions in factories and mines, low wages, and so on called forth reaction eventually. As their counterparts in Europe had done earlier, so did American workmen begin to organize. An early expression of this was the group called the "Molly Maguires," formed among the Irish miners in the anthracite coal country of Pennsylvania and West Virginia. Commencing in 1862, they at first attempted to seek higher wages and safer conditions in their very dangerous work peacefully. Unable to do so, and inspired by the Fenians in Ireland, they formed the Molly Maguires (named after an 1840s widow who led anti-landlord agitation in Ireland) as a secret society. They indulged in sabotage and assassinations as a result. In the end they were infiltrated and broken, although conditions did improve somewhat in their coal fields. But the major problem was not rectified either there or anywhere else in the U.S.:

> ...the same gulf that gave employers a sense of superiority over their men also kept them ignorant of the workers' condition and needs, and therefore incapable of dealing with labor-related industrial problems intelligently. Employers who condemned their men for squandering their wages on drink generally knew little about the grinding toil that drove men to seek comfort in alcohol, or the squalid tenement homes and dreary boardinghouses that led them to look for comfort and sociability in saloons. They became furious when workers placed loyalty to a union above loyalty to the company, not understanding why the ordinary hired hand had little reason to identify with a corporate employer. Repeatedly men were fired for trying to organize unions, even for presenting the grievances of their fellows to their bosses. "[If] a man employed on this railroad...is appointed on a committee to adjust a grievance," a Texas and Pacific worker told a congressional committee in 1886, "he is likely to be discharged for it." In 1886 the managers of the Chicago, Burlington, and Quincy Railroad decided to fire every man who belonged to the Knights of Labor, "inasmuch as the Knights of Labor owe allegiance to somebody else, and not to the railroad." They saw no contradiction between the

demand for employee loyalty and their declared policy, enunciated by general manager Henry B. Stone: "If I wanted boiler iron I would go out on the market and buy it where I could get it cheapest, and if I wanted to employ men I would do the same." In 1883 the Western Union telegraphers struck for a 15 percent wage increase. They did so, however, only after the company had several times refused even to respond to petitions. The direct result of the strike, one telegrapher testified, "was the insult offered to our executive committee by the officials of the Western Union Telegraph Company.... If our committee had been met in a gentlemanly manner... there would probably have been no strike (John A. Garraty, *The New Commonwealth 1877-1890*, pp. 148-149).

The Knights of Labor herein referred to was in fact the first important national labor organization. Founded in 1869, the Knights were originally a secret society; the secrecy was intended to protect the membership from the sorts of reprisals just described. The Knights were actually in favor of reorganizing society along what would later be called the corporate state—shopkeepers and farmers were held to have the same interests as workers, and the idea was that cooperatives of these would become the framework of the state.

This *Syndicalism* as it was called, owed a great deal to the pre-Marxist Socialists of Europe, but nevertheless also bore more than a small resemblance to what Catholic social theorists in Europe like the Baron von Vogelsang and the Marquis de La Tour du Pin were advocating. Moreover, since many more Catholics in America were workers than farmers, the question of Catholic membership in the Knights of Labor was much more pressing than the Grange or other Populist or Farmer groups (whose often public and vocal anti-Catholicism in any case reduced the interest of individual Catholics in such organizations). As we shall see, the Knights became a major source of dissension within Catholicism.

Regardless of this, however, the Knights and organized Labor became synonymous in many people's minds with newly imported Socialism. Here was a real conundrum; on the one hand, the majority of Americans were doubtless resentful of the Plutocrats. On the other, being assured that Socialism involved atheism, free love, and sundry other terrible things, they did not look too kindly on Labor organizers—the more so after the bloody Haymarket Square riots in Chicago in 1886 (which led to the secession of more conservative labor folk who in turn formed the American Federation of Labor). In succeeding years, railroad, mine, and factory strikes were often suppressed by Federal troops.

While all of this went on, however, less visible reformers worked, not to change the system, but to ease its more objectionable features. Part of the same reformist thrust that brought about Prohibition agitation also worked for the suppression of abortion, contraception, child labor, impure food, and the like, as well as civil service reform. Most of the laws against abortion in the various states date from this era; there were then Societies for the Suppression of Vice established.

One of the most visible (if less important) means of government corruption was the giving out of civil service jobs to political allies—the famed spoils system. In 1883, the Civil Service Act required competitive examinations for entrance into the Civil Service, thus going far to keep out incompetents with friends in high places. Four years later, the Interstate Commerce Act was passed. This set up the Interstate Commerce Commission to regulate railroad traffic and fees. In 1890 Congress passed the Sherman Anti-Trust Law. This declared illegal "any contract, combination in the form of trust or otherwise, or conspiracy, in restraint of trade or commerce among the several states or with foreign nations." Heavy penalties in the form of fines and imprisonment were set up, the whole to be enforced by the Federal Department of Justice. The result was that such combines as Standard Oil were broken up.

Here, however, we are faced with a problem which dogs us yet. The depredations of the Trusts and spoilsmen and railroaders and robber barons and so on defied local action. Yet in calling the Federal government in to fight them, it was necessary to grant that government powers never envisaged by the framers of the Constitution. Further, one must presume that the Federal government would discharge its new found activities with due respect for liberty of its citizens. This extension of power began erecting into the law of the land what the Civil War had de facto established—that the Federal Government was superior to any other force in the nation.

It is not too much to say that without the precedents established by this legislation, the subsequent expansion of the government into so many facets of life would have been impossible. Yet to oppose such an extension would be in essence to declare one's adherence to the spoils system in the Civil Service, to robber barons running the railroads as they pleased, and to plutocrats turning into monopolists and ruining both their workers and customers with ease. The easy solution to any problem in America has always been passage of a law; yet the laws themselves have often precipitated worse results, even while palliating the specific evils.

In addition to the Farmer, Labor, and Reform questions, the Monetary question also agitated Gilded Age America. From the beginning of the Republic, America had been Bi-metallic; that is, the dollar was pegged at once to gold and to silver, thus fixing an exchange rate between the two as well. The system's proponents declared that the two metals expanded the nation's monetary reserves, and so the money supply; there would be more stable prices as a result (important to the farmers, for whom a large money supply meant higher prices for their products as against their expenses); and there would be greater ease of exchange among nations.

The need on the part of farmers for high prices—that is, inflation, had led them after the Civil War to advocate the continued use of greenbacks—paper money unbacked by anything save the government's guarantee. The utility of this for Lincoln's regime was that it gave the government unlimited spending money; the farmers were pleased very much at the rise in food prices and their resulting prosperity.

The deflation in prices after the War led to what was called the Panic of 1873; as a result of it, many farmers helped organize the Greenback Party which was one of the organizations which formed the Populists. In 1879, the government had begun once again redeeming currency in gold and silver. After this, the extension of silver and preservation of Bimetallism became an important part of the Agrarian movement's platform. In 1890 the Sherman silver purchase act was passed which required the government to buy 4,500,000 ounces of silver (about the annual national production) monthly, and paper money to be issued on its value. The result was that the government's gold reserves were soon severely depleted. Three years later, the British Indian government ceased to coin silver to keep it from going to the U.S.; the government's shortage of gold caused a lack of public credit, and the result was the Panic of 1893—almost forgotten today, but similar in its result to the Stock Market Crash in 1929.

The silver purchase law, although advocated by the Democrats, had been passed under the Republican administration of Benjamin Harrison (1889-1893). Even so, Harrison's Democratic successor (and predecessor, being the only President to serve two non-consecutive terms), Grover Cleveland, persuaded Congress to repeal it. The purchase of silver was ended, and the issuance of bonds to replenish the gold reserves was enacted.

The next year was grim, indeed. J.P. Morgan and various other millionaires agreed to furnish gold to the government; the free silver advocates were outraged. The great coal strike affected six states, and the militia was called out; a band of unemployed called "Coxey's Army" marched on Washington; the American Railroad Union called a general strike, and threatened to bring the country to a standstill. It was crushed with Federal troops. In a word, 1894 was as traumatic a year as constitutional government in this country had ever faced in peacetime.

Despite the actions of President Cleveland, the Democratic Party as well as the Populists remained committed to free silver. The Republicans, on the other hand, were convinced of the necessity of the gold standard—linking the dollar solely to gold. Although the minting of silver coinage would continue, every dollar would be backed by one hundred cents of gold, freely accessible. This would limit the amount of money in circulation, and so stave off inflated credit collapses like the Panic. It would also stabilize international trade.

This question of inflation and deflation, of hard currency versus soft is yet another which plagues us still today, just like that of free trade or protection. Deflation benefits the consumer (unless his salary falls faster than his expenses) but it can ruin the farmer. Similarly, inflation will aid the farmer, but ruin the urban dweller. Protection benefits the industrialist (and to a greater or lesser degree the worker) but hurts the farmer, while free trade can benefit him (unless foreign food becomes cheaper thereby). In a system like ours, with no higher interest than the economic and little pretension to social solidarity, neither side is interested in aught but its own benefit, and so no mutually acceptable compromise is possible.

There is, however, another question to be considered; the role of monetary questions in the growth of oligarchic power. During the Gilded Age, the major expression of the rulership of this country were the plutocrats, whose control of the larger amount of gold made the gold standard a perfect consolidation of their economic and political power. But in later days the ruling class would shift again, just as it had from the northern patricians to the plutocrats. This second shift would result in the creation of an essentially synthetic oligarchy, based more upon manipulation of government, credit, and media than upon actual production of anything, industrial or otherwise. For them, the gold standard would be an impediment which must be done away with. (This, by the way, shows the futility of attempting to chart the course of power in American history purely by adherence to a given stand on an issue or several issues). That development, however, lay in the future at the time of the election of 1896. Oddly enough, 1895 saw the Supreme Court rule as unconstitutional what has since become one of the major means of Federal control over its citizens: the Income Tax.

At the Democratic National Convention, the Bourbon Democrats who had supported Cleveland were swept out of power in the party by the nomination of *William Jennings Bryan* (an event paralleled by Tillman's defeat of Hampton in South Carolina). He declared that the Republican Party, committed to the gold standard, would not be allowed to "crucify the country on a cross of gold." The Populist Party likewise endorsed him.

The Republicans, in the meantime, had nominated William McKinley. The Republican platform came out for high tariffs and the gold standard, and declared that Bryan was a dangerous radical. In the event, Bryan did well only among the silver-mining states, the South, and the plains; the midwest was divided, and Bryan carried no state East of the Mississippi nor North of the Mason-Dixon Line. He lost.

The radicalism of the 1890s drifted off into local party politics, big city machines, and labor agitation. Although it would remain a large factor of discontent, the political power of the Agrarians was broken. The future lay in the hands of the urban, industrial plutocracy, the latest expression of the nation's ever-changing yet ideologically stable rulership. It ought to be borne in mind also, that while both farmers and labor challenged the more obnoxious symptoms of that rulership, they never challenged the national ideology which made that rulership possible—indeed, inevitable. Actually, they were among its fiercest proponents, even as Colonel Shays and his farmers had been.

The End of the Indian Wars and the Frontier

All the while that these events had agitated the East, settlement in the West was continuing. Successive gold, silver, and copper strikes resulted in an ever-increasing influx of settlers. The completion of the transcontinental railroad in 1869 meant that these were no longer restricted to wagon trains.

The great tribes of the West—the Sioux, the Cheyenne, the Flathead, the Commanche, the Arapaho, the Apache, and so on, quite naturally opposed this westward movement, relentless as it appeared to be. There had been a lull during the Civil War, in the course of which the Sioux of Minnesota had revolted and slaughtered many settlers until finally suppressed. "The only good Indian is a dead Indian" was a saying etched in blood on the frontier, and atrocity bred atrocity.

The Five Civilized Tribes in the Indian territory had been allies of the Confederacy during the War, and had lost half of Indian Territory as a result. But in the rest of the Great West, the tribes continued their conflict with the whites.

While the Federal authorities saw the Indian primarily as an impediment to settlement, the Church saw him as a potential convert; rather than desiring his ruin, she sought to preserve him. Under the French and Spanish, of course, missionary activity was supported by the State; to a degree this was also the case in Canada. In the United States (although a small amount of government money would be made available eventually for Catholic mission schools) this missionary activity had to take place with no assistance from the secular authorities, and sometimes hindrance—to say nothing of the fact that soldiers and settlers alike often embittered the tribes against the White Man's religion. Nevertheless, a great deal of progress was made.

One of the first and most important missionaries to the Indians on U.S. territory was Bishop *Frederic Baraga* (1797-1868). A Slovene, he worked among the Chippewa and Ottawa Indians of Michigan and Wisconsin. Eventually he became Bishop of Marquette, presiding over his Indian charges and English, French, and German-speaking Catholics. Much of his work has survived to our own day, as may be seen in Appendix I, alongside WPA accounts of other such Missions of the same period.

The Jesuits had been major Indian converters prior to their abolition in the 18th Century; it made sense that they should reassume the work interrupted then. One of the most illustrious of the Jesuits who came to the American West to do this was *Fr. Pierre Jean De Smet*. In him the spirit both of St. Ignatius and St. Francis Xavier dwelled. Like the latter, his great desire was the salvation of souls, and thus their conversion to Catholicism. Like him also, his path was lit by many miracles.

He was born to a pious family in Termonde, Flanders, in 1801. His father, Joost, had resisted the French Revolutionaries; an elder brother, also a priest, had been exiled for his refusal to take the oath to the revolutionary constitution. The De Smets were a family in which all the traditions and beliefs of Flemish Catholicism were maintained—and acted upon.

Meeting in 1817 Fr. Nerincx, the missionary in Kentucky, the young and athletic De Smet was fired with a resolve to evangelize the Indians whom Nerincx described. Despite parental opposition, De Smet left for America in 1821. He entered the Jesuit novitiate at Whitemarsh, Maryland. Shortly thereafter, it was transferred (with the young De Smet and 19 other novices) to Florissant, Missouri. Nearby was the convent of the Madames of the Sacred Heart, led by St. Rose Philippine Duchesne, whom the Indians called "the woman who prays always." Both orders watched over a school to which Indian children from other parts of Missouri were sent by their parents to study. This was De Smet's first encounter with the people he would serve the rest of his life; he was ordained at last in 1827. He assisted two years later in the founding of the school which would become St. Louis University.

From 1834 to 1837, he was in Belgium raising funds. The year after his return, a group of Pottawatomis who had left their lands in Michigan for Kansas and Nebraska, asked the Jesuits for missionaries. Fr. De Smet was assigned to them, and arrived at what would become the town of Council Bluffs; the following year, another mission was founded for them at St. Mary's, Kansas. Not only was De Smet able to firmly implant the Faith among the Pottawatomis, he also negotiated a peace treaty between themselves and the Sioux. Soon, neighboring tribes like the Omahas were asking for priests. De Smet, however, was to be sent elsewhere.

In the northern Rockies and the headwaters of the Columbia dwelt a number of tribes: the Kalispells, the Coeur d'Alenes, the Chaudieres, the Spokanes, the Kootenais, the Nez Perces, and the Flatheads. These latter, between 1812 and 1820, received into their midst a band of Catholic Iroquois from Caughnawaga near Montreal, led by a chief called Ignatius La Mousse, or Old Ignatius; he had been instructed and baptized by Jesuits there. He taught the Flatheads the Catholic faith, and baptized many of them. Soon the neighboring Kalispells and Nez Perces were interested in embracing this religion. Old Ignatius realized the need for Blackrobes. Although he knew they were to be found around St. Louis, to reach them would require a journey of 3,000 miles through every kind of terrain and territory held by hostile tribes. Three unsuccessful attempts were made, in the course of one of which Old Ignatius was killed by Sioux. But at last a group made it, and in 1840 De Smet returned with them. Among them he opened St. Mary's mission, and began to plan for the future.

He looked to his order's glorious past: once before they had been faced with a large number of Indian tribes, living outside the boundaries of colonization. There, free to order things as they wished, these early Jesuits formed the famous "Reductions" of Paraguay. Sandwiched between Portuguese Brazil and Spanish America, they created an entire Indian mission-state. At its height, it comprised 32 cities inhabited by 40,000 families. Even antagonistic writers of the time (like Voltaire) declared that Paraguay under Jesuit rule was as close to Paradise as the Earth afforded—a Paradise which ended with the expulsion of the Jesuits and the destruction of Paraguay in 1767.

De Smet declared that "The little nation of the Flatheads appear to us to be a chosen people, out of which a model tribe can be made; they will be the kernel of a Christianity that even Paraguay could not surpass in fervor" (E. Laveille, S.J., *The Life of Father De Smet, S.J.*, p. 126). The rules he drew up for his missions were modeled as closely as possible on those of Paraguay; like the Jesuits who created that model settlement, he knew that success for this plan could only come if contact with immoral, irreligious, or exploiting whites was kept to a minimum or avoided entirely.

The Virgin herself appeared to a little Flathead orphan named Paul; she informed him that the new village should be named St. Mary's, and practically the whole tribe, as well as many of those neighboring converted. At St. Mary's the day began with the Angelus, and was organized within a few months according to the daily Office of the Church.

The Kalispells and the Coeur d'Alenes were visited in 1842; most of the latter were already informed of Catholic doctrines because of an Iroquois who had come among them. After the visit of this Indian to them in 1830, an epidemic had broken out. One of their braves, dying, heard a voice which said, "leave your idols, adore Jesus Christ, and you will be cured." He did so, and was; thereupon he began preaching to all the tribe, with the result that they were ready for Fr. De Smet.

This was a pattern which was repeated among many tribes and villages. Wherever De Smet's journeys took him—Oregon, Washington, Wyoming, Montana, or anywhere else in the Northwestern quarter of the country, miracles occurred:

> During the summer of 1868, immediately after the close of the war over the Bozeman Road, Father Pierre Jean De Smet preached the first Catholic sermon in the vicinity of Sheridan, before a large gathering of the Crow Nation. A legend of a miracle the "Black Robe" (as Father De Smet was called by the Indians) performed to illustrate the potency of the white man's God is still repeated in the valley. Because white men had brought war and pestilence with them into the West, the Indians regarded their God with suspicion and mistrust. When De Smet arrived in the Crow camp, a chieftain pointed out an aged buffalo bull near by and commanded the priest to approach him and place his hand on the head of the enraged animal. De Smet, the legend says, approached the bison warily, expecting to be gored. But the sun glistened on the silver crucifix that hung from the Black Robe's throat, and the bull was hypnotized by the reflection; he stood very quiet while the priest reached out and scratched his head. Then De Smet returned to accept the homage of the tribesmen (WPA, *Wyoming*, p. 208).

Despite his great successes, the influx of white soldiers and settlers into the West meant that many Indians would be more concerned with defending their lands than saving their souls. Although he became a friend of the great war-chief, Sitting Bull, his friendship could not make up to the Sioux and Cheyenne, for example, the line of broken treaties made by the government in Washington. Apart from the ever-growing conflict with U.S. soldiery, alcohol and immorality picked up from traders also hampered De Smet's efforts. By the time of his death in 1873, he knew that his dream of a North American Paraguay would not be realized.

Nevertheless, his work was far from vain. At his death there were seven missions among the tribes, some of which survive today. The WPA Guides covered a number of them:

ST. IGNATIUS..., is a subagency almost at the center of the Flathead Reservation. The village is dominated by Indians. Like the ROMAN CATHOLIC MISSION, established here in 1854 by Fathers De Smet, Hoecken, and Menetrey, the town was named in honor of St. Ignatius of Loyola, the Spanish priest who founded the Society of Jesus.

The MISSION SCHOOL, CHURCH, and HOSPITAL are the results of nearly a century of patient, conscientious work among the natives. Early paintings used in teaching the Indians are on view (WPA, *Montana*, p. 296).

In De Smet is the SACRED HEART MISSION which was founded by Fr. De Smet in 1842. Another of Idaho's historic buildings, the Father's house, built in 1881, was burned to the ground in 1936, and only a few of its more valuable possessions were saved. Among these was a communication from Pope Pius IX in 1871, believed to be the only papal brief ever addressed to an Indian tribe. Fronting the Mission, also partly destroyed by fire, is a group of one- and two-room shacks, which are occupied only over week ends when Indians come in from the countryside for the Sunday services. Around De Smet is an area cultivated by the Kutenai Indians. Comparing favorably with those of white men in both their manner of operation and in living conditions, these farms suggest the progress that these Indians have made (WPA, *Idaho*, p. 210).

Sitting Bull always cherished a cross given him by Fr. De Smet. It is noteworthy that many of the Sioux and Cheyenne braves who fought under him against General Custer at the 1876 battle of the Little Big Horn were Catholics. One of Custer's subordinates, Colonel Keogh, had been a Pontifical Zouave in the army of Pius IX. After the battle, the Indians discovered the Papal medal on his corpse; as a mark of respect his body was not robbed or mutilated, but wrapped in skins and treated with respect.

Despite this great victory, the unrelenting forward march of the whites could not be stopped. It was not merely a question of ever more settlers and railroads; as a matter of policy, the buffalo were exterminated in large numbers, thus cutting off the Plains Indians' main food source. By 1885, they were confined to reservations, and completely defeated. The Apache in the Southwest were reduced about the same time.

But De Smet was not the only one to dream of a Catholic nation in the West. So too did *Louis Riel*, the greatest of the Metis. These last are a fascinating folk, as may be seen from their description in Appendix J. Although the Metis had settlements in the United States, the Red River region of what is now Manitoba was their center. By the 1860s they had set up a community, their roughly 6000 people living in farms along the

Red River, with priests and parishes of their own. Even while their brightest were educated in Quebec (whence came their priests) they kept in touch with the Chippewa, Cree, and other Indians to whom they were also related.

For time out of mind they had lived under the benevolent and loose rule of the HBC. But in 1869 the Company surrendered its territories to the two-year-old Dominion of Canada. Henceforth, and without warning, the Metis were to be ruled by a far away government of which they knew nothing. One of the things the Dominion government wished was to send English-speaking farmers into the fertile land of the Red River to offset French influence there. They would survey the land and subdivide it, without regard to Metis farm boundaries. A team of surveyors trespassed in the autumn of 1869, and were repelled by a band of 16 Metis, led by Riel.

Born in 1844, Riel had studied for the priesthood in Montreal. Although lacking a vocation, he nevertheless became an educated man and thus a leader of his people upon his return to the Red River. James Morris describes him thusly:

> He was a passionate patriot, emotional, volatile, often naïve, and was to prove one of the most poignant figures of the imperial story, moving through the pages of Canadian history in a mist of tears. He was like a child. Quick to temper or to forgive, vain, oddly guileless, his touchiness was partly a sense of racial humiliation. His religion was mystic (*Heaven's Command*, p. 287).

The Metis under Riel refused to accept the governor sent out from Ottawa. They raised a flag over Ft. Garry (now Winnipeg) which featured a fleur-de-lys and a shamrock on a white field, and on December 27 elected Riel provisional president of "Rupert's Land and the North-West." After agreeing to send delegates to Ottawa to negotiate, the Metis executed a Protestant for treason against the new government.

The Metis requests were met; a new province, named Manitoba, was to be established, in which French would have equally official status with English in education, just as in Quebec, and where the Metis would have 1,400,000 acres reserved to them forever. Riel ran up the Union Jack next to the provisional flag. It seemed that he was to achieve his dream of an autonomous Catholic Metis and Indian nation under the ultimate authority of the British Crown—a notion similar in some ways to De Smet's. But it was not to be.

The execution was considered murder; the Orangemen in Ontario demanded that the death be avenged and Riel's government suppressed. A small army was dispatched into Manitoba, and the Metis government collapsed. Riel nevertheless proved his loyalty to the Queen on August

4, 1871, leading 300 of his people against a Fenian attack from the U.S. Via gerrymandering, the French and Metis lost control of Manitoba in 1874.

From 1878 to 1884, Riel taught at various Indian Mission schools in Montana. In the latter year, however, in response to appeals from the Metis who had migrated westward to Saskatchewan where both the buffalo they depended on and the land they had settled were again being seized by Anglophone settlers, he returned to Canada to lead them. In January of 1885 he led them in revolt; madness came upon him, and he declared himself a virtual messiah (turning against the priests).

Indians joined him; some of the Cree were pagan, and on April 2 killed two missionaries. Troops rushed in, and a month and a half later, Riel surrendered. His mind had collapsed under the strain of the revolt, but the government insisted on both prosecution, and when convicted, execution.

Although while in the grip of madness Riel had uttered heresies, he retracted them before his death; his vision of the Northwest remains, like De Smet's, an intriguing might-have-been.

But if such grand attempts failed, smaller ones were not without some effect. The missionaries who had come with Fr. De Smet were similarly made of tough stuff:

> Near Bowesmont in the spring of 1860 occurred an event illustrative of the hardships suffered by the missionaries to this region. The Reverend Joseph Goiffon, assistant at the Pembina Catholic Mission, returning from a trip to St. Paul, left his party behind in an effort to reach the mission in time to conduct a certain Mass. A driving rain had been falling and this suddenly turned into a swirling snowstorm. In a short time the ground was covered with six or seven inches of snow, and the driving wind made it impossible for him to continue. The blizzard did not abate, and in two days his horse had died from exposure and his own legs had frozen so that he was unable to walk. For five days he remained on the prairie, living on the flesh of his horse, until the storm subsided and a passer-by heard his feeble cries for help. It was found necessary to amputate parts of both legs, but in spite of this he returned to the Pembina mission and was later transferred to St. Paul and Mendota, where he served until his death in 1910 (WPA, *North Dakota*, p. 185).

After the Indians, in the wake of the Little Big Horn, were restricted to reservations, it became obvious to the regime in Washington that merely military solutions would not be enough in the long run; even the slaughter of the buffalo would simply reduce Indian spirit, not subdue it. Thus it was decided under President Grant to subsidize denominational schools, and to put religious and educational life at the various Indian agencies under the control of different Christian bodies. It was further decided that the only missionaries permitted at these agencies would be those of the first denomination to have reached the tribe concerned. Under these provisions, the Church was entitled to the oversight of 38 agencies. But the bureaucrats concerned permitted priests to take up only eight of the number. The result was that 80,000 Catholic Indians in 72 agencies passed under the temporal and spiritual rule of Protestant ministers.

The bishops organized a Catholic Commission of Indian Missions to press the government to permit Catholic Indians religious freedom—a goal achieved in 1883. The next year, Msgr. Joseph A. Stephan became Director of the Bureau of Catholic Indian missions. He organized the opening of mission schools, with a success that the following examples culled from the WPA guides in Appendix K will illustrate.

Miss *Katherine Drexel*, of an old Philadelphia family, took a great interest in the welfare of both Indians and Blacks; in 1891, at the invitation of Leo XIII, she founded the Sisters of the Blessed Sacrament for Indians and Colored People, whose purpose was "...the complete consecration of the Sisters to the service of Our Lord in the Blessed Sacrament, so that through Him they may lead the Indian and Colored races to the knowledge and love of God" (Thomas McCarthy, C.S.V., *Guide to the Catholic Sisterhoods in the United States*, p. 15). Presiding over the order until her death in 1955, Mother Katherine was beatified by Pope John Paul II—the first native-born cradle-Catholic to whom this has been done.

The work of the Missions came even to Alaska:

> HOLY CROSS is a Jesuit mission and school at the mouth of the Innoko about 400 miles from Fairbanks. The mission was established in 1887, and is operated by the Jesuit fathers and the Sisters of St. Ann. There is a boarding school for Natives, a boarding house for visitors, general store, and a farm with cows and horses where sixty tons of potatoes and seven tons of vegetables are raised annually (WPA Guide, p. 210).

It is very fashionable today to attack the work of the Church among the Indians. Usually, Catholic missionaries from the time of Columbus until Vatican II, whether in North or South America, are presented as having stolen from the Indians their deeply spiritual beliefs. Always, the natives of this continent are presented as having a much deeper connection to the spirit than their evangelizers, who imposed the white man's God on them. Perhaps the Bible of such people is a book filled with sayings of a Sioux medicine man—*Black Elk Speaks*. Therein the old Sioux paganry is explored, and made by its white author to appear superior to Christianity; from it has come much of the ideology which underlies both the Native American movement and such films as *Dances With Wolves*. It is a pity that this book, which sells well even today, does not include Black Elk's testament. We have included it in Appendix L.

So the great dream of Fr. De Smet was not without fruit. Yet one cannot help but wonder what the result would have been had he had his way, or Riel his. Some indication of what the West would have been like might be gleaned from this description of a shrine revered by Indian and Metis alike in North Dakota:

> BELCOURT,..., agency headquarters for the Turtle Mountain Indian Reservation, lies in a shallow valley on the southeastern border of the hills. It was named for the Reverend George Antoine Belcourt, a priest prominent in the establishment of the community. The Indians, about 95 per cent of whom are of mixed Chippewa Indian and French blood, make their homes in crude cabins on small farms out in the reservation....
>
> Since 1896 the week of St. Ann has been the occasion of a retreat at Belcourt for the people of the mountains, for whom St. Ann is the patron saint. Many of the Indians bring their tipis in which they live during the retreat. The week is culminated with the feast of St. Ann (*July 26*). On the feast day a procession is held, with hundreds participating. Many cures... have been attributed to the shrine at the Belcourt church (WPA, *North Dakota*, p. 229).

Perhaps something more will come of it.

THE CHURCH IN THE GILDED AGE

While the missionaries were working in the West, the Church was growing in more settled areas also. As we saw earlier, the rapid growth of mines, factories and railroads required enormous amounts of cheap labor. Catholic Germans and Irish continued to come, of course, but they were augmented by many other peoples.

In New England, the cotton mills and other industries attracted droves of French Canadians from the province of Quebec. French Canada had not been affected by the overthrow of Catholic and Royal France in 1789, nor by the subsequent upheavals in the mother country in 1830 and 1848, save to be disgusted by them. The rise of Liberalism in Europe and North America called forth defenders of the truth from among both clerics and laity in Quebec.

One of the most notable was *Louis-François Lafléche* (1818-1898), who began his priestly career as a missionary in the Red River country among the Metis. Consecrated a bishop there, he directed the defense of

50 Metis against 2,000 Sioux near Turtle Mountain in North Dakota in 1851. Made bishop of Trois Rivieres in 1870, he was a zealous defender of Catholic principles without regard to other considerations. In 1866, he laid down the principles of French-Canadian national ideology—*La Survivance:*

> I. A nation is constituted by unity of speech, unity of faith, uniformity of morals, customs, and institutions. The French Canadians possess all these, and constitute a true nation. Each nation has received from Providence a mission to fulfill. The mission of the French-Canadian people is to constitute a center of Catholicism in the New World.
>
> II. Authority derives from God. The best form of government is a moderate monarchy (the Church and the family are examples of it); the most imperfect is democracy. Liberalism commits the fundamental error of seeking to build society on other than religious principles. Electors not only exercise a right; they fulfil a duty for which they are responsible before God. The priest thus has a right to guide them.
>
> It is an error condemned by reason, by history, and by Revelation to say that politics is a field in which religion has no right to enter, and in which the Church has no concern (F. Mason Wade, *The French Canadians 1760-1945*, p. 346).

Obviously, while these sentiments were in complete accord with the teaching of Pius IX in his *Syllabus of Errors* (joyfully received in French Canada), they could not be expected to find favor with either Canadian Liberals or most non-Catholic Americans. Nevertheless, the first sentence summed up the three foundations of La Survivance: the Faith, the Language, and the Customs. This survival, however, was not merely for the sake of the French Canadians themselves; rather, they were to serve as a vessel for the conversion of the continent.

A great lay Apostle of the time was *Jules-Paul Tardivel*, who started a paper in Quebec called *La Verité* in 1881. A disciple of the great French journalist Louis Veuillot, he knew of the value of La Survivance through intimate knowledge of its opposite; born in the United States of a French father and an English mother, at age 16 he started at a minor seminary in Canada not knowing a word of French. He stands today as giant of Catholic journalism on this continent.

The French-Canadian leadership saw their struggle with both Anglophone and Francophone Canadian Liberals as merely a part of the worldwide battle between the Church and her Masonic and Socialist enemies. Hence in 1867 a large party of Quebecois youth volunteered to join the Pontifical Zouaves and defend Rome against Garibaldi.

Quite apart from the integral Catholicism of French Canadian leaders, the life of the people was suffused by their religion. Not only was the church the center of village life, and the liturgical year the pattern for the secular, but the customs associated with holy days, as in other Catholic cultures, were the guideposts of life. Advent with its prayer, fasting, and elaborate preparations for the coming of Our Lord; Christmas carols, midnight Mass, after-Mass feasting, visiting, and collections for the poor; New Year's, with its blessing of the children by the father; Epiphany, with its Twelfth Night cake and selection of Epiphany King and Queen thereby; Candlemas, with its distribution of candles which protected the home, and its pancake parties; St. Joseph's Day, upon which fireworks were set off in his honor; Carnival, during which feasting and consumption of soon-to-be-prohibited foods prepared one for Lent; Lent itself, with its strict fasting and abstinence; Passion Sunday, whereon many people brought fruit cuttings indoors, putting them in water so they would bloom on Easter; Holy Week was much as it is among all Catholics—but on Holy Thursday, when the bells were silent, children were told they had gone to Rome to report to the Pope for a blessing; On Easter Sunday, many would rise before dawn to fetch water from the nearest stream, when it was said to have miraculous powers; St. Mark's Day would see seeds brought to the church to be blessed; the whole month of May was given up to Marian devotions. Corpus Christi was celebrated with processions of great splendor:

> The feast was very popular in rural French Canada. The entire parish would take part, either as members of one of the men's, women's, or children's organizations moving solemnly through the village streets and nearby countryside, banners displayed, or as spectators joining in the singing of hymns and repeating prayers as the procession went by. Houses and streets were embellished with bunting and other ornaments. The spectacle of the priest in dazzling cope and velum bearing the monstrance under a canopy carried by the marguilliers inspired everyone with awe and fervor.
>
> At one or two points along the way—different places each year—a temporary altar was set up in front of someone's home, and the honor of decorating the site with flowers, greens and tree boughs was conferred upon the occupants. A benediction was held here before the procession returned to the church. The event, which generally occurred in front of one's own house only once in a lifetime, was considered to be one of the great moments in a family's history (Gerard J. Brault, *The French-Canadian Heritage in New England*, p. 28).

So too was St. John the Baptist's Day celebrated with parades; All Saints and All Souls were kept in honor of the dead.

In New England, the French-Canadians maintained the ideas of La Survivance. In 1869, Bishop of Burlington Joseph Louis de Goësbriand declared that the French-Canadian flood into New England was God's way of converting the region to the true Faith. Moreover, La Survivance was adapted to a specifically American context:

> According to this view, Franco-Americans may have ignored the call of the land—that is the agrarian life for which they were supposedly destined—and left their native country, but they would continue to exist and prosper as a people if they cherished and safeguarded the other elements of their French-Canadian heritage, namely their mother tongue, Catholic faith and customs. To do this, it was important to remain attached to traditional ways, and it was absolutely essential to combat the godlessness, materialism, and promiscuity they believed existed all around them (Brault, *op. cit.,* pp. 65-66).

Obviously such beliefs were subversive to what was considered the American way of life. But they found echoes in other Catholic nationalities. These latter were moving not only into New England but into such states as New York and Pennsylvania. The situation across the country is well described by the excerpts from various WPA Guides in Appendix M. The efforts of these brave colonists from so many different nations, united solely by their religion, reflected a type of Faith which, while happy to be in the new land, had no intention of simply being merged and lost. It will also be noticed that, for the most part, these settlements were organized by individual priests and laymen, or by companies organized for the purpose, or even by the railroads. But in some places Catholic colonization was the stated policy of the local bishop. One such man and place was bishop John J. Ireland of St. Paul, Minnesota.

The then Fr. John Ireland became President of the Minnesota Irish Emigration Society (founded under the patronage of Bishop Grace) on May 12, 1864. Although nothing came of this immediately, Ireland retained his interest in Catholic colonization as a means of both opening the West and ensuring that the Church would be strong there, and also of rescuing Catholic families from the squalor of the Eastern slums. Once he became bishop on December 21, 1875, he set to work almost immediately. Three weeks after his consecration, he concluded an agreement with the Northern Railroad that he would undertake to settle two thousand Catholic families along 75,000 acres of railroad land. On January 22, 1876, he announced the formation of the Catholic Colonization Society of St. Paul, to replace the IES.

The property he initially acquired from the railroad comprised four townships in Swift County; therein was one railroad station, called De Graaf. It was platted, alongside another, of which the WPA Guide tells us:

...CLONTARF... In a widely circulated pamphlet entitled *Invitation to the Land* (1876), the site of Clontarf was described by Archbishop Ireland as "wide open opportunity-waiting spaces of the west." Oratory, advertising, and brochures in the "poverty stricken and demoralized crowded centers of the East" brought an Irish-Catholic "prohibition colony" from Pennsylvania to Benson. Thence they proceeded north by ox cart to the 117,000 acres that were under the jurisdiction of Archbishop Ireland. They named their settlement Clontarf, for an Irish watering-place near Dublin, scene of Brian Boru's victory over the Danes. Churchmen of the colony protested against killing the grass-hoppers that devoured their crops the first year, believing the pests were "heaven's punishment for the people's sins."

About 2 miles north of the village Clontarf Industrial School was established by Archbishop Ireland to instruct Indian boys in the Roman Catholic faith and to teach them the arts of husbandry. The several buildings had a capacity of 80 pupils, although the average attendance at first did not exceed 40. The school was taken over by the Federal Government in 1897; in 1898 it was closed and the students were transferred to the Morris Industrial School nearby (WPA, *Minnesota*, p. 387).

Although founded for the Irish, Clontarf would soon attract large numbers of French-Canadian and Belgian settlers. Then came "AVOCA... founded in 1878 by Roman Catholics, was named for a river in Ireland" which in turn gave birth to

FULDA..., in an excellent farming territory, is predominantly German, and was named for the ancient city in central Europe. The coming of the railroad and the settlement in the early 1870s by Bishop Ireland's colonists started the growth and development of this community (WPA, *Minnesota*, p. 450).

In 1881, Irish Nationalist John Sweetman selected a site near Avoca, called Currie, upon which he settled with a number of his tenants and friends from County Meath.

Two years previously, Ireland had set up a colony for English and Irish settlers at Minneonta; many Belgians took up land there also. Many more of these, at the same time as Sweetman's effort, established Ghent. Primarily Flemish, these colonists founded St. Eloi parish there, and preserved much of their culture up to our own time.

There were other colonies established under Ireland's benevolent eye, if not necessarily as his projects. Such were

...GENTILLY... Most of the inhabitants are of French-Canadian origin. Their parish priest for many years was Father Eli Theilon, born near the town of Limoges in France. He urged his parishioners to organize a co-operative plant and make Limoges cheese from the recipe he had obtained from his old monastery in France. Within a year of its founding in 1895, the Gentilly Dairy Association produced 15,000 pounds of Limoges cheese; by 1927 its output was 150,000 pounds, most of which went to eastern markets. Prosperity came to farmers and town alike. Father Theilon served as president of the association and manager of its factory until his death. He refused any personal reward, but his grateful parishioners built for him the impressive CATHEDRAL that stands on the outskirts of the village (WPA, *Minnesota*, p. 338).

and

...SILVER LAKE... Here Czechs settled in 1874 and established their own churches and library. In Silver Lake small boys still go from house to house early Easter Monday, in Czech called *Dyngus*, with whip and baskets to collect Easter eggs from the girls and threaten to switch those lying abed... The women make apple strudels and potato dumplings and grow their own poppies—to insure plenty of seed for their *kolacky* buns. This town, small as it is, has given the State several noted scholars and has a fine group of women singers (WPA, *Minnesota*, p. 393).

But it must be understood that all of these settlements, Ireland's and the others, had one main goal in mind: the fervent practice of the Faith. "Working on the land, these people acquired a deep appreciation for the role of Divine Providence in their lives. As they said the prayers for a good harvest at Vespers each Sunday, as they followed Bishop Ireland in the procession of the Blessed Sacrament through the streets of De Graaf during the grasshopper plague of 1876, and as they sang their jubilant *Te Deums* after a successful harvest season, these pioneers gave evidence of their faith in God. These Minnesota colonists were not a random group of individuals who had merely been born and reared as Catholics. They were persons who had deliberately elected to make an extraordinary effort to live in a community in which their religious life could be fulfilled" (James P. Shannon, *Catholic Colonization on the Western Frontier*, p. 175).

As might be expected, the sheer diversity of immigrant nationalities gave the Church difficulties in serving them all properly, even liturgically. Some interesting ways of meeting the problem were devised:

CADOTT, ... has a curious conglomeration of racial strains. It was perhaps named for the father of Michael Cadotte..., Jean Baptiste Cadotte, a French-Indian trapper who settled here on the Yellow River in 1838. Later other Frenchmen came from Canada; Germans, English, Irish, and Norwegians arrived after the passage of the homestead law of 1862; and many Czechs and a few Slovaks came about 1900. This mixture of nationalities created a problem in the churches. In the local Roman Catholic church a single service was conducted in French, English, and German, and later even in Czech, so that on Sundays the devout spent four hours in kneeling, standing, and sitting, until the polyglot devotions were ended (WPA, *Wisconsin*, p. 475).

The immigrants of the various nationalities, scattered across the nation, soon began to form mutual assistance societies to help them succeed. The Irish founded in 1836 the Ancient Order of Hibernians. Its "avowed purposes" were "promoting friendship, unity, and Christian charity among its members and the advancement of the principles of Irish nationality." Its branches provided insurance and scholarships for its members, as well as aid to the Gaelic League in Ireland for the purpose of reviving the nation's ancient language. The Irish Catholic Benevolent Union was founded sixty years later with similar aims. For the French-Canadians the Association Canado-Americaine was founded in 1896, and the Union St. Jean Baptiste (a merging of a number of earlier groups) in 1900. The German Central-Verein was founded in 1855, and during our period became the foremost disseminator of Papal social teachings in the country, under the leadership of *Frederick P. Kenkel*. The Magyars formed the Catholic Hungarian Association in 1896, while the Italians formed hundreds of local ones (and were served by *Mother Cabrini*, the first American citizen to be canonized, who came on their behalf). For Czechs, The Bohemian Roman Catholic Central Union was founded in 1877. The National Croatian Union, the Greek Catholic Union, the Ruthenian National Union, the Slovak Catholic Union, and the Slovene Catholic Union all served to give their respective nationalities unity and mutual protection within the new land. Less recent arrivals also banded together. In New Orleans, white Creoles organized the Athénée Louisianais to preserve French culture in their city. In the New Mexico territory starting in 1867, the Hispanos attempted to retain political control of the region under the leadership of Colonel J. Francisco Chaves (whose father had sent him to school in St. Louis and New York, telling him "the heretics are going to overrun the country. Go and learn their language and come back prepared to defend your people"). Here too, the stories of the priests and layfolk who organized them ought to be immortalized.

On a less wholesome note, perhaps, the pressures of life in a foreign and often hostile urban environment often led the immigrants to organize for less high-minded purposes. The Irish, for example, often came to dominate or create local political machines in cities like New York,

Boston, Philadelphia and Chicago—of which the most famous was New York's Tammany Hall. Among the Italians, secret societies which had flourished for years in Italy, like the Mafia, the Camorra or the Black Hand, originally sprang up here to protect Italians from harassment. Later, they turned to organized crime.

The growth of the Catholic body, dedicated as it was to a culture and a world-view completely alien to that of the Puritans, the Founding Fathers, and indeed, Masonry, could not help but arouse opposition. Immediately after the War, such opposition could be found openly in the country's highest circles:

> As the saliency of wartime and Reconstruction issues faded and the hard times of the seventies sapped Republican strength, party leaders became more outspokenly anti-Catholic. The Indiana Republican platform of 1876 declared: "It is incompatible with American citizenship to pay allegiance to any foreign power, civil or ecclesiastical, which asserts the right to include the action of civil government within the domain of religion and morals." Rutherford B. Hayes, locked in a tight and nationally significant contest for governor of Ohio in 1875, made the question of Catholic influence in the public schools an important part of his campaign. He explained to James G. Blaine why this was necessary: "We have been losing strength in Ohio for several years by the emigration of Republican farmers and especially of the young men who were in the army. In their place have come Catholic foreigners... We shall crowd [the Democrats]...on the school and other state issues." James A. Garfield struck a similar note in campaign speeches supporting Hayes: "It is evident that the Catholic Church is moving along the whole line of its front against modern civilization and our fight in Ohio is only a small portion of the battlefield." The former soldiers (and future Presidents) were joined by Ulysses S. Grant. In September 1875, a week before the Ohio balloting, the chief executive warned that the next great struggle in America would be between "patriotism and intelligence on the one side, and superstition, ambition, and ignorance on the other." In his December 1875 message to Congress, Grant called for the outright prohibition of public aid to church-related schools. James G. Blaine sponsored a constitutional amendment designed to implement Grant's proposal. The House approved by a margin of 180 to 7, but the Senate vote of 28 to 16 (on strict party lines) fell short of the two-thirds margin necessary to send the amendment on to the states (Morton Keller, *Affairs of State*, p. 141).

In time, this opposition on the part of the oligarchy became muted. Partly because public display of such prejudice was becoming unrespectable; partly because (as we shall see) much of the American hierarchy was behaving in such a manner as to demonstrate to the satisfaction of the country's rulership that, whatever the beliefs of Pope and foreign bishops, American Catholics were no threat to the establishment. This realization did not, however, trickle down to the oligarchy's nominal opposition, the lower and middle class supporters of Populist ideas:

> ...many Americans, particularly in the Middle West, viewed with mounting alarm the rapid accretion of Catholic power. They took amiss the agitation to secure public funds for parochial schools and regarded even the labor encyclical of 1891 as a sinister move by the Vatican to gain American working-class support.
>
> As in the 1830s and 40s, the fear and misunderstanding took the form of organized bigotry, embodied this time primarily in the American Protective Association, a secret oath bound order founded in 1887 by H.F. Bowers, a sixty-year old lawyer of Clinton, Iowa. Cradled in the heart of agricultural America, the anti-Catholic animus was vaguely mingled with the long-standing rural antagonism toward the great cities where, of course, the citadels of Romanism were to be found. The A.P.A. gained adherents slowly at first, having only seventy thousand members in 1893. Then, spurred by fear of immigrant competition during the hard times and a sudden flaming resentment on the part of urban dwellers against Irish machine politicians, the movement had a mushroom growth in the cities, probably commanding a million members in 1896. [note—In Chicago in 1894 the mayor, chief of police, fire chief, city attorney, a number of judges, forty-five aldermen, nine out of ten policemen, four fifths of the fire department and two thirds of the school teachers were said to be Catholics... It was alleged that the municipal offices of New York, St. Louis, New Orleans, San Francisco and other important cities were also under Catholic control.]
>
> All the familiar phenomena of the earlier Know-Nothing movement were reproduced. The members of the order swore not to vote for or employ Catholics. "Escaped nuns" and "converted priests" told their harrowing tales to anyone who would listen. Forged documents were circulated to expose the designs of Rome against free America, one of them, an alleged papal encyclical, ordering the faithful to "exterminate all heretics" at the feast of St. Ignatius of Loyola (July 31) in 1893. In a similar spirit, stories were whispered of the gathering of arms in the basements of Catholic churches; and in at least one instance, that of the Toledo council of the A.P.A., a quantity of Winchester rifles was purchased as a measure of self-defense—a fact revealed by the dealer's suit for non-payment. At Dallas, Keokuk and elsewhere mob outrages occurred, the riot in East Boston on July 4, 1895, causing the death of one man and the injury of 40 others (Arthur Schlesinger, *The Rise of the City 1878-1898*, pp. 346-347).

In truth, they need not have worried. Some of the most important bishops in the country were resolved to make American Catholics as little different from their neighbors as possible.

Americanists, Cahenslyites, and Ultramontanes

Shannon's book, *Catholic Colonization on the Western Frontier*, to which reference has been made, has an intriguing note on p. 191, which is important as an introduction to the role that Ireland, whom we have seen up to now as a zealous proponent of Catholic culture, would be more famous for:

> Several decades later (1917), the Minnesota Commission of Public Safety investigated the extent to which foreign languages were being used in private and parochial schools in the state and found that a considerable number of them were "using a foreign language wholly or in part as a medium of instruction, and that some 10,000 children receiving their education in these schools were being brought up as aliens and foreigners." Folwell, *A History of Minnesota*, 4, 166. Undoubtedly this criticism referred to Catholic schools, and quite probably to German-Catholic schools. And it is reasonable to suppose that in the early years of the western colonies there was similar criticism of the German language used in Fulda, the Flemish spoken in Ghent, and the French used at Clontarf. However, the most articulate opponent of foreign language in America was John Ireland himself. If his colonists were labeled as foreigners, he was doing all in his power to teach them the English language and thus relieve them of the stigma of being called "aliens."

Indeed, he and his close associate, Cardinal Gibbons, were and are renowned as the foremost proponents of Americanism, a heresy which requires close examination. We have already touched upon it in the introduction to this series; we mentioned it again in connection with Archbishop Carroll. With Carroll, it was simply the notion that the Church in America must be more or less independent of Rome, so as to completely identify with the non-Catholic nation. This attitude went underground during the years after Carroll's death in 1815, simply because the rush of missionaries and immigrants had no use for it. But it revived after the Civil War, very much along the lines of Orestes Brownson's view in 1866. Men like Gibbons and Ireland adopted these views, but unlike Brownson, failed to repent of them.

Americanism in the 1880s was particular affliction of the Irish clergy in this country. The reason is not difficult to find: it is simply because, of all the Catholic immigrants, the Irish were the only ones who arrived speaking the language and, as it were, already a part of the Anglo-Saxon mindset. The Gaelic culture of the nation, although severely damaged by the Penal laws, had nevertheless survived. But the Potato Famine, which reduced so much of the population of the Island to absolute starvation, practically confined it to the Western fringes of Ireland, the *Gaedhealtacht*. As Fr. Cahill, S.J. put it so well, "...the old Catholic Irish tradition of the Gaedhealtacht, where alone the Irish Catholic tradition lives, is one of the nation's best bulwarks against the materialism of the English-speaking world by which it is surrounded" (*The Framework of a Christian State*, p. 666). It is precisely this linguistic bulwark which was lost to the Irish who came here—and which the French-Canadians, Germans, Poles and so on still maintained. Because they knew the language well, Irish clerics were quickly promoted after the Civil War to Episcopal Sees. Many of them were divided from their non-English-speaking flocks and fellow bishops not merely on national but on religious grounds, though as we shall see there were indeed some Irish bishops who were quite orthodox. In any case, the Third Plenary Council of Baltimore in 1884 laid down several rules which were intended to establish a unique "American" identity for the Church in this country. One was the establishment of the Catholic University of America in Washington; the second was the replacing of all previous catechisms in use, like St. John Neumann's and Deharbe's (which in common with their European counterparts put the Faith and its necessity rather strongly) with the somewhat softened "Baltimore Catechism"; and thirdly, the prohibition of proper clerical dress for American priests, substituting the clerical suit in its place to propitiate the Protestants. This Council succeeded in assuring the powers that were in the U.S. that Catholicism was no threat. Certainly such prelates as Ireland and Gibbons were concerned with assimilating all the non-English-speaking Catholics as quickly as possible. But in their desire to do this they soon came into conflict with the Germans.

Because in such cities as St. Louis and Baltimore German parishes had been made canonically inferior to English-speaking ones, there was a great deal of discontent among the Germans. Fr. Peter Abbelen, a priest of the diocese of Milwaukee (which had both a German majority and a bishop of that nationality) went to Rome in 1886 to seek such things as German priests being given jurisdiction over German layfolk. At the same time as Abbelen's trip, which roused fears among Americanist bishops of direct Roman intervention in America, Gibbons was able to successfully delay appointment of an Apostolic Delegate. Just as non-Catholic Americans feared that the Catholics were servants of a foreign Pope, so too did Gibbons, Ireland, and company.

In 1887, one Fr. John Gmeiner, a priest of Milwaukee who would soon transfer to Ireland's See of St. Paul, published a pamphlet called

The Church and the Various Nationalities in the United States. Are German Catholics Unfairly Treated? Therein, he declared that German culture in the United States was doomed, and in any case was not required for retention of Catholicism.

The result was an enormous pamphlet war. One of the most inflammatory against Gmeiner's position was that of Nicholas Gonner, editor of the *Katholischer Westen*. Gonner made a number of extreme statements. However,

> In the final section he pointed out that with the loss of Gaelic customs and language the Irish had been weakened in their religion [which claim was later made by Fr. Cahill, himself an Irishman]. The same would happen to German Catholics if they were considered as second-class Catholics (Colman Barry, O.S.B., *The Catholic Church and German Americans*, p. 81).

Moreover, the French-Canadian Charles F. St. Laurent seeing the application of La Survivance beyond his own nationality, supported the Germans in his *Language and Nationality*. But the best known was Cincinnati priest Fr. Anton Walburg's *The Question of Nationality in Its Relation to the Catholic Church in the United States*. While giving due honor to the part the Irish had played in establishing the Church in the U.S., Fr. Walburg pointed out that the English language itself was pervaded by Protestant ideas. While the old mainline Protestant sects' influence was on the wane, American culture was still

> ...a hotbed of fanaticism, intolerance, and radical ultra views on politics and religion. All the vagaries of spiritualism, Mormonism, free-loveism, prohibition, infidelity, and materialism, generally breed in the American nationality. Here we also find dissimulation and hypocrisy.

He then asked:

> And now we are asked to assimilate with this element, to adopt its usages, customs, feelings, and manners? That cannot but prove detrimental to the Church. Are we going to lead our simple, straightforward, honest Germans and Irish into this whirlpool of American life, this element wedded to this world, bent upon riches, upon political distinction, where their consciences will be stifled, their better sentiments trampled underfoot?
> But it will be said, religion will keep them from rushing to this end, will sustain them in the path of virtue and rectitude. Nonsense! Denationalization is demoralization. It degrades and debases human nature. A foreigner who loses his nationality is in danger of losing his

faith and character.... Like as the Indians coming in contact with the whites adopted the vices rather than the virtues of the latter, so the effort to Americanize the foreigner will prove deteriorating.

There were, however, other Catholics whose critique of national life, while just as severe, was not directly related to the nationality question (although these other were generally sympathetic to non-English-speaking Catholics). They took as their yardstick such documents as Pius IX's Syllabus of Errors and Leo XIII's encyclicals *Libertas* and *Immortale Dei*. Among these were *Michael Corrigan*, Archbishop of New York, and *Bernard McQuaid*, Bishop of Rochester. Layfolk included *Arthur Preuss* of the St. Louis *Review* and *Condé Pallen* of the St. Louis *Church Progress*.

At the same time, there lived in Germany a gentleman named *Peter Paul Cahensly*. Cahensly was a wealthy German businessman, and a member of the Prussian Lower House for the Catholic Center Party from 1885 to 1915 (he would be elected to the Reichstag, the national parliament, in 1898). Born in 1838, the wealthy Cahensly had been a Catholic activist early on. Joining the St. Vincent de Paul Society while studying trade at Le Havre in 1861, as part of his work for the Society he visited emigrant ships waiting in the harbor to leave for America. Horrified by the conditions he saw, Cahensly gathered information on them which he submitted to the annual convention of German Catholic organizations in 1865. Under his aegis, the St. Raphael Society (placed under the patronage of the Archangel of travelers) was formed in 1871.

The Society was soon hard at work in major European ports. Agents were assigned to each of these, chapels, lodging houses, and express agencies built. A banking and credit service was instituted, as well as a postal service. Beyond this, the spiritual aids of the Church were made available to comfort the emigrant before he left. It was for organizing all of this that Cahensly was called "The Father of the Emigrant."

But in the course of his work, Cahensly made the unpleasant discovery that one third of all German Catholics lost their faith after arrival in the States. This led him to try to make some provision for the emigrants once they had reached their new home. To do this adequately, however, the Society must become international in scope. A branch was opened in New York in 1883, and a Belgian section in 1887. The agency in Antwerp began to care not only for Germans, but for Austrians, Poles, Italians, Czechs, and the rest. In 1889, Austro-Hungarian and Italian branches were set up, and the next year Swiss and French groups began to organize. The need for the work was shown by the figures estimated by Fr. Alphonse Villeneuve, a French-Canadian priest in New York State. Pointing out that twenty-five million Catholics had emigrated to the United States from Europe and Canada, and that in 1890 the Catholic population of the country was a mere five million, the conclusion to be drawn was obvious. For all that Ireland and Gibbons talked about the necessity of adjusting to the American environment, that environment had seduced 20,000,000 Catholics from their Faith.

The leadership of the various St. Raphael Societies were seasoned Catholic activists, veterans of the struggle for Catholic social teachings in their own nations. Moreover, many were noblemen, with a strong sense of Noblesse Oblige. It was imperative, they believed, that this loss of souls be stopped. The result was a gathering of the leadership in Lucerne, Switzerland on December 9-10, 1890. They drew up a memorial to the Holy Father, dated February 1891, which proposed a thoroughgoing reorganization of the Church in this country, in order to preserve both the Faith and the cultures of the emigrants (the text of which is in Appendix N). This appeal was signed by, apart from Cahensly, nine other German directors; nine Austro-Hungarians; eight Belgians; eight Italians, and one each from the French and Swiss Societies, then in the process of formation. Moreover, once drafted it was signed by Henri Mercier, Prime Minister of Quebec, and fourteen other prominent Canadian Catholics.

Much of what it called for was in due time applied: in certain dioceses, national parishes were erected, with equal standing with English-speaking ones. In such places, parochial schools were erected wherein half the day such topics as religion, history of the homeland, and the national language were taught in the mother tongue; the remainder would find English used (in addition to grammar and that sort of thing) for American History, civics, math, and science. My own father was the product of such a school in New England, and emerged therefrom both perfectly bi-lingual, proud of his French-Canadian heritage and his country of residence, and eager to see Catholicism extended through the latter. Further, this author attended High School with boys who had been to a local Lithuanian parish school; they were by far the most devout in our grade, as well as the best students. Some of their number went back to Lithuania to help rebuild the country after Communism's fall. There is in Los Angeles, over the parish hall of St. Peter's Italian Catholic Church, an interesting inscription: "To Enrich American Life With Italian Culture." One might substitute, if one wished, any Catholic nationality's name with equal justice; add Faith to culture and you have a perfect sentiment.

If one should wonder why these things were so important, there are three reasons: first, as we have seen, they would have served to keep many more of the immigrants in the Church; although different statistics were offered, the retention of 10 to 20 million immigrants and a large number of their descendants would have made a great difference in the history of the Church in this country. Secondly, although such men as Gibbons and Ireland complained that retention of the immigrant cultures would have retarded the conversion of America, the reverse is actually true. For in a country like ours, there is always a yearning on the part of many for something deeper and truer than what the mainstream offers; this is particularly true among writers and artists—the shapers, after all, of public opinion. The Catholic revival in Great Britain between the World Wars, for example, shows this. Had it not been for subsequent liturgical and doctrinal upheaval, the likelihood was that the revival would have continued to grow—but of course, such a lay effort was dependent in the end upon the vagaries of clergy. In any event, as convert writer Walker Percy observed in his *Lost in the Cosmos*, English-speaking writers tend to gravitate to such centers of Catholic culture as France, Italy, Spain, or on an American level, Taos and New Orleans. Yet as he also pointed out, Catholics in Cleveland are less Catholic culturally than Protestants in New Orleans. This is a defect which has without a doubt lost many who would have joined, had they been subjected to the attractions of an integrally Catholic culture mingled with purest orthodoxy. The third benefit which would have resulted was the most important; it would have been impossible for the heresy of Americanism to survive. The key to the whole thing was the appointment in America of foreign bishops who would be resolutely orthodox.

As might be expected, reaction to the Lucerne Memorial was swift. In such official publications as the *Catholic Review* and the *Northwestern Review*, the Lucerne Memorial was branded a conspiracy to subject the Church in America to a vaguely defined coalition of "foreigners." Much the same rhetoric was used against German and other non-Irish Catholics as the A.P.A. used of the Church as a whole—with as much justice.

Asked by the AP correspondent in St. Paul to comment on the Memorial, Ireland replied that "American Catholics" resented any interference by foreigners in the affairs of the Church here; only the Pope would be listened to. He received overwhelming congratulations from non-Catholic media and leaders all over America. But the way he really felt was expressed in a telegram to Monsignor Denis J. O'Connell, rector of the North American College in Rome: "GREAT DISTURBANCE, DANGER OF SCHISM AND PERSECUTION UNLESS ROME DENOUNCE CAHENSLY, AND DENOUNCE ONCE FOR ALL, AND FOR TIME BEING NAME NO GERMAN BISHOPS" (Barry, *Op. Cit.*, pp. 142-143).

It was not just a question of threatening the Holy Father; Ireland and Gibbons had a powerful friend in Rome—the Secretary of State,

Cardinal Rampolla. Rampolla always attempted to influence Leo XIII to favor various Liberal schemes; one of his greatest triumphs was to convince the Pontiff to order French Royalists—the most devout Catholics in that nation—to support the anti-clerical Third Republic, with the result that the French laity split. Rampolla was suspected of being a Freemason, and was only narrowly prevented from becoming Pope in 1903 by Franz Josef of Austria-Hungary exercising the ancient right of veto of the Holy Roman Emperors. From this controversial action emerged the election of St. Pius X. The Gibbons-Ireland party could always look to Rampolla as a powerful defender of their interests with Leo XIII; to his influence may be attributed much of the Pope's indecision on American affairs.

The Americanists went on a campaign of insult and libel against Cahensly and his associates in the Catholic and secular press, saying among other things that Cahensly plotted to put America under the thumb of the Kaiser. Never mind the fact that the Germans who signed the document were veterans of the *Kulturkampf*, and had fought the Imperial government very strongly, or that they were part of the parliamentary opposition to the cabinet, or that they stood for federalism in internal German affairs, as opposed to the government's Prussian centralism. Never mind also, that, as Barry shows us, non-German American support for Cahensly was forthcoming:

> The *Catholic Record* of Indianapolis on August 2, 1891, maintained that Americanism was pharisaical: "What has America that has not been brought and planted from Europe?" Population, religion, language, cities, customs, art, economics, law, population, all came from Europe, the editor stated, and accordingly it was pure imagination to fear European influence. America was rather a mixing of Europe. *L'Observateur*, of New Orleans, on August 6, 1892, advised French Catholics that only a political bond had been broken with the fatherland, but not their bond of love, blood, morals, soul, mother tongue; and that their children must preserve these traits. *Le Travailleur*, of Worcester, on July 11, 1892, blamed fanatics for wanting to wash away from the soul of the immigrant all remembrance of his fatherland, and introduce an Anglo-American system which would quickly lead to apostasy (p. 152, n. 28).

This sort of sense, common and Catholic, might be expected from these organs, the first being produced under the eye of Bishop Francis Chatard, a close ally of Corrigan; the second as a register of educated Creole opinion; and the third having been founded by the redoubtable *Ferdinand Gagnon* (1849-1886), the "father of Franco-American journalism" in New England. For all of these folk, America was the land they loved, but as a country only; not as a new religion, nor as a sort of Messiah of the nations—this is where they differed from the Americanists.

In any case, Rampolla convinced the Holy Father not to act on the proposals of the Lucerne memorial, but rather to leave everything in the hands of the American episcopate. In a word, where a local bishop saw fit to apply part of the program, he might, as we have seen. But where the bishop wished to force Americanization, there would be no hindrance. Certainly bishops would not be appointed on the basis of nationality.

Shortly after a letter arrived from Rampolla to Cardinal Gibbons detailing this, on July 11, 1891, the latter met President Benjamin Harrison at their mutual vacation spot, Cape May, New Jersey. There the President assured the Cardinal of his happiness at Gibbons' victory; in the course of the conversation, Harrison said, "This is no longer a missionary country like others which need missionaries from abroad." Surely as natural a sentiment might have been expressed by a Brahmin priest to St. Francis Xavier, or by a Crow medicine man to Fr. De Smet. It is highly unlikely, however, that such men would take the word of an infidel that their unconverted country did not need evangelization.

In any case, the smear campaign went on; even Archbishop Corrigan was convinced of Cahensly's fault, although His Grace was head of the St. Raphael Society in New York. In the end, Cahensly's reputation was cleared with Corrigan and his friends. But his proposals were not implemented nationally and wholeheartedly; this, in the end, proved to be a great loss to both Catholicism and America.

In any case, the Cahenslyite controversy was soon subsumed into the larger struggle between Americanists and Ultramontanes, as they were called. These latter, headed by Corrigan and McQuaid, as well as Milwaukee's Archbishop Katzer, comprised those Catholics who wanted the Church in America to be an integral part of the Church Universal, rather than some sort of autonomous national church, bearing the same relation to Rome that the Episcopalians do to the Church of England.

The opening salvo in this battle, not directly connected (although not completely divorced from it, either) was the schools controversy. As earlier pointed out, first Noah Webster and then Horace Mann had designed the American Public School to be an instrument of ideology, rather than education. To protect Catholic children from its influence was a major concern of every devout Catholic parent or clergyman. So convinced, however, that Catholicism and the national religion were the same thing, were Gibbons and Ireland, that they advocated the merger of Catholic and public schools. Addressing the National Education Association in St. Paul in July of 1890, Ireland developed this theme, ending with the rousing call: "The Free School of America! Withered be the hand raised in sign of its destruction."

In August of 1891, he negotiated an agreement with the schoolboards of Stillwater and Faribault, whereby they took over the local parochial schools, but permitted religious instruction for Catholic students on school grounds after hours. At the same time, Cardinal Gibbons asked Fr. Thomas Bouquillon, professor of moral theology at CUA to write a pamphlet on education; entitled *Education: To Whom Does It Belong?* it declared that the state had the right to control education. When more traditional Catholics replied that parents were the primary authority in education, Ireland exploded. Such arguments were outmoded, and most of those who said so were Germans who were out for vengeance, so Ireland maintained. Both sides appealed to Rome, and Ireland went there to present his case. He further reiterated his position that opposition to his merger of the schools was part of the Cahenslyite plot to "Germanize" America (an unusual charge given, as we have seen, the support given Cahensly's position by French and French-Canadian sources, who could hardly be seen to wish "Germanization"). Ireland's subsequent record in sparking major schisms with Polish and Ruthenian Catholics over similar questions make his statements appear even more questionable.

In the meantime, the Holy Father sent a delegate to the New York meeting of the Archbishops in November of 1892. This man, Archbishop Satolli, was at the time a friend of Ireland. The meeting was filled with discord and recrimination; in reply, on January 23, 1893, Satolli was made Apostolic Delegate to the United States, a post which Gibbons had fought against being created.

Satolli's friendship with Ireland, however, was ended when Gibbons and Ireland attended the World Parliament of Religions in Chicago in September. Today, when the appearance of Catholic prelates at such gatherings is considered matter of course, this may not seem like a great battle. But in those days prelates still believed that the Catholic Church was the One True one. Fr. William Tappert, a pastor in Kentucky, commented during a speech at the National Conference of Catholic Societies in Cologne, at which he had been invited to speak on the Church in America:

> Since our enemies keep up their sorry courage by concentrating their criminal attacks on a man from the Center [Cahensly], who has been highly useful to the German emigrants, you will permit me to explain our attitude toward the ecclesiastical and religio-political questions which have so prominently occupied the Catholic mind in the United States of late.... Our great enemy is liberalism, the denial of the social kingdom of Christ on earth. This great heresy of our time

is threefold: first, avowed unbelief; second, social rationalism; last, but not least, an ecclesiastical liberalism which here and there blocks our way. It holds sway over certain Catholics who have inscribed on their banner: "Union of the Church with modern ideas, with Americanism." Hence the extolling of modern liberties, not as a requisite for a justified tolerance, but as the ideal of political and ecclesiastical wisdom; hence the cautiousness of preaching Catholic truth, under which truth and Catholicity suffer; hence the more than sparing attitude of this third kind of liberalism toward secret societies; hence the unreasonable backing away from some Catholic traditions in the temperance and liquor questions; hence, finally, that coquetting with a more or less general all-embracing christianity to which a far-reaching expression was given at the Chicago parliament of unholy memory. From the same source originates those fulsome praises for the public schools...and that ridiculous boastfulness about Americanism, which is not ashamed to reproach foreign-born co-religionists with an attachment to the language and customs of their fathers, and brand them publicly as being opposed to the English language and devoid of love of country" (Barry, op. cit., p. 221, n. 62).

What is intriguing about this passage is that, despite the ignominy heaped upon its author after his return to his home in Kentucky, a century later his words ring true. One may argue until one is blue in the face about the intentions of Ireland and his clique; but the results of their handiwork are clear.

The year 1895 saw two major setbacks for the Americanists; one was the adherence of Satolli to Corrigan's group. While warm toward Ireland initially, residence in this country showed him the folly involved in Americanism. The other defeat was the sacking of Msgr. O'Connell as head of the North American College. This latter was due entirely to O'Connell's mismanagement of the College and his continual working on behalf of the Americanists. The next year, Americanist Bishop John J. Keane was removed as head of CUA.

The last major skirmish in this saga came with the publication in Paris of a French translation of an American life of Fr. Isaac Hecker, founder of the Paulists, in 1897. Hecker was of course an Americanist, as both of his friends Brownson and McMaster came to realize. The foreword to the new publication was written by a liberal French priest, Abbé Felix Klein. In it, Klein extolled Hecker's methods—praising the active virtues at the expense of the passive, teaching potential converts only the bare minimum of the Faith so as not to offend them, and the like, and seemed to canonize Hecker. The Liberal French Catholic Press (including the Sillon, later condemned by St. Pius X) lined up behind Klein. Both in Europe and America, the work was denounced as heretical. Finally, there appeared in 1899 an apostolic letter from Leo XIII, *Testem Benevolentiae*, which although originally much stronger in its condemnation of the heresy of Americanism (the original named names—like Gibbons and Ireland, an unpleasant feature Rampolla persuaded the Pontiff to delete), remains strong to us even in its weakened state. After saying that there are said to be some in America who desire that the Church there be different than it is in the rest of the world, he continues, saying that these teach that:

> ... in order the more easily to bring over to Catholic doctrine those who dissent from it, the Church ought to adapt herself somewhat to our advanced civilization, and, relaxing her ancient rigor, show some indulgence to modern popular theories and methods. Many think that this is to be understood not only with regard to rule of life, but also to the doctrines in which the Deposit of Faith is contained. For they contend that it is opportune, in order to work in a more attractive way upon the wills of those who are not in accord with us, to pass over certain heads of doctrines, as if of lesser moment, or so to soften them that they may not have the same meaning which the Church has invariably held. Now, beloved Son, few words are needed to show how reprehensible is the plan that is thus conceived, if we but consider the character and origin of the doctrine which the Church hands down to us. On that point the Vatican Council says: "The doctrine of faith which God has revealed is not proposed like a theory of philosophy which is to be elaborated by the human understanding, but as a divine deposit delivered to the spouse of Christ to be faithfully guarded and infallibly declared... That sense of the sacred dogmas is to be faithfully kept which Holy Mother Church has once declared, and is not to be departed from under the specious pretext of a more profound understanding..."
>
> ...Far be it, then, for anyone to diminish or for any reason whatever to pass over anything of this divinely delivered doctrine; whosoever would do so, would rather wish to alienate Catholics from the Church than to bring over to the Church those who dissent from it. Let them return; indeed, nothing is nearer to Our heart; let all those who are wandering far from the sheepfold of Christ return; but let it not be by any other road than that which Christ has pointed out.

Strong indeed it is to us; but each side got what it wanted. The Americanists were a little chastened; no more World Parliaments or school mergers would take place for quite some time. But neither Gibbons nor Ireland were mentioned, let alone deposed. Keane became Bishop of Dubuque, while O'Connell received Richmond. On the other hand, the Ultramontanes were satisfied that they had won, and so relaxed their vigilance in the face of the exciting events that lay ahead. This was a signal mistake, as we now know.

A NEW WORLD POWER 1866-1921

FOREIGN POLICY AND IMPERIAL AMBITION

The end of the War Between the States found the U.S. in a rather strange position regarding Latin America. As we have seen, the government inevitably lent its prestige and whatever assistance it could give to the anti-clericals in those countries; when filibusters like William Walker struck in Central America during the 1850s, it was always in support of the Liberal faction. The War provided a break.

Indeed, it was the War which permitted the creation of the Empire of Mexico. Although Maximilian had taken up his throne after a French invasion of the country, it must be remembered that this occurred in the aftermath of a bloody Civil War, in which the triumphant Liberals had received assistance from the U.S. French intervention was seen by the Conservatives as redressing this injustice. The notion of bringing over a European prince to serve as Emperor went back to independence and Iturbide. During the subsequent years, men like diplomat and former cabinet minister Jose Gutierrez d'Estrada kept the hope of a Mexican monarchy alive. Gutierrez well understood the threat that the U.S. posed not only to Mexico and the rest of Latin America, but to Europe also. At the outbreak of the Mexican War he had written to Metternich,

> If the European powers persist in ignoring America's aggressive policy toward her neighbors and allow it to go unchecked, still regarding this growing giant as a child, how will they be able to defend themselves against America's encroachment in the field of industry and commerce? The triumph of America is only possible at the expense of Europe, who will have to pay dearly for her lack of foresight.

At length, Napoleon III listened to Gutierrez and other Mexican Conservatives. Although trounced in 1861, they were avenged the next year when the French invaded and defeated Liberal leader Benito Juarez. In 1863, Maximilian, brother of Franz Josef of Austria-Hungary, accepted the throne of Mexico. Apart from the French, and the Austrian and Belgian (his wife Carlota was a princess of that country) legions, Maximilian depended upon his Mexican army, led by such valiant veterans of the Conservative Party as Miguel Miramon, who had both led the Conservative army and had been President, and Tomas Mejía, an Indian general.

Maximilian's reign, though short, was, as far as a regime can be so while fighting a vicious civil war, just and humane. But from the beginning he was opposed by Benito Juarez's sponsors, the Americans. The U.S. Consul was withdrawn just before Maximilian's arrival at Vera Cruz on May 28. The American Congress made it clear that they would never recognize the Empire, and continued to consider Juarez president, for all that he controlled little of the country.

In an attempt to assuage the U.S., Maximilian decreed religious toleration. While this doomed any chance of a concordat with the Holy See, and cost him needed support in Mexico, it did nothing to affect the opinions of the American government or press. In August of 1865, the American ambassador in Paris delivered a note from Washington asking when French troops would be withdrawn from Mexico, "where their continued presence may end in undermining the cordial relations between our two countries." The message was clear; if France did not pull out and leave Maximilian to face Juarez—to whom the U.S. was rushing aid—there might be war. Assistance in the form of smuggling arms and raiding over the border was encouraged by the American commanding the forces on the U.S. side of the border, General Phil Sheridan. Years later, in his memoirs he admitted, "Juarez would never have been victorious without the help of the United States."

Under diplomatic pressure, Napoleon III decided to withdraw his troops at the end of 1865. As they began to withdraw, the ever more heavily armed Juarezistas closed in behind. When at length the inevitable happened after the French left, Maximilian and his army were left with little more than central Mexico. Through treachery his last position was taken by the Juarezistas, and with Mejía and Miramon, Maximilian was captured. On June 19, 1867, he was executed:

> The troops on the top of the hill were drawn up in three sides of a square, the fourth being formed by a low adobe wall. The prisoners were led into the square and placed with their faces turned toward the town. For the last time Maximilian looked out over the tiled domes and baroque steeples, the orange groves and gardens of Queretaro, where he had found so much loyalty and devotion. An order was given and the seven men of the firing squad moved into line. Father Soria said a short prayer and the Emperor embraced his two companions. Miramon was as proud and composed as always but Mejia, who could still hear the heart-rending cries of his young wife, could hardly stand upright. The officer in charge of the firing squad appears to have been so moved by the Emperor's behavior that he offered a few words of apology, but Maximilian answered, "you are a soldier and it is your duty to obey." Then he handed a gold ounce to each of his seven executioners, asking them to take good aim and not deface him, so that his mother could

look upon him again. The young officer was about to wave his sword when Maximilian stepped forward and called out in Spanish: "I forgive everybody. I pray that everybody may also forgive me, and I hope that my blood which is about to be shed will bring peace to Mexico. *Viva Mexico! Viva Independencia!*" The last words had hardly been spoken when a sword flashed in the air and seven shots rang out simultaneously. The Emperor fell backwards, his body still twitching convulsively on the ground, though later it was ascertained that he had died instantaneously. The young officer stepped forward and pointing to the heart, ordered a soldier to give the *coup-de-grâce*. Now came the turn of Miramon and Mejía, both of whom died as heroes crying, "God bless the Emperor!" (Joan Haslip, *The Crown of Mexico*, p. 498).

So died the last Emperor of Mexico, and with him any hope that Mexico would be a truly independent Catholic nation. With short intervals, every government the country has had since then has been more or less dominated by the United States—which always favors anti-clericals.

As indeed it did in the rest of Latin America. For the next decade saw the assassination of one of the most brilliant Catholic leaders on this or any continent, aided and abetted by the American ambassador: Jose Garcia Moreno.

Born in 1821 to an aristocratic family of Ecuador's capital, Quito, Garcia Moreno studied theology in the university there. Thinking he had a vocation to the priesthood, he received minor orders and the tonsure; but his closest friends and his own interests convinced him to pursue a more worldly career. Graduating in 1844, he was admitted to the bar. Starting his career as both lawyer and journalist (opposed to the Liberal government in power) he made little headway. In 1849 he embarked on a two year visit to Europe to see first hand the effects of the 1848 revolution. He made a second trip in 1854-56. Louis Veulliot (himself a great champion of the Faith in the press) described what these trips did for Garcia Moreno:

> In a foreign land, solitary and unknown, García Moreno made himself fit to rule. He learned all that was necessary for him to know in order to govern a nation, formerly Christian but now falling fast into an almost savage condition... Paris, which is at once a Christian and a heathen city, is the very place where the lesson he needed would best be acquired, since the two opposing elements may there be seen engaged in perpetual conflict. Paris is a training school for priests and martyrs, it is also a manufactory of anti-Christs and assassins. The future president of Ecuador gazed upon the good and the evil, and when he set out for his home afar, his choice was made.

He returned home in 1856 to find his country in the grip of strident anti-clericals; he was elected a senator and joined the opposition. Although himself a Monarchist (he would have liked to have seen a Spanish prince on the throne of Ecuador) he bowed to circumstances and allowed himself to be made president following a civil war the year after his return—so great had his stint in the country's Senate made his reputation. In 1861 this was confirmed in a popular election for a four year term. Unhappily, his successor was deposed by the Liberals in 1867. But two years later he was reelected, and then again in 1875. During his period in office, he propelled his nation forward, all the while uniting her more closely to the Faith.

Personally pious (he attended Mass, daily, as well as visiting the Blessed Sacrament; he received every Sunday—a rare practice before St. Pius X—and belonged to the Workingmen's section of the Sodality, in which he was quite active), he believed that the first duty of the State was to promote and support Catholicism. Church and State were united, but by the terms of the new concordat, the State's power over appointments of bishops inherited from Spain was done away with—at Garcia Moreno's insistence. The 1869 constitution made Catholicism the religion of the State and required that both candidates and voters for office be Catholic. He was the only ruler in the world to protest the Pope's loss of the Papal States, and two years later had the legislature consecrate Ecuador to the Sacred Heart.

In more worldly things, he came to office with an empty treasury and an enormous debt. To overcome this, he placed the government on stringent economy and abolished useless positions, as well as cutting out the corruption which siphoned off tax dollars. As a result he was able to provide Ecuadoreans with more for less. Slavery was abolished, but there was full compensation for the owners; (thus neither former slaves nor masters suffered economically). The army was reformed, with officers being sent to Prussia to study, and illiterate recruits taught basic skills. Houses of prostitution were closed, and hospitals opened in all the major towns. Railroads and national highways were built, telegraphs extended, and the postal and water systems improved. City streets were paved, and local bandits suppressed. Garcia Moreno further reformed the universities, established two polytechnic and agricultural colleges and a military school, and increased the number of primary schools to 500 from 200. The number of students in them grew from 8,000 to 32,000. To staff the enormously expanded health-care and educational facilities, foreign religious were brought in. All of this was done while expanding the franchise and guaranteeing equal rights under the law to every Ecuadorian.

But the Liberals (with contacts and support in the American Embassy) hated Garcia Moreno; when he was elected a third time in 1875, it was considered to be his death warrant. He wrote immediately to Pius IX asking for his blessing before inauguration day on August 30:

> I wish to obtain your blessing before that day, so that I may have the strength and light which I need so much in order to be unto the end a faithful son of our Redeemer, and a loyal and obedient servant of His Infallible Vicar. Now that the Masonic Lodges of the neighboring countries, instigated by Germany, are vomiting against me all sorts of atrocious insults and horrible calumnies, now that the Lodges are secretly arranging for my assassination, I have more need than ever of the divine protection so that I may live and die in defense of our holy religion and the beloved republic which I am called once more to rule.

Garcia Moreno's prediction was correct; he was assassinated coming out of the Cathedral in Quito, struck down with knives and revolvers. So passed from the scene one of the greatest Catholic statesmen the world has ever seen. He showed that making Catholicism the basis of public policy will not doom a country to poverty, but quite the opposite; all Catholic Latin American politicians who have followed since owe him a great debt. Similarly, the American officials who assisted in his murder (partial planning for which was done in our embassy) thus have blood on their hands. A blood which, like Maximilian's, only a change of policy can begin to wash off.

But another triumph awaited us in Brazil. That nation had become independent from Portugal in 1822. Nine years later, the Portuguese Crown Prince, who had proclaimed himself Emperor Pedro I, sailed for Portugal to take up his father's crown leaving his five-year-old son and heir to be Emperor under a council of regency. The period of the regency was unstable, however, and the Emperor Dom Pedro II was proclaimed of age at 14.

His was a Liberal Monarchy, like that of Louis Phillipe of France. He was a Freemason (as were a number of the bishops and priests; a divisive issue indeed was the Pope's condemnation of the Order). Although a practicing Catholic and regular Mass-goer, he not only observed the religious liberty clause of the constitution, but subsidized Protestant schools and missions. During our Centennial year of 1876, he visited the States and fell in love with them. In a word, he was up to date and Liberal.

But he was still a Monarch, still a descendant of an ancient race, still a Catholic. No matter how much he might like the U.S. (and be liked by individuals here) the American oligarchy and government could never see him save as an obstacle. Like Maximilian, like Garcia Moreno, he wished to see his country strong and prosperous, and did much to encourage immigration, good government, railroads, and all that sort of thing. But if a strong and independent Catholic Mexico, or a strong and independent Catholic Ecuador could not be tolerated by the rulers of America, how could such a Brazil be?

The example of America was much looked up to by some Brazilians, particularly those who had become Positivists, a religio-philosophical creed which, taking advantage of the religious liberty law, had become quite powerful in Brazil. When the Emperor's daughter (regent for her father when he was out of the country for medical treatment) signed a bill in 1888 abolishing slavery, the die was cast. The next year Positivists and a clique in the army pulled off a coup and expelled Dom Pedro II and the Imperial family—not without encouragement, once again, from our embassy. Just as Maximilian was revered by the Indians, particularly the Mayans in Yucatan, so too was Dom Pedro by the poor blacks in Brazil, and there were several risings on his behalf—but of course, these were easily suppressed. Brazil entered into a period of chaos.

We may next turn our attention across the Pacific to Hawaii. This group of islands had been united into a single Kingdom by Kamehameha I in the late 18th Century. For a short period the nation had been a British Protectorate, which is why the Union Jack was (and is) in corner of the Hawaiian flag. With increasing European and American influence came Congregational and Episcopalian missionaries from New England. Their descendants acquired a great deal of power and influence. By the time Queen Liliuokolani ascended the throne in 1891, they were a much bigger power than the native Hawaiians or their monarch. Two years after her accession, they engineered a revolt against her, and took over the country, proclaiming a republic under the presidency of Sanford B. Dole (whose family would become famous for the production of pineapples). Although President Cleveland refused to accept the new republic into the U.S., it was annexed in 1898. As with Alaska, bought from Russia in 1867 (much to the chagrin of the native Aleuts, who were by this time all Russian Orthodox), this was a bloodless conquest.

But if bloodless, it was not without tears. The Queen journeyed to Washington to plead her people's case. At the same time she wrote a book to explain the situation to Americans; in it she makes this heart-rending appeal:

> Oh, honest Americans, as Christians hear me for my down-trodden people! Their form of government is as dear to them as yours is precious to you. Quite as warmly as you love your country, so they love theirs. With all your goodly possessions, covering a territory so immense that there yet remain parts unexplored, possessing islands that, although near at hand, had to be neutral ground in time of war, do

not covet the little vineyard of Naboth's, so far from your shores, lest the punishment of Ahab fall upon you, if not in your day, in that of your children, for "be not deceived, God is not mocked." The people to whom your fathers told of the living God, and taught to call "Father," and whom the sons now seek to despoil and destroy, are crying aloud to Him in their time of trouble; and He will keep His promise, and will listen to the voices of His Hawaiian children lamenting for their homes.

It is for them that I would give the last drop of my blood; it is for them that I would spend, nay, am spending everything belonging to me. Will it be in vain? It is for the American people and their representatives in Congress to answer these questions. As they deal with me and my people, kindly, generously, and justly, so may the Great Ruler of all nations deal with the grand and glorious nation of the United States of America (Liliuokolani, *Hawaii's Story by Hawaii's Queen*, pp. 373-374).

We know, of course, just how we dealt with her and her people.

At any rate, we were in search of new worlds to conquer; one lay just off our doorstep: Cuba. The loss of most of her New World Possessions had reduced Spain's Empire to Cuba, Puerto Rico, the Philippines, Guam, and what is now Micronesia. During most of the 19th Century, Civil Wars had raged in Spain; these were primarily between the Carlists who fought for the restoration of Spain's traditional Catholic Monarchy, and the Cristinos who wanted a Liberal monarchy, as Louis Phillipe or Dom Pedro had. Masonic lodges spread like wildfire, both in Spain and the colonies. At home these bodies supported mere anti-clericalism; in the colonies they favored both that and independence. This last was particularly the case in Cuba (In the cemetery at Key West there are buried a number of 19th Century Cuban revolutionaries; all their stones bear the Masonic square and compass). Through their successive revolts they had been aided by the United States. After the election of 1896, spurred on by such newspaper magnates as William Randolph Hearst, the public began to feel a need to "do something" about Cuba. The Spanish looked to the rest of Europe for help in defending Cuba against the Americans.

The latest revolt was put down in 1897; to this was added the promise of Constitutional reform. Nevertheless, U.S. papers kept all sorts of supposed Spanish "atrocities" in front of the public eye. Tensions mounted, until the battleship U.S.S. Maine blew up in Havana harbor on February 15, 1898. To this day no one really knows how it happened, or who was responsible. But the papers and annexationists declared that it was the Spanish, and that we must go to war immediately. War was declared (although President McKinley, who would be assassinated two years later refused to sign the declaration), and off we went.

In short order, Cuba, Puerto Rico, the Philippines, and Guam were taken. The Philippines were a bit of a problem, because the insurgents there apparently wanted us no more than they had wanted the Spaniards. Nevertheless, we were there to stay. Spain ceded our conquests in return for a cash payment, and the war was over.

Cuba we were resolved to give up. But in the remaining territories, work immediately began on shedding the Spanish ethos—including religion—and making them over. Church and State were of course separated immediately; this provided a bit of a problem, because the Spanish government paid the clergy and supported the church buildings in lieu of moneys from ecclesiastical properties seized by the government during various 19th century anticlerical binges. But in Puerto Rico, especially, the new American government simply kept the property and did not pay any money, invoking separation of Church and State. It would take some court battles to get the money paid in a lump sum.

In the Philippines, things were even more serious. During the course of the insurrection against the Spanish, a schism broke out. The schismatics, led by a man named Aglipay, were able to secure from the anti-Roman American authorities the keys to many churches. Again, it took a lot of legal fighting to regain the property. The Pope obligingly replaced the Spanish clergy with Irish and Americans.

The most severe treatment the Church received, however, was on Guam. The U.S. military Governor, Leary, set about the systematic de-Catholicization of the island. In August of 1899, he forbade religious processions, requiring feasts to be celebrated purely within churches or homes; ordered all couples to marry at once in civil ceremonies; outlawed the ringing of church bells at 4 am, when most Guamanians rose to work; and ordered all crucifixes removed from the classrooms and catechism instruction ended. At last, he expelled all the priests from Guam save one. Finally, he legalized divorce. While his reign of terror lasted only a year and most of his religious laws were abrogated after he left, it does show the sort of American who would be building a U.S. Empire.

When trying to garner support for Spain in 1896, foreign minister Carlos O'Donnell made some salient points in an instruction to his ambassador in London:

> It is requisite that you stress the effects which the Cuban insurrection may have on the monarchy in Spain, on the Regency, and on the monarchical principle in general. You should also stress the consequences of a war with the United States, which may be forced upon us in defending our rights and our national honor.
>
> ...Under the circumstances, the government of Her Majesty would regard themselves as faithless to their duty, if they did not place before

the consideration of the cabinets of the Great Powers of Europe, the special dangers which they see looming in the near future, and which, though especially affecting Spain, hold also a threat to colonial and maritime nations in general, and may even compromise other very important European interests.... There is inherent in the Cuban question a problem supremely European, affecting not only the development of Spain, but also the general interest of Europe, because very grave international consequences may result from the Cuban insurrection, and the daily more absorbent Monroe Doctrine.

Commenting on this passage, George O'Toole says perceptively:

Thus, O'Donnell had formulated a kind of "domino theory." If America intervened, Cuba would be lost. If Cuba were lost, the monarchy would fall. If the monarchy fell, then what of Czar Nicholas, Kaiser Wilhelm, Emperor Franz-Joseph, Queen Victoria, and the other crowned heads? Would their own thrones remain secure? (*The Spanish War*, p. 72).

A good question indeed; one which would be answered by the events of the next two decades. One thing is certain; by their refusal to stand by Spain, the European powers helped to make Gutierrez d'Estrada's words to Metternich come true.

Meanwhile, however, the acquisition of Puerto Rico, Hawaii, Guam, the Philippines, and possibly Cuba (it was not certain yet) led to a great deal of impassioned debate about the morality of the United States, founded as it was in revolution from an Empire, building one of its own. The question of the Philippines was quite pressing, because the insurrection there had just switched target from the Spanish to ourselves. Of course the Imperialists won out. One of the most influential of these was Senator Albert J. Beveridge, a Republican from Indiana who rose on January 9, 1900, to give a speech in the Senate, "In Support of an American Empire."

In his opening remarks, Beveridge informed his colleagues that the Philippines were "ours forever." Further, "We will not abandon our opportunity in the Orient. We will not renounce our part in the mission of our race, trustee, under God, of the civilization of the world." We were to move forward with "thanksgiving to Almighty God that He has marked us as His chosen people, henceforth to lead in the regeneration of the world." Beveridge described the Filipinos as

...Orientals, Malays, instructed by the Spaniards in the latter's worst estate. They know nothing of practical government except as they have witnessed the weak, corrupt, cruel, and capricious rule of Spain... What alchemy will change the Oriental quality of their blood and set the self-governing currents of the American pouring through their Malay veins? How shall they, in the twinkling of an eye, be exalted to the heights of self-governing peoples which required a thousand years for us to reach, Anglo-Saxons though we are?

Commenting on the importance of the question, the Senator declared:

> It is elemental. It is racial. God has not been preparing the English-speaking and Teutonic peoples for a thousand years for nothing but vain and idle self-contemplation and self-admiration. No! He has made us the master organizers of the world to establish system where chaos reigns. He has given us the spirit of progress to overwhelm the forces of reaction throughout the earth. He has made us adepts in government that we may administer government among savage and senile peoples. Were it not for such a force as this the world would relapse into barbarism and night. And of all our race He has marked the American people as His chosen nation to finally lead in the regeneration of the world. This is the divine mission of America, and it holds for us all the profit, all the glory, all the happiness possible to man. We are trustees of the world's progress, guardians of its righteous peace.

One might be excused for considering all of this blasphemous. Yet it is what the New Nationalism, with its grinding out of local and state liberties to create a synthetic nationality led to. Moreover, if it sound blasphemous, compare it with another individual we have met in the previous chapter:

> For me this is not simply a question of Cuba. If it were, it were no question or a poor question. Then let the "greasers" eat one another up and save the lives of our dear boys. But for me it is a question of much more moment:—it is the question of two civilizations. It is the question of all that is old and vile and mean and rotten and cruel and false in Europe against all that is free and noble and open and true and humane in America. When Spain is swept off the seas much of the meanness and narrowness of old Europe goes with it to be replaced by the freedom and openness of America. This is God's way of developing the world. And all continental Europe feels that the war is against itself and that is why they are all against us, and Rome more than all because when the prestige of Spain and Italy will have passed away, and when the pivot of the world's political action will no longer be confined within the limits of the continent; then the nonsense of trying to govern the universal Church from a purely European standpoint—and according to exclusively Spanish and Italian methods, will be glaringly evident even to a child. (Gary Potter, *In Reaction,* p. 84)

Sounds similar, eh? Indeed it does! It is from a letter written by our old friend O'Connell to Archbishop Ireland in May of 1898. The Americanist clergy treated the Spanish War as a holy crusade, just as the Imperialists did, and for the same reason—they shared the same religion, when all is said and done. Because they were not dealt with properly in 1899, they came to dominate the Church in this country—and to shackle her to the latest opinions of the oligarchy. It is the mark of the liberal Catholic that he believes politically whatever the rulers do. So Ireland was a Republican and a jingo; during the Depression many prominent prelates were devout New Dealers; after that, in the 50s, they were resolutely anti-Communist; and today are interested in Gay Rights and the environment. But just as with our temporal rulers the issues themselves do not matter, so too with the liberal Catholic. The ideological ground shifts continually; all that matters is the reality of power.

So by 1899, the one truly independent and counter-cultural force in the country was muzzled. Economically and politically the outlines of the centralized state we know today had been laid down, the whole put at the service of the national ideology. A foreign Empire had been conquered, and that which had bred here for such a long time was at last ready to be released into the world.

But of course, little of this was discernible to most people. Instead, on New Year's Eve, 1899, as the revelers clinked their champagne glasses, they looked at the technological advances, the growth in reform acts and liberal institutions, and thought they were embarking upon a bright spanking new century of progress.

NEW TECHNOLOGIES, NEW CHALLENGES

The popping of champagne corks subsided, leaving these United States to face the new century. The first decade of that century saw the rise of revolutionary technologies which would alter the face of the globe even more than steamships and railways had done in the 19th. Although *Alexander Graham Bell* invented the telephone in 1876, it was not until 1891 that Edison and Berliner perfected the carbon microphone and telephone transmitter; these allowed the phone to become the instrument we know today.

The eminent Serb inventor, *Nicola Tesla*, developed the use of electrical alternating current the next year. This would permit the spread of electrical power to homes throughout the world. The same year, *Otto Daimler* invented the first gasoline automobile engine. The phone, the automobile, and electricity were beginning to make themselves felt when the 20th Century began, and during the first decade they spread tremendously, making *Thomas Edison* and *Henry Ford* household names.

Between 1903 and 1905, *Wilbur* and *Orville Wright* perfected the aeroplane; by 1910, photography had progressed to such a point that moving pictures made their debut as mass entertainment, albeit silently.

The impact of telephone, electricity, automobile, aeroplane, and the movies was tremendous. Electric lights would doom gas lamps, candles, and oil lamps (thus contributing to the demise of both Yankee whaling and "the old lamp-lighter of long, long ago"). They would also isolate modern, urban man from his ancestors' fear of the dark—thus adding in a way to the growing climate of disbelief and the notion that "science can do everything."

Instant communication via phone revolutionized human relations; in time it would thin the number of telegraph delivery boys tremendously. The automobile gave mobility to its owner. No longer need his horizons be confined to the village or neighborhood of his birth. In time, his car would require the brick and cobblestone street paving to be done over with the blacktop now so familiar to us. To manufacture these motor cars, the assembly line dominated factories.

The aeroplane (or airplane, as it came to be called) answered one of man's greatest and deepest desires—flight. No more need he be physically earthbound; moreover, in time he would be able to circle the earth if he wished, without resorting to time-consuming ships and trains.

It is difficult for us, weaned as we have been on technological cinematic marvels, to appreciate when we see them today the enormous impact of the first movies on our great-great-grandparents. To us they are crude things; but to those who saw them first, they were an entrance into wonderland. The movies awoke in many a heart yearnings never felt before, for adventure, for romance—yearnings, alas, rarely achieved in this world. For some the movies were a joyous escape from labor-intensive existence. For others they sparked abiding discontent with their lives, loves, and jobs.

Together these and other inventions altered the face of the nation and much of the world in a very short time. Moreover, they brought about for many an enormous change of attitude. Everything pre-electric was old-fashioned and not to be trusted. Utopia seemed deliverable now through technology—one of our national obsessions appeared to be just around the corner. For some, religious faith was shaken, for others, morality. The new inventions at first clustered in the city, so that the movement there from the country was accelerated.

These inventions tended thus to break down cultural and other distinctions between regions and ethnic groups. This was not a short process, but it continued the work done in the political sphere by the Civil War, and in the economic and social by the Gilded Age.

It is remarkable that after the Civil War, up to and including the First World War, regional writing emerged with a vengeance, as if in defiance of the long slow process of homogenization. So *Kate Chopin* and *George Washington Cable* wrote of the Louisana Creoles, *Edward Arlington Robinson, Sarah Orne Jewett*, and *William Dean Howells* of the New England Yankees, *Helen Hunt Jackson* of the Spanish *Californios*, and *Mark Twain* most notably of the dwellers along the Mississippi River. Yet all of these groups were passing away; from this time on, regional writing in America has counted decay among its major themes. Once the local customs and manners of the nation's regions were of importance— the very life of the country. But that importance, already doomed perhaps by Appomatox, the Public School, and the Trusts, diminished with every telephone line laid, every car purchased and driven across new vistas, and every movie house opened showing the same silents viewed in similar movie houses across America. Folk-lore, crafts, and music, once simply the natural products of the people's way of life, would make way for cheaply made products and entertainment radiating from a few manufacturing centers; such lore, crafts, and music would become ever more the property of either museums or enthusiasts, rather than the masses. Can it be that said masses were culturally enriched thereby?

Regardless of how much traditional culture and religion might have been battered by the new developments, traditional secularized Puritanism was, if anything, accentuated. As a nation where progress was hailed, the coming of these inventions was sign of our election to—well, to whatever secular puritans are saved by and through; further, the importance of these things was proven by their wide profit margin.

Mark Twain is perhaps one of our most truly American authors. His great gifts are indisputable; but he was not merely a mourner of past times and ways, like some of the other folk just listed. He welcomed the changes and all their implications wholeheartedly, and saw technological progress as a sign of treading the upward way—wherever that way might lead. In his fiction, he contrasted the can-do American mentality with what he conceived to be European backwardness in his comic *A Connecticut Yankee in King Arthur's Court*; in essays and speeches he did so both more seriously and more bitingly. Yet for all his self-identification with things progressive, his world view had not in essence gone far beyond Plymouth Rock, as *H.L. Mencken* pointed out in a 1917 essay, *Puritanism as a Literary Force*:

> Mark Twain, without question, was a great artist; there was in him something of that prodigality of imagination, that aloof engrossment in the human comedy, that penetrating cynicism which one associates with the great artists of the Renaissance. But his nationality hung

around his neck like a millstone; he could never throw off his native Philistinism. One ploughs through *The Innocents Abroad* and through parts of *A Tramp Abroad* with incredulous amazement. Is such coarse and ignorant clowning to be accepted as humor, as the best humor that the most humorous of peoples has produced? Is it really the mark of a smart fellow to lift a peasant's cackle over *Lohengrin*? Is Titian's chromo of Moses in the bulrushes seriously to be regarded as the noblest picture in Europe? Is there nothing in Latin Christianity, after all, save petty grafting, monastic scandals, and the worship of the knuckles and shinbones of dubious saints? May not a civilized man, disbelieving in it, still find himself profoundly moved by its dazzling history, the lingering remnants of its old magnificence, the charm of its gorgeous and melancholy loveliness?

In the presence of all beauty of man's creation—in brief, of what we roughly call art, whatever its form—the voice of Mark Twain was the voice of the Philistine. A literary artist of very high rank himself, with instinctive gifts that lifted him, in *Huckleberry Finn*, to kinship with Cervantes and Aristophanes, he was yet so far the victim of his nationality that he seems to have had no capacity for distinguishing between the good and the bad in the work of other men of his own craft. The literary criticism that one occasionally finds in his writings is chiefly trivial and ignorant; his private inclination appears to have been toward such romantic sentimentality as entrances schoolboys; the thing that interested him in Shakespeare was not the man's colossal genius but the absurd theory that Bacon wrote his plays. Had he been born in France (the country of his chief abomination!) instead of in a Puritan village of the American hinterland, I venture that he would have conquered the world. But try as he would, being what he was, he could not get rid of the Puritan smugness and cocksureness, the Puritan distrust of new ideas, the Puritan incapacity for seeing beauty as a thing in itself, and the full peer of the true and the good.

It was not really Twain himself that Mencken was attacking so much as the culture of Puritanism around him—a culture which, as HLM pointed out a few paragraphs before the passage cited, encompassed even its apparent opponents:

> The literature of the nation, even the literature of the enlightened minority, has been under harsh Puritan restraints from the beginning, and despite a few stealthy efforts at revolt—usually quite without artistic value or even common honesty, as in the case of the cheap fiction magazines and that of smutty plays on Broadway, and always short-lived—it shows not the slightest sign of emancipating itself today.

The new technology would, via movies and later forms of entertainment rebel against such restraints—but strictly according to the patterns of Mencken's "cheap fiction magazines" and "smutty plays on Broadway," a rebellion firmly a part of the mind set it was supposedly opposing. Yet the ever-increasing pervasiveness of such entertainment could not help but lower high and banish folk culture more and more.

Mencken saw clearly the effect of this sort of Puritanism on political life:

> The chief concern of the American people, even above the bread-and-butter question, was politics. They were incessantly hag-ridden by political difficulties, both internal and external, of an inordinant complexity, and these occupied all the leisure they could steal from the sordid work of everyday. More, their new and troubled political ideas tended to absorb all the rancorous certainty of their fading religious ideas, so that devotion to a theory or candidate became translated into devotion to a revelation, and the game of politics turned itself into a holy war. The custom of connecting purely political doctrines with pietistic concepts of an inflammable nature, then firmly set up by skillful persuaders of the mob, has never quite died out in the United States. There has not been a presidential contest since Jackson's day without its Armageddons, its marching of Christian soldiers, its crosses of gold, its crowns of thorns. The most successful American politicians, beginning with the antislavery agitators, have been those most adept at twisting the ancient gauds and shibboleths of Puritanism to partisan uses. Every campaign that we have seen for eighty years has been, on each side, a pursuit of bugaboos, a denunciation of heresies, a snouting up of immoralities...

The latest political crusade of the time was for Prohibition of alcohol; but the effect of the new technology upon politics was to exacerbate this situation, to inflame it. For quicker means of communication did not mean merely that one received news faster; it also put the receiver of news more at the mercy of the sender, and reduced the time in which he could reflect on said news. Moreover, as the average individual came more and more to rely upon newspapers and movies for his view of the world, and correspondingly less upon the religious and cultural traditions from whence he sprang, the less connected to actual reality he became. A chill presage of this was the part played by great newspaper magnates like William Randolph Hearst in pushing this country into the 1898 war with Spain; as radio and then television were invented and spread decades later, this sort of manipulation became an accepted commonplace.

So too did the mad, blind, Puritan faux religiosity of politics. Even as professedly Puritan standards were overturned, and rebellion against them then enforced with a ferocity which would have pleased the witch-hunters of Salem, so too did politics change their emphasis from "moral reform" like Prohibition and the Mann Act, only to pursue an almost opposite agenda in our own time (the famous Political Correctness) with insane vigor.

Yet despite the damage done by the spread of the new inventions to traditional modes of life and belief in this country, their impact was, as we have said, compounded by the deepest roots of our national psyche. As George Santayana put it in 1920:

> The discovery of the New World exercised a sort of selection among the inhabitants of Europe. All the colonists, except the Negroes, were voluntary exiles. The fortunate, the deeply rooted, and the lazy remained at home; the wilder instincts or dissatisfaction of others tempted them beyond the horizon. The American is accordingly the most adventurous, or the descendant of the most adventurous, of Europeans. It is in his blood to be socially a radical, though perhaps not intellectually. What has existed in the past, especially in the remote past, seems to him not only not authoritative but irrelevant, inferior, and outworn. He finds it a rather sorry waste of time to think about the past at all. But his enthusiasm for the future is profound; he can conceive of no more decisive way of recommending an opinion or a practice than to say it is what everyone is coming to adopt. This expectation of what he approves, or approval of what he expects, makes up his optimism. It is the necessary faith of the pioneer.
>
> Such a temperament is, of course, not maintained in the nation merely by inheritance. Inheritance notoriously tends to restore the average of a race, and plays incidentally many a trick of atavism. What maintains this temperament and makes it national is social contagion or pressure—something immensely strong in democracies. The luckless American who is born a conservative, or who is drawn to poetic subtlety, pious retreats, or gay passions, nevertheless has the categorical excellence of work, growth, enterprise, reform, and prosperity dinned into his ears: every door is open in this direction and shut in the other; so that he either folds up his heart and withers in a corner—in remote places you sometimes find such a solitary gaunt idealist—or else he flies to Oxford or Florence or Montmartre to save his soul—or perhaps not to save it (*Character and Opinion in the United States*, p. 166).

So fled Henry Adams and *Henry James*, and in later years *T.S. Eliot* and *Ezra Pound*. But for the millions left behind, the combination of Puritanism, blind optimism, and materialism, both amplifying and amplified by rising technology, would produce a people infinitely manipulable; any leader who knew how to push the right buttons would get majority support no matter what he stood for, or how much of remaining popular freedom would be eroded.

Internal Politics

President McKinley faced 1900, an election year, with confidence. Although against the Spanish War, he had prosecuted it vigorously, it was a quick victory, and so the credit redounded to him. Since he had become President, the United States had acquired Guam, Puerto Rico, the Philippines, Hawaii, and the Eastern half of Samoa (a treaty bestowing the other half on Germany had been signed with that country and Great Britain on December 2, 1899). Not only was the U.S. now the major Caribbean power, she was also an Asian-Pacific power practically overnight. Sure enough, McKinley defeated Bryan again on November 6.

The internal challenges which had faced the nation before the Spanish-American War, however, had not vanished: the monetary problem, the agrarian and industrial unrest, the growth of Trusts; all these remained to plague the McKinley administration.

The first named was dealt with on March 14, 1900. On that day was passed the Gold Standard Act; this ordered that all paper money would be redeemable in gold, that a gold reserve was to be maintained, and that circulation of national bank notes was to be expanded. Thus the Free Silver Movement and Bi-metallism were defeated.

On February 2, 1901, one of the key elements of the independence of the several States was done away with. An act reorganizing the army was passed, which permitted a maximum number of 100,000 troops. But one of its most significant provisions was to put the state militias under Federal supervision. Henceforth to be called the National Guard, these units would remain under state control, but would have their training and equipment supervised by Federal authorities; they could be taken under Federal control (Federalized) without the permission of the governor and state legislatures at any time, even in peacetime. Thus passed from the states one of their most important claims to sovereignty (and incidentally, had there been any real fear of it, any chance of secession or armed resistance to the Washington government). If the states wished to have armed forces entirely under their own command, they must form State Guards at their own expense.

On the economic front, a similarly important event occurred 23 days later. On that day the United States Steel Corporation was founded, the "Billion Dollar Steel Trust." Many other combinations were formed, both in industry and railroads. Although some would be challenged under the Sherman Anti-Trust Act, there would be little effect in the overall picture, except to force the large combinations to diversify their interests.

McKinley was shot by an anarchist on September 6; he lingered for a few days, dying on September 14, 1901. His Vice President, Theodore Roosevelt, assumed office. Roosevelt had made a name for himself as both an opponent of the Trusts when he was governor of New York, as a war hero (with his Rough Riders he charged up San Juan Hill, near Santiago, Cuba), and as an outspoken believer in the New Nationalism and Manifest Destiny. Roosevelt, a grinning moustachioed figure, brimming over with vitality, was at once a symbol of the new confident world power, and an easy target for cartoonists. The "Teddy Bear" was named after him, since the first samples of that sort of stuffed animal were made to resemble him.

Serving out McKinley's term, and being reelected for one of his own in 1904, Roosevelt stood for the Gold Standard, high tariffs, building up of the merchant marine, and the restriction of trusts. The shoddy conditions in food preparation disturbed him greatly, particularly after the publication of Upton Sinclair's novel *The Jungle*, about disgusting conditions in Chicago's meat-packing industry brought public attention to them. Roosevelt pushed through Congress the Pure Food and Drugs Act, and the Meat Inspection Act, which established Federal regulations for those industries. The day before, June 29, 1906, Congress passed the Hepburn Rate Bill, giving the Interstate Commerce Commission the power to fix rates for interstate commerce. As under his predecessors, real problems were answered with an extension of Federal power to oppose them. Regardless of their actual effect upon the evils involved, the power of the central government continued to grow ever stronger. But it was in foreign affairs and colonial administration that Roosevelt left the greatest mark.

The World's Policeman

The civil organization of the conquered territories was a pressing problem for the McKinley administration. Guam would, due to its size and position, remain under Naval administration. The Philippines, however, were a different story.

Although the Americans conquered Manila in 1898, the Filipinos under Aguinaldo, (whose rebellion against the Spanish in 1896 had been suppressed by them that same year) demanded independence. Fighting broke out between the occupiers and the occupied on February 4, 1899; within a year Aguinaldo's army was broken, and he was captured in April, 1901. Meanwhile, a commission was sent to the islands to establish a civil government in 1900. Its first act was to separate the Catholic Church from the State. A Governor-General was appointed, and a cabinet. The first Governor-General, William Howard Taft, connived with a group of schismatics called after their leader Aglipay, Aglipayans, to deliver into the hands of the latter many of the churches in the islands. The new codes inaugurated American-style public schools, whose curriculum (particularly in history) was very anti-Catholic. As education was made compulsory, most Filipino children had to attend these schools. Moreover, the properties of the Friars, earlier seized by anti-clerical Spanish governments which nevertheless paid rent to the Church for them, were simply appropriated by the new regime. It was apparent to casual observers that de-Catholicizing the islands was part of the American agenda; pressure was successfully placed upon the Holy See to replace all the Spanish bishops with American or Irish ones.

The new bishops pursued a policy of accommodation. As a result, the properties seized by the Aglipayans were returned legally in 1906-07; a lump sum was paid for the Friars' properties, and the dioceses of the islands allowed to incorporate in accordance with American business law. Henceforth, the Church would cooperate with the new regime loyally.

Puerto Rico found herself in a similar situation. There too the Church was separated from the State, and Church-properties appropriated by the government (and compensation only achieved after long court struggles). Immediately steps were taken to Americanize education and de-Catholicize and de-Hispanicize the country. *Luis Muñoz Marin*, born in 1898 and later the island's first native-born governor, wrote an article ("The Sad Case of Porto Rico," *The American Mercury*, XVI, No. 62, February 1929) which described pungently the existence of Puerto Rico under the Spanish and changes under the American occupiers:

> The American flag found Porto Rico penniless and content. It now flies over a prosperous factory worked by slaves who have lost their land and may soon lose their guitars and their songs. In the old days most Porto Rican peasants owned a few pigs and chickens, maybe a horse or a cow, some goats, and in some way had the use of a patch of soil. Today this modest security has been replaced by a vision of opulence. There are more things that they can't get. The margin between what they have and what they can get has widened monstrously. While there are many more schools for their hungry children and many more roads for their bare feet, their destiny is decidedly narrower now than it was when they were part and parcel of one of the most interesting and incompetent nationalities in the world.
>
> In 1898 Porto Rico was a semi-feudal country, typical of the old Spanish provinces in America, willing and capable of assuming with a natural grace and a natural awkwardness its position in the Spanish Commonwealth of provinces, or to venture into a simple, old-fashioned Latin-American national form. Its economics were those developed by

> Spain in the tropical New World: fiscally rotten, socially humble and sound. Culturally, it was a slow, calm place...
>
> Spain had recently granted Porto Rico an autonomous form of government. The island was run by Porto Ricans under a responsible Cabinet system, and the Governor-General, barring his military command, was as purely ceremonial as his colleague of Canada. Porto Rico had control of her customs, a measure of treaty-making power, sixteen representatives in the Madrid Cortes. She was empowered to develop her economic life as best suited her tastes and interests. Her statesmen and politicians had the future in their hands. Theirs was the responsibility for molding this quiet lovely place into an image of unassuming prosperity and justice...

Muñoz then went on to describe the results of the American take-over:

> Then the tariff wall was thrown around the island. Sugar became the chief beneficiary and cane spread over the valleys and up the hillsides like wildfire. The Spanish economy had been somewhat haphazardly predicated on small-landholding. The American economy, introduced by the Guánica, the Aguirre, the Fajardo and other great *centrales* was based on the million-dollar mill and the tight control of surrounding countryside.
>
> By now the development of large absentee-owned sugar estates, the rapid curtailment in the planting of coffee—the natural crop of the independent farmer—and the concentration of cigar manufacture into the hands of the American trust, have combined to make Porto Rico a land of beggars and millionaires, of flattering statistics and distressing realities. More and more it becomes a factory worked by peons, fought over by lawyers, bossed by absent industrialists, and clerked by politicians. It is now Uncle Sam's second largest sweat-shop.

Grim words indeed, but far from unjustified. The effect of the American ethos upon the Hispanic Catholic Philippines, Guam, and Puerto Rico was little short of catastrophic in many ways. Roads and schools were brought, indeed; but the things brought in by those roads, the curriculum taught in those schools vitiated many of the improvements the new regime brought. Certainly the secularization fostered by liberal Spanish regimes was speeded up tremendously.

In Hawaii the situation was a bit different, though not much. The Crown lands and Government lands of the Hawaiian Monarchy were taken over by the Federal government; the Hawaiian language was forbidden in the new Public Schools, and political and economic dominance passed into the hands of the owners of a few large sugar firms—the "Big Five."

Cuba was a different case entirely. Since the U.S. had gone to war against Spain ostensibly to free Cuba, annexation was out of the question. American occupation lasted from 1899 to 1902. During that time a constitutional convention was held, which designed a government modeled after that of the U.S. Separation of Church and State was hotly debated, but it was clear that the Americans wanted it; it was done. To this was added the "Platt Amendment" which provided "That the government of Cuba consents that the United States may exercise the right to intervene for the protection of Cuban independence, the maintenance of a government adequate for the protection of life, property, and individual liberty..." In other words, the U.S. government was given veto power over the Cuban—a tacit surrender of the nation's sovereignty to her northern neighbor.

Already in 1900, America's position as an Asian power had required her military intervention in the affairs of China. That Empire for the preceding half century had been increasingly enfeebled. Three Opium Wars fought with France and Britain, and a crushing defeat in 1895 by Japan had shown that the antiquated technology of the Middle Kingdom was no match for that of the West, which had been so successfully accepted by the Japanese. As a result, Treaty Ports through which trade was funneled with the outside world existed under European supervision; concessions in various major cities were administered by foreign powers; extraterritoriality ensured that the citizens of no less than 18 foreign nations were liable to be tried for crimes only under their own consular courts; there were ceded various ports outright to Great Britain, Russia, France, Germany, and Japan; and there was the dividing up of the country by those nations into economic and political spheres of influence, making a mockery of Chinese sovereignty, and seeming to threaten the very existence of the nation. To be sure, modern trade, industry, and above all, Christian missionary work of various sorts had been made possible by these developments; moreover, the U.S. had decisively intervened on China's behalf in 1899. This was the McKinley administration's backing of the *Open Door Policy*, which aimed at preventing spheres of influence from becoming outright colonies.

In 1898, the Chinese Emperor, Kwang-su, with a group of advisers (most notably *K'ang Yu-wei*, arguably one of the most interesting philosophers China has produced in centuries) wished to repeat the work of the Emperor Meiji in Japan. That ruler had overthrown the shogunate in Japan in 1867, beginning the "Meiji Restoration." Apart from restoring the role of the Emperor in the life of the nation, this involved ending the unequal treaties imposed upon Japan by the Europeans after the country was opened in 1854, and adopting enough of the new technology to make Japan a great power. All the while, however, the Japanese retained as much of their national tradition as they could.

This effort of Emperor Kwang-su was resisted by the Dowager Empress, who had the Emperor imprisoned and assumed direct control. Thus the last chance for China to modernize and retain cultural and political integrity was lost. Rather than attempt to use Western technology to bring China into equality peacefully and gradually, she resolved to attempt to eject the "Foreign Devils" militarily. Backing a secret society resolved to this end called "The Society of Harmonious Fists" (known more commonly in the West as "the Boxers"), the result was the Boxer rebellion.

On the eve of the Rebellion, Catholics in China had just received an important concession from the Imperial Chinese government. Negotiated by the French Legation (which held the protectorate over Catholic missions in China), the agreement conceded to Catholic bishops equal status with government mandarins. Thus Catholic missionaries and Chinese were the object of especial hatred by the Boxers. The beginning of the Rebellion was signaled by the murder of the German Ambassador, von Ketteler (a relation of the great Bishop) by a mob of Boxers in June 1900. The Foreign Legations at Peking and the Catholic Cathedral were besieged for 55 days, while foreigners and Chinese Christians were murdered throughout Northeast China, and their homes and churches sacked and burned. The defense of Bishop Favier and 3,400 lay Catholics (all save about a hundred of these being Chinese) shut up in the cathedral by 30 French and 13 Italian sailors is an epic of Catholic arms equivalent to anything in the pages of chivalry. Commanding this handful of sailors and the Chinese men they trained was a 23-year-old Breton officer named Paul Henry. Mortally wounded on July 30, he ought to be remembered as a true hero. There were no serious attempts to storm the cathedral after his death, although the bombardment continued.

At last, a 20,000-man international relief column set out from Tientsin. In its ranks were Japanese, Russians, French, British, Germans, Austrians, Italians, and 2,000 Americans. The siege was broken, the Boxers defeated, and the Imperial Court sent scurrying out of the city. Peace was negotiated. Among other things, twelve places between Peking and the coast were to be occupied by allied troops. Some of these would be American Marines; this would be our first permanent contingent of troops on the mainland of Asia—but not the last.

Much of Roosevelt's attention was taken up by events in Latin America. Internal unrest and successive incompetent regimes in various of those countries (often led by American-backed Liberals) had resulted in excessive debts to various European powers. As these last had carved up Africa and were doing so with Asia, so too did Latin America appear to be yet another avenue for expansion. Thus, Roosevelt declared the "Roosevelt Corollary to the Monroe Doctrine," which stated simply that the U.S. would intervene in any Latin American country to forestall occupation by outside powers.

The first test of American resolve was in December of 1902, when in response to Venezuelan dictator Cipriano Castro's attempt to renege on his foreign debt, Great Britain, Germany, and Italy blockaded the country's ports. Castro called on the United States, which prevailed upon the powers to withdraw and submit the problem to international arbitration. Three years later, when the Dominican Republic appeared to be similarly threatened, Roosevelt agreed by treaty to collect the customs and pay off the country's debts with them. When Congress refused to ratify the treaty, the President simply made it an executive order. The next year, Roosevelt and Mexican President Porfirio Diaz mediated a war between Guatemala, El Salvador, and Honduras.

But American intentions did not always appear so benevolent. In 1901 Colombia signed a treaty with the United States allowing the Americans to dig a canal across the isthmus of Panama, similar to that possessed by the British at Suez. But two years later, the Colombian Congress rejected the treaty. Immediately, an American inspired revolt broke out in Panama, and independence was declared on November 3, 1903. A convenient American gunboat prevented the landing of Colombian troops, and three days later the U.S. recognized Panama. A short twelve days after, a treaty was signed with the new government giving the U.S. the right to dig the Canal. A scant five years later, the Panama Canal Zone was given over to the United States. Coupled with the occupation of Cuba in accord with the Platt Amendment, Latin American opinion began to resent the United States tremendously.

Typical of anti-American critique was that of the Uruguayan *José Enrique Rodó* (1872-1917). In his 1900 work, *Ariel*, he contrasted the spirituality and culture of Latin America, which he likened to Shakespeare's Ariel, with what he considered to be U.S. materialism—Caliban. The Nicaraguan *Rubén Darío* (1867-1916) sounded a similar warning in his 1905 poetry collection, *Cantos de vida y esperanza* ("Songs of Life and Hope"). In this period, whether for religious, cultural, or political reasons, much of educated Latin America began to become anti-U.S. This would have far reaching political effects later.

Regardless of Latin American opinion, however, for the moment nothing was succeeding like success. Two occurrences pointed up America's new status as a world power. The first was Roosevelt's mediation of the Russo-Japanese War in 1905. His negotiation of the Treaty of Portsmouth allowed him to act as "honest broker" between

Russia and Japan (which peace, incidentally, marked the first defeat of a European power by an Asian one in modern war).

The second was our intervention in the affairs of Morocco. That nation being in a state of perpetual anarchy, the French, Spanish, British, and Germans were jockeying for position within its boundaries. In 1904 the American consul at Tangier, a Mr. Perdicaris, was kidnapped with his stepson by a Berber chieftain, the Raisouli. Roosevelt threatened to send in American troops, and popularized the slogan, "Perdicaris alive, or Raisouli dead!" In the end, 800 French troops took Tangier and secured the release of the captives (although a highly fictionalized 1975 movie about the incident, *The Wind and The Lion*, has Roosevelt actually sending in the Marines). Trivial as this episode might have been, when conflicts in Morocco between the powers seemed about to lead to war in 1906, American envoys were invited to the Algeciras Conference as a result. War was averted, but the U.S. appeared to lean toward the British and French, and against the Germans.

William Howard Taft

Roosevelt would not run in 1908, and so his Vice President, former Philippine Governor-General William Howard Taft accepted the Republican nomination. Running against William Jennings Bryan, Taft won easily. In foreign affairs, his administration continued Roosevelt's policies. Among other things, Nicaragua became a U.S. protectorate in 1911.

On the domestic scene, however, there were a number of differences. June 18, 1910 saw the passage of the Mann-Elkins Act, which extended the power of the Interstate Commerce Commission over telephones and telegraph, as well as increasing Federal control of railroad rates. But Roosevelt's skirmishing with the Trusts was called to a halt. A group of Republicans called Insurgents, and including such men as Senator La Follette of Wisconsin, stood for continued attack on the Trusts, creation of a Federal Income Tax as a way of tapping the wealth of the millionaires and corporations, and the like—many of which concerns they shared with the Democrats. As Taft's administration careened toward the election of 1912, relations with the insurgents grew ever more strained.

On a less controversial note, 1912 saw the admission of Arizona and New Mexico, both now with comfortable Anglo majorities, as states of the Union. There can be little doubt that their admission was so long delayed precisely so that they would not be Hispanic-majority States.

At the Republican Convention in Chicago on June 22, 1912, the Insurgents bolted the party; Taft was renominated by the remnant. Constituting themselves the Progressive Party, the Insurgents nominated

Theodore Roosevelt as their candidate for President. Meanwhile, the Democrats nominated *Woodrow Wilson*, former President of Princeton University, on a ticket advocating, among other things, Federal Income Tax and anti-trust legislation. Although the two Republican candidates between them garnered the most popular votes, Wilson had more than either, and as a result trounced them both on November 5.

THE REIGN OF WOODROW WILSON

Woodrow Wilson was, in terms of setting his mark upon the world, possibly the second most important president in our history, only behind FDR. Committed to a policy of strengthening Federal power at home and abroad, he was certainly one of the most successful; even things he failed to achieve later folk would obtain.

Even prior to Wilson's inauguration on March 4, 1913, an event occurred which would have far reaching effects on the country's future: this was passage of the Sixteenth Amendment to the Constitution, permitting the Federal Government to "lay and collect taxes on incomes from whatever source derived." Living as we do in a time when the Income Tax is so much a part of our lives; when April 15, the annual deadline for its filing, is a day which rivals Christmas, Thanksgiving, and Independence Day (although not, perhaps quite in the spirit of any of those days) for our attention; when wage-earners work 167 days a year to pay it; when the Internal Revenue Service is perhaps the single most spoken of governmental office, and the one with which we have most concern; that the Income Tax did not begin to exist (save as a measure of questionable legality during the Civil War) until 1913. Strange to say, government was able to go on somehow before its blessed emergence upon the scene.

It had been discussed during debate on the amendment, whether or not a ceiling of 10 percent ought to be put on this tax; the notion was rejected as being too high. Shortly after passage, Congress imposed a tax of 1 to 7 percent on income above $3,000 per individual. Income Tax was off and running, and would never look back. Although failing perhaps to do much save make life rather more frugal for segments of the Middle Class, it did at least give the Federal Government lots of extra cash which would soon be put to all sorts of creative uses. The irony is that while Wilson's administration was ostensibly committed to fighting trusts, it helped build the biggest and most powerful of them all.

The next great change in government was caused by the passing of the Seventeenth Amendment on May 31. This provided for direct election of Senators by the people, rather than by the state governments; this measure had been sought by professional reformers for some time.

In appearance democratic, it was instead the final nail in the Constitution's coffin.

Why? To begin with, the whole point of the Senate had been to give the then-sovereign states a check on the power of their instrument, the Federal Government. Removal of this last bit of power from them destroyed this. Moreover, where Representatives, responsible as they are to 20,000 or fewer individuals, are susceptible to pressure by them (and also have them as support in the face of special interests and lobbying), the popularly elected Senator would have to look to the entire population of a state. In practical terms he would be alike free from their pressure and bereft of their support. Since State government was no longer a stepping-stone to the Senate, fewer men of ability bothered with it, preferring to play a larger role in Washington. Thus the Governor's Mansions and Statehouses began to attract even more of their share of demagogues, incompetents, and ignoramuses. Of course, the change in the Senate also ensured that men rooted in their communities and states, with high ideals (whatever they may have been) like Calhoun, Webster, and Clay were less likely to run for the Senate. After all, such men often do not have the charisma necessary to be elected.

The last great event of 1913 was the passage on December 23 of the Federal Reserve Bank Act, which established the institution giving the bill its name. This would be a central bank, made up of member banks, which as a private institution (rather than a part of the government) would have control of the nation's money supply—in a word, of one of the most important parts of a government's sovereignty. Thus Congress surrendered to private bankers its right to coin money, an act plainly unconstitutional. From that day to this, the basic tone of the economy is in the keeping of folk who are not elected by nor responsible to the people of this country.

The results of these three acts would not be apparent for years, and even decades to come. But the Federal Government which rang out the year 1913 was quite a different entity from that which rang it in. Had Wilson's administration been unmarked by further activity, it would yet have carved its mark in our history. Nevertheless, further adventures waited in the wings.

Foreign Entanglements

Although Wilson had pledged himself to dealing honestly with the Latin Americans, he felt it necessary to order the occupations of Haiti in 1914 and the Dominican Republic the next year. In both cases civil government had broken down and payment of debts ceased. American forces were intended to keep the peace and reorganize those countries' political systems.

More fearsome was Wilson's dealing with Mexico. In 1913, Mexican anti-clerical President Francisco Madero, heir to the revolution which forced Porfirio Diaz into exile, was murdered during a coup, and succeeded by General Victoriano Huerta (who was somewhat friendlier to Catholics). Wilson much objected to Huerta's manner of obtaining power, and refused to recognize him.

Tensions mounted, and after an incident at Tampico, Wilson ordered the American fleet to bombard the port of Vera Cruz (where German arms were to be landed for Huerta) on April 21, 1914. The Marines then seized the city amidst much bloodshed. Argentina, Brazil, and Chile offered mediation, which Wilson accepted. In July, Huerta was deposed.

Mexico fell into ever deeper anarchy, however; raiding bands terrorized the countryside. One such, led by Pancho Villa, crossed the border and killed 18 Americans in Columbus, New Mexico on March 9, 1916. Public outrage was enormous, and Wilson sent cavalry after Villa, commanded by General John J. Pershing. They failed to get Villa, but they did manage to show the usefulness of cavalry in modern guerrilla warfare when accompanied with aerial reconnaissance. In any case, all such concerns were about to be subsumed in a greater struggle.

The World at War

Since 1890, Europe had been polarizing around two blocs: the Triple Alliance, consisting of Germany, Austria-Hungary, and Italy, on the one hand, and the Triple Entente, Great Britain, France, and Russia, on the other. Germany and Britain opposed each other in Africa and on the high seas, where German naval expansion was threatening British supremacy; Germany and France had unsettled business remaining from the 1870-71 Franco-Prussian War (most notably German occupation of Alsace-Lorraine), as well as colonial conflicts; and Austria-Hungary and Russia were jockeying for position in the Balkans. Italy's adherence to the Triple Alliance was purely in hopes of gaining in any partition of the tottering Ottoman Empire, whose Sultans vied with the Chinese Emperors in ever-weakening response to European encroachments.

While the French Third Republic was anti-clerical and Freemasonic, the five monarchies involved had governments and bureaucracies which, apart from being subject to many of the same influences as dominated the French, were increasingly difficult for those countries' traditional rulers and nobility to dominate. In the case of Italy there was no attempt to, the House of Savoy being established on a Liberal base anyway. In Great Britain, of course, the King had long been a figurehead; 1911 saw the final deliverance of governing power into the hands of the professional politicos and bureaucrats by the stripping of the veto from the House of Lords.

The peoples of Europe, in addition, had become extremely nationalistic, ready to be led into warlike conflict as a result of the same sort of journalism which contributed so heavily to our entering the Spanish-American War. They were ready for excitement, for action. They soon would have it.

The assassination of the Archduke Franz Ferdinand, heir to the Austrian throne, and his wife on June 28, 1914, set in motion a series of events which seemed unstoppable. They were killed by Serb nationalists in Sarajevo, Bosnia. It should be borne in mind that Serbia was an anarchic state in those days. King Alexander and his Queen had been murdered in a 1903 coup. The man responsible for the coup (and chief of Serbian intelligence) was behind the recalling from exile of King Peter I, head of a rival dynasty. This same intelligence chief was the guiding force behind the Black Hand, the group which killed the Archduke.

Having determined this, the Austrian government presented Serbia with an ultimatum on July 23. It required that within 48 hours, Serbia: suppress publications hostile to Austria; dissolve organizations propagandizing against Austria; eliminate such propaganda from their schools; remove all officials from the government whom Austria charged with distributing such propaganda; collaborate with Austrian officials sent to Serbia for the purpose of suppressing these groups; initiate judicial action against the plotters of June 28; arrest two Serbian officials; prevent arms from crossing the Austrian border; and apologize. The Serbs agreed to all conditions save the sending of Austrian officials, without which Vienna believed no real investigation would be undertaken.

Through the months of July and August, events moved quickly; Serbia refused to accept the Austrian officials, resulting in a declaration of war by Austria. Russia, Serbia's ally, then declared war on Austria. Germany, Austria's ally, replied in kind, only to have Russia's ally France do the same. The Germans had long planned, in the event of war, to invade France through Belgium, as their common frontier was heavily fortified on both sides; the one catch was that Prussia (Germany's predecessor in diplomatic affairs) had agreed to safeguard Belgium's neutrality in 1830. So had Britain, which gave the British a reason to declare war on Germany. The intricate network of European alliances, the desire of lesser cogs in the military-industrial complexes of each nation to solve internal social stresses through warfare, and, one suspects a grand strategy on the part of certain unnamables, all coalesced to bring about the conflagration so narrowly averted over the past two decades in

Morocco and the Balkans. Franz Josef of Austria-Hungary, Wilhelm II of Germany, George V of Great Britain, and Nicholas II of Russia all looked on in horror as the governmental structures over which they nominally presided carried them and their subjects into a general conflagration.

German troops crossed the Belgian frontier on August 3; by September 6 they had arrived at the Marne river outside Paris. Forced back from this highwater-point, they took up entrenched positions, and settled down into trench warfare. In the trenches, all the 19th Century panoply of war was dissolved by mud and barbed wire, and ever newer and more devilish inventions—machine-guns, poison gas, tanks—each of which was supposed to end the deadlock, and did not. Aeroplanes and dirigibles brought warfare to the skies, and rained death down upon innocent civilians; submarines brought the same terror to the high seas. To a European population schooled in the optimism and decorum of the Edwardian era, sure that the growth of technology could only bring a better life, the disillusionment was perhaps unthinkable to those of us who have grown up watching such things every night on television.

Moreover, in the first weeks of the war, the finest young men in every country rushed forward to join the colors. They in turn were the ones sent "over the top," in fruitless attempt after fruitless attempt to break through enemy trenches. *Rupert Brooke*, a handsome English poet, was seen in his death to represent the death of the flower of his generation. But it was not only he; so died the Frenchman, *Charles Peguy*; the Italian, *Giosué Borsi*; and innumerable other writers and artists. Many who survived were embittered by the experience; those who lived through it would often later feel a camaraderie (and a corresponding hatred of the politicians who had sent them) which transcended national boundaries.

The fight was not confined to the Western Front. Austria and Germany together fought Russia in Poland, Galicia, and East Prussia. Bulgaria would join them in defeating Serbia, while Italy entered the war on the side of the Allies in hopes of taking Tyrol and Dalmatia from Austria. The Ottoman Empire came in for Germany and Austria, and would suffer Russian invasion on her northern border, and the conquest of Iraq, Palestine, and Syria by British Empire and French forces. Seeking to take Constantinople, British, Australian and New Zealand (Anzac), and French troops landed at the Gallipoli peninsula, gateway to the Turkish straits. It was a dismal failure; but from this debacle emerged Australian and New Zealand national identities.

Elsewhere in the world, war raged. The German colonies in Africa were conquered by British, French, and South African troops—although Von Lettow-Vorbeck, commander in German East Africa (now

Tanzania), driven out of his own territory, led the Allied forces a merry chase down through Mozambique, back up through the Belgian Congo, and back at last to German East Africa (in the end, he held out until after the Armistice, becoming the only German general never to surrender). Anzac forces seized German New Guinea and the Solomon Islands, while the Japanese drove them from their Chinese city of Tsingtao and the Pacific Islands of Micronesia. Above all, German U-Boats menaced Allied shipping.

Both Germans and British had declared war zones around the territorial waters of their opponents, through which neutral shipping would not be permitted to pass. This was in clear violation of the laws of neutrality accepted by all civilized nations. After August, 1914, the British began to seize American ships.

While German and Irish Americans were desirous of maintaining neutrality, the fact remained that we were an English-speaking nation, and the sympathies of many were with the British. Certainly Wilson's were, as were those of his chief adviser, Colonel *Edward Mandell House*. Nevertheless, officially at least, Wilson had to maintain an appearance of impartiality toward the two sides, particularly since both were interfering with our shipping. This was why in 1916 legislation was passed that would make our navy "second to none."

The United States exported badly needed foodstuffs, munitions, and other things to the Allies. The result was that in 1916, America ceased to be a debtor nation and became a creditor nation. New York succeeded the City of London as the major gold center and exchange market of the world. This change meant that the world's economic focus had shifted from Europe to this country. A new era in the world's history had begun.

In the meantime, however, Wilson and House were desirous of entering the war against the Central Powers:

> It is apparent that the United States drifted into war with Germany because the Department of State condemned German submarine warfare as inhuman and illegal. It is not so well known that Robert Lansing, the counselor of the Department of State, was badly confused in his controversy with the German Government concerning this submarine warfare. On February 4, 1915, the German Foreign Office announced the establishment of a war zone around the British Isles. In this war zone after February 18 all "enemy merchant vessels" would be destroyed without much regard for the safety of the passengers and the crew. In a sharp note of February 10, 1915, the Department of State protested against the sinking of any merchant ships without the usual preliminary visit and search, and it gave a distinct warning that the German Government would be held to a "strict accountability" for every injury inflicted upon American citizens.

Professor Borchard has clearly demonstrated that this acrid note of February 10 was based upon an incorrect interpretation of international law. After discussing the background of the submarine controversy, he remarks: "It is thus apparent that the first American protest on submarines on February 10, 1915, with its challenging 'strict accountability,' was founded on the false premise that the United States was privileged to speak not only for American vessels and their personnel, but also on behalf of American citizens on Allied and other vessels. No other neutral country appears to have fallen into this error."

It is remarkable that Mr. Lansing, as the counselor of the Department of State, should have drafted a note so patently incorrect in its interpretation of the law of nations. Before entering upon his official duties in the Department of State, he had for many years been engaged in the practice of international law. He was quite familiar with American precedents and practices, and it is quite mystifying to find that at one of the great crossroads in American history a presumably competent lawyer should give the President and the Secretary of State a legal opinion that would have shamed a novice.

Having made a fundamental error in his interpretation of international law with reference to submarine attacks upon *unarmed* merchant vessels of the Allied powers, he then hastened to make another error with regard to attacks upon *armed* merchantmen. It was Mr. Lansing's contention, and therefore that of President Wilson, that German submarines should not sink Allied armed merchant ships without first giving a warning that would permit the passengers and crew ample time to disembark with safety. The German Foreign Office hastened to point out that armed merchantmen would take advantage of this procedure to fire upon and destroy the undersea craft. For a brief period in January and February, 1916, Mr. Lansing, Secretary of State since June 1915, accepted the German contention and the Department of State was ready to insist that Allied merchant ships either go unarmed or take the consequences. But Lansing, upon the insistence of Colonel House, retreated from the sound position he had temporarily assumed and once more asserted with vehemence that armed merchantmen were not vessels of war that could be sunk at sight. Thus, by reason of Secretary Lansing's final opinion, the President "and the House and Senate also, were misled into taking a position which had no foundation either in law or common sense. Yet on that hollow platform Wilson stood in defending the immunity from attack of British armed merchantmen and of American citizens on board."

It is thus clear that America drifted into war in 1917 either because the chief legal adviser in the Department of State made fundamental errors of interpretation which a mere student of international law could have avoided, or because the adviser wanted a war with Germany and therefore purposely wrote erroneous opinions. These facts completely destroy the old popular thesis that America went to war in protest against German barbarities on the high seas (Charles Callan Tansill, *Back Door To War*, pp.7-9).

Wilson came up for reelection in November of 1916. With the catchy slogan "He kept us out of war," he retained his hold, defeating Republican Charles Evans Hughes. Although some Dominicans, Haitians, and Mexicans (particularly those of the latter who had "heard Woodrow Wilson's guns," as Warren Zevon put it in his song, *Vera Cruz*) might have found the President somewhat less pacific, it was primarily on his record as a peace-keeper and the presumption that he would so continue that he was returned to office.

He had other intentions, however, as did Col. House. House is a key figure to understanding the Wilson Administration. Where Wilson appears to have been a college professor in love with high-sounding slogans, House appears to have had a genuine agenda. So much, indeed, does he seem to have had one, that conspiracy theorists of all sorts have depicted him as the evil genius of the administration, whose desire was simply to put the huge resources of the United States completely at the disposal of those who would destroy traditional values both at home and abroad. It would be useful (particularly in the light of House's connection with Lansing's alteration of opinion just mentioned) to look at the description of House's novel (in which he sets forth his political ideals) given by noted historian and philosopher John Dos Passos, a man whose interest in the truth of the matter can scarce be doubted:

> This fantasy, a daydream remarkably boyish to be the work of a man of fifty, was eventually published, anonymously of course, by Ben Huebsch under the title of *Philip Dru, Administrator*.
>
> It is a rather awkward story, set ten years forward in the nineteen-twenties, of a civil war between progressive and reactionary forces in the United States. The hero is a lithe young West Pointer named Philip Dru whose army career is cut short by a case of heat prostration contracted while riding out in the Mexican Desert with a highly imaginary young lady named Gloria. During his convalescence the hero lives over a hardware store on the lower East Side of New York and absorbs the mystique of the coming European revolution from a Jewish idealist who escaped from Polish pogroms to take refuge in America. Meanwhile Gloria, who has taken up settlement house work, tells him of a Senator Selwyn's conspiracy, backed by a fund raised by a thousand multimillionaires, to take over the United States Government in the interests of the rich.
>
> Senator Selwyn bears a more than accidental resemblance to Senator Nelson W. Aldrich of Rhode Island who, as sponsor of the Payne-Aldrich Tariff so hated in the south and west, was the bugbear good Democrats and Progressives used to frighten naughty children

with. Senator Aldrich, able, ruthless, and thoroughly convinced of the Godgiven right of the Moneymen to rule, led the standpat forces which had taken over Taft's indecisive administration. In the story, House, as a science fiction touch, has his Senator Selwyn imprudently dictate his conspiratorial plans into a dictaphone. Dru, who has become a journalist for the muckraking press, gets hold of the guilty cylinder and forms a committee to fight for freedom and right. With Gloria raising money from the Pinchots and Walter Perkinses among the millionaires, Philip Dru becomes the leader of outraged democracy. Civil war breaks out. Transformed into a general of Napoleonic scope, he defeats the army of capitalist privilege and marches on Washington.

Wearing Dru's fictional cloak, House simplifies the legal code and repeals unnecessary laws. He institutes a graduated income tax. He borrows a land tax on unimproved land from Henry George. He centralizes government administration, takes the currency out of the hands of the bankers, regulates public utilities and bans holding companies.

For the benefit of the workingman he sets up state employment agencies, old age insurance, workingmen's compensation for accidents. Labor is to be represented in management and to share in the profits of industry.

He institutes cooperative financing and marketing for the farmer.

He rewrites the Constitution. The President with a ten year term becomes a mere head of state but an Executive is chosen by the House of Representatives and is responsible to the House. Party government in the English style. Senators are elected for life subject to recall every five years.

Having reformed the government to Colonel House's satisfaction the hero resigns his powers and fades away in a rosy haze with the beautiful Gloria (*Mr. Wilson's War*, pp. 61-62).

This novel illustrates well Col. House's agenda; it became Wilson's as well. Beneath the high-sounding phraseology, the objects were clear: revolution abroad, and the overthrow of monarchy and all traditional life there; domestic centralization and the reduction of all Americans to dependence upon the Central Government—guided by "enlightened" figures. Such was the policy of our government—and it included perforce war with the Central Powers.

The War in the meantime was demanding of the belligerents on both sides oceans of blood and mountains of treasure. In Russia, perhaps least suited of all the combatants to modern war, conditions were so bad that revolution was ignited. On March 12, 1917, Tsar Nicholas II abdicated, and the Provisional Government of Russia (headed first by Prince George Lvov and then by Alexander Kerensky) took power, promising to continue their country's participation in the war. That same month an alleged telegram to the German ambassador in Mexico from the German

Foreign Office proposing a German alliance against the U.S. with Japan (which had conquered so many German possessions in China and the Pacific), and Mexico (which had collapsed in anarchy) was delivered to Wilson. Although the doubtful possibility of such an alliance has led many to question the reality of the Zimmermann Telegram, it was seized upon by President Wilson as a cause of war. Together with the attacks on merchant shipping, it was used by him in his address to Congress on April 2, asking for a declaration of war against Germany.

For four days, the Senate debated. In the end, six senators voted against war, one abstained, and the remainder voted for it. Two of those against were Progressives George W. Norris of Nebraska and Robert M. La Follette of Wisconsin. Norris pointed out in his April 4 speech that both sides had behaved similarly toward neutral shipping, but that the Wilson Administration's one-sided reaction had done little to restore freedom of the seas. Moreover, he added, war would only benefit Wall Street, whereupon he quoted a letter from a prominent member of the stock exchange contending that war would be good for business.

La Follette, in turn, spoke of the wishes of most Americans not to enter into the conflict. He added:

> Any war with Germany, or with any other country for that matter, would be bad enough, but there are not words strong enough to voice my protest against the proposed combination with the Entente Allies.
>
> When we cooperate with those governments, we endorse their methods; we endorse the violations of international law by Great Britain; we endorse the shameful methods of warfare against which we have again and again protested in this war; we endorse her purpose to wreak upon the German people the animosities which for years her people have been taught to cherish against Germany; finally, when the end comes, whatever it may be, we find ourselves in cooperation with our ally, Great Britain, and if we cannot now resist the great pressure she is exerting to carry us into the war, how can we hope to resist, then, the greater pressure she will exert to bend us to her purposes and compel compliance with her demands?

Where La Follette made one error, however, was to suppose that Wilson was being forced or cajoled to bring the U.S. into the war. As would soon be made evident, our entrance into the conflict would make us masters of the peace, and end the dominance of old Europe. In bringing the United States into Europe, the Allies were dooming themselves quite as much as their enemies.

Although the first American troops would not reach the trenches in France until October, Wilson almost immediately became the effective leader of the Allies. This was shown in August, when Pope Benedict XV issued an appeal for peace, which may be read in Appendix. The response of the various governments to this proposal is most instructive. The Germans showed some interest; the Austro-Hungarian Emperor-King, Charles I (who came to the throne the previous year after the death of Franz Josef) was extremely enthusiastic—he immediately began to attempt peace negotiations. But Wilson would have none of it. In the words of Dos Passos:

> The gist of [Wilson's reply] was that although he refused to believe that the word of the present German Government could be trusted, he hoped to help negotiate with some eventual German Government which really represented the German people, an equitable peace.
> "The object of this war," Wilson wrote, "is to deliver the free peoples of the world from the menace and actual power of a vast military establishment controlled by an irresponsible government. The enemy was not the German people but their "ruthless masters." (pp. 281-282).

Supposedly, our reason for going to war had been to ensure freedom of the seas; Wilson transformed it into a holy crusade which would not end until the Government of Germany was deposed. Although we have become used to such things, the fact remains that at the time such a war to the finish was unheard of. So the war must go on, and the Pope could whistle.

What was the reaction of America's Catholics to this cavalier disregard of the Papal peace plan? None. As in all this nation's wars, Catholics flocked to the colors. The "fighting 69th," a mostly Irish regiment of New York Infantry served gallantly in France, chaplained by the famed Fr. Duffy. In its ranks fell Catholic convert poet, *Joyce Kilmer*. On August 11 and 12, 1917, a general convention of Catholics was held in Washington under the auspices of the hierarchy to organize the National Catholic War Council, which would mobilize Catholics behind the war effort. Intended as an emergency organization for the duration, it would become (as the National Catholic Welfare Council) a permanent fixture. One day, it would outrank the hierarchy.

American troops at last arrived in France and were deployed. Although relatively few in number, they were enthusiastic combatants, and demonstrated their bravery in places like the Argonne Forest. Despite its size, the American Expeditionary Force under General Pershing decisively tipped the balance in favor of the Allies.

Meanwhile, the continuing conflict brought the new Russian government to the breaking point. On November 7, Kerensky was deposed in Petrograd by the Bolsheviks led by *Vladimir Lenin*. Within the month, the new regime began negotiations with the Central Powers for peace.

On January 8, 1918, Wilson at last unveiled in a speech before Congress a set of principles for negotiation: the fourteen points, as seen in Appendix P. The last point, dealing with the establishment of what became the League of Nations, Wilson claimed, was "the moral climax... of the culminating and final war for human liberty."

Although Russia had collapsed, with the Ukraine, Finland, Poland, the Baltic States, and various other sections seceding, and although a draconian treaty would be signed by the Bolsheviks with the Central Powers on March 3, those same powers were teetering toward economic collapse.

The result was to lead both Germany and Austria to attempt to negotiate on the basis of the 14 points. November 1917 saw Germany's first Catholic Chancellor, philosopher and politician, *Georg Count von Hertling*, appointed. In his first speech he indicated a willingness to conclude a peace based upon Wilson's points, and the integrity of the Empire. Charles of Austria proposed turning his Empire into a federation, in accord with Point X; to no avail. Wilson was determined that the war must go on.

At last, the Bulgarian front collapsed, and it was apparent that the separatists of Austria-Hungary and the Republicans of Germany alone had Wilson's ear, and alone would thus be able to bring peace to their shattered nations. Meanwhile, Civil War between Reds and Whites had broken out in Russia, and American and many other troops were dispatched there.

The Emperors Charles and Wilhelm left their countries, and Austria-Hungary dissolved. On November 11, at 11 A.M., 1918, an Armistice came into effect. But although the hostilities were over in the West, they were just beginning in the East. The withdrawal of German troops meant that all the emerging nationalities there would fight one another and the Red Russians; boundaries would not settle down until 1922, amid incredible carnage.

Still, November 11, ("Armistice Day" in British Commonwealth countries, and among us until after World War II, when it became "Veterans' Day") would be marked in many nations by the wearing of orange poppies (often of paper), minute silences, and ceremonies at Tombs of the Unknown Soldier which were built. It is a good thing to mark this day, even if one did not lose an ancestor in this war; in it died, alongside ten million people on both sides, what remained of Christendom; Wilson and his allies insisted upon four things. One was exclusion of Benedict XV, with his quaint religious notions of forgiveness from the peace process. Secondly, Germany's republican status, thus ensuring in that country a political power vacuum. Third was enormous territorial reductions of that country, as well as cash reparations which simply could not be paid; the bitterness this fostered would not soon go away. These two points would keep Germany a potential source of future conflict.

The fourth point was the dismemberment of Austria-Hungary, and insistence that the Habsburgs could never again rule any portion of their ancient lands. In this we see the ideology of Colonel House; for the League of Nations, based as it was upon a purely humanistic (not to say Masonic) basis, as the prototype of the Universal Republic so beloved of the Founding Fathers, was unalterably opposed to the kind of unity represented by the Habsburgs: the *Res Publica Christiana*, Christendom, the Sacred or Holy Empire. Gary Potter defines it admirably in modern terms (*In Reaction*, p. 55):

> Words express ideas, and some of them now being quoted signify notions likely to be totally foreign to anyone unfamiliar with history prior to a few decades ago: "world emperor," "imperial office," ... This is not the place to lay out all the history needed to be known for thoroughly grasping the notions. However, the principal one was adumbrated by Our Lord Himself in the last command His followers received from Him: to make disciples of *all* the nations. In a word, the idea of a universal Christian commonwealth is what we are talking about.
>
> To date it has never existed. Today there is not even a Christian government anywhere. However, from the conversion of Constantine until August, 1806—with an interruption (in the West) from Romulus Augustulus in 475 to Charlemagne in 800—there was *the* Empire. It was the heart of what was once known as Christendom. Under its aegis serious European settlement of the Western Hemisphere began, and the Americas' native inhabitants first baptized, which is why the feathered cloak of Montezuma is in a museum in Vienna. After 1806 a kind of shadow of the Empire, the Austro-Hungarian one, endured until the end of World War I, when its abolition was imposed as a condition of peace by U.S. President Woodrow Wilson. Since 1438, when Albert V... was crowned Roman Emperor, all the Emperors were Habsburgs. The last was Archduke Otto's father, Charles.

The wearing of poppies on Armistice Day serves as well to mourn for Christendom, as for Grandpa John, or Great-Great Uncle Albert.

Thus far, we have seen few great leaders in connection with this war. But seeing that one of them may have been a saint, it would be wise to take a closer look at him, in Appendix Q.

The Aftermath in America

On July 10, 1919, the Versailles Treaty was submitted to the Senate. Wilson took his case to the people in a series of speaking engagements. But the ruin caused by the war and our part in it spurred a backlash. The idea of becoming a permanent fixture on the European and world scene via the new League of Nations was repugnant to the majority of the people. Wilson faced much opposition; the strain took a toll on him, and he was taken ill on September 25. He would be unable to meet with his cabinet until April 14, 1920; his wife and Colonel House were the virtual regents until then.

Meanwhile, the Prohibition Movement had gathered strength during the war. While Wilson was being lionized as a victor at Versailles, the 18th Amendment had been passed, prohibiting the manufacture and sale of intoxicating liquors (which had already been done as a war measure; allegedly the alcohol was required for explosives); the so-called "noble experiment" had begun. A year to the day it took effect.

On March 19, 1920, the Versailles Treaty was rejected by the Senate. The country was in no mood to deal further in European affairs. Indeed, so fearful were Americans of foreigners in general that the Ku-Klux-Klan revived to combat them, blacks, Catholics, and Jews. Industrial strife, complete with strikes and lock-outs grew ever more serious. Exhausted, mainstream America wanted to return to the days before the war.

Of course, this was not possible. To deal with changed conditions, the Catholic bishops of the United States issued a Program of Social Reconstruction. Written by Msgr. John Ryan, it attempted to apply the social teachings in an American context. Hence it called for, among other things, labor participation in industrial management, housing projects for the working class, minimum wage, reduction of the cost of living, social insurance, and an end to child labor. The program concluded in the following manner:

> "Society," said Leo XIII, "can be healed in no other way than by a return to Christian life and Christian institutions." The truth of these words is more widely perceived today than when they were written more than twenty-seven years ago. Changes in our economic and political systems will have only partial and feeble efficiency if they be not reinforced by the Christian view of work and wealth.
>
> Neither the moderate reforms advocated in this paper nor any other program of betterment or reconstruction will prove reasonably effective without a reform in the spirit of both labor and capital. The laborer must come to realize that he owes his employer and society an honest day's work for a fair wage, and that conditions cannot be

substantially improved until he roots out the desire to get a maximum of return for a minimum of service. The capitalist must likewise get a new viewpoint. He needs to learn the long-forgotten truth that wealth is stewardship, that profitmaking is not the basic justification of business enterprise, and that there are such things as fair profits, fair interest, and fair prices. Above and before all, he must cultivate and strengthen within his mind the truth which many of his class have begun to grasp for the first time during the present war; namely, that the laborer is a human being, not merely an instrument of production; and that the laborer's right to a decent livelihood is the first moral charge upon industry.

The employer has a right to get a reasonable living out of his business, but he has no right to interest on his investment until his employees have at least obtained living wages. This is the human and Christian, in contrast to the purely commercial and pagan, ethics of industry.

So far, so good. But where the Bishops' Program differed from Papal teaching was in its silence regarding the proper place of the Church in society. What was here proposed was fine; but the values it promoted, if ever they are to be more than pious aspirations, require an explicit recognition—not of some vague Christianity—but of the One True Church. The problem for Msgr. Ryan and those for whom he wrote this program was the same problem which must assail anyone who attempts to embrace both Christendom and Naturalism—driving a round peg into a square hole.

Whatever the concerns of Catholics, however, most residents of the now dry country wanted only to forget the horrors of war, for all that they had touched us but little. In November of 1920, they elected Warren Gamaliel Harding, a Republican who promised a return to "Normalcy." After his inauguration on March 4, 1921, he declared that he would enforce economy in government, lower the tax burden, and raise tariffs.

But the America which Harding presided over was quite different from that of Wilson's first inaugural. Not only had thousands of Americans been uprooted from their neighborhoods and thrown together, here and abroad; women had achieved the vote with the Nineteenth Amendment, and radio had been developed in the war to the point where it would soon join the movies as a means of mass entertainment. In Russia, the Whites had been defeated, and the Reds promised to export their revolution all over the world. Ties of blood, rank, and locale were weakened tremendously.

If the new administration did not care to use the leverage in world affairs given them by the country's new found economic supremacy, that supremacy was not about to cease. In truth, Britain and France had lost the World War almost as badly as Austria and Germany. This would become apparent in the years to follow.

Most Americans, though, were not that concerned about such problems. Of greater importance were the daring new fashions and dances; the Gibson Girl with her long hair done up, her long full-figured dresses, and her lady-like bashfulness was about to be replaced by the boyish, breezy flapper. Above all, in 1921, most of America wondered where their next drink would be coming from. They need not have worried; men like Al Capone and Joe Kennedy would soon be supplying their requirements.

ISOLATION AND THE RISE OF FASCISM
1922-1929

THE ROARING TWENTIES

The post-war world (and these United States which formed an important portion of it) are inscribed in our cultural memory. The Charleston, bathtub gin, raccoon coats, jazz, Betty Boop, "Bright Young Things," and much beside have all contributed to an image of wild frivolity and sudden liberation. There was, to be sure, some truth to this notion, but only some.

The experiences of the War had led many to question the accepted beliefs of their raising, as ever war will. The ideas of *Sigmund Freud,* the Viennese psychologist who claimed that all mental illness was the result of sexual repression (this is a crude oversimplification, to be sure, but it adequately represents what many people *thought* Freud was saying) weakened the morals of many, and gave justification to many more who were looking to have them weakened.

The gaining of the vote for American women launched the "New Woman." Self-reliant, wise-cracking, equal to men in every way, the New Woman bobbed her hair, shortened her skirt to her thighs, and flattened her figure, all the while smoking cigarettes. From the ashes of the Gibson Girl emerged, phoenix-like, the Flapper. Hard-drinking and hard-living, she embodied the "Jazz Age," as the era was called. In the wild abandon of the Charleston, she found her element. A softened amusing send-up of the type may be seen in the 1968 musical comedy, *Thoroughly Modern Millie.*

Prohibition, intended as it was to cure drunkenness by outlawing demon rum, had in fact the opposite effect. For a whole new class of criminals arose, the bootleggers, to provide America the alcoholic relief she required. Although some of this activity was undertaken by light-hearted amateurs out for fun, bootlegging established such organized crime figures as *Al Capone.* Rival gangs in cities like Chicago fought for control of liquor-sales and gambling, shooting one another and buying off police and politicians. The Mafia was launched, and an element of lawlessness entered into American life which had not been seen since the settling of the frontier, and which has not yet left it.

The growth of the automobile, the radio, and the movies contributed to national conformity, while post-war prosperity gave a feeling of excitement to the big cities. During the Twenties, Hollywood emerged as a center of entertainment, and Valentino led his short but wild career. Writers and actors of a leftish cast thronged New York's Greenwich Village, while nearby Wall Street boomed. It was the age of *F. Scott Fitzgerald, Damon Runyon,* and *Thorne Smith.*

But in the midst of all the fun, darker currents flowed. The revolution in Russia, horror at the horrors of war, fear of the labor movement, and more such events caused not only fear of Communist infiltration, but a hatred of all things foreign. In 1921 and 1923, laws were passed virtually eliminating immigration from abroad. This, however, hardly affected "furriners" already here. To combat their influence, the Ku-Klux-Klan revived.

Just as big in the North as the South, the newborn Klan disliked foreigners of all sorts, blacks, Jews, and of course, Catholics. A delicate rhyme of theirs from the era sums up their opinions in the latter case:

> I'd rather be a Klansman, in robes of snowy white,
> Than be a Roman Catholic, in robes as black as night.
> For a Klansman is an American, and America is his home;
> But a Catholic owes allegiance to the Dago Pope of Rome.

So great was their power and influence in the early 20s that President Harding himself (ever a joiner of groups like the Elks and the Red Men) was initiated into the Klan in the White House. So too was a future Supreme Court Justice named Hugo Black.

The 20s, however, were far from being a pure amalgam of gangsterism and Klansmen. Perhaps the most representative figure to emerge from the period's literature was Babbitt, from the novel of the same name by *Sinclair Lewis*. A resident of the "up-and-coming" Midwestern town of Zenith, Babbitt was held up as an example of the loss of individuality and creativity supposed to result from thinking solely about business, the Rotary Club, and conformism. The word passed into English; "he's a real Babbitt" still implies that a person is at once a boor and a bore.

Babbitt was, to be sure, a proud descendant of the Puritans, at least in spirit. 1920s criticism kept up a continual barrage against the hapless Puritan, albeit often for the wrong reasons. H. L. Mencken continued to lambaste the "Booboisie," as he referred to the Babbitts and Puritans, first in the pages of *The Smart Set*, and then from 1924 to 1933 as editor of the *American Mercury*. His trenchant criticisms of the follies of the day remain excellent examples of fine essay-writing.

Mencken was one of thirty three contributors to a 1922 collection of essays edited by *Harold Stearns*, entitled *Civilization in the United States:*

Page after page detailed a shallow community life, the absence of democracy, the lack of fit between techniques and ideals, a culture that failed to engage the best minds, and a business-dominated civilization that sanctioned acquisitive materialism. Although in his introduction he denied a muckraking intent, Stearns drew three major indictments. First, the ideals and practices of the culture did not coincide, producing not a general feeling of hypocrisy but a fear of being found out. To this sure sign of decadence Stearns added the widespread delusion that the nation ws predominantly Anglo-Saxon. Since Stearns used "Anglo-Saxon" as a term of derision, a synonym for dull, predictable, stodgy, limited, and repressed, the pretense of cultural uniformity by his lights had disastrous consequences for valuable diversity. Finally, Stearns saw social life as "emotional and aesthetic starvation, of which the mania for petty regulation, the driving, regimenting, and drilling, the secret society and its grotesque regalia, the firm grasp on the unessentials of material organization of our pleasures and gaieties are all eloquent stigmata. We have no heritages or traditions to which to cling except those that have already withered in our hands and turned to dust. One can feel the whole industrial and economic situation as so maladjusted to the primary and simple needs of men and women that the futility of a rationalistic attack on these infantilisms of compensation becomes obvious" (Daniel H. Borus, ed., *These United States*, p. 19).

These criticisms were echoed in various ways by the contributors. Interestingly enough, where Lewis was considered a liberal, Stearns was deemed conservative. He was in any case a product of Harvard, and a school of criticism which had developed there about 1910; this was the much ballyhooed "New Humanism."

Led by such men as the ironically named *Irving Babbitt, Paul Elmer More, Norman Foerster*, and *Robert Shafer*, the New Humanists considered that every civilization needed to strive for the ultimate good (although they could not agree as to what that was—Babbitt, for example, seeking refuge in a kind of neo-Buddhism). Art, so long as it was oriented toward that good, had moral authority in a culture. The New Humanists believed in what they called "Classical" restraint, as against "Romantic excess." While Mencken lampooned them mercilessly, they did influence one other important figure besides Stearns—*T.S. Eliot.*

Heavily influenced by both Babbitt and Santayana, Eliot emigrated to Great Britain in 1914. There he attempted with *Ezra Pound* and others to develop a new sort of poetry; this was called *Modernism* (not to be confused with the heresy of the same name). His 1922 poem, *The Waste Land*, relying as it did on both an ultra-contemporary mode and the symbolism of the Holy Grail, was seen by many as a perfect mirror of modern man's condition. Others were not so impressed. However that may be, Eliot's conversion to Anglo-Catholicism and taking British citizenship in 1927 completed the process begun when he left the St. Louis of his birth for the Boston of his ancestors. In later years he described himself as an Anglo-Catholic in religion, a Royalist in politics, and a Classicist in literature. In a word, he came in his own life to disown the American ethos. His later friendship and admiration for *Charles Maurras* (of whom more presently), and avowed Papalism, completed this process.

Further South, some of the notions of the New Humanism affected the formation of a group of poets and critics at Nashville's Vanderbilt University just after World War I. The leader of this group, called the Fugitives after their magazine of the same name, was *John Crowe Ransom*. Associated with him were men like *Donald Davidson*, *Andrew Lytle*, *Merrill Moore*, and *Robert Penn Warren*. Originally, these men protested against the "backwardness" of Southern culture. But as the 20s progressed, the Fugitives, like so many other of the time's artists and writers, began to protest against the materialism and crassness of the contemporary American life they saw to be given over to the pursuit of profits—ignoring all religious and aesthetic aspects of life. They began to re-examine the history and culture of their own region, which would come to appear as one which had, at great cost to itself, resisted domination by the industrialized and money-oriented North.

In that north, however, in Providence, Rhode Island, dwelt a writer named *H.P. Lovecraft* (1890-1937). Lovecraft was a pioneer in the writing of horror fiction; his strange short stories dealing with odd entities and decaying New England towns appeared from 1923 on, primarily in the pulp magazine *Weird Tales*. He too shared a dislike of the materialism and cheap boosterism prevalent in his day, and sought refuge not only in horror, but in contemplation of the traditional lore and customs of New England (all the while both condemning Puritanism, the American Revolution, and various other stand-bys of that tradition). Although he claimed to be an agnostic materialist for most of his life, his letters show an increasing sympathy for Catholicism which one may hope bore fruit.

Richmond saw the arrival on the scene of a similarly inclined figure, fantasy writer *James Branch Cabell* (1879-1958). Cabell set most of his novels in the fictional French Medieval province of Poictesme. While he avoided the use of realism, his work showed a dark view of the human condition.

What all of these writers had in common was a deep distrust of and disillusionment in what they considered to be the materialism and sheer crassness of the life of the nation; added to this was a rejection of the national cult of progress, itself a secularized version of Calvinistic predestination. But during the 1920s, while there were pockets of poverty, to be sure, the general prosperity rendered all such complaints seemingly inacurate. After all, if the majority prospered under the current system, what were all these criticisms save the whinings of maladjusted and alienated intellectuals? Only mass disillusionment, of the sort that financial ruin brings, would give the protests of the intelligentsia any hearing amongst the majority of Americans. Otherwise, such complaints against a system which, whatever its faults, managed to provide a good living for the majority of its residents could not possibly be true. Could they?

Between 1922 and 1925, the liberal magazine *The Nation* hired 48 writers of varying opinions and backgrounds, from Mencken to pro-Communist Johan J. Smertenko, to write articles on each of the states. From these can be drawn an intriguing picture of a nation in transition; transition, however, from bucolic boredom to industrialized conformity. Few of the writers were quite as nasty as Edmund Wilson in his description of New Jersey:

> But the smarter communities come even further from fostering an independent local life. It is either a question of well-to-do commuters who are fundamentally New Yorkers and who never really identify themselves with New Jersey as citizens of that State or of people with country houses who merely come down to New Jersey for a few months in the summer. And they do not even carry smartness to a particularly brilliant point. Rich brokers and powder manufacturers build houses like huge hotels, where their families go about the familiar business of motor and country club. There are the regular tennis, golf, and polo, and, occasionally, a half-hearted fox-hunt. Scattered fragments of a local squirearchy live in the country all the year 'round, accustomed to the society of their horses and dogs and not greatly missing any other. The children of both these elements, rather unusually stupid flappers and youths, pursue a monotonous round of recreation of which they never seem to tire. They are neither very sprightly nor very wild and between the beach club, the tennis club, and the country club attain a sun-baked, untroubled comeliness of healthy young solid animals. They have not even much of a heritage of snobbery to give them the distinction of a point of view (Borus, *op. cit.*, p. 244).

While Wilson was perhaps more snappish than was usual among his colleagues, his sentiments were echoed in most of the articles. From C.L. Edson's jolly observation of his native state that: "Arkansas has its own popular motto and it is this: 'I've never seen nothin', I don't know nothin', and I don't want nothin',' These fundamental aims the people of Arkansas have achieved in every particular;" to Leonard Lanson

Cline's maintaining that Michigan had gone from being "...without identity, without community of purpose or past, without tradition..." to taking on an air "...of newness, of hardness, of thin varnish, faking up what passes for prettiness," in a word, to becoming the "...consummation of the salesman's ideal;" the same themes are played upon. Alongside these, of course, were coverage of local questions like the control of Montana by the Anaconda Copper Co. or of Delaware by the du Pont clan. Yet, in the dreary picture so painted, a few locales were looked at as islands of sanity. San Francisco, New Orleans, and Baltimore were highly commended by their assigned authors for their having escaped the deadness of the rest of the nation. The reason for this, so it was said, was the close connection of those towns to Europe; we might say, even if they would not, to cultural Catholicism.

Harlem Renaissance and the First Black Power Movement

New York City, however, remained the Great City of America. Center of theater, of publishing, of trade and commerce, on the little island of Manhattan was encapsulated the whole of the American experience from the penthouses of Park Avenue to the tenements of the Lower East Side. One of the city's most well-known areas between the wars, however, was newly-black Harlem.

Before World War I, Harlem was a primarily German settlement which had been engulfed by New York City as the metropolis, during the course of the 19th Century, crept up the island and spilled over into Westchester County (eventually annexing the region called The Bronx). But after the War, Harlem underwent a great change.

Many blacks had come North during World War I from the impoverished South, exchanging the grinding life of poor sharecropping for the grinding life of factory work. After the War, many more made the trek, leaving behind the poverty and post-Reconstruction Jim Crow laws for the chance to make real money and to live with fewer restrictions (and, so they hoped, less prejudice). In Chicago, Boston, Philadelphia, and many other major Northern cities, black neighborhoods or ghettos developed. The best known of these was Harlem.

To Harlem came black artists, musicians, writers, and intellectuals from all over the nation. Many of these had served in the army during the war and were exposed to the relative color-blindness of French society. Returning to an America where the newly re-emerged Ku-Klux-Klan had singled them out with Catholics and Jews as enemies, and where anti-black riots and lynchings had taken place during and just after the war in several Northern cities (perpetrated mostly by white workers who feared an influx of cheap labor), such folk were understandably resentful. In Harlem they would attempt to carve out an enclave where the black man would come into his own.

In great part, Harlem between the wars fulfilled much of this dream. Mingling with poverty were black-owned businesses and newspapers; such places as the Cotton Club and the Apollo Theatre figured strongly in the growth of Jazz. Thereat would play such great names as *James P. Johnson, Willie "the Lion" Smith, Thomas "Fats" Waller*, and *Edward Kennedy "Duke" Ellington*. Singers and dancers like *Josephine Baker* (who would go on to be the toast of Paris), *Bessie Smith* and the Catholic convert *Billie Holiday* (who made her debut in 1931) were accompanied by them. To hear these performers, well-to-do whites came uptown to Harlem in the 1920s and 30s, dressed in their finery; one of the reasons "the Lady is a Tramp" in the song of that name is her refusal to go to Harlem "in ermine and pearls."

But achievement in Harlem was not restricted to music. This was the era of the *Harlem Renaissance*. Prior to the 20s, books about black life and culture were written primarily by whites, employing a great deal of dialect—like Joel Chandler Harris' Uncle Remus stories. But the writers of the Harlem Renaissance wrote about these topics as insiders; further, they did not depict their topic as an amusement, but in an attempt to foster pride among their co-racialists. In one sense, they were part of a large movement; the scientific study of American folklore in general dates from about this time, and as we have seen, regional writing was flourishing. But the fact of intelligent writers dealing with the situation of what remained basically a subject people was without parallel. That Jim Crow could easily survive when the majority of blacks were illiterate field hands and domestic workers was obvious; but in the face of articulate opinion, just how well could legal segregation and so on continue?

At any rate, the writers of the Harlem Renaissance were an interesting lot, indeed. Chief among them were *James Weldon Johnson*, best known as the author of the 1927 book *God's Trombones*, a presentation of seven sermons in free verse, showing the style and concerns of black preaching, a major element in the culture; *Claude Mckay*, a Jamaican immigrant poet, and novelist (most notably 1928's *Home to Harlem*); *Countee Cullen*; and *Langston Hughes*. But perhaps the most remarkable among them was *Zora Neale Hurston* (1891-1960).

Hurston was the first black woman writer to achieve prominence in the United States; in her relatively short career she produced two books of anthropology (*Mules and Men* and *Tell My Horse*), four novels (one of which, *Seraph on the Suwannee*, represents perhaps the first time in a novel a black author wrote about white characters exclusively), a play, and an autobiography (*Dust Tracks on a Road*, perhaps the most incisive and rhetoric-free description of the black experience in America as yet written). Her work was excellent taken on its own merits, and portrayed people—black and white—sympathetically, but without either sentiment or animus. Without doubt she was one of the greatest writers this nation has produced in the 20th Century.

All of the Harlem Renaissance writers had this much in common: they wished the black man to take his place in America alongside the white as an equal partner. But just as the Klan called for the separation of the two races, so too (for completely different reasons) did a black leader who rose to prominence in the Harlem of the 20s: *Marcus Garvey*.

Garvey, born in Jamaica in 1897, had founded in his native land in 1914 the Universal Negro Improvement Association (UNIA). Its aims were to foster black pride of race and economic power, and to reclaim Africa from the colonial powers; all blacks would return thereto, and an independent black nation would be established. Finding little support in Jamaica for these goals, Garvey arrived in Harlem in 1916. Within three years he had garnered 2,000,000 supporters in Harlem and the other Northern ghettos. That year of 1919, in order to stimulate black economic power within the white system, he founded Negro Factories Corporation and the Black Star Line of steamships. UNIA's businesses included restaurants, grocery stores, a hotel, and a printing press. Garvey's power was at its apex in 1920, when his international convention brought together delegates from 25 countries. The high point was a parade of 50,000 through Harlem's streets.

The next year he proclaimed himself president of the "Empire of Africa;" he went so far as to approve the Klan, precisely because it too favored the separation of the races. He soon feuded with established black leaders, like W.E.B. Du Bois of the NAACP. In 1922 he was indicted and convicted of mail fraud, receiving a sentence of 5 years, which was commuted by President Coolidge in 1927 to deportation. His movement did not long survive him.

The importance of this episode, however, is that it points up an enduring question of American racial relations—what is the goal toward which white and black Americans ought to strive for together? Separation or integration? Given that there is an inequality between the two races, and antipathy on either side, what is the proper role of government in dealing with the problem? Given that the government does not operate under a clearly defined moral or religious code, how far should it be allowed to take charge of the question? Above all, what does justice demand in this case? Unfortunately, these are questions which, while recurring throughout our history, seem as far from a solution today as ever.

Three Presidents and Their Adventures

Warren Harding was an amiable man, if not too discerning. His associates, however, were not always of the highest caliber. Committed as he was returning the nation to normalcy, Harding pursued a laissez-faire approach to business. So too did various of his cabinet secretaries. Most notable of these was Secretary of the Interior Albert B. Fall.

On May 31, 1921, Harding transferred control of the Naval oil reserve lands from the Department of the Navy to Fall's control. On April 7, 1922, Fall secretly granted control of the Teapot Dome oil reserves in Wyoming to Mammoth Oil Company head Harry F. Sinclair. Shortly after this, a friend of Sinclair's gave Fall over $200,000 (roughly 2 million today). Fall asked Papal Count Edward Doheny of California for a $100,000 non-repayable loan. Not long after, Count Doheny received leases of parts of the Elk Hills and Buena Vista reserves in his native state. Naval Secretary Edward Denby innocently signed all the transactions.

News of these shenaningans leaked out; Congress ordered President Harding to quash the deals, and nullified the transfer of the reserves from Navy to Interior, after the Supreme Court ruled against all of it. Fall was convicted of accepting a bribe, while Sinclair and Count Doheny were acquitted. Various other folk involved were imprisoned or committed suicide.

Harding was crushed by what he regarded as wholesale betrayal by his most trusted appointees. The public at large was shocked, and lost confidence in him. While no one accused Harding himself of any wrongdoing, it was nevertheless clear that his laxity in monitoring his staff had been partly to blame for the affair. While we have grown somewhat used to these sorts of goings on in high office, at that time there had been nothing like it since the days of President Grant. The effect on public trust, coupled with all of the Prohibition-related events (which featured so many local officials in the pay of bootleggers) contributed to a tremendous breakdown in public life.

Exhausted and broken-hearted, Harding died in the midst of a national tour at San Francisco on August 2, 1923. Staying at his father's farmhouse in Plymouth, Vermont, Vice President *Calvin Coolidge* was awoken in the wee hours of the morning; his judge father administered the oath of office to him, and Coolidge became the 30th President of the United States.

The new chief executive was the very picture of a stern old Puritan father. Thin and harsh-appearing, he looked, in the words of Alice Roosevelt Longworth, as though "he had been weaned on a pickle." He was felt by his new electorate to encompass all the virtues of thrift and frugality summed up in *The Old Farmer's Almanac*. Although his party was rent by factional strife, the administration was stained by scandal, and Congress was in rebellion, he moved swiftly and quietly to exert control. He was easily nominated by the party in 1924.

Using the motto, "keep cool with Coolidge," he was reelected, announcing in his inaugural address that "the business of America is business." As president (save for Latin America, as we shall see) his method in both foreign and domestic affairs was nonintervention. For the former reason, he refused to join in any "entangling alliances" in Europe; for the latter, he opposed both a bonus to World War veterans, business regulation, and farm relief.

The name "Silent Cal" was earned through keeping his public statements to a minimum. The story is told of a female reporter who informed him that she had a bet with the others in her office that she could get him to say more than two words. "You lose," was his reply. Similarly, upon his return from church services one Sunday, he was asked what had happened.

"The preacher preached."

"What about?" asked his wife.

"Sin."

"What did he say about it?"

"He was against it," came the magisterial repy. Coolidge won musical renown, of a sort, when the hit 20s song, *Crazy Words, Crazy Tune*, included the immortal line, "You all heard, yesterday, what did President Coolidge say? Vo-do-de-o-do-do-deo-do!" Rarely in history has a leader so well matched his time and his people.

For the 20s were a time of change and excitement, and in such times, we Americans always look to a father figure. What silent Cal performed would be done again by a much more active figure shortly after his term ended. In any case, so long as Calvin Coolidge was on the job, Middle America (a phrase which can mean either the Midwest, the Middle Class, or whatever bedrock group one wants to mention) felt relatively unthreatened by changes in society, by the upward spiraling credit cycle, and even by the gangs which were coming to give so much power in places like Chicago and New York—to say nothing of the political machines which dominated them.

But storm clouds were gathering, and Coolidge did not intend to face them. In 1928, he informed the Republican Party Convention that "I do not choose to run again..." This led to the nomination of *Herbert Hoover*, who had served in many capacities, most notably as organizer of famine relief to Allied Europe during and after the Great War, and as chairman of the Colorado River Commission; through his work, Hoover Dam was built. Hoover squared off against the Democratic nominee, New York

Governor *Alfred Emmanuel Smith*. The first practicing Catholic ever to be nominated for the presidency, Al Smith was called "the Brown Derby", after his habitual head-gear. Apart from this, he was outspoken in his opposition to Prohibition; worse yet in a country which still to a large degree suspected urban life, Smith was a New Yorker's New Yorker.

A product of Tammany Hall, Smith was nevertheless renowned as being scrupulously honest. Easy-going and straightforward, he knew how to work a political machine without selling his soul to it. In 1926, Broadway habitue and composer *Jimmy Walker* won election as mayor of New York on Smith's recommendation. The Brown Derby had become the best-known Democrat in the nation, and favored to win nomination in 1928. As soon as this became well-known, the assault on his religion began.

In August of 1926, the president of the New York Anti-Saloon League, Methodist Bishop Adna W. Leonard of Buffalo, declared: "No governor can kiss the papal ring and get within gunshot of the White House" (*New York Times*, August 9, 1926). After handily winning at the 1928 Convention, Smith had to endure continued attacks on his Faith:

> [Smith's Catholicism] far outweighed every other issue in the campaign. There was a long history of anti-Catholicism in American politics. It was always a powerful force at the polls. Even an impressive old Progressive like William Allen White was upset by Smith's nomination: "The whole Puritan civilization which has built a sturdy, orderly nation is threatened by Smith."
>
> The Protestant churches led the attack on the governor. It was not unusual for a church to try to influence American politics. The Baptists in the South and the Methodists in the North had been major political instruments for more than a century. And six moths before the Houston convention, a Methodist Bishop, James Cannon, was touring the South trying to organize an anti-Smith bloc to deny him the nomination. On the eve of the election the *Memphis Commercial Appeal* carried an advertisement urging, "Vote as You Pray." At the request of the Republican National Commitee, Mabel Walker Willebrandt, assistant attorney general, went to Cincinnati to address a gathering of Methodist ministers. Hoover had studiously avoided any mention of religion. Mrs. Willebrandt, however, was carried away by the sight of 2,000 divines at her feet. "There are 2,000 pastors here," she exulted. "You have in your charge more than 600,000 members of the Methodist Church in Ohio alone. That is enough to swing the election" (Geoffrey Perrett, *America in the Twenties*, pp. 313-314).

It is interesting to note, in looking at this passage, that there was no question of "separation of Church and State," to be found here.

Catholics, as we shall see, were accused of desiring to break this separation; but of course, it did not really exist, save when convenient for the enemies of the Faith to evoke it:

> Then, too, there was the matter of Smith's religion. Stronger even then the agrarian myth in America was the Protestant myth. According to it, the United States always had been and must forever remain a dominantly Protestant country. Never before Smith's time had a Catholic seriously sought a presidential nomination. Anti-Catholic prejudice was an old American heritage that dated back to colonial times and had flared up again with every major accretion of Catholic immigrants. To most Americans religious prejudice was principally a matter of feeling rather than of reason, but with Smith's candidacy some intelligent questions began to be raised. Would a Catholic President of the United States owe a double allegiance, to a foreign potentate, the Pope of Rome, as well as to the American nation? Would he be free to support such fundamental principles as the equality of all religions before the law, the separation of Church and State, and the American system of free public schools? Debate on these subjects reached a high plane in two *Atlantic Monthly* articles of 1927, one contributed by Smith himself, who asserted eloquently that his church loyalty left him free from any of the restraints alleged or implied and denounced with fervor the injection of the religious issue into politics. But only those were convinced who wished to be convinced, and Smith's nomination brought out anew every scurrilous anti-Catholic charge that had ever been made. Particularly in the South, where Protestantism was still militant, Smith's religion cost him many votes (John D. Hicks, *Republican Ascendancy 1921-1933*, pp. 206-207).

If America was Protestant, then of course allegiance to Methodism or Baptistry implied nothing more than adherence to the spiritual side of the American ethos. But if it was not, then surely such adherence implied a double allegiance just as great as that of Catholics vis-a-vis the Pope. Today, when believing Protestants are as much a minority in the country as Catholics, we see the logical result: Evangelical Christians who run for office are similarly accused of the same "crime" with which their fathers charged Al Smith. Equality of religions before the law, separation of Church and State, and the Public Schools, these principles which the Catholics were accused of wishing to destroy, have been the means of driving all religion—indeed, morality, from public life. Hence, one might say that their preservation has done little for those who considered them in 1928 to be dogmas of the true national religion. At any rate, the course of the campaign was very dirty, indeed. Robert Leckie well describes it, as well as Smith's reaction:

One of the chief reasons for Al Smith's defeat was the vicious and sometimes obscene attacks made upon him by the Klan and similar nativist groups. Much of the old literature of No-Popery was reprinted and circulated, and it was charged, among other things, that after President Smith handed the United States over to the Pope, His Holiness would issue a decree bastardizing all non-Catholic children. [In Catholic folklore there is a probably spurious but nevertheless very funny anecdote which claims that after Smith was defeated he sent the Pope a one-word cablegram which said: "Unpack."]. If this were not absurd enough, there were actually people who expressed their alarm that the tiny ceremonial cannon outside Georgetown University was pointed directly *at the Capitol.* Unfortunately, in minds disposed to think ill, nothing is too ridiculous to be believed, and much of this arrant if scurrilous nonsense was taken for truth. In fact, Governor Smith himself complained that the Republican party was not above issuing campaign literature "of a nature other than political." Smith's remark came during his celebrated speech in Oklahoma City. Aware that Southwestern states such as Arkansas and Oklahoma were particularly frenzied in their hostility, so much so that there was "real concern for Smith's personal safety" in Oklahoma City, he courageously decided to beard the lion in his den and bring the religious question into the open.

"I have been told," he said, "that politically it might be expedient for me to remain silent upon this subject, but so far as I am concerned no political expediency will keep me from speaking out in an endeavor to destroy these evil attacks."

The first myth which Smith demolished was the charge that as governor of New York he appointed practically no one but Catholics to office. "What are the facts?" he asked. "On investigation I find that in the cabinet of the Governor sit fourteen men. Three of the fourteen are Catholics, ten are Protestants, and one of Jewish faith. In various bureaus and divisions of the Cabinet offices, the Governor appointed twenty-six people. Twelve of them are Catholics and fourteen of them are Protestants. Various other State officials, making up boards and commissions, and appointed by the Governor, make a total of 157 appointments, of whom thirty-five were Catholics, 106 were Protestants, twelve were Jewish, and four I could not find out about." What Smith could but did not add was that in New York State was located the country's largest concentration of Catholics, and that his co-religionists had not fared quite so well under him as under non-Catholic governors. Having gone on to detail other examples of bigotry in his campaign, Smith concluded:

> *I here emphatically declare that I do not wish any member of my faith in any part of the United States to vote for me on any religious grounds. I want them to vote for me only when in their hearts and consciences they become convinced*

that my election will promote the best interests of our country. By the same token, I cannot refrain from saying that any person who votes against me simply because of my religion is not, to my way of thinking, a good citizen...

The constitutional guaranty that there should be no religious test for public office is not a mere form of words. It represents the most vital principle that ever was given to any people. I attack those who seek to undermine it, not only because I am a good Christian, but because I am a good American and a product of America and of American institutions. Everything I am, and everything I hope to be, I owe to those institutions (American and Catholic, pp. 291-292).

Here, in a word, was the tragedy of Al Smith, and of American political Catholicism in the 1920s. For as we see, the accusations against Smith and American Catholics in general were completely false. No single group were more committed to the secular faith of the country than were the Catholics—although this meant tacitly abandoning everything in the Church's social teaching which might clash with the American secular cult.

By their tactics, we have seen that even the self-appointed watchdogs of American liberty did not believe in it as much as the Catholics did. This is unfortunate indeed, because, after all, they are now as much that cult's victims as are the Catholics. Had Catholics in politics remained firmly committed to the principles of such Papal encyclicals as Gregory XVI's *Mirari vos*, and Leo XIII's *Immortale Dei* and *Rerum novarum*, the heirs of Smith's Protestant opposition in 1928 might not be a universally reviled minority in the 1990s.

Had that been the case, however, it is doubtful that Catholic politicians could have obtained anything like the influence which they did. There would have been no Smith campaign in 1928, and surely no Kennedy victory in 1960. But ballot-box victories for Catholics have done little for either Church or State in this country. If, perhaps, all that energy had been put into converting the nation, rather than merely getting Catholics elected to office, there would have been much beneficial and fundamental change here: surely the only way of putting Catholic political principles into practice in the U.S. is by making them a Catholic nation. What is saddest about the election of 1928 is that Smith, like most American Catholics, really and sincerely believed that, as may be seen by the first two sentences of Leckie's quotation from his speech, "religious grounds" and "the best interests of our country" could be separated. In truth, separation of the two is like separating soul from body—the exact definition of death, and one which our present status seems to exemplify.

In any case, Hoover won handily. The only lasting result of the campaign was to make the Italians and French-Canadians of New England, long staunch Republicans in opposition to the Irish-ruled Democrats, willing to vote with the Irish. Catholics continued to conform politically, and, as we shall see, frequently did so at the expense of their co-religionists.

The Church in the 1920s

Despite the opposition to Catholicism inherent in national life (and exposed once more for public viewing, as we have just seen, in the 1928 election), in the 1920s the Church continued to grow in this country. Although immigration had slowed to a trickle, those who had arrived in the preceding few decades consolidated their lives in the new land, building ever more grandiose and beautiful churches. Although Margaret Sanger (a fallen-away Catholic) had founded the forerunner of Planned Parenthood in 1921, the vast majority of Catholics in this country still agreed with Church teaching on the matter. As a result, the numbers of Catholics continued to rise through childbirth. (Interestingly enough, the 1920 Lambeth Conference of all the world's Anglican Bishops condemned birth control; that of 1930 reversed this position). There were in addition some few converts made.

In truth, the material position of the Church in America could not have been better. New orders of sisters were springing up to staff ever more schools and hospitals; many other orders were imported. Catholic universities and colleges grew in numbers also.

Nor was spiritual life unaffected by all this growth. Devotion to St. Therese, the newly canonized Little Flower, spread rapidly; sodalities and confraternities of all sorts were founded. Holy Name Society Communion Sundays, the early First Communions advocated by Pope St. Pius X, numerous choirs inspired by the motu proprio on Church music issued by the same Pontiff, and all sorts of other efforts were evidence of this.

The crowning achievement of the American hierarchy in this decade was, without doubt, the financial rescue of the Holy See by Chicago's Cardinal Mundelein in 1928. The signing of the Lateran Treaty with the Italian government the next year would obviate any need for further loans from American bishops—at least for a while. But a precedent was established.

Yet under all of this apparent prosperity, religiously and temporally, the Church in America was becoming ever more Americanist. The

Bishops' Program for Social Reconstruction referred to in the last chapter, was tacitly abandoned, although the Catholic Central Verein in St. Louis continued as a strong voice for the Church's social teaching. *Fr. Joseph Husslein, S.J.*, among others, continued to labor to make the Church's doctrines in social, political, and economic matters well known. Two episodes illustrate in what direction the American Church was going.

The first was the Sentinelle Affair among the French Canadians in New England, a sort of Gallic reprise of the Cahenslyite controversy. The roots of the affair lay in France, where *Charles Maurras* had founded in the late 19th Century an organization called *l'Action Française*. In his youth a positivist, his studies of history and literature convinced him that the Monarchy and the Church were what had built France's glory, and so must be restored to their former state if France were ever to again be the great nation it had been.

Although Maurras himself was for most of his life an unbeliever, all but a few of his comrades were fervent Catholics. Cardinal Billot, the Jesuit theologian, Cardinal Charest of Rennes, and Cardinal Dubois of Paris were all vocal supporters of the movement. Its influence was felt all over Europe, and such luminaries as *Hilaire Belloc, Arthur Machen*, and T.S. Eliot expressed their admiration thereof. Men like *Salazar* in Portugal, *Fr. Groulx* in Quebec, *Denis Jackson* in Australia, *Saunders Lewis* in Wales, *Stuart Erskine* in Scotland, *Fernand Neuray* in Belgium, and many others throughout the Catholic world were much influenced by *Action Française*.

In Quebec, the aforementioned Fr. Lionel Groulx founded a similar organization, called also l'Action Française, and inspired by Maurras' group, albeit in a Canadian context. Summing up this ideology, Fr. Groulx declared in the newspaper of the same name's January 1921 issue:

> Our doctrine can be contained in this brief formula: we wish to reconstitute the fullness of our French life. We wish to reconstitute in its integrity, the ethnic type which France left here and which one hundred and fifty years of history has shaped. We wish to remake an inventory of moral and social forces, which in itself will prepare their flowering. We wish to purify this type of foreign growths in order to develop in it intensively the original culture, to attach to it the new virtues acquired since the Conquest [of Canada by Great Britain from the French], above all to keep it in intimate contact with the forces of its past, in order to let it go henceforth its regular and individual way. And it is this rigorously characterized French type, dependent on history and geography, having ethnical and psychological traits, which we wish to continue, on which we base the hope of our future; because

a people, like all living things, can develop only what is in itself, only the forces whose living germ it contains.

This germ of a people was one day profoundly strickened in its life; it was constrained, paralysed in its development. The consequences of the Conquest weighed heavily upon it; its laws, its language were hamstrung; its intellectual culture was long hobbled; its system of education, deviated in some of its parts, sacrificed more than was fitting to English culture; its natural domain was invaded, leaving it only partially master of its economic forces; its private and public customs were contaminated by the Protestant and Saxon atmosphere. A distressing make-up has gradually covered the physiognomy of our cities and towns, an implacable sign of the subjection of souls to the law of the conqueror.

This evil of the Conquest was aggravated after 1867 by the evil of federalism. Confederation may have been a political necessity; it may have promoted great material progress; for a time, it may even have given Quebec a greater measure of economy. But it could not prevent the system from turning notable influences against us. Our particular situation in the federal alliance, the isolation of our Catholic and French province amidst eight provinces in majority English and Protestant, the imbalance of forces which ensued, sometimes increased by the hostile policy of some rulers, led federal legislation little by little towards principles or acts which endangered our fundamental interests. The political system of our country, such as it is by way of being applied, leads not to unity but straight to uniformity.

But Fr. Groulx was far from entirely negative; in the same article, he offered a way out of the dilemma:

> For our intellectual élite we ask Roman culture and French culture. The first will give us masters of truth, those who furnish the spiritual rules, which make shine on high the principles without which there is no firm direction, no intangible social basis, no permanent order, no people assured of its goal. In the natural order, the culture of France, the immortal educator of our thoughts, will achieve the perfecting of our minds. And when we speak of French culture, we mean not in the limited sense of literary culture, but in the broad and elevated sense in which the French mind appears to us as an incomparable master of clarity, order, and subtlety, the creator of the sanest and most humane civilization, the highest expression of intellectual health and mental balance. And equally we mean not an initiation which leads to dilletantism or to alienization, but a culture which serves without servility, which safeguards our traditional attitudes before the truth, which become a real and benificent force, will permit our next élite to apply itself more vigorously to the solution of our problems, to the service of its race, its country, and its faith.

For Fr. Groulx, as for Tardivel and Laflesche before him, the French Canadians ought to have the goal of being "a Catholic and Latin people, of being absolutely and stubbornly ourselves, the sort of race created by history and desired by God." Moreover, whatever quarrels they might have between one another, the French-Canadians would serve as a sure defence in the struggle shared by Anglo-Canadians to prevent the Dominion from being absorbed by the colossus to the South: "The more we preserve our French and Catholic virtues, the more faithful we remain to our history and traditions, the more we remain the element impermeable by the American spirit, the strongest element of order and stability."

As might be expected, such an ideology found support among the French-Candians of New England, a group of whom launched in 1922 a newspaper, *La Sentinelle*, of Woonsocket, Rhode Island, which was inspired by Fr. Groulx's thought, and whose editor was the redoubtable *Elphege Daignault*. In an American context, this meant the safeguarding of French-Canadian religion and culture through the maintenance of national parishes and schools. When, in the mid-twenties the Irish bishop of Providence, having appointed an Irish pastor to St. Louis church in Woonsocket, demanded a financial assessment of French parishes for an English-language High School (in departure from previous practice), the struggle was on. Petitions, protests, pew rent strikes, and finally, a mass rally of 10,000 in Woonsocket culminated in a civil suit against the bishop; in response, the next year Bishop William Hickey excommunicated 62 Sentinellistes connected with the suit.

It was a struggle which divided Franco-American New England. Like the *ralliement* in France, which saw the French Church cut in two over Leo XIII's call for Royalist French Catholics to abandon their King and rally to the anti-clerical republic, so too did this battle pit two elements—national tradition and loyalty to the hierarchy—which had always been in accord, against each other. Just as some rallied behind the Sentinellistes, and saw compromise with the Bishop as a betrayal of the ancestors, their opponents among their co-nationals saw defiance of that same Bishop as the same treason. Of the two major organizations, the Association Canado-Americaine in Manchester, New Hampshire, sided with the Sentinellistes, and the Union St. Jean Baptiste with the Bishop. The struggle spread throughout the French communities of New England: Central Falls and Pawtucket, in Rhode Island; Manchester; and Worcester, Massachusetts. After the excommunications, it was threatened that a French-Canadian version of the Polish National Catholic Church would be set up. Another schism seemed imminent.

A mediatrix was found in the person of "Little Rose" Ferron. A native of Sherbrooke, Quebec, Little Rose was a stigmatized mystic, whose cause has since been introduced at Rome. Accepted by the Sentinellistes as one close to God, she was able to convince them to make submission to the Bishop in 1929, after which the movement, for the most part, died away.

While its influence lingered (the fiery anti-assimilationist Wilfrid Beaulieu, a disciple of the Sentinelle, launched his Worcester paper *Le Travailleur* in 1931; this journal proclaimed the same message until it ceased publication in 1978, the year before Beaulieu's death) the end of the *Sentinelle* meant the end of independent Franco-American critique of the U.S. system, and was a corresponding victory for the Americanists. This victory was echoed in Louisiana, where in 1918 the Catholic schools had banned the use of French by students, a move echoed a few years later by the state public schools. The year 1926 saw the closing of the last daily French paper in New Orleans.

The second great episode was the American Catholic reaction to the 1926 *Cristero* rebellion in Mexico, of which we shall see more shortly. For our present purpose, what counts is the welcome given by American churchmen to four emissaries of the Catholic Mexican revolt:

> The four anticipated great success; Eamon de Valera had successfully appealed to American Catholics for aid against Ireland's oppressors, and they would do the same on behalf of Mexico. But at their first stop, Corpus Christi, the bishop rebuffed them with the comment that people in his diocese didn't like Mexicans. In Galveston, the bishop took a ten-dollar bill from his wallet and gave it to Rene, ending the interview. Houston, Dallas, and Little Rock were much the same—they got twenty, thirty, fifty dollars. Sleeping outdoors at night and eating as little as possible to economize, they believed the northern states would be different—de Valera had succeeded there. The Archbishop of St. Louis was outraged by conditions in Mexico as described by Capistran Garza; he gave one hundred dollars. At the next seven stops—East St. Louis, Indianapolis, Dayton, Columbus, Pittsburgh, Altoona, and Harrisburg—they got even less. In Columbus, the bishop expelled them from his residence without even hearing them out. In New York, without warm clothing, they nearly froze. Friends said Boston was promising. They went. There, Cardinal O'Connell examined their credentials carefully and listened without interrupting. Then, in a fatherly tone, he urged Rene to suffer patiently the trials God was sending and told him to urge those who had commissioned him to do likewise. He advised Rene to get out of the whole business, to look for a job; he would be happy to give him a letter of introduction to the Massachusetts Knights of Columbus, who might be able to help him find work (David C. Bailey, *Viva Cristo Rey!*, p. 103).

At first sympathetic to the Cristero plight, prominent and wealthy laymen like Count Nicholas Brady and William F. Buckley, Sr., appeared disposed to aid their brother Catholics financially. But intervention by American bishops (as well as fear for American oil holdings in Mexico) put their sympathy to rest. As Bailey puts it,

> The American bishops deplored the persecution in Mexico and extended hospitality to exiles and refugees; but they drew back in horror from the suggestion that they help bankroll a rebellion. Some, like Archbishop Drossaerts, might lambaste the [U.S.] administration for supporting [Mexican anti-clerical President] Calles, but they would never dream of violating the neutrality laws. Knights of Columbus leaders and a few Catholic Congressmen protested vigorously and demanded withdrawal of U.S. recognition; but, after their complaints had been duly lodged and reported in the press, and after State Department officials had explained to them that it would be unwise to take extreme action, they ceased their badgering (*op. cit.*, p. 308).

Surely, this bland inaction in the face of the martyrdom of a neighboring Catholic nation is one of the most inglorious events in the history of the Church in the United States. But it shows what that Church had become by 1929. What is most pathetic is that, as we shall see, intervention by the U.S. government on behalf of anti-Catholic factions remained as much a part of our relations with Latin America as it had been before. One would think that America's Catholics might try to change this, but, alas, they did not.

We need not be too surprised at this, given the lukewarm reception accorded in this country to *Quas primas*, the encyclical of Pius XI establishing the feast of Christ the King. It was not, of course, the feast itself which was ignored, for it was immediately and grandly observed. Rather, it was the teaching of the encyclical on that Kingship itself which was politely allowed to drop down the memory-hole:

> 18. Thus the empire of our Redeemer emraces all men. To use the words of our immortal predecessor, Leo XIII: "His empire includes not only Catholic nations, not only baptised persons who, though of right belonging to the Church, have been led astray by error, or have been cut off from her by schism, but also all those who are outside the Christian faith; so that truly the whole of mankind is subject to the power of Jesus Christ." Nor is there any difference in this matter between the individual and the State; for all men, whether collectively or individually, are under the Dominion of Christ. In him is the salvation of the individual, in him is the salvation of society. "Neither is there salvation in any other, for there is no other name under heaven given to men whereby we may be saved." He is the author of happiness

and true prosperity for every man and for every nation. "For a nation is happy when its citizens are happy. What else is a nation but a number of men living in concord?" If, therefore, the rulers of nations wish to preserve their authority, to promote and increase the prosperity of their countries, they will not neglect the public duty of reverence and obedience to the rule of Christ. What we said at the beginning of Our Pontificate concerning the decline of public authority, and the lack of respect for the same, is equally true at the present day. "With God and Jesus Christ," we said, "excluded from political life, with authority derived not from God but from man, the very basis of that authority has been taken away, because the chief reason of the distinction between ruler and subject has been eliminated. The result is that human society is tottering to its fall, because it has no longer a secure and solid foundation."

True enough; but in an America engulfed by prosperity, the Pope's words seemed faint to the ear, indeed—and any attempt to implement them would inevitably arouse to fever pitch the forces which had made themselves obvious in the election of 1928. Rather than suffer such abuse, Catholic America burned incense before the social clichés of their countrymen.

The United States and Latin America

In 1922, American troops were on guard in Haiti, the Dominican Republic, and Nicaragua. In the first two countries, American troops had intervened to prevent European occupation, as we saw in the last chapter. In 1924, the Dominican Republic was returned to local control, but another decade would follow before Haiti would be evacuated.

Nicaragua was a different story. There, after withdrawal in 1923, the pro-Catholic Conservatives under the leadership of *Emiliano Chamorro* rose against the Liberal government. The revolt was successful; President Coolidge refused to recognize the new regime. In the face of American opposition, the Chamorro government resigned and the country lapsed again into chaos. Coolidge had the country reoccupied in 1925, and appointed the Liberal leader *Somoza* as president.

But it was in Mexico (as usual) that the real nature of U.S. Latin American policy became manifest. The country had suffered Revolution continually from 1910 to 1920. When the dust cleared, a thoroughly anti-clerical regime was in the saddle. In 1917 it passed a series of laws based upon the French 1904 code. Religious orders were expelled, as were all Spanish priests. Churches became the property of the State, and religious rites confined to their interiors; outside of them, clerical dress was not permitted. Schools, hospitals, monasteries, orphanages, and so on were all seized and given over to other uses or sold.

While these laws were initially only half-heartedly applied, the ascension to power of Plutarco Calles in 1926 saw their application made rigorous. In retaliation, the Vatican ordered all Mexico's priests to cease functioning: if the State wanted the Churches, they could have them! But Mexico's laymen were not far behind. The National League for the Defence of Religious Liberty organized an economic boycott—Catholics would not travel, nor buy anything but absolute necessities. The loss of governmental revenue in terms of sales and other taxes was tremendous. Yet Calles would not relent.

After the expulsion of the Apostolic Delegate in July, sporadic Catholic uprisings began to occur. The League, with the tacit approval of the Mexican episcopate, began planning a nation-wide revolt. The Catholic political party, the Union Popular, decided to join them. Its leader, Anacleto Gonzalez Flores, addressed the membership thusly:

> I know only too well that what is beginning for us now is a Calvary. We must be ready to take up and carry our crosses... I, who am here responsible for the decision of all, feel a sacred obligation not to deceive anyone. If one of you should ask me what sacrifice I am asking of you in order to seal the pact we are about to celebrate, I will tell you in two words: *your blood*. If you want to proceed, stop dreaming of places of honor, military triumphs, braid, lustre, victories, and authority over others. Mexico needs a tradition of blood in order to cement its free life of tomorrow. For that work my life is available, and for that tradition I ask yours. (Navarrete, Heriberto, S.J., *Por Dios y Por la Patria*, pp. 123-125).

In early 1927, the revolt blazed throughout a dozen Mexican states. By the end of the conflict two years later, over 40,000 men had served in the ranks of the Cristeros, as they were called from their battle cry, *Viva Cristo Rey!* —"Long live Christ the King!" Despite lack of much weaponry beyond what they could capture from government troops, despite lack of funding from abroad, despite official U.S. support of Calles, they fought on, nearly to victory.

The Calles regime replied with unspeakable atrocities. Perhaps best known of their victims was *Blessed Miguel Agustin Pro, S.J.* But for all the killing, more Cristeros emerged from the countryside. Nor, despite the support of the United States for the government, did the Cristeros initially go unheard by the Pope. Pius XI issued another encyclical, *Iniquis afflictisque,* in which he declared (cap. 27) that "...We can scarcely keep back Our tears, some of these young men and boys have gladly met death, the rosary in their hands and the name of Christ King on their lips. Young girls too were imprisoned, were criminally outraged..."

While the fighting continued, most of the bishops left the country (although some, like the Archbishop of Guadalajara, took to the hills with the Cristeros). Despite the fact that by 1929, victory appeared to be in Cristero grasp, Vatican Secretary of State Gasparri was anxious to come to an accord with Calles. Using two Mexican bishops for the task, through the mediation of American Ambassador to Mexico Dwight Morrow, an accord was signed with the Calles regime on October 11, 1929. A month later, Jose Manriquez y Zarate, bishop of Huejutla, addressed the faculty of Belgium's Louvain University:

> The Mexican people, preserving the pure, integral faith of their fathers look on the Pope as the Vicar of Christ on earth. Knowing this fact the enemies of Christ were very astute to betake themselves to Rome in order to break the immovable wall of armed resistance. Very soon they had the satisfaction of seeing the people surrender their arms at the first signal from the Pope. Those in the government who consented to a settlement offered all kinds of promises verbally but never afterward removed a single comma from the monstrous laws that have wounded Holy Church in Mexico and strangled the most sacred rights of men and society.

The rebellion collapsed. Priests who did not abide by the settlement were to be suspended. The government treated the accord as a surrender by the Church, and despite the promised amnesty, mass executions of Cristeros went on sporadically, even as late as the 1950s. The churches were reopened, but the anti-clerical laws remained until 1991. Even with their lifting, all church property built prior to 1991 remains in government hands. The ideology of the ruling party has not changed since the days of Calles. The fact that they are willing to abolish these laws merely indicates that Catholicism is no longer a threat—which is certainly a rebuke to us. We have in any case already seen what American Catholic response to the Cristeros was at the time.

Europe and the Rise of Fascism

The smoking ruins of Europe were not magically restored by the Armistice on November 11, 1918. The Russian Civil War, a bloody conflict, indeed, had resulted not only in millions of atrocities and an athiestic inhuman regime coming to power in an ancient Christian land; it had also produced a stream of White Russian refugees, who soon became fixtures of society in London, Paris, Istanbul, Berlin, Buenos Aires, New York, San Francisco, Shanghai, Harbin, and many other cities across the world. Beyond this, temporary or abortive Red regimes repeated the atrocities of their prototype in Hungary, Slovakia, Bavaria and other parts of Germany. The new Soviet state was bent on world domination, for all that it was in terrible shape internally. In every country Communist cells were organized under the paternal eye of Moscow's Comintern—the Communist International.

The presence of the White Russians in so many cities ensured that news of what Communist rule would mean was widespread. The Red Scare of which we spoke earlier was not without justification, despite often being ignorantly directed.

Communism appealed to many in Europe, particularly proletarians and intellectuals, whose beliefs in the certainties of pre-War religion and politics had been shattered. Prior to the War, it was assumed that the ruling circles in each nation knew best; this notion was shattered in the muck of the trenches, and the blood of the Eastern Front. All hope that existing abuses in society would be gradually ameliorated by imposition of Liberal progress was destroyed. The great urban mobs became seemingly living beings, ready to follow anyone who promised solutions. These the Communists claimed to have in plenty.

But the old politicians, the industrialists, the great landowners, were not without resources of their own—with which they would be quite happy to reward anyone who could harness the power of the mob, and keep it away from Communism and from bloodshed.

The Church, for her part, surveyed the wreck with dismay. The first encyclical of the new Pope, Pius XI, *Ubi arcano Dei consilio*, published on December 23, 1922, well described the situation:

> 11. Public life is so enveloped, even at the present hour, by the dense fog of mutual hatred and grievances that it is almost impossible for the common people so much as freely to breathe therein. If the defeated nations continue to suffer most terribly, no less serious are the evils which afflict their conquerors. Small nations complain that they are being oppressed and exploited by great nations. The great powers, on their side, contend that they are being judged wrongly and circumvented by the smaller. All nations, great and small, suffer acutely from the sad effects of the late War. Neither can those nations which were neutral contend that they have escaped altogether the tremendous sufferings of the War or failed to experience its evil results almost equally with the actual belligerents. These evil results grow in volume from day to day because of the utter impossibility of finding anything like a safe remedy to the cures of society, and this in spite of all the efforts of politicians and statesmen whose work has come to naught if it has not unfortunately tended to aggravate the very evils they tried to overcome.

In such circumstances, millions of Europeans felt alienated from their leadership, from Capitalism, and from Communism as well.

Moreover, there was a spirit abroad in Europe, bred partly from the experience of soldiers in the War, and partly from the youthful idealism of High School and College students too young to have served themselves. In Germany, Austria, and Hungary, the onus of defeat lay heavily on these two groups; in Allied nations, veterans felt themselves shortchanged in return for all their wartime sacrifices, and students objected to being ruled by the same "old men" who had made their fathers and older brothers serve in a pointless and bloody conflict. Everywhere, the ex-soldiers yearned for the unity, brotherhood, and sense of purpose they had experienced at the front, in the face of a dull, indifferent, divided peace-time country to which they returned. The students, on the other hand, thrilled at once by the adventures of the soldiers and by their own idealism, regarded the society in which they found themselves as stifling and mediocre. A vague, indefinable mysticism with a political edge developed out of this, a search for exaltation and ecstacy which somehow would transform the shell of Europe into the green land of the past, the shining realm of tomorrow, or both at once. In a word, it was a form of Romanticism, produced from the War's killing of the smug Age of Liberalism—even as the original Romanticism was the child of the Age of Reason's death at the hands of the Revolution.

In every nation of Europe these elements produced movements which aimed to strike at Capitalism and Communism alike; some were Catholic, most were not. Those which were not looked to find mystical fulfillment not in Christ but in the nation or the race. Authors have come to call some or all of the groups after the first of them to come to power in a European state (Italy) by the name *Fascism*.

To our own time, Fascism (with which, in America, we tend to lump German National Socialism—the Nazis) remains a powerful symbol of oppression, and a pejorative which may be leveled at anyone whom we dislike. The greatest estimate of those who met their ends at the hands of the Nazis is 11 million, a large number, to be sure. Inevitably, the Fascists and Nazis are conjured up as examples of the ultimate evil.

Eleven million is a large number, to be sure; but Stalin was responsible for the deaths of 70 million, to say nothing of his predecessors and successors at the helm of the Soviet Union. While the German Concentration Camps, which lasted in their classic sense but five years and have been shut for 50, are continually evoked, the Soviet Gulag's seven decades and recent closure have been forgotten. In China, where as of this writing Mao's system remains in place, over 200 million lives were snuffed out by command of the Father of Chinese

Communism. Yet as of the moment, that regime retains Most Favored Nation status with these United States. One cannot help but wonder why.

We shall not speculate, however. Suffice it to say that we must look at Fascism not for its current symbolic value, but as disinterestedly and impartially as we would be expected to look at Soviet and Chinese Communism. Hitler ought not repel us more (or less) than Stalin or Mao. That having been said, let us consider the facts.

Firstly, let it be said that the different groups lumped together as "Fascist", often did not have much in common. Where the National Socialists considered Germans racially superior, Italian Fascists believed that their nation's superiority was strictly cultural. Where Nazis feared and hated Jews on grounds of blood, the Romanian Iron Guard opposed them for religious and cultural reasons—and the Italian Fascists, until World War II, did not oppose them at all. The same variety of attitudes characterized every issue with which such folk were concerned. The problem is neatly stated by H.R. Kedward:

> The tempting conclusion may well be that there is no such thing as fascism, only a number of groups and parties which showed similar characteristics but were really quite distinct. There would certainly be some truth in this view, but it would tend to ignore the conviction of most Fascists that they were part of a general movement designed to change not merely their own nation but the whole of society (*Fascism in Western Europe 1900-1945*, p. 5).

The same author accurately portrays the complexity of the issues involved:

> It is essential to see that the ferment of ideas presented here was the basis not only for Fascism but also for modern art and music, modern science and technology, the growth of psychology and a new theology. Fascist ideology was one particular synthesis made up of ideas which had a variety of influence. When it is analysed and broken down into its component parts it is found to contain much that in a different setting would be excitable. For this reason the label "Fascist" must be carefully used and "potential Fascist" not at all, for may not a "potential Fascist" turn his violence into art, his rhetoric into the pulpit or his wish to control people into advertising? (*Op. Cit.*, p.7).

Kedward identifies several conflicting pairs of ideas from the synthesis of which he maintains that Fascism arose. Let us examine them in turn, and make our own judgment of each.

The first was the aforementioned conflict between Capitalism and Communism. As observed earlier, many Europeans felt that neither the greed and rapacity of the one, nor the godless cruelty of the other, fitted either of them to be the guiding philosophy of a civilized nation. Such folk sought for a "Third Way" between the two. One of the most common solutions to the problem of economic organization was called variously "Corporatism," "Syndicalism," or Guild Socialism. While there were very many different variations thereof, all versions agreed in calling for representation of the people on a class or professional basis, rather than geographically, as was and is done in most of the world's Parliaments. There was envisaged the organization of "Corporations" or "Syndicates" in each trade, encompassing employers as well as workers. These in turn would be represented in a "Chamber of Corporations" or the like, which might either replace or supplement the existing legislature. Some variants of the notion took the Medieval Guilds as inspiration—due to the place of the Church in those organizations historically, some Corporatists converted to Catholicism, and many Catholics interested in social problems became Corporatists.

Another allied notion in Great Britain and the Commonwealth countries was "Distributism," the child of G.K. Chesterton and Hilaire Belloc. This called for the widest possible distribution of property and business among the people of a country: in place of large agribusinesses and industrial conglomerates, Distributists favored small farmers and local business. They too wished the restoration of Guilds, and so also looked to the Church for inspiration. More concerned with questions of banking and money circulation was Social Credit, proposed by Col. C.H Douglas. It advocated taking control of the money supply out of the hands of the banks and putting it into those of the government. All of the advocates of these ideas opposed as well international banking and high finance. Corporatist economics were generally adopted as part of their program by Fascist parties. But not all Corporatists, etc., were Fascist. One general distinction was that non-Fascist Corporatists believed that the Corporations should be organic bodies, built up from the grass roots and to whom the government should bear some responsibility; Fascists, on the other hand, saw the Corporations as being regime-directed and controlled. Moreover, where Fascists saw the ideology of the party as the animating spirit of such institutions, their opponents preferred something else—often Catholicism. But the apparent resemblances in structure, as well as shared antipathy to international finance has led to many commentators lumping all Corporatists together as "Fascists."

The next dichotomy examined by Kedward is that of "Rationalism" versus "Irrationalism." These two are to be found in every heart, of course, but in the 19th Century they assumed an ideological function. Order, authority, control—these were the earmarks of the historic European right. Men like Maurras, for instance, laid great stress on the need for order in the State, and maintained that the modern crisis was the result of these having broken down. Contrarily, irrationalists (ranging from Nietsche to the Anarchists to Freud) charged that the structures of society, and indeed rational thought oppressed Man; according to such theorists, only living for the self, and in the moment, with no regard for society's strictures could provide true happiness. Beyond politics, this was a movement which declared that the human urge to unrestricted sex and violence was not an expression of his lower nature, but his higher. To a greater or lesser degree, this was an attitude associated with the historic Left.

These two notions were fused into one by Fascism. The Fascists managed to be at once the party of order and of violence, of restraint and revolution. In this, as in their economic policy, they transcended the traditional Right/Left division. In this way, large elements of virtually every stratum of society could find a place for themselves in the Fascist spectrum.

Akin to this last was the division between civilized and primitive. Throughout the 19th Century, one current of thought, often identified with the Romantics, like Scott, Chateaubriand, and Novalis, looked to Europe's Medieval past and folk present for inspiration. Identifying again with the historic Right, these saw the Continent as having abandoned a glorious past for a dry, spiritually dead present. Opposed to this was the idea of progress, of evolution. Applying Darwin's theory to political and social life, and associated with Liberalism and Socialism alike, this cult of progress looked to a hypothetical future as the goal. Here too, Fascism managed to be both at once; declaring itself to be at once rooted in the nation's or the race's past, it claimed also to be the party of the future, leading the community ever forward into a glorious new age. Yet what the party was uniting was essentially a pagan past and a godless future; barbarism joined with scientificism. The Catholic ethos of Europe was almost entirely left aside.

Kedward's last opposition is that of the mass and the elite. Here too, the categories were associated with the traditional Right and Left. On the Right, it was held that Monarchs and Aristocrats had a God-given duty to rule. By virtue of blood and birth and training, they were most suited to governance. The Left, of course, believed (or claimed to) in the common man—Marx's teaching was allegedly intended to pave the way for mass rule. But here too, Fascism managed to combine the two. For the Fascists, leadership would rest in a single charismatic individual, who would wield all effective power in the state; his word would be law, like an absolutist monarch of the 18th century. But unlike a monarch, he did not owe his position to God (nor was he responsible thereto) but to the "spirit" of his people—he was, in a word, the incarnation of the folk he ruled. Opposition to him was not, therefore, a crime against God, but against the sovereign people (whose sovereignty, however, would only be exercised through the ruler; it neither protected nor legitimized any single individual of that people). Hence Nationalism became an important part of the Fascist mix. The influence of Nationalism spread through Europe, not only leading to the exaltation of existing nations, nor solely in ethnic conflict in the racial crazy quilt of Eastern Europe, but in the revival of such peoples as the Scots, Welsh, Bretons, Basques, and Flemings. Fascism's influence versus that of Christianity could be seen in how far each of these movements saw themselves as either a) an important part of the European quilt, or b) a good solely unto themselves, with the right to oppress or vanquish other nationalities. Here too, Fascism would substitute for the religious virtue of old-fashioned patriotism—love of country—a Nationalism which was neither religious nor really so much love of country as hatred of the foreign. Unfriendly observers have characterized such Nationalism as an attempt to persuade Europeans to regard their country or ethnic group in the same way that Americans do theirs.

At any rate, both Traditional Right and Left found much to sympathize with in Fascism, and much to oppose. For the Left, the aspects of imposed order, of exaltation of the past, and of a ruling elite and leader were repellent. Right-wing criticisms of Fascism were the opposite: its love of violence, its belief in evolution, and its appeal to the masses all disgusted old-style Royalists and the like. What then, was Fascism? In the end, if we wish to characterize it one way or the other, its this-worldly emphasis, its basic opposition to Christianity must line it up alongside Marxism. But this is an identification neither easy to make, nor true of all groups commonly identified as Fascist (though certainly it was true of the Italian Fascists and Nazis). An interesting confirmation of this is the fact that often strongholds of Communism in Italy and Germany (the Po Valley and Saxony, for example), were staunchly pro-Fascist during the years of Mussolini's and Hitler's ascendancy, only to return to their prior allegiance after those leaders' demise.

Italy, after the War, was torn between Nationalists and Socialists in the Chamber of Deputies, and an extremely militant Communist Party, which appeared to be headed toward power. To prevent this from happening, Pope Benedict XV lifted the *Non expedit* (the decree forbidding Catholics to take part in Italian political life after the 1870 loss of the Papal States). Don *Luigi Sturzo*, a Sicilian priest, founded the Popular Party. Based firmly on Catholic social teachings, and advocating Corporatism, the *Popolari* won in the November 1919 election 99 of 508 seats in the Chamber of Deputies. The new party was second to the Socialists' 151 seats.

In the years 1919-1922, Socialist and Communist gangs worked to destabilize the country—intimidating and even murdering their opponents. Mussolini, himself an ex-Socialist who had broken with the Party over World War I, organized the *squadritisi*. Formed of veterans and students intent on saving their country from Communism and in revitalizing Italian life, these groups engaged the gangs of the Left in precisely the same manner. Public order began to break down all over Italy; the country seemed on the verge of total anarchy.

There then occurred the famous "March on Rome." On October 26, 1922, the Fascists began to occupy public buildings in different parts of Italy. The next day they began a mass movement on Rome, only to find out that King Victor Emmanuel III had appointed Mussolini as Prime Minister, with emergency powers. The Fascists were in control; yet they had not seized power—they had filled a vacuum.

Mussolini quickly eliminated Socialism, and began to alter the shape of the country's political structure. It must be emphasized that many of his measures were good in and of themselves: the Corporate restructuring of the economy, family protection laws, and repression of groups (like the Mafia and the Grand Orient) which had always been problems for the Church were in accord with the Social encyclicals. But these things were not done out of a love of Christ and the neighbor, but rather out of a basically non-religious ideology. "Everything for the State" was Mussolini's motto. Certainly, the continued existence of the Popular Party would have allowed pressure to be applied to Mussolini, forcing him to emphasise the better parts of his program.

But guided by Secretary of State Pietro Cardinal Gasparri (disciple of that Cardinal Rampolla we met making mischief under Leo XIII) Pius XI was content to leave politics to the State, if the rulers thereof simply allowed the Church to pursue her mission unmolested. It appeared to the Pope that if the Popular Party continued, at once representing Catholic interests and opposing Mussolini, there would be much unnecessary friction. Since a priest led the party, and many more acted as local organisers, the answer was simple. On February 1, 1924, he forbade priests to belong to political parties. Catholic Action was to be entirely separated from the *Popolari*. Sturzo resigned from the Party in July, whereupon it collapsed. Its founder went into exile. In return, Catholic Action was recognized by the government. Peace settled over the land, for the moment.

But it was only for the moment. Based on an essentially atheistic outlook, Fascism soon clashed with the Church on the educational front. While religious instruction had been reinstated in State schools, it was made optional in the higher grades, where the philosophies of Kant and Hegel were to be taught. The struggle heated up, and both sides were anxious for a solution to this as well as the Roman Question (the illegal occupation of the Papal States by the Italian government). 1928 became 1929, and the stage was set for a Concordat, similar to the one Pius VII made with Napoleon.

This was a particularly beneficial arrangement for both parties. The Church received the independence of the Vatican (to which Mussolini had been prepared to give much more territory than was settled for); financial reparations for the lost Papal States; acceptance of Catholicism as the State religion; revision of things like the Law of Marriage in accordance with Church teachings; and numerous other items of that sort. Catholic Action was given official status, and in a flash of Papal honor, the Black Nobility (those Roman nobles who had continued to recognize the Pope as sovereign of Rome after 1870, as opposed to "Whites," who accepted the House of Savoy) were given Vatican citizenship. In return, the State received the blessing of the Church, and Mussolini the credit of closing a fault-line which had impeded Italy since 1870.

Yet, as subsequent events showed, Mussolini was not to be trusted. Still and all, the question must be faced. Given the anarchy into which Italy was sliding, and Communist revolution imminent in 1922, what are we to make of Mussolini's rise to power? It would be difficult to argue with the opinion of Arthur Cardinal Hinsley, Archbishop of Westminster, who would distinguish himself as a fervent opponent of Fascism:

> To speak plainly, the existing Fascist rule, in many respects unjust, is one example of the present-day deification of Caesarism, and of the tyranny which makes the individual a pawn on the chess board of absolutism. I say that the Fascist rule prevents worse injustice, and if Fascism—which in principle I do not approve—goes under, nothing can save the country from chaos: God's cause goes under with it.

It would soon be apparent, however, that if God's cause would go under if Fascism did so, it would have a tremendous fight on its hands if Fascism succeeded.

Benito Mussolini was a forceful personality, who knew how to use radio and newsreels to unite and inspire his countrymen. He soon set the economy to booming, and restored confidence in government. Under his rule, there was an appearance of class unity, and the fear of Red revolution was dispelled.

In the meantime, the prosperity of the 20s had spread through most of Europe. In France, Great Britain, Spain, Czechoslovakia, Germany, and elsewhere, parties more or less committed to Liberal Democracy succeeded one another in office, while the majority of their citizens happily enjoyed enhanced standards of living, and docilely went to the ballot-box at the appointed times. It was a period when, as popular wisdom had it, Communism would be kept out of Europe by four factors: the Papacy, the British House of Lords, the *Academie Française*, and the German General Staff. Yet this was a stability which depended upon one thing—continued prosperity. In the meantime, however, every detail of the Jazz Age now reigning in New York (save, of course, Prohibition) was reproduced in the great cities of Europe. Thither fled expatriate writers like Hemingway and Fitzgerald.

Not everyone believed that the current situation could last. Devoted adherents throughout Europe of the Old Right or the New Nationalism looked at Mussolini's Italy, and dreamed of reviving their own nations in similar wise. In Vienna, Budapest, Madrid, Bucharest, and elsewhere small groups formed with the idea of adapting Fascism to their own traditions. These men and women varied much from one another—and from a mustered-out Corporal in Munich, one Adolph Hitler who was, however, likewise a fervent admirer of il Duce.

Back in the U.S.A.

How was Mussolini seen in the untouched-by-war-or-revolution United States? With few exceptions, throughout the 1920s, publications as diverse as the *Saturday Evening Post* and the *New York Times* endorsed both his takeover and his internal policies. He was seen as "the Man who made the trains run on time." Nativists applauded him for restoring Italian traditions (though an endorsement from Klan types could hardly be seen as a bright mark for him!). The general run of folk viewed him as the savior of his country from Communism—this at a time when the United States was having its own "Red Scare." Above all, he was seen, at his worst, as a necessary evil, needed to force an indolent and ignorant people into the modern world. They would be impressed by all his posturing. Hard-working, hard-headed Americans, on the other hand, were supposed to have no requirements for national father figures and flashy dictators. They were a free nation of rugged individualists, full of republican virtue. Indeed, American freedom, rugged individualism, and republican virtue were all three to receive their greatest test since the War Between the States.

The Boom of the 20s simply could not last; credit was highly inflated, and the mass practice of buying stocks on borrowed money, then repaying the loans with dividends, built an economic house of cards. In October 1929, the bubble burst. On Black Monday, the New York Stock Exchange plummeted. Within a few weeks, stocks had lost 40% of their value. Prices fell, some wealthy and many middle-class folk were financially ruined, and banks and industries failed. Thousands were thrown out of work; with every bank closure and industrial failure, the process accelerated. On the farm, runaway deflation destroyed the value of crops, while in those states affected by the Dust Bowl, it was the crops themselves which were destroyed.

In short order, this Great Depression, as it was called, sped round the World, spreading the same swath of economic destruction. This storm would challenge every government and every institution on earth; many would crack under the strain. In all nations, the system was severely challenged. It would be so in Europe and Asia, in Latin America and the British Dominions. It would be so in the United States.

THE GREAT DEPRESSION AND THE ONSET OF WAR 1930-1941

A WORLD TURNED UPSIDE DOWN

The effect of the Great Depression on the World's peoples was catastrophic, not merely in an economic sense, but in a psychological one. Almost everyone everywhere, it seemed, was affected. As banks failed and businesses went bankrupt; as tumbling farm prices made beggars of the farmers and factory closures did the same for industrial workers, it seemed that the whole edifice of modernity was doomed. The complex structures of finance and industry, credit and bureaucracy which had emerged since the 19th Century (and which were little understood by the masses of people who lived under them) seemed about to collapse. Never, perhaps, since the Barbarian invasions which brought down the Roman Empire had life seemed so fearful and bleak.

Despite this, however, two inventions emerged which brought the embattled folk of the 1930s much solace: commercial radio and sound pictures. Despite the atmosphere of gloom which pervaded both this country and the rest of the world, the Depression was in many ways the Golden Age of both media.

Radio brought a steady stream of news and entertainment into every home, directly linking the listener with the outside world. While this did much to end rural isolation in those places where electrification had taken root, it also bred discontent. One can only imagine the longing for the unattainable a family in say, drought-ridden Oklahoma, would feel listening to the glamorous sounds of Guy Lombardo and his Royal Canadians, "live from the Grand Ballroom of the Astor Hotel in New York City." Without a doubt, however, the Big Bands who are so legendary today were the creation of the combination of records and radio.

The medium lent itself to the production of radio plays; soon a neverending stream of series—mysteries, comedy, soap operas, and the like were being churned out. From *The Shadow* and *The Whistler* through *Little Orphan Annie* and *The Easy Aces* to *My True Story* and *The Columbia Theatre of the Air*, there were shows of every imaginable description. Being strictly audio, these programs made the listener a sort of co-creator, inducing him, through the use of sound effects, to conjure up in his own imagination the appearance of the action described.

Radio also revolutionized advertising, as various companies sponsored these shows in order to promote their products.

The advent of sound was revolutionary in the world of movies. Many an actor or actress' career was ruined because, however appealing their appearance, their voices were unsuitable. But some did make the transition, and many more replaced those who could not. *Mae West, Frederic March, Errol Flynn, Clark Gable,* and *Myrna Loy* were only a few of the names who came to prominence in this period. In its infancy, the industry produced such classics as *Dracula, Robin Hood, Little Caesar,* and *Treasure Island.* Musicals were invented, wherein such as *Fred Astaire* and *Ginger Rogers* would transport their impoverished and despairing viewers into a never-never land of song, dance, and romance.

This was also the age of the Movie Moguls: men like Louis B. Mayer at MGM, Darryl F. Zanuck at 20th Century-Fox, and Jack Warner at Warner Brothers produced some of the finest pictures ever made, but ran the industry like the Robber Barons of the 19th Century. Big-name actors and Moguls both were able to command wealth unheard of to most Depression-era audiences. Where Old Money and Industrial Tycoons alike took pains to conceal their wealth from the impoverished crowds, Hollywood flaunted it. What would be intolerable activity on the part of a factory owner became expected in an actor: people loved to read and hear about the scandalous lifestyles of the stars, and so a new kind of journalism was born—the Hollywood gossip column. The battling queens of the profession during the Depression were public enemies and secret friends, *Hedda Hopper* and *Louella Parsons*.

While all of this may seem a bit unimportant, it introduced into our culture an element which has been present ever since. The effect of entertainment media on molding societal attitudes has been enormous; at the same time, the influence is reciprocal, since the media must make a product that will sell. Nevertheless, what is portrayed onscreen approvingly is halfway to acceptance by the general public. The frequent divorces and other irregularities of some of the Stars contributed, in the long run, to legitimizing such behavior. It was a process which could be measured only over decades, and which continues today.

One other important note about the Depression concerns a style of both architecture and interior decoration. Old techniques, taste and style came in the 1920s to meet new ones; it was considered that the world stood on the edge of a new age, and so required a new look. Thus was born Streamline Moderne, or as we call it today, Art Deco. At the time it was seen as the coming thing, and everything from glasses to churches (most notably the Shrine of the Little Flower in Royal Oak, Michigan, and the Catholic Cathedral in Salina, Kansas) were designed in it. Its original name gives some impression of the style. Streamlined it certainly was. Whether bric-a-brac or posters, things designed in this mode gave the impression of straining either for speed or upward-reach.

There are two things to remember about Art Deco: 1) it defined the 1930s; and 2) despite being thought of as "Moderne," it was perhaps the last truly human style this century. Where a procession can be seen from Romanesque to Gothic to Renaissance to Baroque to Rococco and so on, up to Art Deco, the line stops there. There were reasons for this, as we shall see.

The Depression Under Hoover

The first reaction to the Crash was one of optimism. Throughout history, events have rarely been seen in their true light; so it was in this case. As Robert S. and Helen M. Lynd wrote of Middletown (actually, Muncie, Indiana), a typical Midwestern city, in their 1937 study, *Middletown in Transition:*

> Middletown entered 1930 prepared for the best. There had been a stock-market crash to be sure but... local bankers were predicting a boom in the spring...
> One of the most illuminating aspects of this early period of the depression was the reluctance of Middletown's habits of thought to accept the fact of "bad times" ... one does not like to admit that the techniques and institutions which one uses with seeming familiarity and nice control are really little-understood things capable of rising up and smiting one. The local press... became... a conscious and unconscious suppressor of unpleasant evidence. Hopeful statements by local bankers and industrialists... tended to make the front page, while shrinkages in plant forces and related unhappy news commanded small space on inside pages or were omitted entirely.

There were in fact a few spasmodic upswings in the economy in the months following the Crash which appeared to justify such optimism. But in May 1930, another downturn crushed such hopes.

It is a common myth to suppose that President Hoover did nothing in the face of the Depression. This widely-held notion (fostered afterwards by adherents of his successor) is ably summed up by Leo Gurko:

> Part of the country believed confusedly with President Hoover that the surest way to save the country was to imitate the techniques of the Puritan pioneers: reduce costs, tighten belts, close all the windows, bolt the shutters, and generally make oneself as small and inconspicuous a target as possible for the slings and arrows of misfortune. Politically, this took the form of cutting the budget, holding frequent conferences with the leaders of commerce and labor, issuing periodical statements that prosperity was just around the corner, declaring moratoria on foreign debts, praying, suggesting to factory owners that they not lower

wages, and trusting that the system would get back on an even keel of its own volition. This program was attractive to a great many people because it involved them in the least possible effort and encouraged them to keep moving in familiar, hence more or less comfortable grooves (*The Angry Decade*, p. 43).

So deeply held was this view that in the eyes of many, Hoover himself became personally responsible for the Depression. As it ground on, and millions were reduced to beggary, selling apples, and the like, the tent-and-shanty villages which the now-homeless constructed on the outskirts of major cities came to be called *Hoovervilles*. The same feeling was reflected in a popular song, whose best-known line runs: *Mr. Herbert Hoover says now's the time to buy; so let's have another cup of coffee, and let's have another piece of pie!* But in fact, after time, Hoover began to fight the Depression strongly, as we shall see.

Although perhaps most people in 1930 thought that the American economy would pull through intact, a few voices were raised declaring that mere economic recovery was not enough; that a more thoroughgoing regeneration was in order. Two of the best-known groups of this sort had been saying the same things in the previous decade; but prosperity had severely limited their audiences. In hard times, as is ever the way in America, more were willing to listen.

The first group to enter the fray were the New Humanists, with the publication in February 1930 of a group of essays entitled *Humanism and America: Essays on the Outlook of Modern Civilization*. Editor Norman Foerster opened his preface with the words:

> "Life's a long headache in a noisy street," sang the poet Masefield in *The Widow in the Bye Street* seventeen years ago. Since then we have all come to live in Main rather than Bye Street, and our headache has grown apace despite the best efforts of the physicians of the age. The noise and whirl increase, the disillusion and depression deepen, the nightmare of Futility stalks before us in the inevitable intervals when activity flags. Heroically or mock-heroically we distrust or reject such stimulants and anodynes as religion, moral conventions, the dignity of manners, the passion for beauty, and even our recent faith in democracy, in liberalism, in progress, in science, in efficiency, in machinery. At length revolt and scepticism themselves have ceased to be interesting. The modern temper has produced a terrible headache.
>
> In vain does our Chief Executive assure us that "we have reached a higher degree of comfort and security than ever existed before in the history of the world." Like Mr. Punch when it was announced that the government would soon be broadcasting intelligence by radio, we wonder "Where will the government get it?" All governments, all nations, are to-day in this predicament (p. v).

The fourteen following essays proposed rather similar theories: that modern man had given himself up to his own whims, that he was urged by his opinion molders "to live as unconsciously and mechanically as possible," in the words of Gorham B. Munson (p. 243). From this had resulted all our current problems. The answer, thought the New Humanists, lay in self-discipline, in reason, and in acceptance of "transcendent values." As noticed in the last chapter, they disagreed (in a most gentlemanly manner) among themselves as to what these latter were, Irving Babbitt declaring for whatever spirituality was common to Christianity and to Buddhism; T.S. Eliot cleaving to external religious authority. To Babbitt, having commented on the joint Humanist and Catholic veneration for, say, Aristotle, "It follows that the Catholic and the non-Catholic should be able to co-operate on the humanistic level" (p. 44). Eliot, however, had a rather more interesting view of the Church:

> The great merit of the Catholic Church, from the worldly point of view, is its Catholicity. That is to say, it is obvious that every religion is effectively limited by the racial characteristics of those who practise it, and that a strictly racial or national religion is certain to hold many irrelevances and impurities, from lack of an outside standard of criticism. When the Catholic Faith really is catholic, the aberrations of one race will be corrected by those of another. But it is obviously very difficult even for the Roman Church, nowadays, to be truly Catholic. The embarrassment of temporal powers, the virulence of racial and national enthusiasms, are enormous centrifugal forces. The great majority of English speaking people, or at least the vast majority of persons of British descent; half of France, half of Germany, the whole of Scandinavia, are outside of the Roman communion: that is to say, the Roman Church has lost some organic parts of the body of modern civilisation. It is a recognition of this fact which makes some persons of British extraction hesitate to embrace the Roman communion; and which makes them feel that those of their race who have embraced it have done so only by the surrender of some essential part of their inheritance and by cutting themselves off from their family (pp. 106-107).

In all of this, there is much talk of the cultural and the spiritual, but little of the supernatural and the salvific. The New Humanists were severely hampered in dealing with the Church, as for them it was merely a generally positive force for cultural and spiritual values, rather than a supernatural one bound up with their own individual salvation. This is certainly in part due to the fact that their New England Yankee (whence most of them had sprung) heritage disposed them to think of the Church as something for other people; especially for one's Irish maids. But the greater responsibility lies with American Catholics. Men like the New

Humanists knew the Catholic Church simply as the source of Gregorian Chant, Scholastic Philosophy, and Gothic Architecture—an impression which their Catholic contemporaries, having fallen far below the cultural level of their ancestors, did not try to replace with the notion of the Church as the saving Mystical Body of Christ. The fact that she sometimes also produces wonderful things in the artistic realm is secondary—both to the role she plays in saving individuals, and the role she may play in saving their society. At any rate, because of this lack of realization of the Church's mission, the New Humanists could not realize her true place in the reconstruction of society or their obligation thereby.

The second drawback they faced was that they were literati and academics, not men of action. Hence they could produce no concrete program, or even a vision of the America they would like to see. Indeed, they scorned such as mere "legislationism." Their true sphere was criticism of the arts and education. But in a society such as ours, where such things are seen as being beyond the average individual's interests, their insights could have, ultimately, only a small audience.

All that having been said, however, it must also be pointed out that the New Humanists, if they were not offering real solutions, were at least asking questions which had not been asked; questions which, heretofore, *ought not* to be asked, at least not by true blue Americans. By their insistence that the life of the mind and spirit had a proper role to play in national life, they were defying the American religion. Given their antecedents, that was something.

More specific were the Southern Agrarians, most of whom had been part of the Fugitive Movement in the preceding decade. Twelve of them authored a joint manifesto entitled *I'll Take My Stand: The South and the Agrarian Tradition*. In many ways, it was a reply to *America and Humanism*:

> The "Humanists" are too abstract. Humanism, properly speaking, is not an abstract system, but a culture, the whole way in which we live, act, and feel. It is a kind of imaginatively balanced life lived out in a definite social tradition. And in the concrete, we believe that this, the genuine humanism, was rooted in the agrarian life of the older South and of other parts of the country that shared in such a tradition. It was not an abstract moral "check" derived from the classics—it was not soft material poured in from the top. It was deeply founded in the way of life itself—in its tables, chairs, portraits, festivals, laws, marriage customs. We cannot recover our native humanism by adopting some standard of taste that is critical enough to question the contemporary arts but not critical enough to question the social and economic life which is their ground (p. xliv).

Their basic contention was that the very things which the New Humanists decried were the product of Industrial and Banking civilization; further, that the South had resisted this to a greater degree than any other part of the nation, even despite its military defeat in the War Between the States. At long last, they believed, the South itself was succumbing. But if the country as a whole was ever to become a decent nation again, it would have to regain an agrarian culture. By this the Southerners (who included such men as Robert Penn Warren, Andrew Lytle, John Crowe Ransome, and later Catholic convert Allen Tate) meant not a pure farming society, "that has no use at all for industries, for professional vocations, for scholars and artists, and for the life of cities." Rather, it would be "one in which agriculture is the leading vocation, whether for wealth, for pleasure, or for prestige—a form of labor that is pursued with intelligence and leisure, and that becomes the model to which other forms approach as they may." Yet in this first collection, the Twelve themselves admitted that they had no practical means to bring about this necessary goal, only the conviction that it could and must be done.

If Conservative intellectuals were considering such things, the Comintern in Moscow was doing so also. Like the New Humanists and Southern Agrarians, they believed in the need for thoroughgoing change; unlike them, they had a practical program for doing so. From 1930, Comintern ordered Communists around the world to penetrate the arts, the clergy, trade unions, and the like. Where formerly they had tried to build their own unions and declare themselves openly, henceforth they would practice a tactic called United Front. It is hard to realize since the fall of the Soviet Union, but Communism presented a real threat to American society. The Depression called forth, particularly among writers, artists, and actors, very many folk who saw in the rhetoric of the Communist Party a real solution to the horrible misery around them. In 1930, it was not so obvious that this misery would be around for a while; but it became so as 1930 passed into 1931.

The second full year of the Depression saw its destabilizing results around the world. In the Far East, the Japanese government, whose population was on the brink of starvation at the best of times, believed that only overseas expansion could relieve the pressure on them. One faction of government felt that this expansion should be aimed at Soviet Siberia; another that the European colonies in Southeast Asia were easier targets. But both areas would require considerable military strength. Manchuria, on the other hand, nominally linked to the weak Chinese government of Marshal Chiang Kai-Shek, would be a more tempting target. An incident was provoked, Manchuria invaded, and after Shanghai was occupied to force Chiang to negotiate, the war ended.

Manchuria became the Empire of Manchukuo, under the last Chinese Emperor, although the country was of course ruled by the Japanese.

Already, in the rest of the world, liberal democracies were judged by many of their citizens to be incapable of either staving off the Depression or the increased Communist threat. Under Mussolini, Italy had been able, after a brief economic downturn, to shrug off the Depression raging elsewhere. It was thought that if traditional party politics could be suppressed, and all a country's political and social forces mobilized under a single leader, the Depression could be defeated. In a pattern which would be repeated throughout the world, Mussolini's skill in protecting his nation's economy was much admired by Argentine general *Jose Felix Uriburu* (1868-1932). It must be understood that Argentina at this time was considered at once democratic and advanced; Bueno Aires had well earned its nickname of "the Paris of South America." The anti-clerical Radical Democratic Party had held power since 1916. Seeing the helpless floundering of the civilian government, Uriburu led an army coup against it in September of 1930. Installed as president in September, he abrogated his predecessor's labor legislation two months later. He then proceeded to remove Radical Democrats from national and state offices, and finally dissolved the National Assembly itself. Reformation of the constitution followed, decency and order were restored, and Catholic Action introduced. Uriburu then stepped down to allow for a presidential election. Although Argentina was far from removed from the Depression, its worst effects were muted.

In the other major South American nation, Brazil, the Depression had similar effects. On October 30, 1930, a military revolution ousted the civilian president and installed *Getulio Vargas* as president. Unlike Uriburu, but like Mussolini, Vargas had no real ideology of his own; rather, he cooperated with leftists and rightists alike, with anyone whose support would cement his power. Similarly, he was not a practicing Catholic like Uriburu, but knew how to speak to Catholics, like Mussolini. Eventually, he introduced the *Novo Estado*, the "New State," which like Mussolini's Fascist state, was essentially power- rather than ideology-oriented.

As in Latin America, so too in Europe, the notion took root of mobilizing all national resources in the fight against the Depression. Germany saw Catholic Centre Party chief *Heinrich Bruening* become Chancellor. Assuming office on March 28, 1930, he increased taxation, reduced government expenditure, raised tariffs on agricultural imports, and cut salaries and pensions. When the Reichstag (Parliament) rejected much of his legislation, he persuaded President Paul von Hindenburg on July 16 to push it through using the emergency powers given him by the

Constitution's article 48. Unwittingly, he had prepared the way for Hitler:

> [Former Chancellor Hans] Luther who began it and Bruening who repeated this stratagem were not evil men. The result of the precedent was all the more damaging for the very reason that Bruening was a man of unimpeachable integrity. He was doubtless the ablest German statesman of the whole period, save perhaps Stresemann, and even that exception may not stand. He was a man of singular probity of life, a devout Catholic, a deeply patriotic, patient, prudent, and courageous intellectual. He had devoted much of his life to editing and leading the Catholic Trade Union Movement in Germany. As Chancellor he lived with becoming modesty in a few rooms of the chancellery, using the public taxi instead of an imposing limousine, conducted himself with exacting frugality as an example of high citizenship in a period that called for high sacrifices from everyone, and gave numerous exhibitions of his purity and strength of character. He of course believed that he could save Germany from the danger that hung over her. (John T. Flynn, *As We Go Marching*, pp. 144-145).

Ultimately, Bruening hoped to establish a Corporate State with a restored Monarchy; but, as will become apparent, Germany instead received a parody thereof.

In neighboring Poland, the government had been dominated since 1926 by Independence leader *Josef Pilsudski*. A fallen away Catholic, Pilsudski had ruled with the help of the Socialists. But under the stress of the Depression, Pilsudski and his left-wing allies parted company. In the Summer of 1930, Pilsudski moved against his erstwhile friends and established a rightist "Government of National Unity," which however left out the Catholic National Democrats.

The same desire for governmental unity became apparent even in Britain; not only was a mixed Conservative-Labour-Liberal National Cabinet established under Ramsay MacDonald, but similar regimes (like the South African "Fusion") took power elsewhere in the Empire. This was not considered enough in some quarters, however, and 1931, which saw both the formation of the National Government and Britain's leaving the Gold Standard (to conserve the precious substance) also saw the formation of the British Union of Fascists under *Sir Oswald Moseley*. The Depression also spurred interest on the part of British and Dominion people in Belloc and Chesterton's *Distributism*. This latter advocated the breaking up of large industrial and agricultural combines, and their replacement by many small holders. Colonel Douglas' *Social Credit*, with its advocacy of credit-free money distributed in large enough quantities to end deflation and bring both wages and prices up to an acceptable level gained many adherents in both the British Empire and the United States.

As the first months of 1931 passed by with little financial relief in sight, Pius XI wrote an encyclical dealing with economic questions. Marking the anniversary of Leo XIII's *Rerum novarum*, it bore the name *Quadragesimo anno*— "Forty Years After." It comprised three major objectives: 1) to show the benefits brought by Leo's encyclical to the World at large and to the Church; 2) to defend that pope's social teaching and to develop it more fully; and 3) to examine the roots of the current social unrest, and to suggest a cure.

In addition to a reform in morality, and recognition of Christ the King, as he had recommended already in the 1926 *Quas primas*, Pius called for wide distribution of ownership—even as did the Distributists. He went further to declare that the State must withdraw from many functions which it had usurped since the French and Industrial revolutions. Echoing Leo XIII, Pius decried the fact that:

> Things have come to such a pass that the highly developed social life which once flourished in a variety of prosperous institutions organically linked with each other, has been damaged and all but ruined, leaving thus virtually only institutions and the state.

To remedy this situation, the Pope called for the formation of Vocational Groups. Uniting both employers and labor in each given profession, they would be represented in some sort of governmental body, and have the highest amount of autonomy possible. It would be the job of the State to coordinate these bodies.

The ideas in this encyclical were suggested to the Pope in great degree by two German Jesuits: *Oswald von Nell-Breuning* and *Heinrich Pesch*. Having lived through the see-saw interwar history of Germany, and being grounded strongly in the German Catholic social tradition, the ideas here presented were called in their ecclesiastical form *Solidarism*. As might be guessed, the Vocational Groups resembled the Guilds of English Guild Socialism, and the Corporations already being erected by Mussolini. But the Pope criticized these latter as being too State-dominated; rather than drawing their power from the grass-roots up, they appeared to be mere organs of governmental domination over each employee.

Interestingly, Solidarism, under that name, only found much favor among Russian emigres—specifically, the organization called NTS (National Union of Solidarists). As expressed by Walter Laqueur:

> Solidarism saw itself as the antithesis of the class struggle. Relations between classes were to be harmonious, with a strong state

as supreme arbiter. This implied the rejection of both "excessive" liberal individualism and Western pluralism. There was to be freedom in the future Russia, but not unlimited freedom; nor did the NTS envision a multiparty capitalist system. Key industries were to be state-owned. Lastly, religion was to be of central importance in the future order, with the Orthodox church in a dominant position (*Black Hundred*, p. 81)

Although, as Laqueur observes in the preceding paragraph, "This doctrine was by no means identical with the social teachings of the Catholic church which went by the same name," the divergence was primarily cultural rather than ideological. Similar ideas were espoused by the Romanian Legion of the Archangel Michael (or Iron Guard) led by *Corneliu Codreanu*.

The encyclical had the effect of galvanizing Catholics around the world in support of Distributist and Corporatist ideas. One such was Antonio Salazar of Portugal, who had become Prime Minister of that country in 1926. In 1932 he gave the nation a Corporative constitution. In this document, the ideas espoused by Pius XI were erected into law. The result was called (as in Brazil, although it was quite different from Vargas' Brazilian edition) the *Estado Novo*, the New State. Corporations representing labor and capital in every branch of industry were erected.

The economy of Portugal had been in foreign hands for a long time; Salazar restored the position of the Portuguese fishermen, farmers, and artisans. The Church reassumed her rightful place in the national life. He declared that when the country was ready, he would bring back her King. Above all, Salazar tried, as had La Tour du Pin, von Vogelsang, and the other Corporate theorists, to put an end to the rule of party and faction. In his own words:

> ...we seek to construct a social and corporative state corresponding exactly with the natural structure of society. The families, the parishes, the townships, the corporations, where all the citizens are to be found with their fundamental juridical liberties, are the organisms which make up the nation, and as such they ought to take a direct part in the constitution of the supreme bodies of the state. Here is an expression of the representative system that is more faithful than any other.

Another attempt to inaugurate a Catholic, Corporate state took place in Austria. The rump remaining from the German-speaking areas of the former Empire was always in a rather precarious position economically. The Depression hit the country badly. The rise of the Nazis to power in Germany in 1933 caught the country in a vise; to stave off Hitler, successive Austrian governments had to turn to Mussolini. Moreover, the Socialists and Communists were very active. Surrounded by dangers internal and external, Austrians looked for strong Catholic leadership. They found it in *Engelbert Dollfuss*.

Born in 1892, Dollfuss had studied law and economics at Vienna. He became secretary to the Lower Austrian Peasant Federation, and in 1927 director of the Lower Austrian chamber of agriculture. In 1931 he became chancellor. At the Christian Social party conference in April 1933, the need to reconstruct Austrian society if it was to stave off its enemies was of paramount concern. At that conference, Dollfuss' assistant, Kurt von Schuschnigg declared that the "reconstruction of the state" was "indivisibly connected with the reform of society," and that *Quadragesimo anno* was the guide. A new Corporative constitution was adopted on June 19, 1934.

It is a remarkable document. Its preamble reads: "In the name of almighty God from Whom all justice emanates, the Austrian people receives for its Christian, German Federal State on a corporative foundation this constitution." In keeping with this, the Concordat with the Holy See was elevated to Constitutional law. Corporative legislative bodies like the Federal Cultural Council and the Federal Economic Council were erected. Dollfuss, lover of Austrian institutions that he was, favored a Habsburg restoration. But although he gave his country a good constitution, he did not see it in operation for long.

The Austrian Nazis were fearful that Dollfuss' activities would prevent the country's being annexed by Germany. On July 25, 1934, a group of 150-200 Nazis seized the chancellery, and murdered Dollfuss. Although the attempted coup was put down, it was nevertheless a great blow to Austrian independence.

Dollfuss' constitution did survive him—for four years. At last, abandoned by the West, Austria submitted to her northern neighbor. For the short period that Dollfuss' reforms were in effect, they produced some excellent results.

Lithuania also attempted a similar solution to the problems of the Great Depression, Communism, and Nazism. After a pro-Communist government was deposed in 1926, Antanas Smetona, who had led the nation to independence in 1918, returned to power. Under his sponsorship, a new constitution in 1931 made Catholicism the religion of the State, and established Chambers of Commerce and Agriculture to function in typical corporative style. A 1935 law created a Chamber of Labor to safeguard the workers' cultural, economic, and social interests. Here again, only four years would pass before Soviet troops ended the experiment—but what was accomplished in the meantime showed great promise.

The next year, Lithuania's neighbor to the north, Latvia, adopted a Corporative government; this even though only 29% of Latvians were Catholic. Still, it conformed to the general pattern otherwise:

> A corporative form of government came into effect with the formation, in January 1936, of a National Economic Council, made up of the elected boards of the newly created chambers of commerce, industry, agriculture, artisans, and labor. A State Cultural Council was also created, consisting of the boards of the Chamber of Professions, and the Chamber of Literature and Art. These councils were allowed to collaborate with the respective government departments, individually and jointly. The two National Councils constituted the Joint Economic and Cultural State Council, which was convoked by the President of the Republic, and worked in close collaboration with the Cabinet of Ministers. The Joint State Council represented all sections of the nation, including the national minorities. It passed resolutions by a simple majority vote of its members.
> The reorganization of the producing population on a guild basis was paralleled by a readjustment in municipal and rural self-government, where elections were now held along guild rather than political lines. A new communal law provided for an organic coordination between the various corporative chambers and the self-governing territorial administrations. It was generally conceded at the time that the direct participation of every producing socio-economic group in the governmental machinery ensured that national unity which both public opinion and the men in office sought as a remedy for the current ills and a new foundation for the future security of the state (Alfred Bilmanis, *A History of Latvia*, pp. 360-361).

Needless to say, the Soviets put an end to all of that also in 1940.

Quadragesimo anno made such an impression in the Netherlands that Corporations were actually formed at the behest of the minority Catholic party, and endowed with a certain amount of governmental power in the 1938 constitution; World War II and German occupation ended this experiment. In Belgium, Robert Poulet, a journalist, played an important part in the Réaction group. This consisted of men of letters, war veterans, corporatists, etc. Established in 1932, its organ for the next two years was the *Revue Réactionnaire*. It tried to foster a "powerful current of opinion against parliament and democracy;" it felt that the old parties must disappear and "abdicate their sovereignty into the hands of the king." The king, who would govern with the help of a corporatist system, would be given the most extensive powers, including legislation. In 1935 the *Revue Réactionnaire* was succeeded by the *Revue de l'Ordre Corporatif* (1935-1940) which continued the struggle for a "corporate monarchy." The previous year, Poulet and various other Réaction members took over the *Nation Belge*. This latter held that the Parliamementary regime was dying, and should be replaced by a corporatist state organized around the king. Of similar views were Pierre Nothomb (b. 1887), writer and orator, founder of the weekly *L'Action Nationale* (1924-1930), and Paul Hoonaert, who was executed by the Nazis.

In Ireland, Corporatism inspired the work of Fr. Denis Fahey and Fr. E. Cahill; it also had some influence on the 1937 constitution. Quebec and Latin American nations outside Brazil and Argentina showed interest in the same ideas.

Beyond and alongside the Guilds, Corporations, or Vocational Groups ending class struggle, as envisaged by Pius XI, Catholics and others confronted by the Depression looked to certain other common motifs in reconstructing the social order. These included a strong national leader who would direct reforms: he might be the legitimate King, as advocated by the Action Française, the Belgians whom we have just mentioned, Dollfuss, and Chancellor Bruening—and as put into practice by Yugoslavia's Alexander and Bulgaria's Boris III; or else a purely self-made charismatic leader like Mussolini or Salazar. This leader would undertake the coordination of the nation's economic interests. National traditions would be the guiding ideology, and party strife would be removed or lessened. Above all, the country's financial system would be removed from the vagaries of international finance and run for domestic interests alone.

These basic ideas lent themselves to a dizzying multiplicity of interpretations, both from country to country and within each of them. Mussolini claimed to be a Corporatist, and his program had a certain resemblance to the Pope's. But the Popolari under Don Luigi Sturzo, his earliest opponents (and whom he managed, as we saw in the last chapter, to reduce in 1923) had as their motto, *Libertas*, a liberty which was not "the liberal, individualist, antiorganic atomic conception, which is based on the [false] conception of the sovereignty of the people." Similarly, in Germany, Bruening's support for the Corporate State was echoed by his Nazi enemies. What separated Sturzo and Bruening from Mussolini and Hitler was their belief that the executive should be a legitimate Monarch, that the Corporations should be directed from the bottom up, and that Catholicism, rather than the Nation or race should be the defining element in social morality. With Hitler's advent to power in 1933, however, the strong attraction of a charismatic leader to a people made desperate by poverty and hungry for security at any price, became manifest.

Bruening had been unseated by a cabal of short-sighted politicians, who prevailed upon the aged von Hindeburg to dismiss him. His place was taken by the Catholic Franz von Papen; he in turn was replaced by General Kurt von Schleicher. At last, confident that they would be able to restrain Nazi excesses, Conservative leaders agreed to the appointment of Adolph Hitler to the Chancellorship. Von Papen became Vice Chancellor, but the old guard was woefully mistaken in his belief that he could control the Nazis.

Communist agitation and street battles between Reds and Nazis (to say nothing of economic hardship) had made the Germans think that security for freedom was a good bargain. When, on the night of February 27, 1933 the Reichstag building was set ablaze, it was suspected that the Communists had done it (to this day it remains unknown whether it was in fact started by them or by the Nazis). The next day, Hitler prevailed upon von Hindenburg to issue a decree "for the Protection of the People and the State." This had the effect of voiding constitutional protection for personal, property, and political rights. Although the Nazis failed to gain an outright majority at the March 5 national elections, Hitler persuaded the Reichstag to pass an Enabling Act which transferred legislative power to the cabinet. Shortly thereafter, the first concentration camps were built and given prisoners; Communists first, but others later.

As with the Fascists, the National Socialist movement was designed to be attractive to both Right and Left. The Left wing of the party, under Ernst Rohm, began to press Hitler for radical social and economic changes and the abolition of the army. This began to worry both industrialists and military men, whose tacit support the regime required. The traditional Right felt threatened on grounds of freedom. In a Dresden speech delivered in July of 1933, von Papen declared:

> Who among us would have imagined it possible that within four months the National Socialists would have taken over the entire German Reich, that all the middle-class political parties would have disappeared, that our democratic institutions would have been eliminated as with one stroke of the pen, that the new chancellor would have assumed a degree of power that no German Emperor ever possessed.

Von Papen's concerns were borne out by Nazi actions over the following months. Ever more incidents of terrorism occurred, with Rohm's SA attacking opponents of the regime. But the wily Hitler used that time to ingratiate himself with von Hindenburg, by showing the old man that through the Nazi program of rearmament and voiding the Versailles Treaty, Germany would again become a great nation. He further assured the highest leaders of the army and navy that he would muzzle the SA (paramilitary militia—the Storm Troopers or Brownshirts) and make the German war machine something to conjure with.

Von Papen, who had helped convince von Hindenburg to appoint Hitler in the first place, began to seriously cast about for some way to restrain the Nazis:

> By early June 1934 Papen had concluded that since Hitler was unwilling or unable to control his SA, he, the vice-chancellor, would have to move the government into action by calling public attention to the regime's misdeeds. As a forum for this challenge, he chose the auditorium of Marburg University, one of the few German universities that had shown any reluctance to give the Nazi regime an intellectual stamp of approval. On June 17, before what he called "the intellectual aristocracy of Germany," Papen delivered a speech written for him by the Christian Conservative intellectual Edgar Jung. Papen began by defending the Christian Conservatives' role in helping Hitler to power, explaining that they had hoped to "reform" the discredited Weimar democracy by "unifying" the divisive party system under the banner of National Socialism. They had meant this to be a "temporary" measure designed to clear the way for a creation of a "new spiritual and political elite." They had certainly not intended to introduce an "unbridled dictatorship" and a "revolution against order, law, and church." After cataloging more precisely the ways in which the Nazis had violated fundamental values and institutions of "European civilization," Papen appealed to Hitler to distance himself from those of his followers who were "falsifying" his ideas. "No people," he warned, "can live in a condition of perpetual upheaval; perpetual dynamism can create nothing. Germany must not climb aboard a train traveling into the void, no one knowing where it might finally stop" (David Clay Large, *Between Two Fires*, pp. 120-121).

Hitler was much disturbed by the favorable reaction this speech received. The result was the June 30 "Night of Long Knives." Leaders of the Party's Left wing like Rohm were killed. But the Right felt Hitler's wrath as well. Jung was murdered, as well as Erich Klausener, the German head of Catholic Action. The purge extended outside of Berlin. In Munich, old Gustav von Kahr, the Catholic Monarchist leader who had thwarted Hitler's 1923 putsch was hacked to death with axes; his body was then dumped into a swamp.

Yet, when it was all over, the army, reassured by the downfall of their SA rivals, ordered each soldier to take an oath of personal loyalty to Hitler. Hindenburg died; his Presidential office was merged with that of Chancellor into the new post of *Fuehrer*— "Leader." Hitler's grasp on the country was complete.

But however uncomfortable his takeover, Hitler, through his public works (such as the construction of the autobahns) and rearmament programs, made good on his promise to lead Germany out of the

Depression. Many Germans still distrusted and feared him. But as in Italy (and unlike Russia), so long as it produced economic results, regardless of whatever freedoms were lost, the majority would give the regime tacit support.

As will now become apparent, although subsequent events have led us to look at Hitler and Mussolini as simply evil men, and their peoples dupes, the Germans and Italians made a deal which was uncomfortably like that which Americans would soon make.

Although Hoover in the beginning of the Depression was little disposed to major action, his mood changed as the situation worsened. The country had tightened its belt to be sure; do-it-yourself shoe repair kits were all the rage among those who could still afford them. Dance marathons offered hard-earned money to those whose feet could survive the strain. Agencies and private organizations offered relief, but it began to run dry after three years of Depression. Since cities and towns were going bankrupt, many could not afford to feed the poverty-struck. Moreover, those who could do so were withdrawing money—preferably in gold coin—and hoarding it. In response, Hoover sponsored through Congress the Reconstruction Finance Corporation, which lent 1.5 billion by the end of 1932 to help rebuild the devastated economy. In May and June, 17,000 World War veterans arrived in Washington urging passage of a bill which would allow them to cash their bonus certificates early. When the Senate defeated the bill, the government offered the vets money for their return trips to their homes; but the last 2,000 of the "Bonus Army" had to be driven out by troops led by General Douglas McArthur.

At the 1932 Democratic Convention, Al Smith was defeated for the nomination by his successor as Governor of New York State, *Franklin Delano Roosevelt*. "FDR," as he was popularly called, was a product of what is considered America's aristocracy. Cousin of Theodore Roosevelt (whose niece, Eleanore, he married), he combined a refined and individual accent with the same impression of energy his cousin had possessed. Charming, assertive, with a jauntily placed cigarette holder seemingly hermetically attached to his teeth, he radiated confidence. Well he might; having inherited from outgoing Governor Smith a budget surplus of 15 million, he would manage to leave the Albany Statehouse with a deficit of 90 million. Despite this he was able to speak convincingly of the need for radical economizing in government.

No matter. He fought the 1932 campaign against Hoover on just this point, as well as demanding States' Rights. He beat Hoover handily; his campaign song was the upbeat ditty, *Happy Days Are Here Again*. Despite this, it would take a lot more to quiet the loud chorus of *Brother Can You Spare a Dime?*

In those days, since the inauguration took place on March 4, the outgoing president faced a four-month-long lame-duck period. In January, more and more banks failed. When, on February 14, 1933, the two largest banks in Detroit closed and Governor Comstock ordered a bank holiday for Michigan, Hoover decided that something similar must be done on a nation-wide basis, with the flow of gold out of the country being stopped as a corollary. As a lame-duck president, thoroughly discredited, who faced a Democratic Congress, he did not feel able to carry out such a sweeping measure without the support of the President-Elect. He sent a note to Roosevelt on February 17 outlining the situation, asking him to do so publically. Although FDR laughingly showed the note to friends, he did not reply to it. John T. Flynn tells the story:

> At the beginning of February, Hoover proposed to the Federal Reserve Board that every bank in the country should be closed for just one day. Each bank would then submit a list of its assets and liabilities. It would list its live assets and its dying or dead assets separately. The Federal Reserve would accept each bank's own statement. The next day all solvent banks would be opened and the government would declare them solvent and would guarantee their solvency during the crisis. That would stop the runs. As to the banks with large amounts of inactive assets, the live assets would be separated from the inactive ones. The banks would be reopened, each depositor getting a deposit account in proportion to his share of the active assets. The inactive assets would then be taken over to be liquidated in the interests of the depositors. This was an obviously sound and fair solution. Had it been done countless millions in deposits would have been saved and the banking crisis at least would have been removed from the picture. However, the Attorney-General ruled that the President did not possess the power to issue such an order unless he could have the assurance of Congress that it would confirm his action by an appropriate resolution, and that this, as a matter of political necessity, would have to be approved by the new president who would take office in a month. It was some such plan as this that Hoover had in mind when he wrote Roosevelt on February 17. It had one defect from Roosevelt's point of view. It would not do to allow Hoover to be the instrument of stemming the crisis before Roosevelt could do it (*The Roosevelt Myth*, p. 22).

In accordance with this last, FDR refused to reply to Hoover until they actually met on March 2, at which time he refused to approve the plan. Although hundreds of millions in gold had flowed out of banks in the intervening period, closing thousands of banks and businesses and sending unemployment through the roof, Roosevelt would not act until he was inaugurated, and might take care of the problem himself. In a manner of speaking, the bank crisis would be Roosevelt's Reichstag fire.

A nation desperate for some solution would invest him with near total power, would look to him as an economic savior.

THE NEW DEAL

Roosevelts's inaugural address showed that he viewed himself as America's savior quite as much as did anyone else. After a great deal of lovely high-flown rhetoric, including the famous phrase, "the only thing we have to fear is fear itself," he got down to brass tacks. If Congress failed to support his programs,

> I shall not evade the clear course of duty that will then confront me. I shall ask the Congress for the one remaining instrument to meet the crisis—broad executive power to wage a war against the emergency as great as the power that would be given me if we were in fact invaded by a foreign foe... The people of the United States have asked for discipline and direction under leadership. They have made me the present instrument of their wishes.

Of course, seeing that the Tenth Amendment to the U.S. Constitution declares that "The Powers not delegated to the United States by the Constitution, nor prohibited to it by the States, are reserved to the States respectively, or to the people," one might wonder if even Congress had the right to invest such control in one man. But never mind. Roosevelt chose to take the fact of his election as a sort of Enabling Act.

Indeed, "The Hundred Days," as the period of time following his assumption of power were called, saw an unprecedented rush of legislation; after it passed, the old notion of governance in America had passed forever. At least Prohibition was ended; the newly legal alcohol had been seen as a possible source of tax money. When the 18th Amendment was repealed, the country went drunk with joy.

Once firmly in the saddle, Roosevelt convened an extraordinary session of Congress and ordered a bank holiday at last. In the same order, all trading in foreign exchange or transfer of credit abroad was forbidden under pain of fine or imprisonment—effectively confining to these shores anyone who might be tempted to leave with his money. On March 9, the Representatives and Senators gathered to consider a bill approving all that FDR had done. Unfortunately, the bill had not yet been prepared, so a folded newspaper was made to do duty until it was written up. Roosevelt then sent it on to the legislative branch who then passed it and gave the President full power over foreign exchange. The bill also authorized FDR to seize all gold held by individuals and corporations; failure to do so would result in a fine equal to twice the value of the gold held by the recalcitrant. Congress had signaled its willingness to join the Reichstag and the Italian Chamber of Deputies in becoming a rubber stamp.

April 5, 1933 saw the presidential decree requiring all gold to be turned in, adding to the authorized fine the threat of prison. This was an extraordinary event; residents of the alleged freest nation on earth would not be permitted to own (apart from jewelry or coin collections) gold. All gold coins would be withdrawn from circulation: the $20 Double Eagle, the $10 Eagle (in those days an "Eagle" was a basic currency unit, like the dollar and the cent), the $5 Half Eagle, and the $2.50 Quarter Eagle, all would go. Each gold dollar would be exchanged for its equivalent in paper money. Sold to the American populace as a purely temporary measure, it in fact remained illegal for Americans to own gold until 1974.

Had gold remained in private hands, the government's monopoly of banking and credit, its total control of money supply, would have been challenged. As it was, the citizenry were told that their gold was being held in trust. Gold had been exchangeable always dollar for dollar, and would surely be so again when the emergency had passed. The Secretary of the Treasury, after all, had declared that "Those surrending the gold of course receive an equivalent amount of other forms of currency and those other forms of currency may be used for obtaining gold in an equivalent amount when authorized for proper purposes." Nothing was said either about devaluing the dollar or going off the gold standard—had it been, the surrender of gold would probably not have been accomplished so easily.

In the meantime, the treasury was empty. Treasury bonds were therefore issued, retaining the engraved promise of the United States Government to pay the interest and redeem the principal "in United States gold coin of the present value."

Then was passed, as a rider to the Emergency Farm Relief Act, the Inflation Amendment. This required the Federal Reserve Bank System to issue three billion dollars of Treasury Notes at the President's order, and gave him discretion to devalue the dollar by one-half. On June 5, Congress repudiated the gold redemption clause in all government obligations. Henceforth, the government would be able to redeem bonds or bank notes in whatever sort of money it chose. The same sort of clause in all private transactions was declared invalid. Then a new banking act gave the Federal government the power to tell banks how to lend their money, on what kinds of collateral; and in what proportions. Above all, under the act, banks might be cut off from the Federal Reserve System by government fiat: from the origin of the Federal Reserve to the act in question, the law read that the Federal Reserve Banks "shall" lend to a private bank on suitable security. This "shall" was amended to "may," thus making the transaction a privilege rather than a right, and giving FDR the effective power to strangle any bank he wished to.

Most interesting was Roosevelt's effort to force the dollar into inflation. Because the dollar was still quite strong, it did not fall in value when cut loose from gold by the inflation amendment. So, in FDR's words:

> I am authorizing the Reconstruction Finance Corporation to buy newly mined gold in the United States at a price to be determined from time to time after consultation with the Secretary of the Treasury and the President. Whenever necessary to the end in view we shall also buy or sell gold in the world market. My aim in this step is to establish and maintain continuous control. This is a policy and not an expedient.

From that time on, the government announced every day how much it would pay for gold: one day 30 paper dollars per ounce, the next 32, two days later 34. This meant of course that the value of the dollar fluctuated daily, and had the effect of halting loans; no bank could make a long-term loan if it had no idea what the money with which it would be paid back would be worth. But the Soviet regime was strengthened by our purchases of Siberian gold.

FDR then put the government into the loan business in a big way. Through the Reconstruction Finance Corporation and the newly created Farm Credit Administration and Home Owners Loan Corporation, easy credit was extended to all. Since these bodies were not too concerned about being paid back, they could lend money on very easy terms indeed. Whence came the money for the loans? Apart from taxation, it came through the Inflation Amendment and an appropriation of $3.3 billion put into FDR's hand to fight the Depression any way he wished.

Next, on January 30, 1934, Congress passed a law giving the Federal government outright ownership of all the gold which folk had turned in, believing it would be returned. When Roosevelt asked Congress for the law, he declared that "I do not believe it desirable in the public interest that an exact value [of the dollar] be fixed." Nevertheless, the day after passage of the law, he did so, at 59% of its former gold value. The dollar was devalued by almost half.

But this was far from all that the New Deal encompassed. Roosevelt was a master of propaganda, insistently denouncing "the Old Order" as in "We cannot go back to the Old Order." Symbolic as he made it out to be in his voluble radio "Fireside Chat," the dreadful Old Order had been nothing more than the three evil demons he conjured up: the "Economic Royalist," the "Brigand of the Skyscrapers," and most evocative of all, the "Modern Tory." A steady stream of antibusiness propaganda was necessary if the next part of the New Deal was to succeed. This was nothing less than the complete subjection of every basic segment of the economy to Federal supervision.

One dilemma facing FDR was how to redistribute the national income. With control of banking and credit, he could do it; but in order to attach both the farmer and laborer to his banner he had to avoid favoring one at the expense of the other. If he simply raised the farmer's income, labor would be annoyed. If he raised incomes equally, the farmer would not benefit. What, then, to do!

> The solution was a resort to subsidies. If the prices the farmer received were not high enough to give him that share of the nation's income which he enjoyed before the worldwide depression of agriculture, the difference would be made up to him in the form of cash subsidy payments out of the public treasury. The farmer on his part pledged himself to curtail production under the government's direction; it would tell him what to plant and how much. The penalty for not conforming was to be cut off from the stream of beautiful checks issuing from the United States Treasury. The procedure was said to be democratic. It is true that a majority of farmers did vote for it when polled by the Federal county agents. The subsidies were irresistible. More income for less work and no responsibility other than to plant and reap as the government said. Nevertheless, it led at once to compulsion, as in cotton, and it led everywhere to the compulsion of minorities (Garet Garrett, *The People's Pottage*, p.49).

Something similar was done with labor. By spending billions on employing young men in Federal labor projects, eight to ten million of them were taken off the labor market, thus preserving the wage structure and the union monopoly of labor.

In addition to these measures, there came the establishment of the "Alphabet Soup" Agencies, so called from their acronyms. In toto, they covered every element of American life. Keystone of the system was the NRA, the National Recovery Administration. Established in June 1933, the NRA was to administer industry wide codes which would end unfair trade practices, reduce unemployment, establish minimum wages and hours and guarantee collective bargaining for labor. In the end, some 765 codes were established, governing the lives of 22 million workers. Companies which accepted the codes displayed the blue eagle symbol of the NRA. The NRA had the effect of binding both larger companies, which application of its codes favored, and union leadership, to the New Deal.

The AAA (Agricultural Adjustment Administration) after its Mary 1933 debut administered the subsidy program; the CCC (Civilian

Conservation Corps) provided jobs for young men (18-25) in a paramilitary camp atmosphere. For a dollar a day plus food and shelter, they worked in the woods and fields, planting trees, stocking streams, protecting wildlife, and rebuilding historic sites. But of the many other agencies, the one which left the greatest tangible imprint on America was the WPA.

The Works Progress Administration, headed by *Harry Hopkins*, went to work on a number of tasks that formerly either local government or private donors would have provided before. A dizzying array of public buildings and roads, parks, playgrounds, and bridges sprang up all over the land. Many of them are still in use today (often in modified Art Deco).

But in addition to these sorts of projects, the WPA also funded artists in the Federal Art Project, which subsidized the decoration of hospitals, post offices, and schools—giving work to teachers, librarians, historians, draftsmen, and scientists; musicians in the Federal Music Project, which brought bands and symphonies to towns which had never enjoyed their benefits; actors in the Federal Theater Project, which put on performances of social protest plays; and the writers of the Federal Writers Project.

To this last came such great names as Conrad Aiken, Saul Bellow, Zora Neale Hurston and Lyle Saxon. Like many of the WPA projects, Communists were to be found in large numbers among its members, and hacks rubbed elbows with men and women of real talent. Set up on a state by state basis, the major work of the Project was the composition of the American Guide series—this latter offered guidebooks for each of the 48 states, Alaska, and Puerto Rico. Each was divided into three parts: the first would contain essays concerning general topics—natural setting, history folklore, the arts, and so on; the second was always a profile of the major cities in the state; the last part would be description of the towns and villages to be seen on various automobile tours. Taken together with the added published material—regional guides, ethnic groups descriptions, and so on, it must be said that the Project was able to portray America as it existed in all its rich diversity in 1938. In previous chapters we have incorporated material from these guides, which remain the most thoroughgoing survey of these United States ever attempted. In the words of project member Jerre Mangione:

> In addition to what they could do for themselves, the Project members, without realizing it, provided a powerful antithesis to the widespread obsession with proletarian writing that dominated the literary atmosphere of the thirties—the obsession which produced an outpouring of didactic writing that told and retold what was wrong with the country and what Marxist-Leninist solutions could save it from the

evils of capitalism. The project writers, during this same period, simply told their countrymen what their country was like. As Louis Filler put it, "the Communist-minded writers could only talk about the bad time here and the good time coming, but the Federal writers could write about *their* country, *their* government: its present sorrows, weakness, and promise" (*The Dream and the Deal*, p.373)

In any case, the New Deal faced some legal challenges, no matter how much FDR might trample on the Constitution.

Congress had become a rubber stamp in the first year of the New Deal, and never regained its power while FDR was President. When it opposed him, it was severely denounced in the Press. Power, once given up, is never easily regained.

The Supreme Court at the beginning of Roosevelt's reign was chaired by Chief Justice Charles Evans Hughes. When the "gold cases," with their bait-and-switch treatment of the American public and obvious governmental fraud came up, the Supreme Court ruled that what the government had done was immoral but not illegal; since the government had the sovereign power to commit an immoral act, it must be borne. But they ruled the NRA unconstitutional on May 31, 1935, thus arousing Roosevelt's ire at the destruction of one of his favourite programs. In 1936, the AAA was struck down. But on April 12, 1937, (after Roosevelt's re-election showed his popularity), the Wagner Labor Relations Act, making the Federal government the supreme judge of labor through the National Labor Relations Board was upheld. Chesly Manly's summation of this event may seem a trifle harsh:

> When the Supreme Court upheld the Wagner Labor Relations Act on April 12, 1937, the United States ceased to be a Republic with a government of limited powers, expressly enumerated in the Constitution, and became a welfare state on the European model, in which the national legislature has the power to regulate industry, agriculture, and virtually all the activities of the citizens. This concept of government was not completely established until the court upheld the Social Security Act on May 24, 1937, and the compulsory marketing quotas of the new AAA on April 17, 1939; but the New Deal principle of unfettered legislative authority was accepted when the court pronounced the Wagner Act constitutional. We still have the Bill of Rights, which safeguards the fundamental liberties of the people, but even this protection could be destroyed by treaties (*The Twenty Year Revolution*, pp.68-69).

In 1938 there was FDR's famous and unsuccessful attempt to pack the Court outright. In this he failed, but in time through death and replacement, he came to have a majority on the Court. From that time to this, the Court has rarely struck down Federal laws, preferring to interfere in State and local affairs instead.

Although the States were immortalized as cultural and historical entities in the American Guides, Roosevelt relieved from them much of their political identity. First, Roosevelt imposed Federal standards on the State social security systems, and made old age pensions and unemployment insurance a Federal thing. Then, huge grants in aid were made from the Federal Treasury to the States on condition they accepted Federal policies; since the citizenry clamoured for what appeared to be free Federal money, it was a difficult offer to refuse. Thirdly, since the WPA, the Tennesee Valley Authority, and other such agencies were organized on a regional basis (the Writers' Project was a notable exception to this rule), State political and property rights were ignored. Fourthly, the Interstate Commerce Clause was extended into all sorts of areas not obviously under its sway.

Roosevelt's first term was conducted in a flagrantly unconstitutional manner, a fact not lost on his contemporaries, as the Supreme Court challenges make clear. But why, then, was there so little outcry? Caroline Bird provides an answer:

> There was something for everybody. For families, price supports. For the unemployed, Federal relief. For bank depositors, Federal insurance against bank failure. For investors who had bought worthless securities, Federal policing of security issuance and trading. Debtors took heart because the President was given power to inflate the currency, and mortgages were extended. Creditors were reassured by the pay and pension cuts. Business got protection from wage and price chiselers. Labor got protection for unions. In a crisis, mortgages could be stayed, gold impounded, banks closed, veterans deprived of their pensions and private parties of their property.
>
> No one really worried about whether all this was constitutional. Lawyers knew the powers were too vague to stand up in court, but no one had the heart to push the point. When someone asked Fiorello LaGuardia, the dynamic representative from New York City, whether it was constitutional to prevent foreclosure of a mortgage, he pointed to my father, who was serving on a citizen's committee drafting a mortgage moratorium law, "Ask Mr. Bird, he's the lawyer here." Father and the lawyers just laughed. The idea was to get something going and get it going fast (*The Invisible Scar*, pp.126-127).

Thus, in the end, Americans showed themselves quite as willing to barter freedom for security as either Germans or Italians. It is a sobering thought.

The Church and the Depression

Like the rest of America and the world, the Church was hard hit by the Depression. Church building ground to a halt for a few years, while the hierarchy concentrated on relief projects. *Quadragesimo Anno* prompted a huge outpouring of Catholic social thought and action around the world. In America, the Depression was seen as confirmation of the criticisms of capitalism contained in the Bishop's Program of 1919. In the intervening years, *Fr. Joseph Husslein, S.J.* and *Msgr. John Ryan*, among others, had worked hard to make the Church's view of society well-known, not merely among non-Catholics, but Catholics as well (who are often just as ignorant of it). In this they were assisted by such Catholic journals as *The Commonweal*. But while, in America as abroad, almost all Catholics who know of these teachings accepted them, they differed sharply on their concrete application. The result was that, in country after country, Catholics found themselves in conflict with one another; the cause was generally the nature of whatever non-Catholic allies this or that Catholic group had chosen to assist in accomplishing one or another of Pius XI's objectives.

In the beginning, the vast majority of Catholics (generally Democrats anyway) hailed FDR's assumption of power:

> Roosevelt presented to the nation what he called "a new deal," and for the most part the editors of *The Commonweal* were pleased with it. So were the great majority of Catholics and Catholic publications. Bishop Karl Alter of Toledo stated that the president's inaugural address "breathes the spirit of our Holy Father's recent encyclical." When speaking to Catholic audiences, Roosevelt himself referred to *Rerum Novarum* and *Quadragesimo Anno*. Richard Dana Skinner, drama critic for *The Commonweal* and an interested Democrat, wrote privately to party leaders that if Catholics "once understood clearly the identity of idea between the administration's efforts and the Pope's recent program of social justice, they would be more likely to give it enthusiastic support through thick and thin." Another staunch friend of the administration who was affiliated with *The Commonweal* was Father John A. Ryan, who had accepted an invitation to join *The Commonweal* editorial council in 1930. In later correspondence, Ryan would refer to Roosevelt as "the Miracle Worker in the White House" (Roger Van Allen, *The Commonweal and American Catholicism*, p.43).

But as the New Deal continued, it became apparent to many Catholics that it was not all it was claimed to be. One of the first to dissent was none other than Al Smith. The Brown Derby had this caustic comment on the first year of FDR's reign: "Check the Constitution."

Although originally a political ally of Roosevelt's, Smith would become one of his bitterest opponents.

On a level deeper than that of mere government, some Catholics began to realize that, beyond the obvious question of the Depression, America's ills required deep and spiritual solutions. A radical renovation of the nation's spirit would be necessary if there were to be any real change. One theorist of this sort was the French immigrant, *Peter Maurin.* Having come to this country in 1911, Maurin sought to spread the teachings of Leo XIII among the masses of people. In December of 1932, he met Dorothy Day, a former socialist convert, who had similar interest in bringing the Church to the Depression-struck. Although like her he wanted change, he hated what passed for much of social agitation at that time:

> I did not like the idea of revolution... I did not like the French Revolution, not the English Revolution. I did not wish to work to perpetuate the proletariat. I never became a member of a union, even though here in America I did all sorts of hard labor. I was always interested in land and man's life on the land.

In her forward to his *Easy Essays,* Dorothy Day describes his thought rather well:

> "People are just beginning to realize how deep-seated the evil is," he said soberly. "That is why we must be Catholic Radicals, we must get down to the roots. That is what radicalism is—the word means getting down to the roots."
>
> Peter, even in his practicality, tried to deal with problems in the Spirit of "the Prophets of Israel and the Fathers of the Church." He saw what the Industrial Revolution had done to the common man, and he did not think that unions and organizations, strikes for higher wages and shorter hours, were going to be the solution. "Strikes don't strike me," he used to say when we went out to a picket line to distribute literature during a strike. But he came with us to hand out the literature –leaflets which dealt with man's dignity and his need and right to associate himself with his fellows in trade unions, in credit unions, cooperatives, maternity guilds, etc.
>
> He was interested in far more fundamental approaches. He liked the name "radical" and he had wanted the paper to be called *The Catholic Radical.* To him *Worker* smacked of class war. What he wanted was to instill in all, worker or scholar, a philosophy of poverty and a philosophy of work.
>
> He was the layman, always. I mean that he never preached, he taught. While decrying secularism the separation of the material from the spiritual, his emphasis, as a layman, was on man's material needs, his need for work, food, clothing, and shelter. Though Peter went

weekly to Confession and daily to Communion and spent an hour a day in the presence of the Blessed Sacrament, his study was of the material order around him. Though he lived in the city, he urged a return to the village economy, the study of the crafts and of the agriculture. He was dealing with this world, in which God has placed us to work for a new heaven and a new earth wherein justice dwelleth. Peter's idea of justice was that of St. Thomas—to give each man what is his due.

The pair founded *The Catholic Worker* in New York, and the first issue appeared on May 1, 1933. Day's journalistic interests were in the social and industrial evils of the day—Maurin dwelled in his *Easy Essays* upon what ought to be done with them. His answer was threefold: Round Table Discussions, which would seek "clarification of thought" through discussion of the Church's teaching and its application; Houses of Hospitality, which would provide havens for the urban poor, and give them places to live, work, and discover the Faith in the midst of poverty—these would include soup kitchens and so on; and Farming Communities, where the same urban poor could be reintroduced to the land, and where a nucleus of a truly Catholic economy could be formed. Moreover, he advocated guilds. In addition to this, *The Catholic Worker* opposed both usury and modern war. Their stance on the latter was motivated not by pacificism pure and simple, but by the belief that modern weapons made a "just war"—by the Church's standards—simply impossible. In all of this, there was nothing too groundbreaking in Catholic terms: Distributism, Guild Socialism, Social Credit, Solidarism, Corporatism—all had similar messages. What made *The Catholic Worker* unique was its desire to put these things in practice, not by capturing the organs of government, but by exposing the poor to them. As Maurin wrote in one of his quasi-poetic *Easy Essays*, (*op.cit.*, p.3):

> Writing about the Catholic Church,
> a radical writer says: "Rome will have to do more
> than to play a waiting game;
> she will have to use some of the dynamite
> inherent in her message."
> to blow the dynamite
> of a message is the only way
> to make the message dynamic.
>
> If the Catholic Church
> is not today
> the dominant social dynamic force,
> it is because Catholic scholars
> have failed to blow the dynamite
> of the Church.

> Catholic scholars
> have taken the dynamite
> of the Church
> and wrapped it up
> in nice phraseology,
> placed it in an hermetic container
> and sat on the lid.
> It is about time to blow the lid off
> so the Catholic Church
> may again become
> the dominant social force

In the years that followed, *The Catholic Worker* built up a network of hospitality houses in many of the nation's cities, as well as a number of farms. In subsequent wars in which this country was involved, they have inevitably protested (and been arrested for so doing) our involvement in them. Such work has brought them much into contact with radical leftist groups—thus leading many to consider them a left-wing group themselves. But in truth, although many times such associations have appeared to seem more important to various Catholic Worker members than their religion, this was certainly not the case with the founders; for that matter, in recent years their opposition to abortion has led to rifts with many whose company they had enjoyed on the barricades. After all, Maurin declared himself to be a man of the Right—but of course, he meant that in a European sense.

As at *The Catholic Worker*, so too at Baroness Catherine De Hueck's Friendship and Madonna Houses in Harlem, Toronto, Hamilton, Ontario, and elsewhere, it was considered that each poor person who came to the door should be given food and shelter as a right, not as a privilege. The Baroness moreover cultivated a special apostolate toward Harlem's blacks, to show them that real liberation would be theirs only through the Truth of the Catholic Faith. Both *The Catholic Worker* and Friendship House did not believe in just filling the mouth of the hungry, nor yet in spreading the Faith alone. Rather they tried to educate those who came to them in the Church's social teaching. In his *Easy Essays*, as in his conversation and lectures, Maurin revealed to the poor the teachings of such as Chesterton and Belloc, Alphonse Lugan, Eric Gill, Southern Agrarian Andrew Lytle, Gothic Architect Ralph Adams Cram, Economist R.H. Tawney, Guild Socialist Arthur Penty, and many others. The response of the poor was enthusiastic. Baroness De Hueck had a similar experience:

> The door of Toronto's Friendship House library opened with a band and three men walked in. Two were still in their working clothes,

their faces smeared with coal dust. They were engineers in a nearby factory. The third looked tired and thin, and his clothes bore the obvious stamp of city relief supplies.

They called out a cheery "Good-afternoon" and asked if any new copies of their favourite magazines had come. By "their favourites" these particular three meant *The Commonweal, The Sign, America* and *The Catholic Worker*. Some new copies had just arrived and the three settled down to enjoy them. An hour or so later, they announced they had to go. Before they went, they asked to borrow some books.

With the card index file before me, I marked off the volumes just returned. Christopher Hollis, *The Breakdown of Money*, was the first. I noticed with gratification that it had been out four hundred times in the last year. Arnold Lunn's *Now I See*, was next. It had been out three hundred and seventy-five times. Fanfalli's *Catholicism, Protestantism, and Capitalism* was the third. It had been out three hundred and forty-two times. Naturally, we had several copies of each.

Before I had time to ponder further on the significance of the popularity of this type of writer, my three friends had made their selection. Again as I checked I felt there was much food for thought. For before me lay *Selected Papal Encyclicals*, Dawson's *Religion and the Modern State*, and Berdyaev's *The End of Our Times* (Baroness Catherine De Hueck, *Friendship House*, pp.17-18)

With the apparent collapse of the American system, there was a hunger in the land for a replacement—hence the easy acceptance of the New Deal. But the New Deal could not alter the fact that something was hollow in the country's heart. That something was the lack of the Catholic Faith. Where *The Catholic Worker*, Friendship House, and similar apostolates tried to work on individual souls in hopes of changing the country in the long run, others attempted quick projects. Hence Msgr. Ryan, dubbed "The Right Reverend New Dealer," attempted to baptize Roosevelt's programs simply by saying they were in accord with Papal teaching, and then by defending them against all comers.

In a more constructive vein, the National Catholic Rural Life Conference, founded at the behest of the bishops in 1923, extended its work in the face of the Depression eleven years later. This operated to help the Catholic farm population retain its position in the face of the economic disaster, and to assist Catholic urbanities in resettling on the farm.

These and many other efforts made some local impact. But the one Catholic voice heard most loudly throughout the dark years of the Depression was the cultivated tone of Canadian-born *Fr. Charles E. Coughlin*, pastor of the Shrine of the Little Flower in Royal Oak, Michigan, outside Detroit.

Fr. Coughlin had in 1926 been assigned Royal Oak in the face of dominance of the town by the Ku Klux Klan. They burned down the church he built; as he stood over the charred embers, he looked skyward, and vowed that he would build a church "with a cross so high... that neither man nor beast can tear it down." He did so. Additionally, in order to raise public knowledge about the Church, and to fight bigotry, he took to the radio airwaves, making his first broadcast on October 17, 1926. For the succeeding three years, he kept to doctrinal themes, with occasional blasts against birth control (just then becoming popular) and the Klan. On January 12, 1930, he addressed politics for the first time, denouncing Communism.

Coughlin had always had a great love of the poor, and had been a member of the Basilians, an order dedicated to social work. The Archbishop of Detroit, Michael J. Gallagher, had moreover studied in Austria during the 1890s when Leo XIII's teachings were first enunciated. The Depression having broken out, nothing pleased the Archbishop more than the idea of having social teachings on the air.

In his broadcasts, Fr. Coughlin reiterated the fact that Capitalism had bred the conditions necessary for the growth of Communism. He declared in the fall of 1930, "The thoughtful American is now convinced that the most dangerous communist is the wolf in sheep's clothing of conservatism who is bent upon preserving the policies of greed, of oppression and of Christlessness." In all his speeches, Fr. Coughlin assured his audiences that the beliefs of Christ and the Founding Fathers were the same; when he spoke of the Cross or the Saints, the Flag and Washington and Lincoln were never far behind. Like most Catholics in the U.S., he was an Americanist—the more so, perhaps, because he was an immigrant. In any case, he always avoided proselytization and indeed came out for religious liberty.

In any case, he met FDR in 1932, and became his staunch supporter. During the election he coined the catchy phrase, "Roosevelt or Ruin." Certainly, with his national audience, the Detroit priest was a figure to be cultivated by the new President.

Throughout 1933, the radio priest urged the remonetization of silver as an alternative to the now absent gold. Although FDR declared his appreciation of Coughlin's advice, he followed none of it. For his part, Fr. Coughlin began to find the behaviour of the Alphabet soup agencies—the subsidies for crop destruction by the AAA and the monopolization encouraged by the NRA, for example—distasteful. Although still protesting his loyalty to FDR, he began to let drop such statements as, "I am for *a* New Deal." On November 11, 1934, he started the National Union for Social Justice, whose preamble and principles may be read in Appendix R. While it is obvious that point one contradicts

Pius IX's *Syllabus of Errors*, points six, seven, and eight put Fr. Coughlin on a collision course with Roosevelt. For while FDR had captured control of the country's credit and banking, it had not been for the sake of the population; indeed, the powers of the Federal Reserve had been immeasurably strengthened by New Deal measures.

The open break with FDR came over the proposed entrance of the United States into the World Court, a proposal favored by the administration. Senate debate on the treaty came to an end on Friday, January 25, 1935. On Sunday, Fr. Coughlin delivered a stinging attack on the notion, declaring that it would end American sovereignty and put the country under the thumb of international financiers. He urged his audience to flood Washington with telegrams; they did so. Over 200,000 telegrams featuring one million names came into Senatorial office. The measure was defeated, and FDR, who had staked much personal prestige upon his treaty, was heavily stung.

The rift was unbridgeable. Fr. Coughlin would, with such men as *Fr. Edward Lodge Curran* of Brooklyn, (head of the Catholic Truth Society there), eventually organize the Christian Front, which would be a source of opposition to administration policies until the beginning of World War II. To the same end would be turned his newspaper, *Social Justice*. But Fr. Coughlin's greatest battle with FDR would already have been fought by then; the election of 1936, which he would wage with the aid of non-Catholic allies. After that he would make common cause with right-wing groups of more or less respectability. In a word, he became a mirror image of *The Catholic Worker's* leftist trend.

What strikes the observer, decades later, was the reluctance of either the official hierarchy (represented by such as Msgr. Ryan) in their zeal for the New Deal, Fr. Coughlin and his connection with certain right-wing factions, or *The Catholic Worker* with their socialist allies, to break entirely free of the Americanist trap. Based upon common compartmentalizing ideology, they still would not see the need for an effort to convert the nation to *authentic* Christian religion. Instead they tended to take the easy way out of purely or mainly political activity, accepting uncritically the notion that the American civic religion was somehow Christian and compatible with Catholicism. Only Peter Maurin warned that "Christian Democracy is not possible without Christian Aristocracy." But his criticisms would be echoed primarily outside Catholic circles.

Opponents of the New Deal

If most Catholics happily accepted the New Deal immediately, many other folk did not. The first active source of opposition to FDR was a group of industrial and financial magnates (including J.P. Morgan, the Du Ponts, Andrew Mellon, and General Motors) who organized in September 1934 the American Liberty League. Al Smith was a prominent member of it, and it included a great many folk who feared that the New Deal was simply Socialism under another name. At one point, its leaders even contemplated a military coup against FDR. But when, after the election of 1936, its big business sponsors decided to make peace with Roosevelt, the American Liberty League was disbanded by them. Their opposition to Roosevelt was not ideological at all, but purely fiscal. Their piece of the pie assured, their enmity vanished.

The opposition of others to the New Deal was rather more serious. In April of 1933, Seward Collins, editor of *The Bookman*, a journal primarily influenced by the New Humanists (Collins was a disciple of Babbitt in the beginning) replaced it with a new periodical, *The American Review*. In his opening editorial, he stated:

> The *American Review* is founded to give greater currency to the ideas of a number of groups and individuals who are radically critical of conditions prevalent in the modern world, but launch their criticism from a "traditionalist" basis: from the basis of a firm grasp on the immense body of experience accumulated by men in the past, and the insight which this knowledge affords. The magazine is a response to the widespread and growing feeling that the forces and principles which have produced the modern chaos are incapable of yielding any solution; that the only hope is a return to fundamentals and tested principles which have been largely pushed aside. Fortunately, there is no lack of able men to represent this traditionalist point of view, although they have been forced to work in isolation from each other and have achieved nothing like the influence to which their stature entitles them. It should be obvious that a periodical aiming to bring these groups and individuals together is particularly needed in this country, where tradition took little root before it was overridden by the disruptive forces that are now threatening Western civilization. In Europe the spokesmen for sanity and order are more numerous and more solidly entrenched: they have built up such a weighty mass of indictment and prescription that they can be said to have their modernist foes already on the defensive. For this reason we shall frequently be drawing on European contributors, but the editorial emphasis will be directed to the needs of this country.

He went on to describe some of the groups that would find a voice in his magazine. The New Humanists would find their niche, of course. But the Distributists would also be represented, and in fact both Chesterton and Belloc contributed to this and subsequent issues. In this way they were introduced for the first time to the non-Catholic American public. Then too, the Southern Agrarians were present also, as were the Neo-scholastics, those folk who repopularized St. Thomas Aquinas, T.S. Eliot, Christopher Dawson, Charles Maurras, Henri Massis, and various other Europeans of like mind would also add their input. In a word, Collins hoped to produce a "forum for the views of these 'Radicals of the Right' or 'Revolutionary Conservatives.'"

As the journal developed in the years of its life from 1933 to 1937, all these views and many more—Monarchist, Corporatist, Guild Socialist, and so on, were encountered in an American context. One eminent writer brought to public view by the Review was *Ross J.S. Hoffman*, a convert. His essays in Collins' magazine were published in 1935 as *The Will To Freedom*; his 1938 *Tradition and Progress* and 1939 *Organic State* elaborated the Catholic view of social reform.

Above all, *The American Review* brought together these varied folk in a way that would have been impossible without it. One product of this conjunction was the publication of a volume two years before *The American Review's* demise, *Who Owns America?* Subtitled "A Second Declaration of Independence," it was edited by Herbert Agar and Allen Tate. Although conceived of as a sequel to *I'll Take My Stand*, it offered in addition to the Southern Agrarian writers the Ohioan Willis Fisher, who argued for the integrity of non-Southern regions against the ever-centralizing state; Hilaire Belloc, who of course put forward the Catholic editor of *The English Review*, who would the next year fly General Franco from the Canary Islands to Spanish Morocco in his private plane (thus doing his part in the Spanish Civil War). As Agar wrote in his introduction:

> Among the authors of this book there are Protestants, agnostics, Catholics, Southerners, Northerners, men of the cities and more who live on the land. There are two Englishmen who give the European background of the problems which afflict our country. Our common ground is a belief that monopoly capitalism is evil and self-destructive, and that it is possible, while preserving private ownership, to build a true democracy in which men would be better off both morally and physically, more likely to attain that inner peace which is the fruit of a good life (p.ix).

Like its predecessor, and like the journal in which many of its authors encountered each other for the first time, *Who Owns America?* offered a cogent criqitue of both the New Deal and the American system which spawned it. But all these protests were (despite their inherent value simply in being uttered) ultimately of no effect. Certainly, FDR lost no sleep over them, any more than he did over the fulminations of the

Technocrats (who wished to beat the Depression by turning control of the country over to scientists, who they thought could best figure out something so complex), or Upton Sinclair's EPIC (End Poverty In California) movement, which would have established the Golden State as a vaguely Socialist entity. None of these folk came remotely close to achieving power in any area of the country. The only individual who offered a real challenge to the New Deal was "the Bonaparte of the Bayous," *Huey Long* of Louisiana.

Elected Governor of Louisiana in 1928 as a Populist opponent of big business, Long soon had the entire state completely under his thumb, He ran Louisiana more like a Latin American dictatorship than like a state. But while in office he made many improvements, particularly in roads and education. The result was that to this day people in the Creole State are severely divided over him.

But there were similar folk elsewhere in the country who ran states or regions more or less like benevolent despots. Frank Hague, mayor of Jersey City, dominated the whole of New Jersey with the support of local Catholic organizations like the Knights of Columbus; Mayor James Curley of Boston; Governor Eugene Talmadge of Georgia, Governor Bibb Graves of Alabama, and many others fit the bill. In a time when the Depression-wracked populace were looking for economic salvation, the same impulse which had brought FDR to power was at work on the state and local level, and had similar results.

What set Long apart was his ability to project an ideology, and to become a national figure. It would have been impossible to think of Hague or Talmadge as President; by 1935, it was not impossible to think that way of Long.

Having broken all opposition in Louisiana, Long was able to secure a puppet's election as governor in 1930, and in that year went to the Senate in Washington (although when at home in Baton Rouge he would still conduct sessions of the state legislature). The next year he was able to procure the election of an ally as Senator from Arkansas; it was a first sign of his influence beyond state boundaries. He used that influence to help win first the nomination and then the election of 1932 for Franklin Delano Roosevelt.

But Roosevelt soon tired of Long as he had of Fr. Coughlin. The rift took place in 1933. Long took to the airwaves as Fr. Coughlin had, and like the radio priest soon built up a national movement. This was centered upon his "Share Our Wealth" plan, first enunciated in his autobiography, *Every Man a King*. The basis of it was the limiting of all incomes to one million dollars a year, the remainder to be given to the government and distributed among the rest of the populace. It was a program which, while not directly threatening class warfare, was revolutionary enough to make the wealthy fearful and the poor hungry. By 1935, Long was beginning to look like a real threat to FDR in the election to be held the next year. He insouciantly published a "novel," *My First Days in the White House*, describing the beginning of a Long presidency (in which he magnanimously gives a cabinet seat to his defeated predecessor, FDR).

Fr. Coughlin, in the meantime, began to look forward to allying his supporters with Long's; this grouping would be completed by the adherence of Dr. Townsend, a social theorist who advocated a revolving pension for old people; they would be required to spend all the money they thus received—the economy would be stimulated and their lives bettered. This threeway conjunction appeared to have a chance of propelling Long right into the White House.

Luckily for Roosevelt, this possibility was stilled by an assassin's bullet on September 7, 1935. Dr. Carl Weiss, the murderer, was killed immediately by Long's guards at the Statehouse where the shooting occurred. The perpetrator dead, rumors of outside conspiracies abounded; to this day in the bayous and small towns of Louisiana, some whisper that FDR, "mus' a' had sompin' to do wid it." Whether or not that is so (and political assassinations with dead assassins are always fonts of conspiracy theories) this was not a death Roosevelt could have been too hurt by.

With Long dead, his machine turned inward, toward retaining their grip on Louisiana (which they managed successfully to do, thus staving off Federal corruption charges which would have sent many of them off to jail had they not agreed to end all activities outside their own state). Long's national organization, presided over by one Gerald L.K. Smith, was thus cut off from its base of support and left to fend for itself. Nonetheless, Smith, Townsend, and Fr. Coughlin decided to go ahead as planned. They formed the Union Party in May of 1936, and nominated Representative William Lemke of North Dakota as their Presidential candidate. The three backers prepared to fight the election.

Fight it they did, as did the Republican nominee, Alf Landon of Kansas. But the Union Party, bereft as it was of the charismatic Long, for all the letter writing and radio broadcasting received only 892,378 out of 45 million votes—less than two percent. Despite the support of the Liberty League and stalwart campaigning on his behalf by Al Smith, Landon did worse than any major candidate had up to that time; failing to carry even his native Kansas, he had to be content with just Maine and Vermont. Up to that time, Maine had been a bellweather of elections, consistently electing the victor; hence the prevalent saying, "As Maine goes, so goes the nation." Roosevelt triumphantly quipped, "As Maine goes, so goes Vermont."

Triumphant FDR well might be. With the thrashing of all his foes at the polls, there was now no significant challenge to him; he was at last in complete control. Fr. Coughlin and the tattered remnants of various movements remained, but they were no threat. He yet had one major problem, however. For all the rhetoric and posturing and New Deal legislation and sound and fury, the Depression, despite occasional flurries of prosperity, still retained its icy grip upon the land. If he was to retain power, he must somehow break that grip. Luckily for him, hope—in the form of war clouds—was on the horizon.

Countdown to War

In the great world outside, things were indeed going from bad to worse. The Far East saw the continued attempts by both Japan and the Soviet Union to dominate ever more of China. While Manchukuo was being formed into a Japanese puppet state, the Soviets were completing similar work with Outer Mongolia. The Japanese, who as earlier noted felt compelled to dominate China for economic reasons, were now forced to redouble their efforts in the northern part of the country to stave off the Soviets. On November 16, 1933, FDR recognized the Soviet Union; the policy of non-recognition was applied to Manchukuo, and the impression given Japan that while Soviet colonization of China was all right, Japanese was not. After all attempts at renewing the traditional US Japanese alliance failed in 1934, Tokyo began to draw close to the new regime in Berlin.

Meanwhile, Germany reoccupied the Rhineland and Italy seized Ethiopia in the year of 1936. American response to the latter was to apply sanctions and hold aloof from any negotiation. But the big event of the year was the outbreak of the Spanish Civil War.

After Alfonso XIII had been forced out of Spain in 1931, a parliamentary republic established in his exile tottered ever leftward. Violence against Catholics and Conservatives rose, and by mid-1936 it became apparent that either the Right-wing army or the Communist militias would revolt; the army struck first. General Francisco Franco was flown from his command in the Canary Islands to Spanish Morocco by Douglas Jerrold. There he raised the standard of revolt, led his troops into the Spanish mainland, and began a three-year conflict which would end with the extinction of the progressively more Communist Republic.

The Falange, one of several political factions within Franco's national coalition, maintained the following point along with the 27 others in their program:

25. Our movement incarnates a Catholic sense of life—the glorious and predominant tradition in Spain—and shall incorporate it into national reconstruction. The Clergy and the State shall work together in harmony without either one invading the other's domain in such a way that it may bring about discord or be detrimental to the national dignity and integrity.

The others dealt with the regeneration of Spain and the establishment of a Corporate State.

Given this sort of ideology, the two sides soon attracted foreign volunteers. France, Britain, and the US followed a policy of "non-intervention" which meant that they would not sell arms to the "Loyalists," as the Republican government's adherents were called; the Soviets armed them, and foreign leftists flocked to their banners. Germany and Italy sent troops, and several thousand Portuguese joined Franco's ranks. But the conflict was a world war in miniature. Two brigades of Americans—the Abraham Lincoln and the George Washington—fought with the Loyalists, as did such luminaries as later Bulgarian dictator Dimitroff. On the Nationalist side, in addition to the three nations named, six hundred Irish "Blue-shirts" under General Eoin O'Duffy served, as did a number of others. About 1,000 foreigners of other nationalities served with Franco in the winter of 1937-1938. These included some French *Camelots du Roi*, White Russians, Latin Americans, Romanian Iron Guardists, a handful of English, Canadians, and Americans, and a few interesting characters like South African Catholic poet, *Roy Campbell*.

The victory of the Nationalists was a Godsend to like-minded folk throughout Latin America and elsewhere; but the tacit support of the Loyalists by Roosevelt, as well as the continued support by our government for anti-clerical groups and regimes, was not forgotten. At a time when Catholic Spain seemed again a strong nation, her descendants in South America rallied to her. In Colombia, *Laureano Gomez*, leader of the Conservative Party, provided a focus of Catholic and Hispanic loyalty, as this quote from a Colombian paper of the time shows:

> We were born Spanish.... We speak the tongue of Castile because we can speak no other.... The twenty cowardly governments of Latin America have put themselves into the hands of foreign nationals, dedicated to false liberalism and to Masonic, atheistic democracy.... The panorama is desolate... we are still conquered territory...
>
> *Hispanoamerica*, the land of vassalage... Each day the yoke of Saxo-Americana is drawn tighter around our throats. Sometimes the yoke is of steel, sometimes of silk, soft and perfidious...

But—all is not lost. There is still heard the voice of Laureano Gomez to tell the truth about the future, to direct us to the road of tomorrow, the Catholic Hispanic Empire.

And we will go back to Spain. The five arrows of Ferdinand and Isabella, the symbol of Catholic unity, will be our symbol also. It is written in the future of America by the inscrutable hand of Providence.

In Ecuador was a similar group led by Jacinto Jijon y Caamaño. In Lima, Peru, such opinions were expressed by the newspaper *El Comercio*, and its owner Carlos Miro Quesada Laos. Havana boasted the paper *Diario de la Marina*, whose editor Jose Ignacio Rivera continued the Carlist traditions of his family. Even in the American-held Philippines, a branch of the Falange existed, organized by Andres Soriano and Enrique Zobel. Puerto Rico had a similar organization.

But most interesting of all were the Mexican Sinarquistas. Wanting to set up a Catholic Corporate state in Mexico, the April 1939 issue of their journal, *El Sinarquista*, declared:

> All those who have been concerned with dignifying the life of Mexico, as well as those who have wanted to point the way to the real aggrandizement of Mexico, speak of Spain. To put it more concretely, they speak of the work done by the Mother Country during the historical colonial period. She showed us the road and gave us our bearings. So Mexico must cling to its traditions to find the meaning of its future. Thus, those who feel the desperate uncertainty that today hangs dense and heavy over the nation, want to return to Spain.

By 1941 they were well-established throughout Southern California and South Texas, thus giving more than abstract interest to Fr. Coughlin's observation in *Social Justice*:

> Advocates of Christian social justice in America, Christian Americans who once dreamed of a national Union to effect a 16-point reform, and who have watched the progress of the Christian states headed by Salazaar, De Valera, General Franco... will want to hear further from Mexico's Sinarchists with their "16 principles" of social justice.

But in truth, there could be no triumph of Catholic principles in Latin America without a similar triumph in Europe; Spain, Ireland, Portugal, and Poland put together would not be enough to shield our southern neighbors from the US governnment's habitual pressure. Who then could they turn to in Europe? Not Britain and France, who were, in any case, weak and distracted. That left only Germany and Italy, who, as a result of the Ethiopian sanctions, were drawing closer to one another. Many a Latin American Conservative thus made the mistake of turning pro-Axis.

Meanwhile, collusion between Hitler and Mussolini led to the snuffing out of Austria, and its absorption by Germany. This led to the encircling of Czechoslovakia by the Reich, and the Munich crisis. On August 18, 1938, FDR gave a speech at Queen's University, Kingston, Ontario, in which he declared that the Monroe Doctrine covered Canada, and by extension, the entire British Empire. This was taken by the French and British as a pledge of alliance should war break out. However, the menace was averted by the famous appeasement of Munich, and so Roosevelt would have to wait for events to develop in his favour. Unfortunately, the economy, which had been stable, took another dive.

The Sudetenland having been absorbed, Hitler shocked Europe by his takeover of Prague and the remaining Czech lands on March 15, 1939; Slovakia became independent under Msgr. Tiso, and Ruthenia did likewise, preparatory to being absorbed by Hungary.

Outright war had broken out between Japan and China in 1937. Rapidly the Japanese had seized Shanghai, Peking, and the capital at Nanking. Chiang Kai-Shek was forced to retreat into the country's interior, and to rely heavily on the Communist guerrillas who had been his longtime foes (and would be again). On October 5, the President gave a speech in Chicago, abandoning his policy of taking no sides in the conflict and suggesting a need for economic sanctions against Japan. Apparently an economic downturn and the revelation that newly appointed Supreme Court Justice Hugo Black was a former Klansman required a speech that would get everyone's mind off troubles at home. While a large bloc of newspapers supported the President's new stand, the Catholic Press did not. The Jesuit *America* stated (October 16, 1937), the "people of the United States are positively opposed to any foreign imbroglios."

While that was certainly true, it did not affect FDR's conduct. Time after time, in the remaining years leading up to Munich, peace feelers and initiatives sent out by both Germany and Japan were brazenly rejected. It might be objected to this point that both regimes were already guilty of oppressive behavior; however, as noted, Roosevelt had done his best to cultivate friendly relations with the Soviet Union, which under Stalin had carried out yet another bloody purge in 1936. Surely, then, what could little things like atrocities mean to us?

When war broke out between the British and French on the one hand, and the Germans on the other, over the latter's invasion of Poland, Roosevelt, as was customary, invoked our neutrality. Almost as soon as he had done it, though, he began to circumvent it. On September 2, 1940, the famous "Destroyers for Bases" deal was concluded between Britain and the United States. In the words of Charles Callan Tansill:

> From the viewpoint of international law the destroyer deal was definitely illegal. As Professor Herbert Briggs correctly remarks: "The supplying of these vessels by the United States Government is a violation of our neutral status, a violation of our national law, and a violation of international law." Professor Edwin Borchard expressed a similar opinion: "To the writer there is no possibility of reconciling the destroyer deal with neutrality, with the United States statutes, or with international law." The whole matter was correctly described by the *St. Louis Post-Dispatch* in a pertinent headline: "Dictator Roosevelt Commits an Act of War" (*Back Door to War*, p.599)

It would be the first of many. Why not? Had he not shown in the prior seven years in office how little he thought of law? For that matter, since he continued to make speeches pledging to stay out of the war, it is perhaps touching to see that FDR's sense of veracity had not altered since the days of the gold confiscation. The president's activities did however cause a rift between him and the Catholic hierarchy.

On February 1, 1941, the US Navy assumed responsibility for protection of British convoys in the Atlantic; on March 11, the Lend-Lease treaty took effect. If ever there were violations of neutrality, these were they. On April 10, 1941, the US destroyer *Niblack*, which was picking up stranded Dutch sailors from their torpedoed ship, dropped depth charges on the submarine which had done the job. After this, as the US ships escorted convoys, there were ever more such incidents.

But Hitler would not rise to the bait. His ships were instructed not to attack if they saw that a ship was American, and only to fire if fired upon. Undeterred, Mr. Roosevelt looked East.

In November 1940, the Japanese authorities asked Bishop James Walsh of Maryknoll to bring a proposal to Washington; this would include: 1.) an agreement to end their connection with the Axis, and 2.) "a guarantee to recall all military forces from China and to restore to China its geographical and political integrity." His Excellency laid these proposals before FDR and the Secretary of State. He was told they would be taken under advisement. They were never heard of again, much to the chagrin of the Japanese.

After spurning several peace initiatives by Prime Minister Konoye, Roosevelt finally refused to meet with him on August 17, 1941. Finally, stung by his inability to make any arrangement with the US, Prince Konoye resigned on October 16. He was replaced by the less peaceful General Tojo.

On November 15, Secretary of State Cordell Hull handed to the Japanese Ambassador an ultimatum, requiring withdrawal from China. He reiterated those terms on November 26. To a warrior-proud people, who had tried so uncharacteristically long to come to an honourable accord, there seemed, after the final ultimatum, only one way out of the impasse.

The country they were facing across the Pacific had just returned to office for an unprecedented third term Franklin Delano Roosevelt. He was, in November of 1941, at the height of his power. His opponents had failed to unseat him, and those who opposed the warward drift on which he was taking the country were called "Isolationists." Membership in the America First Committee, headed by Col. Charles Lindbergh and John T. Flynn, was considered by many to be tantamount to Fascist Party membership. Yet the Nazis found Roosevelt admirable. According to a *New York Times* dispatch from Berlin (September 26, 1937):

> The German argument contends that democracies like Britain, France, and the United States are inherently weak through lack of an ideology.... [However] President Roosevelt in German eyes already is well ahead of world democratic leaders in his perception of the importance of ideology as a factor in national politics.... He is believed to be more keenly alive to the post-war necessity of imbuing even democratic formulas with new, even radical spiritual values—less violent and robust maybe than those incorporated in the Fascist and National Socialist decalogues.

Certainly, they should know. The Nazis admired strength above all else, and that FDR had in abundance; he was the living embodiment of the will-to-power, American-style. Leo Gurko's words regarding Huey Long are, one cannot help but feel, even more appropriate for his adversary in the White House:

> What is surprising—and of serious import—is how easily one can be seduced away from the democratic idea; how tyrants, even in America, with its endemic hatred of tyrants, can be glamorized during their lifetime and justified after their death. (*The Angry Decade*, p.185)

For Roosevelt was in truth, despite all the Communists and fellow-travelers associated with the New Deal, at heart a Fascist. That may seem a bit harsh; but after all, the American versions of world trends are always softer than the originals. The American and French Revolutions were very close in doctrine, but different in carrying out; the same might be said of Jackson and Bonaparte. So too with Roosevelt and, say, Mussolini. Why are we this way? The temptation is to say simply that we are a nicer bunch of folks than "them foreigners." But it might also be that, as they resist internal subversion much more strongly than we do, perhaps the enemy here need not be so severe. Remember the contrast between Fisher Ames and the Marquis d'Elbee!

At any rate, it were well, before we say farewell to peacetime America, to see what John Flynn had to say about what a Fascist United States would be like:

> Fascism will come at the hands of perfectly authentic Americans, as violently against Hitler and Mussolini as the next one, but who are convinced that the present economic system is washed up and that the present political system in America has outlived its usefulness and who wish to commit this country to the rule of the bureaucratic state; interfering in the affairs of the states and cities; taking part in the management of industry and finance and agriculture; assuming the role of great national banker and investor, borrowing billions every year and spending them on all sorts of projects through which such a government can paralyze opposition and command public support; marshalling great armies and navies at crushing costs to support the industry of war and preparation for war which will become our greatest industry; and adding to all this the most romantic adventures in global planning, regeneration, and domination all to be done under the authority of a powerfully centralized government in which the executive will hold in effect all the powers with Congress reduced to the role of a debating society. There is your fascist. And the sooner America realizes this dreadful fact the sooner it will arm itself to make an end of American fascism masquerading under the guise of the champion of democracy (*As We Go Marching*, p.253)

What the dogged Mr. Flynn, with his idealism, could not fathom, is that we would love our chains. This is the most recent American Revolution, or at least the penultimate one. We all owe FDR a great debt for it indeed.

But here we have merely spoken of ourselves. The war which Mr. Roosevelt so dearly wished us to enter would change not merely American and world politics, it would alter every element of life, down to the last cuff-link.

WORLD WAR AND COLD WAR 1941-1951

WAR AT LAST

On November 19, 1941, the Japanese Foreign Ministry informed its embassy in Washington that if war with the United States was imminent, it would have broadcast over Tokyo's radio station JAP the weather report, "east wind rain." Since the US military and naval intelligence had previously cracked the Japanese codes, this was known immediately to FDR. Armed forces receiving stations were put on the alert for just such a message.

As we have seen, Secretary of State Hull had rejected Japanese peace terms on November 26, demanding immediate withdrawal of all Japanese forces immediately from China and French Indo-China. This ultimatum was obviously impossible to comply with, and on December 4, the east wind message was duly broadcast. Those who intercepted it, a Lieutenant Commander Kramer and a Commander Stafford, reported it to their superior, Rear Admiral Noyes, who in turn passed it on to the President's naval aide. There can be no doubt that Roosevelt was aware that the Japanese intended to commence hostilities.

The historical consensus, however, is that FDR imagined that such an assault would commence in the Philippines and the Dutch East Indies; according to the *Encyclopedia Brittanica*, he was quite surprised when the attack came upon Hawaii.

If that is so, of course, it would simply show the duplicity of FDR's dealing with the American people; the America First Committee had charged repeatedly that Roosevelt wanted to get this nation into the War by hook or by crook. It is, as we saw, a matter of record that when approached on several occasions by the Japanese to negotiate, his administration refused. Thus it is obvious that despite his promises to the American people, Roosevelt was willing to waste the lives of American boys in pursuance of a policy the American people did not want. Call it what you will, this cannot be said to be either democracy or honesty.

There is, however, evidence to suggest that Roosevelt did know that an attack on Pearl Harbor was imminent. For example, having cracked the Japanese codes the Navy Department was in a position to track Japanese naval moves. Moreover, although the old and obsolete battleships were left at Pearl Harbor, ships which would have been little use in modern war (which FDR would have known, having been Assistant Secretary of the Navy in the First World War), the aircraft carriers were sent out to sea and so escaped destruction. There is more. Speaking of the intercepted east wind rain message, Charles Tansill declares:

> It would be ordinarily assumed that the President, after reading this intercepted message, would hurriedly call a conference of the more important Army and Navy officers to concert plans to meet the anticipated attack. The testimony of General Marshall and Admiral Stark would indicate that he made no effort to consult with them. Did he deliberately seek the Pearl Harbor attack in order to get America into the war? What is the real answer to this riddle of Presidential composure in the face of a threatened attack upon some American outpost in the faraway Pacific? The problem grows more complicated as we approach zero hour. At 9:00 A.M. on December 7, Lieutenant Commander Kramer delivered to Admiral Stark the final installment of the Japanese instruction to [their Ambassador] Nomura. Its meaning was now so obvious that Stark cried out in great alarm: "My God! This means war. I must get word to [commanding officer at Pearl, Admiral] Kimmel at once." But he made no effort to contact Honolulu. Instead, he tried to get in touch with General Marshall, who for some strange reason, suddenly decided to go on a long horseback ride. It was a history-making ride.... In the early hours of World War II, General Marshall took a ride that helped prevent an alert from reaching Pearl Harbor in time to save an American fleet from serious disaster and an American garrison from a bombing that cost more than 2000 lives. Was there an important purpose behind this ride?...
>
> When Colonel Bratton, on the morning of December 7, saw the last part of the Japanese instruction to Nomura he realized that "Japan planned to attack the United States at some point at or near 1 o'clock that day." To Lieutenant Commander Kramer the message meant "surprise attack at Pearl Harbor today." This information was in the hands of Secretary [of War] Knox by 10:00 A.M., and he must have passed it on to the President immediately.
>
> It was 11:25 A.M. when General Marshall returned to his office. If he carefully read the reports on the threatened Japanese attack (on Pearl Harbor) he still had plenty of time to contact Honolulu by means of the scrambler telephone on his desk, or by the Navy radio or the FBI radio. For some reason best known to himself he chose to send the alert to Honolulu by RCA and did not even take the precaution to have it stamped "priority." As the Army Pearl Harbor Board significantly remarked: "We find no justification for a failure to send this message by multiple secret means either through the Navy radio or the FBI radio or the scrambler telephone or all three." Was the General under Presidential orders to break military regulations with regard to the transmission of important military information? (*Back Door to War*, pp. 651-652).

If Professor Tansill's inference is correct, then FDR knowingly sacrificed over 2,000 American lives at Pearl Harbor to involve the country in a war which otherwise he could never have managed to get the country into. Had FDR alerted the Japanese to his knowledge of their actions; had he dispatched the navy to interdict them on the high seas; in a word, had he either convinced them to desist, or else defeated them with a minimal loss of American life, it would have been impossible to interest Americans in another war. In the words of then-House Majority Leader John W. McCormack: "We couldn't get a declaration of war through Congress. If Pearl Harbor hadn't happened, in my opinion the intense isolationism was so strong, we never would have entered the war" (Roy Hoopes, *Americans Remember the Home Front,* p. 23). Obviously, had FDR negotiated a settlement with Japanese before they felt forced into war, this would have been doubly true. The course of Japanese actions had been predicted decades before by widely-known American military analyst, Homer Lea.

As it was, the assault fell upon an utterly unprepared Pearl Harbor; the surprise was perfect. Admiral Kimmel's reputation would be ruined for not being better prepared, though obviously he was a scapegoat. Over 2,000 Americans died, including the band of the U.S.S. Arizona; having won a battle of the bands in a Honolulu hotel the night before, they were permitted to sleep in the morning of December 7. So they shall until the last trump when the Earth opens up its graves.

The effect was all FDR could possibly have hoped for. The America Firsters, until now rigidly opposed to a war which did not concern this country, jumped to the colors when as they thought, the Japanese made a totally unprovoked sneak attack. The President's stirring speech to Congress is impressed to this day on our national consciousness: "Yesterday, December Seventh, 1941, a date which shall live in infamy..." As soon as the news reached the various parts of the country, crowds formed in various areas, including Lafayette Square by the White House. Hymns were sung in churches, and the first black outs engulfed America. Fear was especially widespread on the West Coast.

Immediately, long-prepared defense plans went into effect: soldiers, sailors, police, and newly mobilized civilian guards were set to guarding dams, bridges, reservoirs, and the like. Censorship too went into effect, with all cables, letters, and radiograms being sent out of the country made subject to scrutiny. All over America, young men rushed to enlist, while even 81-year-old General "Black Jack" Pershing hobbled on his cane from Walter Reed Medical Center to the White House to offer his services to FDR.

Even more, perhaps, than in 1917, America's entrance into the War in 1941 reflected the European experience in 1914. Unlike that first conflict, when there was no question of foreign invasion, on this occasion there might be. While few mobilized in 1917 actually saw service in the AEF, many thousands of American young people would in the course of this war be transported all over the world; moreover, they would not come back when it was "over, over there" as their fathers had, but would remain even unto this day, as the world's policemen. For Europe, the old order ended in 1914; for us, it was really 1941.

On December 11, war was declared on Japan's allies, Germany and Italy. Roosevelt's primary interest was thus served. But events in the Far East pushed Europe out of the popular mind. The day before, Guam had fallen to the Japanese; little Wake would hold out gallantly until December 22. In the meantime, the Japanese invasion of the Philippines was in full swing. Heavily outnumbered, the American and Filipino defenders of the island of Luzon were pushed steadily back toward their prepared final redoubts of the Bataan Peninsula and Corrigidor.

We will rejoin our forces overseas before long. For now, let us focus on the home front. Almost immediately, automobile production was shut down; General Motors was the last to do so, in early February 1942. At sea, American shipping was in great danger from both German and Japanese subs; this danger soon extended to the coast itself. On February 23, a Japanese midget sub lobbed shells at an oil refinery west of Santa Barbara, California (they missed their target, but did manage to stampede a herd of nearby horses). Two nights later, at 2:25 in the morning, L.A.'s civil defense blacked out the city, air-raid sirens wailed, anti-aircraft guns fired, and searchlights broke the night.

All for nothing. Despite the widespread pandemonium in the streets (including many auto accidents) caused by the black-out, despite the furor and rushing around, the celebrated "Battle of Los Angeles" was a real non-event, caused by war fever and mass hysteria. The only damage caused by weaponry was that to windows and roofs hit by AA shrapnel. Western Defense Command insisted that there had been unfriendly aircraft about, but to this day none has ever been identified by any other source.

Amusing as this incident may seem, it had one terribly serious result: all Japanese-Americans were removed from their homes on the West Coast, from Seattle to San Diego, and placed in detention camps. They were forced to leave all at once, and to leave most of their belongings behind; in hours, one of the most hard-working ethnic groups in America was reduced to absolute penury. Unlike German and Italian Americans, no Japanese American was ever convicted of spying for the enemy; indeed, Japanese Americans were instrumental in cracking the Japanese codes. While their elders, wives, and younger siblings languished in camps like Manzanar and Tule Lake, the youthful Japanese of the 442nd

Regimental Combat Team fought in Europe and became the most highly decorated American unit of World War II. This disgraceful action was all the more ironic because it was approved by California Governor Earl Warren, whom we shall meet again in the next section as a great Liberal.

Civil Defense organizations blossomed everywhere; an Arts Council was formed to mobilize actors, writers, and artists behind the war effort. Melvyn Douglas was appointed by Eleanor Roosevelt to head it. Just as with the New Deal, so too, the Roosevelts saw the War Effort as a cause to further centralize American life under government direction. As head of the Office of Civil Defense, Mrs. Roosevelt was able to indulge all her interests. One was physical fitness, for which she hired John B. Kelly (father of Grace Kelly, noted actress who became Princess Grace of Monaco), former Olympic sculling champion, as head of the PF program. Pushing for everything from golf to mass tap-dancing, the programs issued from his office remind one more than a tad of the Nazi "Strength through Joy" movement, if they were not taken nearly so seriously.

Dancing particularly enthralled the First Lady:

> She proclaimed a "Dance-for-Health Week" that would commence on April third. Then the First Lady set an example by organizing folk dances during coffee breaks and lunch hours in the enameled corridors of OCD headquarters. This was a commandeered apartment building on Dupont Circle, bordering "Embassy Row." She not only arranged the dances; she often led them" (A.A. Hoehling, *Home Front, U.S.A.,* pp. 38-39).

Amusing as these capers were, the torrent of ridicule they and other of her activities provoked led eventually to Mrs. Roosevelt's resignation.

Her replacement, former Harvard Law dean James Landis met a similar fate. Civil Defense hysteria was such that, despite the fact that neither Germans nor Japanese possessed bombers capable of reaching the continental U.S., Landis ordered teams of emergency fire fighters trained everywhere, just in case.

A seemingly never-ending cornucopia of Civil Defense schemes poured from Landis' mind. But:

> The "block plan" was to prove Landis' Waterloo. The catastrophe was not especially surprising since the block warden was heaped with duties and prerogatives which far exceeded his normal role. In addition to calling attention to offending lights or reminding that air-raid drills were in progress, he or she was supposed to encourage housewives to save fats, conserve sugar, help draw up car pools, provide the counsel

of a veteran agronomist on the culture of victory gardens, and even boom the WAVES and WACS to eligible females.

To many legislators, especially Republicans, these wardens appeared to be the American equivalent of block "fuehrers," or leaders, in Nazi-governed towns and cities. The wardens seemed to be assuming an ever-encroaching role in the nation's home life, barely stopping short of changing the diapers of the block's infants. Alarmists feared their next step would be to call the political tune for their captive wards (Hoehling, *op. cit.*, pp. 44-45).

The scheme was stopped, and in the Spring of 1944 the OCD was abolished. But "Alarmists" had reason to be alarmed. Although the Communists had always been present in the New Deal, and while, during the period of the pact between Germany and the Soviet Union they had been loud pacifists, Hitler's invasion of Russia caused them once again to support the pro-war forces. Once we were in, Communist actors, writers, directors, and so on became very powerful in Hollywood, lending their efforts to propaganda films like *Mission to Moscow*. Since Stalin was our ally, the doings of Communists in this country went unchecked and even were tacitly fostered in certain areas by government representatives. In Hollywood, this took the form of an unofficial black list, whereby outspoken anti-Communist film-folk found it difficult to find work during the war. They would remember this afterwards.

More frightening still, however, was the government's use of the emergency to increase its stranglehold on the economy and on political life. The former resulted from a simple fact: war materiel had to be produced. After Pearl Harbor, 20,000 of our best warplanes were shipped to Great Britain and the Soviet Union. Tanks and planes must be turned out to replace them, as well as rifles, oil, military posts, and everything concerning the conflict. Old factories must be converted, new ones built, and housing for workers provided. One result of this and the draft was the immediate dissolution of the Great Depression and the country's unemployment problem; the second was the inauguration in January 1942 of the all-powerful War Production Board. The WPB, working hand in glove with the Justice Department could requisition the entire output of any mine or factory, and direct its use and allocation. To build up the labor pool, convicts were used, aliens given work permits, and above all, women were put to work, as in World War I. But this time, the ladies labored in much larger numbers. This, together with the formation of the first large industrial suburbs began two major social changes which would bear fruit after the war: the flight of American women from the home to the workplace, and the flight of the Middle Class from the cities to the suburbs. This latter would have the effect of increasing housing at the expense of the environment while at the same time spelling the death of the inner cities. Moreover, the creation of such new and artificial towns and cities would have the effect of cutting large numbers of Americans off even further from any of their past traditions.

Like unto the WPB was the Office of Price Administration. Headed by Leon Henderson, the OPA took charge of rationing, which began in March of 1942. Initially, only sugar was rationed, but in quick succession, shoes, coffee, gasoline, rubber, and butter followed. Much of these were sent to sustain our allies. Occasionally the uses they were put to were intriguing: Russians, for example, unused to butter, employed it to grease rifles and other things. More and more items, from radios to car parts to paper to toys, became rationed or scarce. Much of this was to be expected, as the needs of the war consumed an ever-increasing share of production. But, at least as far as the OPA was concerned, there was more involved.

> Controls, [Henderson] declared, should be yet tighter and extend to still more commodities. Underlying much of his philosophy and his efforts was a desire, repeatedly avowed in public by Henderson, to level out society more equally. He alluded to the change in rich homes and habits, especially the anticipated extinction of the multi-servant household (Hoehling, *op. cit.*, p. 66).

Although this latter did indeed occur for the most part (though such places as the White House and the Roosevelt estate at Hyde Park were exempted) Henderson's officiousness resulted in his forced resignation in 1943. His policies continued however, resulting in (among other things) the virtual death of the multiservant estate. This was a great loss.

Why? Amongst other things, it meant the passage of a certain style of life. Amy Vanderbilt describes this in her *Etiquette:*

> The day of the complete staff, of formal entertainment, except in a limited way, is about done. The most exclusive men's tailors in the country say they have no ready-made liveries any more because there are no longer customers to support the department. The very few establishments with permanent men servants must have liveries made to order.
>
> This is the day of the electric dishwasher, the storage wall, the dining ell, the deep freeze, buffet meals, day workers, cleaning services by the hour, unionized bonded help, sitters, the automatic washing machine, the dryer, and nursery school instead of Nanny (p. 476).
>
> Most of us do our own work or make do with occasional or regular part-time help as I've said above. There are indeed, however, some households run with full staff, which have some of the facilities still for the kind of gracious living once quite usual among those who could afford it....

Most of us don't want to live this way any more even if it were possible (p. 504).

While Miss Vanderbilt may not have wished so to live, and indeed, while today's American wealthy might for the most part echo her sentiments, it is truly unfortunate for them as well as for the rest of us. As you may remember from earlier on, it is in fact the landed gentry, with their tenants and staffs of servants, who acted as this country's first governing class. Were they good or bad, they learned from dealing with servants to look beyond their own interests, and to deal on a small scale in the little communities which their homes were, with the problems which afflicted town, province or state, and finally nation. In a word, their experience as paternal employers assisted them in the leadership role their wealth brought them. Today, such folk remain wealthy, and others have become rich; but the idea that wealth has a social use is foreign to them.

Moreover, since such folk were large scale employers in the areas where they lived, they both provided an incentive for local people (whether servants or simply outside suppliers of such households) to remain in rural areas, and carried much weight in local affairs. There they provided something of a counter to the centralizing tendencies of the Federal Government. Although non-Catholic for the most part, to the degree that they could in their cloudy way, they attempted to fulfill the classic role of aristocracy as outlined by Pius XII in his Allocution to the Roman Nobility of January 16, 1946:

> As history will testify, wherever true democracy reigns, the life of the people is permeated with sound traditions, which it is not legitimate to destroy. The primary representatives of these traditions are the ruling classes, or rather, the groups of men and women, or the associations, which set the tone, as we say, for the village or the city, for the region or the entire country.
>
> Whence the existence and influence, among all civilized peoples, of aristocratic institutions...

While such folk, being non-Catholic, had never functioned to the greatest possible good, they yet remained a tenuous connection with old Christendom. Moreover, they served to fulfill in some degree a function which Pius XII in the same allocution declared belonged to such folk:

> ...that of acting for the people, in all the facets of public life to which you might be called, as living examples of an unwavering performance of duty, as impartial, disinterested men who, free of all inordinate lust for success or wealth, do not accept a post except to

serve the good cause, courageous men unafraid of losing favor from above, or of threats from below.

He had already said to the same audience in an Allocution of January 14, 1945 that the excellence their state in life required would be

> ...made manifest in the dignity of one's entire bearing and conduct—a dignity that is not imperious, however, and that, far from emphasizing distances, only lets them appear when necessary to inspire in others a higher nobility of soul, mind, and heart.

In a secularized (and so less effective way) these values were aspired to by the class that the OPA set on its way to extinction. As was said of the founder of the Hotchkiss School, a favored prep school for such folk:

> Though he never came right out and said so, George Van Santvoord was emphasizing the true standards of a true aristocracy—standards of cultivation, of intellect, of duty, of generosity of spirit, standards of doing one's best. The fact is that out of schools like Groton and Hotchkiss, out of even the most hothouse-seeming notions of how the children of the American rich should be educated, would emerge people who, when the chips were down, would manage to rise to occasions and do the things that were expected of them (Stephen Birmingham, *America's Secret Aristocracy*, p. 253).

So they rose, for better or worse, in every one of this nation's conflicts. World War II would be their last major War. Their descendants exist still, and some retain their traditions. But they are no longer a force around which opposition to the regime in power might coalesce. Today the citizenry of this country tolerate things their ancestors would not have; part of the reason for this is the lack of effective leadership—a lack in no small part due to the erosion of the class which once provided it. But because this class had, since the Revolution and the Civil War been consecrated to the ideals of Americanism, there was little they could do when effectively liquidated in the name of that ideology.

All that has been said in regard to the gathering of power in the hands of government might be dismissed as the natural growth of modern government. We have come to accept the notion that, so long as government is "nice," it has a right to all the power necessary to run the country. The idea that a people might run themselves has become foreign. Nevertheless, even under the new scheme of things, most folk would, one supposes, believe that even a modern state has no right to suppress peaceful opposition. But the wartime regime presided over by FDR did just that.

Among other things, the war gave Roosevelt the chance to even old scores. Thus, when Montgomery Ward was plagued by labor disputes, the opportunity was seized by the government to take control of the chain from board chairman and long-time FDR opponent Sewell Avery. In April 1944, Attorney General Biddle flew to Chicago with six helmeted soldiers. On April 26 at 10 A.M., they arrived at Avery's office. When he refused to leave they carried him out bodily in his chair and deposited the 71-year-old on the sidewalk outside.

In Detroit, the new Archbishop, Francis Mooney, a friend of FDR's, silenced Fr. Coughlin and ended the publication of *Social Justice*. In this way, much that befell other opponents of the New Deal was spared the priest.

As noted earlier, there were a number of Italian and German Americans who spied for their former home-countries. The government took the opportunity, while ferreting out treason and traitors, to also discredit or imprison those whose crime was simply opposing the course which this country had taken since 1933. It will be readily admitted that there is a difference between taking a dissenting or even unpopular stand, and aiding and abetting the enemies of one's country. Moreover, as we have seen in the case of natives of Communist countries who assisted our intelligence agencies against the regimes which oppressed their nations, even "treason" can appear justified to its practitioners on ideological grounds. If one is convinced of the evil nature of a regime, and for the sake of the country it rules aids that regime's foreign opponents, where does treason lie? We know that the Nazis and Communists were evil, indeed; but what of those who genuinely thought the same of Roosevelt? To this day we blithely do business with heirs of Mao Tse Tung, who was responsible for the deaths of hundreds of millions of Chinese, and spurn the successors of his opponents on Taiwan. Of what does our morality consist? As the saying has it:

> Treason never prospers;
> For if it prosper,
> None dare call it treason.

One might consider the subversion of a constitution to which a man has sworn allegiance to be treason; if this were true, then such a one might consider FDR a traitor. But in wartime, to think such thoughts would itself be called treason. Confusing, indeed.

On July 22, 1942, Attorney General Francis Biddle secured an indictment against twenty-eight defendants. Some were racists and indeed out and out Nazis, like William Dudley Pelley, leader of a group of would-be storm troopers called the "Silver Shirts." Others, like

Prescott Freese Dennett, an avid America Firster who was well respected by a number of Congressmen and Senators, were quite respectable. But crackpot or respectable, the 28 were all accused by the indictment of treason:

> It being the plan and said purpose of said defendants, and divers other persons to the Grand Jurors unknown, to destroy the morale and faith and confidence of the members of the military and naval forces of the United States and the people of the United States in their public officials and Republican form of government...
> ...the said defendants... planning and intending to seize upon and use and misuse the right of freedom of speech and of the press to spread their disloyal doctrines, intending and believing that any nation allowing to its people the right of freedom of speech and the press is powerless to defend itself against enemies masquerading as patriots and seeking to obstruct, impede, break down and destroy the proper functioning of its republican government under the guise of honest criticism...

Indeed! One cannot help but wonder, given the present assurance that freedoms of speech and the press are absolute—particularly with regard to pornography and so on—if it was a tad disingenuous for the regime being criticized to determine whether that criticism was honest or not. In any case, the sought after convictions were achieved, as were those of many others. One of these was the aviatrix Laura Ingalls, who upon being found guilty declared:

> Your honor, one of the great fundamentals implicit in our Constitution is liberty of conscience. I felt I had a right to follow the dictates of my conscience... I worked individually, and individualism is a real American trait. My motives were born of a burning patriotism and a high idealism...I am a truer patriot than those who convicted me... I salute the Republic of the United States!

With that she was led away. From April to November 1944, another 26 Americans were tried for sedition, including among their number anti-Catholic Gerald L.K. Smith and Catholic Elizabeth Dilling. Treason trials, like any other sort of politics, make strange bedfellows. In the end, the judge died on November 30, and a mistrial was declared. Had they been acquitted, it would have been a black day for FDR; had they been convicted, for America. As it was, little resulted.

Nevertheless, the struggle between the verbiage and the reality of the Americanist ideology was spelled out in detail. Later on, when the

Vietnam War broke out, Americans opposed to it sometimes collaborated with the enemy in ways which would have won them prison during World War II. What had changed?

The War, in any case, altered America in much the same way that World War I changed Europe, despite the fact that we were not invaded. The rush of women to the work place helped destroy the notion of housewifery as a decent occupation. Relaxed morals led to a skyrocketing in the divorce rate, which has continued ever since. We have referred to the political consequences of the ruin of America's gentry. There were purely social ones as well. Where before the War, Americans aspired to "class," to dress and act with style, the emphasis on "democracy" and the demise of that class which formerly set standards replaced this aspiration with a taste for the casual. Male formal wear was seen less and less; in nightclubs and restaurants, the patrons gave up dinner jackets for suit-and-tie—resulting in the curious fact that waiters were and are often better dressed than the clientele. Such relaxation was followed in etiquette, in speech, in a hundred things; taken up by movie actors, these trends accelerated.

Communism, as we have seen, spread in a sympathetic atmosphere. Such men as Harry Hopkins, the President's right hand man, and Alger Hiss, achieved high positions, and used them to help their cause. This would be a grave problem later.

In a nutshell, for all that we were on the winning side, the result on the Home Front was a defeat for all that was best in the country. We shall now see the effect our intervention had on the world outside.

A World at War

Shortly after Pearl Harbor, Roosevelt and Churchill met in Washington to coordinate the war effort. They agreed to concentrate first on Europe, since, as Churchill put it, "It is generally agreed that the defeat of Germany, entailing a collapse, will leave Japan exposed to overwhelming force, whereas the defeat of Japan would not by any means bring the World War to an end."

From the time that Britain and France had declared war on Germany in response to Hitler's attack on Poland in September of 1939, the war had gone badly for the Allies there. Poland fell swiftly, and then in 1940 Denmark, Norway, the Netherlands, Belgium, and most surprising of all, France had fallen to the seemingly invincible German army. The defeat of these liberal democracies brought to the fore in each of them internal divisions which had been brewing for a long time.

In each, the Right wing was divided on how to deal with the occupation, particularly since the invaders had had the collaboration of the Communists (due to the Ribbentrop-Molotov pact) in the invasion. How could one operate under German control? How true was the German rhetoric about building a New Europe and an anti-Communist crusade? Did one trust the new rulers and work with them, or did one work with leftists and with (after the invasion of the Soviet Union in June 1941) the Communists in Resistance? Not an easy call, indeed. In a word, with which despot would you ally, Stalin or Hitler? Which could you trust?

The Sovereigns, ruling and not, of Europe had obviously little to hope for from the Communists; neither, however, did they trust Hitler. The Archduke Otto von Habsburg, son of the saintly Charles I, had many supporters in both Austria and Hungary before the War. Both Dollfuss and his successor were in principle Monarchists. So much did Hitler fear a restoration that he named his planned invasion of Austria "Case Otto." But Otto was not restored, and the takeover was peaceful. When war began, Otto left for New York, and after Pearl Harbor was given charge of a Free Austrian battalion of 500 volunteers authorized by Secretary of War Stimson. However, the outcry arising from anti-Monarchists in this country was great, and the battalion disbanded. So ended a chance for this nation to make some small reparation for the terrible wrong committed in our name by Woodrow Wilson.

In Germany itself, with few exceptions, the Royals had had little use for Hitler. The Kaiser himself, in exile in Holland, refused to acknowledge the Honor Guard sent to his home after the Germans conquered the country. His grandson and heir, Louis Ferdinand was briefly in the Army when the war started. Hitler, fearful that royal princes in the army showing heroism might win popularity, ordered all such gradually put out. Louis Ferdinand then involved himself casually with the plotters of July 20, 1944 (of whom more shortly) and then had to go underground until the war ended. Crown Prince Rupert of Bavaria, an early foe of Hitler, saw his wife Crown Princess Antonia sent to Buchenwald Concentration Camp, where she was cruelly tortured; the Prince was forced into exile in Italy.

The heir to the Russian Imperial throne, Grand Duke Vladimir Cyrilovitch, lived in St. Brieuc, France, when the Germans conquered that country. Hitler offered the Grand Duke his throne if he would assist in the forthcoming invasion. He refused, and went to Spain.

Queen Wilhelmina of the Netherlands, King Haakon VII of Norway, and, after their countries were conquered in 1941, Kings Peter of Yugoslavia and George II of Greece fled to Britain, assisting their Governments in exile in continuing the war against Hitler. In this time of occupation and defeat, they summed up in themselves their respective nations' desire to be free.

This was true also of the two who remained behind: Leopold III of Belgium and Christian X of Denmark. In the case of Leopold, he had known early on that the British intended to withdraw their troops by sea from western Belgium. As Commander in Chief of the Army, he was with his troops in the field; his government informed him that if defeated, it was necessary for King and Cabinet to continue the fight from abroad. He on the other hand believed it to be his duty to share his people's fate. On May 28, he surrendered his army, and addressed them, saying: "I will not leave you in these tragic moments. I shall stay with you to protect you and your families and your fate will be mine." The Royal family were imprisoned in their palace until June 1944, when they were taken into captivity in Germany.

Because Denmark was never at war with Germany, so swift was its conquest, its King and Government remained in place throughout the occupation. But every day and in defiance of German wishes, the King rode a horse through the streets of Copenhagen in Danish army uniform. To his people he carried in his own person their refusal to be other than what they were. So impressed were they by this lone and dangerous deed, that Kaj Munk, a noted Danish resistance fighter executed by the Nazis on January 4, 1944, wrote one of his most stirring poems in Christian's honor.

But for less elevated personages, things were not quite so clear. As General Weygand, who would loyally serve the Vichy regime of Marshal Petain put it: "Any man will do his duty. The tragedy comes when he must make a choice between two sign posts each marked 'duty' and pointing in opposite directions."

The first country whose inhabitants would face this question was Czechoslovakia. From the beginning, the ethnic Germans in the Sudetenland, the Slovaks, the Ruthenians, and the Magyars all faced domination by the Czechs. Among the Czechs themselves, unbelievers and Protestants (like apostate Thomas Masaryk, the nation's first President) were in power, relegating the Catholic majority, whose Party led by *Fr. Jan Sramek* was dedicated to accomplishing the Church's social teachings in the country, to a minor role. The Sudeten German Party, although host to a Nazi element, was until 1938 dominated by members of the *Kameradschaftbund*, followers of Professor Othmar Spann, an Austrian Catholic conservative who was held as a dangerous enemy by the Nazis. The Ruthenians, a branch of the Ukrainians, were led in turn by *Fr. Augustin Volosin*, and the Slovak Nationalists first by *Fr. Andrej Hlinka*, and then by *Msgr. Josef Tiso*. In the beginning, the anti-clerical Czech government helped assist in the formation of a schism in 1920. That year saw a group of Catholic priests, members of a group founded in 1890 to press for things like a vernacular liturgy and the abolition of celibacy, secede to form the Czechoslovak Church. Although at first claiming to retain Catholicity, in short order its adherents abandoned the Apostolic succession, numbered the Bible as only one of many sources of revelation, held reason as the highest religious truth, declared that Christ was God's son only ethically, rejected Original Sin; in a word, they became Unitarians. The government's support for these folk was not lost on the country's Catholics; nor were its centralizing cultural and political methods, nor were the pro-Soviet tendencies of some of its leadership, particularly after Eduard Benes became President. It seemed to many, both Czechs and those of other nationalities, that the leadership in Prague and perhaps the very State itself offered a long-term threat to their religion, their culture, and perhaps (should the government become more dictatorial) their very lives.

Under these circumstances, the rise of Nazi Germany appeared to many of these people to be an opportunity for freedom. To the Sudeten Germans, and to the Magyars of southern Slovakia who were incorporated in Hungary at the same time after Munich, this seemed particularly the case. Another result of that treaty was that Benes left the country, and was replaced as President by Emil Hacha. Slovakia and Ruthenia were each given autonomous governments. When Hacha attempted to suppress Slovakia's in March of 1939, the Germans were appealed to by the Slovaks as guarantors of the Munich accords, and they very happily marched into Prague. Slovakia became independent, Ruthenia was seized by Hungary, and the rump of the Czech lands, still nominally governed by Hacha and his cabinet, became the Bohemia-Moravia Protectorate. Benes formed a Czech government in exile, while Bohemia-Moravia became an integral part of the German War efforts:

> The situation of the Czechs in the so-called Protectorate during the war was not unfavorable. In the first place they were exempt from military service, and worked quite willingly for Hitler's war machine in the Bohemian industries, which were greatly developed by the Germans. Thousands of tanks, airplanes and guns were produced in the factories, many more than could possibly have been destroyed by the Legions which were organized by Benes in France, England, and Russia. The Legion in the West, which consisted of about 5,000 men in the ground forces, never went into action, while the 12,000 men in Russia were engaged in only a few insignificant skirmishes. As Benes himself said, it was a "symbolical army," but propaganda made quite a respectable amount of political capital out of it, and the books and newspaper articles which were written about it during and after the liberation of Prague gave the impression that the war could scarcely have been won without its aid. However, it would be unjust not to

mention here the well-deserved glory earned by some Czech airmen in the Battle of Britain.

Statistics show that Bohemia's war-time industrial and agricultural production were proportionately equal to that of Germany, and food shortages were no worse there than in the Reich. In contrast to Poland active resistance and sabotage scarcely existed in Bohemia until the last days of the war, although arrests were made in Bohemia and Moravia as in the other countries occupied by Germany, and in Germany itself.

The assassination of Heydrich was planned and organized abroad, and the Benes government cleverly exploited the severe reprisals that followed, and especially the shooting of the 168 male inhabitants of Lidice, to influence British and American public opinion in its favor. Care was taken, of course, to avoid mentioning the fact that the reprisals were not the responsibility of the Sudeten Germans but were carried out by German Nazis (F.O. Miksche, *Danubian Federation*, p. 25).

Czechs served in large numbers in the German army, and the Czech clergy supported Hacha because of their fear of both the anti-clericals and the Soviets. The Czech populace as a whole was quiescent, and the result was that Prague came through the war unscathed. It was an odd situation, but who (save those who actually have been in such a spot) can claim they would have been more courageous than the Czechs in their position?

Slovakia was a different question. Where German power meant subordination for the Czechs, it meant independence for the Slovaks. Msgr. Tiso and his government took the opportunity given them to organize:

> The constitution of the Slovak Republic, adopted on July 31, 1939, was that of a typical parliamentary democracy. Legislative and fiscal powers were vested in a one-house assembly elected by universal suffrage, which also chose the president of the republic and approved the ratification of treaties. The president conducted the government with the aid of ministers responsible to the assembly and removable by vote of no confidence. The constitution provided for an independent judiciary and contained a full bill of rights and guarantees of due process of law. Although the government, under constant pressure from the Nazis, was obliged to exercise a certain degree of censorship, there was no violation of basic human rights. Even the postwar Communist-dominated government was obliged to admit that "not a single political execution took place in the Slovak state."
>
> Article 79 of the Slovak Constitution grouped all citizens, regardless of social status, into "six estates"—agriculture, industry, commerce, banking, free professions, and public employees—which

some writers have mistakenly identified with the corporations of Mussolini's fascist state. These estates were not, however, copied from Italian Fascism: they were recommended by Pope Pius XI in his encyclical *Quadragesimo Anno*, and were self-governing bodies in which employers and workers in each branch of the economy could resolve their social conflicts in accord with Christian principle. Another superficial resemblance to fascism lay in the para-military Hlinka Guard, the uniforms of which looked rather like those of Hitler's storm troopers. Here it might be commented that in borrowing some of the panoply of Fascism, Tiso and his associates hoped to distract Nazi attention from the Christian orientation of the Slovak state. The Hlinka Guard conducted frequent drills, parades, and demonstrations, and helped the army and police in tasks of order and defense—it did not indulge in organized smashing of Jewish shops or liquidation of political dissenters (Kurt Glaser, *Czecho-Slovakia: A Critical History*, pp. 57-58).

An American correspondent, Edward L. Delaney, who spent much of the War in Slovakia, gives a similar account in his book, *False Freedom*. But what we are to make of the Tiso regime, which, until a 1944 revolt forced him to call in German troops, pursued an independent and by and large benevolent policy? Were they traitors? To the Czechs? But again, if they were ill-advised to accept German aid, would we have known better?

The case of France is even more complex. Catholics and Monarchists had little reason to mourn the Third Republic; indeed, for such folk the defeat of France in 1940 was a Divine judgment. The only way for France to return to greatness and independence was to atone for her past and shed the decadence which had caused her defeat. Thus traditionalists of all sorts (most notably Charles Maurras and the Action Française) rallied to Marshal Petain and the regime he headed, based at Vichy and controlling the unoccupied south of France and the colonies.

At first, their hopes seemed justified. Petain restored Catholic education to the public schools and public aid to the Catholic ones. Divorce was made much harder to get, and large families were given financial incentives. The lodges of Freemasons were closed. There was talk of restoring the provinces abolished in 1789, and subsidies given families who would reopen and operate abandoned farms. A corporatist economy was set up. It seemed that in time a Traditional Catholic French Monarchy would rise from the ruins.

But this was not to be; the Nazis had no use for that sort of thing. As time went on Petain was forced to replace traditionalists in his government with former Socialists and even Communists like Pierre Laval, Georges Doriot, and Marcel Deat. In 1940, Petain had seemed like the incarnation of France; but the German occupation of Vichy in response to the 1942 allied seizure of North Africa and Vichy's increasing subordination to Berlin led a former pupil of Petain's to acquire the mantle: *Charles De Gaulle*.

Interestingly enough, one Monarchist who never believed that Germany meant to deal honestly with Vichy was the heir to the French throne, Henri, Comte de Paris. Having served in the French Army against the Germans under an assumed name, he left after the surrender for Morocco. There he made clear his preference for the Free French based in London under De Gaulle's headship.

De Gaulle had declared himself leader of the Free French in a BBC broadcast on June 18, 1940, in which he declared that France was undefeated; he called upon all Frenchmen desirous of continuing the war to rally to him. At the time he was a virtually unknown figure. The Marshal had been invested with authority by the last government of the Third Republic, and was recognized as Chief of the French State by all neutral powers, including the United States. At first, the entire French overseas empire rallied to Petain. De Gaulle was without any territorial base from which to carry on his fight. But in a swift series of moves, all of French Equatorial Africa rallied to him from August 26 to August 29. In those three short days, Free France acquired a home.

Flush with victory, De Gaulle and Churchill planned an assault on the strategic Vichy held town of Dakar in Senegal. Much to their surprise, resistance was stiff, and the invaders were beaten off. This was not surprising. At this stage the Marshal's regime appeared truly independent, and De Gaulle was regarded as a traitor by perhaps the majority of Frenchmen, although in September the French possessions in the Pacific—French Oceania, French India, New Caledonia, and the New Hebrides rallied to Free France. This notion, however, would change as the iron grip of the Nazis tightened on France. With the Communists still allied to Hitler, the early Resistance within France was made up of non-Communist left-wing intellectuals and right-wing and Monarchist activists who did not trust the promises the Germans made to Petain about an armistice with honor. After the German invasion of the Soviet Union, the Communists made an about face, and in many districts came to dominate the Resistance. Thus a terrible case of divided loyalties was proffered the average Frenchman: to side with Petain, whose government was ever more under Hitler's thumb, or with De Gaulle, whose men in the field often had to collaborate with Stalin's? It was a microcosm of the European dilemma.

Whatever the case internally, more and more of the empire was slipping from Vichy's grasp. An Anglo-Free French invasion of Syria and Lebanon commenced on June 8, 1941, and concluded, after a surprisingly fierce Vichy resistance, on July 12.

America's entry into the War did not mean a severance of relations with Vichy, even though the Marshal had indicated to the American ambassador on November 18 that he was "a prisoner." Nevertheless, German seizure of strategic Vichy-held colonies was a threat; nowhere was this a more severe threat than on the little French islands of St. Pierre and Miquelon off the coast of Newfoundland. It was FDR's intention to take them over using U.S. or Canadian forces. On December 24, 1941, a small Free French flotilla seized them instead. American Secretary of State Cordell Hull sent an insulting note to the Canadian government virtually ordering them to expel the Free French. The Canadians and the British backed up De Gaulle, and the occupation of the islands was ungracefully accepted in Washington. But the natural dislike between FDR and the leader of the Free French was cemented; Roosevelt, if he must eventually withdraw recognition from Vichy, would find a more pliant Frenchman to run that country's war effort, if he could.

Meanwhile, the Japanese occupation of French Indochina, Burma, Thailand, and Malaya, as well as air assaults on Ceylon, turned Allied attention to the huge French island of Madagascar. Reasoning that Vichy's garrison would offer little resistance to the Japanese, it was decided by Churchill that the island must be taken. But knowing that FDR would be upset at any participation by De Gaulle, he ordered that it would be a purely British operation. On May 6, 1942 the assault began. At that time the U.S. State Department announced that Madagascar would be returned to France after the war. Incensed, de Gaulle demanded satisfaction from Churchill. The result was that a week later the British Foreign Office announced that once the country was secured it would be turned over to Free French administration.

In July of 1942, it was agreed by the British and Americans that, preparatory to landings on the continent of Europe, French North Africa as well as Libya had to be taken by the Allies. It was also agreed that the Free French were to have no part in it, despite their valor in Libya, where their troops had won a great victory at Bir Hacheim against Rommels' Afrika Korps. Operation Torch, as it was to be called, was to be bloodless. To accomplish this goal, Roosevelt would have to find his replacement for de Gaulle:

> Roosevelt's objective was to find a Frenchman who, by lending his name to Torch, would give to an act of aggression the appearance of an act of liberation. He recognized that Vichy might order its forces in North Africa to resist the landings. A Frenchman of great stature, he believed, could persuade the troops that it was in the interest of France to lay down its arms. Roosevelt set out, even before Torch had been decided, to find a Frenchman who could unite all Frenchmen under

United States leadership (Milton Viorst, Hostile Allies: FDR and De Gaulle, p. 97).

There it was in a nutshell. What the New Deal had been to America in terms of subjecting every facet of life to Government control, so would American participation in the War be. Independent Allies (save, as we shall see, the Soviet Union) could not be tolerated. The British Empire through her economic and military dependence upon us and the cession of her bases even before the War had already been reduced to a junior partner. The same should happen to France. For all his failings, De Gaulle was resolved that this would not happen to his country.

General Maxime Weygand, an independent minded old soldier whose German-ordered dismissal from the Vichy cabinet was the occasion of Petain's declaration to the American ambassador earlier cited, was approached and offered the role of leader after the invasion. He angrily refused, and informed the Marshal of Allied plans. The U.S. then turned to General Henri Giraud, who had recently escaped from a German prison and pledged his allegiance to Petain at Vichy.

On November 8, 1942, Operation Torch began. Three days earlier, Giraud had arrived in Algiers, to be ready to take control as civil administrator of North Africa when the invasion was over. De Gaulle broadcast over the BBC an appeal to the French in North Africa to rise up and join the Allies.

Petain, in the meantime, who had warned the Americans after Weygand told him of the plot that he would resist any invasion, gave the following reply to the American ambassador who presented a conciliatory note from FDR:

> It is with stupor and with grief that I learned during the night of the aggression of your troops against North Africa.
>
> I have read your message. You invoke pretexts which nothing justifies. You attribute to your enemies intentions which have never been manifested in acts. I have always declared that we would defend our empire if it were attacked. You knew that we would defend it against any aggressor whoever he might be. You knew that I would keep my word.
>
> In our misfortune I had, when requesting the Armistice, protected our Empire and it is you who, acting in the name of a country to which so many memories and ties bind us, have taken such a cruel initiative.
>
> France and her honor are at stake.
>
> We are attacked.
>
> We shall defend ourselves. This is the order I am giving.

To Petain, the assaults on Algiers, Oran, and Casablanca appeared to be cut from the same cloth as Pearl Harbor.

Meanwhile, Admiral Darlan, commander in chief in North Africa, and formerly Petain's premier (until replaced at German insistence with ex-Socialist Laval) called for a cease fire two days later, while wondering what next to do; the Germans saved him the trouble of further thought by occupying the unoccupied zone of France the next day.

Darlan assumed complete civil control of French North Africa, and accepted Giraud as military commander. The Germans occupied Tunisia with Italian aid, but the French troops in eastern Algeria, now united with the Allies, kept them from advancing further west. Darlan still professed to be subject to the Marshal, with American approval. De Gaulle was obviously to be cut out.

Nevertheless, as 1942 drew to a close, a certain impasse was reached: three factions behind Darlan, Giraud, and de Gaulle kept a sort of uneasy logroll between them. On December 24th, Darlan was assassinated by a young Monarchist army officer, Bonnier de la Chapelle. It was his hope that this would precipitate a coup in favor of the Count of Paris, who was in Algiers (ironically after having returned from trying to persuade Petain to allow the Allies to seize North Africa peacefully). Indeed, there was much support for such a move. The chief of police, Henri d'Astier, was plotting such a coup, but was quickly arrested.

On Christmas Day, General Eisenhower arrived in Algiers. At his behest the French authorities in Algiers made Giraud Darlan's successor. Friction between de Gaulle and Giraud—and so between Churchill and Roosevelt—festered.

But Algeria was not everything. In late November, 1942, the Indian Ocean island of Reunion passed from Vichy hands to de Gaulle. At the same time, half the officers, two thirds of the non-commissioned officers, and all of the men of the Madagascar garrison, after surrendering to the British, joined the Free French. The remainder volunteered for service with Giraud. The next month, French Somaliland with its 8,000 troops joined de Gaulle. General Leclerc led his troops from Chad through the Libyan desert and linked up with Montgomery. Every such victory eroded Giraud's position further.

Most ironic was the fact that, despite acting in great part for Roosevelt, Giraud was committed to the principles of Vichy. In order to justify American support, Giraud had to make a profession of belief in liberal democracy on March 14, 1943. Without bringing him republican support, it lost him his Vichy allies in North Africa. From this point on, he represented only FDR. Rewarding him, the U.S. prevented de Gaulle's representative from taking over in French Guiana when the Vichy administration there was overthrown. Interning him in Trinidad, they flew in one of Giraud's men instead.

When, in early May, Tunis at last fell, both de Gaulle's men and Giraud's were present at the victory. But afterwards, many of the latter went over to the Free French, inspired as much by Leclerc's epic march across the desert as anything else. On May 15th, de Gaulle received from his liaison with the Resistance in France their acceptance of his leadership. Later that month, Giraud gave in and acknowledged de Gaulle as head of Fighting France. Roosevelt was foiled; France had an Allied government which was now in charge of the French Colonial Empire and insisted upon being treated as an equal partner with the U.S., the British Empire, and the Soviet Union.

A number of our allies were not so fortunate. As with Czechoslovakia, Yugoslavia was a creation of Versailles and Woodrow Wilson, and included a number of irreconcilable elements. Serbia had, before 1914, acquired Macedonia, the largest number of whose people were ethnically connected to the Bulgarians. In the region of Kosovo were many Albanians who looked over the border to their independent nation, wrapped in chaos as it was. To this primarily Eastern Orthodox country were added in 1918 Bosnia-Herzegovina (primarily Moslem with Orthodox Serb and Catholic Croat minorities), and Catholic Croatia and Slovenia, as well as ethnically Serb but fiercely independent Montenegro. Over this gimcrack collection of peoples reigned first Prince Regent and then (after the death of his father Peter I) King Alexander. The King desired a centralized state under Serbian control; the Slovenes and Croats wanted a federation. *Fr. Anton Korosec* (1872-1940), was a Jesuit and leader of the Slovene people, who like the Slovaks looked traditionally to the Catholic clergy for leadership.

In Croatia, however, secular nationalist thought had long had a strong presence, as in Poland. Croats and Serbs clashed repeatedly on the political front, making parliamentary government very difficult. The assassination of the Prime Minister in 1928 led King Alexander to take direct control of the country. Rather than reigning as Monarch of all his peoples, it became his policy to "Serbianize" the nation, outlawing Croatian and Slovene national symbols and using exclusively Serb ones. The Croatian opposition as well as the Communists were keenly persecuted by the regime. In 1932, the Croatian nationalists united to oppose the Royal government. Numbers of them were murdered by the secret police, and they retaliated in kind. At last, on October 9, 1934, King Alexander was assassinated in Marseilles by Croat Nationalists.

Since Alexander's son, Peter II, was a boy of 11 years when his father died, a Regency was established, under the King's cousin, Prince Paul. Under the Regent, Yugoslavia returned to Parliamentary rule with its attendant division and low scale chaos. The Croatian Nationalist Movement, the Ustasha, continued its conflict with the government.

In the meantime, war broke out, and France fell in June of 1940. This put Romania and Yugoslavia, traditional French allies, in a very bad position; due to the Soviet German pact, the two powers most desirous of gobbling up the Balkans were allied. Romania in particular was in a bad position. King Carol II, a noted immoralist and indifferent politician, had established a nominally corporatist state under his own control in 1938. During this time the Iron Guard, despite initial persecution by Carol (resulting in the death of founder Corneliu Codreanu) gathered enough strength that the King was forced to appoint Guard sympathizer General Ion Antonescu to the Defense Ministry. After the fall of France, Carol was forced by Germany and the Soviet Union to cede Bessarabia to the Soviets, half of Transylvania to Hungary, and Southern Dobrudja to Bulgaria. So great was the outcry that on September 18, Carol made Antonescu Prime Minister, and two days later abdicated. His 19-year-old son Michael became King, but real power was in the hands of Antonescu. Despite appearances, the now-Marshal Antonescu was so subservient to the Germans that the next year he ordered a bloody purge of the Iron Guard, who demonstrated that their primary loyalty was to Romania and not Germany. In short order, Romania, Bulgaria, Hungary, and Slovakia joined the Rome-Berlin-Tokyo Axis.

Now Yugoslavia's position was tenuous indeed. With Italian-controlled Albania in its rear, and the Italian, German, Hungarian, Romanian, and Bulgarian frontiers all occupied by Axis troops, Prince Paul was easily convinced that his nation's survival lay with the Germans. On March 25, 1941, he signed an agreement bringing his nation into the Axis. This precipitated a coup by Serbian Nationalist Army officers, who resented the Regent's recent accord with Croatian leaders. They denounced the pact with the Axis.

German reaction was swift: on April 6 German, Italian, Hungarian and Bulgarian troops surged across the border; totally outflanked, the Yugoslav army capitulated on April 17. King Peter and his government fled to London, and the country was partitioned. Macedonia was given to Bulgaria, half of Banat and another small district to Hungary, Dalmatia, Kossovo, and half of Slovenia to Italy, and the remaining Slovene portion to Germany herself. Montenegro was placed under Italian occupation, and the rump of Serbia, run by former Minister of War General Nedic, under German. Croatia was declared an independent state under Ustasha leader Ante Pavelic, who then declared the country a monarchy and the Italian Duke of Spoleto (cousin of the Italian King) was given the throne under the title Tomislav I. He never entered his putative realm, however.

The new Croatian state immediately began to settle old scores with the Serbs—these old scores became the murder of 500,000 Serbs, an act condemned by Cardinal Stepinac, Archbishop of Zagreb, as well as by the dean of Croatian nationalists, Vladimir Macek. The latter for his pains spent the war years in jail. But it should be pointed out that many sincere Croats joined the Ustasha simply because it promised a national renaissance.

Resistance to the Germans broke out in their zone of Serbia under Colonel Draza Mihailovic. A staunch Royalist and Serb nationalist, Mihailovic organized his guerrillas under the name of "Chetniks," the name used by similar bands who had fought the Turks centuries before. They soon scored many successes against the invaders.

The Communists, in the meantime, began hostilities after the invasion of the Soviet Union, calling themselves Partisans. Led by Josip Broz (Tito) they soon became the rivals of the Chetniks, who had been recognized by King Peter II as his representatives. But Churchill and Roosevelt came to favor Tito, as did of course, their ally Stalin. Having prevented an attempt by Peter to parachute in and join his men, the Allies in 1943 switched their allegiance from Mihailovich to Tito, and forced Peter to recognize him. When the Italians surrendered in 1943, they were instructed to surrender their arms and territory to the Partisans, thus placing Tito's men in a position to control the country in 1944, when the Germans at last withdrew.

Albania underwent a similar travail. There too, after an initial outbreak by Royalist Resistance loyal to the exiled King Zog I, the German invasion brought forth Communist guerrillas led by one Enver Hoxha. In time, they alone received Western aid, thus ensuring Hoxha's control when the Germans pulled out.

In all the Balkans, only Greece managed to escape Communism's maw and regain its King; this was due to Churchill's actions in the teeth of Roosevelt's opposition. Part of the reason was that Greece's George II was the close cousin of Britain's George VI; added to this was the fact that, as in Albania and Yugoslavia, the only alternative to Communism in Greece was in fact the King. Greece's strategic situation vis-a-vis the Suez Canal had brought British troops when the Germans invaded at the same time as they attacked Yugoslavia. Swiftly conquering the mainland, the Germans took the last Anglo-Greek refuge in Crete. The Royal Family fled to South Africa, where they got to know the country's Prime Minister, Jan Smuts, very well. They then proceeded to London for the duration.

Greece lost Macedonia to Bulgaria and the Ionian Islands to Italy. The remainder of the country was under German occupation, nominally under the control of a Greek General who defected to the Axis. As in the rest of the Balkans, Communist Guerrillas used the War to extend their control over the countryside. Unlike the rest of the Balkans, when the

Germans withdrew in October 1944, British troops arrived to replace them. The Greek government returned to Athens, but opposition to the King's return on the part of the Allied leadership, despite the pleas of General Alexandros Papagos who led the Greek army against the Communists, remained.

Poland, whose territorial integrity was, after all, the alleged reason for the war, faced a similar dilemma. Unlike the other occupied nations, in Poland there was no collaboration; the Poles were all too aware that Nazi racial theory had slated their nobility, priesthood, and intelligentsia for destruction, and the remainder of the populace to serfdom. A proud Catholic people, the Poles did not submit easily, either to their German or their Soviet invaders.

Almost immediately after the defeat of the Polish Army and the establishment of the Government-in-Exile in London, the Polish Underground organized as the Polish Home Army. It functioned in fact as an clandestine Polish Government. After the invasion of the Soviet Union by Germany, the invaders discovered the barbarous murder of Polish Officers by the Soviets at the Katyn Forest. Yet these were the folk whom first Churchill and then FDR directed the Poles to cooperate with!

Polish insistence on an inquiry into the Katyn murders led to a rupture between their government in London and Moscow. The Soviets created their own Polish Communist government, to which the few Communist guerrillas and the Poles fighting in the Soviet Army gave their allegiance. But the Polish Home Army, under its heroic "General Bor" (actually Taddeusz Count Komorowsky) spread throughout the country and gathered ever more strength. When the Soviets had advanced as far as the suburbs of Warsaw, they encouraged the Home Army to rise and take Warsaw, which was done on August 1, 1944. Rather than advance to their aid, however, the Soviets sat calmly by while the Germans besieged the city, eventually reconquering it on October 2. The fighting had destroyed the Home Army, at the time of the Warsaw Rising a powerful armed force which could have served to defend Poland from the Soviets after the War; it also exhausted the Germans, so that in a mere two months after the surrender of General Bor, the Soviets moved into the devastated city.

The War on the Eastern Front typified the reasons for the Nazis' eventual defeat. On June 22, 1941, just before dawn, Germany attacked the Soviet Union. All along the front, from Finland to the Black Sea, the Wehrmacht advanced. Finland, which had lost an unequal conflict (and much territory) to the Soviets in 1939-40, joined the Germans; with them too were Italian, Hungarian, Romanian, and Slovakian troops. Eventually, although Franco refused to enter the War, Spanish volunteers arrived. On that June day the entire nature of the struggle changed. All over the world, the Communist Parties switched sides: from acting as informants for the Germans against the Resistance in occupied countries, they became "patriots;" in the U.S., they abandoned isolationism and insisted on American entry into the conflict. Stalin felt personally betrayed, since Hitler he had always regarded as a kindred spirit.

At first, the advance was easy going, indeed. The Red Army, devastated by purges in 1936, was no match for the invaders. Moreover, since the German government's rhetoric about Communism was taken at face value (even as Petain and other "collaborators" had taken its talk about European unity) the advancing troops, after the initial battles were over, found themselves greeted in many towns and villages by children with flowers. Had the Nazi racial theory not interfered, the War in the East could have been won.

But it did so interfere. When General von Leeb, Commander of the Northern Group of German Armies, had surrounded Leningrad, he was in a position to march right into the city. He was stopped by Hitler's personal order:

> Years later in Washington [German General] von Boetticher told [American General Albert Wedermeyer] that Hitler wanted von Leeb to continue his siege of the city so that its two million inhabitants would slowly starve. This tied down important elements of von Leeb's forces. Eventually von Leeb's reserves were taken away and moved to hard-pressed southern areas with the result that he no longer had sufficient forces to capture Leningrad. Thus Hitler's demographic sadism kept von Leeb from delivering a decisive blow to Russian resistance. Today the Communists celebrate justifiably the heroic defense of Leningrad, but it was probably the intercession of Hitler that prevented professional German military leaders from taking the city (Albert C. Wedemeyer, *Wedemeyer Reports!*, p. 415).

In matters of tactics and strategy, Hitler interfered; but also in matters of internal administration. The familiar apparatus of oppression was imported, and a marvelous chance to truly unite the peoples of the East lost. Instead of Latvia, Lithuania, and Estonia being freed, they were lumped with Byelorussia in the Reichskomissariat of Ostland; the Ukraine was similarly constituted a Reichskomissariat. Alfred Rosenberg, chief racial theorist of the Nazi Party, was placed in charge of these two areas; he was to supervise Germanization of the regions and the rounding up of slave-workers for the Reich industrial machine. In his *Myth of the Twentieth Century*, he had set forward the Party's racial theory. Most interesting for our point of view was Rosenberg's opinion of Catholicism:

Rosenberg denounced Christianity as a dangerous product of the Semitic-Latin spirit and a disintegrative Judaistic concept. Christian churches, he wrote, especially the Roman Catholic Church, are "prodigious, conscious, and unconscious falsifications." The Old Testament should be abandoned as a book of religion, because it was responsible for "our present Jewish domination." For the Old Testament cattle breeders Rosenberg would substitute the Nordic sagas and fairy tales. Instead of what he called the murdering messiahship he would have "the dream of honor and freedom rekindled by the Nordic, Germanic sagas." The true picture of Christ, he asserted, had been distorted by Jewish fanatics like Matthew, by materialistic rabbis like Paul, by African jurists like Tertullian, and by mongrel half-breeds like St. Augustine. The real Christ, Rosenberg insisted, was an Amorite Nordic, aggressive and courageous, a revolutionary who opposed the Jewish and Roman systems with sword in hand, bringing not peace but war. Popes and Jesuits, in Rosenberg's view, had made Christianity unrecognizable, and the heroic Luther and Calvin had been frustrated by their followers.

Rosenberg reserved his utmost contempt for the Roman Catholic Church. It had kept civilization in slavery, and it remained a pitiless force working against the Nordic ideal. Roman Catholicism, he wrote, was an even greater menace than Judaism because its roots were tenacious in history. It had made the fundamental error of taking into its fold any human being regardless of his racial origin—a crime against the ideal of racial purity. The Catholic doctrines of love and pity were directly contrary to the Germanic virtues of heroism and honor. There were irreconcilable differences between the Catholic and Christian mentalities. Catholicism sprang from Oriental races in Judaea and Syria and was therefore alien to the spirit of Nordicism. Spiritually, the Catholic clergy was a continuation of the old Etruscan priesthood. The Pope was merely a medicine man, and church history only a series of atrocities, forgeries, and swindles.

As a Nazi ideologist, Rosenberg demanded that the "white race" be freed from the disruptive Etruscan-Syrio-Judaic-Asiatic-Catholic influence. This influence was, he charged, a monstrous perversion of truth. The German people must turn away from the medicine man Pope and his voodoo practices, from mongrelized Catholicism, from the Old Testament, from the decadent morals of the Sermon on the Mount, and from the doctrine of sin and salvation. These should be replaced by the swastika as the living symbol of race and blood (Dr. Louis L. Snyder, *Encylopedia of the Third Reich*, p. 301).

This was the chap who would determine policies in the two Reichskommissariaten. Polish Galicia was given over to the Government General, that body which administered the rump of Poland not directly annexed to Germany. Romania was allowed to reoccupy the territory the Soviets had taken, and a bit more besides. Outside of the Romanian zone, however, German treatment of the civilian population led directly to the formation of partisan groups directed from Moscow.

Despite such ill-treatment, thousands of Cossacks, Ukrainians, Kalmucks, Tartars, Lithuanians, Latvians, Estonians, Byelorussians, Armenians, Georgians, and Turkestanis, were recruited into the German military. Moreover, a million Russians were recruited, most of whom were ultimately commanded by General Vlassov, an ex-Soviet General. The poor usage of his men—and that of the anti-Communist eastern volunteers as a whole—was seen only too well by the German liaison, Colonel Claus Count von Stauffenberg. A pious Catholic and hater of both Bolshevism and National Socialism, Stauffenberg saw in Hitler's and the Nazi machine's treatment of the East, Germany's doom.

So it would prove. The resistance which Stalin was able to mount, reinforced by America after Pearl Harbor, tied up enormous amounts of Axis men and materiel. In 1943, the Allies crossed over into Sicily; that island seized, they attacked the mainland of Italy itself. At last, the Allies having taken Naples, on July 25, King Victor Emmanuel III dismissed and ordered imprisoned Mussolini. The King's own description of the event is worth quoting:

> This morning [July 25th, 1943] Mussolini asked me for an interview which I fixed for this afternoon at 4.00 P.M. at this villa. When he arrived Mussolini told me that a meeting of the Fascist Grand Council had been held and had passed a vote of censure on him, but he believed that this resolution was not in order. I replied at once that I did not agree with him; the Grand Council was an organ of state which he himself had created by means of a law which had been passed by the Chamber and Senate; therefore every decision of the Grand Council was valid. "Then according to Your Majesty I ought to resign," he said with considerable violence. "Yes," I answered, and told him that I forthwith accepted his resignation.

He appointed Marshal Pietro Badoglio as Prime Minister. Hitler struck fast; German troops seized all territory not held by the Allies, despite a spirited resistance by Italian soldiers. The King and his government were forced to flee to Bari in the South. Mussolini was sprung from jail in a daring raid, and given headship of the Italian Social Republic (which consisted of all Italian soil occupied by the Germans). Yard by bloody yard the Allies (now including the Kingdom of Italy) pushed the Germans up the Italian peninsula.

At about the same time, the wily King Boris III of Bulgaria died shortly after a visit to Hitler. He had sheltered Gypsies, Jews, and other folk the Nazis wanted; had refused to send troops to Russia; and in all things preserved as independent a policy as he could. His mysterious death has been ascribed to both Nazis and Communists, both of whom stood to gain. His six-year-old son, Simeon II, succeeded him under a regency led by Boris' brother, Prince Cyril. The boy-King's mother, Queen Giovanna, was the daughter of Victor Emmanuel, and feared that after her father changed sides, they would be menaced. Sure enough, Hitler demanded to be made Simeon's guardian. The Queen Mother smuggled herself and her royal child out of the country to Turkey.

The Eastern Front continued to deteriorate, and in June 1944, D-Day opened a third front in France. It was obvious that Germany was about to be defeated. Thus it was that on July 20, 1944 the famous Stauffenberg coup was attempted against Hitler.

The German Resistance was a varied one. From the beginning, however, it was in particular dominated by Army Officers, nobles, Catholic and Protestant churchmen, and the like. Its greatest organizer was Karl Goerdeler, sometime Lord Mayor of Leipzig, and its theorists Helmuth von Moltke and the diverse members of the "Kreisau" (his county estate") circle. The ideology of the most active members of the Resistance is very enlightening:

> An examination of the ideas and programs of the leading conspirators against Hitler reveals the existence of two concerns: limitations on political participation by the masses, and moral reconstruction of the "mass man". Naturally, the ideas of the Resistance were in no sense identical with all the grotesque variations of the anti-Weimar ideology. Above all, the conspirators had in good measure broken with nationalism, which had been the basis and the cement of the Conservative Revolution [the Right-Wing opposition to Weimar]. Nevertheless, both major concerns of the Resistance were derived from the Conservative Revolution. Moreover, despite the presence of a few persons of old-fashioned liberal persuasions, and of a few Socialists, the anti-Nazi Resistance was borne by heirs of the conservative anti-Weimar movement. Their attitudes and interests determined the flow of events in the conspiracy. Their ideas—thoroughly reminiscent of the tone and content of Conservative longings during the Weimar period, though now increasingly betraying a turn from the realm of politics to the realm of religious and moral transformation—molded the programs for the future (George K. Romoser, "The Politics of Uncertainty: The German Resistance Movement," in Hans-Adolf Jacobsen, ed., *July 20, 1944: Germans Against Hitler*, pp. 72-73).

Time after time, the Resistance plotted either coups or assassination attempts against Hitler. The first named collapsed time after time because the contemplated Allied victory—over the Rhineland, Czechoslovakia, or wherever—never materialized. When FDR entered the War, and made it clear that Unconditional Surrender was all that would be acceptable to him, the chances of the Resistance were reduced even further: they could not offer prospective supporters even the assurance that Hitler's overthrow would result in a negotiated peace.

But as the situation became ever more desperate, it was realized that desperate measures would have to be taken. A figure arose willing to do what must be done to do away with Hitler and inaugurate a new regime: Colonel Claus Count von Stauffenberg, whom we met in Russia. Wounded (losing a leg, part of a hand, and an eye) in North Africa, Stauffenberg believed that God had preserved him purely to rescue his Fatherland. Handsome, stalwart, a good father and husband, von Stauffenberg was truly a figure of Chivalry. As co-conspirator Axel Baron von dem Bussche recalled three years later: "Only under three assumptions can Claus Stauffenberg be understood: his origin from a family of Swabian knights, his Catholic upbringing, and his own intellectual world in the environment of Stefan George, with whom he was closely associated."

Had the Coup succeeded, the new government, headed by General Ludwig Beck as Regent (a new Kaiser—probably Louis Ferdinand—would be established afterwards) would have looked for a negotiated peace in the West, and a successful completion of the War in the East. It was the stated desire of the plotters to

> ...establish a state in accordance with the Christian traditions of the Western World, and based upon the principles of civic duty, loyalty, service, and achievement for the common good as well as on respect for the individual and his natural rights as a human being" (Fabian von Schlabrendorff, *The Secret War Against Hitler*, p. 213).

The new government would press for a united Christian Europe.

The plan was for von Stauffenberg to leave a bomb next to Hitler in his East Prussian headquarters, then quickly return to Berlin and direct a coup against the surviving Nazi personnel in the capital from the Army Headquarters on the Bendlerstraße. In the event, Hitler was not killed, the coup collapsed, and von Stauffenberg and three others were shot in the courtyard of the Bendlerstraße building. In the months that followed, some 2,000 people were judicially murdered in connection with the plot.

Today, the building where the four men died is located on the now-named Stauffenbergerstraße. In the courtyard is a memorial in the form of a naked man manacled. On its pedestal are the words:

> YOU DID NOT TOLERATE SHAME,
> YOU DEFENDED YOURSELVES AGAINST IT,
> YOU GAVE THE GREAT AND WATCHFUL
> SIGNAL FOR THE CHANGE,

SACRIFICING YOUR ARDENT LIFE
FOR LIBERTY, JUSTICE, AND HONOR

With them died the most recent chance for a Europe patterned after the old Holy Empire. But it is not a dream that can ever wholly die.

The Nazi Party became ever more tight-handed in the diminishing territories left them. In the West, almost all of France was cleared of German troops, and the Allies took Belgium and began to push into Germany. Although the Battle of the Bulge signified a short-lived exercise of German strength, no one believed now that they would win. In September, the Soviets arrived at the Romanian border; the 23-year-old King Michael overthrew Antonescu in a daring maneuver at great personal risk, and the new government joined the allies, as did the Regency in Bulgaria. October saw the German withdrawal from Greece, Albania, and Yugoslavia. The next month, Hungary's Admiral Horthy attempted to pull his nation out of the Axis; he was overthrown by the Germans, who occupied the nation until the Soviets rolled over it. Relentlessly, the Italian, Western, and Eastern fronts pushed toward one another until the Third Reich was a bunch of scattered pockets.

The Battle of Berlin ended in April 1945; when it was over, Hitler was dead, and the city shattered; the thousand-year Reich would survive its Führer by mere days. On May 8, 1945, the War in Europe ended. The Nazi Regime, which had claimed the lives of such as St. Maximilian Kolbe, Bl. Titus Brandsma, Bl. Rupert Mayer, and Bl. Benedicta of the Cross, as well as innumerable other priests, religious, and lay folk (to say nothing of the many Gypsies, Jews, and others who were done to death), was over. In their reign over Europe, the Nazis had raised and dashed the hopes of numerous nationalities, from the Bretons to the Ukrainians, for independence. They raised and dashed the hopes of those in every country who hoped for a renewed Europe, one in Faith and aspiration, which would again fulfill the role of the Holy Empire. Those who longed for such things either cooperated with the Axis and were destroyed or discredited by their association with them, or else joined the resistance and found themselves either destroyed by Communist colleagues or co-opted by Social Democratic ones. Hitler, Roosevelt, and Stalin shared a disdain for Catholic claims, for Monarchy and nobility, for all that Old Europe had been, however much their "positive programs" may have differed. For all that Hitler hated the fate of the Nazi Party in 1945, he could not have been too upset by the downfall of altar and throne. For the first time since the year 800, the Holy See was completely without temporal allies (save Spain and Portugal).

The War in Asia had followed a somewhat similar course, in that there were the same factors of collaboration and resistance, of nationalism and dominance, as in Europe. To reign alongside Pu-Yi in Manchukuo, the heroic Mongol Prince Teh was given headship of Inner Mongolia under the Japanese; former left-wing Kuomintang man and colleague of Chiang Kai Shek, Wang Ching Wei, was given nominal headship of those sections of China under Japanese occupation. Because these men led regimes whose primary rhetorical focus was opposition to Chinese and Soviet Communism, they are dismissed as mere collaborators.

Thailand was the only pre-existing independent nation to ally with Japan, and so received portions of Laos and Cambodia in return. After Pearl Harbor, Japanese forces steadily unseated the Europeans and Americans from their territories: French Indo-China, the Philippines, the Dutch East Indies, British-held Burma, and Malaya. On February 14, 1943, the British General Perceval surrendered the last bastion at Singapore. The losses to the British Empire numbered in excess of 166,600 men.

In their conquered territories, the Japanese installed various nationalist leaders to preside over allied governments: Jose Laurel in the Philippines, Ba Maw in Burma, Sukarno in Indonesia, and so on. These would change sides at the last minute, and claim recognition from the Allies as co-combatants. The Communists among their adherents—and among the anti-Japanese resistance—grew in strength and position, in hopes that after the War they might dictate the peace. In China the Reds under Mao Tse Tung used the War to consolidate their gains in the countryside, so that they would be able to commence again their fight against the Nationalist government afterwards.

While the Allies valiantly fought their way back through Island chains, Burma, and so on, and although such battles as Iwo Jima and Okinawa are tributes to the valor of the American fighting man, the War against Japan (as against Germany) was waged very much through bombing. Just as the Germans launched the Blitz against targets in Britain, so too did the Americans and British carpet bomb Germany; such cities as Hamburg, Berlin, and especially Dresden were hard hit. Over ten times the number of German as British civilians died as a result of bombing raids. The Allies made a specialty of what was called "Baedeker Bombing;" selecting targets particularly for their cultural or historic rather than military value.

Much the same occurred in Japan, culminating in the dropping of the newly-invented atom bomb. Hiroshima felt the first one on August 6, 1945, while Nagasaki received one three days later. James Bryant Conant, President of Harvard and inventor of poison gas employed by the AEF in World War I, declared that the Japanese were subhuman and ought to have six more dropped on them. The Japanese Empire, at the insistence of Emperor Hirohito, surrendered on August 14. The greatest conflagration Mankind had known since the Great Flood was over.

What sort of world would result? This had been a matter of great contention throughout the War. For Stalin and his minions, the answer was obvious: Communists the world over worked to make the globe one Soviet Republic. FDR had his own ideas, which his successor, Harry Truman, attempted to put into practice after Roosevelt's death on April 12, 1945.

There had been a number of conferences between Churchill, Stalin, and Roosevelt. That at Teheran had mostly to do with the conduct of the War and refusal to deal with any German government save on terms of unconditional surrender. At Yalta, The Soviets were promised suzerainty over Eastern Europe, and, in return for their entry into the War against Japan (with whom they were not then belligerents) control of Manchuria. The result of this latter was their establishment of a safe haven for the Chinese Reds after the War, as well as their equipping them with captured Japanese weapons. As a final note, Stalin was promised that all Soviet born prisoners taken from Axis forces would be turned over to the Red Army; thus was born the infamous "Operation Keel Haul," in which thousands of men, women, and children were turned over to their enemies. All were slaughtered, often in the hearing of the American or British troops who turned them over. With Truman replacing FDR, the three confederates met again at Potsdam after the War ended, and finalized such things as the occupation zones of Germany, Austria, and Korea.

The Cold War Begins

The Communists immediately began reorganizing their conquests. In Yugoslavia, Bulgaria, Albania, and Hungary, rigged plebiscites abolished the Monarchy. Romania's King Michael with his sterling record of anti-Axis activity held on until the last day of 1947, when he too was at last driven out. In those countries and in Poland, Czechoslovakia, and Eastern Germany, the pattern was for the most part the same. The industrialists and landowners would lose their properties and often their lives. Coalition governments dominated by Communists would become ever more restrictive, abolishing freedom of speech and the press. The Church would be persecuted, and many of its most active people driven underground. A Secret Police would ferret out and destroy opposition to the regime. By handing Eastern Europe over to Stalin, we played our part in this horror which has only recently lifted.

In China, we refused to arm Chiang Kai Shek as we had promised; this was fine payment for his three times refusing a separate peace with

Japan, which would have freed his nation at the price of unleashing 1,000,000 men of the Japanese Kwangtung Army against the West Coast. After a particularly bloody Civil War, the Nationalists were driven from the mainland to the large island of Taiwan in 1949. The year before, Churchill (defeated by Labour candidate Clement Attlee in 1945) had made his famous speech regarding the new order of things in Europe: "From Stettin, in the Baltic, to Trieste, on the Adriatic, an Iron Curtain has descended across the Continent." That phrase, "Iron Curtain" came to be universally known as the border between Communism and the rest of Europe.

But just what was the rest of Europe and the World to be like? It would be a grave mistake to think that the ruling circles in Britain and America were far different in their vision, ultimately, from the Soviets. Proof of this comes from what was done in those sections of Europe under their sway. The Communists executed thousands of Frenchmen and women as collaborators, with Allied tolerance; most of these, in the event, were not German sympathizers but simply the same sorts of folk eliminated by the Communists in countries where Soviet armies gave complete control to them. When order was restored under de Gaulle, this activity ceased. Similarly, the Communists of Belgium made it clear that if Leopold III returned as King to Belgium, they would make the country ungovernable. To preserve peace, Leopold abdicated in favor of his son, Baudouin.

But on a less bloody note, the war against traditional institutions, beliefs, and practices was as great in the West as in the East. The experience of Greece shows this. When Greece was liberated in October 1944, its King wished to return; this was blocked by the Allies, and it in fact took a plebiscite after the War to reinstate him. George Heaton Nicholls, wartime High Commissioner to Great Britain from South Africa (where, as we saw, the Greek Royal Family had spent time and made the acquaintance of Prime Minister Jan Smuts), commented upon this in his memoirs:

> When I arrived in London, the King of Hellenes had a suite of rooms at Claridge's and on occasions I was the bearer of messages between the King and Smuts. As the channel through which these communications passed, I found myself in a most peculiar and somewhat embarrassing position. The King was striving hard to induce the British government to allow him to return to Athens where he felt his presence on the spot, as the constitutional head of the country, would overcome much of the hostility in the political field and would rally the Greek people as a whole to defence of the constitution.
>
> On the other hand, Churchill, as head of the National Government, found himself placed with many who believed that any support given

to the King of Greece would damage the reputation of the British Government. Thus it was that Churchill was being pushed to overthrow the King and support the mob law which called itself democracy. The King of Greece told me that he had been talked to like a hireling by Churchill on this subject.

The policy of the British Government was, therefore, to restrain the King and I found myself the bearer of messages from Smuts to him which I knew were in direct conflict with the policy of the British Government. Once, when I pointed out to the General the compromising position I was in, he said: "give my message to the King. The British Government is aware of my attitude." The result of the plebiscite which later voted overwhelmingly in favour of the return of the King, showed that Smuts' prescience throughout was correct.

The opposition to the return of the King existed just as strongly in the United States, Australia, and New Zealand, as it did in some political circles in the United Kingdom. The outcome of the plebiscite betrayed the failure of all these people to understand the deep spiritual significance and mysticism which surrounds a hereditary ruler fulfilling his predestined task and how curiously unaware they were of the loyalty for a crowned head which exists among all common peoples who have not been influenced by revolutionary propaganda. Those of us who have had experience in the administration of native tribes in Africa, know with what a deep sense of satisfaction an hereditary chief is accepted as their spokesman to the world. Centuries of tradition and ritual are not easily erased by the arguments of the London School of Economics, however logical these may be (*South Africa in My Time*, pp. 372-373).

So it was in Italy. Robert Gayre, who served as a sort of Minister of Education for the Allied Military Government of Italy after the deposition of Mussolini in 1943 wrote graphically of the attitudes of his American colleagues in that regime:

We are well aware of the attitude of vast sections of the American people to the war. It was not to restore Poland from German aggression solely. They had dreamed up for themselves a mission of removing "oppression" everywhere, putting the underdog on top and pulling down "privilege" —and bringing the blessings of American "civilization" to the "barbarians," beyond their own frontiers. The intense nationalism of many of the Americans easily allowed such an atmosphere to develop (*A Case For Monarchy*, p. 41).

In a note on the same page, Gayre goes on to say:

In pursuance of this self-appointed role of the "Great Republic of the West," I was solemnly assured by some Americans that it was not necessary for me to retain the teaching of Latin and religion in the school text-books of Italy—and that what Italy needed was the introduction of a technological civilisation such as existed in America—of which jeeps, refrigerators, and mass production generally were the outward and evident tokens. When one remonstrated, and talked of European culture, of the part that Italy had played in the Renaissance, the need to retain cultural subjects in an age becoming all too rapidly mechanised, and the importance of religious instruction to youth who had been dragged up in the condition of collapsing standards of life as a result of war, one was met by the completely unassailable reply— "Geez! These Wops burn me up!"

As this author records, the U.S. authorities were hell-bent on "reforming" Italian life. Their desire for an end to the Italian Monarchy

> ...was probably the most decisive force in overthrowing the House of Savoy. A new international world was said to be in the process of shaping itself. The Stars and Stripes were bravely fluttering at the head of the column, and all who wanted to feel that they belonged to that brave new world were tempted to fall in and march with it (Gayre, *op. cit.*, p. 42).

King Victor Emmanuel III, feeling himself tainted by his association with Mussolini, had abdicated in favor of his son, Umberto II. In 1946, a plebiscite (held by many to be rigged) found a wafer-thin majority for a republic. Although there were cries of "treason" on the part of the King's supporters, and the armed forces offered to void the plebiscite, Umberto realized the position of the United States and feared the outcome of a bloody civil war. He went into exile, and an Italian republic, renowned since for its corruption and instability, was called into being.

That this Americanization was not reserved merely for the vanquished but for our Allies as well, may be seen from this quote from the *Catholic Herald* of 6 February 1942:

> Two wars are being waged against England. The first we know all about. It is being fought in Europe, in Africa, in Asia. But the second is no less important and no one bothers about it. On this front the outlook is much darker. It is the war against the spirit and traditions of England, and the enemy lies within our gates. Well may German propagandists exclaim that on one side we are being Americanised and on the other Sovietised. Open any paper or pamphlet, and you will look in vain for a mention of "God and My Right," of the ideal of St. George, of the Monarchy, of our constitutional heritage, of our Christian foundations and Faith, of our literature, of our homes that were castles, of our squires, etc., etc., or, if you will find them mentioned, it will generally be with an open or veiled sneer.

What 1945 and subsequent years saw, in a nutshell, was the triumph of Americanism over half the World. The Soviet menace threw many European Catholic Conservatives completely into our ideological camp, just as before the War it had pushed many to the Fascists and Nazis. For the most part, Catholic politicians formed themselves into various parties of Christian Democrats, accepting electoral democracy and economic liberalism and abandoning the Church's social teachings to a greater or lesser degree to merit American aid in fending off the Soviets. To a degree this strategy was echoed even by Pius XII.

The Marshall Plan rushed American aid to the obliterated economies of Western Europe; the North Atlantic Treaty Organization ensured the presence of large U.S. forces in Europe to "contain" the Red menace.

But while we maintained our Allies' security in the Mother continent, we cooperated with Communists and local Nationalists in ejecting them from their colonial empires. The most obvious example of this was in the Dutch East Indies. There, the Netherlands attempted to restore their position after the War. Confronted by guerrilla warfare in the colony and American diplomatic and political pressure at home, they gave up after a four-year struggle. In 1949, Sukarno presided over the birth of Indonesia. To repay the U.S. for its aid, he followed a steadily pro-Soviet line all the years of his rule. This was the beginning of a pattern which would become drearily familiar over the next two decades.

At Home

Many Americans wanted, after V-J Day, simply to return to peacetime patterns. But there could be no return to normalcy. Although initial demobilization was rapid, the result was a recession. Apparently, a wartime economy could only conceal the Depression, not exorcise it. The assumption by America of leadership of the Free World and resultant stepping up of production to arm opponents of Communism rescued us from the economic morass of peace. Defense industries became a large sector of the economy, and paved the way for the great boom of the 1950s, a time when America would reach a prosperity unequaled before or since.

At the same time, the threat of Communist infiltration came to the public eye, particularly as their deeds in Eastern Europe and China gradually became better known. In Hollywood, members of the Entertainment industry, "blacklisted" for anti-Communism during the War, exposed their confreres with links to the Party. The result was the famous Hollywood Ten case, when a number of such folk perjured themselves regarding their affiliation before a Congressional Committee. The famous black lists ensured that many Communists would not work again for years in the Industry. What is not so well known is that the careers of those who testified against them were similarly ruined.

Spy cases came to the fore, such as that of Julius and Ethel Rosenberg, who were accused of passing nuclear secrets to the Soviets, thus helping them to acquire the Atom Bomb and commence a balance of terror which remains with us yet. They were found guilty and later executed, much to the dismay of many who protested their innocence. It is only in recent years that their guilt has been proved by the Russians since the fall of the Soviet Union.

There were voices raised against maintenance of the National Security State created by FDR. Nor were all of these Communists. Such were men like John T. Flynn, true to the same principles he had held when he led the America First Committee. Moreover, the Republican Party was once again in control of Congress after the 1946 elections (in similar wise as their success after World War I). But the work of FDR had its effect. Where Wilson had had to contend with the likes of Henry Cabot Lodge and Warren Harding, with the Republican Party solidly behind them, the threat of Communism had split the Republicans this time. An interventionist wing of the Party had grown up as a result. Led by Thomas Dewey, its foreign policy was virtually indistinguishable from the Democrats'; in domestic policy it was somewhat less activist, but accepted the huge growth of government Roosevelt had fathered.

Opposed to such people was the more traditional wing of the Party, led by Senator *Robert Taft*. Taft opposed NATO and the UN, using such slogans as "Fortress America," and "The Free Hand." He maintained that acceptance of the permanent role of world policeman could only lead to the loss of liberty at home. He lost the presidential nomination to Dewey in 1948. This signaled (together with Taft's loss again to Eisenhower in 1952) the end of the Republican Party as a significantly different voice in America.

Truman, Dewey's opponent in that year, had of course been FDR's last Vice President, as well as Grand Master of the Masonic Lodge of Missouri. It was his choice of cities which had led the Atom Bombs to drop on Hiroshima and Nagasaki (by sheerest coincidence the two centers of Catholicism in Japan). Although the far left and right wings of the Democratic Party each fielded separate candidates in the election, Truman squeezed past Dewey. The man from Independence was President in his own right.

Still, the debate about America's place in the world went on, just as it had in 1914 to 1917 and 1939 to 1941. Just as on those occasions, the argument was won, not by reason or appeal to truth, but by force of arms.

The country of Korea, after its liberation from the Japanese, had been divided at the Thirty-eighth parallel between American and Soviet zones in the South and North, respectively. The idea, as in the case of Germany and Austria, was that after a period the halves should be reunited into one democratic Republic of Korea. Each side had their own idea of what those words meant, however, and the result was the establishment of two different governments. By 1949, most American and Soviet troops had been withdrawn. On June 25, 1950, the North invaded South Korea. The UN Security Council, from which the Soviets had walked out, called on all members to assist in repelling this aggression. Two days later, without asking Congress for a declaration of war, Truman ordered U.S. forces into Korea as part of a UN "police action." Where FDR had maneuvered this country into a War without sanction of its people's representatives, Truman simply entered one. As in all our other major wars, the constitution took another beating. At least this time, we were fighting atheists.

ARSENAL OF DEMOCRACY 1952-1969

THE FABULOUS FIFTIES

The War in Korea saw over the two years of its existence the wildest ups and downs, followed by stalemate. After the North Koreans drove the South Koreans and Americans into the small "Pusan Perimeter" in the extreme South-East of the country, they were halted. The perimeter was reinforced massively, and after a counter attack began, the North Koreans were outflanked by the landing at Inchon.

General McArthur was put in command, and soon drove the North Koreans back to the Yalu river, marking the border with China. On November 24, 1950, 180,000 Red Chinese troops poured over the Yalu. By December 15, the UN forces were driven back to the pre-war border of South Korea. Soon, the Reds had captured Seoul, but they were pushed back again, and a stalemate developed.

It was McArthur's desire to carry the war over into Manchuria by bombing Chinese bases there. President Truman, committed as he was to the "containment" of Communism, had no intention of rolling it back. McArthur was fired on April 11, 1951. The stalemate dragged on for two more years, and at last, a truce was negotiated which continues at the time of this writing.

In the meantime, the United States had a new president. The country had been under Democratic rule for almost twenty years, and it was obvious that a Republican would win the White House in 1952. The important question was, what kind of Republican? The traditional wing of the party was led once again by Senator Taft; the internationalist, interventionist wing, committed to essentially the same foreign and domestic programs as the Democrats, rallied behind General Dwight D. Eisenhower.

Indeed, Eisenhower epitomized all that Americans held most dear; a World War II hero, he gave a feeling of deep-seated comfort, much in keeping with the economic prosperity of the time. Although the public might be tired of the Democrats, they were not really too interested in dismantling the National Security State which had been developed in response to the Depression, World War II, and the Cold War. Above all, Eisenhower reflected the religious sense of the American people:

> The central symbol of the nation's political piety was the President himself. Though not an official church member until after his election,

Eisenhower more than made up for this with his frequent religious pronouncements. Ike's faith was a simple one; it was just faith. "Our government makes no sense," he declared during the 1952 campaign, "unless it is founded in a deeply felt religious faith, and I don't care what it is." On another occasion he told the people, though "I am the most intensely religious man I know, that does not mean I adhere to any sect." In still another speech the President assured Americans that this nation was "the mightiest power God has seen fit to put upon his footstool." In 1954, Ike told the nation to spend July Fourth as a day of penance and prayer. He himself went fishing in the morning, played 18 holes of golf in the afternoon, and bridge at night (Douglas T. Miller and Marion Nowak, *The Fifties*, p. 90).

Peace and prosperity made such can't sound good. It certainly was a time of prosperity for this nation, unequaled either before or since. Most American families could eat meat every night of the week. They could realistically plan to live well, travel on vacations, save for their retirement, and plan to pay for their children's college. Automobile ownership soared, and huge gas-guzzling machines, tail-finned to reflect the atomic age, roared down the nation's highways.

Above all, the 1950s were the Golden Age of Television. The new medium mushroomed throughout the country, until by the end of the decade the vast majority of households were equipped with them. It was and is a powerful tool. So compelling was it that whereas before its advent many activities competed for people's leisure time, afterwards it was always a question of doing anything else or watching TV. The viewpoint of the majority was shaped by what they saw on the tube, something which would have tremendous effects in American public life.

More and more, politicians and other public figures tailored their actions and speech to the TV cameras. TV news more and more came to shape reality as well as to report it. Where in the beginning, television situation comedies ("sitcoms") served to reinforce conformity (a la *Father Knows Best, Make Room For Daddy, Leave It To Beaver,* and *Ozzie and Harriet*), in time, all sorts of perverse behavior would be popularized and made acceptable thereon. Even such as the aforementioned series raised impossible examples of family life for countless thousands of Americans—causing, if such tales can be believed—lots of neuroses which would become manifest in the next decade.

On a more tangible note, the center of family life shifted from the dinner-table or the fire place to the black box. Frozen TV dinners saved housewives time for important viewing. Even local cultures in such places as Pennsylvania and Louisiana were threatened, as time spent chatting with neighbors in the evenings in Pennsylvania Dutch or Cajun

French were replaced with sitting passively in front of the English-spouting tube. In America and all over the globe, singing in pubs was replaced with gawking at ball-games on the bar TV.

There developed also a particular world for children. The Baby Boom carried on through the last half of the 40s all the way to 1960. In the face of vast numbers of children, kiddie shows on Television (like *The Mickey Mouse Club, Howdy Doody,* and *Davy Crockett*) echoed the creation of ever more child-oriented amusement spots, like Disneyland.

If there was a keynote to the 50s, it was homogeneity. Business was good, and America was the wealthiest and most powerful nation in the world. Anyone who thought otherwise might well be a Communist.

And yet, there were Communists about. Senators *Joseph McCarthy* and *Hamilton Fish, Sr.* conducted a campaign against Communists in government via the Senate Government Operations Committee. While they did indeed turn up many well-concealed Reds, their often-slipshod methods laid them open to charges of impropriety. At last, McCarthy got into a dispute with the Army leadership. The result was predictable: he was censured by the Senate on December 2, 1954. From that day until the demise of the Soviet Union, any opponent of Communism was liable to be called a "McCarthyite," who indulged in "McCarthyism."

The Soviet Union's acquisition of the atom bomb added to the strange atmosphere of fear which co-existed with the national mood of self-congratulation. The prospect of atomic war led to the proliferation of home bomb shelters, of "drop and cover" drills in schools, and air raid sirens in the rapidly proliferating suburbs. In these synthetic living spaces, the 50s achieved their epitome.

Education fell ever more under the influence of the ideas of *John Dewey* (1859-1952), last of the triad of great American educators (Horace Mann and Noah Webster being the other two). He carried their ideas even further. Education was no longer to be about imparting literacy at all; rather, it was primarily intended as a means of socialization, a way of integrating the pupil into the educator's vision of what society should be. Although various voices were raised throughout the 50s to protest the progressive de-emphasis on academic skills, such protests came to nothing in the end. Public Education in the US would become woefully inadequate, although it did manage to contribute to the destruction of morality among the young.

Despite it all, the image of the 50s remained The Man in the Gray Flannel Suit: the martini drinking, back-yard barbecuing, association-joining 1950s successor to Babbitt. His sons and daughters were in the scouts, attended dutifully with their parents the church of their parents' choice, and enjoyed the standard-of-living their fathers bestowed on them—a standard far in advance (as he was always happy to tell them) of his during the Depression. Trick-or-treating for UNICEF, watching TV shows, and going off to Summer Camp were some of their rituals. Surely, this new generation, better educated and better fed than any which preceded it, would be happy and glad to inherit and continue the manner of life their parents would leave them. Time would tell.

Voices of Dissent

Not everyone was convinced that Americans lived in the best of all possible worlds. On a lighter note, *MAD Magazine*, with its non-stop parody of American life, soared to popularity among the young. But not everyone was content merely to poke fun at American mores.

American ideological Conservatism, in the sense of a real intellectual alternative to Eisenhower Republicanism, appeared to be virtually dead after his election. Conservatism, in the sense of attachment to the status quo was of course dominant. But of a conscious opposition to the New Deal and its heirs, there seemed to be none when Eisenhower was inaugurated.

Nevertheless, that very year there appeared a remarkable book by a remarkable man: *The Conservative Mind, From Burke to Santayana*, by *Russell Kirk*. This survey of foreign and American right-wing thought, brought together in an attempt to find some commonality between them, marked a change in American ideas. For Kirk, an admirer of Edmund Burke, there *was* a connection between Anglo-American Whiggery and both the Euro-Latin American Right and Southern Agrarianism. An admirer of the English system, Kirk nevertheless maintained that the American Revolution was a development of the British Glorious one, and like that event essentially a "Conservative happening."

But Kirk was responsible for bringing to the attention of the American public such folk as Roy Campbell, the South African Catholic convert poet who had fought for Franco. A few years later, young *William F. Buckley, Jr.*, author of the 1951 *God and Man at Yale* (which exposed the "anti-Americanism" of the Ivy League colleges), founded the magazine *National Review*. At its inception, it was reminiscent of Seward Collins' *American Review*, and provided space for such as the surviving Southern Agrarians and John Flynn. European writers like *Erik von Kuehnhelt-Leddihn* and *Thomas Molnar* were given place, as were native Americans like *Frederick Wilhelmsen* and *L. Brent Bozell*. Save Kirk (who would later convert) all these men were Catholics, although many other contributors to NR were not. In any case, throughout the 50s and into the next decade, the magazine provided the most cogent criticism of the status quo the non-Catholic press offered. But it could not solve the abiding problem of American Conservatism: the revolutionary nature of the very national fabric American Conservatives wished to conserve. The strain would show later.

In the meantime, the newly resurgent Conservative movement focused upon several problems with contemporary America. Southern Agrarian sorts kept up their criticisms of the ever more centralized state; such as John Flynn likewise carried on their crusade against the decay of constitutional government. Similar in outlook, the opposition of the first group of men was based on cultural grounds, the second on political.

More English-oriented sorts took the whole notion of democracy to task, declaring that the "Republic" of the Founding Fathers was Aristocratic rather than Democratic. These kinds of people attacked the whole American mythology of the virtue of the "masses." The Conservative virtues of anti-ideologism and preservation of continuity were praised continually by these folk, chief of whom was Kirk.

The criticisms of Catholics involved with the movement were often even more to the point. In *Liberty or Equality?*, Erik von Kuehnelt-Leddihn argued that these two qualities were incompatible, the quest for equality bringing forth both Nazism and Communism. Thomas Molnar argued in *The Counterrevolution* that lack of conviction on the part of the Right was responsible for the victory of the Left, more than any other single factor: the Left believed in what it was doing. The Carlist supporter, Frederick Wilhelmsen, was a stout defender of Catholic social teachings, without any nod to Americanism. Not surprisingly, these men were all Monarchists; just as unsurprisingly, they had little connection, despite their religion, with most American Catholics, whether clerical or lay.

The one thing which truly united these folk to one another and to the remaining Taft Republicans was their common opposition to Communism, which at the time looked about ready to swallow the Earth. That message was listened to; but their espousal of excellence against the complacent conformity of the majority fell on deaf ears at a time when the White House was occupied by its most popular holder—who happened to be, in appearance, habits, and beliefs, a dead ringer for Babbitt—fell on dead ears.

Another, and seemingly diametrically opposed field of dissent was that of the "Beat" movement. Like the more Europeanized wing of the Conservative movement, the "Beats" rebelled against the dull, gray, conformism of the 50s—which, after all, was only standard American Calvinism made triumphant over the world by victory in the Second World War. Featuring in its number such odd folk as *William Burroughs, Allen Ginsberg, Lawrence Ferlinghetti,* and *Gregory Corso,* The Beat Generation's solutions to the dryness and deadness of American life were often bizarre, to say the least, and involved a great deal of incoherent poetry, "alternative" lifestyles, unemployment, Eastern religions, drugs, and alcohol. In a word, they offered rebellion, pure and simple.

Yet all the evil, squalor, and plain looniness encompassed by the Beats ought not to blind the observer to the fact that much of the criticism of American society which they expressed was quite valid:

> The Beats, and such literary fellow travelers as the Black Mountain poets, shared a unity of purpose. They all wished to restore literature and the arts to the people, to bring literature back from its dull sleep of obscure academic poems and alienated, apathy-inducing novels. Many of the most important Beat works themselves reflect a deep alienation from American society: *Howl's* denunciations of materialism and sexual repression, and the scorn for the middle class in *On The Road*, are only two instances. The romantic fascination with criminality that permeated much of Beat life also was a sign of its estrangement. But these were not simply statements of alienation. The Beats went beyond alienation to emphasize the need for a new American community. They tried to burst through (rather than simply reflect) a world of deadening politics, sexual hypocrisy, TV-induced numbness. As Allen Ginsberg would later put it, the Beat movement meant "the return to nature and the revolt against the machine.... it's either that or take that mass-produced self they keep trying to shove down your throat" (Miller and Nowak, *op. cit.*, p. 384).

If their solutions were mad, the problems they posed were not. Indeed, many of their criticisms of American society (save the sexual ones; this is an area where folk are always likely to confuse chastity with repression—they are in fact as different as temperance and prohibition) would have seemed quite apparent to Southern Agrarians or to the Euro-Conservatives. But with the partial exception of the latter, the Beats shared with Conservatives one major blind spot: they would or could not see that the solution lay ultimately in the conversion of America to the Catholic Faith; that Catholicism alone could reconcile order and liberty, art and life. But in large part this was due to the distorted Americanist Catholicism which they saw around them.

All of this is made manifest in the life of the most interesting of the Beatniks, *Jean-Louis (Jack) Kerouac* (1922-1969). Born and raised a French-speaker in Lowell, Massachusetts, and author of *On The Road*, Kerouac left Lowell at the age of 17. First joining the Merchant Marine during World War II, he eventually studied for a time at Columbia University (where he met Ginsberg) before publishing his first novel in 1950. After that he began his vagabond-like existence. But apart from the snatches of French he often uses in his novels, his religious and cultural upbringing at once separated him from mainstream America, and sparked the mysticism (including, alas, a fascination with Buddhism) which marked most of his literary career.

For a man of his type, there can be no doubt that the immigrant community in which he was raised was terribly confining; yet it is just as obvious that his flirtation with the East and his joining "a widespread subterranean culture of poets, folk singers, hipsters, mystics, and eccentrics..." (*Encyclopædia Brittanica,* "Kerouac, Jack") were attempts to find, once more as an adult, the Faith and folk he had known through a child's perceptions. Certainly, in his last few years he became quite Conservative indeed; many of his utterances would not have been out of place in the pages of Fr. Lionel Groulx's *Action Française Canadienne.* At any rate, although he died in Florida, he was buried in his childhood parish in Lowell. God rest him.

Conservatives and Beats alike had little practical influence on the public at large during the 50s, although in the next decade the influence of both groups would dramatically increase. In the meantime, however, one faction did rise to prominence and accomplished several key goals: this was the Civil Rights Movement.

As we may recall from previous chapters, Blacks in the North generally lived in decaying ghettoes; those in the South found their lives circumscribed by the Jim Crow laws. The rhetoric of "freedom and equality" which was bandied about during World War II had the effect of raising hopes among Black intellectuals and clergymen that such things would soon be applied to their people. Although Truman ordered the integration of the Army, for the most part Blacks and Whites dwelt in separate, unequal worlds.

The progressive wing of the Democratic Party assured Blacks that, once back in the White House, they would put an end to Jim Crow; Southern Democrats replied that this would not happen. As the decade progressed, the issue of Civil Rights loomed ever larger on the national scene, with Southerners divided over Jim Crow, Conservatives divided over States' Rights, and Blacks divided over the best way to bring about change.

For Black intellectuals like Ralph Ellison and Richard Wright, it was apparent that forcing an end to Jim Crow and to segregation in general was the only way. Most leadership in the community agreed with them; together with white sympathizers, the result was the Civil Rights Movement. But they found themselves faced with opposition: the Conservative Republican, Zora Neale Hurston.

Miss Hurston was bitterly opposed to the Civil Rights Movement and its leadership. The reason why is most important:

> Part of Hurston's received heritage—and perhaps the paramount received notion that links the novel of manners in the Harlem Renaissance, the social realism of the thirties, and the cultural nationalism of the Black Arts movement—was the idea that racism had reduced black people to mere ciphers, to beings who only react to an omnipresent racial oppression, whose culture is "deprived" where different, and whose psyches are in the main "pathological." Albert Murray, the writer and social critic, calls this "the Social Science Fiction Monster." Socialists, separatists, and civil rights advocates alike have been devoured by this beast.
>
> Hurston thought this idea degrading, its propagation a trap, and railed against it. It was, she said, upheld by the "sobbing school of Negrohood who hold that nature somehow has given them a dirty deal." Unlike [Langston] Hughes and Wright, Hurston chose deliberately to ignore this "false picture that distorted..." Freedom, she wrote in *Moses, Man of the Mountain*, was something internal.... "The man himself must make his own emancipation." And she declared her first novel a manifesto against the "arrogance" of whites assuming that "black lives are only defensive reactions to white actions." Her strategy was not calculated to please (Henry Louis Gates, Jr., "Afterword," in Zora Neale Hurston, *Mules and Men*, p. 291).

Nor did it; in practice, despite the long-term sense of her beliefs, Miss Hurston's influence would be nil until our own time.

A major strike for the Civil Rights cause was the decision of the Supreme Court under Chief Justice Earl Warren (whom we last met packing off the Japanese to camps during the War) in the case of Brown vs. the Board of Education of Topeka, Kansas. This verdict, handed down on May 17, 1954 reversed the 1896 Plessy vs. Ferguson ruling, which had permitted "separate but equal" educational facilities. Rather, the Court found, segregated schools were inherently unequal, and violated the Fourteenth Amendment, which says that no state may deny equal protection of the laws to any person within its jurisdiction.

Meanwhile, the nascent Civil Rights establishment was gathering strength. A move beyond writing and into action was the result of an occurrence in Montgomery, Alabama, in December of 1955. At that time, a middle-aged Black woman, Rosa Parks, refused to give up her seat to a white man and move to the back of a municipal bus, as was then required. The Black community in the town rallied around Mrs. Parks, and a boycott of the municipal bus lines was called for, and led by, a minister named *Martin Luther King, Jr.*

King, whose birthday is now a national holiday, was an equivocal figure. Communist or Christian, he set his mark upon the Civil Rights movement. A Baptist minister, he had served in his Montgomery church for a year prior to the boycott. A charismatic organizer, he used the action to put together the Southern Christian Leadership Conference, (SCLC). The SCLC was soon in a position to coordinate similar actions throughout the South.

The boycott lasted through 1956; meanwhile the SCLC and the NAACP led anti-segregation drives in hotels, restaurants, schools, and elsewhere.

Opposition was not long in coming, and was motivated by two basic principles. The first was racism pure and simple. Its adherents believed that Blacks were inherently inferior and best kept at a distance. The second opposed Jim Crow's abolition out of a belief in States' Rights; that is, they may not have supported Jim Crow, but believed that neither the Federal Government nor outside opinion had any right to force the majority of a given state's citizens, or their state government, to abolish segregation. Obviously, some individuals were pure racists, other pure States Righters. But in practice, in varying degrees, the two motives were present in differing proportions in most of the Southern opposition. More respectable people formed the White Citizens' Councils, which were pledged to fighting integration legally and peacefully. The more rif-raffish elements joined the latest incarnation of the Ku-Klux-Klan.

But the State governments in the South were not unaware of the threat to their sovereignty the Supreme Court decision provided. The year 1956 saw a barrage of action on their parts. On January 19, the Alabama Senate passed a nullification of the Supreme Court's ruling in Brown; a similar "resolution of interposition" was adopted by the Virginia Legislature on February 1; they then closed the Commonwealth's public schools. March 7 saw the same legislature alter the law to allow public aid to private schools. Five days later, 101 Southern representatives and senators published a manifesto calling upon the states to disobey and resist the Supreme Court's ruling by all lawful means.

School segregation was not the only issue at stake. In the South, large numbers of Blacks had been effectively disenfranchised around the turn of the century. Having successfully intervened in schooling, the Federal Government would deal with the franchise in the South. Despite a filibuster of over 24 hours by South Carolina's Senator Strom Thurmond, Congress passed on August 29 a Civil Rights Bill creating a Commission to investigate denial of voting rights because of religion and race. It further made denial of voting rights in national elections a federal offense.

Meanwhile, the education front was heating up again. After a 1957 ruling by the local U.S. District Court forcing Central High School in Little Rock to integrate, Governor Orval Faubus of Arkansas defied the Court. President Eisenhower in response federalized the Arkansas

National Guard and dispatched 1,000 paratroopers to the school on September 24. The next day, nine heavily guarded Black schoolchildren began classes. A year later, the Supreme Court ruled that it was the duty of local officials to integrate as soon as possible. On January 19, 1959, the Virginia Supreme Court invalidated the legislature's anti-integration laws; two weeks later, the Norfolk and Arlington schools were integrated peacefully.

Starting in February of 1960, sit-in demonstrations held to desegregate lunch counters and the like were launched throughout the South. Congress passed on April 21 the Civil Rights Act of 1960, despite the 121-hour long filibuster mounted by Southern senators. It allowed Federal authorities to step in whenever they considered state registration practices questionable. By this time, the legal machinery was in place to force the Southern states to accept the abolition of Jim Crow.

What are we to think of all of this? On the one hand, there can be no doubt that Jim Crow encompassed many injustices, indeed. It was not just that Blacks were subjected to many indignities on account of race; their natural abilities were stymied artificially, and they simply lacked the opportunity to compete with whites.

However, it also ought to be remembered that Jim Crow was the son of Reconstruction; its notion of basing rights and restrictions upon group membership rather than individual citizenship carried over into Civil Rights legislation. Moreover, the way in which legal segregation was abolished was done by transforming the Supreme Court from an apolitical judicial body into a political quasi-legislative one. It is also interesting to note that since the days of FDR to this, the Supreme Court has only once struck down a Federal Law as unconstitutional; rather they have concentrated on State and local measures. Thus it has become a mere instrument for expansion of the Federal prerogative and destruction of State and local autonomy—a patently unconstitutional development.

The remaining shreds of States' Rights were destroyed during the Civil Rights' controversy. It must be said, that in using them to defend a manifestly unjust system, the Southern politicians showed a criminal blindness. Having lost over integration, there was nothing they could do about fighting abortion, when the time came. Just recently, both Louisiana and Guam fought the Federal government on this key issue. The precedents established in forcing integration were used to beat them down.

Catholicism in the 1950s

As noted before, the rise of Communism had forced Pius XII into a de facto alliance with the United States. Moreover, the devastation of

World War II had made the American Church the most important segment (financially) of the Church as a whole.

A further difficulty was raised by the fact that the Church had just suffered a great deal under the Nazi and Fascist dictatorships, so many of whose policies had borne a purely external resemblance to some of the social and economic teachings of the Church. Above all, having just undergone a struggle with dictators who forbade dissent, and still suffering under Communists who forbade dissent, many churchmen became enamored of the notions of religious tolerance and political democracy:

> A Church so schooled in resistance to oppression, remembers that it is a Church of the people, rather than of rulers; and, whenever it regains its freedom, its temptation is to resort to new alliances with popular movements, or with parliamentary parties and pressure groups. This is the doubtful tendency today of "Catholic Action" and of the "Christian Democratic" parties in the new republics of Italy, France, and Western Germany (Lord Percy of Newcastle, *The Heresy of Democracy*, p. 231).

From the Vatican to the local parish, the doctrinal struggle between Modernism and Orthodoxy, and the socio-cultural struggle between Americanism and Ultramontanism, was supplemented by a political struggle between Liberalism and Traditionalism in terms of separation of Church and State, rights of unbelievers, and so on.

On the one side in the latter struggle were the generality of the hierarchies of the United States, France, Germany, Italy, Belgium and the Netherlands; on the other, most of those of Spain, Portugal, and Latin America.

In Spain, the traditional Catholic and monarchical nature of which had been preserved only at the price of a long and bloody civil war, General Franco had placed in article 6 of the *Fuero de los Españoles*, the country's constitution, the declaration that: "The profession and practice of the Catholic religion, which is that of the Spanish State, shall enjoy official protection." The same article went on to say that: "Nobody shall be molested for his religious beliefs in the private exercise of his cult. Ceremonies or external manifestations other than those of the Catholic religion will not be permitted." They would not be permitted to proselytize. By the terms of the Concordat, teaching in colleges, universities, state and private schools had to conform to Catholicism, and the State would pay clerical salaries and pensions, as well aiding churches and religious houses financially.

In Salazar's Portugal, separation of Church and State had been retained in the 1933 Constitution (it having initially occurred after the revolution of 1910). Divorce was recognized by the State for the marriages of non-Catholics, who enjoyed religious freedom (including proselytization). But in the 1940 Concordat, it was agreed that only Catholic ceremonies would be permitted at State functions, and no official government representatives would attend non-Catholic religious rites.

In Latin America, a number of countries retained something of the ancient organization of Church and State. In Peru, although civil marriage and divorce were permitted in 1930, article 232 of the 1933 Constitution stated that: "Out of respect for the sentiments of the majority of the nation, the State protects the Catholic, Apostolic, and Roman religion. Other religions enjoy freedom for the exercise of their respective worship." Clergy were forbidden from holding office, but were exempted from military service; their salaries were paid by the State. The President could present candidates for the episcopate to the Holy See, while Congress could create or suppress dioceses.

The Panamanian constitution in article 36 "recognized that the Catholic religion is that of the majority of Panamanians. It shall be taught in the public schools, but its study and assistance at its acts of worship shall not be obligatory for students, when their parents or guardians so request..." In Paraguay there was constitutional union between Church and State. The Haitian Constitution stated in article 20:

> All the religions and all the denominations recognized in Haiti are free. Everyone has the right to profess his religion and to carry on his form of worship as long as he does not disturb the public order. The Catholic religion, professed by the majority of Haitians enjoys a special position because of the Concordat.

In Colombia the Constitution of 1887 in no less than eleven articles detailed the privileges of the Church of which the first sets the tone:

> Art. 1: The Catholic Apostolic Roman Religion is that of the Nation; public authorities will protect it and cause it to be respected as well as its ministers, preserving it in the full exercise of its right and privileges.

In Bolivia also the Catholic Church was the State religion. Argentina's 1947 Constitution required that the President be a Catholic, and required State financing of the Church. In all of these nations, of course, those elements who looked either to New York or Moscow favored Separation of Church and State, and continually sought to erode the Church's position.

Such folk had succeeded in Chile, Mexico, Nicaragua, Uruguay, Venezuela, Guatemala, El Salvador, Ecuador, Costa Rica, Honduras, and Brazil—all countries where the anti-clericals had been openly supported by the U.S.

In all constitutions of those nations which retained the union of Church and State, two separate currents might be seen. In such countries as Colombia, Catholicism was the religion of the State, pure and simple. In others, such as Peru and Panama, that recognition was based solely on the fact that the Faith was professed by the majority of citizens. There was a subtle but important difference: in the first case, Catholicism being true, it simply *is* the religion of the State. In the second, that status is based solely upon the will of the people. The Irish case shows the consequences of these differences.

The Irish Constitution of 1937 stated the following in "Article 44: Religion:"

> 1. The State acknowledges that the homage of public worship is due to almighty God. It shall Hold his name in reverence, and shall respect and honour religion.
> 2. The State recognizes the special position of the Holy Catholic Apostolic and Roman Church as the guardian of the Faith professed by the great majority of the citizens.
> 3. The State also recognizes the Church of Ireland, the Presbyterian Church in Ireland, the Methodist Church in Ireland, the Religious Society of Friends in Ireland, as well as the Jewish congregations and the other religious denominations existing in Ireland at the date of the coming into operation of this Constitution.

By American standards, this is a rather radical statement, as indeed those in all the constitutions we have just looked at are. But from an integrally Catholic point of view, it is not so. During the 1950s, there flourished in Ireland an organization called *Maria Duce*, organized by the redoubtable Fr. Denis Fahey, whom we met with during the Depression. In the *Irish Times* of March 7, 1950, J.P. Ryan, Secretary of Maria Duce, critiqued article 44 from a purely Catholic viewpoint:

> For a Catholic, religion is a matter of dogmatic certitude. For him there is only one true religion. In consequence, all non-Catholic sects, as such, are false and evil, irrevocably so. While a Catholic must always respect the non-Catholics' personal rights and liberty of conscience, he may never regard their beliefs as other than false, "may never connive in any way at false opinions, never withstand them less zealously than the truth allows" (Leo XIII). For a Protestant, on the other hand, religion is a matter of private judgement, a question of opinion. Moreover, since no Protestant claims the prerogative of

personal infallibility (as Catholics do for the Pope in matters of faith and morals), it is evident that for a Protestant, thus deprived of dogmatic certainty, the only sane attitude towards those who disagree with his religious opinions is to regard such opinions with a certain respectful deference. Hence the Protestant notion of "religious toleration," the "one-religion-is-as-good-as-another" philosophy which is the logical outcome of private judgement. Toleration for a Catholic always implies that what is tolerated is an evil, and that the toleration of this evil is itself justified only when such toleration is necessary to avoid a greater evil—that is, it is justified by the application of the principle of the double effect. Religious toleration for the Protestant, on the contrary, has no such implications. It is merely the "broadminded," "liberal," admission that people are entitled to their opinions.

What then must be the attitude of Catholic States, such as Spain and Ireland, towards Protestantism and non-Catholic sects in general? The ideal (as outlined in the Syllabus of Pius IX, *Ubi arcano* and *Quas primas* of Pius XI) is that the Catholic State, while extending full liberty and official recognition to the Catholic Church alone, should not only not connive at the proselytism of non-Catholic sects, but should suppress them as inimical to the common good. This attitude is quite logical, since for a Catholic State the vitality of Catholic life is the chief good of society. Such intolerance of error is the privilege of truth. Nor does it entail any violence to the liberty of the individual conscience, for "the Church is wont to take earnest care that no one shall be forced to embrace the Catholic Faith against his will." (Leo XIII—*Immortale Dei*).

Nowadays, however, this ideal, such as was realised in Catholic Spain under Ferdinand and Isabella, is not encountered in practice. In many countries predominantly Catholic, the Church, while never abdicating one iota of her sacred rights, is, nevertheless, obliged to be content with an imperfect recognition. In such circumstances the suppression by the State of falsehood and false sects, however desirable, is not feasible. The principle of toleration (in the Catholic sense already explained) may then be invoked as a temporary expedient, a concession to adverse circumstances, by no means a compromise with error itself. The principle is explicitly laid down by Leo XIII in *Immortale Dei*. There it is clear that this toleration is justified only when the Catholic State in question, while extending official recognition to the Catholic Church alone, has a proportionately grave reason for permitting the evil of heresy to survive within its borders.

We proceed to point out that the liberalism of Article 44 of the Constitution stands unequivocally condemned for giving equal recognition to all forms of religious belief, since it is contrary to reason and revelation alike that error and truth should have equal rights (Leo XIII). From repeated Papal pronouncements, it is abundantly clear that the Catholic Church not only does not condone, but vigourously condemns, the much-vaunted "toleration" of most modern constitutions.

That this kind of talk sounds radical to us is a measure of how far we have fallen from Catholic principles. But the fear of Maria Duce of the Irish Constitution's liberalism was duly demonstrated by subsequent events. Even the modest recognition given the Church was removed from the text in 1976, the referendum campaign being fought under the notion that such a move was necessary if Ireland was to "catch up" with the rest of the Common Market, which the country had joined three years previously. Catholic influence waned until the first half of the 1990s saw the nation's history textbooks ignoring most of the contribution of the Faith to Irish culture, and implying that the privations suffered by the Irish during the Penal Times were mythical. The President was a pro-abortion feminist named Mary Robinson, who in turn was married to a Protestant gentleman who happened to be a high-ranking Freemason. Most telling (if purely symbolic) was the fact that in the early 1990s, Dublin Castle, symbol of rule in Ireland, saw its Chapel Royal (Anglican until 1942, when it was made over into the Catholic Church of the Holy Trinity) turned in the latest renovation into a non-denominational chapel.

Even in countries where the hierarchy supported Liberalism, large numbers of layfolk and some priests continued to profess the Catholic traditions of that nation. Many of these in France were aroused by the struggle over Algeria, of which more shortly. A hostile American commentator said of such folk:

> The Church has many chapels; one of them preserves the memories of the *ancien régime.* Its old saints are De Maistre, Chateaubriand, Albert de Mun; its latter-day saint, Charles Maurras. Not Maritain. The worshippers are of all age groups and professions, military and civilians. We find there Alphonse Juin, the marshal, and an old acquaintance, General Chassin. There is also General Jouhaud. Not all the faithful can attend, but they send flowers: Generals Zeller and Salan, De Beaufort, De Bonneval, and Gardy; many more. All the king's men in their uniforms, and next to them, the members of the other army in *their* uniform: the cloth.
>
> Meet the Other France, attempting, once more, to convert This France. The sacred language fills the room with irresistibly majestic sounds; the visions of the saints, the words of great churchmen are recalled with loving care. But listen closely, and you hear the guns of the Algerian war sound through the thunder from Mount Sinai. *Propaganda fide* blends with the theories of revolutionary war: the army must be given a good conscience (James H. Meisel, *The Fall of the Republic*, p. 244).

Despite his mocking tone, the truth of their position emerges; these were folk whose Faith inspired them to fight for Catholic order, in this case in France and Algeria.

Nor were this sort of people lacking elsewhere. In Italy, the great Catholic philosopher of history, *Attilio Mordini* (1923-1966) and his disciples went so far as to "reject the Risorgimento and exalt the Habsburgs as heirs of the Holy Roman Empire." Similar views were espoused by the *Neues Abendland* group:

> There is a castle in South Württemberg, near Liechtenstein, the Schloss Zeil, the ancestral home of the princely family of Waldburg-Zeil, which is the headquarters of a group calling itself *Neues Abendland*, and the honorary President is the Archduke Otto of Habsburg. The word *Abendland* generally signifies Christian Europe as against the *Morgenland* of the pagan East, and was used as early as the Crusades. In its present particular context it means a land which preserves European monarchist traditions and virtues, especially the Catholic virtues, against the Russian and conceivably even the American menace (Bocca, *op. cit.*, p. 136).

Despite the fact that such folk faced opposition from both their bishops and most of the leadership of their respective national Christian Democratic parties, their very existence was a testimony to the continuing power of the Catholic tradition.

In America, things were a bit different, as we shall see presently. But occasionally, a Catholic would stand up against "the American Way." In January of 1953, for example:

> Anna Collazo, an employee of the Puerto Rican Department of Education, refused to swear allegiance to the entire constitution. She would defend all the laws of the Commonwealth, she said, except those opposed to divine law. Father Arroyo, director of the Confraternity of Christian Doctrine, defended her action, declaring it the duty of all Catholics to make a mental or written reservation against birth control, sterilization, and the secularist school laws when pledging to defend the Puerto Rico commonwealth laws (1954 *Catholic Almanac*, p. 717).

Little enough, one might say, when weighed against all that Catholics were doing elsewhere at that time. But for the United States, it was just the sort of thing to unleash a new wave of anti-Catholicism.

Already, in 1947, Chicago's Methodist Temple played host on November 20 to the founding of an organization with the catchy title, Protestants and Other Americans United For Separation of Church and State (POAU). Its founders drew their membership from Protestant groups, Scottish Rite Freemasonry, the National Education Association, humanist societies, and the American Jewish Congress:

> The "big three" of the founding fathers were Glenn L. Archer of the NEA; Paul Blanshard, a Congregationalist minister and former employee of the U.S. State Department; and the last, C. Stanley Lowell, a Methodist minister. Archer called the Catholic Church a tyranny behind the purple curtain of Roman clericalism; Blanshard described Catholicism as "a dictatorial society within America's democratic society;" and Lowell averred that a Catholic education might qualify a person for citizenship in a totalitarian society but not a free country, adding that "I do not want my child in a school directed by officials who are under control of a foreign potentate" (Hurley, *op. cit.*, p. 35).

Throughout the 50s, POAU would keep up a steady assault against the Church, and particularly against her schools, which John Dewey described as "inimical to democracy." Having dropped "Protestant" from the title, AU soldiers on in our own time.

Rather more successful (both in getting a hearing and raking in the cash), Paul Blanshard continued his crusade via book writing. In his first effort, *American Freedom and Catholic Power* (1949), Blanshard outlined the "Catholic problem" as he saw it:

> There is no doubt that the American Catholic hierarchy has entered the political arena, and that it is becoming more and more aggressive in extending the frontiers of Catholic authority into the fields of medicine, education and foreign policy. In the name of religion, the hierarchy fights birth-control and divorce laws in all states. It tells Catholic doctors, nurses, judges, teachers, and legislators what they can and cannot do in many of the controversial phases of their professional conduct. It segregates Catholic children from the rest of the community in a separate school system and censors the cultural diet of these children. It uses the political power of some thirty-five million official American Catholics to bring American foreign policy into line with Vatican temporal interests (p. 2).
>
> But the Catholic problem is still with us. Primarily it is not the problem of assimilation of the Catholic *people*; they have been absorbed into the American community as completely as could be expected in view of the attitude of their priests. Essentially the Catholic problem in America is what to do with the hierarchy of the Roman Church. The American Catholic *people* have done their best to join the rest of America, but the American Catholic hierarchy, as we shall see in the course of this survey, has never been assimilated. It is still fundamentally Roman in its spirit and directives (pp. 13-14).

This was followed by a whirlwind of tracts exposing Catholic crimes against freedom in Spain, Portugal, and Ireland. Blanshard's tactic was to examine Papal and other documents (like the quote from J.P. Ryan above) and to presume that they represented the goals of the American hierarchy for this country, thus subjugating the States to a dictatorship equally as bad as Communism. In this analysis he made two major errors.

The first was that the American ethos he rightly saw Catholicism as threatening was worth defending. This was the dry, conformist horror the Beats so decried; this was Babbittry. It comprised freedom for heresy, which must always mean slavery for Truth; freedom for divorce, contraception, abortion, and sterilization—in a word, freedom to wallow in the mire of degradation. This was what Blanshard equated with America, and hated the Church for trying to prevent.

His second error was in supposing that the American Churchmen really wanted to save their countrymen from this fate. There were some few who did, to be sure; but Americanism was ever more triumphant, and found its latest champion in one *Fr. John Courtney Murray, S.J.*

Fr. Murray tried in numerous books and articles (such as *We Hold These Truths*) to prove that the Americanist ideology, particularly in the Constitution, actually enshrined Catholic principles, rather than denying them. At first (in response to Blanshard) obliquely, and then ever more boldly, he declared that Separation of Church and State on the American model was superior to the traditional concept of Church establishment. He soon came into conflict with Msgr. Joseph Fenton, editor of the *American Ecclesiastical Review* who defended the traditional view. These two would carry on the fight throughout the 50s.

From merely defending the American Separation of Church and State as a legitimate good, Murray's thought, as it developed, became ever more radical. He came to positively despise old Christendom in words fitting for Bishop O'Connell in 1898: "Catholicism in turn now feels that certain of its past unities were something of a scandal; we now reject, for instance, the specious unity asserted in Belloc's famous thesis that 'Europe is the faith and the faith is Europe.'" He then came to affirm the rights of the individual as being superior to the rights of Truth:

> ...it is granted at the outset that rights may not be founded on error, but only on truth. The first immediate affirmation, however, is that rights are inherent in persons. Rights are founded on the dignity of the person, which is the first truth of the social order—the order in which rights are affirmed and exercised. The dignity of the person is a basic constituent element of the objective moral order, the order on which society itself and its laws and processes must be based.

Thus, based upon his dignity as a person, every man had the inherent right to choose error for himself. Just as the American Republic, by ignoring God and religion in its constitution, practically denied that public life could be touched by questions of the Supernatural order, Murray would have the Church regard the individual in the same way, looking not at his eternal end, but at his temporal state.

But Murray was not a revolutionary; he was simply articulating that which had been the working doctrine of the American Church for a long time.

It was a hard doctrine to argue with, simply because the American Church under its guidance had become so wealthy and successful; not merely in terms of churches, religious houses, schools, universities, and hospitals, but in associations as well. From the Knights of Columbus to the Auto League of the Sacred Heart, there were organizations designed to appeal to Catholics of every interest. There were books and magazines published, and all sorts of goings on. Nor were the spiritual elements neglected: mass Eucharistic and rosary rallies testified to the strength of Catholic sentiment in such places as Boston, New York, Chicago, and San Francisco. *Archbishop Fulton Sheen's* TV show was extremely popular: its comforting and non-denominational message that "Life is worth living," consoled but did not challenge.

Such was Catholic growth that Blanshard and his cronies grew ever shriller. They might have saved their breath. For the average Catholic in the 50s was interested purely and simply in sharing the general prosperity and conformity. People flocked, for example, to the morning Masses of those priests who could rattle off the Tridentine Mass in 15 minutes. As among Protestants, holiness and respectability were seen as interchangeable qualities, and anything beyond making money a waste of time. Religion was important merely as a moral system, rather than a means of Grace, of transcendence, of eternal ecstasy. The Church's only function, really, was to serve as cheerleader for secular change; hence, when the Archbishop of New Orleans illegally (in terms of Canon Law) excommunicated Judge Leander Perez and several other layfolk for their opposition to integration in schools, he was hailed as "far sighted" (although the POAU crowd did not loudly object to this particular intervention of a Bishop in politics, oddly enough).

There were some noteworthy attempts, however, to lead a fully Catholic life. The Catholic Worker and the Madonna and Friendship Houses continued, of course. But in 1946, Carol Robinson and Ed Willock founded *Integrity* Magazine.

In the decade it survived, *Integrity* raised important questions, and pricked the conscience of Catholic America. In one of its most powerful articles, it addressed the national ideology which Blanshard defended:

The prevailing practical philosophy of Americans is liberalism. Since its spirit pervades the very atmosphere we live in it is not surprising that most Catholics are practical liberals in their daily lives.

Think of liberalism as a vacuum, a chaos where men are guided by principles of expediency rather than absolute morality, as absence of order, as inconclusive and indeterminate, and you get its mark. It served to destroy the Christian order, not by contradicting it so much as by diluting and confusing it, by nullifying it at every turn. For the Christian absolute it did not substitute another absolute, but an absence of any absolute, an indeterminism, a tolerance of good and evil, truth and untruth, not in a prudential way, as allowing certain evils to exist rather than stir up worse evils in trying to eradicate them, but as not really preferring one to another. Liberalism used good words ambiguously, so that gradually they were drained of their Christian implications and then gradually again were charged with meaning antithetical to Christianity. It enshrined liberty, equality, and fraternity, but as ultimates, not as means and not as by-products of absolute things such as truth and goodness, not as related to morality but as isolated from God. It worshipped democracy, which is only a means of government, which depends on basic ideals for its real worth. It talked endlessly about freedom, and it was easy to persuade people that this was the same freedom that Christians cherish, but was it? Christ said, "You shall know the truth, and the truth shall make you free." His freedom is a result of knowing the truth—the result of what the liberals like to call "intolerance" and "dogmatism." The liberal's freedom is quite different. It is the freedom to search for truth. Of course, it is a good thing for the men who do not know the Truth to be able to look for it. The trouble with the liberals is that they will not let anyone find it. If anyone claims to find it, he becomes an outcast from their society. They are, it turns out, dogmatists in their own curious way. They know there is no truth, or if there is, it's not knowable.

We have a liberal government, without any real principles, paying lip service to God, and talking more and more about democracy and freedom, while both of these are vanishing for lack of roots in something deeper. We have, or did have until a few years ago (things are rapidly changing), a system in this country of liberal economics, which meant free competition and the legal right to abuse the moral right of private property. It also involved freedom from sanctions against usury. Our system of free compulsory education is also, or was until recently, liberal. Liberal means undogmatic, which means remaining undecided about all the important truths (except that one is allowed his private opinion) while attaching an exaggerated importance and a thousand dogmas to matters of art, literature, science, hygiene, and civics.

The effect of liberalism, economic, philosophical, and cultural, over a period of centuries, has been to destroy all norms. It has no moral code of its own and has endured only as long as Christian morals have survived to hold society together—not only Christian morals but Christian standards of all sorts. The end of liberalism had to be dog-eat-dog because the philosophy itself has no backbone, nothing wherein to construct a life or society. We are in the last stages of it now, and we find everything in ruins. Western society, indeed the whole world, has become one great big vacuum, one vastness empty of all positive content (Carol Robinson, *My Life With Thomas Aquinas*, pp. 34-35).

Quite a powerful passage, indeed! Yet, should anyone consider such a message too negative, this reply on the part of the magazine's editors might be instructive:

When accused of negativism, we used to object that to see that the world is ordered against Christ is at least to see something, and that it is so far true. It is better, for instance, than saying a bad thing is a good thing, just to be cheerful. Yet if our readers are to make over society, we need to see through the disaster to God's use of this adversity, through the modern despair to the hope that lies in Christ. Hope doesn't lie anywhere else except in Christ. That is the vision which is becoming blinding. That is the only source of a "positive viewpoint."; The only constructive program is toward a Christ-centered society. We were right, we think, not to have lavished flattery on any scheme whatever from which the supernatural has been strained out, or to which the Redemption was accidental. We now see, dimly, but certainly, that our elevation to the order of grace must act as the integrating principle in the transformation of the world (*Integrity*, 1949, vol. 3, no. 2).

As might be expected, this vision led them out of the editorial office and into the world—or more exactly, back to the land. Ed Willock and a number of other like-minded men, mostly Irish Catholics from the Bronx, decided they wanted to put their beliefs into action. In 1949 a tract of land was found where the dream might be carried out. A parcel of rural land was found in West Nyack, in then-rural Rockland County about twenty miles northwest of the Bronx. For $600 apiece, heads of families were entitled to one-acre homesteads and corporate ownership of a large common field where cattle might be herded and grain raised. Although the settlers would build their own homes, an architect and a master builder were hired to give advice.

By the late 1950s, some twelve families were settled, with 79 children. Inspired by Fr. Francis X. Weiser's excellent series of books detailing Catholic paraliturgical customs, they set to work to lead a truly Catholic life. Willock wrote later:

...it matures a man to drive hundreds of nails, lay hundreds of bricks, erect hundreds of studs, apply hundreds of shingles... persons who create together will learn to re-create together and even pray together... Marycrest was the scene of rich paraliturgical ceremony: the fields were blessed by local priests; the entire community gathered for Christian folksinging under the light of the moon; bonfires were lit on St. John's Eve.

The settlers were pledged to voluntary poverty.

But in the end, most of the children drifted away, and the original drive was lost. Why? Because it is never enough for Catholics simply to withdraw from the world. Such a retreat (like the medieval monasteries) in order to survive must expand. Had the Marycresters not merely been content to withdraw, but had raised up their children with the idea of evangelizing—well, at least the neighborhood, if not the nation—the original ideals might have survived. In a sense, Marycrest was a microcosm of Catholic America. Not wishing to reach out, it turned in and at length was assimilated.

The crowning moment of this development was the 1959 declaration of Massachusetts Senator John F. Kennedy, then in the running for the Presidential election to be held the next year, before the Houston Ministerial Association. In front of that august body, he solemnly promised that his religion would not affect his conduct in office. Thus did the man who shortly would be the country's best known Catholic layman agree to give up his freedom of religion, the integrity of his Faith, to gain the whole world—or at least the presidency of these United States.

Foreign Policy in the Age of Eisenhower

To this day, the legend of Eisenhower's stalwart anti-Communism has survived intact. His secretary of state, *John Foster Dulles*, had his method of dealing with the Soviets dubbed by the Press, "brinksmanship" (implying that he would bring the country to the brink of war, if necessary). Certainly, there is much to justify this view at first glance.

Eisenhower not only ended the Korean War, but aided the French financially in their struggle to keep Indochina free of Communism. In 1954, he dispatched troops to Guatemala to assist in the overthrow of a pro-Communist regime there. The next year, he rushed support to the Nationalist Chinese on Taiwan when the Reds threatened invasion and did in fact seize the Tachen islands offshore. In 1956, his administration joined with Great Britain, France, Australia, New Zealand, Pakistan, the Phillipines, and Thailand in forming the South East Asia Treaty Organization (SEATO), which hoped to play the part of NATO in its region. Similarly, he lent a benevolent eye to the Baghdad Pact (later the Central Treaty Organization—CENTO) which united Great Britain, Turkey, Iraq, Iran, and Pakistan for the same cause, thus completing a circle of anti-Communist organizations around the periphery of the Communist world.

On March 7, 1957, Congress approved the "Eisenhower Doctrine," which declared American aid and troops would be sent anywhere in the Middle East where called upon by a country threatened by Communist aggression. Under its provisos, 5,000 marines were dispatched to Lebanon in July of 1958, at the same time that the King of Iraq was overthrown and murdered by army officers (his cousin, the King of Jordan, called in British troops to escape that fate).

So from that time on, we have been used to thinking of Eisenhower as a "Cold Warrior." But the reality was somewhat different. As intimated before, the interest of the United States government was not rolling back the Iron Curtain; nor was its policy elsewhere affected by considerations other than dynamiting its allies from their overseas possessions and influence:

> The process of decolonization after World War II was accelerated under the prod of America. The United States was staking out its own self-interested position in the world, at times unavoidably at odds with Britain and France. The country was in its ascendancy, flexing its power, testing its limits, and finding them seemingly non-existent. It was, exulted Henry Luce in his mass publications, *Time, Life,* and *Fortune,* "the American Century." Americans did not disagree, nor did European colonialists, though most of them were not happy about it, for each new country that emerged was one less bauble on the glittering necklace of empire, another shock to the once mighty power and prestige of Britain and France.
>
> British Foreign Secretary Selwyn Lloyd expressed some of the resentment that Europeans felt in the mid-1950s in his memoirs written two decades later. "The Americans were, on the face of it, loyal and dependable allies but underneath there were in many Americans' hearts a dislike of colonialism, a resentment of any authority left to us from the great days of our empire, and a pleased smile, only half concealed, at seeing us go down" (Donald Neff, *Warriors at Suez,* p. 19).

This led us to grease the skids, so to speak, for the British in Cyprus and East Africa, for the French in North Africa, and for the Belgians in the Congo. It led Eisenhower to assure the British and French of his support when they were engaging the Egyptians (in tandem with Israel) over Nasser's seizure of the Suez Canal in 1956, only to turn against them when the Soviets threatened war. Afterwards, Britain would never defy U.S. policy again, becoming a sort of satellite. But in France, the resulting instability led to the overthrow of the Fourth Republic and the ascent of De Gaulle two years later. Although he in turn betrayed his military sponsors by giving away Algeria, he would defy Washington by pulling France out of NATO rather than give up control to the U.S. of her nuclear arsenal in 1965.

This anti-colonial bias did no one any good. It weakened our allies, of course; but the regimes which replaced them were unstable, and despots often came to power who at once made their peoples' lives miserable, and opened their nations to Soviet influence. But in destroying what remained of these Empires, Eisenhower was showing continuity with American foreign policy since the Monroe Doctrine. Such ideological purity must be maintained, regardless of the suffering it caused.

Similarly, the hollowness of Eisenhower's anti-Communist crusade was made obvious by events in Hungary in October and November of 1956. Egged on by American broadcasts on Radio Free Europe, the Hungarians rebelled against the Soviets and succeeded in driving them out. The Soviets, after a short while, counter-attacked in force, and crushed the revolt. Eisenhower refused to send any aid, ostensibly for fear of igniting a nuclear conflict. When Franco offered to send Spanish troops to assist the resistance, if the U.S. would provide air transport, Ike refused. As eleven years earlier he had turned over Russians and Eastern Europeans to Stalin, so did he do again.

The cynical might be forgiven for suspecting that the real end in all of this was not the defeat of Communism, but simply maintenance of the Cold War, which had made both war-time prosperity and government control carry over.

The Election of 1960

Whatever one might think of Kennedy's performance for the Houston ministers, it worked. He beat out Lyndon Johnson for the nomination of his party, although taking on LBJ as Vice President.

On the Republican side, although the Conservatives (spearheaded by National Review and the Young Americans for Freedom) had made Arizona Senator Barry Goldwater a force to be reckoned with, Vice President Richard Nixon was easily nominated. He could be relied upon, if elected, to carry on Ike's policies.

The campaign saw the revival, for the last time, of the usual anti-Catholic calumnies (although JFK was the least deserving of such, as we have seen). He indulged, with Nixon, in the first ever Presidential TV debates, which he won. Youthful and vigorous in appearance, he was married to the glamorous Jacqueline Bouvier; together they provided quite a contrast to the rather dowdy Eisenhowers. JFK was victorious in the November 8 election, upon which day this writer was born.

CAMELOT, THE HIPPIE ERA, AND THE GREAT SOCIETY

In the course of Eisenhower's farewell speech in 1961, he warned of the evils of the "military-industrial complex," which was odd, considering how much he had contributed to it. But JFK's inaugural speech, consisting as it did of marvelous and stirring phrases (including one pirated from Charles Evans Hughes— "Ask not what your country can do for you—ask what you can do for your country") captured the imagination of a generation coming of age.

Young and glamorous as the new first couple were (indeed, theirs would be the last formal inauguration—cutaway coats, top hats, and striped trousers—for another two decades), they seemed to epitomize what the nation's youth were looking for: a challenge to build a better world, and an attempt to transcend the mundane and dull culture in which they had been brought up. It was the age of Dr. Tom Dooley, the young Irish Catholic doctor whose work in setting up a hospital in Laos similarly caught the youthful imagination. On March 1, President Kennedy established the Peace Corps, which would send young American volunteers to various developing countries.

There is, because of the way the Kennedy administration ended, a sort of collective loss of memory which has descended over it. Because of the glamour, the high hopes, and the general atmosphere, it is remembered as "Camelot." The Civil Rights movement grew in strength and visibility, and young Americans dedicated themselves to various ways of improving things.

But in reality, JFK was not a very successful President. Only about 44% of the legislation he presented to Congress was passed. In foreign affairs, from the Bay of Pigs fiasco, to the Cuban Missile Crisis, to the escalation of American involvement in Vietnam, most of his foreign policy moves were less than helpful. To end the Missile Crisis, he had to withdraw our projectiles from Turkey. He persevered over the Berlin Blockade, thus leading to his famous "Ich bin ein Berliner" speech (intended no doubt to show his solidarity with the people of that beleaguered city, but actually proclaiming that he was a sort of jelly-filled doughnut). In Vietnam, the Catholic President Ngo Dinh Diem was assassinated in a coup, rumored by many to have been ordered by the U.S. If true, it was ironic, because a few weeks later, on November 22, Kennedy was assassinated in Dallas.

There have of course been all sorts of tales about the death of Kennedy. If it truly was some sort of conspiracy, it would have had to have been so large and powerful that detection is extremely unlikely. If there was none, then there is of course nothing to detect. However, it is highly doubtful that we shall ever know the truth. What is certain is that many of the young whose idealism had been inspired by JFK saw in his demise the death also of their hopes for decent change within the system.

Johnson and the Great Society

The new President was much more at home with Congress than Kennedy had been. Much that had been purely conceptual under JFK leapt to life under LBJ. On January 23, 1964, the Twenty-fourth Amendment to the Constitution was approved, forbidding poll or other taxes to qualify voters. While obviously intended as a blow against Jim Crow, it had the effect of destroying a major element of the American voting process, which had been believed in by many of the Founding Fathers as essential to an intelligent electorate.

On March 16, Johnson addressed Congress and called for a "war on poverty." This would include formation of the Job Corps, and similar measures.

Meanwhile, the Civil Rights issue was heating up. After a 75-day long filibuster by Southern Senators, debate over the Civil Rights Bill of 1964 was cut off, and the measure passed. It banned racial discrimination in voting, education, public places, employment, and all federally aided programs. Its passage was the signal for hundreds of young white college students, the so-called "Freedom Riders," to bus down to Mississippi in order to register Black voters. The Klan reacted predictably with floggings, terror, and in a few cases, murder. At the same time the "long hot summer" saw race riots rage in New York, New Jersey, Chicago, and Philadelphia.

The Summer also saw the nominations for the Presidential elections. Johnson easily won his party's; in the Republican Party, Goldwater triumphed over the liberal Nelson Rockefeller. From the beginning, Goldwater was the victim of a smear campaign until then unequaled in American electoral history. The result was predictable: November 3 saw a landslide for Johnson.

LBJ's own term began well enough. It did not end that way. In a speech given at the University of Michigan on May 22, 1964, he outlined his view of the "Great Society:"

> The Great Society rests on abundance and liberty for all. It demands an end to poverty and racial injustice, to which we are totally committed in our time. But that is just the beginning. The Great Society is a place where every child can find knowledge to enrich his mind and

to enlarge his talents. It is a place where leisure is a welcome chance to build and reflect, not a feared cause of boredom and restlessness. It is a place where the city of man serves not only the needs of the body and the demands of commerce but the desire for beauty and the hunger for community.

It is a place where man can renew contact with nature. It is a place which honors creation for its own sake and for what it adds to the understanding of the race. It is a place where men are more concerned with the quality of their goals than the quantity of their goods. But, most of all, the Great Society is not a safe harbor, a resting place, a final objective, a finished work; it is a challenge constantly renewed, beckoning us toward a destiny where the meaning of our lives matches the marvelous products of our labor.

In a word, what he offered was utopia. For a generation looking for more than mere money, they were attractive words indeed. But the Civil Rights movement seemed to lose momentum as riots broke out in ever more cities. After the Gulf of Tonkin resolution planted us squarely in the Vietnam War, America's homes were able to watch it every night on television. As it wore on, seemingly without point or end in sight, it came to sum up for many all that was rotten with the system which they had inherited.

College campuses from about 1965 became hotbeds of political radicalism. The War was against Communism, was it? Then that is what many of its opponents would embrace. Hence new Marxist groups like the Students for a Democratic Society mushroomed. Together with the ideas of the Beats, new forms of rock-n-roll spurred by the arrival of the Beatles in 1964, the Eastern philosophies like Zen championed by such as *Alan Watts*, and hallucinogenic drugs popularized by *Timothy Leary*, this heady brew produced the Counter Culture, or as its adherents came to be known, the Hippies.

Casting off the gray and dark suits and short haircuts of the 50s, Hippy men wore colorful clothes and long hair; their "chicks" wore similarly unconventional attire. A whole new idiom of language, art and the like developed. Standards went out the window in dress, in manners, and much else.

Much of this was simply nonsense, but some was not. Putting to one side the drugs, free love, and crazed politics, what are we left with? A realization on the part of many of the Hippies that there really was something deeply wrong with America. For Theodore Roszak in his 1969 *The Making of a Counter Culture*, the movement at its best was an attempt to break through the arid, dry machine-age and Calvinist culture of the time, which he called the Technocracy:

> Understood... as the mature product of technological progress and the scientific ethos, the technocracy easily eludes all traditional political categories. Indeed, it is a characteristic of the technocracy to render itself ideologically invisible. Its assumptions about reality and its values become as unobtrusively persuasive as the air we breathe. While political argument continues within and between the capitalist and collectivist societies of the world, the technocracy increases and consolidates its power in both as a trans-political phenomenon following the dictates of industrial efficiency, rationality, and necessity (p. 8).

For Roszak, much of what was valuable in the Counter Culture was simply a spiritual (if unguided) rejection of the technocracy. Some support might be garnered for his view when one considers the popularity among the Hippies of a perhaps unlikely book: a trilogy called *The Lord of the Rings*, written by a scholarly Oxford don named *J.R.R. Tolkien*.

Placed in an alternative world called Middle Earth, Tolkien's fantasy about dwarves, hobbits, elves, and the like pitted against the evil dark lord, Sauron, soon became a best seller. It was not just that Tolkien's Middle Earth was magical and pastoral; for one reason or another it seemed to answer some of the deepest yearnings of the young. Peter S. Beagle wrote for many of these in 1973, when he stated:

> I've never thought it an accident that Tolkien's works waited more than ten years to explode into popularity overnight. The Sixties were no fouler than the Fifties—they merely reaped the Fifties' foul harvest—but they were the years when millions of people grew aware that the industrial society had become paradoxically unlivable, incalculably immoral, and ultimately deadly. In terms of passwords, the Sixties were the time when the word progress lost its ancient holiness, and escape stopped being comically obscene. The impulse is being called reactionary now, but lovers of Middle-earth want to go there. I would, like a shot.
>
> For in the end it is Middle-earth and its dwellers that we love, not Tolkien's considerable gifts in showing it to us. I said once that the world he charts was there long before him, and I still believe it. He is a great enough magician to tap our most common nightmares, daydreams, and twilight fancies, but he never invented them either: he found them a place to live, a green alternative to each day's madness here in a poisoned world.

It is instructive to examine the opinions of JRRT himself in regard to the topics we have been discussing. A man of extremely Conservative tastes and views, he nevertheless wrote:

> There are, of course, various elements in the present situation, which are confused, though in fact distinct (as indeed in the behaviour of modern youth, part of which is inspired by admirable motives such as anti-regimentation, and anti-drabness, a sort of romantic longing for "cavaliers," and not necessarily allied to the drugs or cults of fainéance and filth) [*Collected Letters,* p. 393].

All of which having been said, what really was the secret of Tolkien's work's attraction to a generation raised on the dregs of Puritanism? Where was the magic? He wrote it down himself in another letter:

> I think I know exactly what you mean by the order of Grace; and of course by your references to Our Lady, upon which all my own small perception of beauty both in majesty and simplicity is founded. *The Lord of the Rings* is of course a fundamentally religious and Catholic work; unconsciously so at first, but consciously in the revision. (p. 172).
> ...I am a Christian (which can be deduced from my stories) and in fact a Roman Catholic. The latter "fact" perhaps cannot be deduced; though one critic (by letter) asserted that the invocations of Elbereth, and the character of Galadriel as directly described (or through the words of Gimli and Sam) were clearly related to devotion to Mary. Another saw in waybread (lembas)=viaticum and the reference to its feeding the *will* (vol. III, p. 213) and being more potent when fasting, a derivation from Eucharist. (That is: far greater things may colour the mind in dealing with the lesser things of a fairy story) [p. 288].

Which brings one back to the question broached with the Beats. We see that, in veiled form, via Tolkien, the Hippies found the elements of Catholicism compelling indeed, in the face of the materialism and drabness with which they were brought up. Why did they not flock to the Faith, as so many Romantics had in their time?

The answer is that by that time the Church in America had conformed even in externals to the Americanist ethos, as to a degree, the Church Universal had done. We must now examine those circumstances.

Vatican II and the Catholic Revolution

With the accession of John XXIII, Church history entered its present phase. For better or worse, John XXIII is generally considered the author of the tide of change which has dominated Church affairs in our time. One of your author's first dateable memories is watching the Cardinals gathering for Pope John's funeral—on TV, of course.

Out of the blue, this Pope called a Council to no apparent end, then died in the middle of it. This allowed the Council Fathers (more particularly their "expert" assistants or *periti*) to do as they pleased. His changes in the Mass, small as they were, gave added impetus to liturgical vandals. Breaking with the anti-Communist stance of Pius XII, John began immediately sending out feelers to Moscow; in return for the presence of Russian and other Slavic Orthodox observers at his Council, he pledged that Communism would not be condemned there. Kruschev's Son-in-law, an editor of *Pravda*, was received at the Vatican, and John XXIII received the Balzan Peace Prize, awarded by a Swiss-based Communist Front organization.

There, at any rate, is one side of John XXIII. But justice compels us to look at another. On 22 February 1962, the Pope ordered published an Apostolic Constitution, that is, a communication of general authority, a most solemn document. Called *Veterum sapientia*, it dealt with the use of Latin in the Church. In it, the Pope speaks of the value and importance of Latin. It is part of the Church's heritage, and further has great cultural and religious value. Latin is Universal, Immutable, and Non-Vernacular. In regard to this last he says:

> ...the Catholic Church has a dignity far surpassing that of every merely human society, for it was founded by Christ the Lord. It is altogether fitting, therefore, that the language it uses should be noble and majestic, and *non-vernacular* (emphasis his; Cap. 9).

He then goes on to expound its educational value, following which he states the Church's official policy with regard to Latin:

> ...We also, impelled by the weightiest of reasons... are fully determined to restore this language to its position of honor and to do all We can to promote its study and use. The employment of Latin has recently been contested in some quarters, and many are asking what the mind of the Apostolic See is in this matter. We have therefore decided to issue the timely directives contained in this document, so as to ensure that the ancient and uninterrupted use of Latin be maintained and, where necessary, restored. (Cap. 13).

The second section contains detailed instruction on Latin (and Greek) in clerical education. Theology and Philosophy are to be taught in Latin, and seminary professors unable to use it are to be gradually replaced. This is "Our Will."

Four years later, the last scrap of the language disappeared from the Mass. In the orgy of destruction which took place after the Council, every innovation, regardless of how cruel or absurd it was, was cloaked with a pious invocation of "Good Pope John." Oh, ye liars and ye hypocrites! That the man was no angel is as true of him as of every son of Adam; but why besmirch his name in death!

There is too to be considered John's praiseworthy devotions to the Holy Ghost and the Precious Blood. He added "Blessed be the Holy Ghost, the Paraclete," and "Blessed be the Precious Blood of Jesus" to the Divine Praises at the end of Benediction. Further, he augmented the five approved-for-public-use litanies with that of the Precious Blood. But after his death, this devotion was even dropped from the Calendar, supposedly to be subsumed under Corpus Christi; as with the Latin, his wishes meant little to those who came after. As Mark Antony said, "The evil that men do lives after them; the good is oft interred with their bones." So it was with Caesar, so, alas, with Pope John, of that name the Twenty-Third.

In 1960, just after John XXIII called for Vatican II, Dr. Hubert Jedin, Vatican archivist and historian of Trent, wrote an historical survey entitled *Ecumenical Councils in the Catholic Church.* To a degree, it was an attempt to explain the Councils to intelligent Catholic laymen. In the light of what actually transpired at Vatican II, it is interesting to quote his penultimate paragraph:

> It has always been the highest duty of a council to assure the proclamation of the faith by delimitating the Catholic doctrine from contemporary errors. There have been councils which issued no disciplinary canons, but none at which some error was not rejected, or some heretic excluded from the community of the faithful. No error of our time is more fraught with greater possibilities of evil than the atheistic doctrines of communism with their caricature of the ideal of human dignity which they actually seek to destroy, and no truth of the faith is in greater need of definition than the concept of the Church.

So thought Dr. Jedin. James Francis Cardinal McIntyre, Archbishop of Los Angeles, went to Vatican II hoping to get a definition on Limbo. But Vatican II was a Council unlike any other in the history of the Church. Speaking in Santiago, Chile, on 13 July 1988, Josef Cardinal Ratzinger, head of the Congregation for the Doctrine of the Faith characterized it in the following way:

> Vatican II is not seen as part of the living tradition of the Church, but as the end of the Tradition, as an annihilation of the past from which the directions to begin a new path are to be taken. The truth is that the Council itself defined no dogma and expressly wished to speak on a more modest level, merely as a pastoral Council. Despite this many interpret the present Council as if it were almost the superdogma that renders all the rest less important.

(*30 Days*, June 1989, p. 3).

Nor was this mere hindsight. John Cardinal Heenan, one of the participants at the Council, wrote in his 1966 work, *Council and Clergy*: "It deliberately limited its own objectives. There were to be no specific definitions. Its purpose from the first was pastoral renewal within the Church and a fresh approach to those outside."

All the other Councils of the Church met to define, to punish, and to correct. Since this was not to be the case with Vatican II, various of the Council Fathers asked for a decision on the theological status of the Council documents. The Theological Commission of the Council replied on 6 March 1964 that,

> In view of the conciliar practice and pastoral purpose of the Council, this sacred Synod defines as binding on the Church only those matters of faith and morals which it has expressly put forward as such (Flannery, O.P., Austin, ed., *Vatican Collection,* I, p. 423).

Paul VI had this declaration read to the Fathers as they prepared to vote on the Constitution on the Church, *Lumen Gentium*. In his General Audience of 12 January 1966, the Pontiff declared that "in view of the pastoral nature of the Council, it avoided any extraordinary statements of dogmas endowed with the note of infallibility." In his closing speech at the Council, he had already remarked that "the Magisterium of the Church ... did not wish to proclaim an extraordinary dogmatic sentence." Writing in the *Tablet,* 2 March 1968, p. 199, Bishop B.C. Butler said very clearly: "There is no single proposition of Vatican II—except when quoting previous infallible definitions—which is in itself infallible."

All of this is important to realize. The sort of mentality which was a strong minority at Vatican I, was slapped on the wrist by Leo XIII, dove for cover under St. Pius X, was slightly relieved by Benedict XV, and successively liberated and wrist-slapped again by Pius XII, emerged as dominant at the Council. To understand the skullduggery that went on, your author recommends *The Rhine flows into the Tiber* by Fr. Ralph Wiltgen, SVD, and *Pope John's Council,* by Michael Davies. We are more concerned here with results than process.

But if this was indeed a purely "pastoral" Council, would it not address Communism? Instead:

> It may... puzzle some future students of late-twentieth century affairs when, seeking to understand how more than 2000 Church leaders in the late 20th Century viewed the phenomenon of communism, they discover that the word "communism" is not even mentioned. Other significant—and not-so-significant—contemporary

phenomena are discussed in the Council documents: the mass media, the problem of over-population, tax evasion, the need to follow basic practices of good hygiene, even the problem of reckless driving. How can one explain the mysterious absence from the Council's documents of the word "communism," a term of such importance for 20th Century man—or at least for the two billion individuals who live under communist regimes? (Tommaso Ricci, *30 Days*, Sept. 1989, pp. 58-9).

This statement was made in the context of a most illuminating article describing the attempt of 454 Council Fathers from 86 countries, to include an amendment to the Constitution *Gaudium et Spes*, "on the Church in the Modern World." The article includes the text of the amendment, which condemns Communism in strongest terms as "intrinsically perverse." It was brought up by these Fathers just prior to the end of the Council precisely because the set agenda provided did not even mention Communism. Luckily, this intervention was "misplaced" by French Bishop Achille Glorieux (secretary of the sub-commission for the revision of *Gaudium et Spes*) until it was too late to act upon. Ricci concludes:

> Was the Council ever really free to decide on this point? This is what some contend. They argue that Glorieux's "forgetfulness" was intentional and was meant to avoid a "dangerous" vote in the Council hall. And why was it absolutely necessary that the Council not mention communism at all? Had a promise been made to someone?
>
> A promise had been made. In return for the presence of Russian Orthodox observers at the Council, the Holy See agreed not to condemn Communism.

If it was not doctrinal, and if it did not deal with the then greatest pastoral problem facing the Church, what was the point of Vatican II? It was certainly the intention of a group of bishops and *periti* to alter the Church into a new religion. It should surprise no one that the two most influential clerics at the Council were the Modernist Karl Rahner, S.J., and the Americanist John Courtney Murray, S. J. As Fr. Wiltgen informs us, Conservative bishops and *periti*, in order to obtain an orthodox presentation in the documents, often had to compromise with Rahner and his followers and allow ambiguous phrasing (capable of an orthodox or heterodox interpretation) in disputed passages. Some, even of Cardinalatial rank, warned Paul VI that the liberals planned to interpret *Lumen gentium* in a liberal way after the Council:

> But the Pope still took no action because of his great faith in the Theological Commission. Then one of the extreme liberals made the mistake of referring, in writing, to some of these ambiguous passages,

and indicating how they would be interpreted after the Council. This paper fell into the hands of the aforesaid group of cardinals and superiors general, whose representative took it to the Pope. Pope Paul, realizing finally that he had been deceived, broke down and wept. What was the remedy? Since the rest of the schema did not make any positively false assertion, but merely used ambiguous terms, the ambiguity could be clarified by joining to the text a carefully phrased explanation. This was the origin of the Preliminary Explanatory Note appended to the schema. (Wiltgen, *op. cit.,* p. 232)

Similar things were done with the other documents. In *Dignitatis humanae,* the Declaration on Religious Liberty, for instance, whose primary author was John Courtney Murray, S.J., we see a direct refutation of the *Syllabus*. Among the propositions condemned therein are:

> 15. Every man is free to embrace and profess that religion which he, led by the light of reason, thinks to be the true religion.
> 16. In the worship of any religion whatever, men can find the way to eternal salvation, and can attain eternal salvation.
> 77. In this age of ours it is no longer expedient that the Catholic religion should be the only religion of the state, to the exclusion of all other cults whatsoever.

To this, *Humanae dignitatis* answers, "the right to religious freedom is based on the very dignity of the human person as known through the revealed word of God and by reason itself" (Flannery, *op. cit.*, I, 800). The declaration prattles on and on, making hair-splitting distinctions, and implicitly rejecting prior teaching. It concludes by saying:

> It is clear that with the passage of time all nations are coming into a closer unity, men of different cultures and religions are being bound together by closer links, and there is a growing awareness of individual responsibility. Consequently, to establish and strengthen peaceful relations and harmony in the human race, religious freedom must be given effective constitutional protection everywhere and that highest of man's rights and duties—to lead a religious life with freedom in society—must be respected.
> (Flannery, *op. cit.*, I, 812).

Contrast this, dear reader, with these words of Leo XIII in *Immortale dei,* (Cap. 32):

> ...the State is acting against the laws and dictates of nature whenever it permits the license of opinion and of action to lead minds astray from truth and souls away from the practice of virtue.

The declaration rightly reiterated the traditional Church teaching that no one must be forced into the Church against his will. But it went on beyond that to say that no restrictions must be put on the individual's practice of a non-Catholic religion (such as forbidding proseletyzing, employment of Catholic servants, public demonstrations, etc.). Completely absent was any concept of truth versus error—there was only the "search for truth in freedom."

It is often argued (most persuasively by Fr. Brian Harrison in his *Religious Liberty and Contraception*; rather poorly by Likoudis and Whitehead in *The Pope, The Council, and the Mass*) that the Religious Liberty declaration did not in fact attempt to alter the Church's teaching. Fr. Harrison points out the extensive word hedging used, and the fact that the prologue forced onto the document at the last moment by Conservative Fathers reaffirms that the Catholic is the true religion; that the individual thus has a responsibility to seek *Catholic* truth, and that "it leaves intact the traditional Catholic teaching on the moral duty of individuals and societies toward the true religion and the one Church of Christ." He admits that subsequent interpretation and practice (such as the Concordats with Italy and Spain concluded after the Council) reflect a non-traditional understanding of the document, but he insists that an orthodox interpretation of the language employed is possible. This may be so. But the whole point of Church teaching is *clarity*, not *ambiguity*. Saints suffered and were exiled and martyred for upholding '$\mathrm{\acute{o}\mu oουσιos}$ over '$\mathrm{o\mu oιουσιov}$, although the latter might, possibly, be capable of an orthodox interpretation. It is the hallmark of Church teaching that it is clear, not murky. The fact that the Holy See and the Catholic episcopate worldwide has opted on the basis of this declaration for a non-traditional approach to the question must surely count for something.

The decree on Ecumenism, *Unitatis redingratio*, is a similar case. If the Religious Liberty declaration was an implicit rejection of the maxim "Error has no rights," then this one in the same manner dispatches "Outside the Church there is no Salvation." Here too we have the seesawing. "On the one hand, things are white ... but on the other they are black!" Regardless of the opinions of such strongly orthodox writers as Fr. Harrison, your present author must side with the 400 Fathers who refused to sign either document.

But it is not only Conservatives who have problems with Council documents. No, certain documents have been ignored by the Liberals. A typical example is *Sacrosanctum concilium*, the decree on the liturgy. The document orders non-specific revision of the liturgy, laying down ambiguous directions:

36. (1) The use of the Latin language, with due respect to the particular law, is to be preserved in the Latin rites. (2) But since the use of the vernacular, whether in the Mass, the administration of the sacraments, or in other parts of the liturgy, may frequently be of great advantage to the people, a wider use may be made of it.

So, the Latin is to be preserved, eh? With due respect to particular law? Which law? Where, how, and when? As for the vernacular, how could it be of great advantage to the people? The average Catholic in 1963 no more wanted the vernacular in the Mass than he wanted dancers in it. Post-Conciliar experience has shown that it has failed to retain large numbers of Catholics, nor has it recruited new ones. But how did the Church observe the injunction that the Latin was to be preserved? We shall let Fr. Flannery speak himself:

> ...restrictions on the use of the vernacular were progressively lifted in the face of representations by hierarchies from all over the world, until by 1971 the use of the vernacular in public Masses was left entirely to the judgement of episcopal conferences, to the judgment of individual priests for public Masses, and of the ordinary for divine office in private, in common, or in choir.
> Strangely enough, the ruling that translations of the breviary had to carry the Latin text as well was not formally revoked, but it was no longer applied after a while.
> (Flannery, *op. cit.*, I, 39).

So it was with Council orders on retention of Gregorian Chant and polyphony at Mass, and of the teaching of Latin in seminaries. Because the plain fact of the matter was that the staff of most episcopal conferences, the Roman bodies "implementing" the Conciliar decrees, many of the individual bishops, and countless theologians, etc., all had a vested interest in transforming Catholicism into something alien. The result was a burst of legislation which, apparently issued or tolerated by the highest offices in the Church, effectively made the Church unrecognizable in less than a decade.

But where does that leave the Council itself? As was said of the Reformation, "what was good in it was not new, and what was new was not good." Richard O'Connor, writing in the *Homiletic and Pastoral Review* (July 1981, pp. 5-6) put it thusly:

> What is more important is to make clear the *kind* of assent demanded of the faithful...What this means, as Pope John Paul II never tires of emphasizing when referring to Vatican II, is that it is to be interpreted in the light of Tradition, of other Councils, and Papal Encyclicals; and, where found to be in conflict with these, disregarded.

So, you might ask your author whether or not Vatican II was really an Ecumenical Council. Well, all the Catholic bishops were gathered to solemnly deliberate; the fact that it was all for naught in terms of dogma is beside the point. Those who demand that the Holy See one day openly disavow it ignore history. What is more likely to happen is that, after the present crisis is surmounted, it will be flushed down the memory hole with Constantinople II, Constance, and Basel. Present on the lists forever as: "21st Ecumenical Council: Vatican II, 1962-65. Dealt with pastoral problems." There safely filed, scholars in 2567 will breeze over it to look at more impressive and important Councils, just as we breeze by Lateran V to look at Trent.

Unhappily, we are not looking back comfortably from a possibly more contented future; we are living in the midst of these events. "It is all well and good," you may say to me, "to ignore Vatican II, and concentrate on the immemorial teachings and devotions of the Church. But Catholic life is not just reading the Fathers and saying the rosary in front of the family Sacred Heart picture. It is attending a parish, sending my children to school, and performing my civic duties in accord with Church teaching. You say that this is next to impossible outside the declining numbers of conservative parishes, and impossible even there if I want the practices of the immemorial Church *in toto*. What to do?"

Well, as one might imagine, the first reaction would be to appeal to the Pope. Paul VI was not unaware that things were out of control at the Council. He took decisive action there: he wept. Then he added codicils that were ignored.

In response to all the horrible things happening throughout the universal Church, the Pope responded firmly in various well reported 1972 statements:

> By means of some fissure the smoke of Satan has entered the temple of God ... One no longer trusts the Church ... It was believed that after the Council there would be a day of sunshine in the history of the Church .... There came instead a day of clouds, storms, and darkness, of search and uncertainty ... through an adverse power; his name is the devil ... Perhaps the Lord has called me not to govern and save the Church, but to suffer for her, and to make it clear that he and no one else, guides and saves her.

In the face of such unparalleled confusion in the Church, such a declaration could be taken as an effective abdication. His Holiness would do nothing to stem the tide, would not attempt to be the Rock of the Church, but would be terribly upset by it all. There is a Latin maxim; "what is permissible to Jove, is not permissible to an Ox." By the same token, what is permissible to an ox, is not permissible to Jove.

Many have compared Paul VI to Hamlet; for he acquiesced to practically anything, no matter how dreadful. Oh, he might put up a token defense, as against Communion in the hand in *Memoriale domini*. But if enough bishops backed a measure, he generally gave in. He did at least repeat the Church's teaching on contraception in *Humanae vitae* against much (including episcopal) opposition in 1968. What could we say of him? In his day, it seemed (on a practical basis) that there was no one in charge at the Vatican at all. The local hierarchies did just as they pleased, only invoking Papal authority when useful in quashing orthodox resistance to them; in response, droves of Catholics in the developed nations either left or simply dropped out. Hamlet? Nay, this Pontificate reminds your author of Chorus' last speech in *Henry V*:

> Henry the Sixth, in infant bands crown'd king
> Of France and England, did this king succeed;
> Whose state so many had the managing
> That they lost France and made his England bleed:

In the United States, soon after the Council, various voices were raised in protest against the changes which had occurred. Most notable, perhaps, was *Triumph* magazine. Published by Brent Bozell, it featured such writers as Molnar and Wilhelmsen; associated with it also were *John Wisner, Gary Potter*, and *Farley Clinton*, to name a few. Originally closely connected with Buckley (Bozell's brother-in-law) and the National Review, Triumph came more and more to represent an integral Catholic point of view, and so its staff began to see in "Conservatism" simply the Right Wing of the national liberalism. Obviously, a break could not be far in the future.

There were likewise American priests like *Frs. Gommar DePauw* and *James Wathen* who, at an early date, foresaw the problems which were about to fall on the unsuspecting heads of Catholic America.

But all of these prophetic voices were considered eccentric by mainstream Catholics. They preferred to do as they were told; this appeared to be simply imitating Methodists. Given all of this, when the youth of America began to look beyond Americanism for answers, all they could see in Catholicism was more of the same. Thus was a splendid opportunity to evangelize the nation lost.

The Space Program

LBJ, his administration rendered ineffective by national unrest, decided not to run again. In the election of 1968, his place was taken by his Vice President, Hubert Humphrey. Humphrey, however lost to the

Republican, Richard Nixon. Thus, eight years after his defeat by JFK, Nixon found himself President-elect of a very different nation.

During all the political and social turmoil, one thing had gone forward: the nation's Space Program. The National Aeronautics and Space Administration (NASA) had presided over the launching of manned spaceships.

First of these was the Mercury series, comprising a one-man capsule designed to revolve around the Earth. On February 20, 1962, John Glenn successfully completed orbit in Outer Space.

Three years later, the first manned Gemini capsule, with two crew-members, took its place on March 23, 1965. Before the last Gemini was launched on November 11, 1966, astronauts had space-walked. Now the great race to put a man on the Moon, announced by President Kennedy, was on in earnest.

There were a number of mishaps with the Apollo project, as the three-passenger capsule was named. But at last, on July 20, 1969, Neil Armstrong set foot on the Moon. He did not claim it for the United States, since this country had signed an Outer Space convention under U.N. auspices resigning all territory outside the atmosphere. But a great dream had been accomplished, a great triumph for American technology. As long as Man had existed, he had dreamt of the Moon; now he had walked there.

If the Science Fiction movies of the 1950s—*Forbidden Planet, The Day The Earth Stood Still, This Island Earth*, and of course, the incomparable *Plan 9 From Outer Space*—had not precisely predicted the actual event, they had helped create a climate in which the public would support the measure. Were heaven to be cut off from them as myth, they would settle for Space.

Your author vividly remembers the Moon-landing. As a nine-year old, it did not occur to him that it was in fact 25 years after the failure of the von Stauffenberg plot in Berlin. It is perhaps ironic that this extraordinary triumph of technocracy occurred on the anniversary of such a crushing defeat for Christian Chivalry.

AFTERWORD

So at last we have come to the end of our tale. It is not really the end of course, because history, American or otherwise, can have no end until the final trumpet when the graves give up their dead. But we leave off at the utmost triumph of the American idea; Man's conquest of the Moon.

What things we should dwell upon were we to continue! The end of the war in Vietnam, and the agony of Watergate; the Reagan "revolution" and the fall of Communism; the legalization of abortion and homosexuality, and continued decay of Church and State. But in these we enter into the realm of current events.

What is to be made of the tapestry which has gone before? What patterns can be discerned? At times we have made some comment upon them in the course of this history, but having come to the end, let us look at them a little more closely.

American history is the tale of two simultaneous developments: the gradual weeding out of the practices and beliefs of old Christendom on the one hand, and their replacement with an ever more elaborate ethos which promised a purely secular salvation. In place of the organic national life offered by the first, America received, as it were, a simulacrum of nationhood, the artificiality of which was effectively concealed by economic prosperity.

The Puritan Fathers came here originally to establish a commonwealth free of "Papist" influences. Despite this, they were men of a formerly Catholic culture, and sketched out for their heretical conventicles a place in society roughly equivalent to that of the Church in fully-Catholic societies. A whisper of this remains in the location of Congregational and/or Unitarian churches of the village commons of New England, echoing faintly the setting of plazas throughout Europe and Latin America.

When the Enlightenment and its accompanying Masonry hit these shores, they spread most rapidly among the sons of the Puritans, gradually destroying the place even of the Bible in their minds, but leaving their Calvinist attitudes and anti-Catholicism intact. This odd mixture became the intellectually dominant force in the thirteen colonies. Under its influence the ruling circles here joined forces with their Whig equivalents in England, and destroyed in America the second most important institution of Christendom, the Monarchy.

After the Revolution, "Americanism" became a religion of its own. In its name, that third key element of Christendom, local liberties (called "subsidiarity" by the Popes, and "States' Rights" in this country) was at first gradually and then forcefully put an end to. One after another, French and Spanish influences within our boundaries were conquered and then assimilated. The unholy trinity of Noah Webster, Horace Mann, and finally John Dewey, refashioned American education from its original aim to being purely a tool of social engineering. Through it, generations of immigrants from abroad were systematically "cleansed" of their cultures, and made loyal adherents of the Americanist faith.

Interior unity achieved, and financial success secured, the Americanist religion traveled overseas, first to Latin America and thence to the world. In every case, the wealth and power of this nation were committed by her leadership to the destruction of any Catholic political power which remained. Thus did Spain and Austria-Hungary go under, and thus were innumerable gimcrack separation-of-Church-and-State republics ushered in throughout the globe. The rise of Communism permitted the installation of Americanist values under the guise of "freedom" in our allies' societies, even as Communism's fall has allowed the same in the former enemy nations. Pornography is, after all, one of our primary exports to such nations. Now, acceptance of contraception and abortion is a must for any struggling country to receive U.S. aid.

Of the institutions of Christendom, the family is the one which has survived longest under Americanist rule. But having been first undermined via contraception and abortion, it is now the direct focus of attack, via such things as redefining child abuse and recognizing "domestic partnerships" as fully legitimate alternatives to marriage. In truth, all that remains now is the individual.

Nor will he be allowed to remain beyond the reach of the State for long. Through euthanasia, increased government monitoring of such "vices" as tobacco and alcohol, and of course the ever more thoroughly enforced expression of "politically correct" speech and behavior, the individual too must become increasingly the ward of an all-powerful government. In return, however, said individual will have access to ever more refined methods of entertainment. In a word, Aldous Huxley's *Brave New World* appears to be en route—this latter being, of course, the "Universal Republic" dreamed of by the Freemasonry of the Enlightenment.

Over the past few centuries, then, first Church, then King, then local liberties, then family, and at last the individual have been disposed of. What has been the attitude of the Church, then?

When the Church enters a heathen land, it is usually her first interest to convert its people as quickly as she may. This includes baptizing whatever local customs may be compatible with Catholic teaching; the same is done with native institutions. The reason for this (and for the frequent martyrdoms of missionaries and converts which often result) is simply and purely the salvation of souls. When a country becomes primarily or entirely Catholic, the public face of that nation changes; there emerges the Catholic State, which recognizes as its primary duty the assistance of the Church in her Divine mission. Thus it was in old Europe; thus also (although not so well known) in Latin America; thus at last in those parts of Asia and Africa which were thoroughly evangelized.

But in the United States this pattern was in no wise followed. From the first, the Catholic community in the thirteen colonies was a despised minority; its lay leadership by the time of the Revolution was committed to a policy of accommodation with the ruling classes, and its spiritual leadership purely to servicing the needs of those already Catholic. There could be no question of converting the nation.

Independence brought forth new opportunities. The rush of immigrants from abroad increased the numbers of American Catholics tremendously. The response of "native" Americans to this was to be found in such incidents as the Know-Nothing riots. "Nativism" of this sort, although re-erupting periodically, was not put an end to by the growth of Catholicism—quite the contrary. Such men as James Cardinal Gibbons assured Protestant Americans that the Church regarded the United States as perfect *in their current religious and political condition*. In a word, co-existence rather than conversion was the goal of American Catholicism. Any stirring on the part of the Catholic faithful in the direction of more integral Catholicity was sternly squelched by the hierarchy.

Although condemned by Leo XIII, Americanism in its form as a Catholic heresy became in the end the dominant belief in the Church in this country. When Modernism arose in Europe, it was brought over to this country, swiftly germinating in a soil well prepared for it. The efforts of our country overseas left America the dominant military, economic, political, cultural, and social force on the globe—which development was echoed in the Church. Vatican II signaled acceptance of Americanism by the leadership of the Church—particularly as regards Religious Freedom, Ecumenism, and Separation of Church and State. From the beginning, it would appear that Rome had not realized the danger Americanism posed—had not realized until it was too late.

Here we stand then, in the first part of the 21th Century. Many believe the role of the Church to be that of a mere spiritual cheerleader for the New World Order. Certainly, this would appear to be a legitimate extension of the role of the American Church under the headship of such as Cardinal Gibbons and Archbishop Ireland.

All of this having been said, American history appears much of the time as a chronicle of lost opportunities, of victories for the wrong side—in a word, as tragedy. But if tragedy it be, said tragedy is not a result of any especial evil in the American character, but of cowardice and dereliction on the part of the country's Catholics.

Where then, do we stand? In what does true patriotism consist for an orthodox Catholic American? How is he able to love the country of his birth, which has done so much to destroy his Faith at home and abroad, and which incarnates, so to speak, the principles of secularism to which he must ever be opposed?

The first is to identify in the country's history and present state those strands which are most acceptable to the Faith—for in truth, there is much to love and admire in this country. In the settlements of the French and Spanish in the Southwest and the Mississippi and Great Lakes basins; in the towns founded by Catholic immigrants where some of their culture yet remains; and even in those regions such as the Appalachians and the rural South and New England where a bit of the once Catholic ethos of the British Isles survives; in these and other places, folklore and song provide what might one day be a foundation for a truly Catholic culture. On many Indian reservations, one yet finds some of the spirit or at least artifacts of the missionaries, like Frs. Serra and De Smet. Every Catholic American should know something of the original settlers of the spot in this country where he lives, as well as of his own ancestors.

For in these United States, as we have seen, are settled people from virtually every country in the world. In microcosm we can see the building blocks of that "one fair realm of charity" which the hymn for the Feast of Christ the King asks God to create by enfolding "all lands, all tribes." Despite the ever-grinding forces of assimilation, enough remains of the cultures which settled here to offer some alternative to the Americanist vision.

Building blocks, however, are not the finished product, anymore than savage Germanic tribes and the decadent Roman Empire were themselves together Christendom. Then as now, it required the vivifying force of the Faith to give those stones life. What we have is in fact a half-life, as has been said; whether we are to be Pinocchio or Frankenstein depends on how and whether the life-giving sacraments are applied to this nation—not as private practice, but as public act.

We saw that Pius XI declared in his 1926 *Quas primas*: "When men once recognize, both in private and in public life, that Christ is King, society will at last receive the great blessings of real liberty, well-ordered discipline, peace and harmony." The Pontiff goes on to describe what great blessings would result to individuals, families, nations, and the world at large, were this done. But practically speaking, it can only happen if this nation is converted. There is where true patriotism is to be found for the American Catholic. Such a one who blithely accepts the religious status quo in America, as did Carroll, as did Gibbons, as did Spellman, is no friend to his country, its peoples, or their liberty.

For what will happen if the United States is not converted? At the moment, this writer sees two possible futures. Either present trends will continue, or they will not.

If they do, the vision of the Founding Fathers will be achieved, and this nation will be the center of a worldwide and despotic republic which will not only grind down its subjects' humanity, but cause them to love their chains and lose their souls. The unspeakable can become quite comfortable if dwelt with long enough. It might be hard to see a worse alternative.

Still, one might. The other possibility is that this technocracy in which we live will collapse of its own weight, its own sterility, its own lack-of-birth-rate. Then will the denizens of the Third World, stripped of Christian love, but well-educated in secular greed to envy the goods of the wealthier nations, rise up and drown them in blood. Or perhaps, beyond the calculations of our leaders, famine, plague, and natural disaster will shatter our fragile infrastructure. How then would our fellow-citizens deal with the great realities of fear and horror, unshielded by technology nor consoled by the religion which it replaced?

Nor let it be thought that political action alone or even primarily can save the Great Republic. One of our regular errors has been to think that Catholics allied with Protestants in order to win victory at the polls for this principle or against that abuse will affect much in the long run. These battles can be useful in the immediate; but they have tended to take our eyes off the main goal and only true solution for the country's ills: the conversion of America. The stories of Fr. Coughlin, Msgr. Ryan, and the Catholic Worker (to say nothing of today's Pro-Life Movement) should tell us something.

Mr. Paul Blanshard (whom we met earlier), an avid hater of the Church, fully acquainted himself with her social teachings in order to show the difference between Catholicism and Americanism. He, of course, espoused the latter. Nevertheless, his contrasting the two religion's beliefs on important social issues is revealing:

> ***Divorce:*** The Catholic Church says: "The State has no right to grant divorces since it has no authority to annul a valid marriage." The federal and state governments disagree. The American people now permit divorce in every state.

Marriage: The Church refuses to recognize marriages as valid when non-Catholic clergymen or public officials perform marriage ceremonies for Catholics. The people, through the United States government and state governments refuse to discriminate against marriages of Catholics by non-Catholic clergymen.

Birth Control: The Church says that all use of contraceptives by non-Catholics or Catholics is illegal under Church law. The people in all but two states of the United States permit doctors to give contraceptive advice to patients. [In 1967 the U.S. Supreme Court abolished any and all restrictions on birth control].

Education: The Church teaches that Catholic schools should be supported by public (non-Catholic and Catholic) taxpayers and that priests should have the right to censor public school text books. The people have enacted both state and federal laws to make *direct* contributions to Catholic schools illegal, and nominally they reject Catholic censorship in public schools.

Sterilization: The people in twenty-seven states permit some eugenic sterilization of certain insane, feeble-minded, and criminal citizens under certain specific safeguards. The Church says this is illegal and immoral, except as a specific penalty for crime.

Therapeutic abortion: The Church says that therapeutic abortion is murder even if it is absolutely necessary to save the life of a mother. The people in all states permit therapeutic abortion when it is indicated to save the life or health of a mother. [In 1973, the Supreme Court legalized abortion under all circumstances, under any pretext whatsoever. Mean old Church opposed this too!]
(*American Freedom and Catholic Power*, p. 22).

Obviously, Blanshard here identifies the mandate of the rulership with the will of the people; this identification has, through the history recounted, been shown to be false. But in the minds of many Americans, whatever their own views on these topics the same identification is made.

Regardless, all of these topics strike at the very heart of a people; the non-Catholic view has prevailed, and the result has been the near-complete transformation of a Puritanical-Masonic regime into a purely inhuman one—and all in the name of freedom.

As recounted earlier, Blanshard declared that American Catholics had a hidden agenda to "subject" this nation to the Church's social teachings. We have seen the great outrage this brought about in U.S. Catholic circles, and the resulting dispute between Frs. John Courtney Murray and Joseph C. Fenton regarding relations between Church and State. But Blanshard had outlined what he believed would become of the vaunted American Democracy, were the Catholics to gain political power. This was a list of three amendments to the Constitution.

The first he called the "Christian Commonwealth Amendment:"

1. The United States [are] a Catholic Republic, and the Catholic Apostolic and Roman religion is the sole religion of the nation.

2. The authority of the Roman Catholic Church is the most exalted of all authorities; nor can it be looked upon as inferior to the power of the United States government, or in any manner dependent upon it, since the Catholic Church as such is a sovereign power.

3. Priests and members of religious orders of the Roman Catholic Church who violate the law are to be tried by an ecclesiastical court of the Roman Catholic Church, and may, only with the consent of the competent Catholic authority, be tried by the courts of the United States or the states.

4. Apostate priests or those incurring the censure of the Roman Catholic Church cannot be employed in any teaching post or any office or employment in which they have immediate contact with the public.

5. Non-Catholic faiths are tolerated, but public ceremonies and manifestations other than those of the Roman Catholic religion will not be permitted.

6. The First Amendment to the Constitution of the United States is hereby repealed.

This shocker was to be followed up by the "Christian Education Amendment:"

1. American religious education belongs pre-eminently to the Roman Catholic Church, by means of a double title in the supernatural order, conferred exclusively upon her by God Himself.

2. The Roman Catholic Church has the inalienable right to supervise the entire education of her children in all educational institutions in the United States, public or private, not merely in regard to the religious instruction given in such institutions, but in regard to every other branch of learning and every regulation in so far as religion and morality are concerned.

3. Compulsory education in public schools exclusively shall be unlawful in any state of the union.

4. It shall be unlawful for any neutral or non-Catholic school to enroll any Catholic child without permission of the Church.

5. Since neutral schools are contrary to the fundamental principles of education, public schools in the United States are lawful only when both religious instruction and every other subject taught are permeated with Catholic piety.

6. The governments of the United States and of the States are permitted to operate their own schools for military and civic training without supervision by the Roman Catholic Church, provided they do not injure the rights of said Church, and provided that only the Roman Catholic Church shall have the power to impart religious instruction in such schools.

7. With due regard to special circumstances, co-education shall be unlawful in any educational institution in the United States whose students have attained the age of adolescence.

8. The governments of the United States and of the states shall encourage and assist the Roman Catholic Church by appropriate measures in the exercise of the Church's supreme mission as educator.

Then at last came the "Christian Family Amendment:"

1. The government of the United States, desirous of restoring to the institution of matrimony, which is the basis of the family, that dignity conformable to the traditions of its people, assigns as civil effects of the sacrament of matrimony all that is assigned to it by the Canon Law of the Roman Catholic Church.

2. No matrimonial contract in the United States that involves a Catholic can be valid unless it is in accordance with the Canon Law of the Roman Catholic Church.

3. Marriages of non-Catholics are subject to the civil authority of the state, but all civil laws that contradict the Canon Law of the Roman Catholic Church are hereby declared null and void.

4. All marriages are indissoluble, and the divorce of all persons is prohibited throughout the territory of the United States: provided that nothing herein shall affect the right of annulment and remarriage in accordance with the Canon Law of the Roman Catholic Church.

5. Attempted mixed marriages or unions between members of the Roman Catholic Church and non-Catholics are null and void, unless a special dispensation is obtained from the ecclesiastical authority of the Catholic Church.

6. Birth Control, or any act that deliberately frustrates the natural power to generate life, is a crime.

7. Direct abortion is murder of the innocent even when performed through motives of misguided pity when the life of a mother is gravely imperiled.

8. Sterilization of any human being is prohibited except as an infliction of grave punishment under the authority of the government for a crime committed.

This supposed "Catholic Master Plan" for America received much criticism from Catholic and non-Catholic critics of Blanshard alike. But Blanshard rightly defended it, declaring (p. 305):

> I remember a verse from Job which is appropriate at this moment: "If I justify myself, mine own mouth shall condemn me." That is meant for Catholic liberals whose temperature has been rising while they have been reading these three amendments. As most of my readers have doubtless guessed, there is not a single original word in my entire three Catholic amendments. They are mosaics of official Catholic doctrine. *Every concept, almost every line and phrase, has been plagiarized line by line from Catholic documents.* The most important phrases are derived from the highest documents [sic!] of Catholicism, the encyclicals of the Popes. The provisions on education come from Pius XI's *Christian Education of Youth*, and those on family life from his *Casti Connubii*, both of them accepted universally in the Catholic Church as the Bibles of present-day educational and family policy. A few provisions are taken directly from Canon Law, the recent laws of Catholic countries like Spain, and the 1929 Concordat between Mussolini and the Vatican, all of which have been publicly approved by Catholic authorities. Only place-names and enabling clauses have been added to give the Papal principles local application. The sources are listed in the notes.

Needless to say, the principles contained in these "amendments" are inimical to everything most Americans hold dear. What Blanshard could not have realized was that not only were American Catholic Liberals sincere in their repudiation of them, their strength was such that in a mere decade and a half, they and their foreign allies would force the Church (even in Spain, Italy, and Ireland) to *de facto* acceptance of the American way. The authentic social teachings of the Church were presented by the governing circles of the Church as merely the opinions of certain Popes or else the much-attacked Roman Curia. Even so late as 1992, Bishop Mark J. Hurley, former ordinary of Santa Rosa, California, could write:

> These [the cases of Fr. Robert Drinan, pro-abortion Jesuit ex-Congressman; Fr. Charles Curran, former CUA dissenting moral theologian; and Archbishop Raymond Hunthausen of Seattle] and other incidents rightly caused legitimate concern in both Catholic and non-Catholic circles. The Roman Curia, notoriously uninstructed and untutored in things American, and hiding behind the anonymity of a

Byzantine bureaucracy, continued to make mischief right into the 1990s to the despair of many bishops as well as others...

The repressions, quiet censorship, removal from office, and other actions gave non-Catholics, in particular, grounds for concern as to where the Church stood on basic liberties, the American bishops to the contrary notwithstanding.

Thanks in large part to the Roman curial actions over the years, two centuries to be exact, those who viewed the American Catholics with distrust were not fighting straw men. Thoughtful men and women asked fair questions; demagogues ran wild (*The Unholy Ghost*, p.52).

Despite the fact that today the Vatican would be much more likely to discipline a theologian who upheld literally Pius IX's *Syllabus of Errors* or Pius XI's *Quas primas* and *Quadragesimo anno*, here Bishop Hurley identifies the curia's spasmodic efforts to address the most notorious attacks of Catholic dogma and morals with everything anti-Catholics hated in her social teachings. Obviously, so long as the American hierarchy are largely of such mind, the bones of Paul Blanshard may rest as easily as his eternal reward permits.

Yet it is precisely the sort of measures Blanshard describes which are required to save this nation from the twin threats of dystopia and bloody anarchy which appear to await us. Obviously, they are a bare minimum; but think on the benefits which would accrue! Were something like his Christian Family Amendment passed, all the evils which have disrupted the family and reduced the young folk of this country to rootless and selfish eternal children would be alleviated. The birthrate of the native-born would rise, thus saving us from an eroding tax-base (with the threat of Social Security's collapse). If marriages were permanent, the evils and crime resulting from broken homes would be alleviated.

The educational amendment, banishing the spirit of Webster, Mann, and Dewey from the classroom, would accentuate improving conditions for America's children, and so for her future. In place of what was social engineering and has become often a physically dangerous day-care center for adolescents, the classroom would become a place whose products would be able to think rationally, would have the academic and technical skills to compete in the job market (and assist the nation in competing with foreign countries), and would have the moral background necessary for a productive and happy adulthood.

Above all, the Commonwealth amendment would place this country in a position to receive the benefits promised by Pius XI in *Quas primas* in terms of societal harmony and solidarity. It would further lay a foundation for a reorganization of the country's political and economic life along the lines of *Rerum novarum, Quadragesimo anno*, and the rest—in a word, the beginning of a truly just society.

But political action will not achieve this. No party, no political action committee for a major corporation, no lobbyist group, will push for such a program; in truth, it cannot be legislated, it cannot be ordered. Had the first Christian Emperor, Philip the Arabian, ordered the Roman Empire to become thoroughly Christian in every detail—in a word, to become Christendom—it would not have happened. Fiats from from above did not create Christendom, although in time they could destroy it. Rather, the long work of missionaries—lay and religious—over many centuries, and the ever increasing and deeper Catholicism of succeeding generations did so. The Germanic warrior code became chivalry; classical philosophy and literature became Christian; the Roman patricians and barbarian chiefs became the European nobility; and so on.

In this same way must this country be converted. But to do so, we orthodox American Catholics must give up our habitual ways of looking at our country and our places in it. To do less is an insult to God, and (seeing that the survival of this nation depends upon it) a form of treason.

To begin with, let us realize that we do not live in a Christian land. It is a heathen nation, and ever has been. Its political factions and feuds (save where they directly concern Catholic interests or moral issues) are for the most part of no more moment than those of warring tribes in New Guinea. Our primary reason for being here is to make more Catholics, not to push for sound money or a clean environment (although such activity—apart from short term gains for the community—provide exposure to sympathetic people who might be willing to listen to our religious message). Yet here we must beware of the opposite thing happening; cooperation with friendly non-Catholics in the political sphere must not have the effect of legitimizing their religion for us. The danger of the missionary "going native" is an ever present one.

Yet we cannot really be missionaries unless we are integral Catholics ourselves. In part, this is a question of learning everything possible about the Faith: her dogmas, her history, and her practices. The English *Denzinger* and Dom Prosper Gueranger's *The Liturgical Year*, as a bare minimum, should be in every Catholic home. To the study of the Faith should go the energy and interest that are often directed to other, less important goals, such as the memorizing of sports scores.

Beyond this, however, we have to actively reconquer our own minds. Rather than accept what is given us on television or in the movies, we should try to fill our heads with the Catholic legends and tales of valor, like the stories of King Arthur and Charlemagne. The Catholic-inspired folk customs of song, cookery, and celebration native either to our ancestors or the region we live in (or both) should determine the atmosphere of our homes, in addition to the presence of statues and paintings of the saints. Let us keep Advent until Christmas Eve, keep Christmas until the Epiphany, feast during Carnival, and fast during Lent. In a word, to the the degree that we can, we need to make our own homes foretastes of the America that ought to be.

But it is not enough to do this for ourselves. Practically speaking, our non- and fallen-away Catholic friends and relatives are the obvious field for us to work in. Once we begin to think of these people not as folk of whom we are fond yet who are spiritually secure, but as souls who need the light of Faith whom (in all likelihood) we may be the only ones capable of bringing it to, all sorts of methods of doing this will suggest themselves.

One of the most obvious is the sending of religious Christmas cards to all our acquaintances, Jewish, Protestant, or whatever. Fear not that they will be offended; after all, they are not worried about offending you when they send "X-mas" cards bearing pictures of reindeer—which Catholics should find offensive.

Similarly, invite such folk to Baptisms, First Communions, and Confirmations. There is no better advertisement for the Faith to a non-Catholic, than to see someone of whom he is fond participating devoutly in the liturgy and/or in para-liturgical customs. The same goes for your home celebrations of feastdays (and, say, serving Lenten meals when friends pop by during that season. This gives you the chance to explain the whole concept, as they look glumly at their tuna casserole).

Above all, be ready to speak about and defend the Faith under any and all circumstances. When your co-workers are only too happy to talk about their children's bar mitzvahs and Sunday schools, be sure to speak of your own children's catechism classes and Christmas pageants.

It is not an easy task; in truth, if we all do our part, the likelihood is that one day Catholics in this country will be martyred. It is always the case in lands where the Faithful do their job. Martyrdom was presented to us by the Know Nothings and the Nativists; our response was to burn incense on the altars of the gods. We have profited materially, but lost our souls thereby.

When our fathers converted the Empire, through the grace of God they brought off a miracle. We do not think of it that way, but through their work, pagan Gaul and its pagan Frank invaders became France, the oldest daughter of the Church; the wreck of Roman Britain, seized by the bloodthirsty Saxons, became England, Our Lady's Dowry; pagan Spain saw after her conversion her Visigothic invaders embrace the Faith, and when Goth and Spaniard were subjugated by the Moors that Faith sustained them through eight centuries of reconquest and expansion into the Americas. Outside the boundaries of the Empire, the Hungarians,

Poles, Czechs, Slovaks, Lithuanians, Croats and Slovenes formed their national identities at the same time that they accepted Catholicism. Much the same occurred with the Scandinavians and Russians, though we do not think of this because of their later defection. Even in lands long conquered by Islam, the Copts and other Christians of the Near East allow one the chance to see what Egypt and Syria were before that calamity.

Imagine, then, what may lie before our descendants! True enough, if we do our duty, the nearer future will see persecution. But farther off, what are now mere potentials might have at last become real. Think of the regions of our country, with their ways and histories! New England and the South, the Midwest and Prairies, the Great Basin and the Northwest, all of them expressing together experiences of Catholicism that are as ingrained, organic, and natural, as anything in Jalisco, Brittany, or Sicily! We cannot, of course, know what the final result will be, in culture, economics, or politics, anymore than the Apostles could foresee what Christendom would produce. But we can know that something even more important than even the rise of a new Catholic civilization will happen at last: the salvation of countless millions of individual souls—including, if we play our part, our own.

To say again, then, for us, patriotism means evangelization—bringing our fellow citizens what they need both in this life and the next. Our failure to do so, or their failure to receive it, will endanger this country no end. It were well to conclude with words of Orestes Brownson earlier quoted:

> Time was when I paraded my Americanism, in order to repel the charge that an American cannot become a convert to the Church without ceasing to feel and act as an American patriot. I have lived long enough to snap my fingers at all charges of that sort. I love my country, and, in her hour of trial, I and my sons, Catholics like myself, did our best to preserve her integrity, and save her Constitution; and there is no sacrifice in my power that I would not make to bring "my kinsmen after the flesh" to Christ; but, after all, the Church is my true country, and the faithful are my real countrymen. Let the American people become truly Catholic and submissive children of the Holy Father, and their Republic is safe; let them refuse and seek safety for the secular order in sectarianism or secularism, and nothing can save it from destruction (*Brownson's Quarterly Review*, January 1873, pp. 2-3).

Appendices

All of the Appendices are available on our website:

http://www.tumblarhouse.com/puritans-empire-appendix.php

BIBLIOGRAPHY

Adams, Henry, *The Education of Henry Adams,* Boston: Houghton Mifflin, 1971
Adams, Henry, *History of the United States During the Administrations of Thomas Jefferson,* New York: Viking Press, 1986
Adams, Henry, *History of the United States During the Administrations of James Madison,* New York: Viking Press, 1986
Agar, Herbert and Allen Tate, eds., *Who Owns America,* New York: Houghton Mifflin, 1936 (Willis Fisher, Douglas Jerrold, Hilaire Belloc)
Angle, Paul M., *Crossroads: 1913,* Chicago: Rand McNally, 1963
Archer, Jules, *The Plot to seize the White House,* New York: Hawthorn Books, 1973
Arias, Bishop David, *Spanish Roots of America,* Bloomington: OSV Publishing, 1992
Bailey, Thomas A., *Wilson and the Peacemakers,* New York: Macmillan, 1947
Baker, Leonard, *Roosevelt and Pearl Harbor,* New York: Macmillan, 1970
Barck, Jr., Oscar Theodore, Nelson Manfred Blake, *Since 1900,* New York: Macmillan, 1947
Barry, O.S.B., Colman, *The Catholic Church and German Americans,* Milwaukee: The Bruce Publishing Company, 1953
Bauer, K. Jack, *The Mexican War 1846-1848,* New York: Macmillan, 1974
Billington, Ray Allen, *The Far Western Frontier, 1830-1860,* New York: Harper and Brothers, 1956
Blanshard, Paul, *American Freedom and Catholic Power,* Boston: Beacon Press, 1949
Bocca, Geoffrey, *Kings Without Thrones,* New York: The Dial Press, 1959
Bogle, Joanna and James, *A Heart For Europe,* Leominster: Fowler Wright Books, 1990
Bolton, Herbert E., *Wider Horizons of American History,* Notre Dame: University of Notre Dame Press, 1967, 191 pp.
Bonsal, Stephen, *Suitors and Suppliants: The Little Nations at Versailles,* Port Washington: Kennikat Press, 1969
Botkin, R.A., *A Civil War Treasury Of Tales, Legends And Folklore,* New York: Random House, 1960
Bradford, Gamaliel, *Confederate Portraits,* Freeport: Books For Libraries Press, 1968
Brandt, Nat, *The Man Who Tried to Burn New York,* Syracuse: Syracuse University Press, 1986
Brault, Gerard J., *The French-Canadian Heritage in New England,* Hanover: University Press of New England, 1986
Brooks, Van Wyck, *The World of Washington Irving,* New York: E.P. Dutton and Co., 1944
Buck, Paul H., *The Road to Reunion 1865-1900,* Boston: Little, Brown and Company, 1937
Cannadine, David, *The Decline and Fall of the British Aristocracy,* New York: Anchor Books, 1990
Caponnetto, Antonio, *The Black Legends and Catholic Hispanic Culture,* St. Louis: Catholic Central Verein, 1991, 173 pp.

Carter, Paul A., *Another Part of the Twenties*, , New York: Columbia University Press 1977
Coulter, E. Merton, *The Confederate States of America 1861-1865*, Baton Rouge: Louisiana State University Press, 1950
Cousins, Norman, *The Republic of Reason: The Personal Philosophies of the Founding Fathers*, San Francisco: Harper & Row, 1988
Curry, Thomas J., *The First Freedoms: Church and State in America to the Passage of the First Amendment*, Oxford: Oxford University Press, 1986
Davis, Jefferson, *The Rise and Fall of the Confederate Government*, New York: Thomas Yoseloff, 1958
DeConde, Alexander, *This Affair of Louisiana*, New York: Charles Scribner's Sons, 1976
Delaney, Edward D., *False Freedom*, Los Angeles: Standard Publications, 1954
Diggins, John P., *Mussolini and Fascism: The View From America*, Princeton: Princeton University Press, 1972
Dos Passos, John, *Mr. Wilson's War*, Garden City: Doubleday, 1962
Dowdey, Clifford, *Experiment in Rebellion*, New York: Doubleday and Co., 1947
Dowdey, Clifford, *A History of the Confederacy 1832-1865*, New York: Barnes and Noble, New York: 1955
Dudley, Michael Kioni, Keoni Kealoha Agard, *A Hawaiian Nation*, Honolulu: Na Kane O Ka Malo Press, 1990
Eccles, W.J., *France in America*, New York: Harper & Row, 1972, 297 pp.
Eisenhower, John S.D., *So Far From God: The U.S. War With Mexico 1846-1848*, New York: Random House, 1989
Faulkner, Harold U., *Politics, Reform and Expansion*, New York: Harper and Brothers, 1959
Faÿ, Bernard, *Franklin*, New York: Little, Brown, and Co., 1929
Fischer, David Hackett, *The Revolution of American Conservatism*, New York: Harper and Row, 1965
Fitzgibbon, Russell H., *Cuba and the United States: 1900-1935*, New York: Russell and Russell, 1964
Fleming, Peter, *The Siege of Peking*, New York: Harper & Brothers, 1959
Flynn, John T., *As We Go Marching*, New York: Doubleday, Doran abd Co., 1944
Flynn, John T., *The Roosevelt Myth*, New York: Devin-Adair, 1948
Foerster, Norman, ed., *Humanism and America*, New York: Farrar and Rinehart, 1930
Foner, Philip S., *The Spanish-Cuban-American War and the Birth of American Imperialism*, New York: Monthly Review Press, 1972
Foot, M.R.D., *Resistance: European Resistance to Nazism 1940-1945*, New York: McGraw-Hill, 1977
Franklin, John Hope, *Reconstruction: After the Civil War*, Chicago: The University of Chicago Press, 1961
Gadney, Reg, *Cry Hungary*, New York: Atheneum, 1986
Gannon, Michael V., *The Cross In The Sand*, Gainesville: University of Florida Press, 1983, 210 pp.
Garraty, John A., *The New Commonwealth 1877-1890*, New York: Harper and Row, 1968
Garrett, Garet, *The People's Pottage*, Caldwell: The Caxton Printers, Caldwell, 1958
Gautier, Leon, *Chivalry*, New York: Crescent Books, 1989, 499 pp.
Gayre of Gayre and Nigg, Robert, *A Case For Monarchy*, Edinburgh: The Armorial, 1962

Glaser, Kurt, *Czecho-Slovakia: A Critical History,* Caldwell: The Caxton Printers, 1961
Goldman, Eric F., *The Crucial Decade,* New York: Vintage Books, 1956
Gregory, Ross, *America 1941,* New York: The Free Press, 1989
Gueranger, Dom Prosper, *El sentido cristiano de la historia,* Buenos Aires: Ed. Iction, 1984
Gurko, Leo, *The Angry Decade,* New York: Dodd, Mead, and Co., 1947
Halasz, Nicholas, *Roosevelt Through Foreign Eyes,* New York: Van Nostrand, 1961
Hargreaves, Mary W.M., *The Presidency of John Quincy Adams,* Lawrence: University Press of Kansas, 1985
Haring, C.H., *The Spanish Empire in America,* New York: Harcourt, Brace, and World, 1947, 371 pp.
Haslip, Joan, *The Crown of Mexico,* New York: Holt, Rinehart, and Winston, 1971
Hechler, Kenneth W., *Insurgency: Personality and Politics of the Taft Era,* New York: Russell and Russell, 1964
Hendrick, Burton J., *Statesmen of the Lost Cause,* New York: The Literary Guild of America, 1939
Hertz, Solange, *The Star-Spangled Heresy: Americanism,* Santa Monica: Veritas Press, 1992, 187 pp.
Hicks, John D., *Republican Ascendancy 1921-1933,* New York: Harper and Row, 1960
Hoehling, A.A., *Homefront, U.S.A.,* New York: Thomas Y. Crowell Co., 1966
Holbrook, Sabra, *The French Founders of North America and Their Heritage,* New York: Atheneum, 1976, 255 pp.
Hoopes, Roy, *Americans Remember the Home Front,* New York: Hawthorn Books, 1977
Hurley, Bishop Mark J., *The Unholy Ghost,* Huntington: Our Sunday Visitor, 1992
Jacobsen, Hans-Adolf, *July 20, 1944: Germans Against Hitler,* Bonn: Federal Press and Information Office, 1972
Jones, Walter Burgwyn, *Confederate War Poems,* Nashville: Bill Coats, Ltd., 1959
Josephson, Matthew, *The Politicos,* New York: Harcourt, Brace, and World, 1938
Josephson, Matthew, *Infidel in the Temple,* New York: Alfred A. Knopf, 1967
Josephy, Jr., Alvin M., *The Civil War In The American West,* New York: Alfred A. Knopf, 1991
Kedward, H.R., *Fascism in Western Europe 1900-1945,* New York: New York University Press, 1971
Keller, Morton, *Affairs of State,* Cambridge: The Belknap Press, 1977
Kirk, Russell, *The Conservative Mind,* Chicago: Henry Regnery Company, 1953
Klement, Frank L., *The Copperheads in the Middlewest,* Chicago: University of Chicago Press, 1960
Korbonski, Stefan, *Fighting Warsaw,* New York: Funk and Wagnalls, 1968
Kramer, Dale, *The Wild Jackasses: The American Farmer in Revolt,* New York: Hastings House, 1956
Lansing, Robert, *The Big Four And Others of the Peace Conference,* Freeport: Books for Libraries Press, 1972
Large, David Clay, *Between Two Fires: Europe's Path in the 1930s,* New York: W.W. Norton and Co., 1990
Laveille, S.J., E., *The Life of Father De Smet, S.J.,* Chicago: Loyola University Press, 1981
Leckie, Robert, *American and Catholic,* Garden City: Doubleday, 1970
Lees, Michael, *The Rape of Serbia,* New York: Harcourt Brace Jovanovich, 1990
Liliuokolani, *Hawaii's Story By Hawaii's Queen,* Rutland: Charles E. Tuttle Company, 1964

Lord Percy of Newcastle, *The Heresy of Democracy,* Chicago: Henry Regnery Company, 1955
Mahon, John K., *The War of 1812,* Gainesville: University of Florida Press, 1972
Manly, Chesly, *The Twenty Year Revolution,* Chicago: Henry Regnery Company, 1954
Marx, Robert F., *In Quest of the Great White Gods,* New York: Crown Publishers, 1992, 343 pp.
McWilliams, Carey, *North From Mexico,* New York: Greenwood Press, 1968, 324 pp.
Meisel, James H., *The Fall of the Republic: Military Revolt in France,* Ann Arbor: University of Michigan, 1962
Merk, Frederick, *The Monroe Doctrine and American Expansionism, 1843-1849,* New York: Alfred A. Knopf, 1967
Meyer, Karl E., *The New America,* New York: Basic Books, 1961
Middleton, Lamar, *Revolt U.S.A.,* Freeport: Books For Libraries Press, 1968
Miksche, Lt. Col. F.O., *Danubian Federation,* Camberley: privately published, 1953
Miksche, Lt. Col. F.O., *Unconditional Surrender—The Roots of a World War III,* London: Faber and Faber, London 1952
Miller, Douglas T. and Marion Nowak, *The Fifties,* Garden City: Doubleday, 1977
Morgan, H. Wayne, ed., *The Gilded Age,* Syracuse: Syracuse University Press, 1970
Morison, Samuel Eliot, *The European Discovery of America: The Northern Voyages A.D. 500-1600,* New York: Oxford University Press, 1971, 712 pp.
The European Discovery of America: The Southern Voyages A.D. 1492-1616, New York: Oxford University Press, 1974, 758 pp.
Neff, Donald, *Warriors at Suez,* New York: Simon and Schuster, 1981
Nicholls, George Heaton, *South Africa in My Time,* London: Jonathan Cape, 1962
Niven, John, *Martin Van Buren: The Romantic Age of American Politics,* New York and Oxford: Oxford University Press, 1983
Noggle, Burl, *Into the Twenties,* Urbana: University of Illinois Press, 1974
Nowak, Jan, *Courier From Warsaw,* Detroit: Wayne State University Press, 1982
O'Neill, William L., *Coming Apart,* Chicago: Quadrangle Books, 1971
Osman, Percy, *Space History,* New York: St. Martin's Press, 1983
O'Toole, G.J.A., *The Spanish War,* New York: W.W. Norton and Co., 1984
Peck, Anne Merriman, *The Pageant of Middle American History,* New York: Longmans, Green, and Co., 1947
Perman, Michael, *The Road to Redemption: Southern Politics, 1869-1879,* Chapel Hill: The University of North Carolina Press, 1984
Perrett, Geoffrey, *America in the Twenties,* New York: Simon and Schuster, 1982
Petrie, Sir Charles, *Monarchy in the 20th Century,* London: Andrew Dakers, Ltd., 1952
Piekalkiewicz, Janusz, *The Cavalry of World War II,* New York: Stein and Day, 1980
Powell, Philip Wayne, *Tree of Hate,* Vallecito: Ross House Books, 1985, 210 pp.
Randall, J.G., David Donald, *The Divided Union,* New York: Little, Brown and Co., 1961
Rao, Dr. John, *Americanism,* St. Paul: Remnant, n.d., 51 pp.
Ready, J. Lee, *Forgotten Allies,* Jefferson: McFarland and Co., 1985
Ready, J. Lee, *Forgotten Axis,* Jefferson: Mcfarland and Co., 1984
Remini, Robert V., *Andrew Jackson and the Course of American Freedom, 1822-1832,* New York: Harper and Row, 1982

Remini, Robert V., *Andrew Jackson and the Course of American Democracy, 1833-1845*, New York: Harper and Row, New York 1984
Robinson, Carol, *My Life With Thomas Aquinas*, Kansas City: Angelus Press, 1992
Sargent, Daniel, *Our Land and Our Lady*, New York: Longmans, Green and Co., 1939
Schlereth, Thomas J., *Victorian America 1876-1915*, New York: Harper Collins, 1991
Schlesinger, Arthur, *The Rise of the City 1878-1898*, New York: Macmillan, 1933
Schoenbrunn, David, *Soldiers of The Night: The Story of the French Resistance*, New York: E.P. Dutton, 1980

Schriftgiesser, Karl, *This Was Normalcy*, Boston: Little, Brown, and Co., 1948
Shannon, James P., *Catholic Colonization On The Western Frontier*, New Haven: Yale University Press, 1957
Shaw, Richard, *Dagger John: The Unquiet Life and Times of Archbishop John Hughes*, New York: Paulist Press, 1977
Slosson, Preston William, *The Great Crusade and After 1914-1928*, New York: Macmillan, 1930
Smith, Gene, *High Crimes and Misdemeanors*, New York: William Morrow and Company, 1977
Smith, Joseph Burkholder, *James Madison's Phony War*, New York: Arbor House, 1983
Smith, George Winston and Charles Judah, *Chronicles of the Gringos*, Albuquerque: University of New Mexico Press, 1968
Snyder, Dr. Louis L., *Encyclopedia of the Third Reich*, New York: Paragon House, 1989
Sosin, J.M., *English America and the Restoration Monarchy of Charles II*, Lincoln: University of Nebraska Press, 1980
English America and the Revolution of 1688, Lincoln: University of Nebraska Press, 1982
Stampp, Kenneth M., *America in 1857*, New York: Oxford University Press, 1990
Sulzberger, C.L., *The Test: De Gaulle and Algeria*, New York: Harcourt, Brace, & World, 1962
Swing, Raymond Gram, *Forerunners of American Fascism*, New York: Jilian Messner, 1935
Trask, David E., *The War With Spain in 1898*, New York: Macmillan, 1981
Twain, Mark, *The Gilded Age*, New York: Trident Press, 1964
Twelve Southerners, *I'll Take My Stand*, New York: Harper and Bros., 1930
Unofficial Observer, The, *The New Dealers*, New York: Simon and Schuster, 1934
Unofficial Observer, *American Messiahs*, New York: Simon and Schuster, 1935
Vanauken, Sheldon, *The Glittering Illusion:* Washington Regnery Gateway, 1989
Verrill, A. Hyatt, *America's Ancient Civilizations*, New York, G.P. Putnam's Sons, 1953, 334 pp.
Viorst, Milton, *Hostile Allies: FDR and De Gaulle*, New York: Macmillan, 1965
von Schlabrendorff, Fabian, *The Secret War Against Hitler*, New York: Pitman Publishing Corp., 1965
Waterbury, Jean Parker, ed., *The Oldest City*, St. Augustine: St. Augustine Historical Society, 1983, 262 pp.
Wedemeyer, Albert C., *Wedemeyer Reports!*, New York: Henry Holt and Co., 1958
Weems, John Edward, *Death Song: The Last of the Indian Wars*, Garden City: Doubleday, 1976
Wellman, Manly Wade, *They Took Their Stand*, New York: G.P. Putnam's Sons, 1959

Wagenheim, Kal, ed., *The Puerto Ricans: A Documentary History,* New York: Praeger Publishers, 1973
Weymouth, Lally, *America in 1876,* New York: Random House, 1976
White, William Allen, *Masks in a Pageant,* New York: Macmillan, 1928
Woodward, C. Vann, *Reunion and Reaction,* Boston: Little, Brown and Company, 1966

INDEX

abolitionists, 228–35, 237
Adams, John, 135–36, 148, 154–55
Adams, John Quincy, 177, 187–88
Africa, 17
American colonies
 founding, 55–64
 ruling classes, 91–93
American Revolution, 108–27
 causes, 87–108
Americanism, 7, 177, 259, 293, 298–304, 431, 466, 480, 500, 504, 505, 507, 515, 519, 521
 after WWII, 459
America's Secret Aristocracy (Birmingham), 149
Ames, Fisher, 156
Anglicanism, 52
Annali Cappucini (Plunket), 72–73
Anti-Federalists, 146–52
Arizona, 214–15
Art Deco, 380
Articles of Confederation, 129–31, 142
Assizes of Jerusalem, 10
Aztecs, 16–17, 32–33

Babbitt (Lewis), 346–47
Bacon, Nathaniel, 67
Beatniks, 467–69
Beats, 491
Beowulf, 10
Bill of Rights, 147–48
Birmingham, Stephen, 149
Blacks, 38, 47, 77–78
 Civil Rights Movement, 469–72
Blanshard, Paul, 479
Bloch, Marc, 10
Book of Common Prayer, The (Cranmer), 51–52
Brazil, 309–10
British Privy Council, 10

Brown, John, 234–35
Brownson, Orestes, 203, 258, 259

Cahensly, Peter Paul, 296–301
Calhoun, John C., 186
California, 215–16
Calvert, George, 57
Cape of Good Hope, 14
Caponnetto, Antonio, 177
Carroll, Fr. John, 138–40
Cartier, Jacques, 42
Cherokee, 48
China, 325–26
Christmas
 during 1800s, 220
Churchill, Winston, 434, 440
Civil Rights Movement, 469–72
Civil War, 236–56
Clay, Henry, 186, 189
clergy
 abuses, 6
Code Noir, 47
colonies. *See* American colonies
Columbus, Christopher, 14, 16, 17, 18, 25, 26–27
Common Sense (Paine), 114
Communism, 367–69, 370, 385–86, 467
 after WWII, 455–61
conquistadores, 30–35
Constitution, 146
Coolidge, Calvin, 353–54, 365
Cornwallis. *See* Lord Cornwallis
Cranmer, Thomas, 51
Cuba, 311–13, 325
Czechoslovakia
 in WWII, 436–38

Danish Council of State, 11
Davis, Jefferson, 238–39, 245
de Champlain, Samuel, 43

524   *Index*

De Gaulle, Charles, 440–44
de Menendez, Pedro, 34–35
De Smet, Fr. Pierre Jean, 277–80
de Verrazzano, Giovanni, 42
D'Huddeghem, Father Helias, 195
Distributism, 371, 387
Divine Right of Kings, 19
Dollfuss, Engelbert, 390
Dom Pedro II, 309–10
Dorr, Thomas, 191
Douglas, Stephen A., 230
Dred Scott case, 232
Dutch, 62–64, 66

Ecuador, 307–9
Eisenhower, Dwight D., 463, 484
Eliot, T.S., 347–48
Emancipation Proclamation, 250
Emerson, Ralph Waldo, 180, 182
Enlightenment, The, 87–88
Europe, 8–14

Fascism, 369–73
Federal Reserve Bank Act, 330
Federalists, 146–52, 155–59, 160, 164
First Continental Congress, The, 106–7
First Crusade, 12–13
Franklin, Benjamin, 120, 134–35, 138
Freedmen's Bureau, 260
Freemasonry, 150, 242
French, 41–49, 75, 127, 164
    aiding United States, 120–21
    in Canada, 78–82
    in WWII, 439–44
French Canadians, 284–87

Garvey, Marcus, 352
Geography of Witchcraft, The (Summers), 71
Germans, 294–96
Gibbons, Cardinal James, 293–304
Glorious Revolution, 54
Goddard Clarke, Catherine

Our Glorious Popes, 19
Gold Rush, 215–16
gold standard, 275
Gold Standard Act, 321
Great Depression, The, 379–97
Great Schism, 8, 13
Groulx, Fr. Lionel, 360–62
Guam, 312
Gueranger, Dom, 41
    on Spain, 21

Hamilton, Alexander, 107, 147, 151–52
Harding, Warren, 352–53
Hargreaves, Mary, 178
Haring, C.H., 27–28
Harper's Ferry, 234
Hawthorne, Nathaniel, 61, 184
Healy, John, 90
Hecker, Fr. Isaac, 302
Henry, Patrick, 146–47, 148
Hertz, Solange, 6–7
historians
    Catholic, 6
Hitler, Adolf, 392–95, 448, 450–53
Hollywood, 380
Holy Roman Emperor, 9
Hoover, Herbert, 354, 395
Hurston, Zora Neale, 351

immigration, 193, 210, 218–27
In Reaction (Potter), 12
Incas, 16–17
Indian Removal Act, 188
Indians, 16, 48, 74, 75, 160, 276–84
    conversions, 276–80
    in Arizona, 214
    rebellion, 81–82
    removal by Jackson, 188–89
    war, 66–68
    with French, 45, 47
    with Spanish, 276–84, 44
Inscrutabile (Pius VI), 87–88
Intolerable Acts, The, 105–7
Ireland, Fr. John J,, 287–89

Oglethorpe, James, 76
Our Glorious Popes. See Goddard Clarke, Catherine
Our Lady of Guadalupe, 15, 32

Paine, Thomas, 114
Paladins of Charlemagne, 10
Panama, 327
Parks, Rosa, 470
Pearl Harbor, 423–25
Peck, Jesse T., 258
Penal Laws, 56
Peru, 174–75
Petain, Marshall, 439
Philippines, 312
Pierce, Franklin, 230–32
Pike, Albert, 242–43
Pilgrims. *See* Puritans
Plan of Iguala, 174
plantations, 58
Plunkett, Fr. Christopher, 72–73
plutocrats, 267, 273, 275
Poe, Edgar Allen, 184
Poland
  in WWII, 447
Pontiac, 81
Pope Leo XIII, 49
Pope Pius VI, 157
Pope Pius XI, 388
Populism, 270
Portuguese, 14, 20, 26–27
  conquests in Africa, 17
  conquests in Asia, 17–18
Potter, Gary, 12
Program of Social Reconstruction, 342–43
Prohibition, 345
public schools
  origin in the US, 221–22
Puerto Rico, 323–24
Puritans, 51, 53, 59–62

Quadragesimo anno (Pius XI), 388
Quebec Act, The, 105
Queen Elizabeth I, 51–52
Queen Isabella I of Castile, 20–29

Ransome, John Crowe, 59
Renaissance, 8, 19
Republican Party
  formation of, 231
Revolutionary War. *See* American Revolution
Richard, Fr. Gabriel, 199
Riel, Louis, 280–82
Robber Barons, 264–68
Roman Curia, 11
Roman Law, 10
Romanticism, 180–81
Roosevelt, Franklin Delano, 395–97, 423–25, 431–34, 455
Roosevelt, Theodore, 322, 326–28
Rosenberg, Alfred, 448–49
Royal Touch, The (Bloch), 10

Salazar, Antonio, 389
Salem, 71–72
Santa Ana, Antonio Lopez, 174, 190, 205–8, 214
Schlegel, A.W., 180
Sedgwick, Theodore, 158–59
Sentinelle Affair, 362–63
Shays Rebellion, 141
slavery, 38, 187, 237
  Britain's view, 241
  Catholic's view, 236
Smith, Alfred Emmanuel, 355–59
Social Catholicism in Europe (Misner), 58
Solidarism, 388
Sons of Liberty, 100
Spanish, 49, 76, 127, 133, 164, 172–75, 211
  in Canary Islands, 25–26
  in New Mexico, 213–14
  in the New World, 25–41
  Moors, 20, 21, 23–25
  treatment of Indians, 28, 276–84
Spanish Empire in America, The (Haring), 27–28
St. Ferdinand III, 21

Irish, 293–94
Iroquois, 48, 71, 122
Irving, Washington, 183–84

Jackson, Andrew, 172–73, 188–90
Jacobite, 55, 98, 112, 158
Japan, 18
   in WWII, 453–55
Jefferson, Thomas, 115, 135, 151, 153, 155, 159–64
Jim Crow laws, 263
Johnson, Lyndon B., 488–89
Juarez, Benito, 305–6
judicial review, 160
Junipero Serra, 35

Kansas-Nebraska Act, 230
Kennedy, John F., 484, 486
Kerouac, Jack, 468
Khublai Khan, 17
King Arthur's Round Table, 10
King Charles II, 53, 68
King George III, 55, 81–85, 89, 91, 93, 94, 115, 124–29
King Henry VIII, 51
King James Bible, 52
King James I, 52–53
King James II, 53–54, 69–70
King Louis XIII, 44–45
King, Martin Luther, Jr., 470
kings
   decline of, 19
   roles, 9, 10
Kings of Castile, 9
Knights of Labor, 272
Korean War, 463
Ku-Klux-Klan, 262, 346, 471

La Vasseu, Noel, 198
League of Nations, 342
Lewis, C.S., 145
Lewis, Sinclair, 346
liberalism, 475–83
Lincoln, Abraham, 233–34, 235, 237, 245–47, 250
   assassination of, 253

Lord Baltimore, 57, 65
Lord Cornwallis, 125–26
Loyalists, 95–99, 114

Madison, James, 136, 164–66
Magna Carta, 10
Manifest Destiny, 210
Mann, Horace, 221–22
Marco Polo, 17
Marx, Karl, 242
Maximilian, 305–7
Mayans, 15
May-Pole of Merry Mount, The (Hawthorne), 61
McCarthy, Joseph, 465
McKinley, William, 320–22
McLoughlin, Dr. John, 204
Medieval Christendom, 8
Mexico, 190, 331
   Cristero rebellion, 363–64, 365–67
   empire, 305–7
   Mexican War, 204–9
Middle Ages, 8
Miller, Perry, 60
Ming dynasty, 18
Misner, Paul, 58
missionaries, 35–37
Missouri Compromise, 228–31
Monroe, James, 175–76
Moore, James, 73, 76
Moreno, Jose Garcia, 307–9
Mormons, 217
Muñoz Marin, Luis, 323–24
Murray, Fr. John Courtney, S.J., 480–81
Mussolini, Benito, 374–76, 386, 450

Napoleon, 164, 241, 306
Nativists, 203
Nazis, 389, 392–95, 434–37, 450–53
New Humanists, 383–84
New Mexico, 213–14

Star Spangled Banner, 167
Star-Spangled Heresy, The (Hertz), 6–7
Stuyvesant, Peter, 65–66
Summers, Fr. Montague, 71, 75
Supreme Court
   on Civil Rights, 472

Tappert, Fr. William, 301
Tecumseh, 166
Tolkien, J.R.R., 490–91
Tories, 90–91, 121, 124
Transcendentalism, 181–82
Truman, Harry S., 460–61
Twain, Mark, 317–18

Unitarianism, 131, 135, 178–80
Uriburu, Jose Felix, 386

Vatican II, 491–500
Versailles Treaty, 342
Vikings, 15
von Habsburg, Otto, 435
von Papen, Franz, 392–95

Washington, George, 110, 117, 151, 154
   on neutrality, 153
Webster, Daniel, 185
Webster, Noah, 136–38
Whigs, 88–90, 127
Wilson, Woodrow, 329–44
   Fourteen Points, 340–41
witchcraft, 71–72
World War II, 423–61

Zimmermann Telegram, 338

www.ingramcontent.com/pod-product-compliance
Lightning Source LLC
Chambersburg PA
CBHW021137080526
44588CB00008B/89